THE
COOK AND HOUSEWIFE'S
MANUAL

To Sandra

with love

Bob   7. Dec. 94.

First published 1829 by Oliver & Boyd, Edinburgh
This edition 1988 by Rosters Ltd. 60, Welbeck Street, London

Published by Rosters Ltd., 60, Welbeck Street, London W1.

ISBN 0–948032–71–5 (Cased)
ISBN 0–948032–76–6 (Paperback)

TYPESET BY LOVELL BAINES PRINT LTD., HOLLINGTON FARM,
WOOLTON HILL, NEWBURY, BERKSHIRE.

PRINTED AND BOUND BY COX & WYMAN LTD
CARDIFF ROAD, READING, BERKSHIRE.

THE
COOK AND HOUSEWIFE'S
MANUAL:

A PRACTICAL SYSTEM OF MODERN DOMESTIC COOKERY
AND FAMILY MANAGEMENT.

———————

THE FOURTH EDITION

REVISED AND ENLARGED:

CONTAINING A COMPENDIUM OF FRENCH COOKERY, AND OF
FASHIONABLE CONFECTIONARY, PREPARATIONS FOR INVALIDS, A
SELECTION OF CHEAP DISHES, AND NUMEROUS USEFUL
MISCELLANEOUS RECEIPTS IN THE VARIOUS BRANCHES OF
DOMESTIC ECONOMY

———————

BY MISTRESS MARGARET DODS,

OF THE CLEIKUM INN, ST. RONAN'S.

———————

PUBLISHED BY ROSTERS LTD,
60, WELBECK STREET, LONDON W1

Editor's Note

We have reproduced in full the fourth edition of the
COOK AND HOUSEWIFE'S MANUAL. The original spelling
and typesetting has been reproduced so that the book
resembles the original as closely as possible. The page
numbers have been altered where necessary to avoid
duplication.

———————"COOK, SEE ALL YOUR SAWCES
BE SHARP AND POYNANT IN THE PALATE, THAT THEY MAY
COMMEND YOU; LOOK TO YOUR ROAST AND BAKED MEATS HANDSOMELY,
AND WHAT NEW KICKSHAWS AND DELICATE MADE THINGS."

BEAUMONT AND FLETCHER.

INTRODUCTION BY GLYNN CHRISTIAN

Welcome to a real cookery book, a book for people who really like to eat. Those who like to cook will obtain limitless pleasure too, but these days cooking seems ever more divorced from eating. Professionals are specially guilty of believing their job done once their food has been dished. And it is now easy for those at home to buy ready-cooked food, thus losing from the general experience the pleasures of cookery smells, the eager expectations of shopping and preparation, the skill and satisfaction of juggling ingredients and choosing substitutes, based on marketing and what's in the cupboard. Increasingly food has become a subject related more to the plate rather than the palate and we are dangerously close to losing also an understanding of the warmth, fellowship and hospitality that flavours the best of cooking and eating.

For me, Meg Dods helps regenerate the bridges between plate and palate, and stimulates interest in ingredients and what to do with them. She has the added and dual advantage of neatly illuminating the truth of two important cliches – that there is nothing new under the sun, and that we have forgotten far more than we have learned. For here, so long ago, are apposite discussions about which stuffing most suits a turkey and why, complaints about the inroads of 'fast food' (steaks in her time!), and reminders of such simple pleasures as the use of bay leaf to flavour milk for custards.

Meg and her book are dogmatic, insightful, comic and revelatory, tainted in places with good old-fashioned cant and humbug. But oh! how welcome they are in the downpour of hopeless and empty 'new' books with which we are deluged each year. Only by looking back with open eagerness can we ever hope to maintain our standards, let alone move forward. As she has done before, Meg Dods seems just who we need to recover our pride in and enjoyment of cooking food, not as an end in itself, but as a prelude to that more important occupation the eating of it with friends and family . . . .

ADVERTISEMENT TO FOURTH EDITION.

In once more making our acknowledgments to the public, and presenting a new Edition of the COOK AND HOUSEWIFE'S MANUAL, professing to be improved and enlarged, with the single view of increasing its work-day, practical utility, we take leave to state in what manner this object has been accomplished.

The improvements, which run more or less through every section of the Volume, are most apparent in the Chapters, MADE-DISHES, FRENCH and ENGLISH, LIQUEURS, PASTRY, CURING MEATS, and MISCELLANEOUS information, of the kind which is considered important to those for whom the Work is principally intended—descending to the cellar and dairy, and mounting to the dressing-room. These improvements we owe in part to the judicious hints and corrections of practical cooks, but chiefly to the contributions of ladies in different quarters, well qualified, by experience and superior intelligence, to enhance the value of a manual of this nature, both to the young cook and housekeeper. This kind of information, which has been anxiously sought, generally relates to dishes and preparations which have been for some time existing in the kitchens of the better classes in the three kingdoms, but which have not yet found their way into books of cookery; and to modes of cookery adopted from France, or introduced from India, but modified, and, as we think, improved, by English taste and practice. Much of this information lay beyond the powers or opportunities of any single individual, however experienced; and the editors can claim no merit from this, which, together with the COMPENDIUM OF FRENCH COOKERY, forms the distinctive, and perhaps most important feature of this work, save the attempt to class these valuable additions.

In the present edition, numbers have been affixed to each specific receipt, to facilitate references; though there are numerous subordinate prescriptions classed under one head, which it was impossible to bring under this rule; for even in the humble merit of bulk, and quantity of letter-press, this MANUAL ranks at least equally with any of its contemporaries. Some useful tables have been added—and almost every receipt has been revised, both with the view of increasing the sum of information, and of rendering the directions as plain as possible—as every one is aware that culinary directions, like those of surgeons and apothecaries, are liable to be strangely misunderstood.

Those who hate prefaces, may, if they please, stop here; but from the more patient reader we would crave a little farther indulgence.—This Work was originally undertaken under the idea that a FAMILY MANUAL OF COOKERY, suited to the advanced state of the art, and to the change of times and manners, had for some time been wanted. The only books of any note on the important subject of culinary art that had appeared for twenty years, were the COOK'S ORACLE by Dr. Kitchener, admirably adapted to those jovial lovers of good dinners, who would have received as oracles the dicta of Quin or Samuel Foote; and the FRENCH COOK, by M. Ude, a work equally valuable to the men-cooks of splendid establishments, and the keepers of fashionable hotels, taverns, and club-houses, but neither of them, we presumed to believe, much calculated to be the domestic MANUAL of the inexperienced female cook, or of the young and anxious mistress of a private family. The facetious Doctor, and the refined *Maître d'Hôtel* of Crockford's though the very antipodes of each other, seemed both alike remote from the point to which our more homely labours tended. The only work of this kind calculated to be of use as a Family Manual, limited in its object at first to the daughters of one family, had, valuable as it will ever be, in the lapse of years become somewhat ancient; and was besides, we ventured to think, from its original purpose, too exclusively, and perhaps provincially English, to have been at any period adapted to the local necessities and exigencies of a very large class in these three kingdoms.

In all the popular systems, Scotland and Ireland, in whatever was peculiar in their cookery, had been either excluded or overlooked; though there is much in the domestic economy of both countries, so far as regards every-day affairs, worthy of attention; and at any rate important to those who have to conduct families in them. How far the present MANUAL is adapted to supply the acknowledged deficiency, and in the middle of the nineteenth century, to afford a really useful compendium of the culinary knowledge so important to the mistress of every family, it is not for us to decide. We may safely assert, that no pains have been spared, in repeated revisals, to make it all that its name imports.

We would fain venture some apology for our superfluous nonsense, and already take credit for having withdrawn much of it to make way for more solid matter; acting on one of our own favourite maxims, that, on plain ordinary occasions, it is generally most seemly and advisable to serve all accompaniments and garnishes on a separate trencher. What decorations of this kind are still retained, we have endeavoured to keep in strict subservience to their alleged purpose. It would, however, be hard on us, and not very liberal in our judges, to have it believed, that, in making an irruption from our head-quarters at the Cleikum, and crossing the Border, preceded by a flourish of marrow-bones, we might not have a message to deliver as earnest and important as any ever conveyed by the soberest tones of monotonous dulness.

To those who use this book as a Manual of Cookery, we would take leave to recommend the perusal of the prefatory remarks to the chapters, particularly those prefixed to the chapter containing the specific receipt they wish at any time to consult, and also of any notes or references connected with the receipt. Many of the important notices and hints necessary to the success of all culinary processes, will thus be brought under the eye, which it is impossible to repeat in every distinct prescription. The Glossary may also be read with advantage; and the perusal of the syllabus of culinary lectures and advertisements to former editions, can do no harm.

Though we have frequently given our directions in a less implicit form than our predecessors, and have condescended to assign the reason of many of our commands, our fair readers must not on this account imagine them one whit less authoritative. They may at all times walk confidently by the letter of our instructions, but will fall far short of the full advantage, unless exercising their own understandings, and applying their own increasing experience, they learn to apprehend the spirit in the letter, and to act in all circumstances accordingly.

ADVERTISEMENT TO SECOND EDITION.

The present edition of this Work has been retarded beyond the period at which it ought to have appeared, by the time occupied in that careful revision and enlargement of the original Volume, which its favourable reception induced the Editors to undertake. The original Work, though pregnant with solid matter, was thought to savour somewhat of a *jeu d'esprit*. In its improved state, if not much more grave, this Manual will be found more *recherché* on all culinary subjects. It has been carefully revised throughout; upwards of TWO HUNDRED NEW RECEIPTS have been added, besides an entirely new-written and enlarged System of Confectionary, and plates illustrative of the Directions for Carving. But the most important new feature of this Work, is a COMPENDIUM OF FRENCH COOKERY, compiled for this Work, and embodying all in foreign culinary science that is considered really useful to the English cook. Besides this distinct section of the Volume, wherever, in the preparation of any particular dish, the foreign method of dressing appeared of importance, the difference has been pointed out in Observations or Notes appended to the English receipt. (See, as examples, Notes pp. 90, 136, 149.—*Obs.* 168, and *Nos.* 268, 274; Note 292, &c. &c.)

These scattered notices, therefore, together with the Compendium, form a System of FRENCH COOKERY more intelligible and better calculated to enlarge the knowledge of the English cook than any French work that can be obtained. They indeed contain the essence of them all, in the shape best adapted to the uses of the home-bred practitioner.

The vanity and amusing self-importance of the *artistes* imported to teach the refined cookery of France in our barbarian isles, has drawn ridicule upon their art, which ought to be exclusively confined to its conceited professors; for there is much, not only in the actual Cookery, but in the domestic economy of our refined neighbours, worthy of profound attention. In the hope that the foreign graces, transplanted into this Volume, may considerably enhance its value to the practical cook, and in the belief that a culinary system superior to either the French or English may be drawn from the combined excellencies of both countries, the Manual in its improved form is now submitted to the public.

It is proper again to notice at the outset, that in mentioning many enriching ingredients, garnishes, and sauces, the things in common and fashionable use are always pointed out, but not always recommended. It has been the aim of the editors to give as much useful information as possible; but its application must always be left to individual discretion.

JULY, 1827.

ORIGINAL PREFACE.

It would be unnecessary to introduce this Volume, written on a subject of universal interest and acknowledged utility, with any prefatory remarks whatever, were it not conceived, that the novel attempt of endeavouring to conciliate the lovers of what is called "light reading," and to gain their attention to what they may consider a vulgar and unimportant art, might alarm those graver and more prudent persons, who think, perhaps justly, the subject discussed, of that earnest nature, which accords ill with any thing fanciful or discursive; and who may thence conclude the petty details and display of internal machinery in the Work, idle, if not impertinent and out of place. These weighty objections can only be met by the assurance, that the *main business* of this MANUAL has, in no respect whatever, suffered from an attempt to separate the culinary art from its fopperies and technicalities; and to render that branch of economy, in which the comfort and respectability of domestic life is so much involved, more attractive to the young housekeeper.

It has accordingly been the object to make this Volume comprehend every thing to which the mistress of any family, in the numerous gradations of middle life, needs to refer, either for information or to refresh her recollections. The *useful receipts* are therefore as numerous as in any work of the kind. Many of them are original in books, though known in good practice, the result of observation in various quarters; and, with few exceptions, they have all stood the test of experiment among skilful cooks and intelligent mistresses of families, and been approved for the judicious combination of what is elegant, with what is healthful, economical, and agreeable to the palate. The best private sources of culinary knowledge have been applied to,—the most esteemed modern works on Cookery, French and English, diligently compared and consulted, and every hint has been adopted which promised either to increase the mass of information or the practical utility of the volume—whether *economical* or *culinary*.

In exact proportion as the principles of the science of *good living* are better understood, the practice of Cookery is becoming more simple and more rational; and, as it is the design of this MANUAL to promote the diffusion of useful knowledge, in our receipts, health and genuine economy have in no instance been sacrificed either to fleeting fashion or to antique prejudice. The besetting sin of professed cooks has been carefully avoided,— namely, the ordering of *bit* of this, and a *dash* of that, and a *little* of the other high-priced ingredient, on the same principle of liberality which makes a milliner overload her customer with ill-assorted and superfluous finery, that she may glorify herself in her own handiwork displayed at the expense of her employer.

But as works of this kind are most frequently consulted on unforeseen emergencies, and on occasions when sparing would be parsimony, receipts for the preparation of the most fashionable dishes will be found in sufficient variety. The tasteful economist must judge when to spend and when to spare. It may be proper to notice that in wine, essences, eggs, cream, meat, gravies, &c., a good deal may yet be saved—even though Cookery is now so much more rationally understood than it formerly was— and the dishes still be savoury and excellent;

and, as a general principle, the total omission of all costly ingredients is recommended to the young housekeeper, as more commendable than the adoption of the paltry substitutes resorted to by spurious economy, united with the ill-regulated desire of being *genteel*. And yet, as inventive economy, neatness, and good taste cannot be more advantageously displayed by a lady than in *varying* as well as in ordering the arrangements of her table, this rule must not restrict the exercise of a sound discretion, though, in general, female industry and ingenuity will be better directed in turning what is already in the house to good account, than in fabricating substitutes for costly dishes.

It may be thought, that some of the more common processes of the kitchen are too elaborately described in this Work, and that some of the plain receipts are too minute in their detail. But every Manual of Art is presumed to be written for the benefit of the uninstructed; and to the young cook and housekeeper it is impossible too much to magnify the importance of the culinary science and of domestic management, or too carefully to obviate their difficulties.

CONTENTS

PART I.

PART II.

PART III.

PART IV.

INSTITUTION OF THE CLEIKUM CLUB.

After the accomplishment of those passages which are recorded at large in that entertaining and highly-popular history, entitled, "St. Ronan's Well," Peregrine Touchwood, Esquire, more commonly styled the Cleikum Nabob, who had been deeply concerned in these disastrous events, was sorely pricked in mind; and, after a time, became afflicted with melancholy langour, so that his appetite failed, time hung heavily on his hands, and he knew not whereunto to betake himself. This worthy gentleman was, it may be remembered, of a stirring active temper; prompt, nimble, and prying in spirit; somewhat dogmatic and opinionative withal; and fond of having a finger in every pie, though it was alleged, that he sometimes scalded his lips with other people's broth.

The unhappy catastrophe which befell the ancient and honourable house of St. Ronan's occurred about the fall of the year; and by the end of March, Mr. Touchwood, having carried reform as far as was possible in and about the hamlet of Auldtown, was in some danger, as we have distantly intimated, of falling into hypochondria, or what the learned Dr. Cackleben called "fever on the spirits," vulgarly, *fidgets*,—a malady to which bachelor gentlemen, in easy circumstances, when turned of fifty, are thought to be peculiarly liable. It so happened, however, that one of those fortunate occurrences which oftenest befall when least looked for, wrought the deliverance of the Nabob from the power of ennui or hypochondria, and restored him to himself. In brief, he exorcised the blue devils which began to torment him, by an attempt to teach his fair country-women the mystery of preparing culinary devils of all denominations; besides *soups, ragouts, sauces,* and the whole circle of the arts of domestic economy,—an entirely new system, in short, of rational, practical cookery.

An idea of this kind had, among many others, been for some time floating in the brain of the Nabob, which was rather fertile in projects; but it would probably never have gone farther than the tongue, save for one of those fortuitous combinations of events which sometimes produce the mightiest consequences, and which about this time sent to St. Ronan's a personage of no less weight than the celebrated Dr. Redgill. The Doctor had for some months been what his physician called "an incipient invalid." His powers of digestion, though still respectable, were of late rather declining; but his appetite, "he thanked God," was vigorous as ever, his taste more refined, and his knowledge matured and extended in every branch of the science. He had been trying the Cheltenham waters in the previous season; and was now recommended by a Scotch physician, who had been singularly happy in the case of his friend, Alderman ———,to try the St. Ronan's Spa, the virtues of which were just then coming into fashionable repute.

Like the bulk of mankind, attracted by the glitter of appearance, Dr. Redgill, on his arrival, had established himself at the New Hotel. But here he soon became discontented with the accommodation, attendance, but, above all, the cookery; and learning that a wealthy old East Indian—a sort of humourist, who understood and loved good cheer—had fixed his head-quarters in a quiet, comfortable, well-ordered, old-fashioned inn, where excellent small dinners were served, the Doctor ordered his low-hung, well-cushioned vehicle, and on the second morning of his residence at St. Ronan's Well, set out to reconnoitre the capabilities of this land of promise.

The Nabob, unshaved, half-dressed, blue and yellow, fallen off in flesh, and given up to melancholious fancies about bilious attacks and the fall of stocks, the vanity of riches, and the moral impossibility of Scotch cooks ever boiling rice properly, was, when the Doctor drove in sight, lounging at his parlour window, directing the old grey Ostler in currying the older grey horse, but with little of his former spirit and promptitude. The eyes of the three persons—the Doctor, the Nabob, and the Ostler—were now attracted to a spectacle in which all mankind take more or less interest,—a pair of Mrs. Dods' game-cocks, which had lustily commenced a sparring-match. The Ostler staid his currycomb and its hissing accompaniment, and clapped his hands to cheer the combatants; the Nabob flung up the sash; and the Doctor drew up to contemplate the exhibition. The feathered combatants fought it out gallantly,— each, no doubt, animated by the knightly consciousness that "his lady saw him," till one dropped dead, and the other staggered over.—"Well done, Charlie!— bravely fought, Charlie!" cried the Ostler, lifting up the survivor.

"Admirable cock-a-leekie," said the Doctor, touching the deceased with the end of his whip; "all the better for the fight; it would raise the creature's blood.—A fine brood that!" addressing the Ostler, and throwing eyes of love on a set of ducklings, just escaped from the shell, that were innocently disporting themselves in a little puddle, near some goodly rows of green peas in a more advanced state of vegetation than any the Doctor had seen since he had crossed the Border; "these ducklings will, however, be too old before the peas are ready. Strange stupidity, not to have them come together!"*—At this instant the soft treble squeak of a pig of tender days, and then the squall of a full choir, a whole litter of pigs,—Chinese pigs, the Doctor knew by the Orientalism of the infant grunt,—struck his ear; and, like an old battle-horse starting at the sound of the trumpet, the Doctor alighted, (the Ostler instinctively seizing the reins,) and, unheeding the proffered courtesy of the Nabob, who requested him to walk in, pushed forwards.—"Whereabouts, good woman? whereabouts is the piggery? How many days are they littered?"—"Gude woman, ill woman," quoth Mrs. Dods,—for it was Meg herself who, with a pailful of slops, was sallying towards the delicate objects of the Doctor's solicitude, under which office she disguised the latent purpose of taking a nearer view of the new arrival at the Spa,—"Gude woman, ill woman, it can make little odds to you, for they are no for your market;" and Meg passed on,

"In maiden meditation fancy-free!"

The Doctor, not yet wholly discomfited in his expectations, followed with grave and ponderous, though eager steps. The appearance of the Hebe who daily ministered to their little wants, called forth a full chorus of grunters, swelling in triple thrice-confounding din; and the matron of the stye, a full-grown porker, bursting the verge of the sanctuary, ran full tilt against the Doctor, and, getting between his legs, caused him perform a somerset, which made him free of the house ere

---

*We never, for our own private eating, could yet find much to admire in the skin-and-bone ducks of June and July.—P.T.

Meg had time to bless herself.—"Help! hilloa, here, good woman!" exclaimed the Doctor, as the enraged matron of the stye, filled with maternal alarms, began to discover her tusks.

"Ye'll ken the way back to my pig-stye now, it's like," quoth Meg, with a grim smile; and, as a measure of defence, she heaved the whole contents of her brimming pail on the sow, thus allowing a rather copious libation to the Doctor.—"Help here, Jerry Ostler; Lord sake, help here! this battle atween the Scots and English is waur than Bannockburn. Is't you, Mr. Touchwood? This is a worse job than Saunders Jaup's jaw-hole yet; the fat English minister, frae the Waal, is smooring a' my wee grices."

"Your grices will smother him, you mean, dame," said Touchwood. "Here, sir; ay, there you are on end again. This way,—follow me. You shall have your revenge though. They bemire you; you shall crunch their bones."

Reeking and panting from the struggle, the Doctor, even more provoked by the fancied insolence of the landlady, and the ill-timed mirth of the Nabob, than by the assault of the felon-sow, growled forth something that, were such enormity possible, sounded very like wishing the whole party in that place from which it was his duty as a churchman to keep them.

"Neither my swine nor my guests boded themselves on you," said Meg. "Them that come unsent for, sit unserved; but that cannot be said of you; ye contrived to get far ben on short notice. If folks will scrape acquaintance——"

"A scraping acquaintance indeed!" interrupted Touchwood. "Here, Jerry Ostler,—your currycombs here! Soap, water, towels! Uncase, Doctor. Faith,

as you say, dame, a worse job than Saunders Jaup's
jaw-hole yet."

The grumbling Doctor, wise enough to make a virtue of necessity, rallied his natural good temper; for
all gourmands are good-natured, except, perhaps, about
meal-times; though it may be, as Lord Shaftesbury
says of other good-natured persons, "because they
care for nobody but themselves; and as nothing annoys
them but what affects their own interest, they never
irritate themselves about what does not concern them,
and so seem to be made of the very milk of human
kindness."—Such was the Doctor. His rubicund coun-
tenance, soft and swelling as a jelly, generally beamed
easy good nature; his ample bosom seemed a reservoir of the very gravy of human kindness; his full,
moist lips curved over like the ledges of an over-
flowing sauce-tureen.—Having cast his slough, and got
purified from the defilements of the stye, arrayed his
outward man in a scanty suit of brown tendered by the
Nabob, and fortified the inner with the full of one
of Meg's long-stalked, enamelled, antique glasses of
Touchwood's Curaçoa, the Doctor was now so far
mollified as to add to a grateful eulogium on the qualities
of the liqueur an acknowledgment of the attention of
his entertainer.

"Never mind it, man," said the easy Nabob; "I at
least am indebted to the delinquent sow; she abridges
ceremony and idle introductions. You must take a
bachelor's dinner with me to-day. No refusal positively.
A glass of Meg's good wine must atone for short
commons. I vow this brush has done me good."

Nothing was farther from the real intention of Dr.
Redgill than to refuse an invitation, which the savoury
steams, now issuing from Meg's kitchen—"steams that

might have created a stomach under the ribs of death"—rendered irresistibly seductive. With a decent show of hesitation, he yielded; and, snuffing up the incense-breathing vapours which ascended the stair, followed the Nabob to a private parlour, where an old, rich china basin, filled with the balmy and ambrosial fluid, was twice replenished for his solace; first, however, improved by a pin's-point of crystals of Cayenne from a silver pocket-case of essence vials, which had luckily escaped the taint of the stye.

"Excellent hare-soup—*very excellent* indeed I pronounce it, Mr. Touchwood. All the blood preserved—the consistence—the concoction complete—the seasoning admirable. Sir, I abhor the injustice of withholding from the poor cook the praise that is her due. It is bad policy, Mr. Touchwood. This hare-soup, I say again, is excellent; and, to my thinking, though a Scottish mode, the very best way of dressing a hare. Sir, you are in snug quarters here. A sensible, discreet person, your hostess, though a little gruff at the first brush. Sir, all good cooks are so. They know their own value—they are a privileged class—they toil in a fiery element—they lie under a heavy responsibility. But, perhaps, after all, you travel with your own cook—many gentlemen who have travelled do."

"No such thing," replied Touchwood; "never less alone than when alone in affairs of the stomach. I may have written out a few items for my old dame here, and taken a peep occasionally into the kitchen and larder for the first three months; but now, matters go on as smoothly as oiled butter."

"Sir, you write receipts, then!" cried the Doctor, looking on his hospitable entertainer with augmented respect,—"perhaps for this very soup—and perhaps—but it would be too great a kindness to request on such short acquaintance—though hare-soup, sir, I will candidly own it, is only understood in Scotland. Sir, I am above national prejudices; and, I must say, I yield the Scots the Superiority in all soups—save turtle and mullagatawny. An antiquarian friend of mine attributes this to their early and long connexion with the French, a nation eminent in soups."

"No doubt of it, Doctor," replied the Nabob; "but you shall have this receipt, ay and twenty more receipts. To this ancient hostel now—you will scarce believe it —have been confined scores of admirable receipts in cookery, ever since the jolly friars flourished down in the Monastery yonder:

> "The Monks of Melrose made fat kail
> On Fridays, when they fasted."

"You remember the old stave, Doctor?"

The Doctor remembered no such thing. His attention was given to more substantial doctrine. "Sir, I should not be surprised if they possessed the original receipt—a local one too I am told— for dressing the red trout, in this hereditary house of entertainment."

"Never doubt it, man—claret, butter, and spiceries. —Zounds, I have eat of it till——It makes my mouth water yet. As the French adage goes,—'Give your trout a bottle of good wine, a lump of butter, and spice, and tell me how you like him.'—Excellent trout in this very house—got in the '*Friar's cast*,' man—the best reach of the river. Let them alone for that. Those jolly monks knew something of the mystery. Their warm, sunny old orchards still produce the best fruit in the country. You English gentlemen never saw the Grey-gudewife pear. Look out here, sir. The ABBOT'S HAUGH yonder—the richest carse-land and fattest beeves in the country. Their very names are genial, and smack of milk and honey!—But here comes a brother of the reformed order, whom I have never yet been able to teach the difference between Bechamel and butter-milk, though he understands ten languages. Dr. Redgill,— give me leave to present to you, my friend, Mr. Josiah Cargill, the minister of this parish. I have been telling my friend that the Reformation has thrown the science of cookery three centuries back in this corner of the island. Popery and made-dishes, Mr. Cargill,—Episcopacy, roast-bee, and plum-pudding,—and what is left to Presbytery, but its lang-kail, its brose, and mashlum bannocks?"

"So I have heard," replied Mr. Cargill; "very wholesome food, indeed."

"Wholesome food, sir! Why, your wits are woolgathering. There is not a barefoot monk, sir, of the most beggarly, abstemious order, but can give you some pretty notions of tossing up a fricassee or an omelet, or of mixing an olio. Scotland has absolutely retrograded in gastronomy: yet she saw a better day, the memory of which is savoury in our nostrils yet, Doctor. In old Jacobite families, and in the neighbourhood of decayed monasteries,—in such houses as this, for instance, where long succeeding generations have followed the trade of victuallers,—a few relics may still be found. It is for this reason I fix my scene of experiment at the CLEIKUM, and choose my notable hostess as high priestess of the mysteries. But here comes Mr. Winterblossom. —No word of Jekyl? Never mind.—Serve dinner there. I allow five minutes for difference of time-pieces, and wait a half-minute more for my tardy guest—no man shall call me uncivil—and then proceed to the main business of the day,—eh, Doctor?—were King George expected."

"Sir," said the Doctor, earnestly, "I venerate your

opinions and practice in this matter. Sir, our great English moralist, Dr. Johnson, though a fellow of no college yet no mean authority, says,—'The man that does not mind his stomach is a fool: the belly is every man's master.'—Sir, I have known young gentlemen, otherwise of unexceptionable morals, disgrace themselves——sir, I say disgrace themselves, and lose the friendship of those who were inclined to serve them and to promote their views in life, by this infamous practice of delaying dinner; which the elegant, classic Addison truly calls a species of perjury. Sir, he brands it as 'the *detestable* habit of keeping your friends waiting dinner.'—'If such persons did think at all,' says he, 'they would reflect on their guilt in lengthening the suspension of agreeable life,'—that is, in lengthening the hanging-on half-hour before dinner."

The dinner was served punctual to the second; for Meg and the Nabob, though they did not quite agree in harmony, always agreed in time:—a true *gourmand* dinner;—no sumptuous feast of twenty dishes in the *deadthraw*, but a few well-chosen and well-suited,—each relieving each,—the boils done to a *popple*,—the roast to a *turn*,—the stews to the *nick of time*. First came the soup—the hare-soup; Meg called it "rabbit-soup," as this was close-time.

"Sir, if you please," replied the Doctor, bowing to the tureen, and sipping his heated Madeira, as he answered the inquiry of the Nabob, if he would take soup,—"as our great moralist, Dr. Johnson, said of your Scotch barley-broth,—'Sir, I have eat of it, and shall be happy to do so again.'"

Stewed red trout, for which the house was celebrated, —a fat, short-legged, thick-rumped pullet, braised and served with rice, and mushroom sauce,—a Scotch dish of venison-collops,—and, though last, not least in the

Doctor's good love, one of the young pigs, killed since his adventure in the stye:—these formed the dinner. And all were neatly dished,—each dish with its appropriate sauces and garnishings,—the whole in *keeping* that would have done honour to the best city-tavern in London.—"Sir, I say city-tavern," said Redgill; "for I humbly conceive that, in all save flimsy show, business is best understood in the city, however finely they may talk the matter at the West End."

Such a dinner deserved a grace. It was, indeed, part of the *garnish*—indispensable. The Doctor's was short and pithy, delivered in a rolling, sonorous voice, pitched to fill the dining-hall of a college; and then the seats were occupied without farther ceremony;—for though it be true that at large dinners "the post of *profit* is a private station," there was here little to alarm. The stewed trout had ceased to be luxury to Winterblossom or the Nabob; and they both knew that though Jekyl would stand out with the most high-bred politeness, like a very gamester, or a Hotspur, for his full share of the *venison fat, browned outside of veal, belly-slice of salmon, mock-jelly of cod's-head, Pope's-eye, crackling,* due proportion of *stuffing,* and all those epicurean delicacies which gentlemen politely urge on each other when resolved to obtain the dainty morsel for themselves, they also knew, we have said, that they could *do* Mr. Cargill with perfect ease; and he was the only other guest present.

Dr. Redgill, with cranberry-tart and a copious libation of rich plain cream, was concluding one of the most satisfactory dinners he had ever made in his life, though called a chance-dinner—he in general detested *chance-dinners*—when Mr. Jekyl, in his fishing-jacket and wet shoes, lounged into the room. Certain reasons made an absence from the metropolis convenient to the young gentleman at this time. He ws therefore still at St. Ronan's, and was become rather intimate with the Nabob, who, like Sir Peter Teazle, never grudged him his good advice.

The young gentleman bore the rebuke, which his want of punctuality drew upon him, with entire non-chalance, surveyed the board with an air of half-supercilious scrutiny, and ordered the female-waiter to carry his compliments to Mrs. Dods, and say that Mr. Touchwood would be particularly obliged by the re-appearance of the excellent roast-beef he had had yesterday, and a few slices of *cold carrot*. The Nabob and the facetious Winterblossom, who, it may be remembered, was the most pleasant companion in the world, albeit he did not value at a pin's point any creature on its surface, were well accustomed to these flings in the young man, and gave themselves no manner of concern; but Dr. Redgill, who was really, as we have said, a good-natured man, and, after dinner, had bowels even for an unpunctual fisher, took compassion on the gentleman-like young officer, and recommended the stewed fowl, "hot yet, hardly touched,"—the pig the Doctor kept as a special preserve. It was admirable re-dressed *à la Bechamel*. The young man was politely grateful, but invincible. Most elaborately did he mix up a relish, compounded of made-mustard, eschalot-vinegar, catsup, and horse-radish, for his cold regale; and plateful after plateful was swallowed, the Doctor looking on in silent admiration not unmixed with envy, and resolving at supper to try this inviting beef, since, unfortunately, a man that lunches cannot comfortably eat two dinners in the same day. The toper certainly has here advan-tage over the gourmand.

And now the clash of plates had ceased, the ringing of tumblers was no more; and as next in degree to the eating of a good dinner—the digesting is a different thing—comes the pleasure of talking of it, the merits of the several dishes were discussed at large. Winter-blossom suggested "a *very* little more currant-jelly to the venison-sauce;" and the Doctor hinted, that, "had the mustard been mixed one hour earlier, the amalgamation would have been complete;— but *freshness*, after all, was the good extreme; it was very well." Both were deep in the stewed trout, when Jekyl, his solitary meal finished, took the lead with his wonted easy, well-bred assurance; and expatiated so knowingly on the mysteries of the French kitchen, unfolding the intricate combinations of the most complicated ragouts, "familiar as his garter," talking so learnedly of unique flavours, of *braises*, *daubes*, *matelôtes*, &c. the compositions of sauces, their inventors, and the names of modern restaurateurs of celebrity, damning this one and applauding the other, and quoting the maxims and proceedings of the *Caveau Moderne*, that the Doctor began to think that on the shoulders of a young life-guardsman he had discovered the head of a bishop. This was, however, rather a blow that staggered than one which made a lasting impression. "Sir," said the Doctor to Touch-wood next day, "the talk of half these young fellows is mere foppery. In reality they know little and care less about the matter—mere foppery and pretence, sir."

But on the present day the racy flavour of Meg's old claret completed the conquest of Dr. Redgill's affections: and he resolved, if possible, to abide in this land flowing with milk and honey. Moving his nose over his glass, like a beau smelling a nosegay, "Sir," said he, "I pronounce this *wine*:—sir, common wines have taste—*this* has flavour." Amid the smacking of green seals and red seals, the cracking of nuts and of jokes, the Nabob withdrew to sound Mrs. Dods on the affair of Dr. Redgill's establishing himself in her house: and this he did in a manner which evinced considerable knowledge of the trim of his hostess.

"Sick! d'ye say, sir? he doesna look like it," said Meg. "Fond o' a quiet, clean, weel-ordered house. Is there no that at the grand new hottle he gaed to? Deeing! Deil a fears o' him—that I should ban! unless he smore in his creesh; whilk is not unlikely.—A swalled, judgment-like Jeshuran, wi' eyne like to loup with clean fat," cried Meg, who had taken deep offence, first, at the Doctor going to the hotel; second, at the freedom with which he, a guest there, had entered her territories.

"But here he *shall* come, Luckie," returned Touchwood, "ay this very night too. What, woman! would you turn the servant of the Lord—the stranger, from your gates?—An invalid too, that cannot get an hour of rest, nor a morsel he can swallow, poor gentleman, in their gilded-gingerbread pig-stye down yonder!"

"Say ye sae, say ye sae, Mr. Touchwood?" cried Meg, her features relaxing; "not a comfortable meltith o' meat, and him in a dwining way, ye say, Nabob?— though troth he does not look like it! But fat folk are often feckless. There was Mr. Matthew Stechy, St. Ronan's auld butler, that kept the first hottle in Glasgow —there is the cook, if ye speak of cooks! that is for a man-cook, whilk is but a non-natural calling—waxed fatter and fatter to a perfect mere-swine. Weel, he broke, sir—became dyvour—was rouped to the door; took the mill-craft down in the haugh, wrought for his daily morsel, and is now as swack and clean-deliver a man as enters the kirk o' St. Ronan's."

"It will do, by Jupiter and Comus!" exclaimed Touchwood, who had been absorved in a very unusual fit of musing. "The Cleikum Club—myself *President*,

—must keep order amongst them—Redgill, *Vice*; Winterblossom, an old coxcomb, but deep in the mystery; Jekyl, a conceited fop, but has his uses; Meg for the executive, with this Stechy—a practical man— nothing like practical men in business—Meg the paragon of economy and cleanliness.—It will do by the boar and the peacock!"

"And what will do, sir?" replied Meg. "The east chaumer, wi' the red Turk-upon-Turk bed. It can get a slaik o' paint, and the easy-chair brought frae Mr. Francie's room. Puir lad, little he sat in't. The bunker i' the window that looks down through the first to the Shaws Place, was aye his seat in the e'ening. I'll ne'er ha'e a lodger like him!"

"That's all past and gone, dame," cried Touchwood, impatiently: "other matters on hand, woman—but remember the rice-water to mix with your whitening, as I directed you in whitewashing the kitchen."

"As ready wi' your advice as your help," muttered Meg: "but I just took kirn-milk, as I used to do, and the same will serve this turn—but better fleech a fule than fecht him."

"Well, he enters to-night," said Touchwood; "Jerry Ostler must settle the bill, and bring over the baggage along with the Doctor's own man."

The defection of the great Dr. Redgill from the new hotel, after a trial of twenty-four hours, was the most signal triumph Meg had yet obtained over that establishment. But she disdained to crimp a customer; and as Mr. Cargill was at this instant passing out, happier than ever, after this symposium, to escape to his burrow, she called on him to witness the compact.

"He'll get the east chaumer" said Meg; "I cannot spare anither parlour,—breakfast his lane, and ye dine thegither. The Club,—the Cleikum Club, ye ca' it,—

and better a mess than making as much ready for ae
single gentleman as would serve six. I'll mak' ye a'
comfortable, never fear it. But,—and hear me now!
—it's no to be said, thought, or surmeesed, that by
harbouring and resetting a rampant follower o' the
Lethargy o' the Church of England, I'm to change my
kirk for the lucre o' trade and custom. Ye certify
that, Nawbob, on saul and conscience, or a dish is no
cookit for him in owre that door-stane."

"Keep yourself easy, Mrs. Margaret," said Touchwood; "the Doctor is a true son of the Church of
England, I dare say; but he admires your practice too
much to seek to shake your faith."

"Na, wha made me a judge and a divine!" replied
Meg, greatly mollified with the act of delivering her
testimony; "I'm no dooting but the Doctor has the
root o' the matter in him, Maister Cargill."

"Ay, that he has," cried Touchwood, "truffles and
morels, onions and carrots, I'll answer for him."

"That's enough," said Meg.

"Go, woman, scour your saucepans. Send for Stechy;
have the kitchen like a Dutch paradise to-morrow
morning; for then we take the field!"

By the time that Touchwood returned from his
negotiation in the kitchen, the good wine had done its
good office in the parlour. Not that there were any
symptoms of inebriation, either actual or remote; but
the prevailing mood was free, joyous, and, in short,
highly convivial. The Doctor told prosy college-stories
of college feasts, and gave Latin toasts; Winterblossom
related anecdotes of the bon-vivans of another genera-
tion, and hummed catches most vilely; and the young
man smoked his cigar and the whole party at once.

In this happy hour, on which favouring stars shed

prosperous influences, was the CLEIKUM or ST. RONAN'S CLUB instituted. To conclude the entertainment, the Nabob produced a single bottle of choice Burgundy, Mont Ratchet; and a special bumper was dedicated to the new-comer. Coffee, four years kept and only one hour roasted, was prepared by the Nabob's own hands—coffee which he had himself brought from Mocha—in a coffee-pot of Parisian invention patronised by Napoleon.

Mrs. Dods was afterwards courteously summoned to make tea: and the plan of the proposed club was submitted to her judgment. She startled a good deal at first; and was several times in danger of bolting off the course. But once fairly engaged, her zeal was unbounded; and long experience rendered her the most efficient member of the convocation.

An extended correspondence was arranged with known *amateur gourmands*, as well as practical cooks; and also with those clubs, both provincial and metropolitan, of which the eating, rather than the erudite preparation, of dishes, had hitherto been the leading business.

Meanwhile, as every thing requires time, while the kitchen stores and utensils were getting into order, the Nabob, aided by his friend, delivered what might almost be called a COURSE OF LECTURES on the science of cookery in all its branches. For these, though exceedingly valuable from the curious facts they contained, as well as for their philosophical speculations, Meg had not patience.

"Let us to the wark!" she cried; "what business ha'e thae lang ink-horn-tailed words wi' teaching wives and lasses to make COCK-A-LEEKIE, or FRIAR'S CHICKEN?"

"Ay, there it is," cried Touchwood, "the very term stamps truth on my theory."

"Ay, there's Friar's Chicken, and 'Friar's Fish-in-sauce, and Friar's Balsam, too, Nawbob," said Meg; "and my grand-dame, as ye say, was just as good a cook as mysel, and may be a wee thought better at the jeelies and paistries; and for a floating island, or a hedgehog, we could never pretend to any sic grandery at the Cleikum; mair especially in days when every farmer-chield gangs yanking by on his bluid-horse, and keeps his bred cook, with her ten pound a-year and her tea-money. A bonny breed there is o' them! Unless I get the jillets o' my ain up-bringing, I wadna trust them to scour a pot-lid, Mr. Touchwood."

"Meg shall deliver the lecture on breeding and training of female cooks," said the Nabob. "But a beginning must be made; and I have thrown together a few loose hints, which I submit to you, gentlemen. You know my object. It was the saying of a great prince, that he wished every one of his subjects 'had a pullet in the pot.' Why may not I, Peregrine Touchwood, do my best to instruct every fair fellow-subject of mine how to dress her pullet when she has got it? If a Dr. King, a Sir John Hill, a Dr. Hunter, a Sir John Sinclair, and a Count Rumford, have dedicated their time and talents to the service of their species, in this important line, why should plain Peregrine Touchwood disdain the task? No man cares less about what he himself eats than I do, gentlemen. A man who has shared horse-flesh with the Tartar, and banqueted on dog's-flesh with the China-man, is not likely to be dainty of his own gab."

Here the Nabob took from his pocket the introductory lecture, which had been privately retouched by

Winterblossom, as its garnish shewed, wiped his mouth with his ample Bandana, and proceeded:—

———

"Gentlemen,—Man is a cooking animal; and in whatever situation he is found, it may be assumed as an axiom that his progress in civilization has kept exact pace with the degree of refinement he may have attained in the science of gastronomy. From the hairy man of the woods, gentlemen, digging his roots with his claws, to the refined banquet of the Greek, or the sumptuous entertainment of the Roman; from the ferocious hunter, gnawing the half-broiled bloody collop, torn from the still-reeking carcass, to the modern *gourmand*, apportioning his ingredients, and blending his essences, the chain is complete! *First*, we have the brutalized *digger* of roots; then the *sly* entrapper of the finny tribes; and next the *fierce, foul feeder*, devouring his ensnared prey, fat, blood, and muscle!"

"What a style o' language!" whispered Mrs. Dods; —"but I maun look after the scouring o' the kettles."

"The next age of cookery, gentlemen, may be called the pastoral, as the last was that of the hunter. Here we have simple, mild broths, seasoned, perhaps, with herbs of the field, decoctions of pulse, barley-cake, and the kid seethed in milk. I pass over the ages of Rome and Greece, and confine myself to the Gothic and Celtic tribes, among whom gradually emerged what I shall call the chivalrous or feudal age of cookery,—the wild boar roasted whole, the stately crane, the lordly swan, the full-plumaged peacock, borne into the feudal hall by troops of vassals, to the flourish of trumpets, warlike instruments, marrow-bones and cleavers."

"Bravo!" cried Jekyl.

"Cookery as a domestic art, contributing to the comfort and luxury of private life, had made considerable progress in England before the Reformation; which event threw it back some centuries. We find the writers of those ages making large account of an art, from which common sense, in all countries, borrows its most striking illustrations and analogies."

"Only hear till him!" whispered Meg.

"The ambitious man 'seeks to rule the roast;'— The meddling person 'likes to have his finger in the pie;'—'Meat and mass hinder no business;'—The rash man 'gets into a stew,' and 'cooks himself a pretty mess;'—'A half-loaf is better than no bread;'—'There goes reason to the roasting of an egg;'—'Fools make feasts, and wise men eat them;'—'The churl invites a guest, and sticks him with the spit;'—'The belly is every man's master;'—'He who will not fight for his meat, what will he fight for?'—'A hungry man is an angry man;'—'It's ill talking between a full man and a fasting;'—and, finally, 'It is the main business of every man's life to make the pot boil;' or, as the Scots more emphatically have it, 'to make the pot play brown,' which a maigre pot never will do."

"And that's as true," said Meg. "A fat pat boiling, popples and glances on the tap, like as mony bonny brown lammer-beads."

"Hush, dame!—The science, as we noticed, gentlemen, had made considerable advances in England, when the Reformation not only arrested its progress, but threatened for ever to extinguish the culinary fire. Gastronomy, violently expelled from monasteries and colleges, found no fitting sanctuary either in the riotous household of the jolly cavalier, or in the gloomy abode of the lank, pinch-visaged round-head; the latter, as the poet has it, eager to

———Fall out with mince-meat, and disparage
His best and dearest friend, plum-porridge—

the former broaching his hogshead of October beer, and roasting a whole ox, in the exercise of a hospitality far more liberal than elegant.

"But, gentlemen, in our seats of learning, the genial spark was still secretly cherished. Oxford watched over the culinary flame with zeal proportioned to the importance of the trust. From this altar were re-kindled the culinary fires of Episcopal palaces, which had smouldered for a time; and Gastronomy once more raised her parsley-wreathed front in Britain, and daily gained an increase of devoted, if not yet enlightened worshippers."

"Ay, that will suffice for a general view of the subject," cried Dr. Redgill; "let us now get to the practical part of the science,—arrange the dinners,— 'the proof of the pudding is the eating.'"

Touchwood had a high disdain for what he called "the bigotry of the stew-pan" in Dr. Redgill, who, like a true churchman, had a strong leaning to "dishes as they are." Jekyl was to the full as flighty and specu-lative as the Doctor was dogmatic. The young man had French theory,— the *beau ideal* of gastrology float-ing in his brains. His experience in the most fashion-able clubs, and taverns, and bachelor-establishments about the metropolis, had been great; but it was fortunately modified by a course of peninsular practice, under Wellington; and, upon the whole, he was found a most efficient member of the club in all that regarded modern improvements, though rather intolerant of Scottish national dishes.

The culinary lectures of Touchwood, whose eloquence for six long weeks fulmined over the Cleikum kitchen, extended to such unreasonable compass, that a brief syllabus of the course is all we can give, without unduly swelling this Manual, and losing sight of the purpose for which it was intended; namely, a PRACTICAL SYSTEM of RATIONAL COOKERY and DOMESTIC ECONOMY.

SYLLABUS.

Lecture I. Importance of the science:—Its history.

II. ON COOKS.—The name clearly derived from Coquin.—Their self-conceit and prejudices.— Their ignorance.—May be propitiated by a printed Manual when they would disdain advice.—Sly peep into the Manual in the dresser-drawer.—Books of receipts most useful to those who have already made some practical progress in the art.

III. ON THE KITCHEN.—Of kitchens in general.— The Dutch kitchen.—The baronial kitchen, and the corridor communicating with the chambers, whence the lady surveyed the operations below.—The Vicar of Wakefield's kitchen.—Kitchen of a comfortable village inn.—The yeoman's hall-kitchen.—Dark kitchens of great cities.—Importance of light.—The construction and regulation of the fires.—Ovens.—Stoves.—Supply of soft water in kitchens.—Kitchen utensils.—Ought to be provided in proper quantity, as well as of suitable kinds.—Rather numerous than otherwise, to save the distraction and waste of time occasioned by a scanty supply.—A *digester, meat-screen, salting-trough, meat-safe, balnea maria,* &c. indispensable in families where comfort and economy are studied.—Speedily pay themselves by the saving of fuel, labour and provisions.—May be bought on the graduated scale suited to the size and circumstances of the family.—The price, to a young housekeeper, of one couch or looking-glass would obtain all those articles so subservient to domestic comfort and economy.

IV. CLEANLINESS.—Its importance insisted on.— Considered the *first virtue* of a plain cook.—But some difference of opinion among gourmands as to its relative importance.—Female cooks generally considered superior to those of the other sex in cleanliness.—1st, Cleanliness as applicable to all descriptions of culinary utensils.—All saucepans, gridirons, spits, skewers, &c. to be laid away clean, and kept well-tinned and free of rust.—Pickle-jars, casks, troughs, paste-pins, &c. to to be laid aside clean.—Great attention to be given to keep pudding-cloths, tapes, jelly-bags, tammy-cloths, sieves, &c. clean, sweet, and dry.—Kitchen-cloths to be washed *every day* after dinner. Wood-ashes recommended by French artists for this purpose, as soap gives a bad flavour to pudding-cloths, &c.—2d, Cleanliness as applicable to provisions about to be dressed.— Should all be duly washed, trimmed, and wiped.— Attention to be given to skimming, straining, withholding the sediment and lees.—Neatness in dishing without slopping the ledges of the dishes.—Anecdotes of the slovenliness of cooks.—Nobleman who, visiting his kitchen, found the butter required for the made-dishes stuck over the kitchen fire-place.—Mr. F—— of C——, on a similar occasion, finds his man-cook employing the contents of a shaving-jug, which he had just been using, to liquefy a dish of mince-collops!

V. EARLY TRAINING OF COOKS.—Receipts not sufficient to qualify for duty.—The cook, like the surgeon, must put to the hand.—Ought to be duly impressed with the importance of the art, and, above all, with her own individual responsibility.—Method: arrangement: forecast.—The days before a great dinner.—The day of a great dinner:—what to be done.—Soups, jellies, creams, and many made-dishes, to be prepared beforehand.— Vegetables cleaned, and in water: spices ready mixed: thickening prepared: poultry ready trussed: chops trimmed, &c.—Rules for seasoning.—Training of the palate of the cook—indurated by the use of spirituous liquors. —Gentlemen of forty-five and upwards, generally found to require a double allowance of Cayenne, eschalot, garlic, salt, and flavoured wines or vinegars, compared with those under that age, unless the juniors have been bred at Oxford.—Bachelors to be allowed a fourth more seasoning than married men:—the same proportions hold between a military gentleman and a civilian.— For West and East Indians, peppers and all stimulating condiments may be used *ad libitum*.

VI. ON FAMILY MANAGEMENT AND DOMESTIC ECONOMY IN GENERAL.—1*st*, Early rising, importance of.—Where impossible or inconvenient, best substitute an early and diligent inspection and regular enforcement of the orders given the night before, for the employment of the morning-hours.—2*d*, Marketing and laying in family-stores and articles that improve by keeping—as soap, sugar, starch, paper, spiceries, seeds, fruits, spring-made candles, &c.—All best preserved in cool, dry places.—No expense to be grudged that prevents insects and vermin from getting at the stores.— 3*d*, Choice of provisions.—The senses of sight and smell the best guides.—*Fish* of all sorts best when short and thick, well-made, bright in the scales, stiff and springy to the touch, the gills of a fresh red, the belly not flabby,—the eyes and fins to be looked at.— Meat speaks for itself.—The fat of *beef* to be white and pure; the lean, smooth-grained, and of a healthy crimson.—*Veal* should be fat, and white, and young:—the mode of feeding it of great importance.—The kidney to be examined, the state of which will show the feeding and condition of all animals.—*Ram-Mutton* discoverable by the rank flavour and coarse texture of the flesh.—*Mutton* not good under three years' old.—Best above five, but seldom to be got in the market of that age.—The black-faced or *short sheep* best for the table, though more depends on the pasture than on the breed.—*Lamb*.—The qualities of it may easily be known by the inspection of the head, neck, and the kidney; let the neck be fat, the eyes not sunk, the kidney fresh and fat, the quarters short and thick.—*Pork* to be chosen by the colour, and the thickness of the rind. Measly pork easily known by the little lumps and kernels mixed with the fat, which look clammy and greasy.—*All meat* known, if stale, by the eyes being sunk, the kidney tainted, the flesh clammy and livid.—*Venison*.—Thick and firm in the fat,—the lean pure. The age of deer, hares, and rabbits, known by the *clefts* and *claws* being close and smooth in the young animal. —*Game* and *Poultry*.—The age known by the legs and spur.—When smooth in the legs and short in the spur, the animal is young.—Trick of poulterers to cut and shorten the spur.—Stale when the eye is sunk, the vent tainted.—Black-legged fowls often the most juicy:—white-legged look better.—Attention to the breed and form.—The Dorking large breed recommended:—best when short, plump, broad in the breast, and thick in the rump.—Game, if stale, known by the livid colour of the flesh about the vent.—*Hams* and *Bacon* good when the flesh adheres firmly to the bone, the smell fresh, the lean clear and not streaked with yellow. —Very good hams from Westmoreland, Yorkshire, and other parts of England:—if well fed and cured, quite equal to those of Bayonne and West-phalia.—*Brawn*.—If old, the rind thick and hard.—*Salt Butter* and *Cheese* to be probed and tasted. Fresh butter easily known by the taste.—*Eggs* not easily known when stale.—Hold between the eye and a candle in a dark room, and if the yolk be unbroken the egg is not stale.—Rather a doubtful test this.—*Anchovies* and *Pickled Salmon* known by the smell, and fresh colour of the fish.—Their pickle-liquor should be pure and well-flavoured.—The red colour given to anchovy-liquor by artificial means, and no test of goodness. —The best joints of the best meat cost most money at first, but are the most economical.—Utility of purchasing these.—All provisions should be bought with ready money; or the bills settled weekly.—Shown to be a saving of 20 per cent.

VII.   MISCELLANEOUS HINTS AND DIRECTIONS.— Straining to be done twice if necessary, or with a double tammy-sieve.—All jelly-bags to be moistened in hot water, and well wrung:—if used dry, will drink up a considerable quantity of the article strained. —Sauces too much *thickened* can never afterwards be cleared of fat, as the fatty matter will not separate.— Sauces and broths must have time to cook; but if kept too long over the fire, will deteriorate both in colour and flavour.—This is peculiarly applicable to sauces of game. —All sorts of small cakes, pastry and puffs, short-bread, Savoy cake, &c., may be renovated by being laid on paper, and heated on the hob, or hot hearth, or before the fire when to be used.—Pastry kept for days is so much refreshed by this process as to eat nearly as well as when newly baked, from the full flavour of the sugar, butter, and fruit, being brought out.—Great care to be taken that *every* single egg used be fresh, as one stale egg will taint dozens.

VIII.   PRESERVING OF PROVISIONS BY SALTING,

DRYING, PICKLING, PRESERVING.—Importance of *sugar* in preserving meat, fish, and butter;—shown to do so most effectually with only a small proportion of salt. The *pyroligneous* acid, or vinegar of wood,—its uses.— Late discoveries in curing provisions in consequence of the premiums given by the Highland Society.—Meat salts the better of having the bones taken out.—Bacon should always be *twice* salted, and patiently rubbed both times.—All meat salted in pieces and packed must be fully covered with the brine. The process of salting accelerated by occasional rubbing with fresh salt. This important subject fully treated of in the MANUAL, *Art. Salting*.

IX. PREMIUMS TO COOKS FOR DILIGENT DISCHARGE OF THEIR DUTIES AND PROFICIENCY IN THE ART.— For neatness, economy, forecast, preservation of provisions, invention or improvement of cheap family-dishes.—Establishment for decayed cooks, and prospectus of a NATIONAL GASTRONOMICAL BOARD.

X. CAUSES THAT RETARD THE PROGRESS OF THE ART.—Ignorance and prejudices of Cooks.—Inattention of ladies.—Impudence and common tricks of quacks and would-be-gastronomers.

XI. ON FRENCH COOKERY.—The French, as a nation, allowed to be the best cooks in the world.—In what their superiority consists:—wherein worthy of imitation.—Their earthen stew-pans,—wood embers,—small furnaces,—their fire applied above and around as well as under their sauce-pans.—Their cookery of vegetables, and of dishes of *desserte*, that is of cold left things, peculiarly commendable.—Reference made to the MANUAL for the substance of French Cookery.

XII. STATE OF COOKERY IN MODERN EUROPE.— A French dinner described.—Restaurateurs of Paris.— A word to Amphytrions,—to guests.—Petty differences of usages in different countries.—What would be considered *bon ton* at a dinner in Paris, reckoned low breeding in London.—Unctuous dishes of Germany.—*Sour* sauce and currants:—*moist* caviare:—pig's-head and sweet preserves.—Mingled barbarism and refinement of Russian cookery,— Russian *whets* and salads:—the *kistischi* or raw vegetables in quass: *vareniky*:—*buterinia*, or salad of salt-fish.—Spain behind all the rest of Europe in cookery:—the *olla* or *puckero*:—the *guisado*.—Spaniards unshaken in their loyalty to garlic:—their taste for allspice traced to Christopher Columbus.

XIII. ANGLO-GALLICAN COOKERY OF THE NINETEENTH CENTURY:—considered the best the world has ever seen.—Causes which retard its progress:—conceit of French cooks, and affectation of juvenile gastronomers. —Reciprocal influence of cookery and literature on each other:—attention given by the periodical writers and novelists of the day to this important subject creditable to their understandings.—The empire of cookery extended by late travellers.—What the science owes to the Jesuits:—to the White Friars:—to the Trappists:—to Mesdames Maintenon and Pampadour.—Eulogy on Vatel.

DIRECTIONS FOR CARVING.

Carving has long been esteemed one of the minor arts of polite life,—a test at first sight of the breeding of men, as its dexterous and graceful performance is presumed to mark a person trained in good fashion. In the times of chivalry, carving was the duty of the younger squire. "To dance in hall and carve at board" are classed together, by no mean authority, in the list of a young gentleman's accomplishments; and Chesterfield, the great modern teacher of polished life, has made this qualification an object of his pupil's peculiar study. Carving, like heraldry, hunting, hawking, and other sciences of a like important kind, had a language of its own. Treatises were composed to show how the heron was to be *dismembered*, the duck *unbraced*, the crane *displayed*, the swan *lifted*, the goose *reared*, and so forth. The GRAND CARVER was a functionary of some dignity in former times; and till the office is revived, or the oriental, and partly continental, custom, of having the principal part of the carving performed by the cook, is adopted, it is necessary to acquire a knowledge of this art on principles of economy, as well as from respect to good manners.

To carve quickly and neatly requires a good deal of practice, as well as vigilant observation of those who perform the office well. There are awkward grown-up persons, having, as the French say, *two left hands*, whom no labour will ever make dexterous carvers; yet there is no difficulty in this humble but useful art, which young persons, if early initiated under the eye of their friends, might not easily surmount, and thus save themselves much awkward embarrassment in future life. One objection to allowing juvenile practice is, that young people *haggle* provisions; but they might be permitted sometimes to try plain joints and cold things, which would soon bring in their hands. A lady in carving requires an elevated seat, a light sharp knife, and the dish placed near her.

Though no directions can supply the place of practice, it may be useful to tell the young carver how to use his tools, and what is expected from him. What are esteemed the most choice morsels of every dish ought to be known; for "to deal small and serve all" must be the carver's maxim. Venison fat,—the Pope's eye in a leg of mutton,—veal and lamb kidney,—the firm gelatinous parts of a cod's head,—the thin part of salmon,—the thick of turbot and other flat fish, are reckoned the prime bits.—The ribs, neck, and pettitoes of a pig,—the breast and wings of fowls,—the legs and rump of hare and rabbit,—the breast, and thighs of turkey and goose, cutting off the drumsticks,—the wings and breast of pheasants, partridges, and moor-game, and the legs and breast of duck, are also reckoned delicacies. There are, besides, favourite bits highly prized by some gourmands, though it is sometimes not easy to discover in what their superior excellence consists; as dry shank of mutton,—turbot fins,—cod's tongue,—the bitter back of moor-game,—the back of hare,—the head of carp:— in stew-soups, meat, and forcemeat balls are prized. A knowledge of these things will be of use to the carver as a guide in that equitable distribution of good things, which is the most pleasing part of his duty.

It is well known, that a person of any refinement will eat much more when his food is served in handsome slices, and not too much at once, than when a pound clumsily cut is laid upon his plate. To cut warm joints fairly and smoothly, neither in slices too thick, nor in such as are finically thin, is all that is required of the carver of a plain joint, whether boiled or roasted.* For this purpose he must be provided with a knife of suitable size, having a good edge; and it will greatly facilitate his operations if the cook has previously taken care that the bones in all carcass-joints are properly divided. It is impossible for the most dexterous carver to proceed with ease or comfort if this be neglected. In carving game or poultry for a large party, where many look for a share of the same delicacy, what is called "making wings" must be avoided; the first helpings should be cut the long way, and not made too large.

Turbot.—The thick part is the best: the *fins* are *fancied*. Make a cross-cut in the thickest part down to the bone, then make lines from the centre to the fins, and

---

*The modern little instrument called "An instantaneous knife-sharper" is worthy of the carver's attention.

take out slices with a fish-knife, helping part of the *fins* with each slice, along with the appropriate sauce.

Salmon is easily carved, whether crimped or boiled whole. At elegant tables, this fish is usually served on a napkin; a slice of the thick, cut so as to preserve the beauty of the flakes, and a smaller one of the thin, with the appropriate sauces; and a slice of lemon or cucumber is to be helped, if not objected to.

Fried fish.—The thick part is reckoned the best. The fish are to be cut quite through, which is commonly previously done by the cook for her own convenience. The choice is—"Shoulders or tail?" *Iron* should never touch fish at table.

Sirloin of beef.—This favourite joint is all prime. The carver may begin at either end, or in the middle, first cutting along by the bone. This, however, is neither the most economical nor sightly method. If the meat is to be presented again cold, this deep trench— this "forty mortal gashes on its side"—looks very ill, while it drains the joint of its juices. Many like the browned outside slice though dry; but, if not chosen, it is to be laid aside, and, cutting down to the bone, a handsome slice is to be served with part of the soft fat delicately cut, gravy, and horseradish. The inside, or *English side*, may be preferred by some guests; the joint must, in that case, be turned over, and slices cut from thence.

Edge-bone, or H bone of beef, the Scottish Heuck-bane.—In this, and all pieces of boiled meat, the outside, which becomes dry and hard in the salting and boiling, is to be laid aside or sent away. This done, cut handsome, smooth slices of the lean, and with each give a very little of the marrowy and firm fat, for which this piece of meat is prized.

Rump of beef is carved as the above, but horizontally, preserving a smooth, finely-grained surface.

A Brisket of beef is cut down to the bone the long way in rather thin slices, as the piece is fatty and gristly; and all fat meat must be cut delicately thin.

Breast of veal or lamb.—Divide the gristly part from the ribs,—then divide both the cross way. The choice is "Gristles or ribs?"

Fillet of veal.—This is usually, and always ought to

be, stuffed in the flap. Cut it in delicate, horizontal slices; and help either browned outside or inside, as is chosen, with a little of the fat, and a thin slice of the stuffing, some gravy, &c.

Gigot.—This delicate joint is familiar where veal is small. It is either cut in horizontal slices, or as a leg of mutton, but beginning nearer the broad end. *Shoulder* and *loin* of veal are cut as mutton. The kidney fat of the loin is prized, and sometimes sliced at table and kept hot over a lamp.

Saddle of mutton.—Cut thin slices lengthways, dividing them if too long, and helping fat and lean together. Some persons think that, besides being a more economical way of carving, the meat is more delicately-grained, and eats better, if a deep incision is made along the bone, and slices be taken crossways from thence.

Roasted pig.—We could wish that the practice of having this dish carved by the cook were universal; for, in this fastidious age, the sanguinary spectacle of an entire four-footed animal at table is any thing but acceptable. Like the larger poultry, pig is also very troublesome to the carver, who must have a sharp knife, with which the head is to be taken off in the first place: then cut down the back from neck to rump; afterwards remove the shoulder and leg on each side. The ribs are then to be divided into four portions, and the legs and shoulders cut in two. The ribs are, or rather were, esteemed the most delicate part of this dish; now the neck of a well-roasted pig is the favourite morsel. The carver must use his discretion in distributing ear and jaw, as far as these will go; and the cook should enable him to help stuffing and sauce more liberally.

Turkey.—Where the party is not very large, and the dishes are numerous, a good many small delicate slices, with very thin portions of the stuffing, may be helped lengthways from the breast. If this is not sufficient, proceed as directed for a goose, page 48.

Hams are cut in three ways. You may begin at the hock, which is the most economical method; in the middle; or at the broad end. The chief thing to be attended to after an incision is made, is the delicacy of the slices.

Tongue.—The best part is the thick, and the meat is

most delicate when cut across in very thin slices, leaving a
bottom or *sole* for the sake of appearance. It is reckoned
more economical to cut it in thin slices the long way.
Tongue and ham cannot, when cold, be too delicately cut.

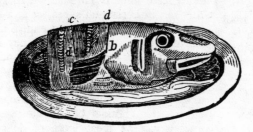

Cod's head and shoulders, if served without a sauce
in the dish, should be served on a napkin over the fish
plate. If sufficiently boiled it is very easily carved.—
Let the back of the fish be placed towards the carver.
Enter the silver fish-carver at *a*, and cut down to the
bone in the direction *a, b, c, d*, and help from this opening right and left at convenience, taking care not to
make a jagged surface by breaking the flakes. The
gelatinous pieces about the neck and head are prized, and
must be helped if asked for; also small slices of the
sound. The palate and tongue may be got at with a
spoon, if it be wished; but these are rather the fantastic
than prime parts. Some cut the fish longways; but
the above is perhaps the fairer mode.

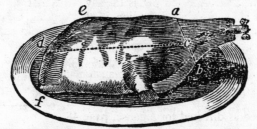

Haunch of venison.—Make an incision quite down to
the bone, in the direction of the line *a b*, to let the gravy
flow. Let the carver then turn the dish towards himself,
and cut down to the bone from *c* to *d*, thus forming, as
it were, the Roman letter T. The most delicate slices
lie to the left of the line *c d*, supposing the joint to lie

endways to the carver, and the broad end of the haunch, *e d f*, next him. From the incision, slices, not too thick, may be cut, which, if too long, can be divided. A thinner and smaller slice of fat must be given with each helping, and also gravy. As the fat of venison freezes very rapidly, the more expeditiously the carver gets though his task the better; or a dish with a spirit-lamp is sometimes brought to the table to keep the gravy and fat, &c. quite hot. Sometimes the cook makes a *chart* of cloves, &c. as a road-post to the carver.

Haunch of mutton is carved exactly as venison.

A boiled gigot or leg of mutton.—A boiled *gigot* or leg is served as represented in the plate; a roast leg is served with the other side uppermost, though they are carved nearly in the same manner: and indeed, whether boiled or roasted, the leg is often served with the same side uppermost. The most juicy part of this favourite joint is about the thick of the thigh. Let the shank lie to the carver's left hand, and let him cut down to the bone, through the *noix* or kernel, called the Pope's eye, in the direction *a b*. Though the most juicy part of the leg is here, some choose the dry knuckle; and others the fatty part about the chump; or small slices that may be found along the back-bone; even the tail of fat mutton is chosen by some. Some modern carvers give horizontal slices, and prefer this mode of cutting.

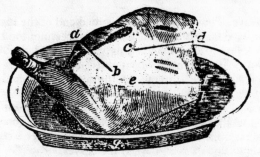

Shoulder of mutton.—This joint is served with the outside uppermost. Cut into the deepest part down to the bone in a slanting line from *a* to *b*; and from this opening take slices of a proper thickness. If more helpings are wanted, some delicate slices may be cut out on each side of the ridge of the blade-bone, in the direction *c d* and *e f*. The most delicate slices are to be found in that part which, in the living animal, lay next to the back-bone; they are to be cut out in rather thin slices, in the direction of the line *g h*. In almost all animals delicate fatty slices are to be found along the back-bone. Good fleshy slices, full of juice, though not very delicate in the fibre, are to be got by turning the shoulder over, and cutting slantwise into the hollow part of the inside. So various are tastes, that some persons prefer the knuckle, though the driest and coarsest part of the animal. Some modern, *straight-forward* carvers prefer cutting slices at once right down from the knuckle to the broad end.

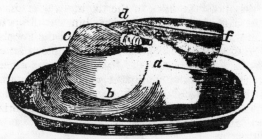

Fore-quarter of lamb.—Separate the shoulder from the ribs, by passing a carving-knife, held nearly horizontally, in the direction *a b c d*. Take care not to make too broad a shoulder-flap, and thus leave the ribs too bare. Some carvers merely make a slight incision into the skin, and tear off the shoulder flap. The shank, which should be twisted in paper, may be held by the carver if it is found convenient. Squeeze a little juice of lemon or Seville orange over the parts separated, and sprinkle them with a little salt. They may also be laid together, and gently pressed down, to make the juice flow; or have a little butter laid between if deficient in juice. Next separate the gristles of the breast from the ribs, in the direction $d\ f$; and the choice is—"ribs, gristle, or shoulder?" though the ribs are esteemed the most delicate part. The shoulder is to be carved as directed for shoulder of mutton; and if the joint is large, it will be found convenient to put the shoulder aside on a plate.

A Goose.—The carver must cut thin nice slices in the lines $a\ b$, down to the breast-bone, helping round as he carves. If there be stuffing, the apron must be cut open in the circular line $f\ l\ g$, and stuffing may be served with each helping. If there be no stuffing, a glass of wine, a little orange-gravy, or vinegar, is poured into the body of the goose at the opening, which the carver, for this purpose, makes in the apron. Orange-gravy or red wine is also often poured over the sliced breast of goose or duck, before the slices are taken out. If the party be so numerous that the breast-slices are not sufficient, the carver must proceed to take off the right leg, for which purpose he must put his fork through the small end, press it close to the body, and, meanwhile, entering his knife at d, jerk the leg smartly back, and the joint will separate, when the leg may easily be cut off in the direction $d\ e$. The wing on the same side is next to be taken off. For this purpose, fix the fork in the pinion, press it to the body, and, entering the knife at c, separate the joint, and afterwards cut off the wing in the direction *c d*. Proceed in the same way to take off the other leg and wing. In helping a goose, the thigh, which is a favourite part, may be separated from the drumstick, and the fleshy part of the wing from the pinion. Fortunately for the carver, the breast-slices are in general found sufficient; as dismembering an old goose or turkey is one of the most laborious and awkward of his duties. They order these things better on the continent.

A Fowl, with the members on one side cut off.— This dish is managed in the same way, whether boiled or roasted. In a boiled fowl, the legs are bent inwards, trussed within the apron, and skewered so till served; in a roasted fowl they are left out and skewered *en long*. The carver may remove the fowl from the dish to his own plate, particularly when there are two (as is usual) served in the same dish. The members and joints, as taken off, are to be placed in the dish, if not helped round as cut off, which is the best way, as the guests are not kept waiting, and the carver sees when he has enough cut. The carver must fix his fork in the breast, and take off slices from the breast on each side of the merry-thought, which are to be helped in the first place, or left till the whole is finished, as is chosen. Next separate the joint of the wing in the direction *a b*; then separate the muscles, by fixing the fork in the pinion, and smartly jerking back the wing towards the leg. Pass the knife between the body and leg, in the direction *b d*, and cut to the joint clear; then, with the fork fixed, jerk the leg back, and the parts will give way. Turn over the fowl on your plate, and take off the other leg and wing; next the merry-thought, in the circular line *f g*. Take off the neck-bone, by putting in the knife at *g; and having*

the fork well fixed, jerk it off from the part which adheres to the breast-bone. The members being thus disposed of, the breast must be divided from the body by cutting right through the ribs down to the rump on each side. This done, turn the back of the fowl upwards on your plate. Lay your knife firmly across it, as if to hold it down, and, with the fork fixed in the rump, give it a jerk, when it will easily divide across; turn the rump from you, and cut off the side-bones, and the fowl is carved. What demands most attention, is to hit the joint of the wing, so as not to interfere with the neck-bone. The prime parts of a fowl, whether boiled or roasted, are the breast, merry-thought, wings, particularly a *livered* wing, and side-bones. The thigh of a boiled fowl is often preferred, if white, fleshy, and fat. Some dexterous carvers can take out a side-bone and leave on the leg and wing, which permits the fowl to be presented cold in good form.*

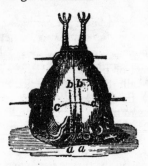

A Pheasant.—Fix the fork in the breast, and cut slices in the lines *a b*. If more helpings are wanted, take off the legs and wings, as directed in carving a fowl, and be careful in taking off the wing to hit the exact point between it and the neck-bone. Next cut off the merry-thought in the line *c d*, and then divide the other parts exactly as a fowl. The prime bits are the same as in a fowl. The brains are *fancied*.

---

* It is an object of economy in carving game and poultry, which are often very high-priced, to cut off no more parts than are required by the guests present.

Pigeons.—To cut them from top to bottom in the line *e d* is the fairest way, as the thigh is esteemed the best part, though some prefer the breast. They may also be divided in the triangular line *b a c*. Ducklings, or very young spring chickens, are carved in the same manner.

A Partridge as trussed for the table.—A partridge is cut up as a fowl or pheasant. The prime parts are the same in them all; but in a partridge the wing, and particularly the tip of the wing, is the most dainty. It is almost needless to mention, that though the *plates* shew the skewers, they must all be withdrawn before any dish is served.

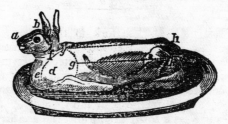

A Hare.—While a hare continues to be sent to table as represented in the plate, the carver must enter his knife at *g*, if the animal be young, and cut fairly along the back-bone to *h*. Then enter his knife on the other side of the back, at an equal distance from it, and cut in a parallel line. The legs will easily be got off, and the shoulders in the circular line *e f g*. Divide the hare into three, or, if a large hare, four pieces, going right through the spine at the joints. The leg, which is too large for one helping, may be divided. The pieces may either be helped as cut off, or laid neatly in the dish till the carving is completed; when they are to be helped round, with stuffing and gravy, to each person. If the hare be old, the carver will succeed better by turning the dish towards himself, and cutting off the legs, entering the knife about two inches below the back-bone, and trying to hit the joint (without which his task will not be easy), and jerking the joint open, as in carving a goose. A few nice slices will be got above the place at which he enters the knife, lying along the back-bone. The back may next be divided into three or four parts, and the fore-limbs cut off. To divide the head, cut it off, place it on a clean plate, and cut the upper from the under jaw. Next cut it down exactly through the middle. The ears and brains are *fancied*. Some care must be taken by papering and basting the ears to have them crisp. Before roasting, they should be singed inside with a hot poker.

Rabbits are carved like *hare*; only, being much smaller, the head is not divided, and the back is only cut in two pieces.

N.B. Every elegant carver will try to cover the unsightly gashes he must make—in fish particularly—by throwing the garnishing over the wreck, or even a fold of the napkin on which the fish is served. Though the remark is somewhat out of place, we must here notice that, in ordinary circumstances, *garnishing* the *ledges* of dishes is rather losing ground. At highly-dressed dinners, garnished by thorough-bred professors, all sorts of ornament are expected. For public breakfasts, collations, and suppers, *garnishings* of coloured jellies, and of sauces iced and moulded in the French style, have peculiar beauty and fitness. And even at small quiet dinners, brain-cakes, forcemeat-balls, small fried fish, or oysters fried, sippets, small sausages, pastry-borders, and those of potato, or rice, are always appropriate when served with the respective dishes to which the best usuages of cookery have attached them; while the fried parsley, the spinage, sorrel, turnip, or other *purees*, on which *fricandeaux*, tongue, or boiled mutton, &c. may be served, is a positive improvement, at almost no additional expense. But as it must ever be more convenient, it is also more agreeable, to see such things as sliced orange or lemon, beet, pickles, scraped horseradish, &c., placed on a small dish near the carver, than tossed awry, soused in the gravy, or sloping the edges of the assets. In this, as in every branch of the art, good taste and discretion must mutually aid each other. There is one cheap and *comfortable* mode of imparting a look of fulness, finish, and neatness, in serving an otherwise insignificant dressed dish, when destined to occupy a principal place, which

OF BILLS OF FARE.

Tables should be like pictures to the sight,
Some dishes cast in shade, some spread in light;
Some should be moved when broken, others last
Through the whole treat, incentive to the taste.
King's Cookery.

As landmarks to the inexperienced housekeeper, we subjoin a few bills of fare, observing, at the same time, that these must, in every instance, be left to individual taste and discretion. Bills of fare may be varied in endless ways,—nor can any specific rules be given for selecting dishes for the table, which must depend wholly on fortune, fashion, the season of the year, local situation, and a variety of circumstances. Neatness and propriety alone are of universal obligation in the regulation of every table, from the humblest to the most splendid. To the credit of the age, it may be remarked, that modern fashion inclines more to a few dishes, well selected and elegantly disposed, than to that heterogeneous accumulation of good things with which notable British housewives used to conceal their table-linen. The culinary tastes of our polite neighbours are imperceptibly undermining some points of our ancient national faith. At genteel tables, fat puddings, very rich cakes, and fat meat-pies, have lost ground. Creams, jellies, and preserved and caramelled fruits or *compôtes*, take their place. Fish is more simply cooked than it formerly was. Putrid game is no longer admired; and the native flavour of all viands is more sedulously preserved by a better style of cookery.

---

merits more general adoption,—namely, serving the dish on a larger one, round which a damask napkin is neatly puffed, thus shewing an agreeable frame-work or border, of which a light paste, bordering round the dish with the viands, may form, as it were, the inner circle. In this manner a turtle course is sometimes served, where the shell is used as a dish.

We hope to see the day when all large troublesome dishes will be taken to the side-table, and carved by the *maître d'hotel*, or whoever waits on the company, as is now the general practice of France, Germany, and Russia. P. T. H. J.

The manner of laying out a fashionable table is nearly the same in all quarters of the united kingdoms; yet there are trifling local peculiarities to which the prudent housewife in middle life must attend. A centre-ornament, whether it be a *dormant*, a *plateau*, an *epergne*, a *candelabra*, or a wine-vase, is found so convenient, and contributes so much to the good appearance of the table, that a fashionable dinner is now seldom or never set out without something of this kind.

It may be assumed, that *utility* is the true principle of beauty, at least in affairs of the table, and, above all, in the substantial *first course*. A very false or defective taste is, however, often shown in centre-ornaments. Strange ill-assorted nosegays, and monstrous bouquets of artificial flowers, begin to droop or look faded among those hot steams, which soon deprive even the more appropriate salad of its fresh and crispy appearance. Ornamental articles of family-plate, carved, chased, or merely plain, but highly-polished, can never be out of place, however old-fashioned, and are the only things of which this can be constantly affirmed. In the same manner we may assume, that in desserts, richly-cut and brightly-washed useful articles of glass can never cease to be ornamental; though we would pause on the adoption of all alum or wax baskets, and all fruits of this last tantalizing substance, with many other things of the counterfeit kind. We are far, however, from proscribing the foliage and moss in which fruits are sometimes seen lightly bedded. These, next to the native dew, and the bloom, are beautiful and appropriate. That sparkling imitation of frost-work, which is given to preserved fruits and other things, is also exceedingly beautiful; as are many of the trifles belonging to French and Italian confectionary. As we are disposed to give the Monks full credit for many of the best French dishes, and for our own antiquated preparations, so are the fair recluses of France and Italy entitled to the merit of much that is elegant in confectionary, of which they long had, and still have, tasteful exhibitions on festivals. To their leisure and taste we owe caramelled and candied fruits, fruits *en chemise*, Chantilly, and caramel baskets, &c. &c. as well as the most delicate lace, needle-work, and cut paper.

Linen well done up, and more cloths than one, with a scarlet baize between, give a table a *clad*, comfortable look.

In all ranks, and in every family, one important art in housekeeping is to make what remains over from one day's entertainment contribute to the elegance or plenty of the next day's repasts. This is a principle understood by persons in the very highest ranks of society, who maintain the most splendid and expensive establishments. Their great town-dinners usually follow in rapid succession; one banquet forming, if not the basis, a useful auxiliary to the next entertainment. But as this has been elsewhere recommended to the attention of the reader, it is almost unnecessary to repeat here, that vegetables, ragouts, and soups, may be *re-warmed*; and jellies and blancmange *remoulded*, with no deterioration of their qualities. Savoury or sweet patties, potted meats, croquets, rissoles, *vol-au-vents*, fritters, tartlets, &c., may be served with almost no cost, where cookery is going forward on a large scale. In the French kitchen, a numerous class of culinary preparations, called *entrées de desserte*, or made-dishes of left things, are served even at grand entertainments.

At dinners of any pretension, it is understood that the first course shall consist of soups and fish, removed by boiled poultry, ham, or tongue, roasts, stews, &c.; and of vegetables, with a few made-dishes, as ragouts, curries, hashes, cutlets, patties, fricandeaus, &c., in as great variety as the number of dishes permits; as a white and a brown, or a clear and a stew-soup. For the second course, roasted poultry or game at the top and bottom, with dressed vegetables, omelets, macaroni, jellies, creams, salads, preserved fruit, and all sorts of sweet things and pastry, are employed,—endeavouring to give an article of each sort, as a jelly and a cream, as will be exemplified in the bills of fare subjoined. This is a more common arrangement than three courses, which are attended with so much additional trouble both to the guests and servants.

But whether the dinner be of two or three courses, it is managed nearly in the same way; and for the advantage of servants, as well as of their juvenile employers, a few particulars may be detailed. In the centre, there is generally some ornamental article, as an epergne with flowers, real or artificial, or with a decorated salad. An ornament, containing essences, is equally appropriate. Two dishes of fish dressed in different ways, (if suitable) should occupy the top and bottom; and two soups, a white and a brown, or a mild and a high-seasoned, are best disposed on each side of the centre-piece: the fish-sauces are placed between the centre-piece and the dish of fish to which each is appropriate; and this, with the decanted wines drank during dinner, forms the first course. When there are rare French or Rhenish wines, they are placed in the original bottles, (uncorked,)* in ornamented wine-vases, between the centre-piece and the top and bottom dishes; or if four kinds, they are ranged round the plateau. If one bottle, it is placed in a vase in the centre.

The Second Course, when there are three, consists of roasts and stews for the top and bottom; turkey or fowls, or fricandeau, or ham garnished, or tongue, for the sides; with small made-dishes for the corners, served in covered dishes; as palates, stewed giblets, currie of any kind, *ragoût* or *fricassee* of rabbits, stewed mush-rooms, &c. &c. Two sauce-tureens, or glasses with pickles, or very small made-dishes, may be placed between the *epergne* and the top and bottom dishes; vegetables on the side-table are handed round. If the epergne is taken away with this course, then a small tablecloth or overlay, which is often placed across, to keep the cloth neat for the third course, is also removed.

The Third Course consists of game, confectionary, the more delicate vegetables dressed in the French way, puddings, creams, jellies,&c.

Water-bottles, with rummers, are placed at proper intervals. Malt liquors and other common beverages are called for; but where hock, champagne, &c. &c. are served, they are handed round between the courses. When the third course is cleared away, cheese, butter, a fresh salad, or sliced cucumber, are usually served; and the finger glasses, where these disagreeable things

---

* If not found troublesome, it is well the corks be left in the bottles—at least they must be returned loosely. A genuine *gourmet* detests previous uncorking and decanting.—H. J.

continue to be openly used, precede the dessert. At many tables, however, of the first fashion, it is customary merely to hand quickly round a glass vessel or two filled with simple, or simply perfumed tepid water, made by the addition of a little rose or lavender water, or a home-made strained infusion of rose leaves or lavender spikes. Into this water each guest may dip the corner of his napkin, and with this (only when needful) refresh his lips and the tips of his fingers. Polite foreigners cannot reconcile the use of finger-glasses with the boasted excessive delicacy of the domestic and personal habits of the English;* yet the custom is now partially adopted even on the continent; whence again some of our young fashionables and veteran men of travel, have caught the filthy practice of eating with their fingers; not merely salads and cheese, but oysters, devils, macaroni, &c. in this disgusting trick far exceeding their French and Italian masters; what in foreigners is an unpleasant habit, being in their imitators bad taste, if not deliberate ill-breeding and effrontery.

The Dessert may consist merely of two dishes of fine fruit for the top and bottom; common or dried fruits, filberts, &c. for the corners or sides, and a cake for the middle, with ice-pails in hot weather. Liqueurs are at this stage handed round; and the wines usually drank after dinner are placed decanted on the table along with the dessert. The ice-pails and plates are removed as soon as the company finish their ice. Where there is *preserved ginger,* it follows the *ices*; being then eaten to heighten to the palate the delicious coolness of the dessert wines. This may all be better understood by noting the following exact arrangement of what is considered a fashionable, though not very sumptuous, dinner of three courses and a dessert.

---

* During the old *regime* the French moved from table to the anti-room to refresh their lips and fingers immediately after the substantial part of their repast. Madame the Comtesse de Genlis appears to consider the abandonment of this practice, and the introduction of finger-glasses, as one of the most flagrant innovations of *parvenu* manners.

A Fashionable Dinner of Three Courses, with Cheese-Course and Dessert.

FIRST COURSE. ★

Turbot boiled.

Lobster sauce.

Wine vase.

Wine. *Wine.*

Wine. *Soupe a la Reine.* *Epergne.* *Soupe Brunoise.* Wine.

Wine vase.

Wine. *Wine.*

Fish sauce.

Soles fried.

SECOND COURSE.

Turkey roast with truffles.

Sweetbreads   Stewed mushrooms.   Currie in rice border

Wine vase.

Wine. *Wine.*

Wine   *Chicken boiled.*   *Epergne.*   *Ham decorated*   Wine

Wine. *Wine.*

Wine vase.

Cutlets   Venison sauce   Patties

Haunch of venison or mutton

★The table may receive a fuller appearance from greater variety of fish sauces, if wished for.

THIRD COURSE.

Roast pigeons.

Jelly.　　　　Sauce tureen.　　　　Small pastry.

Macaroni pudding.

French salad.　Wine vase.　Dressed lobster.

Trifle ornamented.

Wine vase.

Cranberry tart.

Tartlets.　　　Sauce tureen.　　　Italian cream.

Grouse roasted.

Directions for placing the cheese, &c. after dinner.†

British Parmesan or Stilton.

Butter,

In forms, slices, or

pats.

Shred cucumber.　　　　　　　　　　Salad.

Parmesan rasped, and

in covered glass-dish.

(*Next come the finger-glasses*)

------

* In the above Course the jelly and the cream may be placed at the sides. The salad, and a dish of prawns at opposite corners.—or asparagus, pease, or any other nice appropriate vegetable dishes at the other corners. There is no end to the way in which tables may be varied.

† See another way of setting out a cheese-course, page 63; or there may be two small dishes with butter on each side, and a silver bread-basket in the centre, in which rusks or cheese-biscuits are served on a napkin, which it is ever agreeable to see under bread.

THE DESSERT.

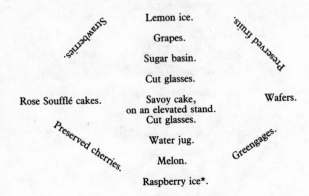

Lemon ice.

Grapes.

Sugar basin.

Cut glasses.

Rose Soufflé cakes.   Savoy cake,
on an elevated stand.   Wafers.
Cut glasses.

Water jug.

Melon.

Raspberry ice*.

Strawberries.   Preserved fruits.

Preserved cherries.   Greengages.

BILLS OF FARE

FOR PLAIN FAMILY DINNERS.

DINNERS OF FIVE DISHES.

Pease soup.

Potatoes browned
below the roast.   Apple dumplings,
or plain fritters.   Mashed turnip
or *pickles*.

Roast shoulder of mutton.

Haddocks baked, *in a potato border*.

Potatoes.   Newmarket pudding.   Rice or pickles.

Haricot, Currie hash, or Grill,

Of the mutton of the former day.

---

* Ice is also handed round, or served, before the dessert. This dessert
may be made more full by a few dishes of wafers, brandy-scrolls, or dried
small fruit.

Knuckle of veal ragout,
or with rice.

Parsnips.   A Charlotte.   Potatoes.

Roast of pork or pork chops.
— *Sage sauce.*

Boiled cod, with oyster sauce.

Potatoes.   Barley broth.   Carrots or turnips.

Scrag of mutton,

with caper sauce, or parsley and butter.

Cod currie, or a fish pie, of the fish of the former day.

Scalloped oysters.   Rice-pudding.   Mashed potatoes.

Roast ribs of beef.

Bouilli, *garnished with onions.*

Marrow-bones.   Soup *of the Bouilli.*   Beef Cecils, of the
roast ribs of the
former day.

Lamb chops, with potatoes.

Vegetables on the side-table.

Potage à la Clermont.

(*Remove*—Fish in brown sauce.)

Stewed celery.   Fruit pie.   Spinage.

Fillet of veal stuffed.

Boiled fowl, or Fricandeau of veal on sorrel.

Currie of veal   New England pancakes.   Pease pudding
in rice casserole.   or greens.

Pickled pork or salted beef.

Crimped cod,

Shrimp sauce.

Pigeon ragout.   Soup.   Carrots or turnips.

Small round of beef with greens,
or breast of beef *à la Flamande.*

Skate, *with caper sauce.*

<table>
<tr><td>Cauliflower,
in sauce blanche.</td><td>Hotch-potch.</td><td>Potatoes.</td></tr>
</table>

Loin of veal roasted.*

Good family-dinners of seven dishes.†

Crimped salmon,
Lobster sauce.

<table>
<tr><td>Mashed potatoes,
in small shapes.</td><td></td><td>Mince pies or rissoles.</td></tr>
</table>

Winter hotch-potch.

(*Remove—apple-pie.*)

<table>
<tr><td>Oxford dumplings.</td><td></td><td>Bubble and squeak
of veal.</td></tr>
</table>

Pickles.

Roast of beef.

Irish stew, or Haricot of mutton.

<table>
<tr><td>Chickens.</td><td></td><td>Mashed potatoes.</td></tr>
</table>

Fritters.

<table>
<tr><td>Apple-sauce.</td><td></td><td>Tongue on spinage,
or a piece of ham.</td></tr>
</table>

Stubble goose.‡

Fried soles.

<table>
<tr><td>Savoury patties.</td><td>Onion-soup.</td><td>Salad.</td></tr>
</table>

(*Remove*—A Charlotte.)

<table>
<tr><td>Macaroni.</td><td>Sliced cucumber.</td><td>Veal sweetbreads.</td></tr>
</table>

Saddle of mutton roasted.

---

* A loin of veal, which is a very common remove of fish or soup, is often sent from the table nearly or wholly untouched; in which case it may be re-warmed in the Dutch oven, or dressed in various ways, as a *ragout, blanquettes,* &c.

† Dinners may be served in two courses where there are so many good dishes; and where there is a high-bred cook, many of the things may be served *en crustades, en timballes,* or as *vol-au-vents.*

‡ The cook must not forget fried or glazed onions, on the sideboard, notwithstanding the apple-sauce for the goose.—REDGILL.

Scotch fish and sauce.

(*Remove*— Cutlets à Chingara.)

Scalloped potatoes.   Apple-puffs.

Marrow-pudding.

Tartlets or sweet patties.   Mashed turnip or green pease.

Gigiot of mutton boiled, with caper sauce.

(*Remove*—Roast ducks.)

A small dinner in courses, with dessert, &c.

FIRST COURSE.

Mock turtle-soup.

Turbot.

Oyster, lobster, or fennel sauce, and cucumber sliced thick, disposed
either on the table or sideboard; and the fish and soup, with
the sauces, and wines, form the whole of the course.

SECOND COURSE.

Pheasant.

Ducklings and pease.   Calves' brains.

Haunch of mountain mutton

THIRD COURSE

Macaroni

Apricot tart.   Cream.   Jelly.

Omelet Soufflé.

CHEESE-COURSE.

Butter in ice,   Silver bread basket.   Small cheese-biscuits,
or moulded.   or sliced roll.

A cream cheese, or grated Parmesan,
in a covered cut glass.

Dinner of two courses, four and five,* for family-dinners or small parties.

FIRST COURSE.
Pike, carp, or eels, baked.

Dutch sauce.

Jerusalem artichokes.   Mashed turnips.

Caper sauce.

Roast leg of mutton.

SECOND COURSE.

Veal cutlets in *Vol-au-vent.*

Young pease.   Ratafia cream.   Dressed lobster,

Ducklings.

PLAIN DESSERT,†

Rennets.

Cut Rummer.

Walnuts.   Water jug.   Spanish nuts

Cut Rummer.   or olives

The wines

Pears.

FIRST COURSE.

Hare-soup.

(*Remove*— Fillets of turbot.)

Stewed cucumber   Dressed turnip.

Roast pig.

---

* Dinners here given in two may in general have the same number of dishes served in three courses, if wished. Spirit-lamps of neat form sometimes very conveniently occupy the sides, at a large dinner, or the corners, as *fill-ups.* Devils, and hot moist *zests,* should alway be served over lamps.

† Zests put down after the dessert is removed, are hot deviled poultry and game, anchovy toasts, anchovies, caviare, olives, deviled biscuit oysters, grated meat, &c. or after a long interval, *Rere-supper* articles, as *Salmis, potted meats, potted shrimps, &c.*

SECOND COURSE.

Sweetbreads fricasseed.

Ginger cream   Calf's-feet jelly.

Roasted pheasant, or game of any kind.

Civet of hare as soup.

Stewed giblets.   Savory patties,
                                                  or calves' ears.

Bread of mutton grilled.

Potatoes and vegetables on the side-table.

SECOND COURSE.

Small ham, *glazed and ornamented.*

Asparagus,   Almond-pudding,   Stewed celery.
with butter sauce.   or Gateau de Riz.
                    Small turkey roasted.

Good dinners of seven dishes—two courses.

FIRST COURSE.*

Oyster soup.

(*Remove*—Slices of salmon with sauce Matelote.†)

Small fricandeau,   Tongue
with spinage, sorrel,   on mashed turnip.
or tomato sauce.

Ducks in ragout.   Partridge pie.   Portuguese
                                              mutton-cutlets.
                    Stewed rump of beef.

SECOND COURSE,

                    Moor-game.
Cranberry tart.   Orange sauce.   Macaroni.

                    Lemon cream.
Cauliflower
in white sauce.   Apricot marmalade
                    Mint sauce.   tart, or pudding.
          Fore-quarter of lamb roasted.

---

* Many will prefer this dinner served in three courses. In three it will still for a small party be a very plentiful dinner.

† Sliced cucumber, (which is eaten with salmon, cod, &c.) on the sideboard, and also other vegetables.

FIRST COURSE.

Fish—*Pike à la Genevoise*.

Sauce.

Veal-cutlets.

Chicken and ham patties.

Giblet soup.

Cod-Sounds.

Curried rabbit in
casserole of rice.

Sauce.
Roast goose.

Veal sweetbreads.

Snowballs, or castle
puddings.

Asparagus,
with butter.

Trifle, or ornamental cake.

Omelet.

Cheesecake.

Roasted birds.

FIRST COURSE.
Mullagatawny soup.

(*Remove*—Fish.)

Macaroni pudding.

Sauce.

Savoury patties

Plateau.

Potato-balls.

Sauce
Roast pig.

Currie of chickens
in rice casserole.

SECOND COURSE.
Green Pease.

Custards in glasses.

Vegetable marrow.

Lemon pudding.

Plateau.

Cranberry tart.

Omelet, or (*Eufs
pochés au jus*.

Cream in glasses.

Duckings.

Dinner of nine dishes.

FIRST COURSE.
Ox-tail soup.

Mashed potatoes
Boiled turkey poult.
Palates.

Boiled rice.
Ham glazed.
Brocoli.

Curried fish.

Haunch of mutton roasted.

SECOND COURSE.*

Black cock.

Small pastry.	Wafers.	Calf's feet jelly.
French beans.	Trifle.	Lobster salad.
Ginger cream.	Wafers.	Meringles.

Hashed hare,
or Venison.

Dinner of eleven dishes.

FIRST COURSE.

White soup,—*à la Reine.*

Stewed pigeons.	*(Remove*—fish.)	Lamb chops and
		Cucumbers.
	Oyster patties.	
Tongue on spinage.	plateau.	Boiled chickens.
	Lobster patties.	
Mutton rumps and		Sweetbreads grilled.
kidneys, or palates.		
	Mullagatawny.	

(*Remove*—Loin of veal, or other roast.).

SECOND COURSE.

Partridge roasted.

Wine jelly.		Dressed lobster.
	Small pastry.	
Stewed mushrooms.	Plateau.	French salad.
	Small pastry.	
Prawns in jelly,		Coffee cream.
or plain.		
	Macaroni.	

---

* If the party is rather large, and the table long, the same number of expensive dishes may do; but they must be arranged down the middle, and at the sides, while a few trifling articles of confectionary fill up the corners.

FIRST COURSE.

Turbot.

(*Remove*—Turkey.)

Melted butter.

| Breast of lamb with green pease. | Chicken and ham patties. | Ox palates. |

Lobster soup.   Plateau.   Brown gravy soup.

Turkey giblets.   Oyster patties.   Macaroni

Lobster sauce.

Fried whitings.

(*Remove*—Stewed brisket of beef, garnished with vegetables, or glazed onions.)

SECOND COURSE.

Veal sweetbreads.

Apricot Charlotte.	Small pastry.	Wine jelly.
Sea kale.	Plateau.	Vegetable marrow
Coffee cream.	Small pastry.	Cabinet pudding.

Woodcocks roasted.

Dinners of nine dishes and eleven.

FIRST COURSE.

Mock turtle.
(*Remove*—Crimped salmon.)

Rabbit and onions.	Lobster sauce.	Scalloped oysters.
Ham braised.	Plateau.	Turkey in white sauce.
Potted eels	Currant jelly. Wine sauce	Stewed pigeons.

Haunch of venison, or of
mutton dressed as Parson's venison.

SECOND COURSE.

Pheasant.

Puffs.	Preserved Cucumbers.	Open tart of apricot marmalade.
Artichokes.	Plateau.	Salad.
Almond cheesecakes	Preserved oranges.	Raspberry cream, in glass cups.

Wild ducks.

(*Remove*—Ramakins.)

Bill of fare for St. Andrew's Day, Burns' Clubs, or other Scottish National Dinners.

FIRST COURSE.

Friar's chicken, or Scotch brown soup.

(*Remove*—Braised turkey.)

Brown Fricassee or duck.	Potted game.	Minced Collops.
Salt cod, with egg sauce.	Haggis. *Remove*—Chicken pie.	Crimped Skate.
Smoked tongue		Tripe in white Fricassee.

Salt Caithness goose, or Solan goose.

Sheep's-head broth.

(*Remove*—Two Tups' head and trotters.)

(*Remove*—Haunch of venison or mutton, with wine sauce and currant jelly.)

SECOND COURSE.

Roast fowls, with *drappit* Egg, or lamb's head dressed.

Buttered Partans.	Small pastry.	Stewed onions.
Calf's-feet jelly.	Rich eating posset, in a china punch bowl.	Blancmange.
Apple-puddings in skins.	Small pastry.	Plum-Damas pie.

A black cock, or three ptarmigan.

*Long Table once covered, with Removes.**

Cod's head and shoulders.

Melted butter.   Oyster sauce.

(*Remove*—Roast turkey and sausages.)

Italian cream.   Charlotte.

Curried chickens   Macaroni pudding.   Grouse pie.
in rice casserole.

Mashed potatoes.   Lobster salad.   Mashed turnips.

Mullagatawny.   Plum pudding.   Onion soup.
(*Remove*—Ham.)   (*Remove*—Boiled fowls.)

Green pease.   French salad.   Cauliflower.

Stewed pigeons.   Savoury patties.   Ox palates.

Cranberry tart.   Calf's-feet jelly.

(1. *Remove*—Round of beef with greens.)

(2. *Remove*—Roast of veal.)

---

* Though a dinner divided into courses is to be recommended, both for elegance and comfort, there are public occasions when convenience and economy make it necessary to place almost all the dishes at once. To arrange them so as best to distribute the several things served up, is all that a dinner of this substantial kind admits of. The soup may be placed either at the top and bottom or at the sides of the table; though when there are large dishes of fish, the latter arrangement seems the more eligible. At a very long table four soups may be placed at the top, bottom, and sides, and the four corners be each furnished with a dish of fish; in which case the stews, boils, and roasts, are to be placed in change for the soups. Such an arrangement will better ensure to each guest a ready supply. The French call this sort of dinner an *Ambigu*: at such dinners they remove only the soups.

Public dinner of two courses, of from thirty-five to forty dishes, arranged in the French style.

FIRST COURSE.

Were this extended to double the number, the dishes are to be extended in the same manner, and large joints introduced accordingly. The centres marked by the asterisks may have another remove according to circumstances, and different sauces may be added. This ought to be attended to throughout the courses.

Rice soup.

Hot pie   (*Remove*—Turbot.)   Oyster patties.
Lobster sauce.

Veal sweetbreads.   Partridge Salmi.

Cold ham pie.

Vegetable pie.

Fowl pie, *or*
Chartreuse d'un*
Salpiçon de Volaille.

Beef palates.   Truffles

Fricassee of chickens.   Chickens.
with cucumbers.

Veal cutlets.

Fillets of Mackerel,
à la Maitre d'Hotel.

Green spring soup.
Remove—
*Roasted lamb.

Plateau.

Brown soup.
Remove—
Stewed beef.

Soles,
à la Ravigote.   Mutton,
à la Ste. Menehould.

Stewed pigeons.   Ducklings ragout.

Mutton cutlets,
à la Soubise.   Pork cutlets.

Cold chicken pie.
Fowl or *capon*   Caper and currant jelly   Mixed ragout.
aux huitres.   Sauces.

Fillets of partridges,
à la Portugaise.   Puddings,
de Richelieu au Velouté.

Patties.   Cabbage soup.   Larks,
in vol-au-vent.

---

* In arranging thirteen dishes upon one side, attention must be had to centres, which may be formed by larger or different shaped dishes: attention must also be paid to their contents.

SECOND COURSE, OF FROM THIRTY-FIVE TO FORTY COVERS.

Partridge pie.

(*Removed by a cake.*)

Spinage in crust border.   Jelly of oranges.

Chicken   Green pease,   Smoked tongue.
with white sauce.   dressed.

Cherry fritters   Tartlets.

Olives.   Herbs.

Rabbits.   Poached eggs
in gravy.
Perches au vin   Fried soles.

Stewed lettuce, or   Young pease.
*Laitues à
l'Espagnole.*

Plateau of Silver,
to be covered with vases and crystal dishes
filled with flowers, confections, or crystallized
fruits and flowers.

Young beans.   Haricots,
à la Lyonaise.

Smelts.   Small pigeons.

Small biscuits.   Ramakins.

Herbs.   Olives.

Apples in rice.   Stuffed cucumbers.

Cauliflower with   Asparagus   Rice fritters.
butter.   with butter.

Blancmange,   Artrichokes,
in small glasses.   *en canapes.*

Glazed ham.
(*Remove—Soufflé.*)

DESSERT.

Preserved pine apple.

Preserved oranges.

Nectarines.   Olives.   Cherries

Preserved Magnum Bonums.   Green-gages. Preserved

Apples.   Peaches.
          Cake ornamented.

Preserved lemons.

Melons preserved.

This dessert, which by some may be reckoned scanty, by others superfluous, and which we submit rather than recommend, may, at little expense, be enlarged by four small dishes, consisting of macaroons, white currants, walnuts, filberts, wafers, &c. &c. nor does it preclude ices, and preserved ginger.

———————

DESSERT OF FRESH FRUIT.

Grapes.

Sugar.

Apricots.   White currants.

Cream.

Almond biscuits.   Macaroons.

Sugar.

Red gooseberries.   Nectarines.

Strawberries.

SUPPERS.

The ingenuity of the genteel economist is as often taxed to contrive supper-things of scanty materials, as in arranging dinners. Dinners admit of less temporizing. Economy, good taste, and neatness, can, however, do much, even with slender means, where the chief organ to be propitiated is the eye; for the lateness of modern dinner-hours has now, almost universally, changed suppers from a solid meal into a slight shewy refreshment.

It is said that ladies are the best critics in suppers, while gentlemen are better qualified to decide on the more substantial business of the dinner table. However this may be, ladies are unquestionably more conversant with the things on which the elegance of a supper depends,—namely, the beautiful shapes and arrangement of china, glass, linen, fruits, foliage, colours, lights, ornamental confectionary, and all the natural and artificial embellishments of the table. These articles, so beautiful in themselves, cannot fail, if gracefully disposed, to gratify the eye, however slender the repast with which they are intermixed.

When a formal supper is set out, the principal dishes are understood to be roasted game or poultry, cold meats sliced, ham, tongue, collared and potted things, grated beef, Dutch herring, kipper, highly-seasoned pies of game, &c. &c., with, occasionally, soups—an addition to modern suppers which, after the heat and fatigue of a ball-room, or large party, is found peculiarly grateful and restorative. Minced white meats, lobsters, oysters, collared eels, and crawfish dressed in various forms; sago, rice, the more delicate vegetables, poached eggs, scalloped potatoes, or potatoes in balls, or as Westphalia cakes are all suitable articles of the solid kind. To these we may add ices, cakes, tarts, possets, creams, jellies in glasses or shapes, custards, preserved or dried fruits, pancakes, fritters, puffs, tartlets, grated cheese, butter in little forms, sandwiches; and the catalogue of the more stimulating dishes, as anchovy toasts, devils, Welsh, English, and Scotch rabbits, roasted onions, salmagundi, smoked sausages sliced, and those other preparations which are best adapted to what among ancient *bon vivants* was called the *rere-supper*.

A supper-table should neither be too much crowded nor too much scattered and broken with minute dishes. Any larder moderately stored will furnish a few substantial articles for supper on an emergency. A few sweet things readily prepared, or purchased, patties, shell-fish, and fruits, will do the rest, if the effect of contrasted colours, flavours, and forms, be understood; and that light and graceful disposition of trifles, which is the chief art in setting off such entertainments. Where small apartments, and crowded parties introduce the unsocial custom of standing suppers, the same *cold* dishes are suitable, served on high tables.

French wines have lately become an article of ambitious display at fashionable suppers, even in families of the middle rank. Where they can be afforded in excellence and variety, nothing can be more appropriate to a light, shewy, exhilarating repast.

DES DÉJEUNERS À LA FOURCHETTE*

That change of manners which has introduced late dinners, and superseded hot suppers, has very much improved the modern breakfast. Besides the ordinary articles of eggs, broiled fish, pickled herrings, Sardinias, beef, mutton, or goat hams, rein-deer's and beef tongues', sausages, potted meats, cold pies of game, &c. &c. a few stimulating hot dressed dishes are, by a sort of tacit prescription, set apart for the *déjeuner à la fourchette* of the gourmand and the sportsman. Of this number are broiled kidneys, calf's and lamb's liver with fine herbs, and mutton cutlets *à la Venetienne*. Receipts for those stimulating preparations of poultry, game, &c. will be found under the proper heads. When the *déjeuner à la fourchette* is an entertainment for company, the articles provided, with the addition of tea, coffee, chocolate, &c. do not materially differ from those of a fashionable supper. The following is an example:—

---

* The same articles will generally answer for luncheons or *comfortable* collations—and those refreshments affectedly termed TIFFINS. A worthy lady of our acquaintance, that we are morally certain never had a family-quarrel in her life, assures us that she regularly *tiffs* with the Doctor and the *bairns* every day, at one o'clock precisely.—P. W.

Marriage, Christening, or Public Breakfast, á la fourchette.

Tea urn.

Lemon cakes.

Butter in ice.

Potted salmon decorated.

Ham in jelly

Partridges, Perigord.

Caramel basket of bon-bons, containing mottoes, &c.

Potted char.

Preserved ginger.

Anchovy butter.

Ginger cream.

Preserved pine, melon, or cucumber.

Strawberry jelly.

Pastry sandwiches, with marmalade jams, &c.

Meringles

Chocolate.   Water urn.

Plateau ornamented; or if for a Marriage or Christening Breakfast, a Brides cake or Christening cake, with flowers, &c. &c.

Milk Coffee.   Water urn.

Tartlets.

Preserved oranges, or West India fruits

Perfumed biscuit.

Almond butter.

Preserved greengages.

Wine jelly.

Caramel basket, filled with confectionary.

Coffee cream.

Potted pigeons. tongue in jelly.

Butter in ice.

Potted lobster. Turkey in jelly.

Orange-flower cakes.

Coffee urn.

---

* N.B.— Cream and sugar in cut glass jugs and dishes may be placed in proper places. Game and Oyster salads may make part of the dishes, and venison is an appropriate luxury. Ice-pails may, in hot weather, be placed on the table. At such entertainments, the lighter dessert wines are used and also liqueurs. Those useful vulgar commodities, buttered toasts, rolls, muffins, boiled eggs, &c. may find a place on the side-table. The articles above, with the addition of fresh fruits, pastry, preserves, and more wines and liqueurs, will afford an elegant cold collation. At the *dejeuneur* of the sportsman, the tea and coffee are not expected to make their appearance till the solids are removed.

PART SECOND

CHAPTER I

BOILING.

O! for some forty pounds of lovely beef
In a Mediterranean sea of brews.
Spanish Curate

Boiling, though not the first invented, is certainly the easiest of all culinary processes; and for this very reason, it is often the worst performed. After what has been said in the introduction, we would disdain to waste words on the careless housewife or greasy Joan, who requires again to be told, that order, arrangement, thorough-going cleanliness, and neatness all but finical, is indispensable in this, as in every other branch of Cookery. Taking it for granted then, that the hearth is neatly swept, that the fire burns clear, that the pots and stewpans, of cast-iron, are of proper size, clean, well-tinned, and fitted with close-fitting tinned lids, we proceed to a few general rules for *boiling*.

All meat, whether fresh or salted, smoked or dried, is best put in with cold water. For fowls or white meats, the water may be a very little heated, and also for salted meat when there is danger of it freshening over much in coming slowly to boil. Gradual heating softens, plumps, and whitens the meat, and, above all, facilitates the separation of the scum, on the removal of which the goodness, as well as beauty, of boiled meat so much depends. Salt also facilitates the separation of the scum. Carefully watch when the first thick scum rises; take the pot from the fire, if necessary, to remove the scum completely; throw in a little cold water, which will check the boiling and throw off what scum remains.—*This is the way in which Soups, Gravies, and Sauces are best cleaned and refined.*—When the pot must be eked, let it be with boiling water from a kettle. Milk and floured cloths as wrappers are often employed in boiling white meats and poultry, to make them look whiter. The practice is questionable; the milk often curdles, and the flour clots; and both fill up the pores and hang about the met, which looks as if it had been poulticed. Soaking in cold or lukewarm water, or, according to circumstances, blanching, careful skimming, and slow boiling, especially at first, are better than any other method. No certain rule can be given for the length of time necessary to boil meat or fish. Dried tongues, for example, or mutton, goat, or venison hams, will take double the time or more to *simmer* which will boil a fresh leg of mutton; and, again, a piece of pork, though a little salted, will take longer to boil than either veal or lamb. Of all meat the hind-quarter, from the solid and compact texture of the fibre, will require longer boiling or simmering than the fore-quarter. The state of the weather, so important in roasting, less affects things that are boiled. As a general rule, liable, however, to many exceptions, from 15 to 25 minutes of time, and a quart of water is allowed by cooks to the pound of fresh meat; and from 25 to 35 minutes for salted meat, with a fourth more water.* But no length of boiling will ever make dried meats fit to be eaten, without sufficient previous soaking. This is emphatically true of goat and mutton hams, rein-deer tongues, dried fish &c. Capital blunders are often performed in this department; and provisions which excel all others for relishes, breakfasts, and luncheons, are made good for nothing but to try the temper, and break the teeth of the eater, who might as well diet upon "spur leather whang." Smoked and dried meats, and dried fish, sometimes require to be soaked from one to four or five days, changing the water often; or, what is better, where there is a run of fresh water, steeping the meat in it, or in the trough of a pump.

When additional saltness is wanted, the meat may be

---

* There is palpable absurdity in this universal culinary rule. A quarter of an hour will not be nearly enough of time to boil one pound of meat, nor a half hour to boil two, still less three quarters of an hour for three pounds. But, again, twelve hours boiling would destroy forty-eight pounds. It must be kept in mind that large joints expose corresponding surfaces to heat, whether in pots or on spits.

wrapped in a cloth dipped in hot water, dusted with flour, and then covered with a layer of salt.—We have but little faith in this method: Meat must have time to imbibe salt; but frequent rubbing and a warm temperature will hasten the process.—In brief, well-tinned clean pots—thick in the bottom to aid in maintaining an equal temperature,—a clear fire, well-washed or soaked viands, gentle boiling, and careful skimming, are all the rules that can be given to ensure well-dressed boiled dishes; for the length of time must, in almost every case, be determined by the size, the condition, and the nature of the provisions.—*Obs.* What goes under the general name of *pot-liquor*, particularly that in which fresh meat or poultry has been boiled, may and should be applied to many useful purposes.

Professed cooks, and works which treat of Gastronomy, uniformly enter a protest against any sort of vegetables being boiled with meat, except carrots,—a rule this which the Cleikum Club thought more honoured in the breach than the observance. Watery vegetables, boiled in water and served in wateriness, find no favour in the French kitchen. Common sense, and, indeed, common practice, discards them.

There is an adaptation, a *natural affinity*, to borrow a learned phrase, between certain vegetables and roots, and certain pieces and kinds of meat. A cook who would excel in her profession ought, day and night, to study this doctrine of *coherence* and natural *affinity*. Who but a fool would dissever from the round of salted beef, the greens or cabbage which become part and parcel of it as soon as it reaches the pot? If, however, from reasons of economy, it is wished to preserve the liquor for other purposes, a quantity of it may be put into a separate vessel, and the greens boiled there. At any rate, the pot may have the top-fat taken off to enrich the water in which the greens are boiled, without any loss of pot-liquor for soup. The grand objection that vegetables spoil the colour of the meat is thus obviated.

Salted beef, with suitable roots and vegetables, is one of these cut-and-come-again family-dishes, which, from November till March, every sensible man hails with pleasure, whether on his own or his friends' table. To dress it in the best manner is therefore well worth the

attention of the cook, the economist, and the judicious
epicure.—*See Salting.*

1.—TO BOIL A ROUND OF BEEF.

A ROUND or buttock of salted beef may either be
boiled whole, divided into two, or cut into three pieces,
according to the size of the meat, and the number of
the guests or family. It is a common error of vanity to
boil too much of a ham or round at once. If boiled
whole, the bone may be cut out; if divided, it is
desirable to give each piece an equal proportion of the
fat. Wash the meat, and, if over salt, soak it in one or
more waters till it be sufficiently softened or freshened.
Skewer it up tightly, and of a good shape, wrapping the
flap or tongue-piece very firmly round. Bind it with
broad strong tape, or fillets of linen. The pot should be
roomy, and the water must fully cover the meat. A fish-
drainer is convenient to boil this and other large pieces of
meat on. Heat very gradually; take off the scum, of
which a great deal will be thrown up, till no more rises,
and throw in some cold water to refine the liquor if needful; cover the pot close, and boil slowly, but at an equal
temperature, allowing about three hours to from 12 to
16 pounds, and from that to four or five hours for a
weightier piece. Turn the meat once or twice in the pot
during the process. Put in the carrot and turnip about
two hours after the meat. If the liquor is to be afterwards
used for soup, these roots instead of hurting will improve
the flavour. Greens may be either boiled in the same
pot, or better separately in some of the pot-liquor.
When the meat is dished, take off, with a clean sponge,
or a cloth moistened in the pot-liquor, any scum or films
which, in spite of the most careful skimming, will often
hang about salted meat; replace the skewer that holds
the flap with a plated or silver one; garnish with large
sliced carrots, (or with greens or cabbage instead,) and
serve mashed turnip and greens in separate dishes.—
Obs. The dry outside slices are to be sent away by the
carver; the meat must be cut in smooth, thin, horizontal slices, keeping the surface level. The soft fat eats
best when the meat is warm, the firm fat when it is
cold; but the taste of the guests must be the carver's
guide. By good management this meat will in cold

weather keep for a fortnight or more. Cover it with several folds of soft cloth, and over these place a dish-cover. Cut off a thin slice from the hard outside before it is again presented at table, or on the sideboard. If underdone, the meat, after keeping some time, may be put into boiling pot-liquor, and get from 15 to 35 minutes slow boiling. This receipt is equally applicable to every piece of salted beef, whether Ribs, Brisket, or Edge-bone, (*Scotticè Heuckbane*,) only, as was said of fore-quarter, these pieces being less solid, require, in proportion to their weight, about a sixth less time in boiling.

2. BOILED BEEF, OR BOUILLI ORDINAIRE.

THIS is another plain family-dish,—boiled fresh beef; but as economy, good sense, and, what is the same thing, good taste, reject this mode of dressing beef but in conjunction with the soup, which forms the better part of it, we leave the *Bouilli* till we give it along with *Bouillon*, though obliged, for connexion's sake, to notice it here.

3. TO BOIL LEG OF MUTTON WITH TURNIP, ETC.

A LEG OF MUTTON—the *gigot* of the French and Scottish kitchen—may be kept from two days to a week before boiling. The pipe, as it is technically called, must be cut out, and the mustiness which gathers on the surface, and in the folds and soft places, rubbed off occasionally. It is whitest when quite fresh, but most delicate when hung a few days in the larder, though not so long as to allow the juices to thicken, and the flavour to deteriorate. Hill wether mutton, from four to seven years old, is far the best, whether for boiling or roasting. Choose it short in the shank, thick in the thigh, and of a pure, healthy, brownish red. Chop but a very small bit off the shank; if too much is taken off, the juices will be drained by this conduit in the boiling.

If you wish to whiten the meat, blanch it for ten minutes in warm water. Boil in an oval-shaped or roomy kettle, letting the water come very slowly to boil. Skim carefully. Boil carrots and turnip with the mutton, and the younger and more juicy they are the better they suit this joint. Be sure never to run a fork or anything sharp into the meat, which would drain its juices. *All meat ought to be well done*, but a leg of mutton rather under than over, to look plump and retain its juices. About two hours of slow boiling will dress it. Garnish with slices of carrot. Pour caper-sauce over the meat, and serve mashed turnip or cauliflower in a separate dish. Some good country cooks serve the turnip as a mash, or *purée*, under the mutton, and as in carving the native juices are all caught by the vegetable sauce, the practice, though not general, is commendable; but where it is followed, the caper-sauce, if served at all, must be kept in a sauce-boat. If chickens or fowls are wanted for the same dinner, they will boil with great advantage along with the mutton, before the roots are put to it, or in some of the liquor in a separate pot.—*Obs.* This joint, above all others, should be boiled slowly to eat well. The liquor in which fresh mutton is boiled is very valuable for broth; and it is a common, and not bad family-practice in Scotland, to make barley or rice broth at the same time the leg is boiled. The broth so made is, however, frequently thin and watery, the pot-liquor being in too great quantity; and before it can be properly boiled down the meat would be spoiled. When broth is to be made, put in the barley at first; lift out the meat after an hour and a half's boiling; cover it up to keep warm; take the lid off the pot, and suffer the liquor to evaporate by rapid boiling, till what remains is strong and good, and the broth of a proper consistence. Cut some of the roots into small slices, and put these, with a head of celery sliced, or a little shred parsley, to the broth; return the mutton, and boil gently for a half-hour longer. A *gigot* is an excellent and most economical joint, capable of being turned to many purposes. It may be dressed as chops, and the best balmy, mellow, barley-broth may be made of what remains. It may also be roasted, or baked, or made into ham, *or*, if a large gigot, a fillet may be roasted, and the knuckle used for barley or rice broth. In French cookery, parsley, onions, and a clove or two of garlic, are boiled with this favourite joint. It is then glazed (a work of worse than supererogation) and served on a Sauce *Espagnole*.—See *French Cookery, Part III, Chap. 2.*

4. TO BOIL SCRAG OF MUTTON, OR BACK RIBS.

WASH, trim nicely, and simmer from three to five pounds of the neck *slowly* for two hours, making broth as in last receipt. Garnish the meat with carrot, or turnips cut; and pour over the meat caper-sauce, or parsley and butter. Serve mashed turnip or cauliflower. —*Obs.* Pouring the sauce over boiled dishes, besides improving their appearance, is to be preferred, because, in carving, the juices of the meat, the natural sauce, flow out and mingle with the prepared relish, "each improving each." But this can only be done when the taste of the company is understood, and the sauce in no danger of becoming cold.

This joint, in a point of economy, comes next to the gigot. The scrag (Captain BOOTH's favourite dish— *vide Amelia*) or neck makes excellent barley or rice broth, or it will stew. The ribs will do the same; or make Chops, Currie, Haricot, or Pie.—See *Made-dishes of mutton*.—French cooks take two necks for this dish, but their mutton, lamb, and veal, are smaller than those of England. They saw off the bones; steep the meat in olive oil, pepper, salt, and sliced onion, and lard it with blanched minced parsley. A boiled *shoulder* of mutton, or of veal, is very good with white onion-sauce poured over it.

5. TO BOIL A LEG OF LAMB.

LAMB is seldom boiled with us, and there is good sense in the omission. It must be boiled slowly to look white; and is served with brocoli, spinage, or cauliflower, according to the season. Garnish with sprigs of cauliflower. The loin may be cut in steaks and nicely fried, and served round the boiled meat with crisped parsley.—See *Made-dishes of lamb*.

6. TO BOIL VEAL.

VEAL, save the gristly parts, plainly boiled is too insipid to be much relished for its own sake. But variety, economy, and veal broth or gravy, sanction this mode of cookery. Boiled veal looks detestable when slobbery and red-coloured; and to prevent this, particular attention must be paid to the boiling. It is eaten with bacon, or *sausage*, like fowls. *Sauce*—Parsley and butter, or onion-sauce of young onions.—See *Made-dishes of veal.*

7. TO BOIL VENISON.*

A NECK, and even a haunch, is sometimes boiled. Let it hang from three days to a week. Boil as mutton. It is eaten with turnip or cauliflower, with which last garnish. *Sauce*—Melted butter, and a little of any of the flavoured vinegars you choose.—See *Vinegars and venison soup; see also Civet de chevreuil, French Cookery.* Part III. Chap. 2.

8. TO BOIL POULTRY.†

Be careful in picking, not to break the skin. Let the fowls hang from two to five days; for the most delicate fowl will be touch and thready if too soon dressed. When to be used, draw, singe without blackening, and wash thoroughly, passing a stream of water again and

---

*It is only in the hunting grounds of America that one could bear to hear of venison so scandalously cooked; but when very plentiful it may be made into soup, which possesses the *wild* flavour so prized by *les hommes de bouche.*

†So little is the proper keeping of fowls previous to dressing attended to in country inns and families, that, warned by experience, the arrival of a stranger is the signal for the whole poultry in some places to run off and burrow among the nettles, to eschew their fate for yet another day. The bounty of a penny sterling, which travellers have sometimes heard offered on the head of "the old cock to make brandered chicken for the gentleman's dinner," is often earned by the galopin loitering about the inn door with the sweat of his brow, so knowing do those old stagers become.—As a house for the wayfarer, and the solitary chance-traveller, poultry was at all times a main article in the larder of the CLEIKUM, where great dinners and numerous dishes were seldom required. So plump, so white, so tender were the fowls, whether boiled or roasted, and the chickens, whether *brandered*, dressed as *howtowdie*, or *Friar's chicken*, that Mr. TOUCHWOOD, so tenacious on other points of the art, gave up this department entirely to MEG herself, reserving only some practical directions for curried fowls, and the feeding and fattening of young poultry, which will be found in another section of this erudite work. "Take the fattest and youngest *eerocks*," (yearlings,) said MEG, "and the whitest, for a white skin is a good sign, whether of beast or body,"—looking graciously to the young man, while the yellow Nabob made a gesture of impatience. But Mrs. DODS was so liable to the infirmity of descanting at large, not only of the St. Ronan's breed of hens, but on the biography of favourite individuals, and the guests that had ate them, that the young man found it necessary to check her vein, and curtail her directions, by at least nine-tenths.

again through the inside. Boiled fowls must be very neatly trussed, as they have small aid from skewers; and nothing can be more indecorous than to see unfortunates on the table—

Whose dying limbs no decent hands composed!

Put them on with plenty of water, a little warmed. Having, as usual, skimmed very carefully, simmer by the side of the fire from twenty-five minutes to an hour, according to the age and size of the fowl. A small tureen of very good barley or rice broth, seasoned with shred parsley and young onions, may be made at the same time, if a shank, or small chops of neck or ribs of mutton be added; which last may be frugally served in the broth. Some good cooks put fresh suet and slices of peeled lemon to boil with fowls; white-legged fowls are most worthy attention, whether for eating or appearance.★

★ MEG'S sauce for fowls was either the national "drappit egg," *egg-sauce*, parsley and butter, or, if the fowls were of a dark complexion, *liver-sauce*, as a veil of their dinginess. TOUCHWOOD chose *celery-sauce* for fowls, and *oyster-sauce* for turkey; JEKYLL preferred *lemon-sauce*, but often joined the Nabob. The best sort of stuffing or forcemeat for poultry was the cause of many disputes. MEG long stood out for sweet stuffing for her turkeys, orthodox *apple-sauce* for her goose, and a sweet pudding in the belly of her sucking pig. After a feud which lasted three days, the belligerents came to a treaty on the old basis of the *uti possidelis*, though the best stuffing for boiled or roasted poultry or veal was agreed to be—"Crumbs of stale bread, two parts; suet, marrow, or fresh butter, one part; a little parsley, boiled for a minute, and very finely shred; the quarter of a nutmeg grated, a tea-spoonful of lemon-peel grated, all-spice, and salt,—the whole to be worked up to a proper consistence, with two or three yolks of eggs well beat." If for *roasted* or *boiled* turkey, pickled oysters chopped, ham or tongue grated, and eschallot to taste may be added. MEG's sweet stuffing was made by discarding the parsley, ham, oysters, and tongue, and substituting a large handful of currants, picked, rubbed, and dried, as for puddings.

A common and an approved smuggling way of boiling a pullet or *how-towdie* in Scotland, was in a well-cleaned haggis-bag, which must have preserved the juices much better than a cloth. In the days of Popery and good cheer, and they were certainly synonimous, though we do not quite subscribe to the opinion of Dr. REDGILL, that no Presbyterian country can ever attain eminence in Gastronomy—in those days of pater-nosters and venison-pasties, stoups of claret and oral confession, a pullet so treated, was, according to waggish legends, the secret regale provided for Mess John by his fair penitents.—Vide ALLAN RAMSAY's "Monk and Miller's Wife," or Friars of Berwick, "Traditions of the Cleikum," and "Bughtrigg's Wife's receipt for 'Ane capon stewed in brewis.'" Butter, shred onions, and spice, were put in the bag along with the fowl, and formed the sauce, *or* else oysters with their liquor strained.

9. TO BOIL BACON.

BRING slowly to boil, and simmer for at least two hours. When ready to serve, strip off the rind, and dry the meat with a red-hot shovel, or set it in the oven to dry up the oozing fat. Strew bread-raspings over it.

10. TO BOIL A HAM. *
(See Curing hams. Section Salting.)

A LARGE ham is very seldom boiled all at once, but whether altogether, or in part, it must be treated in the same way. Pork is so well adapted to salting, that though kept for years, it does not become so hard or tough as beef or mutton would do in half the time. The main point is the *soaking*, which the discretion of the cook must proportion to the hardness and saltness of the meat. If very old, briny, and dry, it will require from three to four days to soften and become mellow. Place it in a run of water, if you have the command of one, or in the trough of a pump-well. By *probing* the degree of freshness may be ascertained. The night before it is boiled, pour lukewarm water over it, scrape it very well, trim off all rusty ill-looking bits. Put it in an oval fish-kettle with plenty of water. Let it soak for an hour or two before coming to the boil,—then quicken the boil, and skim. Let it simmer slowly by the side of the fire for from two to five hours, according to the weight. When done, pull off the skin neatly, and keep it to cover the ham when set by cold; strew bread-raspings over it, and place it on a hot dish set over the pot before the fire, to brown and crisp. It will crisp easier if put in an oven to dry up the oozing fat. Twist writing paper neatly round the shank, if not sawed off, which is much better. Garnish if you choose with greens, or strew raspings in little heaps on the ledge of the dish; *or* dish it over dressed Windsor-beans.—See *Glazing*.

11. HAM WITH MADEIRA.
The French *Jambon Braisé*.

BONE a small nice North of England ham. Saw off

---

* A Hamburgh or Westphalia ham requires longer soaking than one of Bayonne, or one home-made.—We hold a Westmoreland or Yorkshire ham well-fattened, and properly cured, against all the hams in the world.—P. T.

the knuckle. (It may be boned if wished.) Let it soak if old and likely to be briny, and simmer it for an hour; then drain, trim, and dry it. Lay it in a *braising* pan, or oval-shaped nice stew-pan that will just hold it, and in which you have previously put slices of veal, carrots, onions, parsley, and spices. Pour in some good broth (about a pint) and a bottle of Madeira. When done for an hour take off the lid, and let the braise reduce. In a half hour more, probe to try whether the ham is done. Drain and skin, and dry it in the oven. Glaze with *real glaze*; serve the *braise* liquor, well reduced, and skimmed, as sauce.—*Obs.* Ham may be *glazed* by sifting fine sugar over it, and holding a red-hot poker above; but sweet glaze is not suitable to meat dishes. The French often serve *braised* ham over spinage or other vegetables; but this is seldom done in England.

12. HAM WITH WINDSOR BEANS.

BOIL the ham as directed at No. 10, and serve it, trimmed and skinned, over Windsor beans, boiled in salt and water, and tossed up in melted butter.—*Obs*. This, which is just the French ham *à l'essence*, will keep longer than a round of beef, and is an excellent and serviceable article at all hours of the day and night. When cold, keep as directed for a salted round of beef, using the skin instead of cloths. The outside slices pared off before the meat is served can be kept for culinary purposes. The liquor in which the ham was boiled may be strained; and if you manage to have fowls or a knuckle of veal dressed on the following day, the liquors may be rapidly boiled down together, with pepper, mace, eschallot, and herbs, when the result will be a rich and highly-relishing gravy. *Or* pease or carrot soup may be made of these mixed liquors.—See *Potted meats, Pease soup, Ham roasted*, and *Sandwiches.**

---

* JEKYLL was intolerably eloquent on *ham sauce*, and astounded even TOUCHWOOD by anecdotes of a *grand gourmand*, a man of *ultra gout*, who, pursuing the science as one of the fine arts, soaked his Westphalia hams in Rhine-wine, and baked them in fresh wine, with aromatic spices. If ham is tolerably fresh, it will bake very well. It must be soaked as for boiling. The colour will be better than when boiled, and the flavour higher. But Mrs. DODS, who detested that new and unnatural practice, said it was dried to a dander, and TOUCHWOOD dropped the point, as he

13. BOILED BACON OR PORK.

ALL pork to be boiled should lie in salt at least two days previous to dressing. Pork requires more boiling than any other meat. Small pork is the most delicate to boil fresh. Pork throws up a greasy scum during the whole process, which must be constantly removed. *Serve* with pease-pudding, (see *Puddings*,) or parsnips, boiled in the same pot.★

14. A LEG OF PORK TO BOIL.

CHOOSE a nice, small, *well-filled* leg. Salt it, rubbing hard, lay it in pickle; and boil and serve along with pease-pudding, and savoys or green cabbage.

15. TO BOIL RABBITS, PARTRIDGES, PHEASANTS, SNIPES, WILD DUCKS, AND OTHER GAME

BOIL as directed for chickens, or in fresh mutton broth. For Partridges, Pheasants, &c. use the same *sauces* as directed for them when roasted; garnish with crisp parsley, slices of lemon, or green pickles.—*Obs.* Though game of all sorts is occasionally boiled, the

---

could not think of bestowing a libation of Rhine-wine on a Porker of Westphalia (see Ham with Madeira); and distance from the metropolis made it impossible to procure *Essence of Ham*, a high-flavoured commodity sold at the London Eating-Houses, which be not irrationally concluded, might make an admirable substitute for wine, and he afterwards applicable to every purpose for which *Essence of Ham* is used. The experiment is worth trying. In France, hams are boiled deliciously, wrapped in a cloth, with carrots, onions, garlic, cloves, bay-leaves, parsley, thyme, and basil. When enough done, the cloth is tied more firmly, and when cool, the ham is dressed as above, and served on a napkin. The French also *braise* and roast hams, and have the *Pate de Jambon.*

★ Dr. REDGILL, professionally devoted to benevolence and Christian charity, made a long oration on the value of pork liquor for soup to the poor; *charitable* soup, *economical* soup, dealt out in copious libations to old women, as often as very salt and very fat pork was boiled in the Doctor's kitchen. The idea was nauseous to every other member of the committee. TOUCHWOOD asserted that even COBBETT, that enthusiast for hogs flesh, disclaims pork broth. REDGILL on this hard push brought forward his battle-horse, Dr. KITCHENER, in vain,—was left in a minority of one, and the hogs got their natural perquisite. The liquor of young pork not long in salt will, however, make tolerable pease-soup, to which a strong subduing relish of celery and onion should be given. Cabbage may be boiled with advantage in pork liquor. Also pease-pudding.

committee of the Cleikum did not patronize this mode of
dressing, except for rabbits. Stewed rabbits, which must
be neatly trussed, are best smothered with a thick mild
onion sauce, though sometimes a *liver* sauce is made
thus: Boil and bruise the liver; add veal gravy to some
of the liquor in which the rabbits were boiled, thickened
with flour, and a good piece of butter, and some parsley
shred very fine. Season with mace and allspice. Garnish
with sliced lemon. *Onion Sauce* is also used for boiled
goose and ducks, in preference to less piquant compositions. Rabbits will take a full hour of slow boiling;
birds according to their size.—Study page 3.

16. TO BOIL TRIPE AND COW-HEELS.

UNLESS in country places, or where families kill their
own beef, tripe is usually bought ready boiled at the
Tripe or *Cow-heel* shops. It requires very long boiling
—from six to nine hours of *simmering* by the fire-side,
or, as is very good practice where kitchen fires are
gathered, it is left over a slow fire for a whole night.
Tripe requires endless cleaning, and is best managed at
a river side in the first instance. Afterwards, to assist
in the cleaning and blanching, a piece of quicklime may
be dissolved in the water in which it is scalded and
scraped; but tripe so blanched will become ill-coloured
in the boiling. Tripe, like chickens, veal &c. may be
whitened by rubbing it with lemon-juice, where expense
is no object. The scalding must be frequently repeated.
When bought in the shops, choose it thick, fat, and
white, and see that it be fresh. The best way of keeping tripe after it is boiled is to allow it to jelly in its own
liquor. When to be dressed, pare off the fat and films,
and wash it with warm water. Cut it into pieces about
the size of small cutlets, and simmer in milk and water
till it is quite soft and tender, and the sauce thickish.
Peel and boil a dozen white firm button onions. Dish
the tripe in a deep steak-dish or small tureen, and put
the onions to it, taking off the surface-skin if they look
black.* Many persons prefer tripe boiled plainly in

---

* Dr REDGILL to the above added a bit of butter rolled in flour, put
into the sauce half an hour before it was taken off the fire, a large tea-
spoonful of made mustard, or the same quantity of mushroom catsup, and

water, and served with *onion sauce* and mustard; others boil it in veal broth, or put a fresh beef-bone or veal shank to the water.★

Cow-HEELS are generally cleaned before they are bought. They require from five to six hours boiling. *Sauce*,—melted butter, a tea-spoonful of made mustard, and a very little vinegar,—or parsley and butter.— See *Potted heel, Fried and fricasseed tripe, &c. also French Cookery, National Dishes, and Kelly's Sauce.*

CHAPTER II.

ROASTING.

"For what are your soups, your ragouts, and your sauce,
Compared to the Beef of Old England?—
And O, the *Old English Roast Beef!*"

IN a voice between whistling and singing, accompanied by the flourish of the carving-knife, and an occasional rub against steel, it was with the above appropriate stave our brisk old Nabob viewed with high satisfaction the *lordly sirloin*, of a delicate pale-brown, frosted as if with seed pearls, a labour of love which had occupied him for five hours, and now smoked in savouriness on the board of the Committee. In the evening of the same day, and while the process was still fresh in his

---

the onions, previously parboiled, or fried in butter. This original variation was highly approved of.

★ In modern French cookery, tripe, after being boiled and whitened with lemon-juice, is cut in stripes and stewed in white sauce, or strong white broth, for four hours. It is then served either in a sauce à la Poulette or in sauce Italienne blanche. In old French cookery, the tripe, when boiled and cut in bits, was stewed in cullis with all sorts of herbs, onions, and chives, a glass of wine, and a little tarragon. When the sauce was thickened, a little made mustard was added, and the whole strained and poured over the tripe.

The fat skimmings of Cow-heels and Cow-head are the best adapted for frying or basting of all boiled fats. They indeed afford a very rich oil, which is sometimes even burned; and the Perfumers draw largely upon them for some commodities of high name. Calves-feet jelly, so named, is made both of Cow-heels and Tripe; indeed the former affords a much stronger and richer jelly than the article whose name it usurps. A good glaze is made of Cow-heels. It also affords a good cheap soup, if properly seasoned.

head, after sundry disputes with Dr. REDGILL on the *undone* and the *overdone*, the Nabob dictated something like the following discourse on roasting.

No printed rules can make a good roaster. Practice and vigilant attention alone can produce that *rara avis* of the kitchen. In the French kitchen this is a department by itself. He who rules the roast attends to that alone.

No meat will roast to advantage that is not kept the exact length of time; but this in every case must be determined by the weather and the age of the animal. Two days of hot weather is equal to a week of cold in rendering meat fit for the spit.

Even in summer, by proper attention, meat will keep much longer than is generally supposed.* Have the roast properly jointed, which saves much mortification to the carver, and much haggling and mangling of the meat. Let it be well washed with salt and water, and dried. See that the spit be brightly clean. If not, scour with sand and water or Bath brick, and wipe with a clean cloth. If there is too much fat, some of it may be cut off for dripping or puddings. Cover the fat for the first hour with kitchen-paper, fastened on with twine.† A good cook can manage to handle meat very little in the spitting and balancing. In many joints the spit will run along the side of the bone without piercing the flesh. Tie it, or fix with screw skewers. If much handled, baste the joint with salt and water, and dry the dripping-pan, suffering the meat to dry, which it will do in a few seconds by the heat of the fire, before basting with butter. If the joint is not accurately balanced, no horizontal spit will work well.‡

---

* Londoners often roast their beef too soon. In the North of England, and other places, the sirloin is frequently salted, and eaten with vinegar and mustard. A salted sirloin or leg of mutton may eat tolerably well, but they are undeniably a relic of those days when the squire or yeoman killed his own beef and mutton, and his lady found it necessary to keep the holiday joint, however long, to grace the holiday.

† REDGILL insisted upon a warning post here, as the worthy man, in the eagerness of his appetite, had one day a large bodle-pin fixed in his gullet, like a salmon-hook, for a good half-hour, which some of MEG's queans had used in skewering (new reading, *securing*,) on the paper.

‡ A smoke or wind-up-jack or a cradle-spit was considered the best by the Nabob; but Yorkshire jacks, bottle-jacks, Dutch ovens, and

In roasting, the management of the fire is half the battle. Let the kitchen grate be thoroughly raked out in the morning. An hour before the roast is put down, make up a fire suited to the size of the joint; let it be clear and glowing, and free of ashes and smoke in front. A *backing* of wetted cinders or small coal helps to throw forward and sustain an equal radiant heat in front. Place the meat at a due distance, that it may heat through without the outside becoming shrivelled and scorched. To prevent this, baste diligently for the first half-hour. The larger the joint the greater must be the distance from the fire, so that it be not so great as to make the meat tough and sodden by the slackness of the process. A radiant fire, due distance, and frequent basting, can alone ensure a well-roasted joint, of that fine amber colour, crisp, and lightly frothed, which speaks a language that all men understand. A quarter of an hour to the pound of meat is the time usually allowed for roasting, bearing in mind that fat meat takes longer than lean, and Pork and Veal longer than any other kinds of meat. But, as we said of boiling, this must in almost every case be determined by circumstances. Fillets and legs take longer than loins or breasts. A meat-screen, the state of the weather, the kind of fuel, and a thousand things, must be taken into account. A meat-screen contributes so much to good roasting, and is so generally useful, that something of the kind ought to find a place in every family that aspires to comfort. It saves fuel, keeps plates and dishes warm, or makes them so; and, above all, by warding off draughts of air, preserves the temperature in the region of the spit in a state of equality.* Once, or, if the

---

Gipsy jacks, i.e. a nail and a string, and many other contrivances, may all be employed with success, if the *fire be adapted* to the peculiar construction of the implement.

* There was no meat-screen in the Cleikum. MEG said, "She had nae brew of sic new-fangled niceties;" but the Nabob, who, like all men of genius, was handy and full of resource, contrived, with the help of Dr. REDGILL, to erect an immense old japan tea tray upon stools, and barrels. This he substituted till JOHN HISLOP brought a new screen from Edinburgh, for the which JEKYLL had condescended to make a drawing, and which Mrs. DODS, now quite reconciled, has used with great approbation ever since, declaring it the "most comfortable, useful piece of furniture that ever her kitchen saw."

roast be very large, twice during the process, withdraw the spit and dripping-pan, and stir the fire, clear away the ashes, and bring forward the clear burning coals,★ supplying their place with fresh fuel. When the meat is nearly done, which will be known by the length of time, and by the steams, in the language of the kitchen, "drawing to the fire," the paper is to be removed, a little salt sprinkled lightly over the road, and the spit so placed, that the ends of the roast may be browned. The meat must now be carefully basted, and may be placed a little nearer to the fire, if the surface is not yet of a fine clear brown colour. The roast is then frothed, by dredging it very lightly with well-dried flour shaken from a dredging-box, somewhat smaller in the holes than those generally employed.† Fresh butter makes the most delicate froth, but does not improve the flavour of the skin or to the appearance of the gravy, which ought at this stage to be sparkling in the dripping-pan, bright, brown, and transparent as a Caledonian topaz. If much flour is dredged on, let it have time to get crisp.

Fashion and luxury have lately introduced stall-fed oxen and overgrown sheep, which are better fitted for the tallow-chandler than the cook. They are indeed good for nothing, save to obtain premiums at Cattle-shews, and deluge dripping-pans with liquid fat. When meat of this description is to be dressed, it is an object of economy to save the superfluous fat, which makes so much of the weight. Besides what is cut off, the dripping-pan, during the first hour of roasting, may be emptied of its oily contents once or twice, and abundance

---

★ In all departments of domestic life, save the management of kitchen-fires, there is, at least, a plausible show of attention to economy among servants. There the waste is wanton, wilful, and enormous, whether cooking be going forward or not. "The waste of fuel," says Count Rumford, "which arises from making liquids boil unnecessarily, or "when nothing more is necessary then merely to keep them boiling hot, "is enormous. I have not a doubt, that half the fire used in kitchens, "public and private, in the whole world, is wasted precisely in this "manner." To convince a regular cook, or even a kitchen-maid, that she does not know how to manage her fire, is, we confess, quite hopeless; but surely something might be made of young girls by proper instruction in economizing an article of such serious consequence in all families. Fuel is greatly economized by steaming processes of cooking.

† The calibre of Touchwood's dredging-box and that of his pepper-box was precisely the same.

remain for basting. Dripping put aside in this manner will be much fitter for all culinary purposes, whether for pease-soup, pie-crust, or for frying fish, than that which has acquired a highly empyreumatic taste, either from burning cinders, or being exposed to the action of a fierce heat. This disagreeable flavour and the unsalutary qualities which it betokens, make an epicure of any delicacy of stomach reject dripping with abhorrence for any use except frying fish, fritters, patties, rissoles, &c. &c. The improved Cleikum dripping-pan, from a drawing by WINTERBLOSSOM, was made of ample dimensions, and with high sloping ledges. It was furnished with a covered fountain, and a conduit to allow the superfluous dripping to be easily taken away. In the Cleikum kitchen the dripping was immediately clarified for future use. [See *Clarified dripping*.]—If meat is at all of good quality, and roasted with care, it will afford a plentiful supply of good gravy, the natural and best sauce than can accompany it. To the gravy which flows from the meat, the Nabob, after repeated experiments, found, that the best addition was a very little boiling water (a large wine glass full) and salt, poured through the hole from which the spit is withdrawn, and jently laved on the browned outside under bits of the roast. To the gravy of venison and veal, when found scanty, which will sometimes be the case, the Committee ordered a little thin melted butter in preference to drawn gravies. The assets for roasts should be furnished with a gravy-fountain, for comfort as well as neatness. The jelly gravy that flows from young meats, the very essence of meat, ought to be carefully preserved, as it forms the most delicate of all gravies to enrich sauces, ragouts, hashes &c. Of this, veal gravy is the most delicate, and it is accordingly in great requisition among all good cooks; but beef gravy is fit for almost all purposes.*

---

* The Nabob, in the course of his discursive readings, though he was more a practical man than one of research, discovered that many things have been anciently used for bastings which the simplicity of modern practice rejects. Sweet herbs and seeds pulverized, butter and claret, yolks of eggs, pounded biscuit and spiceries, have all been employed. But these antique refinements were all rejected except butter and claret, which, for venison, and all dry meats that sometimes go under that generic

17. TO ROAST A SIRLOIN OF BEEF.—P. S. T., ESQ.

STUDY the above discourse, and bear in mind that next to *broiling*, roasting is the most difficult of all elementary culinary processes; and when well done, is valued accordingly. Instruction may teach even a bungler to compound a tolerable *made-dish*, which, if faulty, may be improved, disguised, or altered. But care alone and a little practice can make a dexterous roaster.

ROAST BEEF is garnished with plenty of horse-radish, finely scraped, and laid round the dish in light heaps, and is served with Yorkshire pudding, or potato pudding, and horse-radish sauce.* The *inside*, or English side,† as it is commonly called in the northern division of the island, is by some esteemed the most delicate. To this the carver must attend, and also to the equitable distribution of the fat. Cold roast beef is very generally liked; but it may be dressed warm in various ways. Slices may be warmed in a Dutch oven, and served with some of the gravy also warmed, and seasoned rather highly with pepper and salt, anchovy, eschallot, or a teaspoonful of eschallot vinegar. Cold beef may also be dressed as Olives, or as a Fricassee, Cecils, Sanders, Bubble and Squeak, &c.—See *Made dishes of beef, and French cookery of beef.*

N.B.—French cooks saw off the large bones, sprinkle the Sirloin with olive oil, and lay sliced onions and bay leaves over it, and leave it thus some days before roasting.—They serve it, when roasted, with *sauce hachée*, that is, chopped gherkins, mushrooms, capers, and an

---

name, were used at the Cleikum with unanimous approbation. Much more did our Nabob, in the fulness of his heart and stomach on this day of his triumph, say on the subject of roasting in general, and this his *Essay* roast in particular, which we must take the liberty to skip, and come at once to the receipts for roasting.

* Dr. REDGILL, who relished a joke after the serious business of dinner was despatched, holding it as a maxim that a moderate laugh aided digestion, was wont to say, that Yorkshire pudding was the true Squire of Sir Loin, and horse-radish his brisk, fiery Page, without which attendants he looked despoiled of his dignity and bearing. Yorkshire pudding is nearly the same as the *Panade* with which it was the ancient custom to baste roast till they gathered a crust before the fire.

† The French distinguish the different parts of the *aloyau* or sirloin as the "*lawyer's* bit and the *clerk's.*"

anchovy thrown into a brown sauce. Sirloin is, we think, better ordered at home. They also *braise* the Sirloin.

18. TO ROAST RIBS OF BEEF.—P. W., ESQ.

THIS piece of beef is garnished, and served with the same accompaniments as the Sirloin. Both the Ribs and the inside part of a large Sirloin may be dressed in a more elaborate way as follows:—Cut out the ribs; beat the meat flat with a rolling-pin; lay it to soak in vinegar and wine for a night; cover it with a rich force-meat, made of minced veal, suet, grated ham, lemon-peel, and mixed spices. Roll it tightly up, fixing with small skewers and tape, and roast, basting constantly with wine and butter. Froth with fresh butter, and serve with *Venison Sauce*. [See *Sauces*.]—*Obs*. A fillet of the loin, larded, marinaded and roasted, makes a handsome French dish, served with tomata sauce, or some substitute, as cucumber sauce.

19. TO ROAST A LEG OF MUTTON.—P. S. T., ESQ.
(*See French Cookery of Mutton.*)

MUTTON intended to be roasted may be kept longer than mutton for boiling, as the colour is of less importance. Cut out the pipe that runs along the backbone, which taints so early; wipe off the mustiness that gathers on the surface, and in the folds and doublings of the meat, and below the flap. This and every other piece of meat may be lightly dusted with flour, or with pepper or pounded ginger, which, by excluding the external air and keeping off flies, helps to preserve the meat, and can be taken off in the washing previous to roasting. A *leg*, a *chine*, a *saddle*, a *loin*, a *breast*, a *shoulder*, and the *haunch* or *gigot*, are the roasting pieces of mutton. Joint the roast well, whatever be the piece. Most of the loose fat should be cut from the loin, which may be stuffed, and must be papered at first, to preserve the kidney-fat.

This roast requires a rather quick fire to concentrate its juices: *onion sauce*, *cucumber sauce*, and currant jelly, are ordered in some Cookery Books to be served with roast mutton; but a juicy leg of mutton requires no sauce save its own gravy. A saddle is roasted as above, tying it to the spit. Some good French cooks serve roast mutton on French beans stewed in good stock, with a couple of onions cut in dice and fried. The crowberry or red bilberry, and even the berry of the mountain-ash, as a thick jelly, makes a good sauce for venison or mountain mutton, and is used for this purpose in Sweden. Many modern gourmands consider sweet fruit jellies with animal food as not merely among the vulgarities but the absolute barbarisms of cookery.

N.B.—Potatoes browned in the dripping-pan, or a plain potato-pudding placed below the dripping, were two favourite accompaniments to this dish at the *Cleikum*. Mashed turnip is another approved accompaniment.—See *Made dishes of Mutton*.

20. TO ROAST A SUCKING PIG.—BY DR. REDGILL.

A SUCKING PIG! *un cochon de lait!* France and England, natural enemies on the relative merits of ragouts and roast beef, are in brotherhood here. The age on which every *gourmand*, whether insular or continental, has set his seal, is, from ten days to double that number. Unlike the ways of other flesh, in this delicate creature —this "ortolan with four feet", as a corresponding member calls it—there is but one step between the *gully* of the butcher and the carver's knife. In short, he must be killed; but that done, the sooner he is roasted and eaten the better is he relished by those in the secret. The ordinary way, after he has received the *coup de grace*, is to take off the hair by scalding.* When

---

* Dr. REDGILL, though apt to be somewhat violent in his prejudices, and entertaining a loyal and laudable hatred of COBBETT and all his ways, paused when TOUCHWOOD communicated to him the method which that demagogue—infallible in hog's flesh, and unequalled in bolting—recommends for removing the hair of grown porkers; "and why not," said the Nabob, "of sucklings?" "The first method (scalding)," says COBBETT, "slackens the skin, opens all the pores of it, and makes it loose and flabby, by drawing out the roots of the hair. The second (singeing) tightens the skin in every part, contracts all the sinews and veins, &c." This is said in reference to bacon no doubt; but it was for talent like Dr. REDGILL's to apply it to young pigs. In a roast pig, where *crackling* is all in all, this burning process is surely worthy of trial. The President, with a meanness of jealousy of which the good Doctor was incapable, where pig of which he was himself to partake, was concerned, had indeed kept this important information secret till the scalded *eleve* of his rival was smoking in the platter; he then referred, with malicious triumph, to the singeing of sheep's head, reasoning on what a *wersh, fusionless* morsel it would make if scalded. The moisture which had overflowed the Doctor's

cleaned from the hair, and the entrails taken out, the pig must be well washed in cold water. Cut off the feet at the first joint, loosening and leaving on the skin to turn neatly over. He is now ready for the stuffing. For this, take a half ounce of mild sage, and a couple of young onions parboiled; chop these very fine, add a cupful of grated bread-crumbs, two ounces of good butter, and a high relish of pepper and salt. Sew the slit neatly up, (this the Doctor did with his own hands,) and baste first with brine, then with the best fresh butter or salad oil, if you would have the *crackling* crisp, which is the true and only test of a well-roasted pig. Some cooks tie up the butter in a bit of muslin, and diligently rub the crackling with this; others anoint that substance with a well-cleaned bunch of feathers, to keep it constantly moist. A pig-iron, or some ingenious substitute, must be placed in the centre of the grate, part of the time, to prevent the middle regions of the animal from being scorched before the extremities are enough done. For *sauce*—clear beef or veal gravy, with a squeeze of lemon, and, if approved, a little of the stuffing stirred into the sauce-tureen.—*Obs.* Apple sauce and currant sauce are still served with roast pig; but sweet sauces for animal food are every day losing favour, if not place. Even currant jelly sauce and venison, which were heretofore considered one-and-indivisible, are now often seen disjoined. The taste of the age is decidedly for the pungent, the sharp, the piquant, and the acid. Another favourite sauce is the liver and brains, and a few sprigs of sage, chopped and boiled up in the gravy. In Scotland, where the pig is too often

---

chops as he viewed his savoury charge reposing, as —— might say, "in the crispness of his beauty," was arrested in its course. But between a singed pig in prospect, and a scalded pig on the table ready roasted, sauce, *crackling*, stuffing, all alike inviting, the Doctor did not long hesitate. This was a young pig of twelve days old; there were still six of the farrow remaining, and, resolving to accept of his stomach's good, even at the hands of a Cobbett, he avowed the intention of making the experiment on one of the others; so that point will be ascertained in time for next year's edition of this our manual.

N.B.—Every cook should be made aware, that, by singeing chickens and fowls, she not only removes the downy feathers, but gives firmness to the flesh, and tenacity to the skin; and that the chickens, if for fricassee, broiling, &c., will cut up much cleaner if well singed.

dished whole, the brains cannot be obtained to enrich the sauce, which, along with the trouble given to the carver, was considered by the Club a capital objection to this mode of dishing. In England the pig is generally cut off the spit down the middle on both sides; the head is cut off and divided, and the jaws are stuck up on each side for ornament, instead of the pippin, which was wont of old to be stuck in the grinning chops of the savoury cherub. Roast pig, when not liked cold, should be cut into neat fillets, and warmed in a strained sauce made of thin melted butter, flour, sweet herbs, chopped mushrooms, and a bay-leaf, or in broth so seasoned, or in *Bechamel*.

For an excellent way of dressing pig, see *French Cookery*,* also Scotch receipt *National Dishes*.

21. TO ROAST A HAUNCH OR SHOULDER OF VENISON IN THE ENGLISH MODE.—BY H. J., ESQ.†

THE meat may be kept from ten to twenty days by proper care, and by observing the precautions formerly

---

* The illustrious members of the *Caveau Moderne*, the most distinguished *gourmet* and *gourmand* association in the world (previous to the establishment of the Cleikum Club), steep their pig in fresh water for four hours; baste him with a *bouquet* of sage dipped in olive oil; and for farcing use fine herbs minced, steeped in lemon-juice, and about a pound of fresh butter. This, though a French, is no bad receipt.—P. T.

† WINTERBLOSSOM and JEKYLL, both men of family and fashion, the former of whom had for forty years, by one means or other, contrived "to sit at good men's feasts," took the lead here. "Nothing," said JEKYLL, "can be more delicious than a fat buck from an English park, a 'hart of grease,' in the proper season. It is food for heroes and princes; but, with the good leave of our hostess, this 'doe or roe, or hart or hind' of the Caledonian forest, would please me fully better bounding on its native hills than smoking on this board. For the greater part of the year these wild animals are as sinewy, lean, and dry as the stalkers who pursue them. Roast it will not,—this meagre hard meat. With all appliances to boot, it makes but indifferent pasty; but after a long morning of shooting, or for a *dejeuner à la fourchette*, I have found a fricassee of it cleverly tossed up—what you Scots call venison collops, Mrs. DODS,—very tolerable eating."

"And what you Englishers lick your lips after," said MEG, not a little offended. "I have had but little handling of English fallow deer; but as gude venishon, haunch and shoulder, neck and brisket, has been roasted in my father's kitchen as e'er coost horn or cloot in an English policy—set them up!"

"For my own private eating," said TOUCHWOOD, "a leg of five-year-old heath wether mutton before all the venison in the world; but

recommended for preserving mutton. When to be used, clean it without much wetting, with a sponge dipped in lukewarm water. Unless venison is *fat* it is useless to roast it; and in roasting, the main object is to preserve the *fat*. For this purpose, butter or rub over with salad oil a large sheet of kitchen paper, tie it over the fat, and butter it on the outside once more. Have ready rolled a coarse paste of flour and water, to the thickness of a half inch, on another sheet of paper, and with this cover the first paper. Tie the whole firmly on, and pour plenty of melted butter over the outside paper to prevent it from catching to the fire. Baste constantly, and keep up the fire, which must be a strong, clear *sirloin* fire to penetrate through the incasements, and roast the haunch. Venison is rather preferred underdone than overdone, as its flesh is naturally dry. A large haunch may be allowed from four to five hours, when wrapped in paste. A half hour before it is ready it must be carefully *unswaddled*, placed nearer the fire, basted with fresh butter, and lightly dredged with flour, to brown and froth. For *sauce*,—Currant jelly melted in red wine, or the jelly roughed in a sweetmeat glass is still usually served.—*Obs*. A glass of claret, with three times that quantity of gravy made of venison or mutton, and a small glassful of raspberry vinegar, all very hot was the sharp sauce most relished by our Club; or a plain sharp sauce made of white-wine vinegar and the finest lump-sugar, heated in a stone jar.

This is the best mode of roasting venison where expense is not grudged. In many cases the paste may be dispensed with,—a double paper will be sufficient. The shoulder, breast, and neck, are all roasted; but the latter is much better dressed as a pasty or as soup.— See also *Pies*.

At small genuine gourmand parties, as the venison fat freezes, it is not unusual to cut off small slices of *fat* and *lean*, and heat them in a silver dish over a

---

on occasions of high festival, this aristocratic dish is indispensable to the fools who preside and the knaves who partake—so about it, Captain. The *dulce* we leave to you and WINTERBLOSSOM; the *utile* is my own peculiar province."

spirit-lamp. Venison can only thus be restored to perfection.

22. TO ROAST RED DEER OR ROE.—BY P. W., ESQ.*

Season the haunch highly, by rubbing it well with mixed spices. Soak it for six hours in claret, and a quarter pint of the best vinegar, or the fresh juice of three lemons; turn it frequently, and baste with the liquor. Strain the liquor in which the venison was soaked; add to it fresh butter melted, and with this baste the haunch during the whole time it is roasting. Fifteen minutes before the roast is drawn remove the paper, and froth and brown it as directed in other receipts. For *sauce*,—Take the contents of the dripping-pan, which will be very rich and highly-floured; add a half pint of clear brown gravy, drawn from venison or full-aged heath mutton. Boil them up together, skim, add a tea-spoonful of walnut catsup, and pour the same round the roast. Instead of the walnut catsup any of the flavoured vinegars most congenial to venison, and to the taste of the Gastronome, may be substituted.†—See *Made dishes of Venison*.

23. TO ROAST VEAL.—P. S. T., ESQ.

THE fillet, the loin, the shoulder,‡ and the breast, are roasted; the back ribs are best used for pie or cutlets; and the scrag should be either cut to pieces and stewed, and served in stew soup, or made into rice-broth. Stuff the flap of the fillet with forcemeat made as directed for boiled turkey, but with rather more lemon-peel; [See No. 8. p. 85.] Sew in the stuffing. Some of it may be worked up with yolk of egg into the shape of pigeons'

---

* This was one of those original receipts on which our old beau plumed himself not a little. This mode of dressing venison, he said, had been invented by the MASTER of the KITCHEN to MARY of GUISE, and had been ever since preserved a profound secret by the noble family of M———, till the late Earl communicated it to himself.

† After the third venison dinner, it was the recorded opinion of the Club, that it is downright idiocy, a wanton and profligate sacrifice of the palate and the stomach to the vanity of the eye, to roast venison when it is not *fat*, while so many more nutritious and palatable modes of cookery may be employed, in soup, pasty or civet.

‡ The *noix*, or large muscle bedded in firm fat near the neck, is the tid-bit of the Parisian epicure.

eggs, parboiled, and fried and browned below the roast, drained, and served as a garnishing or made into a small accompanying dish.* Be careful to brown the outside nicely, which can only be well done by attention to the state of the fire.†

24. LOIN AND BREAST OF VEAL.

A LOIN is roasted and served in the very same way, only the kidney fat, which is so delicate, must be papered, and the roast should be more constantly basted; or the flap part should be rolled in and skewered firm, and the bones chopped off, to give the dish a handsome shape. The SHOULDER is often stuffed; and the stuffing for this piece requires more suet, marrow, or butter, whichever is employed, than the forcemeat for the fillet. The breast must be roasted with the caul on till nearly enough done, which both preserves and enriches the meat. Serve these roasts with their own gravy only.

25. TO ROAST LAMB.

YOUNG lamb, and none other is fit for the use of a gastronome of high *gout*,—a hobble-de-hoy between lamb and mutton being even coarser than a three months pig. Lamb, like pig, and indeed all young meat, should not be long kept, if the flavour, and juices are to be obtained in perfection; time to cool is considered quite

---

* Forcemeat must be left in a great measure to the genius and invention of the cook. Like spiceries and seasoning, it may, in the exercise of good discretion, be used *ad libitum*, bearing in mind, that it is intended to enrich and give piquance to the relish of the more insipid meats. Relishing ingredients of all kinds enter into the composition of forcemeat, such as grated ham or beef, sausage, pickled oysters, caviare, anchovy, sweet herbs, eshallot, mushrooms, truffles, and morells, currie powder, cayenne, &c. &c. "Plodding perseverance," said JEKYLL, "may make a good roaster, and careful observance of rules, a tolerable compounder of a made-dish, but the true maker of forcemeat, like the true poet, must be born."

† "A bit of the brown" is esteemed the most delicate part of this roast. It was with this, liberally supplied from Mr. STRAHAN'S veal, that the demagogue WILKES not only overcame the prejudices, but actually gained the heart of Dr. JOHNSON,—a success which far outdoes that of RICHARD over Lady ANNE. But then he helped a slice of the brown or bitter orange, which formed the garnishing, along with the browned outside. Ever as you would gain the heart of a judicious epicure, garnish your roast veal with slices of lemon.—P. T.

sufficient by knowing gourmands. It is true, the fibre
will be thready, but the flavour will be infinitely
superior to that of lamb killed for days. Lamb is sometimes roasted in a *side*, or in a saddle. In roasting the hind
quarter, the flap of the loin may be stuffed, using the
superfluous fat for the forcemeat.*

Sauce.—The gravy which flows from the meat, with
about a wine glass full of boiling water and a little salt,
run through the spit hole, and *Mint Sauce*. Serve salad,
spinage, French beans, cauliflower, or green peas with
lamb; garnish with crisp parsley, or sprigs of cauliflower.
The fore-quarter may be lightly jointed. Lamb must
be well done. This and the shank or knuckle of all
roasts, or of a ham, ought to have a fringe, or plain piece
of writing paper, twisted neatly round it, as the bare
stump looks ungainly. When the shoulder is removed,
the carver is expected to squeeze a lemon, or to sprinkle
a little salt over the ribs, or, if necessary, to put in a little
melted butter; and to press the separated parts together
to obtain gravy. *N.B.* a friend, who admires French
cookery, recommends a *maitre d'hotel sauce* to be served
under roast lamb. In Parisian cookery the lean parts of
the lamb have thin slices of bacon papered over them
while roasting. When done the shoulder is lifted near
the breast so as not to be perceptible, and a *maitre d'hotel*
sauce is slipped in. A clear gravy is served in the dish,
and the larded parts are glazed.

26. TO ROAST PORK.—DR. R.

PORK takes more of the fire than any other kind of

---

* This is an old Scottish practice, which MEG DODS called "makin
a pouch." Dr. REDGILL, who patronized all receptacles for forcemeat,
wheresoever placed, vowed that "a hind-quarter of lamb should never
again be roasted in his kitchen without *a pouch*." This protuberance
must not be too large, else it might prove offensive to the eye,—an
organ that ought to be diligently consulted in all matters connected with
the table. "Open the mouth, and shut the eyes," the maxim of a
great modern gastronome, had certainly, WINTERBLOSSOM said, been
stolen from the luxurious picture of the Gude Wife of Auchtermuchty's
Sow:—

"And aye scho *winked* and aye scho drank."

Both TOUCHWOOD and REDGILL rebuked the old beau for this
irreverent sally against an authority for which the latter entertained the
most profound respect.

meat. Choose it young, short in the shank, fine in the grain, and smooth but thick in the skin.* Cut a hole in the knuckle, widen it with the finger, and stuff with mild sage and onions parboiled and chopped fine, pepper, salt, grated crumbs, a piece of butter, a tea-spoonful of made mustard, and an egg to cement the whole. With a bunch of feathers rub the skin with salad or sweet oil, or with fresh butter tied up in a muslin rag. Do this frequently to prevent the *crackling* from blistering, and to make it crisp and brown. The crackling must be scored into diamonds twenty minutes before the roast is done; but unless it look *hide-bound*, and scorched or shrivelled, the scoring need not go deep. The roast *loin* should, however, be scored in *stripes*, with advantage both to the eating and to the appearance. Some cooks add pulverized sage to the basting. We only recommend this in roasting the griskin. Pork requires a more pungent sauce than sucking pig; yet apple sauce is still occasionally used. *Onion sauce* we like better, or *sauce Robert*; but confidently recommend Dr. REDGILL's *sauce* for *pork, goose, duck,* or *rabbit.* (See *Sauces.*) French beans or peas-pudding are served with roast pork. The French serve a *poivrade* under a roast chine.—*Obs. Sham* House lamb, when the real is scarce and high-priced, is made by skinning a half-grown porker, and cutting it of a proper shape.—The Cleikum Club countenanced no counterfeits.

27. TO ROAST TURKEY, FOWLS, AND GAME.

A TURKEY will keep a fortnight, a fowl a week. By care they will keep much longer; that is to say, if drawn, hung in a cool, dry air, wiped often, and seasoned with pepper in the inside.† The sinews of the legs must be

---

* If pork is fed in styes, that which has fattened on potatoes and butter-milk we consider much better, both in flesh and flavour, than that which has been fed on drenches of barley-meal and kitchen slops. The use of *scoring* pork is to increase the surface—in other words, that delicious *jaune croquante,* therefore we say *score.*—P. T.

† So dexterously, and with such an air of conscious superiority, did Mistress DODS carry herself, that, except for the new lights which had dawned upon REDGILL in the composition of stuffings, and an affected dandy squeamishness which overcame the young Guardsman about the trussing, in this important branch of the art, the Club would,

drawn, (those of fowls, pheasants, &c., should all be
drawn, especially when the birds are old;) press down the

---

unquestioning, have submitted to her judgment as to an oracle; but
these causes produced open discontents, and vehement debate, and—
"I say sweet stuffing is an abomination for roast turkey," cried
REDGILL, as the knife of WINTERBLOSSOM gave to view MEG's savoury
composition, mottled with Zante currants, and fragrant with what she
termed "a scrape o' a nutmug,"—an immense grater furnished with this
spicy fruit, being, instead of a lady's essence-bottle, generally lodged in
the depths and labyrinths of those strong, blue cloth pockets, with scarlet
walting, of whose multifarious contents JEKYLL one day made a
catalogue. "Oysters! oysters! madam; there is no other turkey stuffing
worth the attention of a Christian eater."—"Or *Dinde aux Truffes et à
la broche*," said TOUCHWOOD, animated by the spirit of contradiction,
and the ambition of displaying his science. "A pound of fresh truffles
chopped, the same quantity of rasped fat white bacon. Soak the
mixture in the stew-pan, with spiceries and a bay-leaf. Stuff the turkey,
and give him three days to take the flavour; covering him with slices of
bacon: Or chestnuts," continued he. "Roast a quarter hundred and
peel them;—leave out ten or a dozen; pound in a mortar, with the liver
parboiled, a quarter of a pound of ham, well grated or pounded, a little
basil and parsley, mace, pepper, salt, our friend MEG's *nutmug*, and a
good piece of butter; stuff and tie the bird at neck and vent:—roast him,
and tell me how you like him. For sauce, the remaining chestnuts chopped
and stirred in a thickened strong gravy, with a glass of old Sherry or
Madeira. Garnish with orange. This, Sir, is a turkey for you; or, better
still, a roast turkey, with rolls of sausage fried, or sausage balls served
with it,—'an Alderman in chains,' as those waggish rogues, the London
sturdy beggars, call it,—their favourite regale at the close of a
prosperous day." REDGILL despised the chestnut receipt; but turkey and
sausage, the ambrosia of the *bousing ken*, seemed worthy of an epicure's
serious investigation; and the next bird was ordered to be dressed
beggar fashion.

"And why, Dame," said JEKYLL, as, thrown back in his chair, he
eyed the roasted turkey with a languid air of half-affected disgust—
"Why produce the unhappy bubbly-jock with his head—forty mortal
gashes upon it—tucked under his wing, while his gizzard and liver,
larger than life, grace his other fin; this affair of dining, after all, has
its *bétise*. Or those rough-footed Scots," pointing to a brace of moorfowl, "in their spurs and pantaloons, with their pretty innocent heads
tucked under their arms, like that of St. Denis in the pictures of a book
of miracles;—nay, worse, I protest," and he lifted up his eye-glass—
"here too are ducks, if I don't mistake; but indeed there is no mistaking
—miserable amphibiae! their saffron web-feet drawn up, and spread in
such goodly sort as if "in act to swim." Our patrons, Drs. KITCHENER
and TRUSSLER, direct, that the feet be roasted *delicately crisp*, as some
people are very fond of them."

"Cut off the turkey's head, Captain JACKALL," broke forth MEG,
with indignant astonishment—"A roasted turkey! Do you tak' us for
born ignoramuses on this side of the border?"—"Cut off the heads,"
responded REDGILL, "of turkey and wild-fowl! Surely, my young
friend, you forget yourself!" The Doctor, a loyal, hearty dining Churchman, had, since the beginning of the French Revolution, seen but too
much of this "off-with-his-head" spirit abroad. "There was no knowing,"
he said, "where its devastations were to stop; it began with anointed
Kings"—"And may safely end with basted turkeys," rejoined JEKYLL,

breast-bone even more than in a fowl, to make the bird look plump; be careful in drawing, to preserve the liver whole, and not to break the gall-bag. For *stuffing* to fill the craw, take a breakfast cup full of stale bread finely grated, two ounces of minced beef-suet, or marrow, a little parsley parboiled and finely shred, a tea-spoonful of lemon-peel grated, a few sprigs of lemon thyme, a little nutmeg, pepper, and salt. Mix the whole well in a mortar, with a couple of eggs.* Do not stuff too full; and, with another egg, work up what remains into balls, to be fried and served with the turkey.

To this stuffing, parboiled sausage meat may be added, or grated ham, or oysters chopped. (The same stuffing is suitable for a large fowl.) Paper the breast. Score the *gizzard*. Season it highly with pepper, salt, and cayenne, and dip in melted butter, and then in bread-crumbs; cover the gizzard and liver with veal or lamb caul, or buttered paper, and roast them, fixing them under the pinion, and basting liberally. A very large turkey will take nearly as long to roast as a sirloin. These are not the most delicate. A moderate-sized turkey will take from an hour and a half to two hours. The fire must be clear and sharp; dredge with flour when laid down. (Fresh butter is always best for bast-ing; but salted butter may be washed and drained.) Keep the turkey far from the fire at first, that the stuffing and breast may be done through. *Sauce*—Bread

---

and he continued, "At all *tonish* tables, Mr. WINTERBLOSSOM, though I do not pretend to think better of mankind than my neighbours, it would be but a well-bred stretch of faith, to take for granted that turkey was not goose, nor pigeon grouse, without such testimony as those bloody heads and feathered heels afford. Why, the panache of his own tail-feathers, which my respected grandmother was wont to stick into the rump of her roasted pheasant, or even the surtout of his entire goodly plumage with which our ancestors invested the lordly peacock, was not more barbarous than this absurd fashion." Loud rose the clamour of cooks, scullions, and amateurs, as this new heresy was broached, and JEKYLL, if not convinced, was at least silenced.

* *An excellent Stuffing for a turkey or hare, French fashion.*—Chop, and afterwards pound in a mortar, half-a-pound of beef-suet, equal bulk (but not weight,) of soaked bread crumbs, lemon peel, parsley, and a sprig of thyme chopped, pepper, salt, two beat eggs, and a little milk or broth. This makes an excellent stuffing. See *also Quesnell's French Cookery.* French cooks are celebrated for their skill in forcemeat; one half of their merit in this department consists in their patience at the mortar.

sauce, with gravy in the dish, oyster sauce, gravy sauce, egg sauce. Hen turkeys are the most delicate, and the whitest; they are consequently preferred for boiling. See *to Hash and Devil* turkey.—Also *Made dishes of Poultry, and French Cookery.*

N.B.—A test of turkey, pheasant, fowl, &c. being ready for the spit, is their falling down when suspended in the larder by a few of the tail-feathers left for this experiment when the birds are picked. For roasting, choose full-fed, white-legged large fowls—smaller ones may do for boiling.

28. TO ROAST A GOOSE.

A GOOSE may, if well cleaned and seasoned inside, with pepper, keep, in cold weather, for a fortnight or more. Geese are in high perfection from Midsummer to Michaelmas. At that season they will improve by keeping in the larder for a week. In Scotland a goose is often rubbed with salt for ten days before roasting. In England, it is often first parboiled. Where they are rank this may be advisable, but not otherwise, as it dries the flesh. After the goose is carefully picked and singed, let it be well washed and dried with a cloth. *Stuffing*—Four well-sized onions, about half their weight of sage undried, and half the liver; parboil slightly, and chop these very fine: Add a bit of butter, yolk of egg, the crumbs of a penny loaf; or, *à la bourgeoise*, an equal quantity of mashed potatoes, and stuff the goose.* Spit the goose; fasten tightly at the neck and rump. Paper the breast, but remove the paper when it has swelled. A goose requires a brisk fire,

---

* All stuffing, containing bread-crumbs, should be allowed room to swell, and indeed all forcemeat whatever, as it expands more or less in the dressing.

The livers of geese and poultry are esteemed a great delicacy by some *gourmands*; and on the continent great pains are taken to procure fat overgrown livers. The methods employed to produce this diseased state of the animals are as disgusting to rational taste as revolting to humanity. The geese are crammed with fat food, deprived of drink, kept in an intolerably hot atmosphere, and fastened by the feet (we have heard of nailing) to the shelves of the fattening cribs. The celebrated *Strasburg pies,* which are esteemed so great a delicacy that they are often sent as presents to distant places, are enriched with these diseased livers. It is a mistake that these pies are wholly made of this artificial animal substance.

well kept up; and will take from two hours to two hours
and a half to roast. The breast must not be allowed to
sink. *Apple sauce* is, by *prescription*, served with goose.
For delicate eating, this bird requires a drawn gravy in
the dish, its own being often rank and oily.—*Obs*. To
apple sauce the Cleikum Club preferred onion sauce;
better still, Dr. REDGILL's sauce for roast pork, duck,
or goose, and sauce Robert.—See *Sauces*. The gravy
may either be poured into the goose by the carver
making, for this purpose, a slit in the apron, or served in
a tureen in thick melted butter. In Scotland it is
customary to garnish with slices of raw onion, but the
practice is on the wane. GREEN GEESE are roasted in the
same manner; but for these thready younglings, the sage
and onion is better omitted. Season them with pepper
and salt, and put a piece of butter into the inside as an
interior basting. Froth and brown nicely. The gravy is
preserved and served, but more gravy must generally be
added. *Gooseberry sauce*, or REDGILL's sauce.—See
Sauces. Garnish with grated crust of bread.* Salted

---

* In England the goose is sacred to St. Michael; in France to St.
Martin; in Scotland, where dainties were not going every day,

> "'Twas Christmas sent its savoury goose."

The Michaelmas goose is said to owe its origin to Queen Elizabeth's
dining on one at the table of an English baronet on that day when she
received tidings of the dispersion of the Spanish Armada; in commemora-
tion of which, she ordered the *Goose* to make its appearance every
Michaelmas. In some places, particularly Caithness, geese are cured
and smoked, and are highly relishing. Smoked Solan geese are well
known as contributing to the abundance of a Scottish breakfast, though
too rank and fishy-flavoured for unpractised palates. They are ate as
whets, or relishes.

The *goose* has made some figure in the English history. The churl-
ishness of RICHARD CŒUR DE LION, a sovereign distinguished for an
insatiable appetite and vigorous digestion, in an affair of roast goose, was
the true cause of his captivity in Germany. The King, disguised as a
palmer, was returning to his own dominions, attended by Sir FULK
DOYLEY and Sir THOMAS DE MULTON, "Brothers in Arms," and wearing
the same privileged garb. They arrived in Almaine, (Germany,) at
the town of Carpentras, where,

> "A *goose* they dight to their dinner,
> In a tavern where they were.
> King RICHARD the fire bet;
> THOMAS to him the spit set;
> FOUK DOYLEY tempered the wood;
> Dear a-bought they that good;"

for in came a *Minstralle*, or she-Minstrel, with offer of specimens of her

geese are, in some parts of Ireland and Scotland, served with a cabbage sauce, or cabbage stewed in good broth. The French roast geese with chestnuts, as in the receipt for turkey, [*Note*, page 105.] The liver is chopped with the chestnuts, and both are fried together in lard before the goose is stuffed with them.* Onions, fried in the goose fat, is a favourite accompaniment with some old-fashioned provincial eaters. Rings of large onions cooked in strong *consommé*, are more delicate, but not better.

29. TO ROAST DUCKS, TEAL, AND WIDGEONS.

KEEP ducks at least three days. If a pair are to be roasted, one may be stuffed as directed for a goose, with about half the quantity of stuffing; and, to suit all tastes, the other done plain, only seasoning with pepper and salt. From three quarters of an hour to a whole hour will roast them. Baste well, and dust lightly with flour to make them froth, and look of a rich, warm brown. Green pease are indissolubly allied to ducks.—*Sauce*,

---

art, in return for a leg of the goose and a cup of the wine. RICHARD, who loved "rich meats," and cared little at this time for their usual accompaniment, minstrelsy,"—

> "—bade that she should go;
> That turned him to mickle woe.
> The Minstralle took in mind,
> And said, ye are men unkind;
> And if I may, ye shall *for-think*
> Ye gave me neither meat nor drink!"

The lady, who was English, recognised the King, and denounced him to the King of Germany, who ordered the pilgrims into his presence, insulted RICHARD, "said him shame," called him *taylard*, probably for his affection for *goose*, and finally ordered him to a dungeon. But RICHARD, a true knightly eater, who besides roast goose, liked to indulge in

> "Bread and wine,
> Piment and clarry good and fine;
> Cranes and swans, and venison;
> Partridges, plovers, and heron,—

was neither dainty nor over-nice. At a pinch, he could eat any thing, which, on sundry emergencies, stood him in great stead. Wax and nuts, and tallow and grease mixed, carried him through one campaign, when the enemy thought to have starved out the English army and its cormorant commander. The courage and strength of RICHARD were always redoubled after dinner. It was then his greatest feats were performed.—*Romance of Coeur de Lion.*

* Query?—Would not a young salted goose answer very well dressed as duck in *sour croute*?—P. T.

Apple sauce, onion, or sage sauce, or Dr. REDGILL's sauce for goose, duck, &c. WILD DUCKS are roasted in the same way, but made very crisp; and as they are smaller, they take less time, from twenty-five minutes to half an hour.—See *Sauces*. The above receipt is also applicable to *Teal* and *Widgeons*.—*Obs*. Some epicures prefer all wild fowl underdone, to have the flavour in perfection; and, to secure this, they eat it without sauce. All sorts of wild fowl require to be longer kept than your "tame villatic fowl," because they are drier in the flesh, for the same reasons that a city Alderman is more abounding in juices than a Backwoodsman, or an Indian hunter.—See *Hashed duck, Made dishes, &c..*

30. TO ROAST PHEASANTS AND PARTRIDGES.*

THESE birds are trussed in the same manner; the craw is drawn out by a slit in the neck, the head is left on,

---

* Necessity and the vanity of producing at a dinner what was rare and far-travelled, must first have introduced among cleanly civilized nations the custom of *over-keeping* game, till in time it came to be considered as essential to its perfection that it be kept till putrid, and that what has not flavour may at least have *fumet*. It is at the same time indispensable that game be kept till *tender*. Game, as we have said before, must be longer kept than domestic fowls, to be in proper condition for the table. A great deal has been said on preserving provisions of late years, but we are afraid little has been done. We are certain that very few of the practices recommended have been adopted, and that chiefly because when tried they were found wanting. Form, colour, and material may be preserved; but flavour, and even nutritious qualities, have fled before the pyroligneous acid, and the genius of Appert; and mummy partridges, and embalmed green pease, survive to please the eye and fill the table—and this so far is highly desirable—but sadly disappoint the palate. Game—we speak not of giving pheasants and grouse to immortality—may be kept good a long time, by drawing, cropping, picking, and (without washing) rubbing with equal parts of salt, pounded loaf-sugar, and a little pepper. It is a great mistake to wet, much less to wash, any thing intended to be kept. Charcoal may also be employed to retard putrefaction. Lay a thin muslin cloth over the birds, and place lumps of charcoal on that. Charcoal baskets and closets may be had on the scale adapted to small establishments. We have no faith in charcoal doing much good in the way of restoring what is much tainted, though this is confidently asserted. The knife applied to the worst parts, scraping and constantly removing the mustiness, and, when to be used, washing with vinegar and water, is the preferable method. Game, when it is wished to be kept to grace a gala day, besides the above precautions, may be parboiled or par-roasted. In

and the legs of the partridge are tucked into each other.★
Baste frequently, and dust with flour to froth; the
fire must be brisk and clear. A partridge will take from
twenty to twenty-five minutes; a pheasant from thirty
to forty-five. Make and butter a toast; having pared
off the outer crust, moisten it in hot water or broth,
soak it in the dripping, and serve the partridge on the
toast. This is lighter than fried bread-crumbs, which
some cooks use for these birds. Pheasants require gravy.
It may be made of scrag of mutton, or knuckle of veal,
but is better of beef, and best of all of game when that
is in plenty.—See *Brown gravy sauce, Bread sauce*, or
Rice sauce.—Obs. We do not recommend the ornament
of the pheasant's best tail-feather stuck in its tail; but
such things are still heard of. *Guinea* and *pea-fowl* are
dressed and served exactly as pheasants; and by a fiction
of cookery, a fowl is converted into a *pheasant* when a
brace cannot be procured.

31. TO ROAST WOODCOCKS, SNIPES, PLOVERS, RAILS,
AND ORTOLANS.

KEEP them till tender. They must not be drawn, as
the intestines are considered a delicacy. [This rule
admits of exceptions. The proverb says, what is one
man's meat is another man's poison.] Tie them on a bird-
spit, and lay them down to a clear brisk fire. Lay slices
of toast in the dripping-pan, to catch the *trail*. These
birds and moor-game require to be deluged with butter

---

short, dipped for *five* minutes in boiling water, or laid to the fire for
seven minutes, which must be made to touch all parts, inside as well as
outside. Then dry thoroughly, and use salt, sugar, and pepper, as
above. Before roasting cleanse from this seasoning, and season with a
little fresh pepper. But the preservation of game depends as much on
the sportsman as on the cook. A bird or hare, much mangled by shot,
will taint far more quickly than one killed in "a gentlemanly way," and
what has fallen into the water, than that which drops on land. For
some seasons back the southern sportsmen, who frequent the highland
moors, have paid great attention to preserving and packing their game.
Packing in *hops* is found to answer better than any other method yet
employed, and is now very generally resorted to.
  ★ French cooks lay slices of lemon over the breasts of the partridges,
on these slices of lard, and above all fasten paper. Dr. Hunter recommends a stuffing of minced beef or veal for a cock-pheasant, the flesh of
which is rather insipid to English palates. This may be more acceptable
than the French practice of enriching these birds by larding.

in basting. Dish them on the toasts, pour clear brown beef gravy very hot into the dish, and set it on a hot table, or over steam, or a chafing-dish. These birds will take from twenty-five to thirty minutes, in proportion to the size.—*Sauce*, Pleydel's sauce for wild-fowl. Garnish with slices of bitter orange, or lemon, and fried bread-crumbs.—*Obs.* French cooks stuff woodcocks with chopped truffles, and either roast them, or dress them with fire under and over the pot.

32. TO ROAST GROUSE, BLACK COCK, AND PTARMIGAN.

TRUSS with the head under the wing. They require a sharp clear fire, must be well basted, and not overdone. Serve on a buttered toast soaked in the dripping-pan, and put brown beef gravy in the dish. In this and the above receipt we recommend plain melted butter instead of gravy, to those who wish to retain the native flavour of the birds.—*Rice sauce*, or Pleydel's *Sauce*, also *Orange gravy*.

33. TO ROAST PIGEONS.

LET them be cropped and drawn as soon as killed, and wiped inside as well as possible. They will be ready for the spit in from twelve-to forty-eight hours, according to the weather; and are in high season from June to November. If kept too long, they lose the flavour. When to be dressed, they must, when drawn, be well washed in several waters; and great care must be taken, as in all birds, not to break the gall-bag. Stuff with parsley parboiled and chopped, and about the size of a nutmeg of butter for each bird, a few bread-crumbs, and the liver chopped, if it is liked. Season rather highly with pepper and salt. Twenty to twenty-five minutes will roast them. Dust with flour, and froth with fresh butter. Parsley and butter, or plain melted butter, is served in the dish, and is more suitable for mild-flavoured birds of all kinds, than meat gravy, which has so strong a predominating flavour of its own.—*Bread sauce, Orange gravy sauce*, or *Rice sauce*. Serve with dressed French beans, or asparagus, or cucumber. Garnish with fried bread-crumbs, or slices of bitter orange.

34. TO ROAST LARKS AND WHEAT-EARS.

WHEN well cleaned, dip them in yolk of egg, and roll them in bread-crumbs. Put a small bit of butter in each bird. Spit on a lark-spit, and fasten that to the spit. Baste with plenty of good butter, which is most essential in roasting all the smaller birds. Strew sifted bread-crumbs over the birds as they roast. From twelve to fifteen minutes will do them. Serve fried bread-crumbs, and garnish with fried crumbs or crisp parsley. —*Obs.* Some good cooks put a thin small slice of bacon between the birds when they are spitted to nourish them. This is good practice.

35. TO ROAST HARE, FAWN, OR KID.

A HARE will keep from a fortnight to three weeks, if properly managed; and is seldom fit for roasting before eight days, though for *soup* it may be used nearly as soon as killed. An old hare is never fit for roasting. A hare keeps best when not opened for some days; and the vent and mouth may be tied, to prevent the air from hastening the process of putrefaction. When kept four days in this state, (if the object is to keep it as long as possible,) it may be paunched and skinned, and the heart and liver taken out and scalded. Wash and soak it in water when to be dressed, changing the water several times. Drip, dry, and truss it. Make a little slit in the neck, and every part where the blood has gathered, to let it out. Even a young hare makes but a dry roast, so that a rich and relishing stuffing is a *sine qua non* when dressing it in this manner. For stuffing, take the grated crumbs of a penny-loaf, a quarter of a pound of beef-suet, or three ounces of marrow, a small quantity of parsley and eschalot, a boned anchovy, a tea-spoonful of grated lemon-peel, and the same quantity of nutmeg; salt and pepper to taste, a little cayenne, and the liver parboiled and chopped if in a sound state.* Mix the

---

* The liver of an animal is often tainted with disease when the animal is otherwise in perfect health. This will be known by the colour and state of the liver. It is surely unnecessary to add, that an unsound liver is not a fit ingredient for stuffing.

ingredients with the yolk of an egg, and the crumbs soaked in a very little claret. Put this in the belly, and sew it closely up.* Baste well with plenty of butter for three quarters of an hour; then drain the dripping-pan into a basin; baste with cream and yolk of an egg well beat, and flour lightly. It will take from an hour and a half to two hours. For sauce, venison sauce, or the drippings of the hare mixed with cream, or with claret, a squeeze of a lemon, some thin slices of bread, and a bit of fresh butter, boiled up with the skimmed drippings, and highly seasoned; also currant-jelly.—See *Hashed hare, Hare collops, Made dishes of hare, &c.—Obs.* In France a roasted hare is always larded on the back, but the French seldom roast this dry animal from choice. For an excellent method of dressing hare, see *Civet* and *Lievre en daube, French Cookery.*

By a fiction of cookery, the lean inside of a large sirloin is cut up, stuffed as a hare, skewered, tied with tape, fixed to the spit and roasted. It requires to be highly seasoned, and in truth eats much better than most roasted hares. In country situations, a hare is often stuffed with mashed potato, grated ham, suet and onion, and highly seasoned with pepper and allspice; nor, though a plain, is this a bad fashion.

36. A young FAWN is treated precisely as a hare, but must not be kept above one day. When somewhat grown, it may be roasted in quarters, or in a haunch or a saddle. Cover with veal or lamb caul in roasting, or slices of fat bacon, and baste well. Froth in the usual manner, and serve with *venison sauce*, and a good gravy in the dish. A KID is roasted as a hare.—*Obs.* These are all, at least hare and kid, very dry meats, and are better dressed, the former as soup or collops, the latter as collops or stew, or both in the French fashion. A RABBIT, when large, may be stuffed and roasted as a hare; when young, baste and dredge as in roasting poultry, and make a sauce of the chopped liver and chopped parsley, stirred into melted butter.†

---

* See also stuffing French fashion, note to page 108.

† A hare's ears are reckoned a dainty by some affected epicures;—they must be singed and cleaned. The Cleikum Club held them in equal respect with duck's feet, but were very tolerant of those who admire them.

37. ON BAKING MEAT.

THE baker's, or the family *oven*, may often be substituted for the cook and the spit, with greater economy and convenience; and for some particular joints and kinds of viands, it is even more suitable. A baking dish ought to be in the form of a trough, and at least six inches deep, that the meat may in fact stew in its own juices, as it gets little or no basting. But a *pig* must be baked in a shallow tin dish;—the dripping-pan of a *Bachelor's* or *Dutch oven* will do very well. Prepare things to be baked as for roasting, but season more highly. A *fillet* or *breast of veal*, if not very high fed, will bake as well as it will roast. The oven is equally suitable to a leg of pork, but a *loin* requires to be *sweated* in roasting—it is too greasy when baked. A *pig*, if not very old, and if the baker is careful to anoint the *crackling* as in roasting, bakes very well. His ears and tail must be put in buttered papers, if you would hope ever to see them return from the oven. Geese and ducks may be baked, if not old and *rank*; in which case they must be *sweated* before the fire, to overcome the flavour. A leg of *mutton*, with potatoes parboiled and peeled, and an onion shred, makes, when baked, an excellent plain family dish, the mucilage of the potatoes combines so kindly with the fat of the meat. The noble *sirloin* disdains to be cribbed in the oven; but a *rump of beef* slightly salted for a few days, washed, highly seasoned, and baked with plenty of butter in a deep covered vessel, is esteemed a delicacy.* A *hare* or *rabbit* may be *baked*, allowing plenty of butter in the dish, and putting a large piece or a rich stuffing into the inside of the animal. *Herrings, sprats, salmon, haddocks*, and *eels*, may all be highly seasoned and baked with advantage.—See *Potted herrings*. Bakers' ovens have one great drawback;—they are accused of being sad suckers in, indeed real sponges for gravy; so that they often indemnify the bakers' apprentices for the trouble saved to the cook. Besides, meat is seldom got home in season from those wholesale receptacles

---

* The Cleikum Club did not prove this receipt.

for all manner of joints; and about the dinner hour, what dismay is often created by the face of the maid,—

"Who comes with most terrible news from the baker,
————————————That insolent sloven!—
Who shut out the pasty when shutting his oven."

Hams are often soaked and baked, where they are used in great quantity, and where the object is to cut thin.* Fish, if baked, must have plenty of butter.

CHAPTER III.

BROILING.

I have no dainties for ye, gentlemen,
Nor loads of meat to make the room smell of 'em;—
Only a dish to every man I dedicate.

BEAUMONT AND FLETCHER.

BROILING is the most delicate manual office the common cook has to perform, and that which requires the most unremitting vigilance. She may turn her back on the *stew-pan* or the *spit*, but the *gridiron* can never be left with impunity.

A valuable and large portion of society is interested in this culinary process. It is the simple mode of cookery, best suited, and generally the most acceptable, to the sickly, fickle appetite of the invalid and valetudinarian. It is also recommended by comfort and economy to solitary diners and small families, as by this means the

---

* A few years since the proprietor of Vauxhall Gardens lost his celebrated carver of hams, when he advertised for a new operator in that department of harmless anatomy. One of notoriety applied, when the worthy proprietor asked him how many acres he could cover with one fine ham; upon which he replied, "he did not stand upon an acre or two, more or less, but could cover the whole of his gardens with one ham." On this he was instantly hired, and told he was the very fellow for this establishment, and to cut away for the benefit of the concern and of mankind at large.

To grow a shoulder or leg of mutton.—This art is well known to the London bakers. Have a very small leg or shoulder; change it upon a customer for one a little larger, and that upon another for one better still, till by the dinner hour you have a heavey excellent joint in lieu of your original small one.—P. T.

smallest morsel of meat can be dressed *hot* as delicately as the largest quantity; and few grown persons relish cold provisions if they could help themselves. The French are admired for their skill in blending flavours, heightening relishes, imparting *sapid* qualities to what is dry or harsh, and giving piquancy to what is naturally insipid. But, as a nation, they are more entitled to praise for that *graduated scale* of cookery which descends to the very lowest class of society, and gives comfort and relish even to the meal of the Parisian tub-woman. Every French man and woman is something of a cook. Hence the proverb, "As many Frenchmen as many cooks." This they owe in some measure to the scale of their utensils, and the tiny furnaces and chafing-dishes, which enable them to deal in all manner of ways with the smallest bit of meat, while their contemporaries in London have too often but the one resource—the Sunday oven—for the large expensive joint, which loses much of its weight and succulence in baking, and, at all events, must be eaten cold by the family till it is finished. Such families seldom see soup, roots, or vegetables, save perhaps a few potatoes on the *hot* day. The cottage cookery of Scotland is much superior to that of their neighbours, from their *canny* skill in the *potage*, and in the use of roots and vegetables; and this they manage with no additional expense of fuel.

Broiling is not, however, the cookery of the cottage economist, and it is of broiling we now treat. The state of the fire is the primary consideration. It must be *clear* and *radiant*, consequently free of smoke. A fire nearly two-thirds burnt is best. The gridiron should rather be over long than too short, and ought to be so contrived that it can be placed at the distance of three, four, five, or six inches above the fire. If a gridiron is well polished at first, there can be no good cause for the bars ever becoming black. Let it be always rubbed when put aside, not only bright on the top of the bars, but clear of soot and grease between them. The bars should be narrowest at top, that they may not intercept the heat of the fire. It is well to have one gridiron for fish, and another for poultry and steaks. The gridiron must be hot through, (which will take five minutes,) before any thing is put on it. It must then be rubbed with a piece of fresh suet, to prevent the meat from being *branded*, or sticking to the hot bars. If for fish, rub with chalk.

There is great convenience sometimes in the perpendicular gridirons; and there is a trifling kind made double, of strong wire, with a hinge, which permits the steaks or fish to be turned by merely turning the implement. On the small scale of cookery, these are very convenient. They go before the fire, or over it.

38. TO BROIL BEEF-STEAKS.—P. T., ESQ.

IN England, the best steaks are cut from the middle of the rump. In Ireland, Scotland, and France, steaks which are thought more delicate, are oftener cut, like chops, from the sirloin or spare-rib, trimming off the superfluous fat, and chopping away the bone. This is the piece of meat usually cut up into steaks in the shops in Edinburgh and Glasgow, rump beef being used for minced collops, sausages, &c. Beef for steaks must be killed for from three to five days, or more, to eat *tender*, but it does not require to be kept so long as a large piece to be roasted. Cut the steaks of equal thickness, (about three quarters of an inch,) beat them out to a level—though much beating is not recommended, as it expresses the juices from the meat. Let them be from three to four inches in breadth, and from four to six in length. *Sirloin* steaks shape themselves. When the gridiron is hot, rub the bars with suet, sprinkle a little salt over the fire, and lay on the steaks. Turn them frequently with steak-tongs, to do them equally, and keep in the juices. When the fat blazes and smokes very much, quickly remove the gridiron for a second, till the blaze is past. From ten to twelve minutes will do a steak. Have a hot dish, rubbed with eschalot, placed by the side or over the fire, on the edge of the gridiron. When turning the steaks with the tongs, if there be on the top any gravy that would fall in turning, drop it quickly into this dish to preserve it. Steaks are generally preferred *underdone*. Sprinkle them with a little salt just before they are dished in the hot dish, in which a little eshalot, finely shred, may be put, a bit of fresh butter, and a tea-spoonful of catsup, if liked. Turn the steaks over with the tongs once or twice in the dish to express the gravy. In Scotland, shred raw onion is still sometimes employed instead of eshalot. Garnish with pickled red cabbage, or cucumber, or horse-radish scraped as for roast beef. *Oyster sauce, Eshalot sauce, Brown onion sauce, Eschalot wine, Carach sauce, General's sauce,* or *Miser's sauce.* Those who enjoy a well-dressed beef-steak★ discard all sauces save the native juices of the meat, with the addition of pepper, salt, and at most, a little minced eshalot or onion.

★ "Ask a dozen healthy men under thirty," said TOUCHWOOD, "what was the very best dinner they ever made in their lives, and I bet from eight to ten of them answer, 'a beef-steak'—and they give you the history of this *unique* regale, generally found on a journey, a pedestrian tour, or fishing excursion. Yes, gentlemen, England may well pride herself on a *bonne bouche* which her rival exhausts herself in vain endeavours to imitate, though she has never yet succeeded in even spelling its Christian name. The *rum'-stick* and *lif-stik de mouton* are not more unlike in orthography than in quality, to the juicy, delicately-browned, hot, tender rump-steak, which has immortalized the name of DOLLY. But I am sorry to say, that beef-*sticks*, literally so, are but too often met with even in our own island. I have calculated, Doctor, that in the cities of London, Dublin, Edinburgh, and Glasgow alone, upwards of sixty thousand young men dine on beef-steaks every day of the week,—students, apprentices, clerks, *'gentlemen of the press,'* and so forth. What a clattering of gridirons here! Now if our receipt, by instructing the thousands of slip-shod wenches who dress those messes, tends to keep said youths from taverns and ordinaries, true to the old sober habits of their country—*home-dinners,* I shall not think this page ill-bestowed, Dr. REDGILL; though you hint that too much space is occupied by simple elementary processes."—The Doctor assured his friend, that he held no such opinion, and suggested, that the girls attending the *national schools* ought to be early initiated into these mysteries, as in the admirable French institution at Ecouen, near Paris, which would be conferring a real kindness on those they were destined to serve in future life. Mr. CARGILL was startled from his silence by this proposal, which he put down with more energy of manner than he was in the habit of displaying; and WINTERBLOSSOM, who loved chat and accordingly detested disquisition, cut the subject by breaking in,—"No spot on earth once like the OLD FLESH MARKET CLOSE of Edinburgh, for a spare-rib steak; and I believe it has not yet quite lost its ancient celebrity. I never ate one in perfection but there:"—and the old beau related, with much vivacity, the adventures of a night, on which he had accompanied to this resort the eccentric Earl of K——, and a party of Caledonian *bon-vivants* of the last age. "But the receipt?" inquired REDGILL, with grave earnestness, corresponding to the magnitutde of the subject, "O! neither more nor less than that those taverns were, and are kept by butchers' wives, so that the primest of the meat found its way there. In the darksome den into which we dived—Luckie MIDDRITT's of savoury memory—hungry customers consumed beef-steaks by wholesale at all hours of the night and day, or rather of the perpetual night. The coal-fire always in prime condition,—and short way between the *brander* and the mouth, Doctor,—served *hot and hot,*—no distance between the kitchen

39. BEEF-STEAKS WITH POTATOES:
An excellent French Dish.

FLATTEN and season with salt and mixed spices, neatly cut rump-steaks. Dip them in melted butter to keep in their native gravy whilst broiling. Have ready a very little blanched and finely-shred parsley, with butter, pepper and salt, in a hot dish. When the steaks are broiled, as directed in the last receipt, lay them on this and quickly turn them over once or twice, and arrange very hot fried potatoes around them, or potato fritters.

40. TO BROIL MUTTON AND LAMB CHOPS, &C.

MUTTON and LAMB CHOPS, RABBIT cut in quarters, SWEETBREADS, and KIDNEYS, may all be broiled in the same way; but particular care must be taken that the fat which drops from mutton does not smoke the chops, —to prevent which turn them frequently, and remove or hold the gridiron aslant when the smoke rises. Kidneys must be stretched on a skewer to prevent their curling with the heat. Each of these things may be higher dressed by dipping them in egg, and then in a mixture of

---

and the hall: before the collop-tongs had collapsed in the hands of the cook, in rushed the red-legged waiting wench with the smoking wooden platter. Every man held his weapon ready, and his teeth set; trencher after trencher followed.—Ay! thus it is to eat a steak in perfection. It can be known but once!" The Doctor compressed his lips, and sighed in accordance with this melancholy view of life. There were times— hours of *crudities* and evil digestion,—when the hand of a child could stagger the strongest principles of his culinary belief. The vision of some three pounds of steaks, consumed at a country inn in Somersetshire, with all the vigour and relish of youthful appetite sharpened by exercise, rose between him and the well-replenished board that now courted his advances; and the Doctor moralized on the vanity and nothingness of all sublunary pleasures, while he handed round the mock-turtle soup.—"No beef-steak, after all, equal to that of my friends the Abyssinians," said TOUCHWOOD. The Doctor anathematized the savage and bloody process,—"Nor any receipt to that of Macbeth," said WINTERBLOSSOM—"not he of the hotel, but of Shakspeare, Doctor;" and he spouted,

> "If it were done, when 'tis done,
> Then 'twere well that it were done quickly!"

"Stolen from the *New Monthly*," said JEKYLL, only half-aside: and the Doctor, more than ever convinced that little assistance for the *great work* could be obtained either from the finical guardsman or the flighty old beau, gave himself in seriousness to the serious business of dining.

bread-crumbs and savoury herbs, which may also be strewed over them as they broil. *Sauces* for Mutton-chops the same as for beef-steaks. For *Lamb*, the *Catsup* is better omitted, and *Cucumber sauce*, or *Sauce Robert*, substituted. *Sweetbreads* and *Kidneys* are better fried than broiled.

41. TO BROIL PORK-CHOPS.

PORK-CHOPS are cut from the neck or loin. They require a great deal of the fire. They must be served broiling hot and a hot gravy, with which a tea-spoonful of made mustard, and a little dry sage pulverized may be mixed. *Redgill sauce* possesses still more *gusto* for thorough-bred pork-eaters.*

---

*PORK-CHOPS.—It is related, that FUSELI, the celebrated artist, when he wished to summon Nightmare, and bid her sit for her picture, or any other grotesque or horrible personations, wont to prime himself for the feat by supping on about three pounds of half-dressed pork-chops.

Though that accommodating Prince, RICHARD CŒUR DE LION, could, as has been seen, eat any thing, all being fish that came in the net when he was sharp-set, he had, like other epicures, his favourite dish. This was *Porkified Saracen, curried*. On recovering in Syria from an ague, his first violent longing was for pork, which is said to approach nearer to human flesh than any other sort of meat. Pork is indeed a "passionate" food. It tolerates no medium. It must be idolized or detested, whether as flitch or gammon, souse or sausage, brawn or griskin. In Syria, where swine's flesh is abhorred, it was not easy to satisfy the longing of the King. But no man durst tell him that pork could not be got for love or money; and in this extremity an old Knight, so much of a courtier as to know that a King's longings are not to be crossed with impunity, counselled thus:—

> "Take a Saracen, young and fat;
> In haste let the *thief* be slain,
> Opened, and his skin off flayn,
> And sodden, full hastily,
> With powder and with spicery,
> And with saffron of good colour.
> *   *   *   *   *   *   *
>
> "When he has a good taste,
> And eaten well a good repast,
> And supped of the *brewis* a sup,
> Slept after, and swet a drop,
> Through Godis help and my counsail
> Soon he shall be fresh and hail."

As the old Knight counselled so it was done. RICHARD *supped* the broth and ate the flesh of the Saracen faster than his carver could supply him, drank wine, slept, and on waking again felt appetized, and accordingly called for

> "The head of that ilk swine
> That I of ate."

N.B.—We would, unless the fire is most temptingly radiant, and the cook dexterous, recommend that pork-chops be dressed in the Dutch oven before a brisk fire, which will prevent their becoming black, and having the smeary appearance which those dressed on the gridiron too often have.

42. TO BROIL CHICKENS AND PIGEONS.—P. T.

A BROILED fowl or pigeon is thought lighter than one roasted, and is at least more expeditiously cooked. It is therefore preferred for the sick, or the hungry and hasty. Singe, as directed in the note, page 98. Pick and truss it; wash it, and cut down the back; season the inside with pepper and salt, and place that side on a gridiron previously heated, and put at a greater distance from the fire than for a steak. This will take a full half-hour to cook perfectly. The birds should occasionally be taken off the fire, and rubbed with butter tied in a muslin rag. Probe with a knife to see if they are done. Particular care must be given to keep every broiled dish warm, as the smallness of the articles exposes them more to the action of cold air than meat cooked in larger quantities. Place your chickens or pigeons in a hot dish. For chickens, serve parsley and butter, or gravy and mushrooms, or sauce *à la Tartare*. Garnish with slices of lemon, and the liver and gizzard (the latter scored) highly seasoned with pepper and salt, and broiled. For pigeons—the *sauce* is melted butter, flavoured with mushroom catsup, or parsley and butter in the dish. Pigeons may be broiled without splitting.

The cook was, it may be supposed, in great consternation at this demand, but was soon relieved by the good humour of his royal master.

> "The *swarte vis* when the King seeth,
> His black beard and white teeth,
> How his lippes grinned wide,
> "What devil is this?" the King cried,
> And 'gan to laugh as he were wode,
> "What! is Saracen's flesh thus good?
> That, never erst, I nought wist!
> By Godes death, and his up-rist,
> Shall we never die for default,
> While we may in any assault,
> Slee Saracens, the flesh may take,
> And seethen, rosten, stew and bake."
> *Romance of Richard Coeur de Lion.*

Truss as for boiling, and flatten the breastbone. Stuff each pigeon with a bit of butter rolled in chopped parsley, and season pretty high with pepper and salt. Tie them close at both ends, and turn them frequently over a clear fire, that they may be nicely browned and equally done; or they may be rubbed with egg, and afterwards rolled in bread-crumbs and chopped parsley, and dredged with this mixture while broiling.—*Obs.* Pigeons are not so light, but more savoury when broiled whole. When a chicken is broiled for an invalid it may be proper to skin it, as the skin is the most tough and indigestible part of the bird, and to use as little butter as possible. It will sometimes be more convenient to dress them as directed for partridges, in the next receipt.

43. TO BROIL PARTRIDGES.

HAVING prepared them, make them firm in the frying-pan, turning them once. Finish on the gridiron; and serve them in a hot dish with *Poor Man's sauce.*—*Obs.* French cooks, after trussing the fowl or chicken, often cut down the back, flatten the breast, break the leg-bones, simmer in butter with white pepper and salt, and finish on the gridiron.—Or a chicken may be par-roasted, cut up, and then broiled.

CHAPTER IV

OF FRYING.

> Passion, O me! how I run on,
> Here's that which should be thought upon;
> The business of the kitchen's great,
> And it is fit that men should eat,
> Nor was it e'er denied.
>
> SUCKLING

THIS, like broiling, is a very convenient mode of cookery to those who wish to unite comfort with economy; and, certain things premised, it is not difficult of management. The frying fat, be it lard, oil, butter, *dripping*, or top-fat, must not be stale, much less rancid; the fire must not be smoky, and the frying-pan ought to be thicker in the bottom than frying-pans are usually made. Fresh butter, clarified from all foreign substances, pure "British oil," is the most delicate substance in which meat can be fried, as it communicates no predominating taste. Oil, lard, or what answers equally well, clarified fresh suet or dripping, (the "kitchen-fee" of the Cleikum,) are better adapted than butter for fish, eggs, or any thing watery. When butter for frying is clarified, it is not nearly so apt to *burn*, which effect is commonly produced by the water or milk it contains. Fritters and sweet things must have either good butter, or good lard, or oil. The fire must not be too fierce, nor yet too slack, as fat is susceptible of that intense degree of heat which will scorch whatever is placed in it before the substance to be fried could be heated through; and, on the other hand, if not hot enough, the fry will be merely sodden in fat, boiled and not fried. If fish, they would be limber, apt to break, of a bad colour, and have no crispness. Fish are far more difficult to fry than meat, from the softness of the fibre. They consequently require a greater degree of attention. Have an oval-shaped frying-pan for fish, as this form requires much less of the frying material than one of a round shape. Ascertain the heat of the fat, by throwing a bit of bread into it, as you try the heat of an oven by a bit of wet paste placed in it. Fat that has fried veal-cutlets, lamb-steaks, &c. may be used afterwards, if allowed to settle, and poured clean from the sediment; but what is used for fish would spoil any sort of meat, though it will answer repeatedly for fish, especially of the same sort, if strained when used. Fat becomes richer from having meat fried in it; and if carefully taken up, may be used repeatedly.*—See *Fritters, &c.*

44. TO CLARIFY BUTTER FOR POTTING OR FRYING, AND SUET AND DRIPPING FOR FRYING.

CUT the butter in slices; put it into a jar, which set in a pan of boiling water; let it melt and heat. Skim it, take it out, and when it has cooled a little, pour it gently off, holding back the milky sediment which will have subsided. Mutton and beef suet and lard may be roughly chopped, have all the skin and fibrous parts

---

A test of the proper degree of heat for frying fish.—Dip the tail into boiling dripping, or whatever fat is used, and if it be crisp at once, the material is ready.

taken out, and either be gradually melted over a slow fire, or before the fire in a Dutch oven, taking away the fat as it drops. In this last process there is less danger of the fat acquiring a burnt taste than when rapidly melted into tallow over the fire. Strain the fat and keep back the sediment.—Dripping and melted suet* are used for pie-crust, for basting and soups, as well as for frying. Their suitableness for all these purposes depends, in a great measure on the way in which they have been melted and preserved. When dripping is to be kept for soup it may be seasoned, not otherwise. It may be very highly purified by twice clarifying. A bit of charcoal or a charred toast will help to remove a rancid taint.

45. TO MELT LARD FOR FRYING, &c., AND TO MAKE LARD.

EITHER melt it as in last receipt, or skin, beat, and boil the caul slowly, and lay it in a little water, working it with the hand. When it will easily break with the fingers, let it cool, and rub it through a search. Keep in bladders in a cool place. *Another way,*—Melt the lard in a stone jar set in boiling water; pour it carefully from the sediment, and keep it in bladders or small jars. For *larding*, rub the lard when taken from the pig with pounded salt. Lay two pieces together, put a heavy weight over them. Let it lie from four to six weeks, then skewer and hang it to dry in a dry cool airy place. It cannot be used *for larding* till it get firm.

46. TO FRY STEAKS.—DR. R.

FRY in butter, for twelve or fifteen minutes, pieces cut of the same size as for broiling. Fry them of a fine brown. The pan may be covered after the steaks are browned, which will render them more juicy. When done, place them in a hot dish by the fire; add to the gravy in the pan a small glass of red wine, and a small anchovy boned, pepper, salt, and a minced eschalot. Give it a boil up, and pour it over the steaks, which, like every fry and broil, must be eaten hot; or fried steaks may be

---

* For an excellent way of using beef suet, see *Paste of beef suet for pies, &c.*

eaten with brown gravy, or onion sauce, or fried onions, served very hot along with them. *Garnish* with pickles or scraped horseradish.* The *wine* may be omitted. Potato fritters are a good accompaniment.

47. SCOTCH BEEF COLLOPS WITH ONIONS, OR COLLOP IN THE PAN.—M. D.

CUT the meat rather thinner than for broiling; make the butter hot, and place the collops in the pan, with about the proportion of a couple of middle-sized onions sliced to each half-pound. If the butter be salt, pepper is used, but no additional salt. Cover the pan with a close lid, or plate reversed. When done, the collops may be drawn aside, and a little oyster-pickle or walnut catsup and boiling water added to the onion-gravy sauce in the pan. Dish, and serve hot.† Ten minutes will dress them.

48. TO FRY VEAL CUTLETS, TWO WAYS.

CUT slices about half an inch thick from the fillet, backribs, or loin. If not equally cut, level them with the cleaver. Have plenty of lard or fresh butter hot to fry them in, not dripping, which is unsuitable to white meats. Keep the pan at a good distance from the fire, if the cutlets be anything thick; when browned on both sides of a light golden-tinged brown, the pan may be held higher above the fire and covered. Have ready some gravy made thus: A quarter pound of the skins, bones, or trimmings of the cutlets, a blade of mace, the head of a young onion, a sprig of parsley, a good bit of lemon-peel, six white pepper-corns, a bay-leave, if the flavour is liked, and a pint of water, which may boil down one-half; add fresh butter, the size of a large walnut, rolled in flour. When this gravy is well thickened, strain, boil again, and pour it hot over the cutlets, which must be served very hot.

---

* Epicures of the modern school begin to dislike the flavour of anchovy in meat-dishes, reserving it for fish. It is certainly, though a high, not a very delicate relish.

† This national dish possessed rather too much *gusto* for JEKYLL; but the Doctor admired it exceedingly, and even suggested that, independently of the collops, this was an excellent method of preparing *onion gravy*, which only required the addition of a little red wine and lemon-juice, to those who like an acid relish, to be a complete sauce.

This sauce may be made *brown*, by the addition of a little walnut or mushroom catsup. *Another way,—Veal cutlets* may also be more highly dressed by dipping the slices in beat egg, and then strewing over them a mixture of bread-crumbs, parsley, and lemon-peel chopped very fine, and a scrape of nutmeg. They must be fried in plenty of butter, and more of the mixture may be strewed over them in the pan. When the *cutlets* are done, place them before the fire in a hot dish covered, and to the gravy in the pan add veal broth or gravy, and a few little bits of butter separately rolled in flour; let it boil and thicken; add a little lemon-juice and white pepper, skim the sauce, and pour it over the cutlets. Where the flavour of lemon thyme is liked, a sprig of it makes a grateful addition to sauce for cutlets. A majority of the Club preferred cutlets as in the first receipt. See, for other ways of dressing cutlets, *French Cookery*. For *Scotch collops*, see *Made dishes of veal*.

49. LAMB OR PORK CHOPS,

ARE fried in same manner, either plain or egged, rolled in bread-crumbs,* and *garnished* with slices of *lemon*, or *crisped parsley*. PORK-CHOPS may be fried as above, dipping them after they are egged† in a mixture of chopped onion, sage, and bread-crumbs.—*Obs*. Care should be taken to have all *chops, steaks*, and *cutlets* of a good shape, neatly *trimmed*, and beat of equal thickness when not cut smoothly and equally.

50. TO FRY FRESH SAUSAGES.—DR. R.

WHETHER pork, veal, or beef sausages, they are best fried in the same way, viz. very slowly, that they may heat to the heart without bursting. Sausages ought to be dressed quite fresh, especially those that are bought at cooks' shops, where it is the practice to put the crumb

---

* *To prepare bread-crumbs*.—Put the grated crumb of stale bread into a slow oven; then beat it well in a mortar, and sift and keep for use. It will keep for some time.

† "To egg,"—to smear with beat egg, or dip in egg,—is an approved kitchen verb, which TOUCHWOOD derived from the Scotch phrase, to "egg up," or "egg on,,, *incite, urge*, or *stimulate*—the appetite. Dr. REDGILL had grave doubts as to this etymology. "To onion" is another buttery verb, which deserves to be more generally known.

of fresh roll soaked in a certain proportion of water into them, which immediately ferments and turns the sausage-meat sour. Very little butter or lard is required to fry pork or beef sausage; veal must have more. If in danger of bursting they may be pricked with a darning-needle; but if gradually heated, unless they are fermenting, this precaution will not be necessary. They must be drained from the fat, laid on a dish before the fire, and dredged with flour to froth them. They are sometimes boiled, and frothed before the fire.—*Obs.* Sausages were wont to be fried with apples pared, cored, and quartered, and garnished and served with the same: the practice is nearly obsolete. Poached eggs and fried bread, mashed, roasted, or scalloped potatoes, or stewed red cabbage, are more suitable to this rich and savoury commodity. With *turkey, fowl,* or *veal,* sausage is often more acceptable than even tongue or ham. To *make sausages* see the Index; also to fry *Fritters, Omelet, &c.*

51. TO FRY EGGS WITH BACON-HAM OR SAUSAGE.—P. T.

BUT for this homely dish many an honest traveller would go without his dinner. The general fault is, that the bacon is too hard, and cannot be cut into proper slices; to steep the slices even for a few minutes in lukewarm water would tend to remedy one defect; they must then be dried in the folds of a cloth. The colour of eggs is very easily hurt, so be sure that the frying-pan is delicately clean. This in all cases is best known, by melting a little fat in it, pouring it out, and wiping hard while the pan is still hot. Let the bacon be nearly fried, draw it aside, and if the fat look in the least dark or burnt, pour it off, and, if nice cookery is wanted, let fresh material get hot before the eggs are broken and gently slipt in. Pour boiling fat over them with an iron tinned spoon. When the eggs are done on the under side, dish the bacon in a hot dish, and either turn them or hold the pan before the fire a minute, to take the *raw* off the upper side of the eggs. Trim them as they lie in the pan; take them up with a slice, and drain the grease off by holding them over the pan a little, before dishing them with the bacon. They are dished either on the slices of bacon, or laid in the dish, with the bacon placed neatly

round them. In nice cookery a separate pan should be
used for frying the eggs.

52. TO FRY SWEETBREADS.

LET the sweetbreads be slightly parboiled when they
come from the butcher. When to be dressed cut them
into oblong slices, and either flour and fry them plain in
butter, or egg them, roll in bread crumbs, and a seasoning of lemon-peel, pepper, and a sprig of basil chopped.
Garnish with crisped parsley: *anchovy sauce*, or melted
butter, and a small tea-spoonful of walnut or mushroom
catsup stirred into it. Serve small slices of crisped
bacon, or slices of sausage done in a cheese-toaster or
Dutch oven before the fire. For *Sweetbreads, see also
French Cookery*.

53. TO FRY LAMB'S LIVER.

CUT a sound fat liver into long thin slices. Soak in
water, dry in a cloth, and flour them. Fry of a fine
rich brown, in plenty of fresh butter. Eschalot, or young
onions, and pepper, may be added to the fry. Serve with
a little hot gravy and stewed cucumbers, or cucumber-
sauce. Garnish with fried parsley.—*Obs.* The liver of
a young animal is seldom unsound. When it is found
either livid, black, or lumpy, it is surely unnecessary to
notice, that, whether for sauce, stuffing, or frying, it is
alike to be rejected.

54. TO FRY CALF'S LIVER AND BACON.—DR. R.

CALF'S liver is fried as above; when nearly done, or
in a separate pan, dress the bacon. Dish with a slice of
bacon laid on each slice of liver; or they may be dished
separately. Serve a little thickened gravy, with a squeeze
of lemon. Garnish with crisp parsley.—*Obs.*Ox-liver
and bacon, done as above, makes a good, *cheap* dish.

55. TO FRY VENISON COLLOPS.—P. W., ESQ.

CUT oblong slices from the haunch, or slices neatly
trimmed from the neck or loin. Have a gravy drawn
from the bones and trimmings, ready thickened with
butter rolled in lightly-browned flour. Strain into a
small stew-pan, boil, and add a squeeze of lemon or

orange, and a small glass of claret:*—Pepper, to taste,
a salt-spoonful of salt, the size of a pin's head of
cayenned, and a scrape of nutmeg. Fry and dish the
collops hot, and pour this sauce over them. A still
higher *gout* may be imparted to this sauce by *eschalot
wine, basil wine*, or *Tarragon vinegar*, chosen as may suit
the taste of the eater. If those flavours are not liked,
some old venison-eaters may relish a very little pounded
fine sugar and vinegar in the gravy, and currant-jelly may
be served in a sweetmeat-glass. *Garnish* with fried
crumbs. This is a very excellent way of dressing
venison, particularly when it is not fat enough to roast
well.—*Venison minced collops*, see *National Dishes*.

56. TO FRY TRIPE.

IT must be boiled till tender, cut in pieces not too
large, and dipped in a batter made of flour and eggs,
with a little salt and minced onion, and fried for seven
minutes of a rich light-brown.—*White Onion Sauce.*—
Obs. COW HEEL is cut into neat pieces, egged, rolled
in crumbs, fried, and served in the same manner. The
CLEIKUM CLUB were not *partial* to these fries. They
to a man preferred boiled tripe, or tripe fricasseed with a
white sauce.—See *Potted heel, Irish tripe, National
Dishes*.

57. TO FRY PARSLEY, HERBS, BREAD-CRUMBS,&C.
For different made dishes.

HAVE the frying-pan well filled with very hot dripping or lard. Have young parsley nicely picked and
washed, drained, and then rubbed lightly between the
folds of a cloth to dry. It must be fried quickly to get
crisp. The moment it is done lift it with a slice, and
place it before the fire on a sieve reversed, to drain and
become more crisp; or it may be crisped in a Dutch
oven before the fire. This is used for garnishing lamb-
chops, liver, or any thing to which the flavour of parsley
is suitable. Many things are served on fried parsley.
—See *Dried Herbs*. BREAD-CRUMBS are fried and drained
in the same manner, taking care that the fat is
perfectly clear and transparent, and that the bread is

---

* Claret, of all the red wines, is that best adapted to the use of the
cook; for higher flavour, Burgundy is preferred.

not burned. Sippets may be cut in the form of stars, the Maltese cross, triangles, diamonds, paper-kites, cocks'-combs, &c. &c., and nicely fried and drained before the fire to serve for *garnishings*. Fried bread is a most useful thing for garnishing, as it never fails to be eaten with the dish it is employed to ornament.

Another Way.—Fry in a colander or net held among the frying fat. The crumbs will thus be easily lifted when dry and firm. Parsley fried in a net may be afterwards dried in the oven.

58. TO FRY HERBS FOR BACON AND EGGS, OR CALF'S LIVER.

TAKE two handfuls of spinage, a bunch of parsley, and a few chives or young onions. Pick, cut, wash, drain, and stew them slowly in a very little broth and butter, taking care they do not burn. They may be fried in a net, floated in the frying fat.

CHAPTER V.

BROTHS, SOUPS, AND GRAVIES.

C'est la soupe qui fait le Soldat.
French Proverb.

SOUP has been termed the vestibule to a banquet. We call it the only true foundation to the principal repast of the day, whether it be a Cottage or a Cabinet dinner. With this belief we hold as maxims, that the French take the lead of all European people in soups and broths, that the Scotch rank second, the Welsh next, and that the English, as a nation, are at the very bottom of the scale; and farther, that if soup be the foundation of a good dinner, it is equally true that *beef* is the only foundation of good *soup*. Whether brown or white, plain or rich, the basis must still be beef,— fresh-killed, juicy young beef, and soft pure water.*

---

* "We of Scotland," said WINTERBLOSSOM, "probably owe our superiority in this department to our long and close alliance with that nation which has ever been most profoundly skilled in the mysteries of

The essential qualities of soup are, that it be nourishing and restorative. It is the food of childhood and extreme old age, of the declining and the debilitated, for whom the soup-pot performs half the offices of the digestive organs. With these invigorating and salutiferous

---

the soup-pot. That Scotland is indebted to France for even the slender proficiency she has attained in cookery, is abundantly evident from the culinary phraseology of the nation. Kitchen—*cuisine*—the word with us comprehends every kind of viand or preparation which may add to the relish of the coarse cake, and decoction of oatmeal and coleworts, which formed the staple of the daily meal. A peasant's butter, cheese, fish, meat, and so forth, all are '*kitchen.*' Then we have the *hachi*—the soup *Lorraine*, the *veal Flory*— or Florentine pie—our *broche* and *turn-broche,* and our culinary adage, '*hunger is gude kitchen.*'"—"If you go on at this rate, you will soon reduce your nation to their original brose and haggis," said JEKYLL, "for you recollect their skill in cabbage and coleworts is attributed to Cromwell's soldiers."—"Little or muckle," put in Mrs. DODS, a true-bred border Scot, who would not yield an inch of the kitchen floor to France or England, "we mak' as gude use o' what little skill is accorded to us, it's like. I have heard them say that should know, and that's the Nawbob himsel there, that there is thousands upon thousands o' hooses in Lunon whar they ne'er saw a broth-trencher, let-a-be a pot o' fat kale:—cauld, comfortless, wasterfu', gude-for-naething gangings on for man, wife, and wean. Their roast joint,—set them up!—scouthered to a cinder in a baker's o'en—a hunger and a burst,—dear bought at first, and a short outcome for a working man's family, compared with two or three pots fu' o' gude barley-broth."

"Even too true, Luckie," interrupted the Nabob; "this must be cared for. The Scots may, and do fail in a grand dinner, Doctor,—no doubt of it; but as a nation they manage better than most of their neighbours, —three hot meals of broth and meat for about the price of one roasting joint perhaps. Then second day's kail,—said I right, dame?—something to warm up to-morrow for the gudeman and the bairns."

"And gude enough too," replied MEG; "sae ye need not cast up puir Scotland, Captain JAYKILL. "Let ilka herrin' hing by its ain head,' as the by-word gangs. We may be easy put by; and the Gude forbid we were belly-gods and pock-puddin Eppycurryeans; though at a Christening, or a Kirn, or on a Sacrament Monday, we may like a bit roast as weel as our nice-gabbit neighbours."—"Ay, thus it is to clip and crib the gluttonizing joys of honest John Bull, 'to some high festival of once a year,'" said JEKYLL. "Call you a wholesome nutritious soup four times a week, clipping the gormandizing joys of John Bull?" dired the Nabob, "instead of his Sunday roast and dilution of porter:—no, Sir, soup is the best as well as the most economical fare a mechanic's family can consume. But I will give him a thousand other preparations."

"Besides the elegant variety of Mr. GEORGE ROSE's salt-herring, and COBBETT's *toujours* fat—very fat—bacon," said JEKYLL, who scented a long prosing harangue and wished to cut it. "But let Mrs. DODS proceed with her discourse."—But here the Doctor called the party to order, and resumed the real business of the day,—*Gravy Soup.*—For many excellent, cheap Scotch soups, see NATIONAL DISHES AND COOKERY FOR THE POOR.

qualities, the mildest, the richest, and the most poignant *relishes* may be combined, by the judicious employment of the numerous ingredients which go to the composition of *soups*. The capital defect of soups is generally not so much the want of meat as of the time necessary to the due concoction of a rich fluid composed of so many ingredients. The defects of soups are vainly attempted to be concealed by the excessive use of pepper and herbs. The following elementary rules, from the French of the chemist Parmentier, were assumed by the Club as practical directions to the cook.

RULES FOR MAKING NOURISHING BROTH.

I. Sound, healthful, fresh viands.
II. Vessels of earthenware in preference to those of metal, as a less degree of heat keeps them boiling; and once heated, a few hot cinders will maintain that slight degree of ebullition which is wanted.
III. Double the weight of water to that of the meat used.
IV. A sufficient quantity of common salt to facilitate the separation of the blood and slime that coagulates under the form of scum.
V. In the early stage of the process such a degree of heat as will throw off the whole scum.
VI. A lower, but an equal temperature, that the soup may *simmer* gently till the substances employed, whether nutritive, colouring, or flavouring, are perfectly combined with the water, according to their several degrees of solubility.

Besides observing these rules, use the softest water that can be obtained, and let the cook read the observations prefixed to the Chapter on Boiling, and attend to the following hints:—Some soups are very good when made the day before they are to be eaten, as the top-fat can be removed in a cake, and they also attain more complete consistence, (*Scotticè*, lithiness,) without losing their flavour; but they need not be seasoned till wanted, and should then be slowly heated to the boiling point: if permitted to boil, most soups will lose part of their flavour; and in soups with meat, the meat will harden.

Excellent judges differ on this point. Many think every hot preparation best when fresh cooked,—and soups of the number. Of the kinds that will keep are brown soup, hare soup, soup of game of any kind, giblet soup, and generally all soups made of the meat of animals of mature growth. Soups into which vegetables and young meats enter in any quantity, are best when fresh made, as these things have a strong tendency to ferment. This also holds of veal and fish soups. This tendency may be partly checked by boiling them up, or changing the vessels. In re-warming all previously-made *soups*, *broths*, *sauces*, and *gravies*, if they cannot be heated completely by the vessel containing them being plunged into a stew-pan of boiling water, particular care must be taken that they are *not smoked*. The fire must be clear, and the lids close; for things re-warmed are much more liable to be smoked than during their first preparation. Soups, gravies, &c. are best kept in unglazed earthen or stone vessels. They must not be covered up till quite cold; and when cold and covered, vegetable soups, &c. may be plunged into a trough or large vessel of spring water.* When soup is to be warmed, take up the cake of fat which settles on the top, and hold back the lees and sediment. Strain before you set it away. Give all soup ample time in the making. From four to six hours is not too much; but the finer flavouring ingredients for soups, gravies, or a made-dish, need not be added, but for the length of time necessary to blend the various *zests* into one harmonious *relish*, without exposing them to that degree of continued heat which drives off their subtle essence. This observation is peculiarly applicable to catsups, aromatic spices, wines, flavouring vinegars, lemon and orange juice. &c.; and a much smaller quantity of these costly ingredients would answer the purpose if this were attended to. In certain cases it is proper to put in the half of these ingredients at an early stage of the process, that the flavour may be intimately blended with the preparation, adding what remains to give

---

* Where there is no ice-house this is a good way to keep cream or milk sweet. The wicker-work boxes or baskets, lined with charcoal, used in hot climates, might often be useful at home to preserve meat, ice, &c. —P. T.

piquance near the conclusion. In all English books on cookery there is too much wine ordered for soups, and sometimes too little meat. The former error is less dangerous, as what is levied from the cellar does not always find its way to the soup-pot. All roots, bread-raspings, barley, and meal, for plain common soups, ought to be put in as soon as the pot is skimmed, when the roots are merely intended to thicken and flavour the soup. When to be cut in pieces and served in the broth, an hour's boiling is fully enough for carrot, turnip, onions, &c. Many things are used to thicken and give consistency to common soups and sauces. The best perhaps is fine toasted oatmeal, potato mucilage, or bread not too stale. When the soup or gravy is too much *boiled in*, the waste must be supplied with *boiling* water or broth; and though we strenuously recommend, in general, close-covered pots, yet when the soup is watery and weak the lid may be taken off till the watery particles evaporate, for *thickening* gives consistence but not strength. It facilitates the operation, if meat for soup or gravy be cut into pieces of about a half-pound each; and improves both the flavour and colour, if the meat, onions, and carrots be stewed at the bottom of the soup-pot or digester, before the water is added to it, with a bit of butter to prevent burning.* The only objection is, that by these means the separation and removal of the scum is not so complete as is necessary to the rock-crystal transparency of clear soups. Broth made of fat meat may have a larger proportion of greens, leeks, cabbage, or whatever *green* vegetable is used, than leaner meat. The best plain *browning* for soups, sauces, gravies, &c. is red wine, soy, or mushroom or walnut catsup. Where these are not admissible, use crusts of bread well browned, browned *flour* or browned oatmeal where thickening is required, the meat browned in the pot, before putting it in the water, and the onions fried a fine deep brown.—(See *Browning for soups and made dishes*.)

---

* To this previous drawing out of the juices without much or any water, we are inclined to attribute much of the superiority of French soups. Some French cooks, to regulate the flavour of soups more exactly, boil the roots, herbs, and vegetables separately to a mash, and then squeeze them and add the juice, till the desired flavour is obtained.

To improve the colour, many cooks sacrifice the flavour of their soups. Burnt meat or bones, burnt sugar or treacle, are all condemned by us.

The cook is entreated to bear in mind, that the elegance of all clear gravy brown soups consists in *transparency*, united with richness and flavour; of white soups, and fish and vegetable soups, in the goodness of the desired colour and in fulness on the palate.

Soup may be made in an infinity of ways. There is no end to the combinations of meat, game, fish, herbs, roots, spices, and mucilage, with water; but the basis of the best soup, where expense is no object, is, as we have said, beef,—fresh, full of juices, young, succulent, and not too fat,—the lean parts of an equally fattened animal. For this *primary* soup we give the following tried and approved receipt:—

59. PLAIN STOCK BROTH, OR PRIMARY SOUP,
The basis of many Soups and Sauces.

IN large families, or if the cook is to have a dinner, let her, on the previous day, prepare the *Stock broth*.—To every pound of fresh, juicy, rump beef, or a shin broken, allow a quart of soft water, and to this add any fresh trimings of lean mutton, veal, poultry, or game, which the larder affords. An old fowl, a rabbit, or a knuckle of veal, are excellent additions, and with these less meat will serve. When the broth is rendered pellucid by boiling, skimming, and clearing, as directed in the observations on boiling, put to it three or four carrots, two turnips, four large onions, four cloves, some good leeks, a faggot of herbs, if you like their flavour, and a head or two of celery.* Let the soup stew slowly by the fire for from four to six hours, according to the quantity. If left too long on the fire, the flavour of the vegetables will become too powerful, and the colour will spoil, and the broth become ropy. When done, let it settle, skim off the fat, (which will be useful for moistening *braises*, enriching vegetables, &c.) pour it from the sediment; strain it through a fine search or wetted cloth, and set it

---

* There are, however, some purposes for which broth is wanted to which this quantity and kind of vegetables may be unsuitable; and this is left to the judgment of the cook.

by for use.—*Obs*. As our object is to unite judicious economy with good cookery, it is proper to mention, that each of the material ingredients of the stock-pot may be turned to good account. The meat may be put on early on the day of the dinner, and may be kept hot, without being overdone, while it affords stock for the soups, sauces, and braises. It may be served in the first course *Garni de choux*, or *Garni de racines*. Or it may be served as a plain *bouilli*, as directed for that dish, by taking it up when just enough done, and placing it in a stew-pan, with a few ladlefuls of the top of the broth, to serve as a sauce. If a fowl is boiled, let it be trussed before boiling, and it may be served with rice, or a suitable sauce, (or *au gros sel*,) so may a knuckle of veal, a rabbit with onions, or a brace of partridges with sauce. In large private establishments, where broth for soups and sauces is constantly required, these articles, of which stock is best formed, may be served at the different tables, or on different days.* The stock being made, the cook is now in possession of a floating capital subservient to many purposes.

60. SECOND STOCK, *the Consommé of the French Kitchen*.

THIS is the same thing, only stronger than the former broth. Take a large old fowl, or a cock, a large knuckle, or a good piece of the leg of veal, a piece of rump-beef, and any game you have to spare; moisten this meat with the first stock broth, and let it boil up quickly till the jelly is drawn; then add more broth or hot water, skim, season with a carrot, two or three onions, two cloves, and some parsley, leeks, and a head of celery. Let the fowl only boil till enough done for the table, and the knuckle of veal till done. Then skim and carefully strain this *consommé* through a gauze search.—*N.B.* Ham is often ordered for these stock broths; but unless for gravies, to enrich ragouts, or to make sauces, it is seldom employed. Indeed, it is more suitable to savoury gravies than to bland elementary broth of which mild soups are to be made.

---

* For hotels, regimental messes, &c., these hints are valuable; for each of these dishes, besides causing no loss, will actually be more rich from the stock-pot than if cooked separately. A fowl *au gros sel* means sprinkled with grains of large bright salt.

61. RICH HIGH-FLAVOURED STOCK.

LINE a well-tinned stew-pan with slices of good ham, over this place slices of veal from the thick of the knuckle, and a fowl or brace of game cut to pieces. When the meat has been *sweated* over a slow fire till the juices have formed a *glaze*, moisten the whole with a quart and a half of good broth, and season with chopped mushrooms, parsley, green onions, a blade of mace, and two cloves. Skim, and let this stew. Thicken it with white or brown thickening, and keep for use.

62. STRONG STOCK, *the* GRAND CONSOMME *of the French Kitchen.*

MAKE this exactly as second stock, but use more veal and poultry and less beef, if convenient. This is the basis of many French sauces, and clear gravy soups.*

63. CLEAR GRAVY SOUP, *the basis of many of the Soups mentioned below.*

HAVE eight pounds of a shin of beef chopped across in two places, and a knuckle of veal or a scrag and some shanks of mutton, with any fresh trimmings the larder can furnish, and a piece of ham, if the ham flavour is admired. Heat and rub hard a nicely-tinned stew-pot; melt in it some butter, or rub it with marrow. Let the meat, with a slice of carrot, a head of celery, onions, the white part of two leeks, and a turnip sliced, *catch*, but not burn, over a rather quick fire; then add four quarts or better of soft water. Carefully skim, as formerly directed. When it is once skimmed, throw in a pint of cold water to refresh it, and take off what more scum is

---

* French cookery is imagined to be a very complicated affair. It is, in fact, more easily understood than our own, because its principles are more fixed, and its language more *scientific*. The Beauvillerian, the *Udean* and *Veryean* systems, are laid down as clearly as the Linnean. Modern French professors have a few grand sounding names which they bestow on elementary gravies and sauces, as *Espagnole, Grand Espagnole, Espagnole Travaillie, Italienne Blanche, Italienne Rousse*, &c.; and these, once defined and properly understood, remain ever the same. Our sauces, like our native melodies, are so overlaid with everybody's variations, that it is difficult for the most correct ear, or the most discriminating palate to recognise them. And with all our culinary deficiencies, our cookery-books give double the number of transmogrified and unintelligible receipts that are to be found in the best French systems. Of their comparative value I do not judge.—H. J.

detached till it become quite limpid. Let the stew-pot simmer slowly by the fire for four hours, without stirring it any more from the bottom, till all the strength is obtained, but not so long as to cause the soup to become ropy. Let it settle on the hearth; skim off the fat, and strain off gently what flows freely through a fine search. —*Obs*. This clear soup (for it must be very clear) is served under many different names; as *Vermicelli*, with this paste separately boiled and put to it; *Carrot-soup*, with carrots cut in straws; *Turnip-soup*, with turnips scooped; *Celery-soup, Asparagus-soup, Green pease-soup*, &c. by adding the ingredient which gives the name.— *N.B.* All these additions must be separately cooked. When all or the greater part of these vegetables, stewed and carefully rubbed through a tammy sieve, are added to this strong gravy soup, you have exactly the French *Cressi* soup. A good French cook would, however, after chopping the roots, &c. stew them in top-fat, or with butter. The French generally have their turnip soup *white*, the carrot soup *brown*. Sippets are requisite to the *Potage à la Cressi*. With chopped lettuce and sorrel this makes *Soupe à la Faubonne*.

64. FRENCH BROWN SOUP, or *La Brunoise*.

To clear amber-coloured gravy-soup put carrots and turnips, cut in dice and straws, and fried and drained if young, but if old blanched. Soak toasted sippets in a basin of broth, and slip them into the tureen after the soup is dished, lest they crumble down and destroy the bright clearness of the soup. This is proper whenever bread is used. Skim off the film of fat from the tureen, and serve.—*Obs*. Cut the leeks and celery in lozenges, the turnips and carrots in ribbands, and you have *Julienne soup*.

N.B.—If gravy-soup is not sufficiently clear, it may be improved by the whites of two or three eggs, well whisked, being boiled up with it before it is strained a second time. But careful cookery is much better than this process of refining any soup.

65. THE OLD SCOTCH BROWN SOUP.

MAKE the stock as directed for clear gravy-soup, but brown the meat a little more, and when ready put to it two pounds of rump-steaks, cut rather small and

nicely browned in the frying-pan, but drained from the
frying fat. Simmer the steaks in the soup for an hour;
strain it; add a small glassful of catsup, with salt,
pepper, and cayenne; slip toasted sippets into the
tureen, and skimming off the filmy fat, serve the soup
with the steaks in it.

66. PLAIN WHITE SOUPS, *or stock for several kinds,—
the French blond de veau, or veal broth.*

HAVE a large knuckle of veal broken, and to this put
any poultry trimmings you have, and a few slices of
lean ham, a carrot, three onions, and a blade of mace.
Moisten these (when laid in a nice stew-pan over which
butter is rubbed) with a little good broth or water.
When the jelly is partly drawn out, and the meat tinged a
little, prick it all over with a sharp knife to let the juices
flow, and add more clear broth or water till you have
enough. Add a bunch of parsley and onions, and white
peppercorns; boil and skim, and when the soup is
ready, skim and carefully strain it. Rice or vermicelli is
put to this soup; or, if a white colour is wished, thicken
with arrow-root, and add, before serving, a pint of sweet
cream, first brought to boil, which will prevent it from
curdling.—*N.B.* Always boil cream before putting it
to any soup or sauce, and stir till it boil.

67. THE OLD SCOTCH WHITE SOUP, *or Soupe à la Reine.*

TAKE a large knuckle of the whitest veal, well broken
and soaked, a white fowl skinned, or two chickens, a
quarter-pound of well-coloured, lean, undressed bacon,
lemon-thyme, onions, carrot, celery, and a white turnip,
a few white peppercorns, and two blades of mace.
Boil for about two hours; skim repeatedly and carefully
during that time. When the stock is well tasted, strain
it off. It will form a jelly. When to be used, take off
the surface-fat, clear off the sediment, and put the jelly
into a tin sauce-pan, or a stew-pan freshly tinned; boil
for a half-hour, and serve on a couple of rounds of a
small French roll; or with macaroni, previously soaked,
and stewed in the soup till perfectly soft; or vermicelli.
This is plain white soup. It is raised to LORRAINE soup
as follows:—Take a half-pound of sweet almonds blanched,
(that is scalded and the husks rubbed off,) the hard-

boiled yolks of three eggs, and the skinned breast and white parts of a cold roast fowl; beat the almonds to a paste in a mortar, with a little water to prevent their oiling; mince very finely the fowl and eggs, and some bread-crumbs. Add to this *hash* an English pint or more of the stock, lemon-peel, and a scrape of nutmeg; bring it to boil, and put to it a pint of boiling sweet cream, and the rest of the stock. Let it be for a considerable time on the very eve of boiling, that it may thicken, but take care it does not boil, lest the cream curdle. Strain through a sieve.

68. POTAGE A LA REINE, *the fashionable white soup.*

TAKE a couple of large or three small fat pullets; clean and skin them: take also two pounds or more of veal cut into pieces; put these together into a very nicely-tinned stew-pan, with parsley, and moisten them with clear boiling veal-broth. Let this stew softly for an hour; then soak in the broth the soft part of a penny-loaf; cut the flesh off the breasts and wings of the chickens; chop and pound it in a mortar with the hard yolks of four eggs, the soaked crumbs, ten sweet almonds and three bitter, all blanched. Rub the compound into the soup; strain the whole, and add a quart of sweet cream brought to boil by itself. COW-HEEL or CALF'S FEET will make a good white soup. Rabbits may be substituted for chickens.

69. PLAIN ONION-SOUP.

CHOP a dozen large onions singly, and stew them in a small stew-pan with butter; stir them about with a wooden spoon; let them cook very gradually and not get brown. Put to this some very strong stock-broth, well seasoned; add pepper, cayenne, and salt, and, if nicer cooking is wanted, strain the soup, and put to it a pint of boiling cream.

70. HIGH-FLAVOURED ONION-SOUP.

HAVE a proper quantity of well-seasoned, clear brown gravy-soup, in which a double proportion of onions and a faggot of herbs has been boiled. To this, when strained, put a dozen middle-sized onions, sliced and nicely fried; let these stew gently in the soup, not to crumble the slices; season with pepper and cayenne, and serve with toasted sippets in the tureen. Button onions, cooked as for garnishing *bouilli*, &c. may be used instead of large ones fried; and for those who like a full-tasted soup, this may be thickened with potato-flour, or the pulp of pease. It must be simmered till the onions, both in substance and flavour, are blended (ready to melt away) with the soup. When very young mild onions are used, more weight must be allowed to obtain the same flavour. —*Obs.* The *gusto* may be heightened and the flavours varied to suit the palate of the consumer. Curry-powder was a favourite addition of the Nabob, and also a spice of ginger, which made a sort of imitation Mulla-gatawny, nothing inferior to the original, at least to those who dislike *fork-soups* and *stew-soups.* Dr. REDGILL heightened the flavour of his onion-soup with mushroom catsup, or eschalot. As the taste for onions,* like that for olives and peppers, increases with age, we do not fix the precise quantity to be used, but merely give the medium in the above receipt. Some cooks thicken onion-soup with the yolk or two or three eggs well beat and stirred into the soup when it is dished, or with cream, as in last receipt; but we see no use for this *liaison*, as French professors term it, in a high-flavoured onion-soup.

---

* Onions are supposed to possess a considerable quantity of nourishment. It is even asserted, that no substance of only equal size affords so much. This is at least doubtful. Onions in their raw state are much relished by some persons, while others find them wholly indigestible: when dressed they are very generally acceptable in soup or sauce. They used to form the favourite *bon-bons* of the highlander, "who, with a few of these and an oat-cake, would," says Sir JOHN SINCLAIR, "travel an incredible distance, and live for days without other food." The Egyptians adored the onion nearly as much as the ox; and the Spaniards have the same fondness for this pungent root, whether to give savour to their rich dishes, or to relish the crust from the wallet, and the draught from the brook, which forms the gay repast of the poor and light-hearted sojourners one likes so much to meet with in the Spanish novels. The Scotch peasants season their *chappit* potatoes with shred onion, and sometimes their *brose*; and the grave and high authority of Mrs. HANNAH MORE recommends "an onion from their own garden, which makes every thing savoury and costs nothing" to the poor of England. "Soupe a l'oignon" is thought highly restorative by the French. It is considered peculiarly grateful, and gently stimulating to the stomach, after hard drinking or night-watching, and holds among soups the place that champagne, soda-water, or ginger-beer, does among liquors.

71. ONION SOUP MAIGRE.

CHOP and fry in clarified butter a dozen large onions, two heads of celery, a large carrot, and a turnip. Pulp the roots through a tammy-sieve, and put them to two quarts of boiling water thickened with six ounces of butter kneaded up with potato-flour, and seasoned with mace and white peppercorns. The crumb of two penny-loaves may be boiled in the water instead of the potato-flour, but it must then be strained. Add bread-sippets fried, and thicken with the beat yolks of four eggs.

72. POTAGE A LA CLERMONT, *an elegant onion-soup.*

FRY a dozen small silver onions cut in rings, of a nice golden tinge, and drain them; cook them lightly in broth, and stew them for twenty minutes in clear gravy-broth coloured with veal-gravy, which is the best material known for colouring soups or sauces. Serve with toasted sippets previously soaked in a little broth.

N.B. Rasped Parmesan is liked with some soups, particularly macaroni. It is grated over the soup-dish. We would recommend that it be served on a plate.

73. VEGETABLE SOUPS, *or Potages Printaniers.**

UNDER this head, which in the French kitchen comprehends a variety of soups, the Scotch *nettle-kail* and *pan-kail* might be included, and also the Welsh leek-porridge when made *maigre*. These mild, healthful, and even elegant soups, are not necessarily *maigre*. The main object of the cook is to have them of a fine clear green colour, which is obtained by the expressed juice of spinach, parsley, green onions, or pease-shell liquor, using the colouring ingredient most suitable to the nature of the soup. Vegetable soups require a good deal of pepper, and are improved by a *spice* of cayenne. They will not keep for any time. If the vegetables are bitter, a bit of sugar will correct that flavour.—*See No.* 75.

74. MACARONI SOUP.

BOIL four ounces of the paste till three-fourths ready.

---

* These *maigre* vernal compositions found little favour in the eyes of the elder members of the Cleikum Club, who thought them only fit for sickly girls and young Cockney poets. They, however, afford an elegant and wholesome variety.

Have a prepared, strong, clear, gravy soup. Take care that the macaroni does not get into lumps. Serve rasped Parmesan in a glass or on a plate.

75. GREEN PEASE-SOUP,—*Maigre*.

HAVE fully three pints of green marrowy pease. Unless the pease are all young and sweet, separate the old from the young. Melt half a pound of fresh butter in a stew-pan, put to it four Imperial pints of boiling water, a slice of bread, a quart of shelled pease, some roughly-chopped green onions, spinage, and green lettuce, salt, and two dozen grains of black and Jamaica pepper. Stew till the pease will pulp back into the liquor from which they are strained; or they may be pounded in a mortar. To this add a pint or more of young pease, the heart of a lettuce chopped, and, if approved, a sliced cucumber, first sprinkling the slices with salt and draining them. If the soup is thought too thin add rice-flour; if too *maigre*, allow more butter; if not green enough, add a little spinage chopped, or a quarter pint of very green spinage liquor, made by parboiling and squeezing the vegetable. Stew for half an hour, but do not let the soup boil, or the green colour will deaden and become a tawny yellow. Green shred mint in a very small quantity may be added to flavour the soup, five minutes before it is dished. Serve with dice of fried bread.—*Obs*. This summer soup may be made from the liquor in which chickens, fowls, veal, mutton, or lamb has been boiled. If the pease are not quite young and sweet, a little sugar may be employed, and consequently less salt.

76. GREEN ASPARAGUS-SOUP.

MAKE this as green pease-soup. Slice and pulp a part of the asparagus; put the other part, cut into nice points, and dressed, into the strained soup before serving; or substitute fried bread cut into dice.

77. AN EXCELLENT SOUP MAIGRE.

MELT a half-pound of butter very slowly, and put to it four onions sliced, a head of celery, and a carrot and turnip cut down. When the vegetables have fried in the butter for a quarter of an hour, and are browned on all sides, put to them nearly four quarts of boiling water, and a pint and a half of young pease, with plenty of un-ground black and Jamaica pepper. When the vegetables are quite tender, let the soup stand to clear from the sediment, and strain it into a clean stew-pan. If not yet sufficiently transparent, let it stand an hour, and turn it carefully over. When it boils, put to it three onions shred, or five young ones. A head of celery cut in bits, carrots sliced, and cut as wheels or stars, and turnips scooped of the size of pigeons' eggs, or turnip-radishes. When the vegetables are enough done without the soup getting ropy from their dissolution, the soup is finished. This and all vegetable soups are the better of a *spice* of cayenne.

78. THE BEST YELLOW PEASE-SOUP.

To a pound and a half of split* pease, soaked and *floated*, to separate the bad ones, and, if very old, soaked again for two hours in a quart of lukewarm water in the soup-pot, add three quarts of very soft water, and three pounds of shin beef, or of any sinewy, lean, gelatinous piece, or trimmings of meat or poultry, a slice of bacon, or a shank of either a bacon or mutton ham scalded (the root of a tongue salted a little, and well soaked to draw out all the slime, does very well), a couple of well-sized carrots, two turnips, and four large or six smaller onions. When this has been skimmed, and has simmered slowly for about an hour and a half, taking care that it does not stick to the bottom of the pot, (Scottice, "*sit on*,") add another quart of boiling water, or any fresh pot-liquor in which poultry or meat has been boiled. Simmer again till the pease are completely dissolved. Pour the soup into a coarse hair sieve, which set over an earthen pan or stew-pot, and pulp the pease through with a wooden, or *tinned* iron spoon, taking back some strained soup to moisten what remains of the pease, till the whole mash is pulped through. Add salt, white pepper in

---

* Whole pease are often sweeter and better than those which are split, but they must be longer soaked. In country families that study economy, pease of the grey kind are often shelled at the mill, and used as white boilers. The colour is not so fine, but the soup is equally good, if not better. Pease will mellow better in the pot, if first soaked a night, and then allowed to dry. By this process they swell in the fibre. They may be broken in a mill.

fine powder, and the onions well pulped, to the strained soup, a head of fresh celery shred roughly, or a dessert-spoonful of the seed (which communicates the flavour in a strong degree) tied up in a bit of muslin rag, which must be lifted out before the soup is dished. Simmer it for a half-hour or three-quarters, if too thin. Pour it into the tureen, and throw in toasted bread cut into dice or diamonds. Carefully remove the film or veil of fat which gathers on the surface when in the tureen, and stir up the soup the moment before it goes to the table. Butter fried with flour may be used to enrich this soup, and toasted oatmeal to thicken it, mixing the oatmeal like starch, and carefully keeping back the grits.—For PEASE-POTTAGE double the quantity of pease is required. —*Obs.* This, though neither the most expensive nor elegant of soups, is a favourite family-dish in cold weather, —that is, nine months of the year,—and is recommended at once by economy and excellence. It can be made of an inferior sort, of any thing that is wholesome. A rump-bone, the bones of meat used for pies, trimmings or a roast, &c., are all excellent. Roast-beef bones, if not stale, nor charred and impregnated with empyreuma, and fresh dripping, answer very well; also the liquor in which salt meat is boiled—or part of it—with the exception of that of fat old pork, which, save in cases of stern necessity, cannot be tolerated by us. When pease-soup is made of shreds and patches of meat, more onion or celery-seed and spice may be used to overcome the flavour of whatever constitutes the basis of the soup. A very convenient way of making a common pease-soup is, to have pease-pudding boiled, ready to mix with the liquor in which meat or fowls are dressed. The above seasonings are then to be added, and the soup may be enriched with butter, or clarified fresh dripping, and thickened with potato-flour or oatmeal, as above directed and finished in a half-hour. Dried mint or dried parsley is sometimes rubbed and strewed into this soup. Withholding* the onions and celery, and substituting asparagus points, makes this an excellent asparagus-soup.

---

* By the addition of curry powder, Dr. HUNTER, the author of *Culina*, makes CURRY PEASE-SOUP. Dr. REDGILL added square bits of fried bacon, cayenne, fried onions or cucumber, and concocted a soup of

79. PEASE-PUDDING.

MARROWY *melters*, whether whole or split, are far the best pease for the cook. Soak the necessary length of time: boil them tied loosely in a cloth till they will pulp through a colander. Add salt, pepper, two beat yolks of eggs, a good piece of butter: tie up firmly, and boil (with pork if boiling) for another half hour.

80. POTATO-SOUP

THIS cheap and generally acceptable soup may be made of the same materials as *Pease-soup*, or of any liquor in which meat has been boiled, or of roast-beef bones, &c.; a hock of ham, or shank of mutton-ham, or anything of this kind, may be advantageously used to flavour and enrich it. Season with onions, celery or parsley, and either thicken with mashed potatoes, or suffer the potatoes, previously pared and parboiled, to fall to a mash in the soup.

N.B.—Where small families kill a sheep now and then for winter-store, what is salted, though it would not make even tolerable broth, will make a very palatable potato-soup with any of the above seasonings. Red-herrings are often recommended to flavour this and other cheap soups: we do not admire them. Cheap potato-soup may be made entirely of dripping.—Cale-cannon and dripping make a good cheap *extempore* soup.

81. TO GRILL CRUSTS FOR SOUPS.

PUT the cut crusts upon a small wire gridiron over hot cinders to crisp. When done, wet the inside with top-fat, and sprinkle a little salt over them, and put them into the tureen; or crisp them over a furnace, wetting with good stock.

N.B.—If you put bread into *boiling* soup, it will swell, crumble, and spoil the appearance of the soup.

---

the composite order, which, in compliment to the inventor, was named by the Club, REDGILL's *Pease-soup haut gout*.

SOUP AND STEW, OR MOUTHFUL SOUPS.

By the above names the reader is to understand all soups in which meat, fowl, or fish, cut in mouthfuls, is dressed and served. Such, for example, are Mock Turtle-soup, Lobster-soup, Oyster-soup, &c. This is a division which we think was wanted in books that treat of the culinary art; as the greatest discoveries which have been made in the English kitchen within the last twenty years are unquestionably in this favourite class of glutinous soups. This important class, be it noticed, comprehends not only the Oriental Mullagatawny and the oleaginous Ox-rump, but even the spicy and luscious Turtle.*

82. MULLAGATAWNY-SOUP.

MULLAGATAWNY differs little, save in the curry powder or other seasonings, from the excellent Scotch dish, "Stewed knuckle of veal." Break and wash a knuckle of good veal, and put it to boil in nearly three quarts of water, with a quarter-ounce of black and Jamaica peppercorns. Place wooden or tinned skewers in the bottom of the stew-pan, to prevent the meat from sticking to it. Put also a few slices of bacon, if the flavour and oily qualities of this meat are admired. Skim this stock carefully when it comes to the boil, and let it simmer an hour and a half before straining it off. Cut three pounds of breast of veal into small bits, adding the trimmings, bones, and gristles of the breast to the water in which the knuckle is put to boil. Fry the bits of veal and six sliced onions in a deep stew-pan, of a delicate brown. Put the strained stock to them; skim carefully, and when

---

* We give no receipt for dressing turtle, an affair on which a volume might be written, so complicated and various are the processes. ROUSSEAU tells of a German who composed a whole volume on the zest of a lemon. What then might not be said on that which comprehends all zests,—"the Sovereign of Savouriness," the Olio compounded "of every creature's best?" As none but thorough-bred *men* of science are ever intrusted with dressing a Turtle, the Cleikum Club did not presume to instruct them, and thought the receipts found in cookery books for this article merely so many make-bulks. Female cooks are excellent in their own way; but no woman ever yet succeeded in writing an epic or dressing a turtle.—P.T.

the soup and meat have simmered three-quarters of an hour, mix two dessert-spoonfuls of curry powder, and the same quantity of lightly-browned flour, to a smooth batter, with salt and cayenne to taste: add these to the soup, and stew and simmer till the meat is quite tender.—*Obs*. This soup may be made of fowls cut in pieces, of rabbits, or mutton cutlets: but is best when made of well-fed veal. For East Indian palates, eschalots, mace, and ginger may be employed, but the quantity must be left to the discretion of the cook.—See *Mullagatawny, as made in India (National Dishes)*.

83. MOCK TURTLE-SOUP.

PROCURE the head of a middle-sized, well-fed cow-calf, with the skin on; scald it, split and take out the brains and the gristles and bones of the nose, blanch it well in several waters, to draw out the slime and blood. Place it in a stew-pan, and cover it with cold water; boil it, and skim without intermission while any scum continues to arise. When the head has boiled gently for three quarters of an hour take it out, and as soon as cold enough to cut, carve it into small neat pieces, in the shape of diamonds, dice, triangles, &c. Peel the tongue, and cut it into cubes of an inch thick. Meanwhile, put the broken bones and trimmings of the head into your stock-pot, with a large knuckle of veal well broken, and three or four pounds of a shin of beef well soaked. Let this boil very slowly, having carefully skimmed it, for at least four hours, and take care it does not stick to the bottom of the pot; then strain for future use, and lay aside a quart of this stock for gravy. Thus much may be done the evening before the soup is wanted. When the soup is to be made, take off the cake of fat which will have formed on the top, and put the stock, holding back the sediment, into a large stew-pan. If the stock is good it will be a jelly, or nearly so. When it is again skimmed, put to it a dozen onions sliced, and browned in the frying-pan, with a half-dozen sprigs of fresh mild sage, also chopped and fried. Thicken the soup with butter kneaded in browned flour, or with brown roux; and season highly with ground black and Jamaica pepper, a little cayenne, two blades of mace, an eschalot, four leaves of fresh basil, and the parings of one large or two small lemons. When the soup is strong and well-coloured, strain it through a hair sieve very gently into a fresh stew-pan, and put the hash of the head to it. Add wine when it is nearly finished, in the proportion of a half-glassful to the quart.* When to be dished, slip in two dozen of small force-meat balls, made of veal or veal-kidney, minced parsley, crumbs, and the seasonings directed for *Quenelles* (*See* French cookery,) well fried and drained; also hard-boiled yolks of eggs, or egg-balls, and the juice of two lemons squeezed through a strainer.—*Obs.* A small piece of bacon used to be put into the stock-pot; and a faggot of sweet herbs, and mushrooms are still often added to the soup. The imitation of the real Turtle-soup was also thought nearer when the soup abounded in pieces of the fat double tripe, gristly bits of veal, or veal sweetbread parboiled, or the belly-piece of pickled pork, cut in mouthfuls, the soft part of oysters, pickled tongue parboiled and cut down, the meat of lobsters, &c. These cloying substances are now very generally discarded. Simplicity is the taste of the day, though much is left to the discretion of the cook in the making of Mock Turtle, and all soups of the *composite order*. The quantity made by the above directions is fully more than will be wanted for any dinner, as it will fill two tureens; but part of the stock may be laid aside for gravy or sauces; and if there is too much *hash* some of it may be highly seasoned and dressed as a *ragout* or *pie*. Mock Turtle may be *greened*, if that is wished, by stewing a large handful of chopped green herbs, such as parsley, young onions, &c. in butter, and putting some of the soup to them; then rubbing this green liquor through a sieve, and putting it to the green soup.

84. A CHEAPER AND VERY EXCELLENT MOCK TURTLE-SOUP.

THIS imitation is made of calf's-feet or cow-heels, gently stewed, the broth strained, and the meat cut down and put to it, with a seasoning of white pepper, allspice, onion, cayenne, a little mushroom or walnut catsup, a squeeze of lemon, and a glass of Madeira. Or

---

* Madeira or Sherry are the wines commonly employed; but Burgundy or Claret may be used, if more depth of colour is wanted.

the wine and expensive seasonings may be withheld, and the soup be very good without them.

85. BAKED MOCK TURTLE-SOUP.

THIS is easily prepared, and generally liked. Put a broken knuckle of veal, or the gristly ends of two knuckles into a deep earthen pan, with two cow-heels, the half of a calf's-head broken, four onions, a dozen of peppercorns, three blades of mace, and a few sprigs of lemon-thyme, an eschalot, or any other flavouring substance that is best relished by those for whom the soup is prepared. Fill up the dish with water or weak broth; tie several folds of paper round the mouth of it, and set it in an oven for upwards of two hours. When it is cold take off the fat from the jelly, cut the meat into mouthfuls, and stew it up with the jelly till perfectly tender. Wine, spiceries, catsup, force-meat balls, or whatever is approved of, may be added, if a soup of *haut gout* be wanted; or it may be seasoned with only a little mushroom catsup, and served plain.*

86. EGG-BALLS FOR MOCK TURTLE-SOUP.

POUND a sufficient quantity of the yolks of hard-boiled eggs in a mortar, with as much raw yolk and flour as will bind the composition. Add salt, and make up in the form of balls the size of a marble. Put at least a dozen to a dish of soup.

87. SCOTCH HARE, OR PARTRIDGE-SOUP.

MAKE a clear strong gravy of from three to four pounds of lean beef cut in pieces, or of a shin, with the trimmings of the hare, a couple of carrots and turnips, a half-dozen onions, a quarter-ounce of black and Jamaica peppercorns, and a faggot of sweet herbs. Cut the hare (or two or three partridges) into small neat steaks.† Wash the pieces, and save the washings, with all the blood,

---

* The French often make their Mock Turtle-soup stock of the trimmings of fish and mutton-shanks, &c., using meat full of jelly. They clarify the stock, and boil it so much down that, when cool, it will bear the Madeira on its surface. They cook the parboiled head in white sauce, and then proceed as above directed, only using more hard-boiled yolks of eggs.

† You may lay aside as much of the fleshy part of a good hare as will make a handsome dish of hare-cakes, or collops, garnished with sippets, or as will make force-meat balls for the soup.

which must be all carefully strained through a fine sieve and afterwards added to the stock, as they contain much of the flavour of the hare. Flatten and season the steaks; dredge them with flour; brown them lightly in a frying-pan, and put them to the strained stock—or merely season and add them with onions without frying. Let the soup stew very slowly for an hour and a half at least. Put in the strained blood, and keep the soup for some time at the point of boiling; but do not let it boil through or the blood will curdle. This soup may be thickened with butter kneaded up in browned flour, or with *roux*, or potato mucilage. Or the fleshy parts of the hare, previously boiled in stock, may be pounded in a mortar with the onions to thicken the soup. Skim it again when nearly finished; put to it a glassful of mushroom catsup and a *point* of cayenne. Serve with the hare-steaks in the tureen.—*Obs.* Red wine, in the proportion of a quarter-pint to a tureen of soup, is reckoned an improvement by some gourmands; and those of the old school still like a large spoonful of currant-jelly dissolved in the soup. *Hare-soup* may be made by cutting down the ingredients and placing them in an earthen jar, in a kettle of boiling water for four hours, and then managing as above. Cold roast hare, not over-done, cut to pieces and stewed for an hour in good and highly-seasoned broth, will make an excellent, but not a highly-flavoured *Hare-soup*.—See *Civet of Hare (French Cookery.)* Cold roast hare, game, or veal, will all of them, if cut down, and slowly stewed for an hour in broth, or boiling water thickened with brown flour kneaded in butter, and rather highly-seasoned with onion, pepper, and cayenne, make a very palatable *Stew-soup*. Many prefer this mode of re-dressing cold meat to either *hashing* or *fricasseeing*. The burnt outside, skins, and every thing unfit for the tureen, should be trimmed away; or, if these are boiled in the soup, it must be strained before the hashed meat to be served is added to it.

88. A MODERN HARE-SOUP.

CUT down the hare into nice pieces, and stew them with four onions, stuck with four cloves, four blades of mace, a bay leaf or two, a faggot of parsley, with two or three sprigs of basil, thyme, and marjoram. Simmer slowly in a little strong stock-broth; and when the juices are well drawn out, put more broth, till the whole quantity required is in. Simmer for another hour at least, and strain the soup. Take the best of the meat from the bones, pound it, moistening with a little of the soup. Pound also some soaked crumb of bread, or the dry mealy part of potatoes, and put this to the soup, which must now be seasoned to your taste with pepper, salt, cayenne, and catsup; *or*, keep the best pieces, if the hare be large, to serve whole in the tureen, cut into mouthfuls, and pound and pulp the others, which will make the soup have quite enough of consistence. The best pieces to serve are the fillets cut off, along the back-bone, which need not be boiled quite so long as the other parts, if to be thus served.

89. PIGEON-SOUP, OR GAME-SOUP.

MAKE a clear gravy stock of four pounds of lean beef, or scrag and shanks of mutton, two turnips, two onions, and four quarts of water boiled down to three. Put to this stock the gizzards, crops, and livers of four or five pigeons or partridges. The birds must be neatly trussed as for boiling, seasoned inside with ground white pepper and salt, and flattened on the breast. Dredge them with flour, and brown them nicely in a frying-pan. Thicken the stock with butter kneaded in browned flour; strain and season it with white pepper, salt, and a little mace, and let the pigeons stew in it for twenty-five minutes, taking off the scum as it rises. Throw a few toasted soaked sippets into the tureen before dishing the soup.

90. SUPERLATIVE GAME-SOUP, OR VENISON-SOUP.

THIS soup is made of all sorts of black or red game, or of venison or wild rabbits. Skin the birds, carve and trim them neatly, and dry the pieces with a few slices of ham, sliced onions, carrots, and parsnips, a little of each. Drain and stew this meat gently for an hour in good fresh veal or beef stock-broth, with a head of celery cut in nice bits, a little minced parsley, and what seasonings you like. Very small steaks of venison may be fried as the birds and stewed in the broth; and if the stock is made of any venison trimmings, it will be an advantage both in flavour and strength.—*Obs*. Jamaica pepper and cloves are suitable seasonings; celery, from its nutty flavour, is a proper vegetable for game-soups. Take out the ham before dishing.

91. OX-HEAD-SOUP, *called Hessian Soup and Ragout.*

CLEAN, rub with salt, and afterwards soak in salt and lukewarm water for four hours, the half of a fat bullock's head and the root of a tongue, or a cow-heel. Wash them, and break and put them into a large pot with seven quarts of water and a spoonful of salt. Skim very carefully, and retard the boiling by throwing in a quart of cold water, which will throw up more scum. When the meat is tender, but not overdone, take it out and strain the broth. When cold take off the cake of fat,* and the oil below it, and put to the remaining soup a pound of white or grey shelled pease. When it has boiled an hour, add (roughly cut) six or eight potatoes, six carrots, four turnips, half a dozen onions, a bunch of parsley, and a dessert-spoonful of celery-seed tied up in a bit of rag; season with pepper and salt, and boil till the vegetables are tender. This makes a very excellent broth, nutritious and palatable, and the meat may either be served in it or as a ragout. But a little more trouble fits this dish to appear at any family-dinner, and entitles it to the appellation of *Hessian Soup and Ragout.* When the pease and vegetables put in the soup, as above described, are soft enough to pulp, strain it, and rub them through a sieve to the soup, which will now be nearly of the consistence of thin pease-soup. If not thickened enough, add rice-flour well mixed, or potato-mucilage, and heat the soup, adding white pepper and cayenne to taste, and a head of celery sliced. The *ragout* or *hash* is made by cutting into mouthfuls the best parts of the head and root of the tongue, or cow-heel, seasoning highly with mixed spices, a little walnut-catsup, and a tea-spoonful of made mustard, with a pint and a half of the clear stock of the head, saved for this purpose when the soup is strained.—*Obs.* Soy, force-meat balls, wine &c., are all ordered for this ragout in some approved books of cookery; but we consider such

---

* This will keep for frying, make a cheap soup, *kail-brose*, or *brewis*.

expensive ingredients quite out of place in a preparation which is cheap, good, and savoury, but never can be elegant. The meat of the head and root of tongue that remains may be eat as a plain stew, or added to the soup, or *potted*, in the Scotch fashion.

92. CALF'S-HEAD-SOUP.

THE half of a large head may be rubbed with salt, soaked for some hours, and, when thoroughly clean, put on with as much fresh water or fresh pot-liquor as will cover it, and with an onion and some parsley. When well skimmed and boiled for an hour, take out the head and strain the soup. Cut the head in nice mouthfuls, about three inches long and one thick, and dress it as ragout, or put it to stew in the soup. Season with white pepper, mace, and herbs.—*Obs.* The heads and the internals parts of animals spoil sooner than the joints; it is therefore important to buy them very fresh. Indeed, all meat for soups ought to be as fresh as possible.—See *dressed Calf's Head.*

93. A PEPPER-POT.*

THIS is now understood to be a sort of clear-larder, Saturday's dinner-dish, composed of all sorts of shreds and patches. It ought properly, if fine cookery is attempted, to be an *Olio*, composed of a due admixture of meat, fish, fowl, vegetables, and roots. To three quarts of water put a couple of pounds of whatever vegetables are plentiful (a good proportion being onions), and a couple of pounds of mutton-scrag cut into three or four pieces; or a fowl, or veal, or a piece of lean bacon, and a little rice. Skim it; and, when nearly finished, add the meat of a lobster or crab, cut in bits, or the soft part of a few oysters, or hard-boiled yolks of eggs. Take off all the fat that rises, and season highly with pepper and cayenne. Serve in a tureen.

94. KNUCKLE OF VEAL SOUP, *an excellent Scotch soup.*

TAKE a large knuckle, or if small add a piece of the scrag. Wash it, and break the bones; place skewers

---

* "Where every thing that every soldier got,
Fowl, bacon, cabbage, mutton, and what not
Was thrown into one Bank, and went to pot."

in the stew-pan to keep the knuckle from sticking; cover it with water and no more; put in a head of celery, a sprig of lemon-thyme, three onions, a carrot, a turnip, a handful of parsley, and two dozen black and Jamaica peppercorns, simmer till the knuckle is tender. Strain the soup. Cut the gristly parts of the knuckle and all that is good, into mouthfuls, and put to it a seasoning of white pepper and mace in powder, and rice-flour to thicken if it is wished. This soup may be made with rice or vermicelli; or the stewed uncut knuckle may be served in the soup; for many like to pick the gristles, a "pleasing toil," instead of having the meat cut for them by the cook.—*Obs.* Some gourmands admire veal stew-soup made of *Staggering-Bob,*—that is an *infant* calf, whose bones are still gristle, and his flesh a jelly. The breast, knuckle, and shoulder-blade, are best for this purpose, and the soup is, when finished, thickened with a *liaison* of the yolks of three eggs, and seasoned with mace.

95. GIBLET-SOUP.*

TAKE from two to three pounds of shin of beef, or of shanks and scrag of mutton, or knuckle of veal, or a part of each, as may be found most convenient; a small faggot of sweet herbs, carrots, turnips, and a little parsley; a quarter-ounce of black or Jamaica peppercorns, and four quarts of water. When this has simmered for an hour, put to it two pair of goose-giblets, or four pair of duck-giblets, scalded and cleaned, and also browned in the frying-pan, if you choose, with minced onion. When the giblets are delicately tender, but not soft and insipid, take them up, and cut them neatly into large mouthfuls. The soup must now be thickened with

---

* This was one of those *pretending* dishes of which Mistress DODS emphatically said, "boil stanes in butter, and the broo will be gude." When plainly made, as directed in the above receipt, it affords an agreeable variety for a family-dinner, and is an economical way of using what might be otherwise wasted, which is always commendable. Wine is ordered for giblet-soup in the most approved cookery books; and we have no wish to restrain the fancies of a gourmand, however extravagant; but Mrs. DODS strongly protested against bestowing Madeira on goosehorns and pinions, French cooks dress giblets as an haricot, wrapping them in layers of bacon, in which they are stewed. When done and drained, the sauce is skimmed and poured over them.

butter kneaded in a large spoonful of flour with *roux*, or with the top-fat gradually mixed with flour, and strained into a fresh stew-pan, into which put the giblets. Boil and skim, and season with a large spoonful of mushroom catsup, salt, and a little cayenne. Serve with the cut giblets in the tureen. Beans, lettuce, and celery, separately boiled, may be added at pleasure. We especially approve of celery.

96. OX-RUMP, OR TAIL SOUP.

Two tails, or, if small, three will make a large tureen of soup. Let the butcher divide them at the joints. Rub them with salt, and soak them in lukewarm water. Place the tails in a stew-pan, with four onions or more, a bunch of parsley, two dozen of Jamaica and black pepper corns, (or a half-ounce if high peppering is wanted,) a turnip sliced, and three quarts of water. When the meat is tender, lift it out, and cut it into small mouthfuls. Thicken the soup with a little browned flour, rubbed up with a ladleful of the top-fat; strain it into a fresh stew-pan, put in the cut meat, boil up, and skim; and finish with a spoonful of mushroom catsup, and pepper to taste.—*Obs.* Ox-tails make a very excellent onion-soup, by adding to it, when strained, a dozen fried onions pulped, and thickening it with potato-flour.

97. POACHER'S SOUP,
or Soupe à la Meg Merrilies.

This savoury and highly-relishing new stew soup, may be made of any or every thing known by the name of game. Take from two to four pounds of the trimmings or coarse parts of venison, shin of beef, or shanks or lean scrag of good mutton—all fresh. Break the bones, and boil this with a couple of carrots and turnips, four onions, a bunch of parsley, and a quarter-ounce of peppercorns, the larger proportion Jamaica pepper. Strain this stock when it has boiled for three hours. Cut down and skin a black-cock, or wood-cock, a pheasant, half a hare, or a rabbit, a brace of partridges or grouse, or one of each, (whichever is obtained most easily), and season the pieces with mixed spices. These may be floured and browned in the frying-pan; but as this is a process dictated by the eye as much as the palate, it is not

necessary in making this soup. Put the game to the
strained stock, with a dozen of small onions, a couple of
heads of celery sliced, half a dozen peeled potatoes, and,
when it boils, a small white cabbage quartered, black
pepper, allspice, and salt, to taste. Let the soup simmer
till the game is tender, but not overdone; and lest it
should, the vegetables may be put in half an hour before
the meat.—*Obs.* This soup may be coloured and flavoured
with wine and two spoonfuls of mushroom catsup, and
enriched with forcemeat-balls.* Soups in which catsup is
mixed should not be salted till that ingredient is added,
as catsup contains so much salt itself.†

---

* The Club were at variance on the above original receipt. JEKYLL
declared for the simple racy flavour of the rude sylvan cheer;
WINTERBLOSSOM liked the addition of forcemeat-balls and catsup; and
the Doctor—hovering between the tureens, like Macheath between his rival
charmers,—laid his ears deeply in both, but when compelled to decide,
from an habitual reverence to the soups that be, voted for the *plain soup*
as originally swallowed with so much unction by Dominie Sampson.

† STEW soups, when not made cloyingly rich nor over-seasoned,
as they always are by those whose trade it is to compound cordials to
stimulate and pamper palled appetites and indurated palates, are, for
common and general purposes, the most easy, wholesome, and nutritious
form in which food can be prepared. This is that combination of fluids
and solids, animal and vegetable substances, with condiments, which
forms the mixture best fitted to the human stomach, and best calculated
to promote health and impart strength. The prejudice which exists in
England against soups as not promotive of strength ought to give way
before Stew soups. It has been gravely contended of late, that human
life cannot be supported on soups, however rich, without solid animal
food; and experiments are quoted where a dog kept on the richest soup
died, while another which was fed on meat boiled to chips, and water,
retained health and strength. To these experiments may be opposed
the living example of the poor of Ireland and Scotland, who hardly ever
see animal food in any form, and yet enjoy health and strength. "The
greatest heroes of antiquity," says Sir JOHN SINCLAIR, "lived on broth."
The liquor in which their mutton or venison was boiled, thickened with
a little oatmeal, and seasoned perhaps with a few wild herbs, formed the
morning tea and coffee in the hall of the chieftain, before the introduction
of these costly foreign commodities. It is impossible to say on what
men will not live, and enjoy health too;—shell-fish, Iceland moss, mushrooms, snails, and an endless variety of substances, have been known to
sustain life and health,—not to mention fricassees of old shoes and leather
breeches, to which shipwrecked mariners have often had recourse. Our
readers cannot have forgotten Sir BEVIS of Hampdoun in his dungeon, of
whom—

> "Rats and mice and such small deer,
> Was the food for full seven year."

This to be sure is solid animal food, and favours the theory of the modern
experimenters; but again, we have Dr. FRANKLIN's old Catholic lady,
who lived solely on water-gruel, and yet enjoyed health. There has lately

98. CHEAP RICE AND MEAT SOUP.

BOIL from three to four pounds of a good ox-cheek, very well soaked and cleaned, in three quarts of water, with four onions, and a small faggot of pot-herbs. Strain it; cut the meat in small pieces, and stew it with six ounces of rice, adding pepper and salt. This cheap stew-soup may be seasoned with curry powder or mace; or made after a finer fashion with knuckle of veal, or two cow-heels.

99. SCOTCH BARLEY-BROTH, WITH BOILED MUTTON, or *Bouilli Ordinaire.*

TO from three to six pounds of beef or mutton, according to the quantity of broth wanted, put cold water in the proportion of a quart to the pound,—a quarter-pound of Scotch barley, or more or less as may suit the meat and the water, and a spoonful of salt unless the meat is already slightly salted. To this put a large cupful of white pease, or split grey pease, unless in the season when old green pease are to be had cheap, a double quantity of which must be put in with the other vegetables, using less barley. Skim very carefully as long as any scum rises; then draw aside the pot, and let the broth boil slowly for an hour, at which time put to it two young carrots and turnips cut in dice, and two or three onions sliced. A quarter of an hour before the broth is ready, add a little parsley picked and chopped,—or the white part of three leeks may be used instead of onions, and a head of celery sliced instead of the parsley

---

started up in England, we are told, a new-fangled religious sect, who from an absurd reading of the commandment "Thou shalt not kill," renounce the use of animal food, and enjoy high health on their vegetable regimen. It is indeed great presumption to limit the powers of the human stomach, in assimilating and turning to healthful chyle; whatever is, in discretion, and without violent and sudden change, submitted to its action. Of this important organ, "the master of the family," it holds as strongly as of the palate, that "what is one man's meat is another man's poison:"

Chaque pays chaque coutume.

The Tartar feeds on horse flesh, the Chinese on dog's, the Greenlander on fish garbage, with the luxurious sauce of train-oil. The Frenchman and German feed on frogs and snails, and the ancients valued *usafoetida* as much as the moderns do curry-powder, or Burgess' fish-sauce.—P.T.

seasoning; but celery requires longer boiling. For beef-broth a small quantity of greens roughly shred, and four or five leeks cut in two-inch lengths, are better suited than turnip, carrot, and parsley, which are more adapted to mutton. If there is danger of the meat being overdone before the broth is properly *lithed*, it may be taken up, covered for a half-hour, and returned into the pot to heat through before it is dished. *Garnish* with carrot and turnip boiled in the broth, and divided; or pour over the *bouilli* caper-sauce, parsley and butter, or a sauce made of pickled cucumbers, or nasturtiums heated in melted butter, or in a little clear broth, with a tea-spoonful of made mustard and another of vinegar. Minced parsley, parboiled for two minutes, may also be strewed over *bouilli*,—or a sprinkling of boiled carrots cut in small dice. Serve the broth in a tureen, removing any film of fat that may gather upon the surface.—*Obs.* The pieces of fresh beef best adapted for barley-broth are the shin, the brisket, the flank, and the veiny piece, —of mutton, the neck, the ribs, and the leg. In some parts of the "land of kail", broth made of fresh beef would scarcely be tolerated,—the meat not at all; and unquestionably the brisket or flank, when salted for a week, makes excellent broth, while the meat eats much better. Many persons, however, prefer the sweetness of *fresh* meat. An economical way of managing where beef is salted for winter-provision, is to boil a piece of fresh and a piece of salt meat together, by which method the broth is not grouty nor yet over salt, which it will be when made wholly of salt meat. In some parts of England, *lean* fresh beef and salt pork are boiled and eaten together. Turkey beans, stripped of their blackening outer husk, are admirably adapted for *lithing* barley-broth.* Barley is very apt to spoil. It becomes *mity*, and, what is worse, this fault is not easily detected. Barley should, if good, no more be wasted than flour; but then it must be fresh and sound, if we would

---

* Mrs. Dods, with her usual sagacity, stated, and it must be owned, with great plausibility of reasoning, that one capital defect of broth cooked by Englishers and other unqualified persons, is produced nine times out of ten by the bad quality of the barley often used in England. Nor does *pearl-barley* give the same consistence as pot-barley.

avoid the glary, ropy decoctions which are sometimes seen on tables where better things might be expected. The quality of flour used in cookery ought also to be attended to. When exposed to air and damp, it becomes musty much sooner than is generally known. English books of cookery order a sauce for meat boiled in broth, of red wine, mushroom catsup, and gravy with cut pickles—a piece of extravagance completely at variance with the character and properties of the better part of the dish,—namely, with the bland balsamic barley-broth of Scotland. But if a fine name is admired, use the French *sauce hacheé*. For cheap and excellent soups and broths, see *National Dishes*.—The above barley-broth will make an excellent rice-broth, by using rice for barley, and omitting the pease. *German* barley-broth is made exactly as above, using a piece of the flank of beef.

FISH SOUPS.

THIS delicate and elegant description of soups has gained on the favour of the gormandizing world very rapidly within the last few years. Cray-fish was the favourite *bonne bouche* of past generations. Oyster and lobster soups are more admired in our day.

100. THE BASIS OF FISH-SOUPS,

The STOCK, as it is technically called,—may either be made of fish or meat. The former is perhaps the more elegant, and is besides suited to *maigre* days; the latter is supposed to be the more rich and nourishing. Beef, veal, or the lean of mutton, may all be used for fish-stock. When made of fish, a skate, a cod's head, haddocks, whitings, eels, gudgeons, flounders, and other white fish, are used, and also the heads, fins, and trimmings of the fish which are to be dressed. As fish-stock soon becomes sour, it should not be made till it is to be used. Boil the fish of which you make the stock, in two quarts of water, with a couple of onions, a piece of lemon-peel, and a faggot of sweet herbs. Skim the liquor carefully, and strain it. If the fish-soup is to be brown, the fish which makes the stock may be browned in the frying-pan before boiling, and catsup is generally put to brown fish-soup.—See *Court Bouillon, French Cookery*.

101. LOBSTER-SOUP.

HAVE three middle-sized, or five small lobsters—*hen-lobsters* if possible—ready boiled, and five pints of good veal-gravy, though beef or mutton stock will answer very well. Break off, and bruise in a mortar, the small claws and fins, with an anchovy, a piece of lemon-peel, and a couple of scalded onions. Put these to the stock, and simmer till you have obtained all the strength and flavour they contain. Strain all the stock. Split the tails, crack without mangling the great claws, and take out the meat, cutting it into small pieces. Pick the meat from the chine, and take part of the coral, the soft part of a few oysters, and anchovy, the quarter of a nutmeg, a blade of mace, a little cayenne, and a tea-spoonful of lemon-peel grated. Put these in a mortar; beat them, and with the yolks of two eggs and a very little flour, make of this a dozen or more small forcemeat-balls for the soup. Next bruise the spawn in the mortar, with a little flour, and rubbing it through a sieve, put this, with the meat of the claws and tails, and the coral left from the forcemeat, into the soup. Fry the forcemeat-balls, or brown them in a Dutch oven, and slip them also into the soup, which may simmer for a quarter of an hour, but must not boil. Test the balls, (See *testing* forcemeat, *Godiveau, French Cookery*,) *or* they may be omitted, and the meat cut in nice bits, put to the strained soup. Foreign substances are sometimes employed to heighten the vermilion tint of this soup, but we do not recommend the practice. Squeeze the juice of a lemon or Seville orange through a strainer into the tureen, and serve the soup, lifting it carefully. Some cooks put a glass of Madeira into it.—*Obs.* This soup is sometimes partly made of sweet cream, or milk thickened with rice-flour and butter, instead of *stock*; but the mixture of milk with fish or meat is less relished every day, and even yolks of eggs, between which and animal substances there is a closer *affinity*, do not gain ground. Wine is a good deal employed by the French in the composition of fish-soups: the rough and dry wines suit most tastes better than cream. In like manner mild ale or beer is sometimes employed in this country. A clear gravy of cow-heels makes an admirable basis for fish-soups, and is believed to be employed extensively by those who deal largely in these compositions in great towns.

102. OYSTER-SOUP.

HAVE two quarts of a good strong clear stock, whether of fish or meat: we prefer it of veal. Add to it the hard-boiled yolks of six eggs, and the hard part of a quart of fresh juicy oysters, previously well pounded in a mortar. Simmer for a half-hour, and strain it into a fresh stew-pan, in which have the oysters cleared of the beards, and very nicely washed from shells and sand. Season with mace and cayenne, and let the oysters simmer for eight minutes, when the yolks of three eggs well beat may be stirred into a little of the soup, and gradually mixed with the whole quantity, drawing aside the stew-pan, and constantly stirring, lest the eggs curdle. When smooth and thick, serve in a tureen, and still stir the soup for a minute, to prevent curdling. Any other flavour that is relished may be given to this luscious soup.

103. ANOTHER OYSTER-SOUP.

AFTER bearding the oysters, dip them in beat egg, dust them with flour, run them on fine wire skewers, and fry and drain them. Place them in the tureen, and pour the prepared soup over them. The beards, nut, (or hard part) and all the oyster-liquor saved, must be put to the soup, and boiled a little before it is strained.—*Obs*. This soup may be thickened with the beat yolks of three eggs; *or* half a half-pint of boiling cream put to it before it is served.

Another OYSTER-SOUP, *maigre*. Have good *Court-Bouillon*, or make some of four pints of water, four onions fried in butter, mace and other seasonings. Put to this when skimmed a pound of fresh butter, and a hundred picked oysters; also a few mushrooms. Thicken with bread-crumbs or vermicelli, and boil slowly a quarter of an hour.

104. CRAY-FISH SOUP.

MAKE two quarts of fish-stock, in which boil a bunch of parsley, two onions, and two dozen of black and Jamaica peppercorns. For this have from two to three pounds of fish fins, heads, &c., all fresh. Boil to a mash, and strain the liquor till clear. Pick from four to five dozen of cray-fish, and stew them in the soup till delicately done: add a little cayenne, and the spawn of a boiled lobster pounded, and stirred into the soup, which it will both thicken and enrich.—*Obs.* Soups are made of *muscles*, *cockles*, and *prawns*. These all require a good stock, (whether *gras* or *maigre*,) plenty of pepper, and careful washing and picking.—As much of the flavour of delicate shell-fish is lost in washing them free of sand, the washings may be kept, strained repeatedly, and put to the stock.

105. FORCEMEAT FOR FISH-SOUPS, OR FOR STEWS OF FISH.

BEAT the flesh and soft parts of a boiled lobster in a mortar, with a boned anchovy, the yolks of three eggs hard boiled, and a head of boiled celery chopped. Put to this a handful of bread-crumbs, cayenne, mace, a spoonful of mushroom catsup, a quarter-pound of melted butter, a large spoonful of oyster-liquor, or some oyster-pickle, and two or more eggs well beaten, to cement the composition. Mix it well, and form into small egg-shaped balls, which fry, or brown in a Dutch oven; or the fish that makes the stock may be pounded for forcemeat. See also *Fish forcemeat, Chapter Fish, and Crappit heads.*

106. EEL-SOUP.

TAKE two pounds of eels, two quarts of water, a crust of bread, six blades of mace, two onions, a few corns of whole pepper, and a bundle of sweet herbs; cut, and boil the fish till half the liquor is wasted, then strain it, and serve it up with toasted bread. This may make both a ragout and a soup. It may be made stronger by boiling it longer, or using broth instead of water.—See *Fish and sauce,* NATIONAL DISHES, also *Fish turtle.*

107. MILK-SOUP.

BOIL two quarts of milk, with a little salt, a stick of cinnamon, and a little sugar; lay thin slices of toasted bread in a dish; pour over a little of the milk to soak them, and keep them hot upon a stove; take care the milk does not burn. When the soup is ready to serve, beat up the yolks of five eggs, and add them to the milk. Stir it over the fire till it thickens; then take it off lest it should curdle, and pour it into the dish upon the bread.—*Obs.* This makes the *Potage de Lait* of French cookery, by the addition of a quarter of a pound of sweet almonds with a few bitter ones blanched, pounded, sifted, and stirred into the boiling soup.

108. PORTABLE-SOUP, *useful for glazing meat.*

THIS soup is best made of shin of beef, but knuckle of veal or cow-heels may be used in a small proportion. Have from ten to twenty pounds of shin of good fresh-killed beef, well broken; and from five to ten of knuckle of veal. Place this in a *digester*, or close-covered pot, and cover it with water. It must heat very gradually, that the fibres of the meat may have time to soften and swell; skim it carefully; retard the boil with a little cold water, and skim till no more scum rises. No roots nor vegetables are boiled with this soup; for although they might improve the flavour, they would both pre-vent, in some degree, the jelly from forming, and make it more difficult to preserve afterwards. The *digester* may be allowed to remain by the kitchen fire all night, if a fire is kept up; and at any rate the soup will require from ten to twelve hours very slow boiling. Strain the broth from the meat, which will be boiled to tatters. When the soup has stood to be perfectly cold, take off the fat carefully, and in turning it out, hold back not merely the sediment, but all that looks muddy. Heat and pour it once more through a sieve, into a thick-bottomed cast-metal stew-pan, well tinned, or into a double-bottomed tin pan, with a quarter-ounce of black peppercorns. Let the fire be clear and brisk, and let the soup boil quickly, which is necessary to drive off the watery particles. Ten minutes' brisk boiling will do more in reducing this soup, or any jelly to be kept, to the proper consistence, than twenty of a slower ebullition. Take off any scum that rises, and when the soup begins to thicken and get gluey, and the quantity is much diminished, it will be safe to pour it into a pan of much less diameter, for fear of burning. Put a little of it in the bottom of a saucer, which may be floated in cold water, or set in a draught of air. If this sets into a strong jelly, it is enough; if not, boil it briskly for a few minutes longer, still trying if it is ready, by putting a little to cool.

This soup is preserved in various ways; the best way, when for family consumption, is to put it into very shallow jelly-pots, to be covered up when cool. But it will be more conveniently kept on a voyage if poured out on a flat asset into tablets, which may be divided when cold, with a paste runner, and when thoroughly dried, packed for use, in bladder or leather, and kept in a dry place. When the soup is to be used as such, to a pint of boiling water, to which parsley, or young onion, or any flavour that is relished, is given in previous boiling, add a little ground pepper and salt, and from an ounce to an ounce and a half of the portable soup. Boil for a few minutes, and serve with toasted bread. A drop or two of catsup will improve the flavour.

N.B.—An excellent *portable*-soup is made of neats'-feet alone. The bones must be broken, and the *oil* carefully removed. French cooks that study economy often use ox-heels in making stock for soup and jellies, both sweet and savoury, and also for sauces. *Liver* is also employed, and is sliced, fried, and stewed for stock for ox-tail or Mullagatawny soup. This is pitiful economy.

109. SPRING FRUIT-SOUPS.

THESE are made of gourds, peeled rhubarb, &c. &c. They may either be made of cream, milk, or good clear gravy; and seasoned to the taste of the eater.

Peel, clean, and blanch a bundle of sticks of rhubarb, cut them in three-inch lengths, and put them to a couple of quarts of good veal or beef gravy, with two or three onions, a few thin slices of bread, crust and crumb together, and salt and cayenne. Skim off all the fat and scum; simmer till tender; strain and serve on toasted sippets. This soup may also be made with a half-pound of butter kneaded in a little flour.

N.B.—For a variety of other fashionable soups, see *French Cookery. For good soups, National Dishes; and Cookery for the Poor.*

CHAPTER VI.

FISH.

All fish from sea or shore,
Freshet, or purling brook, of shell or fin,
And exquisitest name; for which was drained
Pontus and Lucrine bay, and Afric coast.

MILTON.

110. TO BOIL SALMON* *and other fish.*

THERE are many excellent ways of dressing this favourite fish, but perhaps none equal to plain boiling when well performed. Scale and clean the fish without unnecessary washing or handling, and without cutting it too much open. Have a roomy and well-scoured fish-kettle, and if the salmon be large and thick, when you have placed it on the strainer and in the kettle, fill up and

---

* This monarch of the British rivers is in season in some part of the three kingdoms for most part of the year, so that, however the price may vary, the London market—the point which attracts all salmon speculators —is seldom without a supply. The fishing of the river Ness, which the fish visit very early, is opened so soon as the month of December; the Severn fishery even in November; and from that time some fishery is opened every week, till in April the whole are in operation. The salmon of the Thames is that which is most esteemed in London; that of the Tay is the favourite with the inhabitants of the northern metropolis,—probably in both cases, because the fish from those rivers are brought in greater perfection to the respective markets than those of the more distant rivers. We have ever remarked, that the salmon of man's native stream, or of the river of his native province, is to him the best flavoured. Among other marks of degenerate times, is the decrease of salmon on our rivers; and it is perhaps the only one that is undeniable. This fish at one time was so common an article of food, that stipulations were made by hired servants against having it above three times a week for their *kitchen*; and the same conditions were observed in indenturing apprentices in New-castle, Perth, and many other towns. Since Mr. DEMPSTER's discovery, and packing salmon in ice, there has been found no occasion for the enforcement of the clause against salmon-eating in apprentices' indentures. The preservation of this source of wealth and luxury is still an object of legislative investigation, and we doubt not that a subject coming home so immediately "to men's business and stomachs," will meet with all the attention it merits. The destruction of the fry is the chief evil. We have known instances in which whole cart-loads of whitings, or salmon-fry have been used as manure. The poor of London, which draws into its enormous maw all the fish of the kingdoms, still enjoy this luxury, though it must be confessed not in the best state. The introduction of

amply cover it with cold spring water, that it may heat gradually. Throw in a handful of salt. If a jole or quarter is boiled, it may be put in with warm water. In both cases take off the scum carefully, and let the fish boil slowly, allowing twelve minutes to the pound; but it is even more difficult to fix the time fish should boil than the length of time that meat requires. Experience, and those symptoms which the eye of a practised cook alone can discern, must fix the point, and nothing is more disgusting and unwholesome than underdone fish. It may be probed. The minute the boiling of any fish is completed, the fish-strainer must be lifted and rested across the pan, to drain the fish.* Throw a soft cloth or flannel in several folds over it. It would become soft

---

steam-boats has had an influence on the supply in great towns. During the last seasons, a great deal was exported by the steam-boats from Ireland to Scotland and Liverpool, and in the present year the exportation will be still greater. The salmon in its first year, as *grilse*, never bring above half the price of full-grown fish. These are seldom sent to London, though in Paris, where cookery if not more rich than in London, is thought more refined, the trout, from its superior delicacy, is more prized than the ripe salmon. We ought to inform our *gourmand* readers that a fish boiled in the pickling-kettle, where perhaps some dozens of cut fish are preparing for the London market, is superbly done—meltingly rich, and of incomparable flavour. Such a thing is to be procured only at the fishing-stations, at which, it is to be remarked, assizes and presbyteries are always held.

* If meat is ready before the company assemble, take it up as directed above in boiling fish, and it may be kept in good season. Have *all* the dish-covers warmed inside at all times, and the assets well heated. Put a hot cover over the meat, and some folds of flannel over that. If you have a *bain marie*, which is a most useful utensil, or some substitute, you need be at no loss, though the above may tolerably well supply its place—sauces set on a hot table would soon lose both flavour and quality.

The *bain marie* is a flat vessel containing boiling water; you put all your stew-pans into the water, and keep that water always very hot, but it must not boil. The effect of this *bain marie* is to keep every thing warm, without altering either the quantity or the quality, particularly the quality. When I had the honour (says M. Ude) of serving a nobleman, who kept a very extensive hunting establishment, and the hour of dinner was consequently uncertain, I was in the habit of using the *bain marie* as a certain means of preserving the flavour of all my dishes. If you keep your sauce, or broth, or soup, by the fireside, the soup reduces and becomes too strong, and the sauce thickens as well as reduces.

It is necessary to observe, that this is the best manner of warming turtle-soup, as the thick part is always at the bottom of the stew-pan: this method prevents it from burning, and keeps it always good. This *Marie Balnea* does well for melting glaze, or heating up sauces, for the reasons given above.

if permitted to soak in the hot water. Dish on a hot fish-plate under a napkin. Besides the essences to be used at discretion, which are now found on every sideboard of any pretension, shrimp, anchovy, and lobster sauce, are served with salmon; also plain melted butter; and where the fish is got fresh, and served in what is esteemed by some the greatest perfection,—crisp, curdy, and creamy,—it is the practice to send in a sauce-tureen of the plain liquor in which it was boiled. Fennel and butter are still heard of for salmon, but are nearly obsolete. *Garnish* with a fringe of curled green parsley and slices of lemon. The carver must help a slice of the thick part with a smaller one of the thin, which is the fattest, and the best-liked by those in the secret. Sliced cucumber is often served with salmon, and indeed with all boiled fish.

111. TO BOIL SALMON CRIMP.

THIS makes a very handsome dish, and is the way in which salmon is usually dressed in places near the fisheries, where the fish is obtained *quick*; and also at the most fashionable English tables. The fish must be cleaned and scaled without cutting up the breast. Cut off the head, with about two inches of the neck; and the tail, with the same quantity of fish along with it. Cut as many circular fillets of the salmon as you wish for, (according to the size of the fish and the number of the company,) of about three or four inches thick;—the opening of these slices whence the entrails have been taken must be well cleaned from the blood, &c. Throw the whole into cold water made brackish with salt. Place the head and tail on the strainer, and put them in a fish-kettle of boiling water, with a little salt and vinegar—though vinegar rather hurts the colour; let them boil five minutes; lift the strainer, and lay on the slices; take off whatever scum arises, for it is very easy to injure the colour of fresh salmon. Boil from fifteen to twenty minutes. Place the head and tail on end, in the middle of the fish-plate, and lay the circular slices neatly round them. *Sauce* and *garnishing* as in the last receipt. This is salmon in its utmost perfection.

112. TO GRILL FRESH SALMON, OR SALMON CUTLETS.

THIS mode of dressing, though unsuitable for a large dinner where salmon makes a principal dish, is the way in which the solitary epicure best relishes this luxury. Split the salmon and take out the bone* without mangling the fish. Cut fillets of from three to four inches in breadth. Dry them in the folds of a cloth, but do not beat or press them. Have a clear beef-steak fire, and a bright-barred gridiron, rubbed with chalk to prevent the fish from sticking; the slices if not dry may be dusted with flour; turn with steak-tongs. This, like all *broils*, must be served *hot*. The slices may be wrapped in the folds of a hot napkin.—*Anchovy* or *Shrimp sauce.—Obs*. French cooks first *marinade*, i.e. steep the *cotelettes* in oil, seasonings and shred fine herbs; baste them while on the gridiron with the marinade-liquor; take off the skin before serving, and serve with dressed cucumber or caper-sauce. This is good practice. *To fry salmon*,—cut, fry, and serve the fillets as above.

113. TO BAKE SALMON OR TROUT.

PLACE the fish in a deep pan, and stick plenty of bits of butter over it. Season it with allspice, mace, and salt, and rub a little of the seasonings on the inside. It must be basted occasionally with what collects in the baking-pan. If the fish is small, or a grilse, it may be skewered, with the tail turned round to the mouth. A baked salmon, if not too oily, makes a handsome dish, and eats well cold.—*Garnishing* and *sauce* as for boiled salmon.—*Obs*. Many persons think salmon not only lighter but of finer flavour cold than hot. It is, at any rate, too expensive and too good to be lost. Place what is left in a deep dish, with a close cover. To a quart of the liquor in which the fish was boiled put half an ounce of black pepper and allspice in grains, half a pint of the best vinegar, and a tea-spoonful of salt. Boil this with a bay-leaf or two, and a sprig of lemon-thyme. When

---

* A salmon-bone with some pickings left makes an admirable *Devil*. The bone cut out of a *kippered* salmon should be left *rough* for this purpose. Seasoned with pepper and salt, broiled and *buttered*, it is quite an epicure's breakfast morsel. A *kipper* originally meant a black fish. These were *salted*. Now the best salmon are thus managed.

cold pour it over the salmon, which must be kept covered. This pickle will keep the fish good for some days; but if it be necessary to keep it longer, boil up the pickle afresh, adding more vinegar and spice, and when cold pour it again on the fish.*

114. BALLYSHANNON PICKLE FOR SALMON.

VINEGAR two parts, water one, white wine one. Boil in this salt, pepper, allspice, also mace, cloves, ginger, and horseradish sliced, at pleasure; when cold pour this over the boiled cold salmon.

115. TO KIPPER, *i.e.* CURE SALMON.

THE fish must be cut up, cleaned, and scaled, but not washed, and have the bone taken neatly out. Rub with equal proportions of salt and Brazil, or fine raw sugar, with a little saltpetre. Let the fish lie for two days, pressing it with a board on which weights are placed; then hang it up, or, what is much better, smoke it. Lest the folds gather mustiness and spoil, it is a good plan, when the fish is hung, to stretch it open with pieces of stick, that it may dry equally. Peppers in powder may be added to the salt. This forms a favourite addition to a Scotch breakfast, and nothing indeed can be more relishing than fresh kipper, though it soon hardens, when the French mode of dressing grilled salmon may be used with great advantage. It is uniformly dressed by cutting it into slices and broiling. If long hung the slices may be soaked in water a quarter of an hour, which will soften and improve the quality of the fish. If the fish is very large and rich it may be rubbed with salt, and drained for a day before it get the final salting.

116. TO POT SALMON.

SPLIT, scale, and clean, by wiping, for water must not touch it; rub with salt, drain off the moisture, and

---

* N.B.—*Very fresh* salmon is in most places so expensive an article of luxury, that rarity alone has given it a factitious value with many persons; for the fish is in reality much more delicate and sapid when ripened for a day or even more. The same thing holds of turbot and cod, though they too are prized for that crimp harsh freshness, which is in truth no recommendation in the eating, and often a drain on the purse. —P.T. We strongly doubt this. W.W.

season the salmon with pounded mace, cloves, and black and Jamaica pepper. Cut it into neat pieces; lay them in a pan, and cover them with melted butter. Bake it, drain from the fat, and put the pieces into potting-cans, which must then be covered with clarified butter.

117. TO COLLAR SALMON.

SPLIT, scale, and bone as much of the fish as will make a handsome collar of about six inches diameter. Season it highly with beaten mace, cloves, pepper, and salt, and having rolled it firmly up and bandaged it, bake it with vinegar and butter; or simmer in vinegar and water. Serve with melted butter and anchovy-sauce. The liquor in which the collar was boiled or baked may be boiled up with salt, vinegar, and a few bay-leaves, and poured over the fish to preserve it.

118. SALMON CUTLETS.

FRENCH cooks dress slices of fresh salmon as cutlets *en papillote*, by seasoning them with mixed spices, dipping in salad-oil, and broiling. Mustard is considered by knowing gourmands an improvement to salmon when more than ripe.

119. BAKED SALMON-TROUT, *a handsome dish.*

A TROUT of from two to four pounds will make this dish. Having cleaned and scaled it without cutting it much up, stuff with fish forcemeat (see forcemeats), and fix its tail in the mouth. Pour over it a *marinade* made thus:—Boil in vinegar and a good piece of butter, chopped carrots, onions, eschalots, with peppercorns, a bunch of parsley, a sprig of thyme, a bay-leaf, basil, cloves and allspice in grains. Baste with this frequently; when done, drain off the liquor, and keep the fish hot while you boil it down; moisten with a piece of butter rolled in flour, season with a little essence of anchovies, pepper, cayenne, and the squeeze of a lemon. Serve the trout with this sauce strained round it.

120. TO BOIL TURBOT.*

A FISH of the middle size is the best. Choose the turbot thick in the belly, which should be of a cream-

---

* This pontifical fish is found of excellent quality in many parts of the British seas, and also on the Irish coast; but what are still

coloured white, and springy under the slightest pressure of the finger. Unless upon occasions of state, part of this large high-priced fish may be kept by sprinkling a little salt over it, and hanging it in a cool dry place. When to be boiled soak the fish in salt and water, to draw off the slime incidental to all flat fish. When thoroughly clean, score the skin of the back deeply to prevent the belly from cracking when the fish begins to swell in heating; and this done, place it on a fish-strainer with the back undermost. The turbot-kettle must be roomy and nicely clean, as the colour of fish is even more easily injured than that of meat. The fish may be rubbed with lemon to whiten it.* Cover it with cold water, into which throw a handful of salt, which will both improve the flavour of the fish and help to separate the slime and scum. Do not let the fish-kettle come too fast to boil; skim very carefully; and this done, draw aside the *kettle*, and allow it to simmer for from twenty-five to thirty minutes, without that violent degree of ebullition which would crack the skin and spoil the look of the fish. Some cooks, to have the colour fine, and to prevent the skin from cracking, wrap a cloth round it, which is fastened under the strainer. For *sauces*, anchovy, lobster, or shrimp-sauce, or any of the fish-sauces stirred into plain melted butter, may be served in one tureen, and melted butter in another; but lobster-sauce is the favourite sauce. *Garnish* with curled parsley, slices of lemon, or horseradish nicely scraped; covering the cracks, if unfortunately there should be any, with the garnish and a little lobster-coral. These ornaments may be interspersed with fried sprats, or very small flounders fried. Small turbot makes a very delicate dish, cut in slices

---

esteemed the best are caught off the Dutch coast, and brought alive to London in well-boats. This fish is in season, like the haddock, from the time it has had a "leap in the May flood" till Michaelmas. The holibut, which often in Scotland usurps the name of turbot, is in reality a handsomer looking fish, and excellent of its kind, but not equal in richness, and far inferior in flavour to the genuine *Bannock Fluke* of Mr. JONATHAN OLDBUCK. Miss Edgeworth relates an anecdote of a Bishop—and we doubt not that he came to be an Archbishop—who, descending to his kitchen to superintend the dressing of a turbot, and finding that his cook had stupidly cut away the fins, set about sewing them on again with his own Episcopal fingers. This man knew the value of turbot.

* French cooks sometimes boil turbot in milk and water.

and fried, drained from the frying fat, and without breaking, simmered for five minutes in a sauce made of thin melted butter, a few pickled oysters chopped, or a boned anchovy, a tea-spoonful of walnut-pickle, and a dessert-spoonful of mushroom-catsup. Take up the fish with a slice, lay it neatly in the dish, and having skimmed the sauce, pour it over the fish. A glass of claret or port-wine is a great addition to this sauce. Garnish with slices of lemon.—*Obs.* Cold fish of any kind may be cut in neat pieces, and heated up in a white sauce; or *soused*, by placing it handsomely on the dish in slices, and pouring over it any of the flavoured vinegars you choose, or pepper and plain vinegar. If any lobster-sauce is left, it will be found most useful in dressing the left turbot afresh. The French make many *entrées de desserte* of this fish by cutting what remains into fillets or dice, stewing these in a white sauce, and serving in *vol-au-vent*, or dish with an ornamented border made of fried bread cut into diamonds.

121. AN EXCELLENT WAY TO DRESS A SMALL DISH OF TURBOT.

WHEN the fish is cleaned, take off the skin gently, (many like the skin,) and cut the fillets across with a sharp knife. Dip the fillets in beat eggs, then in crumbs, minced parsley, and other seasonings. Dip twice. Place the fillets in a deep dish stuck round with butter, and bake them in a moderate oven, basting from time to time with the butter. Have ready a lobster-sauce made of strong veal-broth, with cayenne, nutmeg and salt; thicken with brown *roux*; letting the lobster meat stew in it first; dish the baked fillets in a hot dish, and pour the sauce over them. Garnish with slices of lemon and curled parsley.—*Obs.* Where the party is not very large, this is a very excellent way of dressing this expensive fish. Fillets of the tail will make a good dish, and allow plenty of an ordinary-sized fish for boiling on another or a previous day. Many persons admire the above more than boiled turbot.

122. TO DRESS A COD'S HEAD AND SHOULDERS,*
Scotch Fashion.

THIS was a great affair in its day. It is still a formidable, nay, even a respectable-looking dish, with a kind of bulky magnificence which appears imposing at the head of a long board. Have a quart of good stock ready for the sauce, made of lean beef or veal, with onion, carrot, and turnip. Rub the fish with salt over night, taking off the scales, but do not wash it. When to be dressed wash it clean, then quickly dash boiling water over the upper side, and with a blunt knife take off the slime which will ooze out, taking great care not to break the skin. Do the same to the other side of the fish; then place it on the strainer, wipe it clean, and plunge it into a turbot-kettle of boiling water, with a handful of salt and a half-pint of vinegar. It must be entirely covered, and will take from thirty to forty minutes slow boiling. Set it to drain, slide it carefully on a deep dish, and glaze with yolks of eggs, over which strew fine bread-crumbs,† grated lemon-peel, pepper, and salt. Stick numerous bits of butter over the fish, and set it before a clear fire, strewing more crumbs, lemon-peel, and minced parsley over it, and basting with the butter. In the meanwhile thicken the stock with butter kneaded in flour, and strain it, adding to it half a hundred oysters nicely picked and bearded, and a glassful of their liquor, two glasses of Madeira or sherry, the juice of a lemon, the hard meat of a boiled lobster cut down, and the soft part pounded. Boil this sauce for five minutes, and skim it well; wipe clean the edges of the dish, in which the fish is crisping, and pour the half of the

---

* Cod is in high perfection about Christmas. It comes into season about Michaelmas, when the other large fish are going out. The Dogger-Bank cod are the most esteemed in the London market, but very excellent fish are now sent from Orkney, and many parts of our own coast. Cod of very good quality are salted in the Hebrides, and a little has been done in Ireland; but the great continental supply of salted fish still comes from Newfoundland. The best cod are such as, with good size and shape, have yellow spots upon a very pure skin. Many persons prefer salt *Ling* to cod; the *Tusk* is much superior to either of them, but is found in very small quantities.

† Many cooks *skin* cod and haddocks. All true gourmands detest *flayed* fish. Where not nicely *crumbed* and browned, they are absolutely horrific and spectral.—P.T.

sauce around it, serving the rest in a tureen. *Garnish* with fried oysters, small fried flounders, and pickled samphire, or slices of lemon. *Cod's head* is dressed with *brown sauce*, by browning the stock with butter nicely browned, and adding a little mushroom-catsup. This sauce is generally made more *piquant* than the white, by the addition of a few boned anchovies.—*Obs.* This Scotch mode of dressing cod is nearly the same as the French *Cabillaud à la Sainte Menehoult*, only the cod is then stuffed with either a meat or fish forcemeat. Cod may be parboiled and finished in the oven with the above sauce.

123. BOILED COD AND SHRIMP SAUCE.

CUT off the tail, which would be useless before the other part is enough done. Rub well with salt inside, without washing; let it lie from one to two days, and wash and boil slowly in plenty of water, with a handful of salt. Drain the fish, serve it on a napkin, and garnish with the boiled roe and liver, or small flounders or whitings, nicely fried,—or with parsley. The tail *cut* may lie in salt for a few days, and be boiled and served with egg-sauce, or parsnips mashed with butter and cream, or it may be broiled fresh, or fried in fillets or slices, and served with *oyster* or *shrimp* sauce; or with a sauce made of half a pint of veal-gravy, a glass of red wine, a boned anchovy chopped, white pepper and salt, and a few pickled oysters, and thickened with a little flour kneaded in butter. Boil up and skim the sauce; place the slices neatly on the dish, and pour it around them.—*Obs.* Cod, if well boiled, should be very white. The French make *entrées de desserte* of cold cod as of turbot, and serve them in the same manner. The fish may be quite fresh.

124. TO BROIL COD-SOUNDS.

CLEAN and scald them with very hot water, and rub them with salt. Take off the sloughy coat, parboil them, then flour and broil till enough done. Dish them, and pour a sauce made of browned gravy, pepper, cayenne, salt, a little butter kneaded in browned flour, a tea-spoonful of made mustard, and one of soy. *Cod-sounds* are dressed as ragout, by boiling as above, and stewing in clear gravy, adding a little cream and butter kneaded in flour, with a seasoning of lemon-peel, nut-meg, and mace. Cut them in fillets. They may be fried.

125. COLD BOILED COD CURRIED.

A LARGE fish that comes in fine flakes is best. Fry the pieces in butter, with plenty of sliced onions, of a fine brown, and stew them in a little white gravy, thickened with butter and rolled in flour, about a glassful of rich cream, and a large dessert-spoonful of curry-powder.— *Obs.* Cream for curries is, we think, the better of being a *little turned*, that is, thick and sourish, but not clotted. Good butter-milk makes an excellent substitute for cream in this and all common made-dishes.— See *Curried Fish*.

126. CABEACHED COD.

CUT the tail part of the fish into slices, and upon these rub some white pepper and salt. Then fry in sweet oil. Take the slices from the pan, and lay them on a plate to cool. When cold, put them into a pickle made of good vinegar, in which some white peppercorns, a few cloves, a little mace, and some salt have been boiled. When cold, mix with the pickle a tea-cupful of oil. Put the fish into a pot, and between every piece put a few slices of onion, and keep the whole well covered with the pickle. In the same manner salmon may be cabeached, but if taken fresh out of the water, it is liable to break, which it will not do after being kept for a few days. *Obs.* Escabeche, in Spanish, signifies, "Fish-Pickle." In the seaports of Spain, they escabeche the fish, which they send inland as presents to their friends. The Spanish preparation is similar to the dish here mentioned, with the addition of a large portion of garlic and some bay-leaves. The Spaniards eat it with ginger and salad, and sometimes stew it lightly.—Dr. HUNTER.

127. TO CRIMP COD.

BOIL very fresh cod, cut or whole, in salt and water for eighteen minutes. Serve instantly with shrimp or oyster sauce.

128. TO DRESS SALT COD, LING, TUSK, &c.

THE fish must be soaked for a length of time correspond-ing to its dryness and the hardness it has acquired. Soak it in cold water for a night; that done, if still hard beat it well with a paste-roller, or brush it with a hard brush, and soak it in lukewarm water. Let it come very slowly to boil. When it has stood for an hour and a half by the side of the fire, take up the pieces; scrape off the tough filmy outer skin, and trim neatly from bones, &c. Place the pieces in the stew-pan, or on the strainer, and pour boiling water over them, which will both freshen and soften the fish. Never allow the fish to boil till it is almost ready. Serve with egg-sauce, or parsnips mashed with plenty of butter. Mashed potatoes are also served with salt fish, and mustard must never be forgotten. Garnish with hard-boiled eggs in circular slices, yolks and white.—*Obs*. At sea, salt fish is dressed after a very palatable, if not refined fashion, by pulling it, when boiled, into flakes, and beating it up with mashed potatoes and butter. In New England, where the management of dry cod is very well understood, it is alternately soaked and laid on a table till sufficiently softened, which is thought a better method of softening than continual soaking.

129. TO DRESS STURGEON.

THIS fish does not eat well boiled. It may be roasted, or baked, basting with plenty of butter, and serving with a rich gravy relished with anchovy, wine, and juice of lemon; or with any favourite flavoured vinegar. Slices of sturgeon are egged, dipped in bread-crumbs, seasonings, and chopped parsley, and broiled *en papillote Sauce*,—oyster or lobster sauce, or melted butter, with a little soy and essence of anchovy. A nonsensical imitation of pickled sturgeon is made of a large Turkey, boned and stewed in a rich pickle made of a quart of port wine vinegar, a pint of Rhenish wine, salt and spices.

130. TEASED SKATE.
From Dr. Hunter's Culina.

TAKE the dried wing of a skate, and after stripping off the skin, cut it into lengths of about one inch in breadth. Put the fish, so prepared, into water, and boil for the space of twenty minutes; after which let it be put into the oven, where it should remain a quarter of an hour, during which time it will become so tender as to permit the bones to be drawn out. The flesh being now detached from the bones, it should be put into a cloth, and well rubbed with the hands till it puts on a woolly appearance, which it will soon do. Take a saucepan, and in it reduce about half a pound of butter into oil, when the teased fish should be put into it, and kept stirring for the space of fifteen minutes. When sufficiently heated, serve up.—*Obs*. Skate, so prepared, may be eaten as salt fish, with egg-sauce, mashed potatoes, or parsnips. The whole wing of a skate will require half a pound of butter, and prepared at a small expense. It improves this dish to stir potato-pudding in it, or more elegantly to serve it in a dish with an edging, or a casserole of mashed potatoes.

131. TO BOIL SKATE.*

IF to be crimp, boil it quite fresh;—if liked tender and sapid, it may, in cool weather, hang from one to three days. *Sauce*,—melted butter, or lobster or caper-sauce. *Skate fries* very well when parboiled, cut in thin slices, and dipped in egg and bread-crumbs; it eats well cold, with mustard, pepper, and vinegar. It is also very good parboiled, and then grilled in slices, serving it with parsley and butter, or caper-sauce.

---

* Skate differs more in quality than perhaps any other fish. It should be broad and thick, prickly on the back, and of a creamy whiteness. We have, however, seen a small kind of skate which is caught along the north-east coast of Scotland, of a leaden-blue colour, called by fishermen the dun skate, which is more delicate than any other kind we have met with. In places where this fish forms a great part of the food of the common people, it is best relished when it is hung till dry, by which time it has acquired so strong a smell of ammonia as to be intolerable to the uninitiated. This fish, in those primitive days when as yet mock-turtle was not wont to be esteemed, was eaten *cold* with mustard and vinegar. It is thought to eat like lobster,—by persons of lively imagination. Skate is said, when out of season, to produce cholera and other violent diseases. The same thing is alleged of salmon in the state of foul or "black fish;" and there is no question but that fish undergoes a change at particular seasons, which renders it for the time exceedingly improper food. There are many instances of seamen dying in consequence of eating dolphin. It is said that accidents of this nature may be avoided by the simple test of putting a piece of silver into the fish-kettle. If it blacken, the fish should be considered dangerous, if not absolutely poisonous.—P.S.T.

132. ANOTHER WAY TO BOÏL SKATE.

MAKE a braise of the trimmings of the skate, parsley, onions, a clove of garlic, a sprig of basil, and a half-pint of vinegar. When this is cooked put in the skate, let it just boil, and leave it twelve minutes covered with a cloth under the lid; put also in the liver. Dish on a napkin. Make a sauce with the brown meat nicely minced, and some of the braise-liquor. Garnish with the liver.—Serve *Caper Sauce*. SKATE is also served with onion-sauce, parsley and butter, and *beurre noir*, or black, i.e. oiled butter.

133. TO CRIMP SKATE.

CLEAN, skin, and cut the fish into fillets, which must be tied with tape to keep them round. Boil these quickly in water made brackish with salt,—drain the fillets,—loosen the tapes,—and serve with caper-sauce, parsley and butter, or shrimp sauce.—*Obs.* The French stew this fish in a marinade of vinegar, salt, pepper, onions, bay-leaves, &c.; and after skinning, serve it with caper-sauce, or cucumbers. As the Parisians seldom have sea-fish fresh, they season more highly than the English and Dutch; on the whole, English cookery of fish is better.

134. HADDOCKS IN BROWN SAUCE.
An excellent Scotch Dish.

CLEAN, cut off the heads, tails and fins, and skin from six to eight middle-sized haddocks. Take the heads, tails, and trimmings, with two or three of the fish cut down, and boil them in a quart of water or broth, with a couple of onions, some sweet herbs, and a piece of lemon-peel; thicken with plenty of butter and browned flour, and season highly with mixed spices and mushroom-catsup; strain the sauce, and when it boils and is skimmed put in the fish cut into neat pieces, and, if you choose, previously browned in the frying-pan. If there be too little sauce, add some good beef-gravy; put in a quarter-hundred of oysters and a glass of their liquor; or some muscles, and a little wine. Take out the fish, when ready, with a slice, and pour the sauce, which should be brown, smooth, and thick, around them.—*Obs. Haddocks may be stuffed* with a fish-forcemeat, and dressed in a sauce, as directed above. Some of the forcemeat may be made into balls for garnishing. Haddocks may also be stuffed, egged, and strewed with fine bread-crumbs, minced parsley, &c., and baked, basting them well with butter. Serve in a white or brown sauce made of a pound or more of good veal, onions, and parsley, and thickened with plenty of butter kneaded in flour. Strain, and add a glass of white wine, the juice of a lemon, white pepper in fine powder, a quarter-hundred of pickled oysters, and a spoonful of the pickle. Pour the skimmed sauce over the fish. Garnish with sliced lemon and pickled samphire. This makes a very handsome Scotch dish. *Whitings* are dressed as above, with a white sauce, and *codlings* with a brown sauce. For *Crappit Heads* see *National Dishes*. Haddocks and codlings may also be dressed in a sauce made of two bottles of clear small beer poured over a half-pound of butter, (nicely browned and dredged with flour,) oysters, and a little of their liquor, mushroom-catsup, spices, and vinegar. Boil the fish in this strained sauce, and serve in a soup-dish. See *Fish and Sauce, National Dishes*.

135. HADDOCKS BAKED, *a good family dish*

CLEAN and season three or four large haddocks, place them neatly on a flat dish, with a border of mashed potatoes neatly marked. Glaze with an egg, and place bits of butter here and there over the fish, and a piece inside of each. Garnish with potato-balls ragout, and bake for a half-hour. Pour a little melted butter and catsup over the dish, as in baking fish gets dry.

136. TO FRY HADDOCKS, SOLES, TROUT, PERCH, TENCH, WHITINGS, FLOUNDERS, HERRINGS, &c.*

CLEAN and skin the haddocks. [Whitings and flounders

---

* It is not easy to know the delicate whiting, at times, from the coarse codling:—the codling has a beard—the whiting is smooth. Flounders differ much in quality;—there is a coarse kind of flounder, with bright scarlet star-like spots, which in reality looks better than the sober-coated *grey-back*, though it is of very inferior quality. This is a surer test than the thickness or firmness of the fish. Haddocks are in season from Whitsuntide to Christmas, and flounders about the same time. Herrings are never long out of season, though the quality falls off at times.

are not skinned by French or Scotch cooks.] If the
haddocks are too large, cut them in two or three
pieces,—or split them, or slit the backs. When the fish
are dried, rub them with flour, and, if to be higher
dressed, rub off the flour, and with a paste-brush wash
them over with beat egg; strew finely-grated crumbs
over them, and fry in a deep pan in plenty of clarified
dripping or lard, heated to such a degree that it may
neither scorch the fish, nor yet stew them. Turn and
lift them carefully, and keep them hot by the fire, on a
sieve and paper, to absorb the fat, till the whole are
finished. The bone may be cut out, particularly in large
fish. Garnish with fried oysters, or a few sprigs of
curled parsley, and sliced lemon, and serve very hot,
with shrimp-sauce, if any is used. If the fish are not
cut down they may be slit either in the back, or slightly
scored;—the same fat will fry more than once, if
strained. Whitings and small haddocks may have the tail
skewered into the mouth. French cooks, and many
English ones serve fried fish on a napkin, which always
looks well if neatly done. In Scotland, herrings are
often dipped in oatmeal, and fried in plenty of dripping,
with sliced onions. In France mustard is served with
fried fresh herrings, and the practice is commendable.
All these fish are occasionally broiled either split (*Scottice
speldered*) or whole. Wipe them very dry, dust them
with flour, and broil over a clear moderate fire.
Haddocks salted and hung for a day or two, split and
boned, are very good when broiled. Skin them, dust
them with flour, lay them on a gridiron, and, if not split,
put the opened part downmost. Turn them a few
minutes on both sides, and they are done. Serve with
cold butter.

137. FINNANS, and Findhorn haddocks, are skinned
and dressed as above. They may be taken from the gridiron when just done, and dipped in hot water if dry or
hard, and wrapped in a cloth to swell and soften them.
Serve wrapped in a napkin.—*Obs.* An imitation of the
Finnan haddock is now made by salting for a few hours,
splitting, and wetting the fish with pyroligneous acid,
and hanging them to dry. Broiled haddocks, whether
fresh, *rizzared*, or as Finnans, are held in great esteem
by those who relish a good breakfast. The latter

commodity is now regularly forwarded from Aberdeen to Edinburgh and London by the mail-coach. They may be very well dressed on a heater before the fire, or in a Dutch oven. They are equally fit for breakfast or supper. An imitation of Finnans is made at many parts of the coast. A tolerable one is made by dipping the fresh split fish in pyroligneous acid as above, and smoking them.

138. TO DRESS SLICES OF HOLIBUT, LING, OR TUSK,
For a maigre dish

FRY the fillets in butter, and stew them in a little fish-stock, seasoned with parsley and celery. Add a piece of butter rolled in flour, white pepper, mace, or a little lemon-peel, and a squeeze of lemon-juice; *or* use a curry sauce.

139. HERRINGS AND MACKEREL.

CHOOSE soft roe Mackerel. When boiled, serve them with mustard. They may be broiled either split or whole, sprinkled or stuffed with herbs chopped, and crumbed, and seasoned with pepper and salt; or collared, by splitting them, taking out the bones, seasoning with mixed spices, rolling up and baking them in a slow oven. Herrings or mackerel are very good baked, and will keep a week without butter. Clean, and season them highly with salt and mixed spices. Pack them neatly, *heads and thraws*, in a deep dish. Fill up with vinegar, and stick a little butter over them. Tie them closely up with several folds of paper, and bake them. They eat very well cold, or will warm up in their own liquor. For pickling highly, bay-leaves, more vinegar and spices may be employed, and the fish may be either baked or boiled;—boil up the pickle, and when cold pour over them, as directed for Salmon, p. 171.—*Obs.* Mackerel must be very fresh. They are served with fennel sauce, or a mixture of fennel and parsley, with melted butter. The French cook mackerel with fine herbs, champagne, and butter.—(*See Maqueraux aux fine herbes.*) Nor in London are the days quite gone by—

When Mackerel seemed delightful to their eyes,
Though dressed with incoherent gooseberries.

140. to stew trout, carp, or perch.

Clean the fish very well; if large, they may be divided, or split. Rub them inside with salt and mixed spices. Lay them in the stew-pan, and put in nearly as much good stock as will cover them, with a couple of onions and four cloves stuck in them, some Jamaica and black peppercorns, and a bit of mace; and when the fish have stewed a few minutes, a couple of glasses of claret or Rhenish, a boned anchovy, the juice of a lemon, and a little cayenne. Take up the fish carefully when ready, and keep them hot. Thicken the sauce with butter kneaded in browned flour; add a little mushroom-catsup and a few pickled oysters, if approved: —the sauce, though less piquant, is more delicate without catsup. Having skimmed and strained, pour it over the fish.—*Obs*. In the French and Dutch kitchen, fish is sometimes stewed with wine, spiceries, and butter, and no meat gravy is used. The dry austere wines are the best adapted for this purpose. The sauce is thickened with bread boiled in it. These fish may all be boiled plain, and served with finely-minced parsley and butter, or fennel, or chervil and butter, or equal parts of each.—See *Sauces*. The fish may be browned previously; but we conceive the flavour better when they are at once put to stew in the sauce. In England fish is sometimes stewed in cider instead of wine, seasoning with cayenne, eschalot, or onion. In Germany carp is sometimes even yet stewed in strong-ale thickened with gingerbread!

141. to stew soles, eels, lampreys, and fillets of turbot, holibut, whitings, cod, &c.

Clean and trim the fish. Eels must be cut in from three to four inch lengths, and rubbed with salt before skinning, to draw out the slime. Wash them very well. The other kinds of fish may be cut into larger pieces; the pieces may be dipped in egg, rolled in grated crumbs, and browned before they are put into the stew-pan. Have a pint and a half of good, clear beef gravy, in which two onions, a carrot, and a few pot-herbs have been boiled. Stew the fish in this gravy very gently, giving a quarter of an hour to the harder sorts, and about ten minutes to whitings or eels. Lift out the pieces, and keep them hot. Skim the sauce, and thicken it with browned flour, *roux*, or rice-flour; add a small glass of red wine, and a large spoonful of mushroom catsup; give it a minute's boiling, and strain it over the dished stewed fish. Stewed fish may be dressed for *maigre days* in the French manner, making the stock strong, either with fish or butter, or part of both, and using more herbs and seasonings. *Lampreys* and *codlings* are the better of having an anchovy and some made-mustard added to the above sauce. Serve with scraped horse-radish, sippets of bread, or fried parsley.

142. TO FRY EELS.*

SKIN and clean them, rub them with salt, and wash them in several waters. Cut them in four-inch lengths, and, having rubbed them with salt and mixed spices, dip them in beat egg, and roll in crumbs. Fry in plenty of boiling lard, drain from the fat on a sieve before the fire, and serve with chervil and butter, or parsley and butter, plain melted butter, or melted butter sharpened with vinegar or lemon-juice.

N.B.—The fat in which eels are fried does not answer well for frying other fish.

143. TO COLLAR EELS.

BONE without flaying a large eel. Season it highly, by rubbing it with mixed spices finely pounded, chopped

---

* The freshness of an eel is known by its vivacity of motion; and its quality by the colour of the skin. The best kind—the silver eel—is that found in the clearest waters. The dingy yellow, and the deep sallow-green, are very inferior to the clear, coppery, brown-backed eel, and even to the bronze-coloured. Fresh-water fish of all kinds are best when found in clear streams. The natives of turbid, sluggish streams are even considered more difficult of digestion. This is said to be peculiarly the case with salmon. If slimy, soak the eels in water in which a piece of alum or charcoal is put.

The cruelty inflicted on eels is proverbial. Instead of skinning and cutting alive, a humane method of putting them to death is recommended by Dr. KITCHENER, which deserves to be generally known. With a sharp-pointed skewer pierce the spinal marrow through the back part of the skull, when life will instantly cease. Mons. Ude gives the following receipt:—"Take live eels, throw them into the fire, and as they are twisting about on all sides, lay hold of them with a towel in your hand, and skin them!"

parsley, sage, and a sprig of lemon-thyme. Roll up and
bind the collar with tape, and boil it in salt and water
till tender. It may be served whole with a sharp sauce,
or it may be cut in slices. It will keep in a pickle of
the liquor it was boiled in, adding salt and vinegar.
Eels may be stewed as carp, but are rather a luscious
dish.

144. TO SPITCHCOCK EELS.

CLEAN them well, and rub with salt and skin them.
Slit open the belly and take out the bone. Wash and
dry them, cut in pieces about four inches long, dredge
with flour, which wipe off, that they may be quite dry.
Dip them, in a thick batter made of melted butter, yolk
of eggs, with a little minced parsley, sage, and a very
little eschalot, with pepper, and salt. Roll the pieces in
fine grated bread-crumbs, or biscuit pounded. Dip and
roll them again, and broil on a clear fire of a fine light-
brown. The eels may be dipped and broiled whole if
they are not too large, or roasted in a Dutch oven.
Serve either anchovy-sauce or melted butter, with any
favourite flavoured vinegar. Garnish with crisped parsley. *Eels* are, by many *gourmands*, preferred when
boiled plain, strewing dried parsley and sage pulverized
over them, and serving with them plain melted butter,
sharpened with lemon-juice. See *Remoulade sauce*.
Eels are dressed as fish-in-sauce also, or as water souchy.
They are also farced.

145. TO FRY SPRATS, SMELTS, AND OTHER SMALL FISH.

CLEAN them well, and when wiped dry, rub them with
flour to absorb any moisture that remains. Dip them
in beat egg, and then in bread-crumbs rubbed through
a colander. Fry them in plenty of oil, lard, or clarified
dripping, making it quite hot. Take care in turning
not to break them. If wanted very nice they may be
twice dipt in egg and crumbs, or in biscuit-powder.
Lay them on a sieve reversed, to drain the fat from them.
These delicate fish may also be stewed in wine, with a
little vinegar and plenty of spice; or in cider. *Garnish*
with fried parsley and lemon sliced.

146. TO BROIL, BAKE, OR FRY SPRATS, SMELTS, &C.

RUN a long bird-skewer or a common knitting-needle through the eyes. Dust them with flour, and have a hot gridiron rubbed with mutton-suet or chalk, and a clear fire. Serve them hot. These fish will pickle, or bake; and eat very well cold. Bake them with butter, and a high seasoning of mixed spices and vinegar. They will keep for a week. *Another way*—Dip them in a batter made of two eggs, and bread-crumbs mixed with flour and seasonings, and fry them. Serve them on fried parsley.—*Obs. Imitation-anchovies* may be made of sprats cured in a strong pickle of bay and common salt, and *sal prunella*, sugar, and pounded pepper, with a little cochineal to colour them. In Scotland, sprats, garvocks, &c. and herrings, are roasted on the *girdle* which toasts the family bread, and this plan answers very well in cottage economy.

147. TO DRESS RED HERRINGS, SARDINIAS, AND BUFFED PICKLED HERRINGS.

SKIN, open, and trim red herrings. If old and hard, pour some hot small beer or water over them, and let them steep a half hour, or longer if hard. Broil them over a clear fire at a considerable distance; or before the fire: rub them with good oil or fresh butter while broiling, and rub on a little more when they are served. Serve them very hot with cold butter; or with melted butter and mustard, and mashed potatoes or parsnips.

Steep pickled herrings from one to two days and nights, changing the water if they be very salt. Hang them up on a stick pushed through the eyes, and broil them when wanted. These are called *buffed* herrings in Scotland, and are used at breakfast or supper.

148. PICKLED HERRINGS, *a French way*.

WASH the herrings; cut off the heads and tips of the tails; skin them; steep them in lukewarm milk and water, and dry and broil them; dish with slices of raw onions and rennets, and serve with oil.

149. TO STUFF AND BAKE CARP, PIKE,[*]
AND HADDOCKS.

HAVING scaled and cleaned the fish without cutting
open much of the breast, stuff them with a *maigre* forcemeat made thus: Beat yolks of eggs, a few oysters
bearded and chopped, and two boned anchovies, pounded
biscuit, or bread grated, minced parsley, and a bit of
eschalot or an onion, mace pounded, black pepper, allspice, and salt. Mix these in the proper proportions;
and having beat a good piece of butter in a stew-pan,
stir them in it over the fire till of the consistence of a
thick batter, adding more biscuit-powder or flour if
necessary. Fill the fish, and sew up the slit. Bake them
in a moderate oven, basting with plenty of butter, and
sticking butter all over them. Serve *pike* with anchovy-

---

[*] *Receipt for Dressing a Pike by* ISAAC WALTON.—"First open
your pike at the gills, and, if need be, cut also a little slit towards the
belly. Out of these take his guts, and keep his liver, which you are to
shred very small, with thyme, sweet-marjoram, and a little winter-savory;
to these put some pickled oysters, and some anchovies, two or three, both
these last whole, for the anchovies will melt, and the oysters should not;
to these you must add also a pound of sweet butter, which you are to mix
with the herbs that are shred, and let them all be well salted. If the pike
be more than a yard long, then you may put into these herbs more than a
pound, or if he be less, then less butter will suffice; these, being thus
mixed, with a blade or two of mace, must be put into the pike's belly;
and then his belly so sewed up as to keep all the butter in his belly if it
be possible; if not, then as much as you possibly can. But take not off
the scales. Then you are to thrust the spit through his mouth, out at his
tail. And then take four, or five, or six split sticks, or very thin laths,
and a convenient quantity of tape or filleting; these laths are to be tied
round about the pike's body from his head to his tail, and the tape tied
somewhat thick, to prevent his breaking or falling off from the spit. Let
him be roasted very leisurely, and often basted with claret wine, and
anchovies and butter mixed together, and also with what moisture falls
from him into the pan. When you have roasted him sufficiently, you are
to hold under him, when you unwind or cut the tape that ties him, such
a dish as you purpose to eat him out of, and let him fall into it with the
sauce that is roasted in his belly, and by this means the pike will be kept
unbroken and complete. Then, to the sauce which was within, and also
that sauce in the pan, you are to add a fit quantity of the best butter, and
to squeeze the juice of three or four oranges. Lastly, you may either put
it into the pike, with the oysters, two cloves of garlick, and take it whole
out when the pike is cut off the spit; or, to give the sauce a hogoo, (*haut
gout*,) let the dish into which you let the pike fall be rubbed with it; the
using or not using of this garlick is left to your discretion.

"This dish of meat is too good for any but anglers or very honest men;
and I trust you will prove both, and therefore I have trusted you with
this secret."

sauce, and *carp* with the following sauce:—Take up the fish on a hot plate; thicken the liquor in which it was baked with butter rolled in flour, boiling it for a few minutes with a faggot of parsley, a few leaves of basil, a sprig of lemon-thyme, and a very little marjoram. Strain and add to the sauce a tea-spoonful of made mustard, and one of Chili vinegar, a glass of red wine, and a little soy, with mace, pepper, and salt to taste. Pour a little of this over the carp, and serve the rest in a tureen. Garnish with curled parsley and slices of lemon, or parsley and scraped horseradish.—*Obs.* A highly-relishing forcemeat for the above may be made of scraped ham or tongue, or bacon fried and cut in little bits, suet or marrow, eschalot, cayenne, salt, a chopped anchovy, bread-crumbs, a little walnut or oyster-liquor, with egg to bind the composition. The meat of a lobster may be substituted for the ham or fried bacon.— See *Crappit heads and fillets of haddocks— French Cookery*.

150. TO DRESS PLAICE.

CLEAN, and without washing wipe the fish, and rub it with salt. When it has lain from six hours to a day, wash it, wipe it very dry, and rub with flour to absorb all the remaining damp. When the flour is rubbed off, brush it over with beat eggs, and dip it in bread-crumbs, with a little finely-minced parsley. Fry it in plenty of lard or good dripping, and when drained from the fat, serve it on fried parsley, with anchovy-sauce, or melted butter sharpened with the juice of a lemon or Seville orange.

151. TO DRESS PIPERS.

CLEAN a very fresh fish without cutting it open too much. Stuff it with a forcemeat of two or three ounces of shred suet, and a large breakfast-cupful of bread-crumbs, mixed with two eggs, chopped parsley, pepper, salt, and a little cayenne. Sew in this stuffing, skewer the tail into the mouth; flour, egg, and crumb the fish; bake it in a hot oven; drain it and serve with Dutch sauce.

152. TO DRESS RED MULLET.

CLEAN and bake or boil the fish. Serve it with lobster-sauce.—*Obs.* French cooks do not gut this fish. It is merely washed, wrapped in buttered paper, and baked to preserve the delicacy of its native flavour.

153. FISH-TURTLE,—*A favourite dish.*

FRY slices of fresh codling or haddock, and drain them. Parboil, skin, and cut into squares a piece of good skate. Have ready some cow-heel, beef, or veal gravy broth highly seasoned with pepper, cayenne, and catsup, and thickened with butter rolled in flour. Stew the fish in this stock with the meat of a lobster, and a few oysters in their juice. Season with essence of anchovy, and a little wine if you like. Serve in a soup-dish.

154. TO CURRY HADDOCKS, CODLINGS, WHITINGS, *Or slices of Cod or Holibut.*

HAVE a quart of good beef or veal stock, in which a carrot or turnip and two onions have been boiled. Thicken it with butter kneaded in lightly-browned flour. Having cleaned, skinned, and boned the fish, cut them into neat bits of about three inches in length. Rub them with flour, and fry them of a fine golden-brown in butter or lard. Drain them, and mix very smoothly with a little of the stock from a dessert-spoonful to a table-spoonful of curry-powder, two onions beaten in a mortar, and a large quarter-pint of good thick cream, if a little sour so much the better. Stew the fish very slowly in the stock till they are tender, which will not take long. Place the pieces neatly in the dish, the largest in the centre, and having skimmed the curry-sauce, pour it over them.—*Obs.* This has become a favourite way of dressing fish, though it finds no place in any book of cookery. It is cheap, convenient, and even elegant. Instead, however, of using curry-powder as obtained in shops, we would advise every cook to keep the several ingredients, each good of its kind, in well-stopped vials, and to mix them when they are wanted, suiting the quantities of the various ingredients to the nature of the dish. Fish, for example, requires more acid than fowl. Some people like a great deal of cayenne, others detest the taste and smell of turmeric, and some are all for ginger. To use curry-powder mixed in the same proportions for every sort of viand and of taste may do very well for those who entertain a mysterious veneration for the Oriental characters inscribed on the packages, but will not suit a *gourmand* of any knowledge or experience. Prawns, oysters, or muscles, may be added to this curry. Dressed fish will make good curry. The curry may be any shade of colour from pale-gold to deep, rich brown, by browning the fish and onions more or less.

155. DUTCH WATER SOUCHY, *maigre*.

EELS, gudgeons, whitings, flounders, &c. are all employed for this dish. Whichever sort of fish you use, clean them well, taking out the gills, eyes, &c. Cut them in neat small pieces. Have a little good fish-stock made of the heads and fins, and seasoned with onion, parsley, a bit of lemon-peel, pepper, and salt. Strain and skim, and stew the cut fish in this for eight or ten minutes. Put in a little catsup; skim, and serve it in a soup-dish. A bay-leaf may be boiled in the stock, and the souchy may be flavoured with essence of anchovy, eschalot, or any flavouring ingredient that is approved.

156. TO DRESS CRAY-FISH.

BOIL them for four minutes in the shell, in wine and water, or in water and vinegar, with herbs, and serve them, hot or cold, on a napkin arranged in form.

157. RICH FISH-PIE,—*a maigre dish*.

CLEAN and nicely trim either soles, trout, salmon, turbot, whichever is intended for the pie, and cut them into handsome fillets. Season the fillets inside with pepper, cayenne, mace, and salt. They may either be turned round or laid flat in the pie-dish, packing them neatly. If to be very rich, the pie-dish may be lined with fish-forcemeat. Put bits of butter below and above the fish, and strew in, if to be very rich, chopped shrimps or prawns, or the soft part of oysters, or lobster-meat. Season nearly a pint of stock made of the heads and trimmings; thicken and strain this over the fish, and cover the dish with a good puff-paste. It will require less cooking than a meat-pie of the same size.

158. LOBSTER-PIE,—*a maigre dish*.

PARBOIL two good lobsters; take out all that is good of

the meat, and cut it in bits, and place it in a small pie-dish. Beat the spawn and shells, and stew them in water, with a blade or two of mace, and a little good vinegar. Strain this over the lobster-meat, and cover with a light paste. A little soy, wine, cayenne, and catsup will make this pie more relishing.—*Obs*. Some knowing gourmands have lobster-pies made of alternate layers of lobster and oyster-meat, and bread-crumbs, with small force-balls of pounded oysters, lobster-coral, and essence of anchovies.

159. AN EEL, MACKEREL, OR HERRING PIE.

SKIN and clean the fish, cut them in handsome pieces, and season highly with pepper, allspice, and salt; stick bits of butter about the fish, and put a little vinegar in the dish. Cover it with a common crust.—*Obs*. The Club did not approve of this pie when covered with a crust. It may however have an edging.

160. A SAVOURY SHRIMP OR PRAWN PIE, *maigre*.

HAVE as many well-cleaned shrimps or prawns as will nearly fill the pie-dish. Season with pounded mace, cloves, a little cayenne and Chili vinegar. Put some butter in the dish, and cover with a light puff-paste. Less than three quarters of an hour will bake these pies.

161. AN EXCELLENT SALT-FISH PIE, *maigre*.

THIS may be made of either cod or haddocks salted, but not too dry. Steep and boil the fish. Trim away all skins, bones, and fins, and cut them into thin handsome pieces. Boil hard, and peel half a dozen eggs, and slice them thin; do the same with as many well-sized onions. Have plenty of parboiled potatoes sliced. Place some bits of butter and a layer of potatoes in the bottom of a large pie-dish, then fish, then eggs, then onions, and again butter, thus filling up the dish, shaking pepper over every separate layer, and putting butter over each. Make a sauce of chopped hard-boiled yolks of eggs, melted butter, a little made mustard, and essence of anchovy, or soy, and pour it over the pie. Cover it with a puff-paste, or with mashed potatoes, scolloped round the edge, and glazed with eggs. This pie will not require much of the oven.—*Obs*. Pies may be made of perch, mackerel, herrings, soles, flounders, haddocks, &c. The tough or oily fish must be previously skinned. Fish-pies may be baked *open*, and in fact are best so.

162. A RICH FISH-PIE OR BAKED FISH.

THREE middling-sized haddocks, mackerels, or soles, will make a pie. They may be stuffed, well-seasoned, and laid in an oval flat dish, with a puff-paste border, and centre ornament, or an edging of mashed potatoes neatly marked. Stick plenty of butter over them, or glaze, and cover with bread-crumbs. Balls of fish-forcemeat, or yolks of hard-boiled eggs, may be employed to enrich the dish; or for plain dinners, potato-balls. If wanted very high-dressed, the fish may be laid on force-meat, and have a rich sauce poured hot over them when baked.—*Obs.* These may be served yet more elegantly, *à la Matelote* or *à la Genevoise*,—See *French Cookery*.

163. SAUCES FOR PIES OR FOR FRESH FISH.

TAKE a quarter-pint of the best vinegar, the same quantity of white wine, a large spoonful of oyster-liquor, and another of catsup, with two anchovies boned and chopped. Boil this sauce for two minutes, and, skimming it, pour it hot through a funnel into the pie when to be served.

164. ANOTHER WAY.

TAKE a half-pint of good thick cream, a dessert-spoonful of soy, two anchovies boned and chopped, and a bit of butter rolled in browned flour. Boil it up in a small sauce-pan, and pour it hot into the pie.

165. TO BOIL LOBSTERS AND CRABS.

CHOOSE lobsters and crabs by their weight, alertness, and fresh smell. The tail of the lobster, when fresh, will be stiff and springy; and so will the claws of the crab.* Fill a large pot with water, and make it brackish

---

* Lobsters and crabs are in high season from March till October; so that they supply the place of oysters, which come in about the time lobsters go out of season. Lobsters are held in great esteem by gastrologers for the firmness, purity, and flavour of their flesh. When they find refuge in the rocky fastnesses of the deep from the rapacity of sharks and fishermen, they sometimes attain an immense size, and have been found from eighteen inches to upwards of two feet in length. Apicius, who ought to be the patron saint of epicures, made a voyage to the coast of Africa on

with salt, (on the coast sea-water is used;) brush and put in the lobsters. Take off the scum, of which a great deal will be thrown up, and let them boil from thirty to fifty minutes, according to the size. If boiled too long the flesh will get thready and coarse; if not long enough, the spawn will not have a good colour. Wipe the lobsters with a damp cloth, then rub the shell with butter, and wipe it off again. Break off the great claws, and crack them at the joints without mangling. Split down the tail, and place them nicely on the dish, serving the following sauce:—The hard yolks of two eggs pounded in a mortar with a little vinegar, and the soft spawn of the lobster. When beaten quite smooth, mix this with a large spoonful of salad-oil and a glassful of the best vinegar, a tea-spoonful of made mustard, and a little cayenne and salt. For crabs the same sauce.

166. TO POT LOBSTERS AND CRABS FOR SANDWICHES, DEVILED BISCUITS, &C.

PARBOIL the fish; crack the claws, &c. and pick out the meat. If for sandwiches, beat it in a mortar with pounded mace, white pepper, cayenne, nutmeg, and salt. If to keep for eating, for a cold relish, mix the meat neatly cut in small bits, and the coral and the spawn in a regular manner in layers or alternate pieces, so that when

---

hearing that lobsters of an unusually large size were to be found there; and, after encountering much distress at sea, met with a disappointment. Very large lobsters are at present found on the coast of Orkney. Some naturalists affirm (OLAUS MAGNUS and GESSNER,) that in the Indian seas, and on the wild shores of Norway, lobsters have been found twelve feet in length, and six in breadth, which seize mariners in their terrible embrace, and, dragging them into their caverns, devour them. However this may be, the lobsters and crabs for being devoured are best when of the middle size, and when found on reefs or very rocky shores. They are found on many parts of the British coasts; and during the summer months there is generally a plentiful supply in the London market. In places where crabs are good and plentiful, a very pretty supper-plate is made of a few pairs of the claws; an excellent substitute for lobster-sauce is made of them, particularly of the small delicate species known in Scotland by the name of *Cavies*. The age of shell-fish may be known as that of a tree is by the bark, from the roughness and incrustations which gather upon the surface. Yet if lobsters cast their shells yearly, how can this be? At any rate avoid the crusted. River lobsters are esteemed more delicate than sea ones. In Germany lobsters are often boiled alive in milk. The Germans are indeed fond of cooking all sorts of fish in milk, and of marinading in milk.—Barbarous cookery!—P.T.

sliced it may have that marbled appearance, that look of mosaic work which so much commends the taste of the cook. Press the layers into a potting-can, and bake covered with butter in a slow oven for about a half-hour. When cold, take off the butter, pack the meat in small potting-cans, and pour the butter clarified over it.—*Obs.* What is left of this butter will be very relishing for sauces. Sometimes *potted lobster* may be dressed as a fricassee in a Bechamel or cream sauce, or eaten cold. Lobsters for sauce, when the fish are dear or out of season, may be well preserved in this way.

167. LOBSTER, HAUT GOUT.—H. JEKYLL, ESQ.

PICK the firm meat from a parboiled lobster or two, and take also the inside, if not thin and watery. Season highly with white pepper, cayenne, pounded mace, and cloves, nutmeg, and salt. Take a little well-flavoured gravy—for example the jelly of roast veal—a few tiny bits of butter, a spoonful of soy or walnut-catsup, or of any favourite flavoured vinegar, and a spoonful of red wine. Stew the cut lobster in this sauce for a few minutes.—*Obs.* This is one of those delicate messes which the *gourmand* loves to cook for himself in a silver dish held over a spirit-lamp, or in a silver stew-pan; the preparation of the morsel being to him the better part of it.

168. TO ROAST A LOBSTER.

WHEN parboiled, rub it with plenty of butter, and lay it in a Dutch oven, or before the fire; baste it till it froth; dredge lightly with flour, and baste again.

169. TO BUTTER LOBSTERS.

WARM the meat cut into nice bits, in a little good brown gravy. Season with spices, nutmeg, and salt; and thicken with butter kneaded in browned flour; or dress them white in clear gravy and a little cream, seasoning with white pepper and salt. *Prawns* and *shrimps* may be *buttered* in the same way, either in white or brown sauce, and served on toasted sippets.

170. FRICASSEED LOBSTER, *an elegant dish.*

DRESS the lobster the same as in the former receipt, but

use more veal-gravy, a little cream, and the beat yolk of
an egg. Dish the fricassee in the middle of a small dish,
and place the claws and tail neatly round it; garnish
with pickled beet-root and sliced pickled cucumber.
This is just a lobster salad.

171. LOBSTER *in the French mode*.

CUT the meat in small dice. Stew it in a little rich
sauce for a few minutes, and serve it in the shell, which
must be nicely cleaned. Strew it twice over with sifted
crumbs, and brown with a salamander. See *Lobster
sauce, &c. and sauce for lobsters,* p. 194.

172-3. TO DRESS CRABS HOT AND COLD, *Or the Scotch Partan-pie*.

PICK the meat out of the claws and body; clean the
shell nicely, and return the meat into it, first seasoned
with salt, white pepper, and nutmeg; with a few
bits of fresh butter, and some bread-crumbs. A small
glass of vinegar, beat and heated up with a little made
mustard, may be added, and a small quantity of salad-
oil substituted for the butter. Brown the meat when
laid in the shell with a salamander.—*To Dress Crabs
cold*. Pick out all the meat, and, mixing it well with a
tea-spoonful of salad-oil, cayenne, white pepper, and
salt, serve it in the shell.—*Obs.* The shell of one crab
will contain the meat of two. The meat may be cut in
fillets for variety, the small claws disposed neatly round
the dish, and the contents of the body pounded, rubbed
through a sieve, seasoned and stewed in a little gravy,
before being returned into the shell.

174. PRAWNS OR CRAY-FISH,—*An ornamental dish*.

MAKE a savoury jelly of calf's-feet or a cow-heel, a
piece of skate, or trimmings of turbot, horseradish,
lemon-peel, an onion, and a piece of lean bacon. When
boiled to a jelly, strain it, and when cold take off the fat,
keep back the sediment, and boil it up with a glass of
white wine, the juice of a lemon, and the whisked whites
of four eggs. Do not disturb it by stirring. When boiled,
let it settle twenty minutes, and run it through a
jelly-bag. Pour some of the jelly into a deep dish;
when it has firmed, put in the cray-fish with their backs

downwards, fill up the dish with the jelly, and when cold, turn the whole out. This jelly may be poured over any sort of cold fish.—*Obs*. A lobster in savoury jelly was one of the fantastic dishes of the old school of cookery. The process was very elaborate, and it seldom succeeded entirely; either a horn was broken or awry, or a claw snapt, or a fracture of the tail took place, to the utter discomfiture of the cook and mortification of the hostess.—See *Aspic jelly or sauce*.

175. MOCK CAVIARE.

BONE a few anchovies and chop them, then pound them in a mortar with some dried parsley, a clove of garlic, a little cayenne, salt, lemon-juice, and a very little salad-oil. Serve on toasted bread or biscuits.

176. A SALMAGUNDI.

WASH and cut open at the breast two large Dutch or Lochfine pickled herrings; take the meat from the bones without breaking the skin, and keep on the head, tails, fins, &c. Mince the fish with the breast of a cold roast chicken skinned, a couple of hard-boiled yolks of eggs, an onion, a boned anchovy, and a little grated ham or tongue. Season with salad-oil, vinegar, cayenne, and salt, and fill up the herring-skins, so that they may look plump and well-shaped. Garnish with scraped horse-radish, and serve mustard with the dish.—*Obs. An ornamental Salmagundi* was another of the frippery dishes of former times. This edifice was raised on a china bowl reversed, and placed in the middle of a dish, crowned with what, by the courtesy of the kitchen, was called a pine-apple, made of fresh butter. Around were laid, stratum above stratum, chopped eggs, minced herring and veal, rasped meat, and minced parsley; the whole surmounted by a triumphal arch of herring-bones, and adorned with a garnishing of barberries and sam-phire.

177. TO STEW OYSTERS,* COCKLES, OR MUSCLES.

PLUMP juicy oysters alone will stew to advantage.

---

* Oysters are conceitedly said to be in season in every month of the year that has an *r* in its name, beginning with September and ending with

When opened, pick them out, beard and wash them in their own liquor, and strain it repeatedly. Put it into a silver or block-tin sauce-pan with a bit of mace, and lemon-peel and a few white peppercorns, a little butter kneaded in flour, and a glass of sweet cream, or

---

April; but the season in many places extends from August to May. Every city has its favourite oyster-bank. In London the Colchester and Milton oysters are held in most esteem. Edinburgh has her "whiskered pandores," and latterly Aberdour oysters; and Dublin the Carlingford, and "Powldoodies of Burran." Venice is celebrated for oysters. Ancient Rome had those of Tarentum. For the convenience of obtaining a ready supply of oysters, they are often transported from their original beds, and laid down on other places of the coast; but these exiles are seldom found in such perfection as those which are called *natives*; that is, such as have never been rudely torn from their native rocks, and sent on voyages of profit. Oysters, when just dredged, may be so packed in small barrels as to keep good for a week or ten days, and in this state they are sent to distant places. Oysters may be dropped out of the shell into a bottle, and kept in their juice for a little time by corking the bottle closely. They may also be preserved good for some time by *feeding*; and custom, which brings *gourmands* to admire game when in a state of putridity, has taught some epicures to relish the flavour of stale oysters better than those recently taken from the beds. The fresher oysters are the better; but when to be kept, lay them bottom downwards in a tub, or any vessel suited to the quantity to be preserved, and cover them with water in which a good deal of salt is dissolved. In this manner Apicius sent oysters to Tiberius when he was in Parthia. Change the water every twelve hours. Most cooks direct that this delicate animal should be fed with oatmeal or flour sprinkled in water; and others, on the principle which leads a mother of the parish of St. Giles to give her new-born darling a drop of gin, are for feeding them with white wine and bread-crumbs! It is said by those who have the charge of fish-ponds, "that fish will eat nothing but what comes out of the sea;" now, though we are not perfectly convinced of this fact, we can at least believe that salt-water gruel is not over well suited to the delicate stomach of an oyster. Those large fat oysters called Pandores, which are so much prized in Edinburgh, are said to owe their superior excellence to the brackish contents of the pans of the adjacent salt-works of Prestonpans flowing out upon the beds,—a subject this worthy of the serious investigation of the oyster-amateur, who may here receive some excellent hints for fattening and improving the quality of his favourite morsel. We have, however, grave doubts on this theory.

Shell-fish, and the oyster above all, have long been esteemed highly restorative, and easy of digestion; they are therefore recommended for the food of the delicate and declining, and of those whose digestive powers have been impaired by excess. When eaten for health, an oyster is best swallowed with its own liquor the moment the shell is opened; or, if found too cold for the stomach, a sprinkling of black pepper may be allowed. Vinegar counteracts the effect of eating oysters to enrich the blood or render it more balsamic, and ought therefore to be avoided by the declining. As there are no reasonable bounds to oyster-eating, it may be useful to notice here, that when too many of these or other shell-fish are swallowed, the unpleasant feeling created may be

of Champagne or Madeira, if for a high relish; in which
case a very little minced eschalot or onion and cayenne

---

removed by drinking half a pint of hot milk. Consumptive persons are
recommended to use hot milk after their oysters at all times.

"Oysters," says the learned author of *Tabella Cibaria*, "were not
common at Rome, and consequently fetched there a very high price; yet
MACROBIUS assures us, that the Roman Pontiffs never failed to have
them every day on their tables. From the fourth century to the reign
of Louis XIV, they were nearly forgotten; but they soon came again into
vogue and from that time have kept up their reputation. Gastronomers,
we know, can swallow from three to four dozen before dinner, and
then sit down and eat perhaps better than if they had abstained from
them. They clear the stomach of accidental phlegm, increase the gastric
juices, and by their natural coolness, condense the air which may be
fixed in the organs of digestion. When good they are wholesome, but
poisonous when bad."—"The Athenians held oysters in great esteem,"
says the same learned authority on matters of the table; and we may
add, that in the Modern Athens they are held in equal regard. They
appear to have fallen into disrepute during the middle-ages. Chaucer's
begging monks *mortified* themselves upon this mean food.

The principal taverns of the Old City used to be called Oyster Taverns,
in honour of this favourite viand; and this name is still kept up by some
modern places of genial resort. "How many celebrated wits and *bon
vivants*, now quite chop-fallen," said WINTERBLOSSOM, "have dived
into the dark defiles of closes and wynds in pursuit of this delicacy, and
of the wine, the wit, the song, that gave it zest. I have heard my
learned and facetious friend, the late Provost CREECH—for it was
rather before my day—say, that before public amusements were much
known in our Presbyterian capital, an *Oyster-ploy*, which always
included music and a little dance, was the delight of the young
fashionables of both sexes."

The municipal authorities of Edinburgh, were wont to pay considerable attention to "the feast of shells," both as regarded the supply and
the price,—and we hope they do so still. At the commencement of the
dredging season, a voyage was boldly undertaken to the oyster-beds in
the Firth of Forth by the public functionaries, with something of the
solemnity of the DOGE of Venice wedding his Adriatic bride. Even
the plodding fishermen of our bleak coasts seem to catch inspiration from
this delicate creature. Instead of the whisky-inspiration which supports
them in dragging the herring-nets, or throwing the cod lines, like
the fishermen of the Sicilian seas, they

"Sing to charm the spirits of the deep,"

as they troll the dredging-nets. There is indeed a poetical notion that
the oyster, among his other *gentle* qualities, is inclined to minstrelsy—

"The Herring loves the merry moonlight,
    The Mackerel loves the wind,
But the *Oyster* loves the dredging-sang,
    For he comes of gentle kind."

The Nabob, emulous of the well-earned fame of Dr. KITCHENER, who
has set the ancient duet between Bubble and Squeak with proper
accompaniments, wished to embellish this volume with the music of the
"Dredging Song," and the shrilling recitative of the oyster-wives,—

may be added. Cover and simmer the oysters very gently for five minutes, lift them with a silver spoon into a deep hot dish, with toasted sippets in it, and strain the sauce over them.—*Obs.* A sort of *deviled* stew is made by adding more seasonings and Parmesan cheese; which high-flavoured cheese the French employ frequently for relishing ragouts, both of meat and fish. If it be true that all fish require silver knives and forks, this holds peculiarly of oysters. A genuine oyster-eater rejects all additions,—wine, eschalot, lemon-sauce, &c. are alike obnoxious to his taste for the native juice.

178. TO SCALLOP OYSTERS OR COCKLES.

HAVING stewed the oysters, as above directed, for two or three minutes in their own juice, have some bread-crumbs moistened with the oyster liquor, a good piece of butter melted, and a little wine. Place some of this in scallop-shapes, and cover with a layer of oysters, then more moistened bread-crumbs, next oysters, and finish with the bread-crumbs mixed with a little grated lemon-peel and finely-shred parsley. Put some bits of butter over the whole, and brown before the fire, or in a Dutch oven.

179. TO GRILL OYSTERS.

BLANCH them in a stew-pan in their own strained juice.

---

those Maids of Honour to the "Empress of the North," who, for miles off, are heard when September evenings begin to shorten—cuckoos of autumn—harbingers of winter—screaming around "her mountain throne"—drowning the summer "babble of green trees," and bringing back the genial associations of "rousing nights," merry tavern-suppers, and "a quarter of a hundred after the play." There is perhaps no spot on earth where oysters were enjoyed in such perfection as at the head of the Old Flesh Market Close of Edinburgh; once,—alas the change!—the cynosure of all the taverns, fish-creels, and booksellers' shops of that learned city: the place where eating, learning, and law sat enthroned side by side. Here, on any evening from October till March, the oyster-*gourmand* took his solitary stand, and enjoyed his delicious regale in its utmost earthly perfection,—*swallowed alive* with its own gravy the moment it was opened by the fish-wife; who operated on the shell with a dexterity of manipulation, a rapidity of fingering which no piano-forte-player we ever saw could compare with,—nothing indeed could be compared with it, except the eager voracity of those genuine lovers of the oyster, to whom these piscatory Hebes ministered. A precious remnant of genuine oyster-eaters still haunt this favourite spot. Dr. REDGILL resolved to visit it on the first night of his sojourn in Edinburgh.—EDIT.

Wash them out of this, and in another stew-pan give them a toss with a bit of fresh butter and a little chopped parsley; but do not let them boil. Place them in their own shells, previously well cleaned, and put some bits of butter over them. Place the shells on the gridiron; two minutes will do them. Nutmeg is added sometimes, both to scalloped and grilled oysters, but we do not approve of it.

180. TO BROWN OYSTERS IN THEIR OWN JUICE.

WASH them in their juice, and dip them one by one in yolk of egg beat up with a very little flour, pepper, and salt. Brown a good piece of butter in the frying-pan, and brown the oysters nicely over a quick fire; draw them aside, and pour their juice strained into the pan; thicken it with a very little flour kneaded in butter, and when it boils stir the oysters among it for a few minutes. This answers for brown sauce to cod's head and shoulders, and for calf's-head, &c.; but when to be served as a stew, it may have a little catsup, bread-crumbs, and minced parsley added to it. Serve in a hot hash-dish on toasted sippets. Lemon-peel and shopped parsley will be an improvement. Muscles may be dressed in the same way.

181. TO SERVE OYSTERS IN THE SHELL.

LET the opener stand behind the eater's chair, who should make quick and clean conveyance. If not so placed, wash, brush, and open and beard the oysters, and arrange them on rows on the tray; or if pinched for room, heap the shells in piles: the fresher from the sea, and the more recently opened the better. The French serve lemon-juice with raw oysters; we serve this, or vinegar, pepper, and toasted crusts.

182. TO PICKLE OYSTERS.

WASH large fat *native* oysters in their own liquor. Strain it, and to every pint of it put a glass of white wine, mace, nutmeg, a good many white peppercorns, and a little salt, if necessary. Simmer the oysters for four or five minutes; but never let them boil, as they will harden; beard them now; wash them from the liquor. Put them in glass or stone jars. Put vinegar in the proportion of a glass to the pint to the liquor, and boil it up. Skim this pickle and pour it over the oysters; and when cold, cork them and tie them close up with bladder. The pickle-liquor may be boiled up occasionally, suffered to cool, and poured over them, which will tend to preserve the oysters: a spoonful of it will be a great addition to any hash or common *ragout*. Add horseradish, parsley, and a little thyme if you like.

183. TO FRY OYSTERS TO GARNISH FISH, *or Oyster-fritters*.

SIMMER them in their own strained liquor for three minutes; drain them; take off the beards, and, dipping in a batter of egg, flour, and white pepper, fry them in lard or butter of a golden brown. The above is the same as *oyster-fritters*, only the fritter-batter must be stiffer, and highly seasoned with mace, nutmeg, and lemon-peel. *Oyster-loaves*, a fantastic sort of dish, is made as oyster-patties, filling the little rolls made for this purpose instead of patty-pans.—See *Patties* and *oyster-sauce, preserved oysters*, &c.*

---

* Fish is a favourite food with the rich and luxurious, but it is not thought to possess much nourishment, though late experiments of men of science in France go far to overturn this opinion. When it is wished rapidly to reduce the weight of jockeys at Newmarket, they are kept on fish. Fish is considered more easy of digestion than flesh, though we are disposed to question the statement. Shell-fish, including turtle, from approaching to the nature of animal jelly, are the most nutritious, but not always the most easily digested. Salmon and salmon-trout, turbot, and sturgeon, are all nutritious, but heavy. Eels are nourishing, but very difficult of digestion. Salt-water fish are considered more wholesome than the fish of slimy lakes and muddy pools. White fish are more easily digested than those of more richness and flavour, such as salmon and herring; and, if less fat, are at least as nutritious. Pike, the water-wolf, is firm in the texture, and a well-flavoured and wholesome, though not a favourite fish. Carp and tench are considered wholesome. Whitings, flounders, and soles, being of a moist, juicy nature, are light, and very easy of digestion. There seems, according to Sir JOHN SINCLAIR, to be a general understanding among mankind, that fish ought to be eaten with butter and acids. "Fish and milk," says the same authority, "are seldom conjoined." Salmon and a dram, he ought to have added, are never separated. "Fish," says Sir JOHN, "do not agree with vegetables, except the potato." Here he is wrong; the people in Orkney and Shetland, who live a great deal both on fresh and salt fish, consume cabbage in large quantities with it, and are entirely free from the scurvy, and those cutaneous diseases which overrun the people of the Hebrides who raise no vegetables. "Among all fish," says Lynch's Guide to Health, "whether of sea or river, the middle-

184. TO STEW MUSCLES FOR FISH-SAUCE.

Do them as oysters, with pepper, butter, and a little vinegar, carefully picking off the beards, which are disagreeable and unwholesome.

185. TO MAKE STORE FISH-SAUCE.*

To an English pint of red port (Burgundy or claret is better,) add fifteen anchovies, chopped and prepared by steeping in vinegar in a close-covered vessel for a week; add to this a stick of horseradish scraped, two onions, and a handful of parsley chopped, a dessert-spoonful of lemon-thyme stripped of the stalks, two bay-leaves, nutmeg, and six blades of mace roughly pounded, nine cloves, and a small dessert-spoonful of black pepper bruised. Pour over these ingredients a large half-pint of port wine vinegar, and simmer slowly in a silver or new block-tin sauce-pan, or earthen pipkin, till the bones of the anchovies are dissolved. Add a few grains of cochineal if the colour is not good. Strain the liquor through a hair-sieve, and, when cold, bottle it for use, securing the vials well with corks and leather. When to be used shake the vials before pouring out the sauce;—two table-spoonfuls will impart a high flavour to four ounces of beat butter, in which it must be simmered for a minute before it is served. *For a great variety of fish-*

---

sized are the best; also those that have not hard and dry flesh, that are crisp and tender, and have many scales and fins." The meat of the turtle, the sea-turtle, is considered not only as a high-flavoured expensive delicacy, but as salubrious and highly nutritious, though those sickly half-dead animals, which are spiced and drugged for city-banquets, may not possess these qualities. Fish were held in such esteem by the ancients, that persons constantly rode post with live fish to Rome.

NOTE BY DR. REDGILL.—"It is strongly recommended to those who may, like me, have the misfortune to swallow a fish-bone, to take four grains of tartar emetic dissolved in warm water, and immediately afterwards the beat whites of four eggs. This mess will instantly coagulate, and will probably bring the bone from the throat or the stomach. The bones of pike, which are sharp and pronged, and so very hard that they will not dissolve in the stomach, ought to be watchfully avoided."

* The CLEIKUM CLUB were favoured with this original receipt from an intelligent Highland lady, who has contributed several valuable original receipts to this volume. This sauce boasts neither the name of BURGESS nor HARVEY, but we would advise those who wish to combine economy with what is healthful and elegant, to make a fair trial of it.

sauces, see *Chapter Sauces*; and for other receipts in *Fish*, See *French Cookery*.

186. TO DRESS PRAWNS, FROM BEAUVILLIERS.

TAKE a pound and half of prawns; cover a dish with a large cup or basin reversed, so that a small damask napkin may be raised like an octagon on it. Cover this with parsley, and dress the prawns on it like a pyramid.

187. JOHN DORY.

THIS hideous-looking but delicious fish is boiled as turbot. Serve with lobster sauce, and cover with plenty of green parsley. *Maids* are dressed like skate, and served with lobster or caper sauce. *Brill* is dressed and sauced like turbot. *Shad* is broiled.

CHAPTER VII.

VEGETABLES AND ROOTS.

————————————THE EARTH HATH ROOTS;
THE BOUNTEOUS HUSWIFE NATURE, ON EACH BUSH
LAYS HER FULL MESS BEFORE YE.
            SHAKSPEARE.

*   *   *   *

Fat Coleworts and *comforting* Pursline,
Cold Lettuce and *refreshing* Rosemarine.
            SPENSER.

VEGETABLES are at their best when just on the eve of being ripe, in their natural season, and when their growth has neither been retarded, nor forced on by artificial means. The vanity, and it is no better, which spurs on people to load their tables with flavourless, colourless, immature vegetables, is ever punished by the expense and disappointment it occasions. Much, however, has been judiciously done of late years, both to improve the quality and to spread the cultivation of vegetables. Where a turnip, a cabbage, or a leek, was thirty years ago the only vegetable *luxury* found on a country gentleman's table, we now see a regular succession of not merely brocoli, cauliflower, and pease, but of the more recondite asparagus, sea-kale, endive, and artichoke; with an abundance of early small saladings. The vegetable-markets of most towns have within the same period undergone a wonderful improvement. The kinds and quantity of articles are more than doubled, and the price, except for early or forced vegetables, has diminished at least a half; so that a healthful and harmless luxury is now within the reach of all classes. But vegetables of the more delicate species are still comparatively such recent acquaintances, that, even at tables otherwise elegantly appointed, they are seldom seen perfectly well dressed, at least in so far as regards colour. That homely chemistry, which does not disdain to descend to the kitchen, has indeed considerably assisted the cook of late in this department. A few general observations will, if attended to, supply the place of long or often-repeated directions for dressing vegetables. Unlike animal substances, vegetables can never be dressed too fresh, though some kinds, such as French beans and artichokes, will keep a few days, and by care all will keep for some time. They must, after being carefully cleared from insects and decayed leaves, or other spoiled parts, be washed in plenty of water; they cannot be too much refreshed. Let them lie in salt and water, head downwards, till they are put to boil. This simple method will bring out every insect that may lurk in the leaves. To preserve their beauty entire, they must be boiled alone, in a perfectly clean and well-tinned vessel, and in abundance of soft water. A teaspoonful of salt wormwood, or a bit of pearl-ashes or soda of the size of a nutmeg, will not only preserve the green colour, but contribute to the tenderness of cabbage, savoys,* &c. A bit of sugar will sometimes be useful. Put in all vegetables with soft boiling water and plenty of salt; with hard water the colour will keep better, but the quality will not improve. Make them boil fast, and do not cover the vessel if you desire to preserve their fine colour. In a former section it was recommended to boil several sorts of vegetables and roots with the meat, when salted, with which they are to be served; and this, though it may injure the colour, will certainly

---

* We know that the Romans used nitre in boiling vegetables.

improve the quality, a point of greater importance. All vegetables should be enough boiled. The cook's rule of having cauliflowers *crisp** is as inimical to health as offensive to the palate. If boiled quickly, which they ought to be, vegetables are ready when they begin to sink in the boiling water, and they will spoil every instant after that. Meat may wait a little, but vegetables will not, particularly the cauliflower kind.

188. BROCOLI AND CAULIFLOWER.

CHOOSE those vegetables close, compact, of a good colour, and from five to eight inches in diameter; strip off the outside leaves, and trim away the tops of the inner leaves; cut off the stalk at the bottom, and pare away the outer husky skin from the branches. Having washed, lay them, head downwards, in a pan of cold water and salt, which will bring out all insects; and boil them on a drainer in plenty of boiling water, with a little salt; some cooks add a bit of sugar. Skim the water well; from ten minutes to twenty will boil them. When the stalks are nearly tender they are ready. If some heads are larger than others, put in the large ones first, dish as one large cauliflower, and if sauce is wanted pour melted butter (*sauce blanche*) about them.—*Obs*. Brocoli is sometimes served at supper, like asparagus, on toast. Melted butter is usually sent to table either about or with both brocoli and cauliflower. Cauliflower is very nicely dressed for a second course by pulling it into handsome branches, parboiling these, and then stewing a few minutes in a sauce of white broth, seasoned with mace, white pepper, and salt, and thickened with a little sweet cream, and a bit of butter kneaded in flour.

189. CAULIFLOWER WITH PARMESAN,
For the second course.

BOIL, and dish, and sauce the cauliflower with *sauce blanche;* strew grated Parmesan over it; then gently pour a little melted butter, then strew crumbs and more grated cheese over all, and colour with a salamander;

---

* If cooks and ladies will have their cauliflowers *crisp*, as they call it, why not serve them *raw*, and the eaters would be aware of them.—P. T.

pour a little well-seasoned *velouté* and fresh butter, well mixed, with grated Parmesan into the dish, or butter melted in cream or milk will do.

190. TO DRESS ASPARAGUS AND SEA-KALE.

SCRAPE the stalks of asparagus nicely clean; throw them into cold water; tie them up in bundles of about three inches thick, with tape or rushes; cut these bundles of equal lengths, leaving about an inch of stalk, and put them into a stew-pan of quick-boiling water, with salt. Notice when the stalks are tender, and take them up before they lose their flavour or colour. Have ready, nicely toasted, a slice of a large round loaf; dip it for a few seconds into hot water, and, laying it in the middle of the dish, serve the asparagus upon it with the heads inward. Serve beat butter in a boat. The same receipt is applicable to sea-kale, except that no bread is served with it.* It should also be well drained, "and dried a little before the fire," says Sir George Mackenzie.

191. TO BOIL ARTICHOKES.

STRIP off the coarse outer leaves, and cut off the stalks. Steep and wash them in plenty of cold water, and boil them with the tops downwards, keeping up the boil, (adding boiling water, when wanted,) for from two to three hours. Float a plate over them to keep them below the water. Try a leaf, and if it draw out easily they are done. Drain them, and serve with melted butter in small cups, a very little in each, or with melted butter in a sauce-boat. Artichoke bottoms, if dry, may be soaked, and then stewed in clear broth, and served with a relishing forcemeat laid in each; or they may be boiled in milk and water, and served with cream-sauce. They are frequently used to enrich ragouts, turtle-soups, pies, &c. The French cut the bottoms raw, and serve them as salad, dipping the slices in oil or vinegar.

---

* So well was the cultivation of vegetables understood by the Romans, that at Ravenna asparagus were raised for the tables of the great, of which three weighed a pound. Nettle-tops, elder-buds, and cliver were among their pot-herbs. Asparagus is thought medicinal. This vegetable is equally a favourite in Paris and London, where enormous quantities of it are consumed. Young buds of the hop form a wholesome substitute for asparagus.—See *French Cookery of Asparagus.*

192. JERUSALEM ARTICHOKES,

MAY either be boiled plain, taken up the moment they are done, and served with melted butter poured over them, or cooked with a rich white or brown sauce. They are very good roasted; they are then served in a napkin, and melted butter is eat with them. They are also mashed, and made in pie.

193. TO BOIL GREEN PEASE.

PEASE should not be gathered, or, at any rate, not shelled, till they are to be used. The younger they are the more delicate; there is also a great difference in the kinds. When the water boils put them in with a little salt and a bit of sugar; skim it, and let them boil quickly for from fifteen to twenty-five minutes, trying when they are ready. Drain them, and put a few bits of fresh butter in the dish, turning them lightly over with a silver spoon till they are buttered. Boil a few sprigs of fresh mint by themselves; chop these fine, and lay in little heaps round the edge of the dish.—*Obs*. Some persons like the flavour of mint boiled with the pease. *Buttered* pease are rather going out of vogue, but *buttering* is a good old commendable English custom. Dr. KITCHENER allows "a peck of pease to two hearty pea-eaters." At this rate pease for a large party would occupy a tolerable space on a modern table. We would, however, allow a peck of *young* pease (*petits pois*) to six or eight persons. *Pease* are sometimes *stewed* in good white broth, with sliced lettuce and onion, or with sliced cucumber. These must be nearly cooked before the pease are put in. Thicken the broth with butter kneaded in flour; season with white pepper and salt, and a sprig of mint, to be taken out before the stew is dished.—See *French Cookery of Pease*.

194. WINDSOR BEANS.

BOIL them in plenty of water with salt. Serve them with or under bacon or pickled pork. Garnish with chopped parsley, and serve parsley and butter.

195. FRENCH BEANS.

CUT off the stalks, and strip off the strings. If the

beans are old, cut them in two slantwise. Lay them in a weak pickle of salt and water for a half-hour. Put them into water that boils quickly, and when done, which will be best known by trying them, drain them, and serve with melted butter.—*Obs*. When old and large they are best split as well as cut aslant.

196. TO BOIL CABBAGE, GREENS, SAVOYS, AND BRUSSELS SPROUTS.

STRIP off the coarse outer leaves, and pare off the coarse husk from the branch-stalks; cut off the stem close to the bottom; wash them thoroughly, and put them on with plenty of boiling water in an open pot, and a little salt of wormwood, or a bit of soda. Divide half-grown cabbages, and quarter large ones, but tie up to keep them whole till served. See that they be well covered with boiling water. They will take from fifteen minutes to an hour, or more, according to the age. Brussels cabbage are boiled as above, and arranged in the dish as asparagus. The French serve a white sauce, and send up a cruet of oil with these small cabbages.—See *Bubble* and *Squeak*, *Boiled beef and greens*, &c.

197. SPINAGE FOR THE SECOND COURSE.

THIS delicate vegatable requires very careful picking and washing. When perfectly clean, put it into plenty of boiling water and salt, and boil very quickly, pressing it down with a wooden spoon; ten minutes will boil it. Then squeeze it, and throw it into a great quantity of cold water to preserve the colour green. Put a piece of fresh butter and a little salt in the stew-pan, and returning the spinage, well squeezed, to heat up, mash it fine. Spread it level on the dish, and scallop with a spoon, or score it in the form of diamonds, or sippets, or press it in a leaf-shaped mould, and turn it out. Cream, the squeeze of a lemon, and mace, or nutmeg, are added by some cooks; and a little rich bland gravy, if to be served under a tongue, fricandeau, or breast of lamb. Spinage is often served with poached eggs. It is then boiled as above, pressed, beat up hot with butter and seasonings, and cut in the form of sippets, with an egg served on each:—it makes a pretty supper-dish. Tender *young spinage*, without any redundancy of vegetable blood or bile in it, may be boiled in a close vessel, with no more water than what hangs about the leaves when washed; but is seldom so free of bitterness as when boiled in water; and we can see no good reson for an omission, which, however, is often recommended in common cookery books.

198. TURNIPS.

PARE off all that would be hard, woody, and stringy when boiled. Boil them in plenty of water, for from three-quarters of an hour to nearly two hours, according to the age and size. Drain and serve them whole, or, if too large, divided, or mashed. A bit of the green top shoot is left on young turnips and on Swedish turnips. Swedish turnip-tops are very delicate greens when young. If boiled in their coats, and then pared, turnips will be more juicy.

199. TO DRESS TURNIPS,
For the second course,—a French mode.

CUT them into cubes, oblong forms, &c. or scoop them out as balls, pears, peaches, plums, &c. and, after boiling in salt and water with a piece of butter, dress them in melted butter, and season with nutmeg.—*Obs.* They are useful to fill up a table when other vegetables are not to be got; glazed or browned in butter or lard they make an excellent garnish to several dishes.

200. TO MASH TURNIPS.

WHEN the turnips are boiled as above directed, drain them and mash them with a wooden spoon through a colander. Return them into a stewpan to warm, with a piece of fresh butter, white pepper, and salt. When mixed well with the butter, place them neatly in the dish, and mark in diamonds or sippets.—*Obs.* The *Cleikum Club* put a little powdered ginger to their mashed turnips, which were studiously chosen of the yellow, sweet, juicy sort, for which Scotland is celebrated,—that kind which, in our days of semi-barbarism, were served raw, as a delicate whet before dinner, as turnips are in Russia at the present day. Mashed turnips to be eaten with boiled fowl or veal, or the more insipid meats, are considerably improved by the Cleikum seasoning of ginger, which, besides, corrects the flatulent properties of this esculent. Yellow turnips, mashed and eaten with milk, are recommended in scurvy and consumption. A small proportion of turnips answers very well mashed with potatoes: they must be boiled for a good while before the potatoes are put in. They eat well with boiled or roasted mutton. The real *navet*, the long-shaped French turnip, is of high flavour, and used to be much employed in soups and turnip dishes.

201. CARROTS AND PARSNIPS.

THESE roots, if old, require long boiling. Wash young carrots, and scrub them with a hard brush. Old ones must be scraped lightly, and when boiled, have the outside peel rubbed off with a coarse towel. They are served with boiled mutton or beef, whether fresh or salted. If large, they may be sliced, either length-ways or across. —*Obs*. Some persons like cold carrot with cold beef; but they taste sweet and mawkish. *Parsnips* may either be mashed with butter or cream, served whole, or, if large, quartered. Turnips, carrots, and parsnips, will all warm up very well in a vessel plunged in boiling water. Parsnips and potatoes mashed together, with butter or fresh dripping, make a good plain dish.

202. CARROTS, *the Flemish way.*

PREPARE (after boiling) in nice forms, as stars, wheels, &c., and stew them in melted butter, with minced parsley, young onions, salt and pepper.

203. FRIED GOURDS.—KITCHENER.

CUT five or six Gourds in quarters, take off the skin and pulp, stew them in the same manner as for table; when done, drain them quite dry, beat up an egg, and dip the Gourds in it, and cover them well over with bread-crumbs; make some hog's lard hot, and fry them a nice light colour, throw a little salt and pepper over them, and serve quite dry.

204. ANOTHER WAY.

TAKE six or eight small Gourds as near of a size as possible, slice them with a cucumber slice, dry them in a cloth, and then fry them in very hot lard; throw over a little pepper and salt, and serve up on a napkin.—*Obs*.

These vegetables are also dressed in milk, with butter and seasonings.

205. SKIRRETS and SCONZONERAS.

THESE are boiled, and then served with melted butter.

SCONZONERA. Scrape off the rind. Steep in hot water, to extract part of the bitter, and then boil or stew as carrots.

206. TOMATAS OR LOVE-APPLES.

THESE have gone down in France, but are just (like other fashions) coming into vogue among us. Tomatas are used both in sauces and soups, and are pickled.—See *Tomata Catsup*.

207. BEET-ROOTS.

THOUGH chiefly used in winter salads, or for pickling, beet-roots may be dressed as parsnips, and served as a garnishing for boiled beef, or with salt fish. Wash, and without touching with the knife, boil them whole, or bake them. If broken, the colour will fly. Parboiled beet-root may be sliced, and stewed with small onions in a little cream or gravy, with seasonings and a spoonful of vinegar. Dish the slices of beet-root with the small onions round them. Beet-root, besides being wholesome and palatable, is exceedingly ornamental in salads, and for garnishing; and makes a cheap and beautiful common pickle. The leaves of the white beet are used as spinage. The juice of the red is used to colour some soups and sauces, by vulgar cooks.

208. TO STEW AND ROAST ONIONS.

SCALD and peel a dozen middle-sized, or four or five large Spanish onions. If old and acrid, parboil them, and stew very slowly for nearly an hour in good broth, with white pepper and salt; thicken the sauce with a little butter kneaded in flour, and, dishing the onions in a small hash-dish, pour it over them. A little mushroom-catsup may be added, and they may be browned. Onions are *roasted* before the fire in their skins, peeled, and served with cold butter and salt. They are eaten either alone or with roasted potatoes, or with red or pickled herrings. In the latter case, we would recommend mustard as well as butter.—*Obs.* Stewed and roasted onions used to be a favourite supper-dish in Scotland, and were reckoned medicinal. The onions were stewed (after boiling) in a butter-sauce, to which cream was put,—the *Sauce blanche* of France.* Onions may be farced, as may several sorts of vegetables with a farce of meat, fish, or poultry. It is seldom however done.

209. VEGETABLE CURRY.

BOIL, strain, and mash, greens or cabbage, stew them in butter, with curry-powder to taste, rubbed down in vinegar, with salt, and pepper. A curry of spinage is made by the addition of vinegar or sorrel, also onions. The sauce is veal gravy or butter, and either bits of meat, or, if *maigre*, prawns, cockles, or oysters, are added to the stew.

210. TO STEW CUCUMBERS AND CELERY.

PARE the cucumbers, and cut them in thin slices; or, if small, divide them the long way. Slice onions in the proportion of one to every two cucumbers. Stew these together in a little good broth, or in melted butter, with cayenne, pepper, and salt. Thicken the sauce with a bit of butter kneaded in flour, and, after dishing the cucumbers, skim it, and pour it over them.—To *stew celery*, clean and cut the heads (the younger the more delicate) in three-inch lengths. Stew them till tender in a little butter. Thicken the sauce with a good piece of butter rolled in flour, add a quarter-pint of sweet cream, and season with pepper, mace, and salt.

---

* "We now," said TOUCHWOOD, "rarely see a dish of onions, yet I have much to say in behalf of this homely patriarchal relish, which is of so much consequence in giving *gusto* to the food of those who cannot reach the costly compound essences that are gradually subverting it in the kitchens of the rich. In the early part of the last century SWIFT sung—

> 'There is, in every Cook's opinion,
> No savoury dish without an onion;

and added, for the benefit of youthful gourmands,—

> 'But lest your kissing should be spoil'd,
> The onion must be thoroughly boil'd,'—

a precaution of no great moment, however, as the period when a man begins to pay much attention to palatic enjoyments is nearly about the same at which the taint of his breath becomes an affair of small concernment either to himself or others, provided he keep a respectful distance. It may be remarked by the way, that one sign of the precocity of the

The French put grated nutmeg or minced parsley to stews of cucumber, and thicken the sauce with beat yolks of eggs. Nutmeg is indeed a very suitable condiment with this watery vegetable, so is cayenne.—*Obs.* Stewed cucumbers are frequently served with lamb-steaks, mutton-chops, or rump-steaks, and with mutton-rumps and kidneys. Some cooks brown the cucumbers and onions before stewing. These vegetables stews may be made into the sauces bearing their respective names, by cutting the celery in smaller bits, and by stewing the cucumber to a mash, and pressing it through a fine sieve. If to serve around veal, veal-kidneys, or fowls, the celery may in cooking be enriched with ham and seasoning herbs.

211. TO STEW RED CABBAGE.

WASH, pick, and shred what will fill a large pint-basin. Melt some butter in a sauce-pan, and put in the cabbage with only the water that hangs about it, pepper, cayenne, salt, and an onion sliced. Stew this, keeping the sauce-pan close covered; and when just ready, add a glass of vinegar, which may just boil up. French cooks add a bay-leaf and two cloves stuck in an onion, which must be picked out before serving. Fried sausages are served on this preparation; or it may be served with *bouilli*.★

---

youth of the age, is their beginning to talk of the business of the table at the years when their fathers were still upon their bread and milk."—"But return we to our onion," said JEKYLL to the Nabob, after delivering this note. "Well, Sir?—and what has consigned this prime root to Parisian *restaurateurs* and London soup-brewers, who are still cunning enough in their art to employ its savoury, cordial, and stimulating qualities, but this same pouncet-box dread of the manly scent of a garlick breath,—another root by the way most vilely neglected? 'Of all plants,' says Sir WILLIAM TEMPLE, 'garlick affords the most nourishment,' and supplies the best spirits to those who eat little flesh.' It clears phlegm, dissipates cold slimy humours."—"Faugh!" interrupted the cornet emphatically; and he continued,—"What a manly odoriferous fellow our friend the Bonassus must be, Doctor, who consumes a bushel of onions a day, they assure me!"

★ The cabbage tribe has ever been a first-rate favourite with writers on diet, whether ancient or modern. Volumes have been composed, not merely in praise of the demulcent cauliflower and brocoli, but of the common white and red cabbage. Besides their use in soups, and in correcting the putrescent qualities of animal food, they are said to be correctives of the consequences of excess in wine. ARBUTHNOT says, the juice of red cabbage baked, is, with the addition of honey, an excellent pectoral; and red cabbage stewed in veal-broth, with calf's lights and

212. TO STEW SORREL FOR ROASTS OF VEAL, LAMB, FRICANDEAUX, &c.

WASH and simmer it in an unglazed earthen or stone jar, very slowly, and beat it up with a bit of butter, or a little salad-oil. Add cayenne, pepper, and salt. A *mixture* of spinage and sorrel is dressed as spinage, where sorrel alone might be thought too strong in acid.

213. MUSHROOMS.

So many fatal accidents happen every season from the use of poisonous mushrooms, and it is so difficult to distinguish between the edible kinds and those that are deleterious, that we would advise our readers either to eat none that they have not examined for themselves, or to be contented with what are raised in artificial beds, though the flavour of these are as decidedly inferior to that of the wild mushrooms as a coop-fed chicken is to the heath-cock.* The small raised buttons are however excellent for pickling.

---

pistachios, is, on the continent, esteemed a specific in consumption,—a malady, by the way, for which a remedy has been discovered in chickens, oysters, jellies, fruits, and every favourite aliment,—in short, in whatever the discoverer fancies he himself could thrive on and live for ever. These discoveries are, we take it, generally made on the principle of the Irish corpse-howl or Ullaloo,—

"Why did you die? Why did you die? Had you not plenty of butter-milk and potatoes?"

* Naturalists enumerate nearly 500 kinds of mushrooms found in England alone, and of these there are perhaps not ten sorts ascertained to be fit for human food. Mushrooms, with coarse bread, form the chief sustenance of the inhabitants of several of the Russian provinces, during a considerable part of the year. They are indeed freely eaten everywhere on the continent, where their properties seem to be better understood than in England. In Russia they are salted, dried, or dressed fresh, and eaten with olive-oil by the better orders, while the poorer classes use hemp-oil. They are also broiled, roasted in the ashes, stewed, and fried, served with meat, chopped with potatoes, turnips, carrots, &c. and form a relishing ingredient in ragouts and sauces. The following is a tolerably accurate description of the wholesome, or, we should rather say, the unsuspected sorts; for, notwithstanding this extensive Russian practice, we question whether mushrooms in substance are ever salubrious. "The eatable mushrooms first appear very small, and of a round form, on a little stalk. They grow very fast, and the upper part and stalk are white; as the size increases, the under part gradually opens, and shews a fringy fur, of a very fine salmon-colour, which continues more or less till the mushroom is a tolerable size, and then turns to a dark-brown.

Mushrooms are safest when pickled or made into cat-sup, because they are then used only in small quantities, and their pernicious properties are also corrected by the acids and spices employed to preserve them. When good, they approach nearer to animal substances than any plant whatever, both in their texture and flavour, and in the gravy with which they abound. Skilful cooks have been known to impose a *ragout* of mushrooms for a meat ragout, even on practised epicures; nor do we know any one flavouring ingredient that the cook could less spare than mushroom-catsup. We by no means, therefore, wish to proscribe this delicacy, but to caution our readers not merely against mushrooms of suspicious quality, but also against consuming many at once, how-ever temptingly they may be dressed.

214. TO STEW *or* RAGOUT MUSHROOMS *in white or brown sauce.*

GATHER the largest button-mushrooms, or the smallest flaps. Trim away all that is mouldy or spoiled, and stew them in their own gravy, in a silver or earthen ves-sel, with a small quantity of water to prevent burning. When nearly done, put in a large spoonful of sweet

---

These marks should be attended to: and, likewise, whether the skin can be easily parted from the edges and middle. Those which have a white or yellow fur should be carefully avoided, though many of them have the same smell, but not so strong as the right sort." The most delicate mushrooms are those found on old close-cropt pastures, or open downs by the sea-shore, where cattle browse. The season in England is, in good years, from about the end of August till October. In Scotland it is a few days later. Mushrooms of good quality are plentiful in Ireland. It is of that country BACON said long ago, "By the favour of the king, Ireland is the soil where *mushrooms* and *upstart* weeds spring up in a night, and do chiefly prosper."

Picking this delicate and singular food forms an agreeable rural amusement; and the ladies, or idle gentlemen of any family, may easily in their walks gather edible mushrooms for pickling, catsup, powder, and for dressing fresh. The ancients, who were delicate in their eating, prepared their own mushrooms with an amber or silver knife.

The following test of the qualities of mushrooms is given, though we do not vouch for its accuracy:—"Boil a peeled onion with the mush-rooms; if it remain white, they are safe; if it become black or livid, there are bad ones among them." It is said, if the water in which mush-rooms are steeped, or the broken parts of them be poured upon an old bed, innumerable young ones will spring up. The mushrooms raised in beds are sometimes of unwholesome kinds, as well as the wild ones. No sort of mushroom will poison a Frenchman.—P.S.T.

cream, a bit of butter rolled in flour, cayenne, white pepper, and salt. Lemon-juice is employed to whiten them. The French thicken this ragout with beat yolks of egg; and this is good and safe practice.—*Mushrooms* are stewed *brown* in good brown gravy, thickened and seasoned as above, with the addition of a little nutmeg. A piece of ham may be put to a *brown ragout*, and also veal, herbs, onions, and parsley.

215. TO GRILL MUSHROOMS, *or Mushrooms à la Bordelais.*

CHOOSE large, firm, fresh-gathered flaps. Skin them, and score the under side. Put them into an earthen dish, and baste them with oil or melted butter, and strew pepper and salt over them. When they have been steeped in this *marinade* for an hour or more, broil them on both sides over a clear fire, and serve them with a sauce of oil or melted butter, minced parsley, young onions, a little garlick, and the juice of a lemon, poured over them; or they may be done in the oven, and a sauce drawn from their trimmings and stalks.

216. POTATOES.

SOME humorous writer pities those people who lived before the publication of the Waverley Novels and the introduction of potatoes,—that root of superlative excellence and unbounded utility, which takes its honoured place on every dining table or stool in the three kingdoms, and goes far to equalize the dining enjoyments of every grade of society.

There are a great many varieties of potatoes, and fully as many ways of cooking them; but when all are tried, as the old yellow mealy kidney is the best potato, so is simple boiling the best mode of preparation. Count RUMFORD, Sir JOHN SINCLAIR, and other writers upon economics, have multiplied receipts for dressing this valuable production; but we would advise such of our readers as are potato-fanciers, rather to follow the practice adopted in the cabins or cottages in their neighbourhood, than any printed formula whatever. Potatoes are rarely seen in their utmost perfection save in such situations, when just ripe and freshly dug they are well washed and scrubbed, suited in size, and boiled in hot-haste, with scanty water, and abundance of salt, and in a vessel to which poverty, luckily for the quality of the potatoes, denies a close-fitting lid. As soon as they are ready, the water is poured off; a few minutes more of the fire evaporates all moisture, and completes the cooking; and there they lie, smoking hot, mealy, and flaky, bursting from their coats, in such guise as potatoes are seldom seen on the tables of opulence. We take it for granted that these potatoes are of the dry farinaceous kinds known in Scotland and Ireland, and not the cheesy, waxy roots which habit has brought the inhabitants of London to relish. A piece of lime the size of an egg boiled with them improves, it is said, those heavy potatoes. *Steaming* is recommended for potatoes by theoretical writers upon the subjects of the kitchen, and certainly, where potatoes must be cooked on a large scale, it is very convenient; but, so far as our experience goes, we will venture to affirm, that the crude, rank, deleterious juice, which makes potatoes so unfit for food in their raw state, is never so quickly nor so effectually extracted as by rapid uncovered boiling. Potatoes ought to be eaten as soon as they are dressed and dried. If they must stand, let it be by the fire, in the sauce-pan, and only partially covered, that the steams may escape as they arise. A piece of coarse calico or flannel kept for this purpose should be laid over the potatoes in folds, and the pot-lid over this. This will not only absorb the moisture, but keep them hot a long while. Young potatoes ought always to be served in their skins;—very little boiling will dress them. They are best when boiled with boiling water poured over them. Young watery immature potatoes are unsafe food if taken in any quantity. After the beginning of April potatoes should be peeled and soaked in water for a short time before they are boiled; or they may be mashed.

217. ROASTED POTATOES.—This is the nicest mode of cooking this root. Let the potatoes be large, of equal size, and well washed and scrubbed; for the browned skin of a roasted potato is the better part of it. They must be *slowly* done before the fire, or in an oven or Dutch oven, or buried in wood or turf ashes. Serve them with cold salt butter scooped, and roasted onions. See *Potatoes browned under roast mutton*, page 97.

218. POTATOES are FRIED or BROILED after being boiled, peeled, and sliced cold. *Broil* on a clear fire, or *fry* in plenty of good clear beef-dripping. They may be dressed as *potato-fritters*, by flouring the slices, dipping them in egg and crumbs, and frying. These form a great addition to sausages, and pickled or red-herrings, with which they may be served. Large potatoes, cut neatly in ringlet-slices and browned, form a suitable garnish to sausages, pork-chops, &c. The French fry sliced potatoes in goose-dripping, which has a very high relish; but before serving, drain them on a towel before the fire.— See *French Cookery of Potatoes*.

219. TO MASH POTATOES.*

THOSE who are more solicitous about the appearance of their tables than the quality of the dishes, have their potatoes mashed, or boiled peeled, all the year round. Wash and skin them, cut out all the *eyes* and specks, boil them with plenty of salt, pour off the water, and put them over the fire to dry for a minute; put in some butter, salt, and a little milk (the less the better, unless they are to be eaten with milk, as it makes them tough and doughy.) Mash them smooth, with the Scottish implement called a *potato-beetle*, or with a rolling-pin, and dish them neatly; score in diamonds or sippets, and brown them before the fire. After the month of March potatoes ought always to be pared before boiling, whether they are to be mashed or served whole.

220. *Mashed Potatoes* may be pressed into patty pans previously buttered, and turned out and browned; or put into stoneware scallop-shell shapes, glazed with eggs, and browned before the fire, sticking a few bits of butter upon them. A few of these make a pretty supper-dish.

221. *Potato-snow, a favourite way of cooking potatoes.*

---

* *There is an admirable receipt for gusty* chappit (i.e. mashed) potatoes in an early volume of BLACKWOOD's Magazine,—the work which, in the mysteries of Comus, takes the lead of all the periodicals of the day. The receipt to which we allude is after the practice of the pastoral inhabitants of Ettrick, Yarrow, and Teviotdale. Before calling the potato-*beetle* into operation, salt, pepper, and *an onion*, finely shred, are sprinkled over the potatoes, with a dash of sweet milk. The *onion* is the *bonne bouche*.

Choose white, mealy, smooth potatoes; skin them; boil them carefully, and when they crack pour off the water, and put them to dry on the trivet till quite dry and powdery. Rub them through a coarse wire-sieve on the dish they are to go to table on; and do not move it or the flakes will fall and flatten.

222. *Potato-balls* is another form into which mashed potatoes may be converted. Roll them up with yolk of egg and a little flour, and fry them in good dripping, or brown them.

223. *Potatoes dressed in a French mode for nursery dinners, &c.*—Stir new milk with pounded potatoes till the mixture is as thin as good cream. Boil this with butter, pepper, and salt, for twenty minutes.

224. *Potato-balls ragout* are also made of mashed potatoes, adding grated ham or tongue, minced parsley and onion, pepper, salt, a bit of butter, and a little of any flavouring ingredient that is suited to the dish they are to accompany. Small *ragout-balls* of potatoes form an agreeable addition to *open* fish-pies, or make a neat supper-plate.

225. *Westphalia loaves, a supper-dish, or to eat with veal, &c.*—Grate four ounces of good lean ham, and mix it with a pound of good potatoes, mashed with butter. Add salt, pepper, and two eggs, to bind the ingredients. Mould this into small loaves, or shape it in patty-pans, and fry and serve in a brown gravy, or without sauce.

226. *A Potato-collar*, rolled handsomely up, scored in diagonal lines, and nicely browned, makes a good potato-dish. Garnish it with potato-balls around it, and a brown onion gravy-sauce, or plain melted butter, which we would recommend in place of the wine-sauce ordered by learned cooks.

227. *Potato fritters, Scotch.*—Parboil waxy long shaped potatoes, dip them (sliced) in egg, bread crumbs, and rasped ham; fry in plenty of dripping, and serve with any sort of steaks and chops, or alone as a supper-dish. They may be dipped in small-beer fritter-batter.

228. *A Potato-pie*, made of sliced potatoes and onions, butter, pepper, and salt, is a good nursery or cottage dish, but a temptation and a trial to the gourmand's temper, and an affront to the cook's puff-paste, when

covered and ostentatiously served up as a savoury pie.—
Obs. There are many other approved ways of dressing
this chief of the esculent roots, either alone or in conjunction with other viands, such as Irish stew, salt-fish-
pie, &c.; and we may mention one or two of them:—
In some parts of Ireland, and in the Highlands and
Islands of Scotlands, where *rizzared* haddocks, pickled
herrings, and dried salt-meats, are regularly served at
breakfast, mashed potatoes, become firm from standing
from the dinner or supper of the previous day, are cut
in *oblong slices*, browned on the gridiron, and to eat with
fish, form a substitute for bread more acceptable than
the principal. In the same situations, a proportion of
hot mashed potatoes is kneaded up with flour or barley-
meal, and, when served hot, makes very palatable break-
fast-cakes. A cheap and delicious mess is furnished in
summer to those healthy and happy children educated
in what are called the *Maiden Hospitals* of Edinburgh.
Good potatoes, boiled, peeled, and roughly broken, are
boiled up with sweet milk, and a small proportion of
butter.

229. *To restore frosted Potatoes.*—This is partially
done by steeping potatoes, or any other frosted vegetable,
in cold water till thawed. A better and more effectual
method has been discovered by a Cumberland gentleman. This remedy is simply to allow the potatoes to
remain in the pits after a severe frost, till the mild
weather has set in for some weeks, and allowed them to
recover gradually. If once exposed to the atmospheric
air, no art will recover frosted potatoes.

230. *Calecannon,* an Irish dish, is made by boiling
and mashing greens, young cabbage, or spinage, and
mixing them with mashed potatoes, butter, pepper, and
salt, pressing it into a buttered shape to be turned out, or
dishing it like mashed potatoes, &c. In this dish two-
thirds should be potato. *Plain Calecannon* is made in
cottages with infinitely less ceremony, and it is quite
as good. Boil the vegetables till nearly done; put the
peeled raw potatoes to them; drain them from the water
when boiled, and with pepper, salt, a shred onion, and
a good piece of butter or dripping, beat them up
together.

231. *Potato-flour,* or *Starch,* is another usual form of

this root, much vaunted of late, for culinary purposes. It is often substituted for arrow-root on common occasions, and is used by many cooks in preference to flour for thickening butter, soups and sauces. It makes pan cakes, and is even prized by nice housewives for pastry, from the purity of colour which may be imparted to it by repeated blanching. It is made thus:—

232. *Potato starch or flour.*—Grate down peeled and nicely-washed raw potatoes into a large dish filled with water. Let this stand for twenty-four hours, occasionally stirring it. When the starch has subsided, pour the water gently off, and put on fresh water. When sufficiently blanched by repeated waters, take up the cake of starch, which will have formed at the bottom, and dry it for future use. A small machine is now in use for this purpose. The flour or starch is also sold very reasonably.

233. OF SALADS.

SALAD herbs are cooling and refreshing. They correct the prutrescent tendency of animal food, and are anti-scorbutic. Salads are at any rate a harmless luxury where they agree with the stomach; and though they afford little nourishment of themselves, they make a pleasant addition to other aliments, and a graceful appearance on the dinner-table. *Lettuce*, of the different sorts, or *salad* as it is often called, is the principal ingredient in those vegetable messes. It should be carefully blanched and eat young; when old, its juices become acrimonious and hurtful. Lettuce possesses soporific qualities, and is recommended as a supper-article to bad sleepers. *Radishes*, when young, are juicy and cooling, but a very few days change their nature, and they become woody and acrid; when not very young, they ought to be scraped. *Cress* and *mustard* are cordial and grateful, and of an agreeable pungency; and *celery*, when young and properly blanched, by its peculiar nutty flavour, contributes much to what EVYLYN calls "harmony in the composure of a sallet." A variety of other herbs mingle in full well-selected salads, such as sorrel, young onions, cucumbers, tomatas, endive, radish-leaflets, &c. Many wild herbs were formerly employed, and are still used on the continent and in America, as saladings. As this is quite a delicate, *jaunty* branch of the culinary art, we would recommend that young ladies residing in the country should gather their own salad herbs, and dress salads for their families, which will give a better chance of a duty being well done, which, in the hurry of the stew-pan, the spit, and the stove, the poor distracted cook must often perform with haste and slovenliness. Never make a salad till near the dinner-hour, as it will flatten and lose its light appearance by standing. Foreigners call many things salads we would merely reckon cold, little, dressed dishes. As this may produce a confusion of ideas in the young housekeeper we notice it here. Our ancestors had the same notion of what *sallets* were that the French still retain.

234. AN ENGLISH SALAD AND SALAD-SAUCE.

LET the herbs be fresh gathered, nicely trimmed and picked, and repeatedly washed in salt and water. Drain and cut them. Just before dinner is served, rub the yolks of two hard-boiled eggs very smooth on a soup-plate, with a little very rich cream. When well mixed, add a tea-spoonful of made mustard and a little salt, a spoonful of olive-oil, one of oiled butter, or two of sour cream may be substituted, and when this is mixed smooth, put in as much vinegar as will give the proper degree of acidity to the sauce,—about two large spoon-fuls; add a little pounded lump-sugar if the flavour is liked. Put this sauce in the dish, and lay the cut herbs lightly over it; or mix them well with it, and garnish with beet-root sliced and marked, rings of the white of the eggs, young radishes, &c. Onions may be served separately on a small dish. Some *knowing* persons like grated Parmesan put to their salad and sauce.

235. *Lobster-salad.*—This is become a fashionable salad. The coral of the lobster is cut, and tastefully disposed among the white and green vegetables, so as best to contrast the colours,—and it also improves the sauce.

236. *Another.*—Dress the lobster and garnish with parsley.

237. *An Italian salad.*—Three hours before dinner, bone and chop two anchovies, mince a small eschalot, and some young cress or parsley. Mix these well in a salad-bowl, add a spoonful of olive-oil, two of vinegar, pepper at discretion, and a little made mustard. To this sauce put

very thin small slices of cold roast meat, or minced breast of cold chicken, or lobster-meat, also veal-gravy; toss them about in the sauce, and let them soak in it, or use *aspic jelly* or *remoulade*. Garnish with curled parsley, boiled white of eggs, or beet-root. Almonds, capers, pickled fruits, or fish, grated cheese of high flavour, and many things of a piquant nature, were formerly mixed with salads, and are still used abroad in their composition. —*Obs*. Salads are likewise compounded of cold oysters, salmon, soles, skate, trout, and cray-fish; but these Gothic mixtures are seldom or never touched.

238. *Boiled salad.*—This, if less agreeable, is more safe than crude vegetables, however they may be compounded. The sauce may be the same as for *English salad*, but the vegetables are previously dressed. It is made of dressed celery, French beans, or cauliflowers. Sprinkle some chopped raw lettuce or endive over it. The jelly of roast veal or lamb blends well with salads instead of oil or cream, and is preferred by many persons. Salad-sauce may be rendered more poignant by the addition of cayenne, minced onion, or eschalot, and any of the herb-flavoured vinegars.

239. A WINTER SALAD.

THE basis of this is the same as any other salad, with the substitution of endive, celery, and beet-root pickled, also pickled red cabbage, hard-boiled yolks, &c.—*Obs*. A very pretty winter salad may be arranged by contrasting the colours, garnishing with the beet-root in slices, and the red cabbage and white celery, cut in delicate straws. Plovers' and sea-birds' eggs are used to ornament salads; and are admired for their *opal* and pearly tints. Salads admit of many elegant decorations of contrasted colour; as scraped horseradish, squirted fairy butter, young radishes, &c. &c.

240. TO DRESS CUCUMBERS.

PARE and slice the cucumbers thin, and with a penknife cut the slices into small skeins (the length of the dish), wound up. Dress these along the dish, and pour vinegar over. Cucumbers thus cut may be served over beet-root sliced. Cucumbers in skeins may also be served cooked.

241. INDIAN SALADO.

SLICE two cucumbers without seeds, a Spanish onion, two rennets, and two chilies. Season with pepper and salt, and stir together, and add two spoonfuls of vinegar, and three of salad oil. The cut meat of a lobster, or of crabs' claws, may be put to this, and cayenne. The onion may be omitted at pleasure.

242. TO PRESERVE ROOTS AND VEGETABLES.

POTATOES are of most consequence. Choose them of the middle-size, fresh from the mould, or the store-pit. Yellow kidneys are for the earlier part of the season; and red or calico potatoes for the spring months, as these keep best late in the year. Keep them in a cellar below ground, where the temperature is pretty equal, and never very low, and defend them well from frost and currents of air with straw or mats. In spring, have them turned over, and the growths carefully picked away, which process must be again repeated later in the season. Keep *carrots* and *turnips, parsnips,* and *beet-roots,* with their native mould about them, in dry sand: *onions* are best preserved strung, or the small ones in nets, in a cool but not a damp place. Use the thick-necked spongy ones first; they may have the germ taken out, with a larding-pin, and then be strung up, or they may be kiln-dried. *Parsley* may be picked, and dried by tying it in bundles to a rope, or drying it in a cool oven; and so may other herbs. French beans will keep by salting and closing them up, and soaking them before they are dressed; but they lose a good deal of their flavour and colour. Cucumbers, kidney-beans, endive, &c., may be parboiled and kept closed up in strong pickle; soaking them to freshen them before they are dressed. *Green pease* are shelled, scalded repeatedly, drained, dried in cloths, spread on plates, and put in a cool oven, and afterwards hung up in paper bags to harden; soak them before they are used. After all this trouble they are but the ghosts of green pease. They may also be scalded, bottled, covered with clarified butter, corked up, and the corks dipped in rosin; but nothing will preserve the sweet flavour and marrowy substance of the young pea. When to be used boil with a bit of sugar. Cabbages, lettuce, greens, endive, leeks, cauliflower, &c. if carefully removed in dry weather from the ground, without injuring the roots too much, and laid in a cold cellar, or on a stone floor, covering the roots with earth or sand, will keep through the winter, even when the frost might destroy them if left in the garden; and this we conceive the best mode of preservation.—*Obs.* Vegetables a little touched by frost may be recovered by soaking in water.

243. TO STORE FRUITS OF DIFFERENT KINDS.

THIS art is now so well understood, that in spring and early summer, apples, and even pears, are seen as plump and fresh as in the autumn when they were gathered.

Gather the fruits when just ready to drop off easily, but not over-ripe,—do not bruise the fruit in gathering, —lay it to sweat* for a week in heaps, covered with mats, or flannels, &c. Wipe each apple or pear, one by one, and wrap in paper:—place them in glazed stoneware gallon jars, bedded in fine sifted sand, dried in an oven: —fill up the jars with sand, which will imbibe the moisture that might injure the fruit. If fruit is frozen, as in all cases of things frozen, steep it in cold water, that it may *thaw* gradually. Pack each sort by itself, label the jars and close them, and keep them in an airy loft, but protect from frost by covering them with a thick cloth.

N.B.—Eggs, fruit, and other things packed in straw, acquire a very musty flavour. This, which is called being *straw-tasted*, may be avoided by using dried fern for packing.

244. HERBS TO DRY FOR KITCHEN USE.

THE herbs which are generally kept dry, are mint, knotted marjoram, thyme, sweet basil, and sage; gather them when ripe, and put in a cool oven, screen, or drying stove; dry them quickly, but do not burn them; when dry rub the leaves off the stalks: pound, sift, and keep them in bottles well corked.

Note.—They are much better flavoured than when dried in the sun.

---

* Some modern horticulturists disapprove of *sweating* fruit.

245. TO SALT VEGETABLES.

FRENCH beans, artichokes, samphire, and olives, may be kept for a long time in a strong brine, taking care that they are kept completely covered.

246. TO SALT BARBERRIES.

GATHER fine full clusters before they are quite ripe. Pick away any dead leaves and injured berries, and keep the clusters in salt and water in jars well covered. When the pickle begins to ferment change it. Red currants may be kept as above.

CHAPTER VIII.

SAUCES, ESSENCES, AND CONDIMENTS.

> "Elements! each other greeting,
> Gifts and Powers attend your meeting!"
>
> *Pirate.*

"IT is the duty of a good sauce," says one of the most recondite of modern gastrologers, the Editor of the *Almanach des Gourmands*, "to insinuate itself all round the maxillary glands, and call into activity each ramification of the palatic organs. If it be not *relishing*, it is incapable of producing this effect, and if too *piquant*, it will deaden instead of exciting those titillations of tongue and vibrations of palate, which can only be produced by the most accomplished philosophers of the mouth on the well-trained palate of the refined *gourmand*." This, we think, is a tolerably correct definition of what a well-compounded sauce ought to be.

The French, among our other insular distinctions, speak of us as a nation "with twenty religions and only one sauce,"—parsley and butter, by the way, is this national relish,—and unquestionably English cookery, like English manners, has ever been much simpler than that of our neighbours. Modern cookery too, like modern dress, is stripped of many of its original tag-rag fripperies. We have laid aside lace and embroidery, save upon occasions of high ceremonial, and, at the same time, all *omne-gatherum* compound sauces and ragouts, with a smack of everything. Yet the human form and the human palate have not lost by this revolution. The harmonies of flavours, the affinities and coherence of tastes, and the art of blending and of opposing relishes, were never so well understood as now; and the modern kitchen still affords, in sufficient variety, the sharp, the pungent, the sweet, the acid, the spicy, the aromatic, and the nutty flavours, of which to compound mild, savoury, or piquant sauces, though a host of ingredients are laid aside.

The elegance of a table, as opposed to mere lumbering sumptuousness, or vulgar luxury, is perhaps best discovered in the adaptation of the sauces to the meats served, and in their proper preparation and attractive appearance. *Plain sauces* ought to have, as their name imports, a plain but decided character; so ought the sweet and the savoury. *All sauces should be served hot,* —a matter too often neglected in the hurry of dishing and serving dinner. Sauces with which cream and eggs are mixed must be diligently stirred after these ingredients are added, to prevent their curdling, and suffered to warm through, but not to boil. The same care must be taken in mixing capers and all acid pickles in sauce. Though it is wilful waste to put wine, catsup, lemon-juice, aromatic spices, and other expensive ingredients, into sauces for more than the time necessary to extract the flavour, yet, on the other hand, these things must be infused or boiled long enough to be properly blended, both in substance and flavour, with the basis of the sauce. The previous concoction must also be duly attended to, whether at the mincing-board, in the mortar, or sauce-pan. As a general rule, brown sauces should be thinner than white. Cream should be boiled before it is mixed with any soup or sauce.

The receipts we have given in this important branch of the art are ample, various, and circumstantial, and have been diligently considered. We do not, however, pretend, either in this chapter or any other, to fix the precise quantities of ingredients; but we have tried to hit the medium, as far as was possible in a matter where men differ so widely and intolerantly, that—

> "The very dish one relishes the best,
> Is tasteless or abomination to the rest."

The basis, or, more correctly, the vehicle of most English sauces, is *butter*, whether melted, oiled, browned, or burnt; or *gravy*, whether clear, brown, or thickened; also water, milk, cream, and wine, or some substitute. A numerous class of sauces is composed of vegetables and green fruits, another of shell-fish, and a third of meat-gravy. There are still other sauces compounded of an admixture of many or all of these ingredients. It will simplify arrangement to take these in regular order; though the philosophers of the kitchen, it must be owned, shake themselves tolerably free of the trammels of system.

247. TO MELT BUTTER PLAIN, *or for sauces.*

BREAK the butter in small bits, and put it into a small sauce-pan, (kept for this and other delicate uses,) with either cream, sweet milk, or water, or a mixture of them, in the proportion of a dessert-spoonful to the ounce of butter. Dredge fine wheat flour or potato-flour over this, and, holding the vessel over the fire, toss it quickly round, till the butter melts into the consistence of a very thick cream. Let it boil up and no more. This is the *sauce blanche.* Some French cooks add a very little vinegar and nutmeg: *Another way*—Make a thick batter of flour with a wine-glassful of water, and six ounces of butter broken. Stir this quickly till it comes to the boiling point.—*Obs.* A spoonful of catsup, and a little vinegar flavoured or plain, converts this *extempore* into a good fish-sauce;—a tea-spoonful of mustard, where suitable, will heighten the relish.

Butter will, from its bad quality, sometimes run to oil in spite of the most vigilant cook. In this case it is the practice to put a little cold water to it, and to pour it rapidly backwards and forwards from the sauce-pan into a basin, which will partially restore it. Melted butter to be mixed with flavoured vinegars, catsups, and thin essences, should be made very thick, and melted with water and flour only, as milk is apt to coagulate; and the vinegars, capers, pickles, &c., must be carefully stirred in, just before the sauce is served, to prevent it from curdling. Butter, on the contrary, into which minced egg, or herbs which thicken, are to be stirred, should be thin when melted, as the other ingredients will thicken it.—*To clarify butter*, see page 124.⋆

248. *Oiled Butter*.—Set the sauce-pan over a slow fire, or at the side of it, and it will oil of itself. Let it settle, and pour it from the milky sediment.

249. *To brown or burn Butter*.—Put a large piece of butter into a small frying-pan, and toss it round over a brisk fire till it becomes brown. Skim it, dredge in lightly-browned flour, and stir it briskly round with an iron spoon, till it boils and is smooth. A little vinegar or lemon-juice, with cayenne, &c., makes this a good plain fish-sauce.

250. TO THICKEN BUTTER *to keep to sauce pease, vegetables, salads, &c.*

COVER the bottom of a wide stew-pan with water. Put to it ten ounces of butter, and let it gradually melt. Take the stew-pan off the fire, and toss it round till the butter becomes smooth. When to be used, heat it in your melting-pan. This and oiled butter answer well for salads to those who dislike oil.

251. *Parsley and Butter*.—Pick and wash the parsley; tie it up in a bundle, and boil it in salt and water, for five minutes if young, or seven if old or preserved; drain it, and, cutting off the stalks, mince the leaves very fine, and stir about a table-spoonful into three ounces of melted butter. This simple English sauce is used with a variety of dishes.

⋆ Butter will sometimes run to oil in spite of the most attentive and dexterous cookery from its own bad quality. Still oftener it is spoiled by ignorance or carelessness. The simple chemical process of making the creamy compound called "volatile liniment," commonly used in cases of sore throat, is familiar to most people. It is merely adding the necessary quantity of hartshorn to sweet oil. By a similar process oiled butter may be recovered, where the appearance of the butter is a matter of more importance than its qualities.

To recover oiled Butter.—Add a little salt of tartar, kept in a close stopt vial for this purpose, to the oiled butter first poured from the milky sediment. Shake them up together, and the desired creamy appearance will be obtained.

252. *To melt butter with cream.*—Melt a half-pound of butter well broken in a glassful of sweet cream. Stir it constantly. This is used for lobster or oyster sauces, for turbot, turkey, &c. when the sauce is to be presented in the very highest style of cookery.

ROUX,* BROWN AND WHITE, TO THICKEN SAUCES, &C.

253. *White Roux.*—Melt some good butter slowly, and stir into it, over embers, the best sifted flour, till it is as thick as a thin but firm paste. Stir it over a slow fire for a quarter of an hour, but do not let it get brown, —a pound of butter will take in nearly a pound of flour.

254. *Brown Roux.*—Melt what quantity of butter you like, very slowly. Stir into this *browned flour*, till of a proper consistence. Small cooking will make the *roux* if the flour is browned previously; and this will prevent the danger of the empyreumatic flavour, which, by the common methods, and even by this French method, is inseparable from browning made of butter.† Pour the *Roux* into an earthen dish, and keep it for use. This thickening will keep a good while, but we conceive the method of having the flour ready *browned* better, as it will keep for ever.

255. *Brown thickening for sauces, ragouts, &c., another way.*—To make thickening properly is one of the most delicate offices of the cook, and a sort of test of skill.‡ It is circumstantially explained, as this is a receipt of general application.

---

* This thickening, or *roux*, as the French term it, comes in place of our *extempore* butter kneaded in flour, and of our hastily-made browning—"a wretched resource," of which the mere name drives a French cook in England *au desespoir*. Jesting apart, the prepared *roux* is certainly superior to our insular, off-hand, kneaded flour, which often communicates a *musty* flavour, at any rate an unpleasant taste of flour to the sauce thickened. We gladly and gratefully adopt the French *Roux*, and warmly recommend it.—P.T.

† We find no account of this simple and useful preparation in the many volumes of cookery which we have perused, though it highly merits the attention of the cook. Where *browning* or *brown thickening* is required for any dish, browned flour may be employed with much advantage. It is easily prepared by laying a quantity of flour on a plate, and placing it in an oven, or before the fire, till it takes the shade desired; for it may be of any tint, from that of cinnamon to the deepness of coffee. Turn it occasionally, that it may colour equally, and keep for use.

‡ We have heard that the button-hole of a *white waistcoat* is what

Throw slices of clarified or good fresh butter into a shallow frying-pan; toss it about briskly till it become of a fine amber colour; skim off the frothy bubbles that float on the surface, and from a dredging-box shake in slightly-browned flour, stirring the composition briskly and incessantly till it become perfectly smooth, and of the consistence of a thick batter. It must be stirred for at least fifteen minutes. Thickening is best when recently made; but it will keep for ten days if poured into small jars, and the surface not broken. Put a little of the sauce to it, and mix by degrees, as in making mustard, till they are thoroughly incorporated. A dessert-spoonful will *thicken* a sauce-tureen of gravy. In spite of the most vigilant attention, particles of fatty and other matters will sometimes, to the great mortification of the cook, be seen floating in sauce. To remove this, throw a glassful of lukewarm water into the thickened sauce, and set the sauce-pan on the hearth, which will drive those crude particles to the top, when they can be removed, and the cook, in serving up a transparent sauce, reap the reward of her toils. This mode of refining may also be employed for soups and white sauces; but be it remembered, that the watery ordeal, while it contributes to the beauty, injures the flavour of those *gusty* compositions. The gravy served with roast ducks, hare, wild-fowl, goose, &c. &c. if clear is generally little better than amber-coloured water. If gravy is required with these roasts, we would advise that the contents of the dripping-pan be strained, (presuming that the first rank greasy droppings of goose, &c. are laid aside,) and thickened with brown *roux*, or potato, or rice-flour, with a little walnut pickle, or catsup. The eye admires clear gravy, (often little more than coloured water,) the palate relishes a savoury thickened gravy, like the above.

---

shews the accomplished tailor; and we know that in our burghs a young member of the worshipful craft of baxters cannot attain burghal honours till he has proved his skill by a "sey-puddin," *pried* and approved by the elder brethren. *Thickening* holds the same distinguished rank in the higher mystery of which we treat.

256. THE BEST BEEF-GRAVY, OR JUS DE BŒUF, *the basis of many sauces for made-dishes.*

FOR *strong gravy* we would once more recommend, in place of all other parts of the animal, the lean and juicy. The gelatinous pieces are better adapted for soup than gravy, which is, in fact, the concentrated *extract* of beef. Ox-kidney is sometimes employed from motives of economy: it makes a strong-flavoured and rich-coloured, but not a very delicate gravy. Cut the gravy-beef, from four to eight pounds, according to the degree of strength and the quantity wanted, into thin slices; score them roughly, and placing a thick slice of lean undressed bacon, in a thick-bottomed stew-pot, lay the cut meat over it, with a few bits of butter, or a cupful of fresh gravy. Slice over this a carrot, a couple of onions, a little eschalot, a head of celery, and, if a high-flavoured gravy for ragouts be wanted, a couple of bay-leaves, and a bundle of sweet herbs of suitable size. Let the stew-pot be deep and very close-covered. Set it over a sharp fire to catch and brown, and shake it occasionally to prevent the meat from sticking. When the meat is drained on both sides, and the juices partially drawn out, which will take about half an hour, put in the proper quantity of boiling water, allowing a little for waste. Skim it well,—check the boil with cold water, and skim it again and again if needful,—wipe the edges of the stew-pot and lid, and, covering close, let the gravy simmer for three hours by the fire. Strain into an earthen or stone vessel, and keep it in a dry, cool place.—See *Consommés, French Cookery.*

257. SAVOURY BROWN GRAVY, *for brown sauces, ragouts, and fricassees.*

THIS brown savoury gravy, or elementary brown sauce, we conceive equivalent to the *Grand Espagnole* or *Italienne rousse* of the French kitchen, for every useful purpose. Line the stew-pan with slices of ham or bacon, or in their place, four or five pounds of a fillet of veal cut in slices, and moisten it with a ladleful or two of good broth, with two carrots and two onions, or double the number, if you for future purposes wish their flavour. The juices will soon form a *glaze*. Take the stew-pan off the fire, and prick the meat all over, to obtain all the juices; moisten with any broth you have made of gelatinous meat, as poultry, game, rabbits; season with a faggot of herbs, (parsley and young onions especially) and mushrooms, if you have them; to this add (according to your own judgment) two cloves, a bay-leaf, a bit of garlic, and a head of celery. When ready, allow this or any gravy to settle a few minutes before straining. This gravy may be very conveniently made *jugged*. Cut down all the ingredients, and put them in a jar; cover it close, and set it in an oven or over a stove for a half-hour; add boiling water, and let the preparation *stove* slowly till wanted. This gravy may be varied and enriched in many ways, by the addition of red wines, flavoured vinegars, eschalot, tarragon, mushrooms, curry-powder, truffles and morells, artichoke-bottoms, anchovy, pickled oysters; in short, whatever is best fitted to improve and heighten the relish of the dish it is to sauce. Thicken it with brown thickening when wanted.

N.B.—Eschalot, a lemon sliced, a bay-leaf, two cloves, and a gill of eating-oil, stewed in a ladleful of the above gravy, with pepper, cayenne, and a glass of white wine, make the *Italienne rousse*; or the *Italienne blanche* is made by using a white instead of a brown savoury gravy.

258. WHITE GRAVY-SAUCE, *the French velouté, or white cullis, the basis of white sauces for vegetables and white fricassees, &c.*

PUT a good piece of the best end of a knuckle of veal into a very well-tinned stew-pan, with some good ham, some beef cut to pieces, and whatever trimmings of game or poultry the larder affords. Moisten this with strong broth, put to it three carrots and four onions, parsley, and thyme, some chopped mushrooms, but no lemon or acid of any kind. Let the meat sweat, but not brown, and prick it to let the juices flow. When the knuckle is done well enough to be served at table, skim the sauce; strain through a lawn sieve; boil it again till well reduced, and add to it, on the fire, as much *roux blanche*, or white thickening, ready prepared, as will make it of a proper consistence, rather thick than otherwise, as it can easily be thinned. Now skim it, and boil it once more, stirring it, and lifting it in a spoon, and letting it fall continually, to make it smooth and fine; do this till it cool. This *skinking* process, which the French call to *vanner* a sauce, has no name in English.

N.B.—M. Ude, a French professor, substitutes cream for *roux blanche* in this sauce, and says it is a great improvement. In appearance it certainly must be so.

259. *Fennel and butter, basil, burnet, chervil, tarragon, cress*, and *butter*, are all prepared for sauce, according to the receipt No. 251.—*Obs*. Tarragon, basil, chervil, rocambole, and burnet, used as parsley and butter, give dishes a smack of foreign cookery. We would, however, recommend a very cautious use of burnet and tarragon, unless the taste of those for whom the sauces are prepared be previously ascertained. Less of these high-flavoured herbs should be employed than of parsley; and it is a good method always to mix a little of this herb with fennel, which is too powerful by itself. *Celery* or *parsley seeds* boiled in the water in which butter is melted will give their flavour when the fresh vegetables cannot be got; they must be strained off. The flavour of these herbs, where acids are admissible in the sauce, may be communicated in a more elegant form to melted butter by the vinegars with which they are tinctured.

260. *Onion-sauce.*—Peel and throw a dozen of onions into salt and water to prevent their blackening. Boil them in plenty of water, and, if they are very acrid, change the water; chop them fine, and with a wooden spoon press them through a sieve; stir them into thin melted butter, and heat up the sauce: or roast the onions, and then pulp them.—*Obs*. For tripe, made mustard may be mixed with this sauce: for smothering rabbits, boiled ducks, &c. cream may be added. Some cooks use veal or clear beef gravy instead of melted butter, and others mash a turnip, or apple, or white beet, along with the onions where the flavour is thought too strong. *Young onions*, when very small, may be served whole in the sauce. The French make onion-sauce with cream or Bechamel as the basis, and season with nutmeg, or mace, and a bay-leaf.

261. *Brown Onion-Sauce.*—This is a highly-relishing sauce, suitable to many different dishes, and a general

favourite with thorough-bred gourmands. Slice large mild Spanish onions, brown them in butter over a slow fire, add good brown gravy, pepper, salt, cayenne, and a bit of butter rolled in brown flour. Skim this, and put in a half-glass of Burgundy, claret, or port, the same quantity of mushroom-catsup; or, if more suitable to the dish the sauce is to accompany, a dessert-spoonful of walnut-pickle, or eschalot-vinegar, to give *piquance*; also essence of ham.—*Obs*. This standard sauce is susceptible of many variations. It may be flavoured with any pungent vinegar, rendered more *poignant* by a little minced eschalot, onion, or made mustard; or more mild by using celery, turnip, or cucumber, instead of one-half of the onions. Onion-sauce, both kinds, may be made at once by stirring small cooked onions into Bechamel or into brown-sauce.

262. *To dress Onions for garnishing, and for bouilli, &c.*—Top and tail small firm silver onions; blanch and peel them; stew them in good broth till they look clear and pulpy.—*Obs*. If to be browned, do not blanch, but at once fry them. If for garnishing *bouilli*, use larger onions; put fire over the stew-pan, and let them fall to a glaze. Pour a little broth into the pan to float off the glaze, which must be poured over the beef. If the onions are not very mild, put a bit of sugar to the broth.

263. *Sage and onion sauce*.—Chop together a couple of onions and eight sprigs of sage; stew them in water with salt, and in a few minutes add bread-crumbs; drain off a little of the water when they are tender, and beat up and stir in melted butter, pepper, and, if for goose-stuffing, a little flour or more crumbs.

264. *Eschalot-sauce*.—Chop of eschalot what will fill a desert-spoon; give this a scald with hot water in a sauce-pan, drain and add a half-pint of good gravy or melted butter, pepper, and salt, and, when done, a large spoonful of vinegar. The eschalots stewed in mutton-broth, with a little butter rolled in flour, and some vinegar, make an excellent sauce for boiled mutton. *Eschalot-sauce* may be made as directed in No. 251 (*Parsley and butter*), by merely stirring a little eschalot-vinegar, or eschalot-wine, into melted butter, with salt; and for roast meat or poultry this is more elegant than sauce of the chopped root. *Carrier sauce* for

mutton is made by boiling chopped eschalots in gravy, sharpened with vinegar, and seasoned with pepper and salt. *Eschalot* enters largely into the composition of most of the high-flavoured compound store sauces, sold by Butler, Burgess, &c.

265. *Garlic-sauce.*—Make this with a spoonful of garlic-vinegar stirred into a half-pint of melted butter; or chop and pound in a mortar two cloves of garlic with a bit of butter, or a very little oil, and, rubbing the paste through a sieve, simmer it in the butter.

266. *Spanish garlic-sauce.*—Slice a pound of gravy-beef and a quarter-pound of ham into thin bits, and lay them in a small stew-pan, with four cloves of garlic, a carrot sliced, and a bit of butter; brown these over a very slow fire, turning them to draw out their juices. When browned, put in a quart of clear broth, a faggot of herbs, a little butter rolled in brown flour, four bruised cloves, and a little cayenne; let this simmer for a long time; skim off the fat, and strain the gravy, which should be reduced nearly to a pint.—*Obs.* This is rather an overpowering sauce for English palates, but it is much relished abroad,* and by middle-aged travelled gourmands at home.

267. MUSHROOM-SAUCE, WHITE, *for fowls, veal, rabbits, &c.*—Wash and pick a large breakfast-cupful of small button-mushrooms; take off the leathery skin, and stew them in veal-gravy, with pepper, cayenne, mace, nutmeg, salt, and a piece of butter rolled in a good deal of flour or arrow-root to thicken, as the abounding gravy of the mushrooms makes this dish take a good deal of thickening. Stew till tender, stirring them now and then, and pour the sauce over the fowls. Those who like a high relish of mushroom may add a spoonful of mushroom-gravy, drawn off by salting a few for a night, or a little mushroom-powder.—*Obs.* The mushrooms may be stewed in thin cream, and seasoned and thickened as above. Mushrooms pickled white may

---

* The invention of the following garlic-sauce is attributed to Mr. MICHAEL KELLY, a musical composer of some celebrity, and possessed moreover of some skill, it appears, in the "Harmonies of Meats."— "For boiled tripe, cow-heels, or calf's-head, take a spoonful of garlic-vinegar and a tea-spoonful of made mustard, brown sugar, and black pepper, stir these into a half-pint of oiled butter."

supply the place of the fresh for this sauce. Lay them in milk for a little, and add some catsup to the sauce if you do not regard the colour.—See *French Mushroom-sauce*.

268. CELERY-SAUCE, WHITE, *for boiled fowls, turkey, &c.*—Wash, pare, and cut down in thin slices, about two inches long, a good head of celery, the younger the better. Blanch or boil it till tender in weak broth or water, and season with pounded mace, nutmeg, grated white pepper, and salt. Thicken with a good piece of butter kneaded in flour. The juice of a lemon is a great improvement, or, for less delicate purposes, a little lemon-pickle.—*Obs.* French cooks stew the celery with suet or fat bacon, and use very little seasoning, which they justly think unsuitable, celery possessing so decided a flavour of its own.

269. *Brown celery-sauce.*—Stew and season as in the receipt 268, thicken with browned flour, and add a glass of red wine and a spoonful of catsup.

270. *Horseradish-sauce, white and brown.*—Grate a tea-cupful of horseradish if for a white sauce, add bread-crumbs and salt, put to this vinegar. For *Brown-sauce* stir the horseradish in brown gravy, and add a little vinegar, salt, sugar, and a dessert-spoonful of mustard; *or* use vinegar alone without gravy.

271. MINT-SAUCE *for hot or cold roast lamb.*—Wash a small quantity of young mint; pick off the leaves, and mince them very fine, and mix them in the sauce-boat with grated sugar and good white vinegar to taste.

272. FOR CUCUMBER-SAUCE, see *Stewed cucumbers*, p. 213.

273. *Sorrel-sauce.*—Stew two handfuls of blanched sorrel very slowly, with a good bit of butter oiled. Season it with pepper, salt, and cayenne; add a little strong gravy, and beat it well. Make it very hot, and serve below lamb, veal, sweetbreads, &c.—See No. 212.

274. *Tomata-sauce.*—Take from ten to fifteen ripe tomatas, or fewer, according to the size; put them into a jar, and set it in a cool oven. When they are soft, take off the skins, pick out the seeds, and mix the pulp with a capsicum, a clove of garlic, and a very little vinegar, ginger, cayenne, white pepper, and salt; pulp this through a sieve, and simmer it for a few minutes. Beet-root juice is used to improve the colour. An

imitation of tomata-sauce is made by roasted apples, properly seasoned and coloured with turmeric.—*Obs*. In this sauce French cooks stew an onion, a piece of ham, a sprig of thyme, and a bay-leaf, and use top-fat, or a rich cullis, to moisten the ingredients. Good practice.

275. *Apple-sauce*.—Pare, core, and slice four or five juicy baking apples, and roast them; or boil them in a sauce-pan, with a little water to keep them from burning, and a bit of lemon-peel and sugar to taste. Let them stew very slowly, taking care they do not burn, and when quite soft, pour off the moisture, and beat them up with pounded sugar to taste, and a small bit of butter. Bread may be added. If for goose or pig, much sugar is objectionable.

276. *Gooseberry-sauce*.—Clip away the tops and tails of a breakfast-cupful of small green gooseberries; scald them, drain them, and stir them into melted butter, with a little sorrel-juice or vinegar. A little ginger may be added; or the scalded gooseberries may be served mashed with sugar and seasonings.

277. *Caper-sauce*.—Take two table-spoonfuls of capers and a little vinegar. Mince the one-half, and stir the whole of them into a half-pint of melted butter, or of strong thickened gravy. To prevent the butter from oiling, stir the sauce for some time. When wanted very poignant, lemon-juice may be added to this simple and tasteful sauce, or it may be flavoured with tarragon or burnet vinegar, instead of plain vinegar. If for fish, as skate, &c. a little essence of anchovy will be found an improvement, with pepper and salt to taste.

278. *Mock caper-sauce* is made of gherkins or nasturtiums cut in bits, with lemon-juice and melted butter; and also radish seed-pods.

279. *Bechamel, or white sauce*.—Cut two pounds of the lean of a breast or knuckle of white veal, and a quarter-pound of lean fresh bacon, into small bits. Melt some butter in a well-tinned deep stew-pan, and put in the meat to draw a little, and to whiten, not to brown. Mix two spoonfuls of potato-flour or fine rice-flour very smooth with fair water, and then put in a quart of clear broth made of veal, or as much pure water or milk. Let this stew very gently with the meat over a chafing-dish, or by the side of the fire, for an hour and a half,

having first seasoned it with a tea-spoonful of white peppercorns, an onion, and a few sprigs of parsley, lemon-thyme, and a bit of lemon-peel. Let the sauce settle, strain it, and stir in rich sweet cream. Bring it to boil, and strain it once more.—*Obs*. A cheaper white sauce to pour over boiled fowls may be made of broth and sweet milk, thickened and seasoned as above, and the yolk of an egg well beat stirred briskly into it when just ready. A few mushrooms will improve this sauce if for fowls. The Bechamel, before the cream is added, is a *white* cullis, fit for white ragouts, fricassees, and hashes of veal. It is also a rich basis for all savoury white sauces, and for dressed vegetables.—See *à la Bechamel, French Cookery*.

280. *Vinegaret for cold meat or fowl.*—Chop young mint, parsley, and eschalot together, and mix them up with salt, oil, and good vinegar.

280. *Sauce à la Tartare.*—Add to vinegaret, chervil and tarragon, with a little made mustard.

282. *Lemon-sauce.*—Pare a lemon, taking off all the white part; cut it in thick slices, pick out the seeds, and on a plate cut the slices into dice, and mix them with melted butter, taking care to stir it up lest it oil.

283. *Miser's sauce.*—Chop two onions, and mix them with pepper, salt, vinegar, and a little melted butter. When made with oil and young onions, add a little parsley and scraped horseradish.

284. Poor Man's Sauce, *to serve with turkey poults or grilled birds,—a French sauce.*—Mince a little parsley and a few eschalots. Stew this in broth or water, and add vinegar and peppercorns.

285. *Carach-sauce.*—Mix pounded garlic, cayenne, soy, and walnut-pickle in good vinegar.

OTHER SAUCES FOR POULTRY AND GAME.

Most of the common sauces for poultry have already been described. These are principally egg-sauce, bread-sauce, rice-sauce, lemon-sauce, celery-sauce, gooseberry-sauce, &c. &c.; but a few of the more rich and elegant still remain to be given.

286. *Bread-sauce.*—Put grated crumbs into a small sauce-pan, and pour a little of the liquor in which mutton, veal, or fowls has been boiled over this. When it has soaked, simmer with a sliced onion, white peppercorns,

salt, and mace; take out the onion, and peppercorns, and add melted butter or cream.

287. *Rice-sauce.*—Stew two ounces of rice in milk, with an onion, white peppercorns, and a little salt. Take out the peppercorns and onions, and rub the rice through a colander. Heat this up with more milk or cream, and flavour it to taste. This looks whiter, but it is not so light as bread-sauce. Butter may be put to it.

288. *Egg sauce for salt fish, roasted poultry, &c.*— Boil three or four eggs for a quarter of an hour. Dip them in cold water, and roll them quickly under your hand to make the shell come easily off. Cut the yolks by themselves into little half-inch cubes, and cut the white of one egg in the same manner. Stir first the white and then the yolks into thinnish melted butter in the tureen.—*For sauces to fish-pies*, see page 193.

289. PLEYDEL'S *Sauce for game, or orange gravy.*— A half-pint of claret, and the same quantity of good brown gravy, see page 233.— Make the gravy boil, put the wine to it, with pepper, salt, cayenne, and the juice of two Seville oranges, or one orange and a lemon. Let them simmer for a few minutes, and pouring some over the game, serve the rest very hot in a sauce-boat.—*Obs.* This makes an elegant sauce for any sort of birds. A French cook would use the thin rind or zest of the lemon and less of the juice.

290. PLEYDEL'S *Sauce for wild duck, teal, pidgeons, &c.*—To a large quarter-pint of savoury brown gravy, put a glass of claret or port, pepper, salt, cayenne, and a dessert-spoonful of finely-shred eschalot. Make this hot, and pour it over the ducks.—*Obs.* In making this sauce for the oily, rank, and fishy-tasted water-fowl, made mustard may be added, and a higher seasoning of eschalot and onion, with walnut-pickle, or a little essence of anchovy. Wild geese, solan geese, mallards, &c. require a very pungent sauce.

291. Dr. HUNTER'S *Sauce for cold partridge, or cold meat of any kind.*—Beat up the yolk of a hard egg with oil and vinegar; add a little anchovy-liquor, some cayenne pepper, salt, parsley, and eschalot, both chopped small.—*Obs.* This is a good extemporaneous sauce, and of small price. It is excellent for cold lobster.

292. REDGILL'S SAUCE *for stubble goose, roasted pork, or pork chops, also called* Dr. HUNTER'S SAUCE.—Make a quarter-pint, or rather more, of savoury brown gravy, or melted butter very hot; thicken it with a little browned flour, and put to it a large glass of claret or port wine, a large tea-spoonful of made mustard, a little salt, pepper, and cayenne. Simmer it a few minutes, and serve it very hot.—*Obs.* For wine may be substituted mushroom or walnut pickle occasionally, and a little chopped green sage may be added. Hard yolks of eggs rubbed smooth make a good variety of the above.

293. SAUCE ROBERT, *for pork cutlets, geese, &c.*— Brown four or five onions very finely shred, in a small sauce-pan, with a good piece of butter. When of a fine rich brown, mix in a table-spoonful of browned flour, one of mushroom-catsup, and another of red wine, with a half-pint of broth, a salt-spoonful of pepper, and one of salt, and a tea-spoonful of made mustard, with the juice of a lemon, or a dessert-spoonful of Chili vinegar.—*Obs.* This sauce is named after the inventor, as we say, cutlets *Maintenon,* or *Sandwiches.* It is a very favourite sauce. Tarragon vinegar will give it the flavour of the French kitchen, which to some gourmands may be a recommendation even as an accompaniment to plain English fare. This sauce is eaten with rump steaks, whether stewed or broiled. Pour it hot over them, and garnish with scraped horseradish, or fried parsley.

294. A CHEAP WHITE SAUCE, *for fricasseed rabbits fowls, veal, whitings, &c.*

To a half-pint of the liquor in which fowls, veal, or trimmings of these have been boiled, put a bit of lemon-peel, an onion sliced, a few white peppercorns, a little pounded mace and nutmeg, and a small bunch of lemon-thyme, basil, and parsley. When the sauce is well flavoured, strain it, add a little rich cream, a bit of butter rolled in flour, and, last of all, a squeeze of lemon, taking care to stir the sauce lest the cream curdle. Pour it over the fricassee.

295. *Lemon and liver sauce for fowls.*—Parboil the liver, having first washed and scored it; mince it very fine. Pare a lemon very thin, as if for punch; take off

the white part, and cut the lemon into small dice, pick-ing out the seeds. Mince about a fourth part of the peel very fine, and put these ingredients, with a little salt, to a half-pint of melted butter. Let them heat up, but not boil, lest the butter oil.—*Obs. Liver and parsley sauce* is a good common sauce, and is made by par-boiling the parsley and liver, and, after they are separately minced, stirring them in melted butter.

296. *The Marquis's sauce for wild fowls.*—A glass of claret, a spoonful of catsup, the same of lemon-juice, a minced eschalot, a few thin slices of lemon-rind, a few grains of the best cayenne pepper, two blades of mace pounded, and a large spoonful of the essence sold at the shops under the name of *Sauce à la Russe.* Simmer these ingredients for a few minutes, and then strain them to the gravy which comes from the wild fowl in roasting. Place the fowl on a dish heated by a lamp, and cut it up, so that the gravy as it flows out may simmer with the sauce.—*Obs.* The above *amateur* preparation is very much admired. The gravy of wild fowl is often scanty; but butter, or even meat-gravy, would hurt the wild flavour. *Game-gravy* may, however, be made by *par-roasting*, and then stewing a partridge, by those who hesitate at no expense in the gratification of the palate. This *essence of game*, French artists procure by slowly stewing the partridges in a vessel closely covered, till they yield a strong *consommé*.

297. VENISON-SAUCES

VENISON may have a sweet, a sharp, or a savoury sauce. *Sharp sauce.*—A quarter-pound of the best loaf-sugar, or white candy-sugar, dissolved in a half-pint of Cham-pagne vinegar, and carefully skimmed.—*Sweet sauce.* Melt some white or red currant-jelly with a glass of white or red wine, whichever suits best in colour; or serve jelly unmelted in a small sweetmeat-glass. This sauce answers well for hare, fawn, or kid, and for roast mutton to many tastes.—*Gravy for venison.* Make a pint of gravy of trimmings of venison, or shanks of mutton, thus:—Broil the meat on a quick fire till it is browned, then stew it slowly. Skim, strain, and serve the gravy it yields, adding salt and a tea-spoonful of walnut-pickle.—*Savoury venison sauces*, see page 100. In the north of Europe a sauce of the whortleberry is used for venison.

298. TURTLE STORE-SAUCE, *to flavour ragouts, hashes, savoury patties, soups, pies, &c.*—A quarter-pint of strong mushroom-catsup, the same of basil-wine and of eschalot-wine, a large glassful of the essence of anchovies, an ounce of lemon-peel sliced thin, concrete of lemon one drachm, and the same quantity of the best cayenne. Infuse for ten days, strain off and bottle the essence, which is very powerful, and very much relished.

299. TURTLE-SAUCE, *for calf's head or feet, stewed knuckle of veal, grisiles, &c.*—To a pint of beef or veal gravy add two spoonfuls of the above turtle store-sauce, and a little essence of anchovy.

300. A STORE-SAUCE, *to flavour the gravy of steaks, chops, or roast meat.*—Infuse in a half-pint of walnut-pickle, and the same quantity of mushroom or oyster catsup, a half-ounce of Jamaica pepper in fine powder, with four grains of cayenne, half an ounce of scraped horseradish, and the same weight of minced eschalot. Let these ingredients steep ten days, and strain and bottle them. A spoonful of essence of anchovy may be added, or a little bruised mustard-seed.—*Obs.* This is a cheap and high-flavoured relish, and will be found useful at all times for seasoning either melted butter or the gravy that flows from chops, steaks, &c.

301. *Curry sauce.*—This sauce is plainly made by mixing curry-powder with melted butter. It is more generally relished if mixed in white onion-sauce; or, if wanted of high flavour, with brown onion gravy sauce. When liked more piquant, Chili vinegar may be added to the sauce.—*Obs.* Imitations of the Indian curry-powder are frequently attempted, and succeed as far as is possible, considering that some of the seeds and spices are used green in compounding the genuine powder, and that in this country they are necessarily all dried. French cooks use saffron to colour curry-sauce, boiling the saffron, and rubbing it through a search. Where a bright colour is desirable, a tincture of saffron is less offensive than an over-dose of turmeric. Saffron is often used to colour cakes, puddings, &c.; but should be used with caution.

302. A CHEAP GENERAL SAUCE *for hashes of beef and mutton.*—Make a gravy from the broken bones, gristles, and other trimmings laid aside when you cut down the meat. In this boil two onions, a faggot of parsley, or a little of the seed, a head of celery, or a little seed, a few sprigs of herbs, and a tea-spoonful of black and Jamaica peppercorns. Strain and thicken this gravy with browned flour, and season with any thing convenient and economical that can be spared; for hash, though it may be good and savoury, is understood to be a frugal dish. Pickle-liquor, whether of onions, mushrooms, oysters, or walnuts, will answer very well; so will a little catsup, or eschalot-vinegar; or a little curry-powder will cheaply give that favourite flavour to the hash. A few chopped pickled walnuts, nasturtiums, or gherkins, are employed by some cooks, though we cannot recommend hard cut pickles in any made-dish. They immediately lose their flavour when mixed with the sauce, and cause a "sharp encounter" of the teeth, which is far from desirable.—See *Hashes*, and *Sauce Hachée.*

303. WHITE HASH-SAUCE, *for veal roasted or minced, or for fowls..*—Take the bones, gristles, and white trimmings of the meat, and stew them in clear, weak broth or water, a small onion, and a good piece of thinly sliced lemon-peel, salt, a blade of mace, or a few white peppercorns. Thicken the gravy with flour or potato-starch rolled in butter, and when it is boiled quite smooth, let it settle, and strain it. A good squeeze of lemon, and a little fresh lemon-grate is the only additional seasoning we could recommend; a spoonful of good cream may be added; and for fowls, a little more mace and less acid. This may be made a *curry-hash*, by adding a small dessert-spoonful of curry-powder, and withholding part of the lemon juice and peel.

304. CUSTARD-SAUCE *for rice, bread, sago, or custard puddings, or fruit pies.*—Stir a pint of sweet cream in a very clean sauce-pan till it comes to boil. Mix into it the beat yolks of two eggs with a drop of cold cream, and some fine-pounded sugar; pour backwards and forwards from the sauce-pan to a basin to prevent curdling, and let it just come to the eve of boiling, constantly stirring it. Serve the sauce in a china

basin, and grate a little nutmeg on the top of it. Butter and flour may be added to thicken it.

305. *Caudle sauce for a plum or marrow pudding.* A glass of white wine, a half-glass of brandy or old rum, or rum-shrub, pounded sugar to taste, the grate of a lemon, and a little cinnamon, stirred into a little thickened melted butter; sprinkle a little cinnamon on the top.

306. PUDDING-SAUCE,—*a store-sauce.*—A pint of canary, sherry, or Madeira, a quarter-pint of old rum, (pine-apple is best,) or of good brandy; a quarter-pint of Curaçoa, a half ounce of good lemon-peel, the same quantity of Seville orange-peel, and half an ounce of mace. Strain it, and add a half-pint of rich clarified syrup. Bottle for use. This may be mixed with wine, cream, thin syrup, *eau sucre*, &c., for a sauce to many sorts of puddings and sweet made-dishes.

307. ESSENCE OF HAM,—*or ham-sauce.*—This may be bought in London and other large cities. In country situations, a highly-flavoured gravy, which makes a great improvement to other gravies for plain purposes, may be made by breaking ham-bones to pieces, and cutting down all the good pickings left on them. Let this just *catch* over a slow fire for a quarter of an hour, adding butter or meat-gravy, (jelly-gravy if you have it,) and stirring it lest the meat and bones burn. When the ham has been treated in this way some time, add broth, a bundle of sweet herbs, and onion and peppercorns; strain it for use.—*Obs. A few receipts for sauces will be found along with the receipts for the dishes they are to accompany. Gravy-sauce for roast-meat, pages 94–97. Sauce for tripe and cow-heel, page 90. Sauce for a pig, page 98. For roast venison, page 100. Sauce for pork-chops, page 121.—See Drappit egg—National Dishes.*

SAUCES OF SHELL-FISH, AND FISH-SAUCES.

308. LOBSTER-SAUCE, OR CRAB-SAUCE, *for turbot, &c.* —For sauce you must have a *hen*-lobster, fresh (alive if possible), and full of spawn. When boiled, pound the spawn and coral with a bit of butter, or a very little oil. In nice cookery reject the coarse outer spawn. Rub through a sieve into a sufficient quantity of

melted butter, and mix it smooth; season with cayenne. Cut the meat of the tail, &c. into small dice, and put these to the sauce, which may be heated up, but not boiled. This sauce is rendered more piquant by ancho-vies, cavice, catsup, spices, walnut or lemon-pickles, &c.; but for fresh fish it is certainly better unmixed with overpowering foreign flavours. Besides, these additions can be made *extempore* at table. A little cream may be put to this sauce, but it must be first boiled.

309. *Crab-sauce* is made nearly as above. Pick the meat from the great and small claws, and a little of the soft inside when not watery; stir this into melted butter.*—*Obs.* Lobsters for sauce may be preserved *potted*, and the live spawn may be kept in brine, or in an ice-house.—*Sauces for lobsters*, page 194. A sprinkling of the red coral rubbed through a sieve makes a pretty garnish to turbot, holibut, or other white fish, especially if they are cracked in the boiling.

310. *Sauce à l'Aurore.*—This kind of lobster-sauce is made of the spawn only. Pound the spawn with butter; rub it through a coarse sieve, and thin it with a little clear broth; season it with salt, pepper, and lemon-juice.—*Obs.* This is served in France with trout or soles.

311. *Oyster-sauce, for boiled turkey, fish, &c.*—Open the oysters when you are just ready to make the sauce; save their liquor, strain it, and put it to them, and give them a scald in it, and a soft boil. Take them up with a spoon with holes, and drain on a sieve (this is proper in pickling oysters). Let the liquor settle: pour off the sediment in melted butter; add cream enough to make it look white and nice; and, after pick-ing and *bearding* them one by one, return them into a stew-pan, in which there must be in the proportion of half a pint of very thick melted butter to two dozen of oysters, or to eighteen large cut ones. Strain the liquor over them;—or letting them come to boil, set them by the side of the fire that they may become tender; for quick boiling hardens oysters. When ready, stir in a little cream. A squeeze of lemon-juice is a simple and tasteful addition. Some cooks add mace, nutmeg, and,

---

* The inside meat of the small crabs, or cavies, makes most delicate sauce, inferior only in name to lobster-sauce.—P.T.

if for fish, anchovy, &c. when a *piquant* sauce is wanted. —*Obs*. In oyster-sauce, it is a frequent and good practice, both from reasons of economy and *palatic* motives, to serve the oysters in one sauce tureen, and melted butter in another. The quantities can then be mixed on the plate of each guest, and the oysters left be afterwards grilled, scallopped, &c. French cooks put flour and milk to oyster-sauce, and very little butter. Our English oyster-sauce is much superior.

312. *Shrimp-sauce and Cockle-sauce*.—Shell and wash the fish carefully, and boil them in very thick melted butter for a minutes. A squeeze of lemon and a little cayenne is the only addition we can recommend for shrimps, though various pungent flavours are often added to this simple, agreeable sauce.

313. *Anchovy-sauce*.—Bone and pound some anchovies very smooth with a bit of butter; stir this into thick melted butter, in the proportion of three anchovies to the half-pint:—*or* melt them in vinegar or wine.—*Obs*. This is a sauce which ought to be *piquant*; the cook is therefore at liberty to make whatever additions she pleases; —cayenne, soy, essence of anchovy, lemon-pickle, horse-radish, mustard, eschalot, nasturtiums, vinegars, in short, the whole circle of the pungent and sharp flavours may be pressed into the service. When a *compound* or *double-relish* sauce is wanted, we would recommend brown gravy-sauce, for the basis, instead of plain melted butter.

314. *Liver-sauce for fish*.—Boil the liver by itself; take away all fibres and black parts that attach to it, and pound it in a mortar. Boil it up in thin melted butter with cayenne, and sharpen with lemon-juice, or lemon cut in dice. If a higher *gout* is wanted, add soy, essence of anchovy, or catsup, instead of lemon-juice, or in addition to it.

315. *A plain sauce for fish*.—Melt some butter in water and vinegar; add the liver first boiled and chopped, and thicken with the yolk of an egg and flour. Mustard, a tea-spoonful of catsup or walnut-pickle, is a cheap pungent addition to the above.

316. *Mackerel roe sauce*.—Boil two or three soft roes; take away the filaments that hang about them, and bruise them with the yolk of an egg. Stir this

into a little thin parsley and butter, or fennel and butter, and add a little vinegar or walnut-pickle, with pepper and salt.

317. *Admiral's sauce.*—Chop an anchovy, a dozen capers, and four or five eschalots or rocamboles; simmer these in melted butter till the anchovy dissolves; season with pepper and salt; and when ready, add the juice of a lemon, and grated nutmeg.

318. *A grill sauce.*—Thicken some good brown gravy with butter and browned flour to the consistence of a batter; add to it a spoonful of walnut-catsup, the juice of a lemon, a tea-spoonful of made mustard, and a dozen chopped capers, a tea-spoonful of the essence of anchovies, a bit of eschalot finely minced, a few grains of cayenne, and a tea-spoonful of grated rind of lemon. Simmer these ingredients for a few minutes, and pouring a little hot over the grill, serve the rest in a tureen. This *compound piquant* sauce will suit several kinds of white fish, such as skate, holibut, &c. to those who like a highly-stimulating relish. It is appropriate to *devils* of all *orders*.

319. *Dutch fish-sauce.*—Equal quantities of water and vinegar, boiled, seasoned, and thickened with beat yolk of egg, and sharpened with a good squeeze of lemon; do not heat it after the egg is added, or it will curdle; but stew it like custard.

320. *An excellent store English fish-sauce.*—A half-pint of claret or red port, a half-pint of mountain or Rhenish, and another of walnut-catsup, a large glassful of walnut-pickle, the grate and juice of two lemons, a dozen well-flavoured mellow anchovies pounded and dissolved by the side of the fire, three eschalots chopped, a good relish of cayenne, four large spoonfuls of scraped horseradish, a few blades of mace, and a dessert-spoonful of mustard, rubbed down with the anchovy-liquor, of which the more you have the better. Boil this composition slowly for a few minutes, mixing in the ingredients according to the delicacy of their flavour and their solubility. Bottle it when cold in small bottles; cork them well, and dip in rosin. This is an expensive but a very rich fish-sauce. It may be made of water in which herbs may be previously boiled, and vinegar may be substituted for wine. It will keep longer if, instead of

fresh lemon-rind and juice, citric acid and dry lemon-peel are used. A tea-spoonful of the above will convert two ounces of melted butter into a well-flavoured extemporaneous sauce; or it may be mixed with the butter on the plate like essence of anchovy, soy, &c.

321. *The General's-sauce, a store-sauce for fish or meat.* —Chop six eschalots, a clove of garlic, with two bay-leaves, a few sprigs of lemon-thyme and leaves of basil, with a few bits of the peel of a Seville orange. Bruise a quarter of an ounce of mace and cloves, a half-ounce of long pepper, and add two ounces of salt, a quarter-pint of vinegar, and a pint of Madeira, with a half-glass of verjuice, and the juice of two lemons. Infuse these ingredients in a stone jar, very closely stopped, and let it stand over embers, or by the side of the fire, or in a *bain-marie*, for a night. Pour it quietly from the lees, and strain it, and bottle as other essences. This is a high compound relish, and must be used in moderation with gravy or melted butter.

322. Dr. REDGILL's *Sauce Piquant, for fish or cold meat.*—Pound a large spoonful of scraped horse-radish, four eschalots, a clove of garlic, a drachm of mustard, and one of celery-seed, with salt and a high relish of cayenne, Jamaica and black pepper. When well pounded, mix with these ingredients a half-pint of cucumber-vinegar, a quarter-pint of eschalot, and the same quantity of horseradish-vinegar. Let these infuse in a close-stopped jar by the fire for a few days, and strain, and bottle in small vials for use.

323. QUIN's* *Fish-sauce, a store-sauce.*—Two glasses of claret and two of walnut-pickle, with four of

---

* Had this great man lived in our day, he would, we think, instead of so much heavy catsup and coarse walnut-pickle, have adopted some delicately flavoured vinegar as a substitute for about the one-half of these ingredients,—such as eschalot or burnet-vinegar, or even fiery horse-radish-tincture. As a mere untravelled practical Englishman, and, moreover, of the old school, QUIN, no doubt, ranks high in the lists of gastronomy. Still he is completely distanced by many moderns, both in love for and knowledge of the science. Among the most noted of the moderns we beg to introduce our readers to Mr. ROGERSON, an enthusiast and martyr. He, as may be presumed, was educated at that University where the rudiments of palatic science are the most thoroughly impressed on the ductile organs of youth. His father, a gentleman of Gloucestershire, sent him abroad to make the grand tour, upon which journey, says our informant, young ROGERSON attended to nothing but

mushroom-catsup; six large pounded anchovies with their pickle, and six eschalots pounded; a half glass of soy, black and cayenne pepper. Let this simmer slowly by the side of the fire till the bones of the anchovies dissolve. Strain it off, and when cold bottle for use.†

324. Dr. KITCHENER's *Fish-sauce superlative, a store-sauce.*—A pint of claret, a pint of mushroom-catsup, and half a pint of walnut-pickle; four ounces of pounded anchovy, an ounce of fresh lemon-peel pared thin, and the same quantity of eschalot and scraped horseradish; an ounce of black pepper and allspice, and a drachm of cayenne, or three of curry-powder, with a drachm of celery-seed. Infuse these, in a wide-mouthed bottle closely stopped, for a fortnight, and shake the mixture every day; then strain and bottle it for use.

---

the various modes of cookery, and methods of eating and drinking luxuriously. Before his return his father died, and he entered into the possession of a very large monied fortune, and a small landed estate. He was now able to look over his notes of epicurism, and to discover where the most exquisite dishes were to be had, and the best cooks procured. He had no other servants in his house than cooks: his butler, footman, housekeeper, coachman, and grooms, were all cooks. He had three Italian cooks, one from Florence, another from Sienna, and a third from Viterbo, for dressing one dish, the *docce piccante* of Florence. He had a messenger constantly on the road between Brittany and London, to bring him the eggs of a certain sort of plover, found near St. Maloes. He has eaten a single dinner at the expense of fifty-eight pounds, though himself only sat down to it, and there were but two dishes. He counted the minutes between meals, and seemed totally absorbed in the idea, or in the action of eating, yet his stomach was very small: it was the exquisite flavour alone that he sought. In nine years he found his table dreadfully abridged by the ruin of his fortune, and himself hastening to poverty. This made him melancholy, and brought on disease. When totally ruined (having spent near £150,000), a friend gave him a guinea to keep him from starving; and he was found in a garret soon after roasting an ortolan with his own hands. We regret to add, that a few days afterwards this extraordinary youth shot himself. We hope that his notes are not lost to the *dining world*.

† Gastronomers will feel a natural desire to know what was considered the "best universal sauce in the world" in the boon days of Charles II; or at least what was accounted such by the Duke of York, who was instructed to prepare it by the Spanish ambassador. It consisted of parsley, and a dry toast pounded in a mortar with vinegar, salt, and pepper. The modern English would no more relish his Royal Highness's taste in condiments than in religion. A fashionable or cabinet dinner of the same period consisted of "a dish of marrow-bones, a leg of mutton, a dish of fowl, three pullets, and a dozen larks, all in a dish; a great tart, a neat's tongue, a dish of anchovies, a dish of prawns, and cheese." At the same period, a supper-dish, when the King supped with his mistress, Lady Castlemain, "was a chine of beef roasted."

A large spoonful of this stirred into a quarter-pint of thickened melted butter "makes," says the Doctor, "an admirable extemporaneous sauce."*—*Obs.* This will be found even more expensive than the fish-sauce of HARVEY or BURGESS; the composition of which, so far as such high mysteries are accessible to ordinary mortals, is not materially different from the piquant fish-sauces for which we have given receipts above, save that more anchovies, cavice, and probably fewer expensive seasonings and less wine are employed. The extensive sales, and the complete apparatus of these *sauce-chemists,* enable them to sell compound essences cheaper than they could be prepared in any private family.

We have been rather diffuse on the subject of fish-sauces, in the persuasion that fish, from its insipidity and softness of texture, requires savoury and stimulating accompaniments more than any other kind of food.†

STUFFINGS AND FORCEMEATS.

RECEIPTS for these are for the convenience of the cook given along with the dishes for which they are employed. See pages 85, 98, 105, 107, &c.; and fish-forcemeat, p. 188. Also *French Cookery, and Crappit Heads.*

---

325. ANCHOVY BUTTER,—*for Anchovy toasts, deviled biscuit, &c.*

BONE, wash, and pound fresh mellow anchovies in a mortar, and pressing into small potting-cans, cover them with clarified butter. If for deviled biscuit, a little cayenne may be added.—See *Aspic* and *Montpelier butter, French Cookery.*

326. ANCHOVY-POWDER, *for flavouring sauces, or sprinkling on anchovy toasts or sandwiches.*—Pound

---

* The above sauce was analyzed with great care by the Cleikum Club at sundry sittings. REDGILL approved of it in *toto,* the NABOB suggested a little more cayenne, and JEKYLL more wine and less catsup, with the elegant substitution of lemon-pickle for walnut-pickle.

† Though so many receipts are given for store-sauces, we do not, when proper sauces can be obtained fresh, recommend them either for taste or economy.

anchovies in a mortar, rub them through a hair sieve, and make them into thin cakes, with flour and a little flour of mustard. Toast the cakes very dry, rub to powder, and keep in well-stopt vials.—*Obs*. Instead of flour of mustard, citric acid and grated dry lemon-peel added when the anchovy-cakes are baked, may be more agreeable to some palates.

327. *Mushroom-powder*.—Peel large, fleshy, button-mushrooms, and cut off the stems; spread them on plates and dry them in a slow oven. When thoroughly dry, pound them with a little cayenne and pounded mace. Bottle, and keep the powder in a dry place.—*Obs*. The dried mushrooms may be kept hung up in paper-bags without pounding. A tea-spoonful of powder will give the mushroom-flavour to a tureen of soup, or to sauce for poultry, ragouts, hashes, &c. when fresh mushrooms cannot be obtained.

328. *Horseradish-powder*.—In the beginning of winter slice and dry slowly before the fire horseradish. When dry rub or pound, and bottle the powder.

329. *Essence of cayenne*.—Steep half an ounce of good cayenne in a half-pint of strong spirits for a fortnight, and strain and bottle it for use.

330. *Essence of lemon and seville orange peel*.—Rub lumps of sugar on the lemon or orange till the lumps are saturated with the yellow rind. Scrape off what is saturated, and repeat the process till all the rind is got off. Press the sugar down close, and cover it up.—*Obs*. *Essence of seville orange* makes a fragrant and most grateful seasoning to custard, rice, or batter puddings. *Quintessence* of lemon or orange peel is made by mixing one drachm of the essential oil of these fruits with a large glassful of rectified spirits, or spirit of wine, and is very convenient when fresh lemons are not to be obtained, though not equal to the fresh fruit either in fragrance or flavour. The oil must be gradually mixed. *Tincture* of lemon-peel may be very economically made when lemon-juice is wanted, by paring the peel off very nicely, and steeping it in brandy. The bottle must be very closely stopped, as the flavour of lemon is exceedingly volatile. *Essence of allspice* may be made in the same way as essence of lemon, and so may *essence of cloves* and *mace*.

331.*Essence of ginger*.—Infuse three ounces of well-bruised fresh ginger, and an ounce of lemon-peel sliced thin, in a pint and a half of strong rectified spirits. Let it be closely stopped, and shaken every day. This preparation is very cordial and grateful.

332. *Tinctures of cloves, nutmeg, allspice, cinnamon, &c.* may all be prepared by infusing a sufficient quantity of the aromatics in strong spirits. They may be converted into plain useful *liqueurs* by the addition of fine sugar; but they must then be carefully filtered.

333. *Cayenne pepper, to make*.—This is made either of ripe chilies or capsicums. If chilies, dry them before the fire, a whole day, turning them till quite dry. Trim away the stalks. Pound the pods in a mortar till they become a fine powder, mixing in about a sixth of their weight of salt. Bottle the powder, and stop the vials carefully. If capsicums are used, dry them in the oven, first mixing them with dried flour; beat them to a powder, and add water, yeast, and a little salt, with which form the capsicums into paste and then in small cakes. Bake these twice; pound and sift the powder, and bottle in vials as usual.

334. MIXED SPICES AND SEASONINGS.—*Cook's or kitchen pepper*.—Dry, and pound or grind to a fine powder, an ounce of ginger; and of nutmeg, black and Jamaica pepper, and cinnamon, half an ounce each, with a dozen of cloves. Bottle these in separate vials labelled and well corked: mix in proper proportions with common salt when wanted.

N.B.—French cooks keep their seasonings mixed, and even pound or mill them together, not from convenience, but to blend the flavours intimately: much may be said for this practice.

335. COOK'S SEASONINGS *for white sauce, fricassees, and ragouts*.—White pepper, nutmeg, mace, and lemon-grate pounded and mixed. Also ginger and cayenne in proper proportions. These may be pounded together.

366. POWDER OF FINE HERBS, *for flavouring soups and sauces, when the fresh herbs cannot be obtained*.—Dry, in summer, parsley two ounces, of lemon-thyme, winter savory, sweet marjoram, and basil, each an ounce; lemon-peel dried, an ounce. Dry slowly and thoroughly; pound, then bottle. The powder should be sifted.

Celery seeds may be put to this useful relish.—See No. 244.

337. HOUSEHOLD VINEGARS.—Vinegar is an article perpetually wanted for various purposes in almost every family; and, compared with the first cost of the materials, it is a very expensive one. Though we are not perfectly convinced that the labour of the *still-room* is at all times what economists would call *productive labour*, we think that vinegar for ordinary purposes may often be made at home. It is easily managed on a small scale, may be made of things that would otherwise be lost, gives little trouble, and would not be adulterated with oil of vitriol. But the pyroligneous acid is now sold so cheaply, and answers so well for ordinary pickles, that vinegar making is becoming more and more a work of supererogation.

338. *Sugar vinegar.*—To every gallon of water put two pounds of coarse raw sugar. Boil and skim this. Put it to cool in a tub, and when sufficiently cold, add to it a slice of bread soaked in fresh yeast. Barrel it in a week, and set it in the sun in summer, or by the fire in winter, for six months, without stopping the bung-hole; but cover it with a plate to keep out insects.

339. *Cider vinegar.*—Put a pound of white sugar to the gallon of cider, and, shaking them well together, let them ferment for four months, and a strong and well-coloured vinegar will be the result.

340. *Gooseberry vinegar.*—To every quart of bruised ripe white or green gooseberries put three quarts of spring water. Stir them well with the water, and let them steep for 48 hours, repeating the stirring. Strain through a flannel-bag, and put two pounds of white pounded sugar to every gallon of liquor. Put it into a barrel with a toast soaked in yeast, leaving the bung-hole as directed above. Keep the barrel in a warm place. *White currants or raspberries* make an excellent vinegar by following the same receipt. Pick the currants from the stalks.

341. *Vinegar of wine-lees.*—Boil the wine-lees quickly for half an hour, skimming well. Cask the lees and add some chervil. Stop the cask, and in a month it will be fit for use as vinegar.

342. *Verjuice.*—Gather some ripe crab-apples, and lay them in a heap to sweat; then throw away the stalks

and decayed fruit, and having mashed the apples express the juice. (A cider or wine press will be useful for this purpose.) Strain it, and in a month it will be ready. This is the best simple substitute for lemon-juice that can be found; it answers still better in place of sorrel. The French, for many dishes, prefer verjuice to lemon. It is even used by *great economists* in preparing lemonade. —*Obs*. It is said that good vinegar may be made in an hour, by steeping green brambleberries in wine. Sour wine will, we have no doubt, be thus made at double the expense of good vinegar; so that this preparation has nothing to recommend it.

343. *Alegar*.—This is often made of stale beer, but is best when made of fresh worts, fermented with sour yeast, and set in the sun till the acetous fermentation takes place.

344. *Raisin vinegar*.—After making raisin-wine lay the refuse in a heap to ferment. Add water in the proportion of a gallon to the pound of raisins and half-pound of sugar. Put yeast to the liquor when strained.—*Obs*. Vinegar makes much more readily if put into a vinegar-cask. A common vinegar may be made of several other things, but the best sorts of vinegar, double-distilled champagne, and red wine vinegar, must be bought. *Ash-leaf vinegar, or crystal acid*, is a very clear and beautiful colourless liquid, but it is reckoned unwholesome. It is, in short, the pyroligneous acid.

345. FLAVOURED VINEGARS.—These are a cheap and agreeable addition to sauces, hashes, and ragouts, and have the convenience of being always at hand, at seasons when herbs are either very costly or not to be procured. They may be coloured with a few grains of cochineal.

346. *Chili vinegar, called pepper vinegar*.—Infuse a hundred red chilies, fresh gathered, in a quart of the best white-wine vinegar for ten days or more, shaking the bottle occasionally. A half-ounce of genuine cayenne will answer the same purpose. This makes an excellent and cheap addition to plain melted butter for fish sauce, &c.

347. *Eschalot vinegar*.—Clean, peel, and bruise four ounces of eschalots at the season when they are quite ripe without having become acrid. Steep them in a quart of the best vinegar, and strain, filter, and bottle.

348 *Garlic vinegar*.—The same as above, but use only half the quantity of chopped garlic.

349. *Celery or cress vinegar*.—Pound a half-ounce of celery-seed or cress-seed, and steep it for ten days in a quart of vinegar. Strain and bottle.

350. *Cucumber vinegar*.—Pare and slice ten large cucumbers, and steep them in three pints of the best vinegar for a few days. Strain and bottle it.—*Obs*. Vinegar of nearly the same flavour may be more cheaply prepared with burnet.

351. *Tarragon vinegar*.—Gather the leaves of tarragon on a dry sunny day; pick them from the stalks, and filling up a narrow-necked stone-jar, pour the best vinegar over them till the jar is full. Let them infuse for ten days, then strain and bottle the tincture.

352. *Basil vinegar* is made precisely as the above. The French add cloves and lemon-rind: we admire this addition.

353. *Horseradish vinegar*.—Pour a quart of the best and strongest vinegar boiling hot on three ounces of scraped horseradish, an ounce of minced eschalot, two drachms of black pepper, and a drachm of cayenne. Strain it in four days, and serve it in a cruet along with cold roast beef. It will make an excellent economical addition to the gravy of chops, steaks, &c.—See No. 270.

354. *Camp vinegar*.—Six chopped anchovies, four spoonfuls of walnut-catsup, two of soy, and a clove of garlic chopped very fine, and two drachms of cayenne. Steep these for a fortnight in a pint of white-wine vinegar, and strain and bottle for use.—*Obs*. This is more properly a *sauce* than a vinegar, as with butter or gravy added, it supplies the place of a store-sauce for either meat or fish. The anchovy should be omitted when the vinegar is to be stored.

355. *Curry vinegar*, may be made by steeping curry powder, in the proportion of two ounces to the quart, in the best vinegar, and straining and filtering for use.

356. *Raspberry vinegar*.—Pour on fresh-gathered raspberries, put in a large stone-ware or china dish, the best champagne vinegar, in the proportion of a bottle to two quarts of fruit. Next day pour off the liquor, and pour a little more vinegar over the fruit: where the fruit is plentiful and cheap, you need not mind expressing the

juice too carefully; strain through a sieve, but do not bruise the fruit. To every pint of the vinegar and raspberry juice, which are now blended, allow a full pound of good refined sugar. Break it in pieces, and dissolve it in the juice. Place the whole in a stone-jar, (not a glazed earthen one,) and put the jar (covered) in a kettle of boiling water for an hour; take off what scum arises; when cool, bottle the vinegar for use. This is an exceedingly pleasant beverage in hot weather. Two spoonfuls mixed with water make a delicious draught; but the large quantity of acid which it contains may in some cases render it an improper one. A cheaper kind is made by substituting pyroligneous acid for half the juice.

357. HERB WINES, &c.

WINE may be impregnated with the flavour of roots and herbs in the same manner as vinegar, and this generous fluid extracts even more of the flavour. The proportions for *Eschalot wine, Tarragon wine, Basil wine,* &c. are the same as when these herbs are steeped in strong vinegar. Eschalot wine is that most used.

358. *Eschalot wine.*—To four ounces of eschalots dried, chopped and pounded, or merely bruised, put a bottle of sherry. Infuse for a fortnight and strain off. If for beef only, horseradish sliced may be added, or rather substituted for part of the eschalots.

359. MUSTARDS.

MUSTARD is best when nearly fresh made. It is prepared in a variety of ways; *plain*, with broth, or boiling water; *mild*, with milk or cream, or with the addition of a little sugar; *pungent*, with water in which garlic, horseradish, &c. is boiled; it is also prepared with the flavoured vinegars, with cayenne, with catsup, and even with spirits.

360. *Good common mustard.*—Mix by degrees the best Durham mustard with boiling water and a little salt, rubbing a long time till it be perfectly smooth. The less made at a time the better; but it will keep for some time in a small jar closely stopt.

361. *Mild mustard.*—Mix as above, but use hot milk or cream instead of water, and sugar for the salt.

362. *Imitation of patent mustard.*—Scrape a cupful of horseradish, and chop a half-clove of garlic. Infuse this with salt, enough to make the water rather brackish in a quart of boiling water. Let it stand for a night; strain and mix with it the best mustard-flour, leaving the mustard rather thick. Keep it close-stopped in small jars:—*N.B.* For mustard-pots always have well-ground close-fitting stoppers.

363. CATSUPS.

MUSHROOM CATSUP is the most esteemed of this class of preparations. Large flap mushrooms, which contain a great deal of juice, and do not answer for pickling or stewing, are well adapted to making catsup. Let the mushrooms be wholesome, (see page 215.) Without washing them, pick off whatever looks dirty or corrupted, and breaking in pieces, lay them in an earthen jar, strewing salt about them. Throw a folded cloth over the jar, and set it by the fire, or in a very cool oven. Let it remain thus for twenty-four hours or more, and then strain off the liquor into a clean sauce-pan. To every quart of strained liquor put a half-ounce of black peppercorns, a quarter-ounce of allspice, a half-ounce of fresh sliced ginger, two or three blades of mace, and a few cloves. Boil the liquor on a quick fire for fifteen minutes; or, if it be wished very strong, and to keep long, boil the catsup till it is nearly reduced a half, adding the spices after it has boiled a full half-hour. Let it settle on the lees, and, pouring it carefully off, bottle what is clear by itself; and bottle the sediment, after straining, in separate bottles, as it will answer very well for fish-and-sauce, hare-soup, game-soup, &c. Dip the corks of the bottles in bottle-rosin. Cayenne and nutmeg may be added to the other spiceries if a very delicate relish is wanted; or all the seasonings may be withheld save the black pepper and salt, of which catsups to make them keep well require a good deal. The longer catsup boils, the better it will keep. In France, *glaze* is put to mushroom-catsup, and the whole is boiled till it be nearly a *glaze* or *rob*; in this state it keeps good for years. *Catsups, sauces, &c. ought to be kept with the bottle lying on the side,* as the cork is best preserved in this manner. It is a general fault with bought *catsups, sauces, &c.* that the bottles are not quite full. A space is left, which, being filled with air, hastens the decay of the contents of the bottle. These things ought to be bottled in very small quantities, as a bottle once opened soon spoils. When a bottle of capers or pickles is opened, it should be filled up with good vinegar, scalded and cooled. Anchovies, bay-leaves, and cayenne pepper, are all sometimes put to mushroom catsup.

364. *Walnut-catsup.*—Gather the walnuts green. Prick them with a bodkin, and throw them into a vessel with a large handful of salt and some water, which will greatly assist in drawing out their liquor. Mash them well with a *potato-beetle* or rolling-pin, and repeat this every day for four days. The rinds will now be soft. Pour scalding water, with salt in it, over the walnuts, and raise the vessel on edge that the walnut-liquor may flow away from the shells. Take it up as it gathers into another vessel, and still repeat the mashing; or pound the walnuts in a mortar, and pour some alegar over them, which will extract all the remaining juice. To every quart of the walnut-liquor, when boiled and skimmed, put an ounce of bruised ginger, an ounce of Jamaica and black pepper, a quarter-ounce of cloves, the same of long pepper and nutmegs. Boil this liquor in a close vessel for three-quarters of an hour, and when cold, bottle the catsup, putting equal proportions of the spices into each bottle.—*Obs.* Anchovies, garlic, cayenne, &c. are sometimes put to this catsup; but we think this a bad method, as these flavours may render it unsuitable for some dishes, and they can be added extempore when required.—See *Pickled walnuts*, p.264.

365. *Lemon catsup or pickle.*—Choose six large, fresh lemons; pare them thinly; rub them well with plenty of salt till they are saturated with it. Make an opening in the end of each, and put in salt. Bed them in a handful of salt and horseradish, and six bruised cloves of garlic for a week; then dry them in the oven till quite crisp; boil them in three bottles of vinegar with a half-ounce of cayenne. Add a cupful of the best mustard-seed. See No. 381.

366. *Tomata catsup.*—Make this exactly as the sauce

page 238; but boil it for an hour, then strain and bottle. A small glassful will flavour any sauce, or, with melted butter, make an *extempore* tomata sauce.

367. *Cucumber catsup.*—Take large old cucumbers and pare them; cut them in slices and break them to a mash, which must be sprinkled with salt and covered with a cloth. Keep in all the seeds. Next day, set the vessel aslant to drain off the juice, and do this till no more can be obtained. Strain the juice, and boil it up with a seasoning of white pepper, sliced ginger, black pepper, sliced eschalot, and a little horseradish. When cold, pick out the eschalot and horseradish, and bottle the catsup, which is an excellent preparation for flavouring sauces for boiled fowls, dishes of veal, rabbits, or the more insipid meats.

368. *Oyster, cockle and muscle catsup.*—Wash in their own liquor, and pound in a mortar, fat newly-opened *native oysters*. To every pint of the pounded oysters and their strained liquor, add a pint of white wine, and boil this up and skim it; then to every quart of this catsup add a tea-spoonful of white pepper, a salt-spoonful of pounded mace, some cayenne, with salt to taste. Let it boil up to blend the spices, and then rub the catsup through a sieve into a clean vessel. When cold, bottle it, and stop the bottles with corks dipped in bottle-rosin.—*Cockle-catsup* is made as above; but as this has less flavour naturally, and is seldom used but for fish, a few pounded anchovies may be added to it.

369. *Browning, or sugar catsup.*—Pound, very finely, six ounces of the best refined sugar, (Hamburgh or exportation loaves,) and put the powder into a small and very clean frying-pan, with an ounce and a half of fresh butter. As it dissolves mix well with a *spatula* or wooden spoon, and withdraw the pan from the fire when the fluid begins to boil violently; keep it thus till it has acquired the rich, dark-brown colour wanted. It may either be seasoned with pepper, salt, cloves, catsup, &c. or not, and is perhaps as generally useful plain. When cold, skim the browning, and bottle it in vials for use.—*Obs.* It is very difficult, nay almost impossible, to prepare browning free of an empyreumatic flavour, which is necessarily communicated to the dish that is coloured with it. Where sauces can be coloured with the catsup,

browned flour, and wine, which may be employed in making the dish, it is better to avoid making *browning;* and soup may generally be made of a sufficiently rich colour by previously browning the meat and onions, and by using toasted bread; for there is scarcely any brown soup into which one or other of these things does not enter. Many cooks boil onion-skins, which contain a yellow dye, to colour their soups; and it is a common, but slovenly practice, where browning is wanted in a hurry, to melt a knob of sugar between the hot bowls of tongs, and drop it into a little soup to colour the rest. This, on an emergency, may be useful, but the necessity ought to be avoided. The refuse of mushroom or walnut catsup boiled in brine, with a bit of Spanish juice, onion-skins, and burnt toasts, makes a well-coloured but very coarse browning.

370. PICKLES.

THESE are an important class of culinary preparations, and one about which the cook and notable housewife make no little bustle, and feel no small pride. Pickles are chiefly intended for a relishing accompaniment to many sorts of made-dishes and sauces, though a few of them are merely ornamental as garnishings.

The only general rules that can be given for the proper and safe preparation of pickles are, to have sound vegetables, not over ripe, and gathered on a dry day. Let the things to be pickled be carefully trimmed and wiped, washing only such thngs as are to be steeped or parboiled previous to pickling. It is miserable economy to employ bad vinegar for pickling, or bad sugar for preserving, or to use either in stinted quantities,—as both the syrup in which fruits are preserved, and the vinegar used for pickles, are afterwards very serviceable to the cook. Pickle-liquor can be at all times conveniently disposed of in seasoning gravies or sauces, or as an accompaniment to cold meat;—the pickle of cucumbers, walnuts, mushrooms, and onions, is especially useful. The vinegar used for pickles, if not boiled, ought to be made scalding hot, as *raw* vinegar is apt to become ropy and thick; but remember that no fermented liquid can be *boiled* without great loss of strength. The spiceries used in pickling are so well bestowed that we give no rule for the quantity, except that it should not be so great as to overcome the natural flavour of the article pickled; for pickles, like every thing else, should be what their name imports,—either *onion* or *cucumber*, &c. and not a hodge-podge of conflicting flavours. Pickles are most safely prepared in stone-ware vessels; but they must, at all events, be kept in small glass or stone jars well stopped, and the corks or *bungs* must be wrapped round with bladder or leather, with an upper covering of the same, if they are to be long kept; or, when well corked, let them be dipped in bottle-rosin. The corks or bungs may be left rather loose for two days, and the jars filled up to the neck with scalded vinegar before being finally closed, as a great deal of the liquor will be absorbed at first by the pickles. When the pickles are used, boil up the liquor with a little salt and fresh spice, and bottle and cork it for future use, either as a sauce, or to pickle nasturtiums and gherkins, where a fine colour is no object. To have *green* pickles of a bright *green*, and yet *safe*, is no easy matter; and we are glad to observe, that there is now at the most refined tables a wholesome distrust of pickles of too brilliant a green. It is, however, very possible to preserve the colour *tolerably good*, and yet prepare the pickles safely, by keeping them for a length of time, first in brine, and then exposed to the steams of vinegar. Potato-plums, elder-flowers in the bud, and several other things, are pickled besides the vegetables in common use; and there is little doubt that many other vegetable productions might answer equally well if spiced and steeped in vinegar. We do not admire them.

371. *To pickle cucumbers.*—Lay fifty firm, young, and very small-sized cucumbers, not too ripe or seedy, on flat dishes, having first rubbed them with salt. Keep them covered, and look at them and turn them occasionally for eight or ten days, and then having carefully drained them, put them in a jar in which vine-leaves or cabbage-leaves are laid, and, pouring two quarts of scalding vinegar over them, cover them with more leaves, and keep them covered by the fire. Next day pour off the vinegar, boil it up, and pour it hot over the cucumbers, again covering them with fresh leaves above and below. A little pounded alum will improve the colour;

but if it be not good enough, scald them once more by placing the jar in a pan of boiling water, or on a hot hearth. When the colour is tolerably good—for it will never be very brilliant—boil up the vinegar once more with a half-ounce of white pepper, the same of sliced ginger, two drachms of cloves, and a bruised nutmeg. Boil the spices for a few minutes with the vinegar, and when cold, bottle them according to the general directions in the preceding page.—*Obs.* A French cook would add a seasoning of tarragon, fennel, and garlic.

372. *French beans*, gherkins, Indian cress, samphire, and other *green* pickles are all to be managed as in the above receipt for cucumbers.

373. *Cucumbers and onions pickled.*—Pare and slice cucumbers, picking out the seeds; and peel and slice large onions in thick slices. Sprinkle salt over them, and drain for a night, then put them into a stone-jar, and pour scalding vinegar over them. Close the jar, and set it by the fire. Scald them by placing the jar over a hot hearth, and repeat this till they become of a tolerable colour; then boil up the vinegar with spiceries, as in No. 371.

374. *To pickle walnuts green.*—Gather the walnuts before they are nearly ripe, and while the shells are still tender. Lay them in a strong pickle of salt and water for nine days. Change the brine twice in that time. Keep a board floating over them, for if they are exposed to the air they will turn black. Drain them, and run a bodkin or a large pin into each walnut in several places. Lay plenty of vine-leaves or cabbage-leaves in the bottom of a pan. Place the walnuts on these, and cover them with more leaves; fill the vessel with water, and give them a scald; let them stand to cool, and repeat this several times, pouring off the blackened water, and supplying its place with scalding water. When the husks become soft, scrape them off with a knife as quickly as possible; and, rubbing the walnuts smooth with flannel, throw them into a vessel of hot water. Boil for three minutes a quart of the best vinegar for every fifty walnuts, with white pepper, salt, ginger, cloves, and cayenne. Dry the walnuts well in a cloth, and pour the vinegar over them. *Walnuts* are pickled *black* in an easier manner, by merely steeping for twelve days in strong brine,

renewed every three days, rubbing them smooth and dry, and pouring boiling vinegar over them, with a seasoning of pepper, horseradish, garlic, and mustard-seed.

375. *To pickle mushrooms*.—Choose small white button-mushrooms, and rub them with flannel or a sponge dipped in a little salt. Put them into a stone-jar, with some mace, ginger, pepper, and salt, and let them stew in their own juices over a slow fire, shaking them well, but not breaking them. Let them remain over the fire till they are almost dry, but take care they do not burn. When the liquor is all re-imbibed by the mushrooms, put in as much hot vinegar as will cover them, and let them just come to boil. When cold, bottle them in jars, and after a week fill up the jars with vinegar, scalded and then cooled, and pour a little oil into the necks of the bottles, which will aid in excluding the air. Cork the bottles, wrapping bladder or leather round the corks, and dip the corks of what is to be long kept in bottle-rosin.

376. *To pickle onions*.—Choose small sound silver onions, as equal in size as may be. Top and tail them, but do not pare the tops very close, as the air will soften and spoil the onions. Scald them with brine. Repeat this on the second day, and when cold, peel the onions as quickly as possible, throwing them into vinegar as they are done, to prevent their blackening. Boil vinegar enough to cover them, with sliced ginger, black and white pepper and mace; when cooled a little, pour it over the onions. Cork them well, as directed for other pickles, and dip in bottle-rosin.—*Obs*. Some cooks peel and scald the onions, a few at a time, take them up as soon as they look transparent, and dry them in the folds of a cloth, covering them carefully to exclude the air. Some cooks scald in brine, and then parboil in milk and water. Pickled onions of the shops look beautifully white, but have little *gout*.*

377. *Red cabbage*.—A firm, deep-purple-coloured middle-sized cabbage is best for pickling. Strip off the outer leaves, cut out the stalk; and, dividing the

---

* In the youthful days of Mrs. Dods onions were pickled in their skins, tops, and tails, and only peeled when to be served at table. The flavour was then very little different from that of a raw onion.

cabbage, cut it down into slices of the breadth of narrow straws. Sprinkle salt over these, and let them lie for two days; then drain very dry, and pour over the sliced cabbage a pickle of boiling vinegar, seasoned with black and Jamaica peppers and ginger. Cover the jar to keep in the hot steams, and when cold, close it up.—*Obs.* A few mild onions sliced is thought an improvement to this pickle. The onion takes the beautiful tinge of the cabbage, thus repaying

"The grace it borrows with the strength it lends!"

378. *Beet-root.*—Wash the beet-roots, but take care not to break the skin or the fibres which hang about it, else the colour will fly. Boil them softly for an hour, or more if they are large, or bake them, and as soon as they are cold enough to be handled, peel them, and, cutting them into slices, put the slices into a jar, and have ready to pour over them cold vinegar, in which black and Jamaica pepper, ginger, cloves, and a little cayenne have been previously boiled.—*Obs.* A few slices of beet-root make a pretty *fill-up* dish for any odd corner on a table, and a very elegant garnish, particularly if contrasted with the brilliant emerald green of pickled samphire. The slices, when to be used, may be cut in the form of leaves, flowers, or nicked round the edges; a few small silver onions, and turnips scooped out to the size of marbles, will take the rich red tinge of this pickle, form an ornamental variety with the beet-root, and cost nothing. Cochineal will improve the colour.

379. INDIAN PICKLE, *or Piccalilli.*—This is a general hodge-podge pickle of all the common *green* and *white* pickles to which the *curry flavour* and *tawny curry tinge* is given. Prepare the pickle-liquor thus:—To every two quarts of the best vinegar put an ounce and a half of white ginger scraped and sliced, the same of long pepper, two ounces of peeled eschalots, one of peeled garlic, an ounce and a half of salt, an ounce of turmeric, a little cayenne, and some flour of mustard. Let this infuse in a close jar set in a warm place for a week; and, in the meanwhile, have ready a white cabbage sliced, cauliflowers cut in neat branches, white turnip-radishes, young French beans, sliced cucumbers, button-onions, and codling-apples, a large carrot cut in round

slices, nicked round the edges, capsicums, bell-pepper, &c. Sprinkle all these things with plenty of salt, mixing it well with them in a large earthen vessel, or pouring scalding brine over them. Let them lie for four days, turning them over, and then take them up, wash them in vinegar, and dry them carefully with a cloth, and afterwards lay them on sieves before the fire, turning them over till thoroughly dried. Next day place them either in a large stone-jar, or in smaller jars, and pour the cooled pickle over them. The jars must be well stopped.—*Obs.* This pickle keeps a long time, and for the first two years will even improve by the keeping. The vegetables do not all come in together, but they may be prepared as for pickling, and added to the general pickle as they come into season. This pickle looks more attractive if the French beans, small whole cucumbers, or melons, are *greened* before they are put to it, as directed in other receipts. When the melons or cucumbers are greened, cut a slit in the side, and scrape out the seeds. Shoots of green elder are also put to this pickle, in imitation of the bamboo in the genuine mango pickle. Instead of being laid in salt, the vegetables may be parboiled in very strong brine, by which means the pickle will be soon ready, but the colour and crispness will be injured, though, on the whole, both for ease of preparation and safety in eating, we think parboiling the preferable method. This pickle is so cheaply bought whether common or nicely prepared, that few families now make it.

380. *To preserve barberries.*—Tie the clusters to bits of sticks and boil them in syrup.

381. *To pickle bitter oranges and lemons for wild fowl* .—Rub the fruit well with salt. Cover them with vinegar, with a handful of coriander-seeds, and some mace. Boil up the vinegar once or twice, and when cool, pour it again over the oranges or lemons.—See No. 365.

382. *To pickle cauliflower or broccoli.*—Take firm, well-coloured vegetables, before they are quite ripe, and cut away the bark of the stems, and all the green leaves. Scald them for four minutes in a pan of boiling brine, and then drain and dry them thoroughly. When dry, pull them into properly-sized branches, cutting the stalks

smoothly, and pack them up in the jars with the same pickle-liquor as directed for onions or beet-roots.

383. *Nasturtiums*, to make either a pickle or for imitation caper-sauce, may be prepared in the same manner; also the seed-pods of the radish which makes a substitute for capers.

384. *To hasten the preparation of pickles.*—Parboil in brine the vegetables you wish to pickle. Drain and dry them, and then proceed as before directed with the respective kinds. The colour will not be quite so good, but the vegetables, besides being less crude, will be fit for use in a few days.

PART THIRD.

CHAPTER I.*

MADE-DISHES.

"When art and nature join, the effect will be
Some nice *ragout*, or charming fricassee."

King's Cookery.

"—— But prudent men will sometimes save their mash,
By interlinear days of frugal *hash*."

Crabbe's Tales.

WHAT is technically called a *made-dish* presupposes either a more elaborate mode of cookery than plain *frying*, *broiling*, or *roasting*; or else some combination of those elementary processes,—as, for example, half-roasting and finishing in the stew-pan, which is a very common way of dressing a *ragout*. All dishes commonly called French dishes are of the class *made-dishes*, such as *fricassees* and *ragouts*, *meat braised*, *larded &c.* and so are *hashes*, *curries*, and generally all viands that are *re-dressed* or *re-made*.

---

* To understand this chapter properly the young cook should first study the directions for *braising*, for cooking in a *poele*, or a *blanc*; also the mixing of peppers and other seasonings, and to make and use all sorts of garnishes, as sippets, fried parsley, casserole edgings, crustades, bread-borders, farce-balls, egg-balls, grilled toasts of all kinds, also serving in *vol-au-vent* in *timballes, glazing*, glazing onions and celery for garnishes, paste-borders, dishing in various forms, and many other matters. She should understand the qualities and uses of the different catsups and flavoured wines and vinegars; and what flavours are best adapted to the several meats, as horseradish with dishes of beef; lemon-peel or juice with veal, &c. These things may all be studied under the respective heads, as pointed out in the Index. See also chap. *French Cookery, and the Glossary of Culinary Terms.*

To dress a *made-dish* properly requires rather judgment and contrivance than great manual dexterity. It is in fact more difficult to broil a chop properly than to dress a ragout, provided the cook knows how to proportion seasonings, and to blend flavours with taste and judgement. Stewing is the common form of dressing made-dishes, and is besides that mode of cookery which is best adapted to dry, fibrous, harsh meats, and to dry salted fish. Its perfection consists in the extreme slowness of the vessel in which the meat is contained. The lid of a stew-pan or digester, after the gravy has been skimmed, ought to be as seldom removed as possible; but the stew-pan may be frequently shaken, to prevent the meat from adhering either to the bottom or to the sides.* Stewing is recommended by Dr. CULLEN as the best mode of cookery for retaining all the native succulence of the meat, thus obtaining from it the greatest quantity of nourishment; and likewise as promotive of digestion,—the last assertion, though of even this great authority, may be questioned.

Made-dishes are valued by the gourmand for their seasonings and piquancy. They are equally esteemed by the economist from the circumstance that a much less quantity of material than would suffice for a boil or roast, will make a handsome and highly-flavoured dish; while, by the various modes of *re-dressing*, every thing cold is, in a new made-dish, turned to good account. The most common fault of made-dishes is, that they are *overdone*. While a large dinner is proceeding, the stew-pans are neglected, because their contents sustain less apparent injury than is instantly visible on roasts, broils, or fries; and also because cooks either do not know, or forget, that meat stewing in its own rich juices is exposed to a more intense heat than in boiling or open roasting before the fire.

The general rules we would give for dressing made-dishes are, that they be not over hastily done, but rather removed from the fire or hot plate, as a very few minutes

---

* It would be a great improvement if the lids of all stew-pans permitted fire to be put over as well as under the meat.

at any time will finish them completely,—that the sauce be smooth and properly thickened, so as to adhere to the meat,—and that the pieces of meat of which they are composed, be nicely trimmed, cut perfectly smooth with a fine-edged knife, and never left clumsily large. This is peculiarly to be attended to in re-dressing cold meat, which sometimes comes to table mangled and lacerated as if it had been gnawed, not carved. Palates, sweet-breads, &c. may be cut into scollops, or other agreeable forms, as is common in French cookery.

The very name made-dish, with us implies something savoury and highly relishing, and though over seasoning is to be avoided, it is proper that *made-dishes* should rather be piquant than insipid.

385. *To glaze tongues, fricandeaux, hams, &c.*—Cut down knuckle of veal, shin of beef, feet and trimmings of poultry, and a few slices of bacon. Let them *catch* over a quick fire, and pour in a little broth made of cow-heels or calf's-head. Stew till this is a strong jelly; strain and pot for use. When to be used, heat the glaze in a water-bath, and brush over the tongue or meat, and repeat this if necessary. An economical cook will seldom need to make *glaze*. She will save it. Glazing is in fact portable soup; it may be flavoured in any way to suit the dish it is to *glaze*.

MADE-DISHES OF BEEF.

386. *To ragout or braise a rump of beef.*—Except for some particular purpose, a rump to be stewed should not be very large, nor above ten inches in thickness, unless it be salted a little. Cut out the bone neatly, and break it; and with that and what trimmings may be made in smoothing the meat, make a little gravy, which season with onions, a carrot, and turnip, and a bunch of sweet herbs. Season the rump highly with cook's pepper and a little cayenne, and skewer and tie it firmly up with tape. Lay skewers or willow twigs in the bottom of a nice clean stew-pot that will just hold the meat, and place the rump upon them, straining over it the gravy drawn from the bones. When it has simmered for an hour or more, turn it over, and put to it three carrots sliced, two turnips scooped to the size of marbles; and in another half-hour onions sliced, and a glass of eschalot-

vinegar, or plain vinegar, with a couple of minced eschalots, and more pepper if required. Keep the lid close the whole time; and before dishing, put in a large spoonful of catsup, and another of made mustard, with *roux*, or butter rolled in flour to thicken the gravy. The rump may be dressed more highly by filling up the hole whence the bone is taken with a relishing forcemeat, egging and browning it before stewing, and putting some wine to the sauce, which may also be enriched with sweet breads or kernels, parboiled and cut into bits. It may be *glazed*, and the *braise* may be prepared with bacon. —*Obs.* A rump salted for four days in summer, or a week in cold weather, washed and stewed plainly, is an economical as well as an excellent dish, whether for company or for family use. It may be divided diagonally, so as to skewer up neatly, and stewed in weak broth with roots, as above. Skim the fat carefully off, and serve the soup, which will be very rich, on toasted sippets, and serve the meat by itself either garnished with cut pickles, or sliced carrot, or with onions prepared for garnishing. See page 236. A rump is sometimes *half-roasted*, and finished in the stew-pot in weak broth, with some mild ale, wine, vinegar, catsup, a faggot of sweet herbs, and onions, mixed spices, pickled mushrooms, &c.—*Obs.* The above is an expensive dish and has nothing to recommend it beyond a plainer-dressed rump, boiled carefully in the stock intended, to make soups and sauces for the same dinner.

387. TO STEW OR RAGOUT A BRISKET OF BEEF.

TAKE four or five pounds of a brisket, with the firm fat; wash and rub it with salt and vinegar before dressing it. Put it into a small stew-pan that will just hold it, with water or broth, and, when well skimmed, let it stew very slowly for an hour, and then put to it cut carrots, turnips, and small whole onions. When it has stewed slowly till tender, draw out the bones, thicken the gravy with butter rolled in flour and a little catsup, with plenty of mixed spices. Serve the meat by itself, with a garnishing of sprigs of cauliflower, and a sauce made of thickened gravy, with more catsup, and a little made mustard.—*Obs.* A haricot of beef may be made of the above, by dividing the meat into about a dozen neat pieces, browning them, and putting in a sliced head of celery and forcemeat balls, in addition to the ingredients ordered above.

388. .—*The French "Bœuf Garni de Choux." an excellent dish.*—Boil firm which cabbage cut in quarters. Finish in any good *braise*, or broth seasoned with roots. Moisten them with a little top-fat. Drain the cabbage, press out the fat, and serve them neatly round the meat. —*Obs.* Tie up the cabbage till served.

389. TO STEW A SHIN OF BEEF, *or bouilli ordinaire.*

HAVE the shin-bone sawed across in three different places. Place skewers in the stew-pot, and lay the meat on them, and as much water as will nearly cover it. When this is skimmed, put in a bundle of herbs, a head of celery cut, four onions, and a dessert-spoonful of black and Jamaica peppercorns in a rag; cover the pot very close, and let the meat stew slowly for three hours, when cut carrots may be put to it, and afterwards cut turnip, with a dozen of small onions roasted and peeled. Make a sauce for the *bouilli*, by thickening and seasoning a pint of the gravy with catsup, spices, and a little made mustard. The French *sauce hachée* is also a very suitable garnish with the onions.

390. BEEF OR VEAL A LA MODE.

THE clod, the mouse-buttock, the rump, or the thick of the flank, may be dressed this way. Take from six to ten pounds of beef, and rub it well with the mixed spices and salt, and dredge it with flour. Lay skewers in the bottom of a well-tinned stew-pan, and on them spread some thin slices of good bacon; place the meat on these, with a few more slices of bacon above, and a small quantity of vinegar and gravy, or good broth. Make the stew-pan very close, and let the meat stew as slowly as possible over embers for two hours. Turn it, and put to the gravy a high seasoning of cloves, black and Jamaica pepper, with a few bay-leaves and mushrooms if in season, or a little catsup, and a few button-onions roasted. Let it again stew very slowly till the meat is tender. Pick out the bay-leaves, and serve the meat in a deep dish with the gravy, which, if slowly stewed, will have thickened to the consistence of glaze. *Veal* is very good dressed in the same manner. The gristly part of the breast is best adapted for this purpose; and lemon-grate may be added to the seasonings, but no catsup. *A la mode* will ever be a good way of dressing beef, for luxurious, healthy stomachs, but it should now be called à l'antique.—*Obs.* The *culotte de bœuf à la geleé* of the French kitchen, called also *bœuf à la royale*, differs very little from beef à la mode, save that it is tied up, and, when half baked or *braised*, is boned. It is glazed, served with its own gravy, and garnished with pickles or parsley, and in *high style*, with different coloured meat-jellies, cut in figures.

391. DR. HUNTER'S RECEIPT FOR A STEWED BRISKET.

Brisket of Beef stewed savoury.—Take eight pounds of the brisket, and stew it till quite tender, in as much water as will just cover the meat. When sufficiently tender, take out the bones, and carefully skim off the fat. Take a pint of the liquor, put to it the third of a pint of red port wine, a little walnut or mushroom-catsup, and some salt. Tie up in a bit of muslin some whole white pepper and mace, and stew these together for a short time. Have ready some carrots and turnips boiled tender, and cut into the form of dice; strew them hot upon the beef, putting a few into the dish. Truffles and morells may be added.

392. *To collar beef.*—Choose the thin part of the flank, or what in Scotland is called the *nine-holes* or *runner.* Let the meat be young, tender, and well-grained, but not very fat, as it is to be eat cold. Rub it with salt, and a very little saltpetre; and when it has drained a night, rub it thoroughly well with a mixture of sugar, salt, pounded pepper, and allspice. Let it lie a week in the salting-tray, turning it, and basting daily with the pickle that will gather. If the weather is cold, it may lie ten days; and then bone it, and cut away all the gristly parts, and the coarse inner skin. Dry it, and strew over the inside chopped herbs and cook's pepper; that done, roll it up as tightly as possible, bind it with broad fillets of strong cloth, and that with tape; press it under a heavy weight, and then undo the bandages and re-fasten them, as the meat will have shrunk, and

make the ends very fast. It will require from three to five hours slow but constant boiling. When done, press it again while still bound; and when cold, undo the bandages. It may be served hot, with savoys or carrot, but it is most valued for slicing down cold.—*Obs.* A large fore-quarter of mutton, with the shoulder-blade cut off, will *collar*, and so will veal, but neither of these eat nearly so well as collared beef.—*Beef is pressed flat* to slice for sandwiches or to eat cold, exactly in the above manner, but then it is not bound up: it eats as well, and is prepared with much less trouble.

393. *To roast collared ribs of beef.*—Take out the bones when the meat has hung till tender, season it highly with spices and herbs, and rolling tightly up roast or bake it, or dress it as HUNTER's beef.—*Obs.* This is an excellent and economical dish, as a soup, much better than what can be made from dripping or roast-meat bones, can at once be made from the trimmings and the bones cut out. A neck or back-ribs of mutton boned, seasoned, and sprinkled with dried parsley and sage, will roast as above, and the bones and scrag make rice-soup or barley-broth; but we would rather recommend this to the economist than to the fastidious eater; for although two good dishes are by this means presented at table, this particular piece of meat eats better dressed as chops, pie, *bouilli* or curry, than as a roast when the *roti* can be dispensed with.

394. *Brisket of beef à la Flamande.*—Take from eight to ten pounds of the gristly nice part of the brisket; trim and season it. Put it to stew in a nice stew-pan with the trimmings, and a slice or two of bacon under and over it. Put to it carrots and turnips cut into the shapes of cocks' combs, pigeons' eggs, &c. and also some cabbage previously dressed in top-fat or good broth. Arrange the vegetables with a few glazed onions round the meat, and thicken a pint of the broth for sauce.—See *German onion beef, National Dishes.*

395. *To dress ox-palates.*—Clean and boil them till the upper skin will easily pull off; and either cut them into long slices and square bits, or merely divide them. Stew them very slowly in good gravy thickened with butter kneaded in browned flour, and season them with cayenne, minced eschalot, or onion, and a large spoonful

of catsup, or the pickle of walnuts, mushrooms, or even of onions, which is very good for plain purposes.—*Obs*. This we think the most suitable way of dressing palates; but they are often more expensively prepared, by adding forcemeat, wine, and mushrooms, or truffles and morells to the sauce; *or* by dressing them as a fricassee in white sauce. Palates are often served with cucumbers, or with *sauce tournée*. In fine cookery they are served in *vol-au-vent* or *casserole*.—See *French Cookery*.—Palates are very suitable to the *dejeuner à la fourchette*, either served *hot* like kidneys, or pickled and eat cold.

396. *Beef-steak with cucumbers*.—Pare and slice three large cucumbers, and as many onions. Fry them in butter, and when browned, add a half-pint of gravy. Beat and season some rump-steaks and fry them. Dish them in a very hot dish, and pour the above cucumber-sauce over them.—*Obs*. This is a good dish for variety, with very little expense.—See No. 39.

397. *To stew a Tongue*.—Trim off the coarse part of the root, but leave on some of the soft fat. Rub the tongue with salt, sugar, and pounded allspice, and let it lie in this for a few days. Stew it in a small close sauce-pan for an hour, and then skin it; strain the liquor, put some fresh broth to it if necessary, a faggot of sweet herbs, three bay-leaves, and a head of young celery sliced. When the tongue has stewed in this very slowly for nearly another hour, take out the herbs and bay-leaves, and season the gravy with cayenne, pounded cloves, mixed spices, and a little walnut-pickle. Serve the tongue in a soup-dish, with the sauce about it, and a few dressed mushrooms (when in season), or small onions previously roasted and peeled. This is an excellent and not an expensive dish; and if any gravy be left, nothing can be better adapted for a sauce to ragouts, &c. The tongue may be cut open the long way, but not quite divided, and so spread out on the dish.—*Obs*. This differs little from the French *langue de bœuf à la braise*, save that the French dish is enriched by the trimmings of game, poultry, or veal, put in the braise, and has a little wine put to the sauce. *Pickled tongues* are frequently *glazed*, after (of course) being boiled and skinned. They are served on mashed turnips or spinage.

Scarlet tongues, cold, may be sliced, and have the slices glazed.

398. *To dress kidneys, or Scotch kidney-collops.*— Cut a fresh kidney in slices of the size of very small steaks, or into mouthfuls. Soak the slices in water, and dry them well. Dust them with flour, and brown them in the stew-pan with fresh butter. When the collops are browned, pour some hot water into the pan, a minced eschalot, or the white of four young onions minced, with salt, pepper, shred parsley, and a spoonful of plain or eschalot vinegar, or of onion-pickle liquor. Cover the stew-pan close, and let the collops simmer slowly till done. If flavoured vinegar is not used, a spoonful of mushroom-catsup put in before the collops are dished will be a great improvement. Thicken the gravy. Garnish this dish like liver with fried parsley.—*Obs.* Some good cooks season this dish with an anchovy and lemon-pickle; others add made mustard.

399. *Beef-kidneys for the dejeuner à la fourchette.* —Mince the kidneys, and season highly with salt, pepper, and cayenne. Fry the mince, and moisten it with gravy and champagne, and serve in a hot dish. Catsup, or lemon, or walnut-pickle, may be used in place of wine. The slices may be first marinaded in vinegar and herbs.—See *French Cookery, Rogons de mouton.*

400. *To dress Ox-tails.*—Let the butcher divide them at the joints. Scald them, dry and brown them in the stew-pan, adding hot water or weak broth, with a piece of butter and rolled in browned flour. Stew them slowly till tender, and season with salt, mixed peppers, minced parsley, and either a spoonful of catsup or eschalot vinegar, or a tea-spoonful of made-mustard. Many will think cayenne an improvement.

401. *Hotch-potch of ox-tails, or, rumps à la mode, a French Dish.*—Have the tails jointed, and blanch as for soup. Cover a stew-pan with trimmings of meat or poultry, and put in the tails, with plenty of onions, two carrots, a faggot of herbs, a bay-leaf, three cloves, and a bit of garlic. Moisten this with two ladlesful of broth, cover it with slices of bacon, then paper, then the lid, and over all a few cinders. Let it simmer for four hours, till the meat part from the bones with a spoon. Serve with a ragout of roots stewed (after boiling) in

the sauce of the tails or in melted butter. Two tails will be required for a good dish.—*Obs*. Ox-tail dressed as above is very good served with a sauce, i.e. *purée* of the pulp of pease, or with *sauce hachée*.

402. *Beef-olives*.—Cut slices from the rump half an inch thick, six inches long, and three inches broad. Flatten them, dip them in egg, and then in a seasoning made of pulverized or finely-shred herbs, bread-crumbs, mixed spices, and salt. If the meat be lean, a little shred suet may be flattened into each piece of meat. Roll them neatly up, and fasten them with packthread: —a little forcemeat may be put in each. The olives may either be roasted on a lark-spit, and served with a drawn gravy, or browned and stewed over embers in a broth made of the skins and trimmings. Thicken the sauce, and season it with catsup and a little walnut pickle, and, dishing the olives neatly, skim it, and pour it hot over them.

403. *Olives au Roi—A favourite small dish*.—Mash two pounds of boiled potatoes; add a quarter of a pint of cream, two yolks of eggs, and one spoonful of flour; season it with salt and pepper; take six long slices of beef, beat out very thin; strew over them a spoonful of chopped onion, the same of parsley, and of mushrooms; spread the potato paste on the olives, and roll up; fry or bake half an hour; glaze them, and put some plain brown sauce under them. Six will make a good-sized, nice dish.—*Obs*. Veal may be done the same way. *Olives* may be baked in a potato border.

404. *Beef marrow-bones*.—Have them neatly sawed by the butcher. Fill up the opening with a piece of dough or paste, and tie a floured cloth over that. Boil them, placed upright, in the soup-pot (keeping them covered) for nearly two hours. Serve upright on a napkin, accompanied with dry toasts.

405. *Beef-heart*.—In England a heart is cut up, soaked to free it from the blood, and has the lobes cut off, after which it is stuffed with forcemeat as a roasted hare, and served with venison-sauce. In Scotland beef-heart is often dressed as minced-collops, with a proportion of beef, or, which we consider the best way of dressing it, is prepared as a cheap stew-soup thus:— Clean and cut the heart in large pieces lengthways.

Put these into a stew-pot with cold water and salt, and carefully skim away the blood, which will be thrown up in large quantities. Take up the parboiled pieces, and carve them into mouthfuls; return them into the strained liquor with plenty of shred onion, a shred head or two of celery, pepper, and allspice, and a dozen peeled potatoes. This is a highly nourishing, well-flavoured, and economical stew-soup, as the half of a good fat bullock's heart will be sufficient to make it.— For *Roast beef*, see page 95; for *Steaks, collops, &c.* pages 118, 120, 125, 126; *Tripe*, page 130.

406. *Beef-skirts.*—These make a nice small dish dressed as palates. The French *braise* and farce them with mushrooms or oysters: they may be served with a ragout of cucumber, or over spinage or fried toasts.

407. *Beef-liver* may be used when sound, and is constantly used on the continent either in a stew-soup with carrot and onion, or slowly cooked in butter or with bacon, as calf's liver: or as directed for *lamb's-liver* in the Scotch mode, page 129.

408. *Beef-udder* may be boiled, sliced, and served with tomata or onion sauce: *udder* is also salted for two days, tacked to a tongue, and they are boiled together. Salted udder is also eat cold with oil and vinegar. It should be very slowly simmered.

409. *To make Hunters' beef.*—Take the bone from a round, and salt it, as directed for a rump of beef, using grated nutmeg, half an ounce, and the same weight of cloves. When to be dressed, wash with a sponge, bind it tightly up, and put it into a tin or earthenware pan that will just hold it, with a pint of melted butter or gravy, and a little butter on the top; cover the pan with several folds of brown paper, or a coarse crust. Bake for four hours or more.—*Obs.* The hole whence the bone is taken may be stuffed with sweet herbs or udder. The gravy in the pan after the beef is baked will be almost equal to ham-sauce for strength and flavour; and is very useful for flavouring soups and sauces. Herbs, coriander-seeds, juniper, and garlic, are all used for this pickled dish by the French. The round is braised with roots, bacon, and wine. The dish is glazed and garnished with pickles and jelly; and thus decorated, when cold, even after being previously served hot, makes a handsome

dormant dish at a great entertainment where there is a long table to cover.

410. *Bœuf de chasse, another form of Hunters' beef* .—Bone a piece of the flank of fifteen pounds. Take two ounces of saltpetre, two and a half of brown sugar, two bruised nutmegs, a half ounce of cloves, and an ounce and a half of allspice, with two large handfuls of salt well dried. Pound and mix these well, and rub them well into the beef. Keep it two weeks in this pickle, turning and rubbing it daily. Bind it up, skewer, and bake it for four hours in a slow oven.

411. *Dutch or Hamburgh beef.*—Rub a rump of beef with brown sugar, and let it lie three days, turning it often; then wipe it, and salt it with four ounces bay-salt, four ounces common salt, and two ounces of saltpetre, well beaten and mixed. Let it lie in this for a fortnight, and then roll it tight in a cloth, and press it under a weight. Smoke the meat in the cloth, hung in a chimney where wood is burned; boil it piecemeal as it is wanted; when boiled, press it till cold, and it will grate or pull like the real Dutch beef.

412. *Hamburgh beef, or Bœuf fumé*, i.e. *smoked*. This is cured in nearly the same manner as No. 411. Take sugar, salt, saltpetre, juniper-berries, and pound them, mix spices with them and aromatics, all in powder. Rub the beef well with this, and leave it for a fortnight, turning it every day, and like all meat pickled keeping it covered; tie up, drain, and smoke it for a week. In Germany, when boiled, it is served on *sour croute*.

413. *Irish beef.*—Proceed as directed for a rump or round, only season with nutmeg and mace, as well as the ingredients mentioned there. Read *Obs., Chap. Salting*.

414. *Fillet of beef with Madeira, a receipt by Beauvilliers.* —Take a nice, fat fillet of beef: cut away all fibres, skins, &c. and lard it equally all over. Line a stew-pan with sliced carrots, onions, and a bunch of herbs. Strew four ounces of rasped lard over them, and place the fillet rolled up on this. Pour a half bottle of Madeira over it, as much good stock, and a little salt. Cover with three rounds of buttered paper, and let there be a very slow fire under, with embers over the lid. When nearly dressed, strain the gravy; and what will not go through a fine sieve return to nourish the fillet, and keep it moist.

Reduce the strained gravy with a large spoonful of *Espagnole* (See *French Cookery*,) put to it, till it comes to the consistence of *glaze*. Drain and glaze the fillet. Season the gravy that remains,—put a pat of butter to it, and pour it over the dished meat.

415. *To press beef.*—Take the bones from the brisket or flank, or the thin part of the ribs. Salt and season it well with salt, sugar, and mixed spices, and let it lie a week; then boil till tender, and press the meat under a heavy weight till cold, when it will either eat in slices or do for sandwiches.—See No. 392.

416. *A porker's and a calf's head* are pressed or collared. A porker's head must be previously salted; for a calf's head the same seasonings are used as when the head is hashed.—See No. 392.

417. MADE-DISHES OF BEEF THAT HAS BEEN DRESSED.

FEW persons come to the years of eating discretion like cold meat; and though the days are quite gone by when the hospitality of the landlord was measured by the size of the joint, it still happens that where a table affords any variety of dishes, a good deal of meat will be left cold. The invention of the culinary artist is thus put on the rack for new forms and modes of dressing, and new names for various dishes which are intrinsically the same. The most common and the best methods of dressing cold beef, are, broiling, heating in the Dutch oven, or hashing. It is served with sippets, and in many ways.

418. *To dress the inside of a cold sirloin.*—Cut the meat in long and rather narrow slices of an inch thick, leaving a little of the firm fat upon each. Season these with salt and mixed spices, dredge them with flour, and heat them, without any thing like violent frying, in the gravy saved from the cold joint, seasoned with an anchovy, an eschalot minced, or a shred onion, and a little vinegar. Garnish with scraped horseradish or fried parsley.

N.B.—The slices may be broiled and served in the sauce.

419. *To fricassee cold beef.*—Cut away all skins, gristles, and fat. Cut the meat into thin small slices. Have ready a sauce made of broth, thickened with butter, rolled in flour, and seasoned with shred parsley and

young onions, pepper, and salt. Strain the sauce when it is well flavoured, and just heat the meat in it by the side of the fire, then add a glass of red wine, the yolk of an egg well beat, and the juice of a lemon. Stir the fricassee for a few minutes, but do not let it boil.

420. *Olives of dressed beef.*—Cut the meat as for fresh beef-olives. Season the slices, and spread thinly over them a forcemeat of bread-crumbs, seasonings, and a little finely shred suet or marrow. Roll them up, and stew them in a relishing gravy saved from the joint, or drawn from the beef-bones, and thickened with butter rolled in flour, and seasoned with an anchovy or a little catsup.

421. *To hash cold beef.*—Cut down the meat either into slices, or mouthfuls, trimming away all burnt outside, fat, gristle, skin, &c. Set aside the meat thus prepared with what gravy you have saved, and draw a pint of broth from the bones well broken, the lean pieces of meat that are not used, or the hard, or overdone. Season this broth highly with pepper, allspice, two onions, and a faggot of parsley, and salt. Thicken it with flour rubbed down as for batter-pudding. Skim all the fat from it; let it settle, and strain it, and heat it up again, putting to it, as additional seasonings, any of the following things:—Walnut or mushroom catsup, or onion-pickle liquor, with a few cut pickles; a little tarragon vinegar, or some shred parsley, made mustard, capers, nasturtiums, &c. &c. in brief, any flavouring ingredient which is agreeable to the taste of the eater, and easily procured. When this sauce is hot, put the cut meat and gravy to it, and let it slowly warm quite through, without boiling; or the sauce may be poured over the meat in the hash-dish, and that set in a hot-water bath, a cool oven, or vessel of boiling water, till the hash is hot through. Place toasted sippets round the dish. A curry hash of beef is generally liked. Fry a few large onions; add the hashed meat and curry seasonings. Garlic may be used if liked.—*Obs.* The varieties of *Hashes* are endless, but the above is conceived the best mode of making this dish, whether the hash be of beef or mutton. Hashes of veal or poultry require a white sauce, a seasoning of lemon-peel, and the juice of lemon; or the flavour of tarragon given by vinegar,

which makes a French-flavoured hash. A *curry hash* of veal or fowls answers very well with plenty of small onions par-roasted, and then stewed whole in the hash-sauce. If meat comes back from the table which you know must be hashed next day, carve it before it get cool; it will then imbibe all the gravy which lies in the dish, and be far more rich than if allowed to remain dry and uncut till next day. This should be particularly attended to in hashes of venison, hare, or mutton.

422. *Beef Cecils.*—Mince the whitest part of the meat very nicely, and mix it up with bread-crumbs, minced onions, a chopped anchovy, and parsley, pepper, salt, and a little onion or walnut pickle. Stir this mince over the fire in a small stew-pan, with a little melted butter; and, when cold enough to handle, make it up into large oval balls with flour; egg the balls and roll them in crumbs; brown them before the fire, and pour hot gravy, seasoned with eschalot and pepper over them.

423. *Cold beef scalloped, or Sanders.*—Mince the meat as in the last receipt, with the same seasonings and a little scraped tongue or ham, moisten it with gravy and walnut-pickle, and fill up the scallop-shapes, laying mashed potatoes thinly, and neatly marked, over the mince. Put some bits of butter over each shape, and set them to warm and brown in an oven.—See *Beef patties* and *Podovies.*

424. *To mince dressed beef.*—Mince the beef finely with a little suet, and warm it up in a small stew-pan, with a little broth or water, minced parsley, eschalot or onion, and a little vinegar, and what meat-gravy you have saved, which is the best ingredient that can enter into the composition of any hash or mince. Dish the mince on toasted sippets, or on poached eggs.

425. *A French mode of dressing cold beef.*—Cut the part most underdone in slices, and stew them over embers in a sauce of weak broth, a glass of red wine, a small spoonful of tarragon vinegar, an onion, two bay-leaves, a sprig of thyme and parsley, pepper, salt, and cloves. Serve, either hot or cold, with the strained gravy, to which, however, more vinegar must be put if the beef is served cold. The wine may be omitted.

426. *To broil cold beef.*—Cut the slices as steaks, broil them over a very clear fire, or in a Dutch oven,

and serve them with fried eggs, or scalloped potatoes, and steak-sauce, grill-sauce, or piquant sauce made hot. —See *Sauces*.

427. *Another way.*—Divide the ribs, and shorten them: leave the meat on the upper side about the breadth of an inch. Sprinkle the steaks well with salt and mixed spices, and place them in a Dutch oven, basting them with the gravy of the roast, bread-crumbs, and chopped parsley. Serve them with *grill sauce.*— See page 249.

428. *Bubble and squeak.*—This dish is made either of cold roast or boiled beef; and is best of salted meat. Cut the slices not too thick nor very large; fry them in fresh butter with plenty of pepper, and keep them warm before the fire. Chop, and fry, or *braise* some boiled cabbage, and lay it on the slices of beef; or heap the cabbage high in the middle of the dish, and lay the meat round it. For sauce, chop and stir a few slices of pickled cucumber and onion into a little thick melted butter, and add a tea-spoonful of made mustard. Fried beet-root, eggs, or apples, may be used. A ragout, of left oysters, mushrooms, or onions, makes this scrap-dish superb.

429. *Bubble and squeak of veal.*—Make this as of beef, but use no mustard.—*Obs.* This deserves to be better known. Spinage may be substituted for cabbage.

430. *Inky pinky.*—Slice boiled carrots; slice also cold roast beef, trimming away outside and skins. Put an onion to a good gravy, (drawn from the roast beef-bones, if you like,) and let the carrots and beef slowly simmer in this; add vinegar, pepper, and salt. Thicken the gravy,—take out the onion, and serve hot, with sippets, as any other hash.

431. *To pot beef, veal, or game.*—Salt a piece of lean fleshy meat for two days. Drain it, season it well, and afterwards bake it in a slow oven, or stew it in an earthenware jar, placed in a vessel of boiling water. Drain off all the gravy, and set the meat before the fire, that all the moisture may be drawn out. Pull it to pieces, and beat it in a mortar, with mixed spices and oiled fresh butter, till it becomes of the consistence of mellow Stilton cheese.—*Obs.* This is mostly made of beef dressed for other purposes, such as beef from which gravy is drawn, or the remains of any joint that cannot

be otherwise used. It may be flavoured with anchovy, mushroom-powder, minced eschalot, chervil or tarragon, dried and pulverized, if the potted meat is not to be long kept. The longer it is beat in the mortar the better it will eat and keep. Put it into small potting-cans, and cover with plenty of clarified butter, which will afterwards be useful for frying meat, pie-crust, &c.— Game to be sent to distant places may be potted as above without cutting up the birds, and will keep for a month.

---

432. MADE-DISHES OF VEAL

VEAL is generally accompanied by *acid* sauces, sorrel, or lemon. It is often the better in made-dishes of a relishing forcemeat; and unless very fat, young, tender, and white generally cooks the better for a slice of good bacon.

433. *To stew a fillet of veal.*—Take off the knuckle either to stew or for soup, and also the square end, which will cut up into cutlets or olives, or make a pie. Stuff the middle part of the fillet with a forcemeat, as directed at No. 23, and, rolling it up tightly, skewer it neatly, and simmer it very slowly in a close nice stew-pan that will just contain it. Lay skewers below to prevent the meat from sticking. When quite tender take it up, and strain and thicken the sauce. Serve with mushrooms parboiled, and then stewed in the sauce and season with white pepper and mace:—or the sauce may be enriched with a few pickled oysters and force-meat balls; season with a glass of white wine and the juice of a lemon, and garnish with lemon sliced.—*Obs.* The fillet may be half-baked and then stewed. For *dividing* the fillet, see *French Cookery.*

434. *To stew a breast of veal, a common remove of fish, or a second-course top-dish.*—Choose thick, fat, white veal. Chop off the neck and the edge-bone, and stew them for gravy. Stuff the thin part of the breast with a relishing forcemeat, made of a sweetbread parboiled and minced, bread-crumbs, lemon-grate, nut-meg, pepper, salt, shred suet or veal-kidney fat, and yolk of egg to bind the forcemeat. Skewer the stuffing neatly in, or sew it in, and stew the meat for an hour in

the gravy made of the neck, first egging and browning it if you choose. Thicken a pint and a-half of the sauce, and put to it a half-hundred oysters cut, a few mushrooms chopped, lemon-juice, white pepper, and mace. Pour this over the stew, and garnish with slices of lemon and forcemeat balls. Cream, wine, truffles, &c. are all put to this dish; also catsup and anchovy-sauce.

435. *To ragout a breast, or tendrons of veal.*— Make a little strong gravy, as above, of the scrag and bones of the breast, and cut the meat into neat pieces, rather larger than if for curry. Brown these nicely in fresh butter; drain them from the fat, and put them to stew in the broth with a faggot of sweet herbs, a piece of lemon-peel, cloves, mace, white pepper, allspice, three young onions, and salt to taste. This, like all stews, cannot be too slowly simmered over embers, keeping the lid of the stew-pan very close. When the veal is quite tender, set the stew-pan to cool, and skim off all the fat that floats on the sauce, which must then be strained and thickened to the degree of thin batter, and enriched just before serving with a glassful of white wine and the juice of a lemon. Dish the veal and pour the sauce hot over it, holding back the sediment. Forcemeat-balls may be used as a garnishing to this dish (they will be more suitable if made with a large proportion of grated tongue, sausage-meat, ham, &c.) also slices of lemon. —*Obs.* Veal, whether the neck or breast, is exceedingly good stewed plainly with a little strong gravy. The meat may be glazed, and covered with white onion-sauce; or stewed with young green pease, chopped lettuce, and young onions chopped, and served *en puit*, that is in a well or space in the middle of the dish, of which the cut meat forms the walls. Celery also answers very well with stewed veal.

N.B. *Lamb or rabbits* may be dressed as above, and served, the former with cucumbers, the latter with white onion-sauce.

436. *Veal-olives.*—See *Beef-olives*, p. 282; or cut, flatten, and spread forcemeat on each slice with season-ings. Roll up each olive tightly, and egg and crumb them, and either roast or stew them in a rich gravy. Thicken the gravy, add to it a few forcemeat-balls, and serve with oyster or mushroom sauce.

437. *Veal-cutlets.*—See pages 126, 289, and *French Cookery.*

438. *Scotch-collops.**—Cut small slices of equal thickness out of the fillet, and flour and brown them over a brisk fire in fresh butter. When enough are browned for your dish, put a little weak veal-broth or boiling water to them in a small close stew-pan, adding, when they are nearly ready, the juice of a lemon, a spoonful of catsup, or the same of lemon-pickle, with mace, pepper, and salt to taste. Thicken and strain the sauce, and pour it over the collops. They may be egged and dipped in crumbs. Some cooks lay the slices in a marinade of vinegar and spices for some hours before frying, but it is bad practice. Serve curled slices of toasted bacon, or mushrooms if in season.

439. *A fricandeau of veal.*—Trim the fat fleshy side of a large knuckle of white veal; *or* take a long thick piece from the fillet; skin it, beat it flat, cut smooth at one stroke, season, and lard it or not with forcemeat. Lay some slices of bacon in a stew-pan, and place the veal on them with more slices of bacon above it. Put in a pint or more of broth, the knuckle-bone broken, or two shanks of mutton, a faggot of herbs, a turnip, a carrot, and four onions sliced; mace, two bay-leaves, some white pepper, and slices of very fat bacon over all. Let this stew for more than two hours over a very slow fire, and keep the stew-pan closely covered (properly there ought to be a fire over it), unless when basting the upper side of the *fricandeau* with the liquor. The gravy will be very rich. Take up the *fricandeau* and keep it hot; skim the fat from the gravy; pour it from the sediment, and boil it quickly down till it thicken,—or, as it is technically called, become a *glaze*, which pour over the meat. Serve with sorrel or tomata sauce.—*Obs.* The lean part of a large neck may be dressed as a *fricandeau*, drawing a glaze from the bones. Truffles and morells, artichoke bottoms, and mushrooms, are all served with this dish. *Fricandeau* is a French dish naturalized, though it does not always succeed in this country. Like many other dishes, it is much improved by having fire put over the stew-pan, especially towards the conclusion

---

* This properly means *scotched*, or scored collops, though the word has come to be understood as above.

of the process; and this is seldom done in England. *Fricandeau* should be so well done as to carve with a spoon; but for English palates meat in tatters does not always suit.

440. *To ragout a knuckle of veal, (an excellent and economical dish.)*—Cut off the meat the cross way of the grain in slices rather thinner and smaller than for cutlets. Draw slowly nearly a quart of broth from the bone broken, the skins, gristles, and trimmings, with a head of celery, an onion, a carrot and turnip, and a small faggot of parsley, with a sprig of lemon-thyme, and basil. Season the slices with salt and cook's-pepper; dredge with flour, and brown them in a small stew-pan; and, pouring the strained broth over them, stew the whole very slowly over embers, or at a considerable distance from the fire, for a half-hour. Thicken the sauce with flour rolled in butter, or white *roux*, and just before serving, add the squeeze of a lemon and pounded mace.—To stew a knuckle with rice, see page 155.

441. *To braise a neck or other piece of veal.*—Cut the scrag in bits, but keep whole, and lard the best end with chopped bacon, minced parsley, pepper, salt, and mace. Lay the larded meat in a shallow stew-pan, with hot water to cover it, and put around it the cut scrag, some slices of bacon, four onions, a turnip, a head of celery, two carrots, and three bay-leaves. Stew till tender, strain off the gravy, and melting some butter in another stew-pan, take the neck gently up, and lay it there to brown. When browned, put as much of the strained gravy to it as will do for sauce, with a glass of white wine, the juice of a Seville orange, white pepper and mace. Dish with the browned side uppermost, and pour the sauce over it.—*Obs.* This is an elegant but a rather expensive dish, with little to recommend it over plain savoury stews of veal save the name and the larding, a resource of cookery, by the way, which does not seem peculiarly suited to English palates, and which is every day less employed even in the French kitchen. Any piece of meat, poultry, or game, may be *braised* as above; or, as another variety, stuffed with forcemeat instead of being larded. *Braising* is, in fact, just slow *stew-baking* in fat, rich, compound juices, with high seasonings.

442. *A Granada (properly* GRENADIN) *of veal,—a naturalized French dish*.—Line a small oval dish with a veal-caul, leaving part hanging over the ledges of the dish. In this, place slices of good bacon, then a layer of forcemeat, next veal-collops well seasoned, and so on alternately till the dish is filled. Tuck the caul over the whole, tie paper over the dish, and bake the *granada*. Turn it out of the dish, and serve with clear brown gravy.—*Obs*. Mushrooms, herbs, &c. may be added at discretion to this savoury dish. This dish may be made in a mould of any shape.

443. *To dress veal à la daube*.—Trim off the edge-bone of a good loin of veal, and cut off the chump.* Raise the skin, season the meat, and fill the cavity with a relishing forcemeat; bind up the loin with fillets of linen, and cover it with slices of bacon; place the loin in a stew-pan, with the bones and trimmings, and veal-broth, if you have it, or jelly of cow-heels. Put in a faggot of herbs, mace, white pepper, and two anchovies. Cover the lid of the pan with a cloth, and force it down very close, placing a weight over it. Simmer slowly for two hours, shaking the stew-pan occasionally. By this time the gravy will be reduced to a strong glaze. Take out the bacon and herbs, and glaze the veal. Serve with sorrel or tomata-sauce; or with mushrooms, which are always a very suitable accompaniment to made-dishes of veal or poultry.

444. *A haricot of veal*.—Shorten the bones of the best end of a neck or back-ribs. Either leave the meat whole, or cut it into chops. Brown it of a fine colour. Stew it in good brown gravy; and when nearly ready, add a pint of green pease, a large cucumber pared and sliced, and a well-blanched lettuce quartered, with pepper, salt, a point of cayenne, and a quart, or what will cover the stew, of boiling broth. Dish the veal in the middle of the soup-dish, pour the stew-sauce over it, and garnish with the *lettuce* and a few forcemeat-balls.

445. *Maintenon-cutlets*.—Cut and flatten the cutlets, season them with mixed spices, dip them in beat egg,

---

* The chump or tail end makes a good family-dish, stewed in broth, with roots, spices, herbs, and a slice of bacon. Serve with its own thick-ened gravy, and the roots that are stewed with it, but take out the bacon.

and then in bread-crumbs and pulverized sweet herbs, with a little grated nutmeg. Broil them over a quick clear fire, turning them quickly, and moistening them with melted butter. Twist each cutlet neatly up in thin writing paper made hot, and serve them accompanied by mushroom-sauce, or catsup, stirred into plain melted butter. These cutlets may be dressed by stewing them for a few minutes with chopped parsley, butter and rasped bacon, and finishing *en papilotte.*—*Obs.* Common books of cookery recommend dressing veal-cutlets, salmon-cutlets, &c. in paper,—a plan which is extremely difficult even in the hands of a French artist, and which requires buttered or oiled paper put on at first, and supplied by fresh buttered paper when the cutlet is nearly dressed. The original paper will look greasy and besmeared whatever care the cook may take, and fresh paper spoils the meat.*—See *Cutlets*, p. 126.

446. *Various ways of dressing veal.*—Prepare as above, and dress cutlets in a Dutch oven, pouring melted butter and mushrooms over them. *Fresh veal minced,* with the grate of a lemon and nutmeg, and a little shred mutton-suet, makes a very good side-dish or supper-dish, and warms up well, or does for patties or scallops. *Veal-rolls,* for a side-dish or supper-dish, may be made of long thin slices of veal flattened, seasoned, and rolled round a forcemeat of bacon or grated ham, suet, eschalot, parsley, and spices. Tie the rolls tight, and stew them slowly in gravy, adding a glass of white wine and the squeeze of a lemon. Serve in a ragout-dish. Stewed mushrooms are a suitable accompaniment to this dish, which is just another name for *veal-olives. Veal* makes excellent *curry* or *pillau.*

447. *To dress a calf's-pluck.*—Clean and stuff the heart with a relishing forcemeat. Spred a veal-caul, or slices of fat bacon, over it, and bake it. Parboil the half of the liver and lights, and mince them rather finer than for a hash. Simmer this mince in a little good gravy, and season it with the juice of a lemon, catsup, white pepper, chopped parsley, and salt. Dish the mince, and place the heart above it, and lay slices of the

---

* Nothing should be dressed *en papilotte* in a kitchen, save a pig's ears and tail.—P. T.

remainder of the liver fried, round it, with fried parsley, or sippets, or bread-crumbs; or the heart, if large and fat, will make a handsome dish if stuffed with a rich forcemeat, roasted with caul or paper over it, and served with melted butter and catsup poured about it, or venison-sauce. The *liver* may be stuffed and roasted as above; but this we conceive one of the absurdities of cookery. The minced *lights* are made into balls, or used for forcemeat, to calf's-head, &c. They must have a good deal of kidney or other fat, or of udder, and the usual veal-seasonings of mace, lemon-peel, &c.

448. *To dress veal sweetbreads.*—Parboil them, but be sure not to boil them much. Divide and stew them in white gravy; thicken, and season this with salt, mace, white pepper, and when just ready, a little hot cream; or, egg the parboiled sweetbreads, dip them in crumbs, chopped herbs, and seasonings, and finish them in a Dutch oven, and serve with melted butter and catsup.

449. *To ragout sweetbreads.*—Cut them in mouthfuls, wash and dry them in a cloth, brown them in fresh butter, and, pouring as much brown rich gravy as will just cover them into the stew-pan, let them simmer gently, adding a seasoning of pepper, allspice, salt, and mushroom-catsup. Thicken the sauce, and, dishing the sweetbreads very hot, pour the sauce over them through a sieve.—See *French Cookery.*

450. *To dress calves'-tails.*—Clean, blanch, cut them at the joints and brown them in butter or soft kidney-fat. Drain, and stew them in good broth seasoned with parsley, onions, and a bay-leaf. Add green pease to the stew if in season, or some small mushrooms. Skim and serve the ragout. Foreigners use garlic in this dish, and dredge it with grated Parmesan.

451. *Calf's-heart.*—Cut down and dress as a plain stew, and season with lemon-grate; or stuff and roast, rolling in forcemeat, as at No. 447.

452. *Calf's-liver.*—Cut a fat white liver into thin slices. Dust flour over these. Fry them for five minutes. Strew minced parsley, and young onions, salt, and pepper over the fry. Moisten it with good broth, and give it a toss for five minutes more; but do not let it boil, or it will harden. Before serving, add the squeeze of a lemon.

Calf's liver may be dressed more richly by stewing it with bacon, herbs, spices, &c. and putting white wine to the thickened sauce.

453. *Veal-kidney* may be minced and fried as sausage, or rolled up in oval balls, mixing the fat and lean together, with a little bacon, onion, pepper, salt, &c. Dressed thus, it forms a relishing accompaniment to plain stews of veal.

454. *To jug veal.*—Cut, flatten, and season slices of veal, and put them into an earthen or stone jar, with a few sprigs of sweet herbs, a roll of lemon-peel, and some bits of fresh butter. Cover the jar very closely, and set it in a pot of boiling water, or in a slow oven, for from two to three hours. Take off the covering, and stir a little thickening and the juice of a lemon into the sauce, and, allowing a few minutes for this to blend, dish the veal in a ragout-dish, picking out the herbs and lemon-peel. Garnish with slices of lemon.

455. *Veal-cake.*—This is rather a pretty fantastical dish to ornament a table than one about which either the epicure or economist cares much. Take the hard yolks of eight or more eggs and cut them in two. Put some of them in the bottom of a small nice tin pan, or earthenware dish. Strew chopped parsley over them, with seasonings; then thin slices of veal and ham, or rather veal and ham separately beaten to a paste in a mortar. Place thus, alternate layers of egg, parsley, and meat-paste, till you have enough. Stick butter over the top, and add a little water or gravy; cover the saucepan very close, and set it in an oven. When done, which will be in about three-quarters of an hour, take off the covering, and press the meat down. When cold and firm, turn it out. It may be baked in an oval or fluted earthenware shape, turned out, and garnished with curled parsley, &c.

456. *To dress a calf's-head plain.*—Wash it and soak it in hot water that it may blanch. Take out the brains, and cut away the black part of the eyes. Boil it in a large fish-kettle, putting it on with plenty of cold water, and some salt to throw up the scum. Simmer it gently for an hour and a half. Take up the head, cut out the tongue; score the head (but not deeply) in diamonds; brush it over with beat egg, and

sprinkle it with bread-crumbs, chopped parsley, and seasonings. Stick a few bits of butter over it, and brown the head in a Dutch oven. Meanwhile, wash, scald, parboil, and skin the brains, and chop them up with parsley and sage (first parboiled and then chopped,) white pepper and salt. Stir this into hot melted butter. Add the squeeze of a lemon, or a little lemon-pickle, a small quantity of cayenne, and a minced eschalot. Skin the tongue, and serve the brains dressed as above directed, around it, as a smaller dish to accompany the calf's-head. Serve also parsley and butter-sauce. Curled slices of toasted bacon, a piece of ham or bacon, a pig's-cheek, or sausage, are indispensable with calf's-head, even when highly dressed.—See p. 155.

457. *Calf or lamb's head and ragout, a Scotch dish.*—Having parboiled a fat head as above, cut down the one-half of it, with the skinned tongue, the palate, &c. into dice and other neatly-shaped pieces. Trim and brush the other half with egg, and strew crumbs, chopped parsley, &c. over it, and set it to brown, sticking butter over it, and basting it with more crumbs. Meanwhile stew the hash in a little good veal-broth, jelly of cow-heels, or any rich fresh stock you have: season this with mixed spices, the grate and juice of a lemon, mace, or whatever seasoning is most approved. Dish the ragout, and place the browned cheek upon it. Garnish with brain-cakes and forcemeat-balls, or fried sippets, or merely with slices of the fried liver.—*Obs.* Pickled oysters, catsup, &c. may be added to this ragout, which may, at the discretion of the cook, be either a white or brown ragout. This we conceive the best way of dressing a calf's-head; though the hash or fricassee of the second day must, by the experienced gourmand, be considered as preferable to any other mode of cookery, and only objectionable from not making so important an addition to the appearance of the table as the full-dressed head. If it be a lamb's-head brown it all: the scrag minced (which is generally cut off with the head in Scotland) will make a great addition to the ragout. The head may be glazed before being crumbed.

458. *To fricassee a calf's-head.*—Clean and parboil the head; cut the cheeks, tongue, palate, &c. into nice bits, and stew them in a rich white gravy, with a little

of the broth in which the head was parboiled, seasoned with white pepper, mace, herbs, onion, and salt. Thicken with butter rolled in flour, and just before dishing the fricassee, add a little hot cream or beat yolk of egg. Simmer this, but do not allow it to boil. Garnish with brain-cakes and forcemeat-balls, or curled slices of toasted bacon, and egg-balls.

459. *To hash a calf's-head.*—Clean and parboil the head; or take what is left of a plainly-boiled cold head, and cut it into slices of a rather larger size than for fricassee. Peel and slice the tongue. Take upwards of a quart of the liquor in which the head was boiled, with the bones, trimmings, and a shank of veal or mutton, and boil these for the hash-stock, with a faggot of sweet herbs, a good bit of lemon-peel, onions, and white pepper. Boil this gravy till it is good and well-flavoured. Thicken it with flour kneaded in butter, and strain it into a clean sauce-pan. Season with pounded mace, catsup, or lemon-pickle, or a little of any piquant store-sauce, and warm up the hash, without suffering it to boil, though boiling will not harm calf's-head so much as it does other cold meat. Garnish with forcemeat-balls, or curled slices of bacon, or fried bread, which forms a suitable accompaniment to all hashes.—*Obs.* This hash may be rendered more piquant by anchovy, pickled oysters, &c. It may be dressed as a curry-hash by the addition of fried onions and *curry-powder*; or receive the flavour of a French dish, from finely-shred parsley, knotted marjoram, and a bit of tarragon, being added to the sauce just before dishing; or a little tarragon-vinegar. It may also be flavoured very agreeably with a little basil-wine. A *brown hash* may be made as above by using fried onion, catsup, soy, a little red wine, &c.; but as all brown made-dishes are expected to be piquant, while those that are white are usually bland and balsamic, seasonings of a more pungent quality are to be used.*

---

* In France, eschalot-sauce is served with a plain-dressed calf's-head; but the favourite mode of dressing this dish is *superbe*. Make a force-meat of a pound of minced veal and two pounds of the fat of beef-kidney, bread-crumbs steeped in cream and dried, and fine herbs minced— namely, mushrooms, parsley, and young onions. Add salt, pepper, and spices. Mix this thoroughly. Stuff the head with it, but keep some for

460. MOCK-TURTLE, OF CALF'S-HEAD.— See also pages 149, 150, and 151.

GET a large fat head with the skin on. *Scald* and clean it well. Soak it in hot water, and, if you wish to have the imitation-dish very rich, parboil it in good veal-broth, with a turnip, carrot, onions, and sweet herbs. Skim this well. In half an hour take up the head, and when cold enough to be firm and easily handled, cut the meat thus:—The eyes into thin round slices, having first picked out the black part; the gristly part about the ears into long narrow stripes, the fleshy part into round slices, the thick of the cheeks into small dice, the thin on the forehead into long stripes, and the peeled tongue into nice square bits. Put the bones and trimmings, with a piece of bacon, back into the stew-pot. Fry some minced eschalot in plenty of butter browned with flour. Put the cut meat to this browning, and give it a toss for a few minutes, then strain a sufficient quantity of the stock over it, to make the dish not much thicker than the stew-soup. Season with mace, pepper, salt, and a half-pint of Madeira. When the meat has stewed very slowly, rather soaking in the gravy than actually boiling, and is nearly ready, put to it cayenne to taste, a small glass of catsup, a very little soy, and a couple of spoonfuls of chopped basil, tarragon, chives, and parsley. When skimmed ready to be dished, add the juice of a lemon. Serve in a large but not deep soup-dish, ornamented with a cut paste-border; and garnish with forcemeat-balls and egg-balls, with a few green pickles intermixed if you choose.—*Obs*. This highly-flavoured dish may be enriched by parboiled sweetbreads cut, oysters, turtle-balls, &c.; if the head be lean or small, a good cow-heel cut down will make an excellent addition to it, but will require more boiling, and must be put into the stock-pot an hour before the head.—For *Potted-head* see *National Dishes*.

461. *To dress calves'-feet*.—Clean and blanch them. Boil them well; divide, and serve them with sauce

---

forcemeat-balls. Braise the head in gravy-broth; put artichoke bottoms, veal sweetbreads cut, truffles, and button-mushrooms, to the ragout, and serve with the farce balls.

Robert, or *sauce à la Tartare*, in the dish; or they may be served as a fricassee like calf's-head, thickening the sauce, and seasoning it with lemon-peel and mace.— For *Calf's brains*, see *French Cookery*.

MADE-DISHES OF COLD VEAL.

462. *To ragout cold veal*.—Cut the cold meat into small cutlets, trimming off all gristles, skins, bones, &c. With the fragments, an onion, a turnip, and carrot, make a little good gravy. Melt some fresh butter in a frying-pan, and flour and brown the slices of veal of a light brown; take them up, strain the made-gravy into the pan, and thicken the sauce to a proper consistence with flour first mixed with butter. When smooth and well mixed, put in the cutlets, and let them simmer very slowly. Season with pepper, mace, catsup, and anchovy, or mushroom-powder, if you choose, bearing in mind that meat re-dressed, having lost much of its native flavour, requires more seasoning than at first. Skim the sauce, and pour it hot over the ragout.

463. *To hash veal*.—Cut the meat in thin small slices, paring away all gristles, skins, &c. Warm it up in a gravy drawn from the bones, as in the former receipt. Thicken with butter rolled in flour, and season with mace, minced lemon-peel, a spoonful of lemon-pickle, or the juice of a lemon; or, in place of these, a glass of basil-wine.—See *Hashed beef*, page 282.

464. *To mince veal*.—Take only the fine white part of the meat,—mince it very finely, and heat it up in a little veal-broth, with white pepper, salt, mace, a good deal of finely-rasped lemon-peel, and a glassful of cream. —*Obs*. Minced veal may be dressed as patties, scallops, or *blanquettes*. It is much more savoury when made of undressed meat.

465. *A Dunelm of cold veal*.—This is made by mixing stewed mushrooms finely minced with minced veal, thickening the fricassee, putting a little cream to it, and serving garnished with toasted sippets, which ought to accompany all *hashes* and minces.

466. *To pot veal*.—A fillet of white veal answers very well potted.— See No. 431. Pounded ham or smoked tongue mixed with the potted veal is a great improvement to it.—For *Potted calf's-head*, see *National Dishes*.

For *Veal sausage*, see *Sausages*; and for severall excellent dishes of veal, see *French Cookery*.

MADE-DISHES OF MUTTON.

467. *A haricot of mutton.*—Cut down the back-ribs into handsome chops, trimming away the fat and bones. Flatten the chops; season them well with mixed spices, (cook's pepper,) flour, and brown them lightly in the frying-pan, over a quick fire, and then put them into a stew-pan with their own gravy, and a quart and a half of strained broth, in which onions, a turnip, a carrot, and a faggot of parsley have been boiled. When the chops have stewed slowly for some time, put in one large or two middle-sized carrots cut into slices and marked on the edges, a dozen pieces of turnips scooped to the size of large marbles, and a half-dozen button-onions either roasted or parboiled and peeled. When the chops are quite tender, skim, thicken, and season the gravy with pepper and salt. Dish the chops in a soup-dish, and pour the gravy and roots over them. What is left of the fore-quarter when a shoulder is cut off to roast, will make excellent haricot or Irish stew.—*Obs.*—Celery or cucumber may be put to the haricot, and also cut pickles, or a spoonful of catsup. *Brown haricot* is made with carrot and yellow turnip, onions, &c. *Haricot* is an excellent plain dish, nourishing and savoury, containing a judicious combination of meat, fluid, and roots, and is one of the best ways in which veal-cutlets, mutton-chops, or rump-steaks, can be used. Haricot may be made of the loin, but not so economically as of the neck or back-ribs. These chops answer well with cabbage *braised* and quartered.—See pages 120 and 126.

468. *Shoulder of mutton with oysters.*—Have a large shoulder, which has been kept till tender, boned, and highly seasoned with salt and pepper. Lay some bearded oysters inside the meat, roll it up firm, bind it with fillets, and simmer in broth, with onion and peppercorns, and a head of celery, till ready. Undo the tape, and pour oyster-sauce over the mutton.

---

* Haricot properly and originally meant French beans. Now with us it signifies stews of meat cut in chops, with vegetables of different kinds.

469. *To dress a scrag of mutton*.—Trim the scrag, and *braise* it in fresh broth with roots, seasonings, and a faggot of sweet herbs, and with a few slices of bacon under and over it, if you wish it rich. Simmer gently for three hours. Skim, and strain the gravy, and serve it with the meat, with dressed spinage, or cucumber sauce.

470. SHOULDER OF MUTTON.—*Receipt by a Scotch lady*.—Keep the shoulder as long as possible without spoiling. Half-roast it. Score it on both sides as for broiling. Melt in the basting-ladle four mellow anchovies chopped; put pepper and salt to this; place a clean dish under the roast, and baste with the following hot sauce:—The melted anchovies, half a pint of port, half a pint of rich gravy, a spoonful of mushroom catsup, the same of walnut catsup, a *point* of cayenne; baste constantly till the mutton is done. Dish on a hot dish rubbed with garlic. Skim the sauce or dropt gravy, and pour it over the mutton.*

471. *To dress a breast of mutton*.—Cut off the fat; parboil the meat; *egg* it, and strew over it shred parsley and bread-crumbs. Stick pieces of butter all over it. Brown it in the Dutch oven, and serve with caper or Robert sauce, or with stewed cucumbers.

472. *Mutton-collops*.—See *Beef-collops*, p. 126, and *Chops* 120.

473. *To grill a breast of mutton*.—Cut off the superfluous fat, and take out the bones. Beat the breast flat, and season and score it in diamonds. Brush it with egg, and strew minced parsley and bread-crumbs over it. Broil it in a Dutch oven, basting it well with fresh butter; and serve with caper-sauce, cucumbers, or sauce Robert.

474. *Mutton-cutlets, Maintenon*.—Cut handsome chops from the loin, or cutlets from the gigot. Fry some chopped eschalot and mushrooms in butter, and in this brown the cutlets. Season them with cook's-pepper, and stew them with crumbs and chopped parsley, and

---

* M. Ude might shrug at this receipt as inadmissible in delicate cookery. But the dish is admirable; and at all events there are so few avowed fair amateurs in Scotland that we like to encourage the breed.— P. T.

twisting them in buttered papers, finish them on the gridiron. Serve with cucumbers, or any sauce that is liked.

475. *Mutton-steaks*.—Cut down the back-ribs, a rib in each steak, and chop the bone short. If very fat trim away some of the suet, and it will answer very well for pie-crust, puddings, &c. Broil them as beef-steaks, and serve hot and hot. Put salt and a bit of fresh butter in the dish, or serve with sauce Robert. They are excellent over potato-pudding, or mashed potato.—See p. 120.

476. *Mutton-collops and cucumbers*.—Pare and slice the cucumbers. Sprinkle them with fine salt and pepper, and pour vinegar over them. Brown the collops in a frying-pan, and then stew them with the drained cucumbers in a little broth. Skim and season the stew, and serve it hot in a ragout-dish.—*Obs*. Lamb chops are excellent dressed as above, but they must not be over fat. Some cooks add slices of onion to the above ragout, and the practice is commendable.—See p. 120, 127.

477. *To roll a loin of mutton*.—Keep the meat till quite tender and just beginning to turn. Bone it, and season it highly with black and Jamaica pepper, mace, nutmeg, and cloves, (all in powder,) and salt. Let it lie a day in this seasoning. Flatten it with a rolling-pin, and cover it with forcemeat as for roast hare. Roll it up, and bind with fillets of linen. Half-roast or bake it in a slow oven. Skim off all the fat when cold, and finish the dressing of the loin by stewing it in the gravy drawn from itself, first dredging it well with flour and more spices. Put to the hot sauce, ten minutes before dishing the meat, a glass of red wine, catsup, an anchovy, and a large spoonful of lemon-pickle.

478. *To dress mutton rumps and kidneys*.—Parboil six rumps (which are the number necessary for a dish) in mutton-broth. Let them cool, and take off the cake of fat from the gravy. Brush the rumps with egg, dip them in crumbs and chopped parsley, and a little lemon-thyme, and brown them. Have six kidneys larded and broiled in a Dutch oven, and stew a little boiled rice in the gravy of the rumps. Dish the rice in a shallow dish, and lay the rumps on it, the points meeting at a centre; place a kidney between each of these, and garnish with cut pickles. See *Kidneys*, No. 399.—*Obs*. This dish is very good dressed plain in the Dutch oven,

and either served on rice stewed in broth, or with stewed cucumbers. Besides the above methods of dressing mutton, a *haunch* may be cut and roasted as venison. A *fillet* may be *braised** by covering it with buttered paper or veal-caul, and then coarse paste, and roasting and glazing it,—serving it on French beans or cucumbers, first stewed in gravy, and placed in the dish below the mutton. Rumps are very suitably served over a *purée* of pease, or of turnips.—See *Rogons de mouton*.

479. *Parson's or Friar's venison.*—Bone the shoulder of mutton, when kept till very tender, and lay it to steep in wine, vinegar, herbs, and spices. Make a forcemeat

---

* *Braising.*—We are afraid that the young beginner in cookery may not find the account of the process of braising which is given in this chapter sufficiently circumstantial. This process, which is of French invention, is, by thorough-bred gourmands, esteemed the *ne plus ultra* of cookery. It is eminently suited to white meats, lean, or what was anciently called "rascal venison," turkey, and domestic fowls. It is not quite so well adapted to delicate stomachs; nor is it relished by those whose unsophisticated palates can still distinguish and enjoy the native, decided flavour of meats. *Braised* turkey, or rather *Dinde en daube*, is a very favourite dish, and, when old and dry in the flesh, braising is requisite for this bird, of which it has been somewhat irreverently sung—

> "Turkey boiled is Turkey spoiled,
> And Turkey roast is Turkey lost;
> But for Turkey *braised*, the Lord be praised."

Braising is comparatively an easy process, and the same rules apply either to meat or poultry. Clean, season, and stuff or lard, where necessary, the article to be dressed. Line a thick-bottomed stew-pan or baking-dish just large enough to hold the meat with slices of good bacon or fat beef, sliced onion, carrot, and turnip. Strew in a few chopped herbs, with salt, mace, and black and Jamaica peppercorns, and a few bay-leaves, a clove of garlic, &c. &c. observing to vary and suit the seasonings to the nature of the preparation. Lay the meat or poultry on this spicy bed, and cover it with a superstratum of the same ingredients. Over this place a sheet of cambric-paper; wrap a cloth about the lid of the stew-pan, and press it closely down, setting a weight over it to keep it so, and to prevent the escape of the savoury steams which the meat or poultry ought to imbibe till completely saturated. Set the stew-pan over embers, have embers above it, and let the process be very slow. Dishes which are *braised* are finished by *glazing*, thus:—Take out the meat and keep it hot; strain the gravy into a clean pan; give it a quick uncovered boil for a few minutes, and brush the meat with the jelly once or oftener till it look well, allowing one coat to firm before another coat of the varnish is put on: *or* you may have a *glaze* ready prepared. French cooks *glaze* every dish. The English relish *varnish* as little on their meat as *rouge* on the cheeks of their countrywomen. The *poele* is much the same. It is used for chickens and white meats; and the cooking process is more rapid than in *braising*.—P. T.

of the trimmings and the kidney, tongue, &c. with oysters or mushrooms. Stuff the shoulder,—cover it with veal-caul; roast or braise it, and serve with venison-sauce. Garlic gives the flavour of foreign cookery, if this flavour is wished.

480. *Sheep's or lamb's trotters.*—Stew in a braise, and serve with sauce Robert.—See *also French Cookery*.

481. *Sheep's tongues.*—Blanch, stew in broth or in the stock-pot, or braise them. Skin and split them; heat them up and dish them round, and pour a *ragout* of turnip or onion over them, or in the centre.

482. *Another way.*—Blanch and stew them, make a ragout of a dozen and a half of small onions, fried in butter with a little minced eschalot, catsup, wine, and white seasonings; add broth. Stew the tongues in this for a half hour. Skim the sauce. Dish the tongues, sauce them, and arrange the onions round, or in the centre.

483. *Made-dishes of cold mutton.*—Dressed mutton may be warmed up either by *hashing, stewing* in broth, or *broiling* in a Dutch oven. The last mode is suitable to a blade-bone, or Poor Man of Mutton, which may be scored, seasoned, broiled, and served with any relishing sauce, or over a hash of the rest of the mutton.

484. *To hash mutton.*—Cut the white underdone parts into thin slices, about the size of a shilling. Prepare a gravy from the gristles and other trimmings, and season it with pepper, salt, and onion. Skim off the fat, and strain it, and putting the meat to it, let it soak till thoroughly warm, but it must not boil.—See *Obs.* No. 421.

485. *Minced mutton with cucumbers.*—Mince the best parts left of a cold roasted leg, and stir this into a mince of stewed cucumbers. Let it heat, but not boil. —*Obs.* Minced mutton may also be served with endive.

N.B.—Almost every dish made of mutton may be prepared of lamb.

486. *Plain casserole of dressed mutton.*—Line a mould with mashed potatoes; fill it with the sliced mutton properly seasoned; cover the whole with more mashed potatoes, and bake and turn it out.

487. *Haricot of cold mutton.*—Cut the cold meat into chops, trimming off all superfluous fat, and simmer it very slowly in any strong well-seasoned broth you may have ready, or may make of the mutton-bones, &c. Add a half-dozen of button-onions, some round slices of carrot,

and a turnip scooped down in bits like marbles.—*Obs.*
This is a good and economical way of dressing cold roast
mutton for family use.*—See also pages 81, 96, 120, 282,
and *French Cookery*.

MADE-DISHES OF LAMB.

488. *Breast of lamb with cucumbers*.—Chop off the
chine-bone, and notching the breast well, stew it in good
gravy for twenty minutes. Take it up, drain and score it
in diamonds. Season it with mixed spices, dredge it with
flour, and finish in a Dutch oven, or on the gridiron.
Serve on stewed cucumbers, or green pease.

489. *Lamb-cutlets with spinage*.—Take cutlets from
the loin; flatten, season, and broil them; and placing
spinage (No. 197) neatly in a dish, lay the cutlets round it.

Lamb-cutlets are also very elegantly served with a
ragout of mushrooms or oysters, the cutlets laid around
the ragout. Asparagus, or asparagus pease, is very suitable to lamb.

490. *Shoulder of lamb stuffed*.—Bone the shoulder,
and fill up the vacancy with forcemeat. *Braise* the
meat very slowly over embers, or a stove; or stew it
plainly in the same manner. Glaze, and serve it either
with sorrel-sauce, tomata-sauce, or stewed cucumbers.

491. *Lamb-steaks ragout*.—Stew them in a little veal-
broth, to which a little sweet milk is put, and season
with white pepper and mace. When nearly ready, thicken
the sauce with a little mushroom-powder, a bit of butter
rolled in flour, and add a large glassful of good boiling
cream.

492. *Lamb-steaks brown*, see p. 120.—Flatten and
season them. Brush them with egg, and roll them in a
seasoning of chopped parsley, bread-crumbs, grated
lemon-peel, nutmeg, and salt. Fry them of a fine light-
brown, and pour over them some good thickened gravy,
in which are put a glass of wine, and either a few
stewed oysters or mushrooms. Skim the sauce, and serve

---

* *A Poor Man of Mutton*.—This Scotch dish is the blade-bone
grilled, or heated before the fire. There is a traditionary story of Lord
————, after a long and severe fit of illness with which he was seized in
London, horrifying his landlord by whining forth from behind his bed-
curtains when urged to choose and eat, "I think I could tak' a snap o' a
Puir man." Swift's scheme for Ireland only went the length of eating
children.

the dish very hot, garnishing it with forcemeat-balls, fried bread, or cut pickles if preferred. These chops, which form a nice side-dish may be served over a *purée* of turnip; or with pease, or stewed cucumbers.

493. *Another way.*—Fry the steaks for five minutes in butter; drain them, dip them in egg and bread-crumbs, and finish them on the gridiron.

494. *Lamb-sweetbreads ragout.*—Blanch what will make a dish with scalding water. Soak and stew them in good clear gravy for twenty minutes, adding white pepper, mace, and salt. Thicken the gravy with butter rolled in flour. Beat up two yolks of eggs and a glass of sweet cream, with a dessert-spoonful of minced parsley, and a little nutmeg. Take off the stew-pan, and gradually mix in the beat egg and cream. Make the sauce hot, stirring it diligently lest it curdle, but do not let it boil. Asparagus points, or cut young French beans, first parboiled, may be stirred into the ragout.—*Obs.* If the sweetbreads are very large they must be cut.

495. *Lamb-chops with potato, a favourite dish.*—Cut the back-ribs of a large lamb into handsome chops, trimming off the bone with a chopping-knife. Season, and brush the chops with a beat egg; dip them in crumbs and minced parsley, and fry them nicely. Place mashed potatoes (made somewhat thin with butter and cream, and again heated,) high in the centre of a dish, score this neatly, and lay the hot chops around, leaning each chop on the side of the adjoining one.—*Obs.* A finely-minced onion may be added to the mashed potatoes if the flavour is liked. This is just a *purée* of potato.

To dress lamb's liver, see p. 129. *To dress lamb's head,* or *calf's head,* see p. 293.

496. *To dress a leg of lamb with vegetables.*—Cut the loin into handsome steaks, and fry them nicely. Boil the gigot slowly, skimming it well, that it may look white and plump. Place the gigot in the middle of the dish, lay the steaks around it, with sprigs of nicely boiled cauliflower on each steak: or it may be served with spinage, sorrel, or stewed cucumber. Pour some hot melted butter over the gigot.—*Obs.* This is an elegant variety in dressing lamb, and is attended with no additional expense whatever.

497. *To grill a shoulder of lamb.*—Parboil, score

in diamonds, and broil (i.e. grill it over a clear fire,) *or* brown it in a Dutch oven. Serve with a clear gravy, or with mushroom, or cucumber sauce.

Besides the above methods of cookery, lamb may be dressed as *ragout, collar, curry, Cutlets Maintenon,* covered with rice, and in all the ways mutton is dressed. Cold lamb, whether shoulder or breast, is best re-dressed in the Dutch oven, by scoring, seasoning, and grilling it; or it may be hashed, though this mode of dressing is not so well suited to lamb as to veal or poultry. For *Roast lamb,* see p. 102.

498. *Lamb's stove, a Scottish dish.*—Clean and blanch the head. Stew it in broth, or along with a scrag of mutton till tender. Add minced parsley, green onions, and some mashed spinage, and serve the stew and head together in a deep dish.—*Obs.* This, nationality apart, we consider a very indifferent preparation. It is but a beggarly imitation of the *Tête d'agneau à la pluche verte* of our old allies the French.—See *Lamb's-head,* p. 293.

499. *Lamb's stove, by a French receipt.*—Clean *two* lambs' heads. Lift up the skin, and cut out the jaw-bones. Let them soak in salt and water; blanch them; rub them with lemon to whiten them. Let them simmer for an hour in a *blanc.** Drain them; split the skull; take out the brains, skin the tongues, and split them; trim the ears. Serve the heads neatly arranged on the dish with a good sauce, and the haslet minced or cut in scollops under the head or heads, as ragout: *or* serve with a green sauce of parsley. One head will make a dish.

500. *Pigs' petittoes.*—Boil the feet till tender; boil also the haslet as directed in lamb's head. Mince the haslet (or pluck), and season, and serve with the feet over it; garnish with sippets. Lamb's trotters, No. 480.

MADE-DISHES OF VENISON.

501. *To Stew a shoulder of venison when too lean to roast.*—Bone the meat when it has been kept long enough. Flatten it, and lay over it thin slices of fat well-flavoured mutton. Sprinkle with plenty of mixed spices, and roll it up very tight. Stew it slowly in rich beef or mutton gravy, in a close stew-pan that will just

---

* See Note in French Cookery for the rich broth called a *blanc.*

hold it. Add, when nearly finished, pepper, cayenne, allspice, and a half-pint of claret or port. When the venison is tender, which will be in about three hours, take off the bandages, and dish it, pouring the strained gravy over it. Serve with venison-sauce.—*Obs.* A few slices of lean mutton, or two or more shanks well broken, may be put to the gravy to enrich the stew. A *breast* may be dressed as above, but is better as a pasty.

502. *Venison-collops, a Scotch dish.*—Cut the meat in thin cutlets, season them highly with mixed spices, and having browned them in the stew-pan, put to them a quarter-pint of strong brown gravy, the same quantity of claret, some fried crumbs, a little fine sugar, and a glass of the best white wine vinegar. Stew slowly in a close-covered stew-pan, and pour over the collops the strained sauce. They may first be marinaded in the wine, vinegar, and spices.—*Obs.* Venison makes the finest flavoured minced collops, surpassing either beef or hare; and excellent *steaks*, when seasoned, dipped in butter, rolled in crumbs, and broiled quickly. But these steaks require a gravy-sauce, unless the venison be very fat.— See Nos. 55, 22, and 21.

503. *Civet of venison.*—Cut the back-ribs, or breast, in small chops. Fry some pieces of good bacon in butter, and when melted, drain off most of the liquid and add flour. Brown the steaks in this *roux*, and then moisten with red wine, (Burgundy or claret,) and good broth. Add parsley, onions, pepper, salt, and also garlic if admired. Let this cook slowly, shaking the pan occasionally. Add small onions and mushrooms. Let the sauce be of good consistence. This is elegantly served *en casserole*. Hare and rabbits make good *civet*.

MADE-DISHES OF COLD VENISON.

504. *To stew cold venison.*—Make a gravy of what remains about the bones after cutting off the meat, a little strong unseasoned mutton-broth, and a bundle of sweet herbs. When this is good, skim it, and add browned butter thickened with flour, also catsup, mixed spices, a little claret, and a spoonful of currant-jelly if it is liked. Boil this till smooth, stirring it well, and put in the thinly sliced venison. Let it heat thoroughly,

and taking out the herbs, dish it, squeezing a lemon into the dish. Garnish with slices of lemon and fried sippets, or with cut pickles.

505. *To hash venison.*—Cut the meat as for other hashes, and warm it in its own gravy. Season and dish it with toasted sippets.—*Obs.* When the hashed venison is very lean, some cooks cut the firm fat of a neck of mutton into thin, small slices, stew them first in wine and sugar, and add them to the hash. A large piece of cold venison, when it cannot be used otherwise, will make a good stew-soup, made as directed for veal stew-soup.—For *Roasting venison*, see p. 99.—*Collops*, p. 129.

MADE-DISHES OF HARE AND RABBIT.

506. *To stew a hare.*—Cut off the legs and shoulders, or wings, as they are sometimes called; chop down the middle of the back, and then chop each side into two or three pieces. Season these with mixed spices, and steep* them for some hours in eschalot-vinegar with three bay-leaves, and some pounded cloves. Make a pint and a half of gravy of the neck, head, liver, heart, trimmings, &c. with onions, a good slice of bacon chopped into small bits, a large carrot split, sweet herbs, and two dozen corns of black pepper and allspice. Strain this into a clean stew-pan, and put the hare, with the vinegar in which it has been soaked, to it, and stew gently till done. Add salt, spices, and a little cayenne. A little catsup may be added, and the stew may be thickened with butter rolled in browned flour.—*Obs.* This is an excellent method of dressing a hare, which makes at best but a dry and ungainly roast. A few par-roasted button-onions may be peeled, stewed in the sauce, and served with the hare. An old hare requires to be either larded, stewed in very rich broth, or, which is still better, *braised*. Garlic, if liked at all, should be used with hare. *Hare* is also stewed in wine, ale, or cider, enriching the liquor with rasped bacon and high seasonings; and also with the blood put in when the dish is taken off the fire; the liver and lights may be dressed as

---

* The propriety of this and of all *marinades*, we must own, is strongly doubted by some gastronomers of repute. They do not consider the flavour imparted as at all equivalent to the native juices withdrawn.

forcemeat-balls to serve with it. Currant-jelly, honey, or sugar may be used with discretion in this dish.—See *Lievre en daube*.

507. *To jug hare*.—Cut it into small pieces; season them, and put them into a jugging-can which will just hold them, with a slice or two of good bacon or beef hashed, a faggot of herbs, a few onions, with a half-dozen cloves stuck in them, a couple of bay-leaves, the rind of a lemon, and a little water. Cover the jugging-can closely, so that the steams may not escape. Set it in a kettle of boiling water, or a slow oven, for three hours. When done, skim off the fat, and strain off the gravy; thicken it; add seasonings if necessary, and, dishing the pieces of hare neatly, pour the hot sauce over them; or, if they have become cold, heat them up in it.—*Obs.* Red wine, instead of water, and the juice of a lemon, may be added to the jugged hare, which will then make a highly-flavoured ragout. Serve venison-sauce; but the natural sauce is the best that can accompany this dish.

508. *To broil a roasted hare for supper or luncheon*. —Cut off the legs and shoulders, and flatten and season them highly; broil them on a quick, clear fire; froth with cold butter, and serve them hot with venison-sauce.—*Obs.* Hare may also be dressed as directed for *braised goose*.—See No. 530.

509. *To hash hare*.—Cut down the cold hare into thin bits, and warm these in a gravy made of the head, bones, &c. Season with mixed spices, an onion, and herbs, and a little wine. Pick out the onion and herbs, and serve the hash with toasted sippets.

510. *Hare-cakes*.—Mince the best parts of the hare with a little firm mutton-suet. Season the mince highly. Pound it in a mortar, and making it up with raw eggs as small cakes or sausage roll, flour and fry them, or do them in a Dutch oven.—See *Gateau de lievre*.

511. *To smother rabbits*.—Truss them and boil them; *smother* them with white onion-sauce, melting the butter with milk or cream that it may look very white.— *Obs.* In Scotland rabbits wont to be smothered in an onion-sauce made with strong clear gravy instead of melted butter, and though the dish looked less fine, it was at least equally good. Rabbits cannot be too slowly boiled. Bring them very slowly to boil, and finish by the side of the fire. Those who dislike strong onion-sauce

for this dish may use a part of apples, turnips, or bread. Celery, artichoke-bottoms, young pease, and French beans, are all used as ragouts for rabbits. Warren rabbits are far before tame ones for the table,—wild ones are better still.

512. *To fry rabbits.*—Cut them in joints, and fry them in fresh butter, with dried parsley and a sprinkling of sage. Serve liver and parsley-sauce. Rabbits may also be fricasseed as directed for chickens. They make an excellent pie, a good soup, and may be potted or jugged.—See *Curry, Pie, Rabbits à la Venetienne, &c.*

MADE-DISHES OF POULTRY AND GAME.—See also
pages 84, 104, and 122.

513. *To boil fowls with rice.**—Stew a large white fowl in a little clear mutton-broth, seasoned with white pepper, onion, and mace, in a close stew-pan that will just hold it and allow it room to swell. When it has stewed a half-hour, put to it a small cupful of clean well-soaked rice. When tender, take up the fowl, keep it hot, and, straining the rice from the broth, place it on a reversed sieve to dry. Dish the fowl, and pile the rice in light heaps around it. Serve parsley and butter sauce. Serve the soup separately.—See pages, 237, 238, 240.

514. *Fowl with mushrooms.*—Season and stew as above in a very strong gravy, with butter rolled in flour, and add a few button-mushrooms nicely picked. Serve mushroom-sauce or a white fricassee of mushrooms.

515. *Fowls with oysters.*—Truss as for boiling. Put plenty of butter and a seasoning of mace and lemon-rind into them; tie them at neck and vent; cover a nice stew-pan with bacon, and put in the fowls. Moisten with broth, and *braise* the fowls slowly. Meanwhile have a very nice oyster-sauce prepared either with butter or cream; dish the fowls on this, and garnish with fried oysters and slices of lemon.–See *Howtowdie, Nat. Dishes.*

516. *To force a fowl,—a favourite, old-fashioned*

---

* *This is quite the French dish, Poularde au riz.* Fowls *à la Turque* are much the same thing too, save that they are stuffed with seasoned rice, in roasting have the breast covered with layers of bacon, and are papered till done. No. 515 is much the same as the receipt in French Cookery, *Poulets aux huitres.*

English Dish.—Having boned the fowl, stuff the inside with the following forcemeat:—A quarter-pound of minced veal, two ounces of grated ham, two of chopped onion and suet, a spoonful of shred sweet herbs, two chopped hard yolks of eggs, a tea-spoonful of minced lemon-peel, mixed spices, and a little cayenne. Let the several ingredients be very finely shred. Beat the whole to a paste in a mortar, adding two eggs to make them cohere. Stuff the fowl, sew it up, keeping it of a natural shape, draw in the legs, and truss the wings. Stew it in white clear broth, and when nearly done, thicken the sauce with butter rolled in flour. When just ready to serve, add a little cream, squeeze a lemon into the dish, and serve the fowl with the sauce around it.—See *Quenelles* and *Gratin, French Cookery.*

517. *To ragout poultry, pigeons, rabbits, &c.*—Half-roast the thing which is to be dressed as ragout. Cut it into joints as at table, and stew in good broth, with a couple of onions, two dozen corns of allspice and black pepper, a few cloves, a piece of lemon-peel, and for some things a slice of celery, for others, a couple of bay-leaves. Skim the stew, and, keeping the lid quite close, let it simmer for three quarters of an hour or more, according to the age and size of the birds. Strain off the gravy, leaving the fowls in the stew-pan to keep hot. Take off the cake of fat which will soon form upon the gravy, and thicken it with butter rolled in browned flour till it is as thick as stiff pancake-batter. Add to it a glass of white wine and the squeeze of a lemon. Dish the fowls, ducks, or rabbits, whichever your dish may be, and pour the sauce hot over them, garnishing with fried bread.—*Obs.* The sauce ought to be smooth, thick, and well-coloured. It may be made without wine.

518. *To braise chickens or pigeons.*—Bone them, and stuff them with forcemeat, as at No. 516. Fry a few sliced onions in a stew-pan; add to these the bones and other trimmings of the chickens, with a broken shank of veal or mutton, a faggot of herbs, a few blades of mace, and a pint of good broth. Cover the chickens with slices of bacon, and then with veal-caul or paper. Wrap a cloth about the lid of the stew-pan, and stew very slowly over embers, or on a stove, for an hour and a half. Take them up, and keep them hot in an oven.

Strain the braise-gravy, and boil it up quickly to a jelly. Glaze the chickens with it, and serve with a brown fricassee of mushrooms.—See *French Cookery*.

519. *A continental method of dressing cold roast fowls.* —Beat up two yolks of eggs with butter, mace, nutmeg, &c. Cut up the fowls, dip them in this, and roll the egged pieces in crumbs and fried parsley. Fry the cut pieces nicely in butter or clarified dripping, and pour over the dish any white or green vegetable ragout (that you may have left) made hot. *Parmesan* grated is used to heighten the *gout* of this dish.

520. *To braise a goose.*—Every thing to be braised is trussed as for boiling. Put slices of bacon over the goose, and line the stew-pan with the same. Put in the goose with the giblets and seasonings. Moisten with stock. Braise as directed, page 300, and serve it above either apple or onion sauce, or onion sauce mollified with white turnip.—*Obs*. A hare may be cooked thus.— Wine is used in braising both goose and turkey, but we see no use for it.—For *Turkey*, see *French Cookery*.

521. *To fricassee chickens white.*—Cut up each chicken into eight parts, as in carving them at table. Wash, dry, flatten, and season the parts with mixed spices, using only white pepper. Take a pint of clear veal or mutton-gravy, or other good clear stock, and put to it a roll of lemon-peel, two onions, three blades of mace, and a few sweet herbs. Stew the chicken in this very slowly for a half-hour, keeping the stew-pan covered. Strain the sauce, and thicken it with butter rolled in flour, adding salt, and a scrape of nutmeg. When ready to serve, add a quarter-pint of good hot cream, and the yolk of one or two eggs well beat. Mix this very carefully, and, lest it curdle, be sure it does not boil. A glass of white wine and the squeeze of a lemon may be put to the fricassee.—*Obs*. Besides the above methods of dressing fowls and chickens, they may be stewed with pease and lettuce in good broth, seasoned with parsley, young onions, salt, and spices. Put in the pease, and a cut lettuce, a quarter of an hour after the chickens. Fill up the dish with the gravy, laying the pease and lettuce over the chickens. If large fowls they may be cut down the back. Young chickens may be trussed as for boiling,

and stuffed.—(See in French Cookery *Fricasee naturel*, and *à la Paysanne*.)

522. *Davenport fowls* are stuffed with a forcemeat made of the hearts, livers, &c., an anchovy, yolk of hard-boiled eggs, onions, mixed spices, and a piece of butter or shred mutton-suet, or veal-kidney fat. Sew up the necks and vents, brown the fowls in a Dutch oven, then stew them in broth, and serve with mushroom-sauce, or melted butter and catsup; a fowl forced in this way may be larded in the breast, and roasted.—See No. 516.

523. *To stew giblets.*—Clean and cut them as directed for giblet-soup, p. 156. Season with mixed spices. Stew them till very tender in a little broth, and before serving thicken the sauce, and add a glass of good boiling cream to it.

524. *To pull cold turkey or chickens.*—Skin them, and pull the meat off the breast and wings in long flakes. Brown these in a Dutch oven, basting with butter, or brown very quickly in a frying-pan, so as not to dry the meat. Drain from the butter, and simmer the pulled meat in good gravy, seasoned with mixed spices. Thicken the sauce. Meanwhile cut off the legs, sidesmen, and back. Season and broil these, and serving the pulled hash in the middle of the dish, place these neatly over and around it. Garnish with fried sippets. Turkey may be warmed as above; but the leg should be scored, seasoned, and grilled, and the hash served under the *devilled leg.*—See No. 27.

525. *To stew pigeons brown.*—Season them, and truss them with the legs inward. Return the livers into them, with a bit of butter and chopped parsley. Lay them in a small stew-pan, with slices of bacon below and over them. Twenty minutes will cook them:—serve well-seasoned brown gravy-sauce with them.—See Nos. 33, 42.

526. *To ragout pigeons.*—Clean and stuff them with a seasoning of mixed spices, salt, parsley shred very finely, a piece of fresh butter, and a few bread-crumbs. Tie them at neck and vent, half-roast them, and finish in the stew-pan in good gravy, to which a glass of white wine, a bit of lemon-peel, and a few nice pickled mushrooms may be put. Thicken the sauce with butter rolled in flour. Dish the pigeons, and pour it over them. Garnish with asparagus laid between the birds.

This is almost the French "*Pigeons en compôte.*"—
Obs. Cream, or the beat yolk of an egg, may be put to
this, and to any white ragout, taking care to prevent
these ingredients from curdling. The pigeons may be
stuffed with a forcemeat of the chopped livers, with
bread-crumbs, minced parsley, butter, spices, and a little
cayenne, and dressed as a brown ragout, by browning
them in the frying-pan previous to stewing, thickening
the sauce with browned flour, and adding to it a spoonful of catsup or a glass of red wine. Some good cooks
stew pigeons with white cabbage, cut as for pickling,
serving the cabbage round the pigeons; or stew them in
brown gravy highly seasoned, adding mushrooms or a
little catsup. Others stew them with a lettuce quartered
instead of cabbage. Pigeons *pot* very well, and are,
though common, excellent as a pie, either cold or hot.
—*N.B.* The cabbage must be first *braised.*—To *Roast*
or *Broil Pigeons*, see pages 112 and 122; *Pigeon Soup,*
p. 153.

527. *Ducks with young pease, a favourite dish prepared
in the best manner.*—Clean, truss, and singe the ducks,
which should be plump and young. Season them
with salt, pepper, cayenne, and mixed spices. Place
them between layers of bacon in a stew-pan that
will just hold them, and moisten them with a little broth.
Stew them from a half-hour to a whole one, according to the size and age of the birds. Meanwhile parboil
and afterwards fry three pints of the most delicate green
pease with a half-pound of good bacon cut in bits. While
the pease still retain their good colour drain off all the fat,
dust some flour over them; add a little water or broth,
a bunch of parsley and young onions, some pepper and
salt, and the ducks carved (if too large) into proper
pieces. Serve the pease over the ducks, and let all fat
be carefully skimmed off. This is much the same dish
as the French *Canard à petit pois.*—*Obs.* The ducks
may be roasted; but stringy summer ducks that come
with green pease are much better dressed as above. Some
persons will prefer the pease fried in butter instead of bits
of bacon; and the dish, if not so rich, will remain at
least as elegant. Take out the parsley and onions.

528. *To stew an old duck with cabbage.*—Stew the
cut cabbage in top-fat with seasonings. Par-roast a

large fat duck, and stew it in gravy well seasoned with herbs, onions, sage, pepper, and salt. Thicken the gravy, and serve the duck with the cabbage under it and the sauce in the dish.—*Obs.* Ducks may be served with mashed turnips, onion *purée*, or *sour crout*.

529. *To ragout ducks.*—Put the gizzards, livers, necks, &c. to a pint of good strong beef-broth, or other well-seasoned good stock. Season the ducks inside with salt and mixed spices. Brown them on all sides in a frying-pan, and then stew them till tender in the strained stock. When nearly ready, thicken the sauce with browned flour and butter.

530. *Another way.*—Clean, and season the ducks with pepper and salt inside. Par-roast them, and stew them in beef gravy, with shred onions fried in the stew-pan before the gravy is put in. When the ducks have simmered for twenty minutes, and been turned, put in a few leaves of sage and of lemon-thyme chopped very fine, or, in the season, a pint and a half of young green pease. When these are tender, thicken the sauce with butter rolled in flour, and serve the ducks and pease together in a deep dish.—*Obs.* When pease are not in season, a dozen or two of button-onions may be first par-roasted and then stewed with the ducks; *or* sliced cucumbers and onions, first fried.*—See No. 527.

531. *To hash ducks.*—Nothing hashes better than a fat duck. Cut it into pieces as in carving at table, and soak these by the side of the fire in a little boiling gravy till thoroughly hot. Add a glass of wine and a sufficient quantity of mixed spices, to give the sauce a high relish: *or*, cut up the ducks, make a gravy of the trimmings and some onions. Thicken it when strained with butter browned with flour. Stew the cut ducks gently till ready, and, having seasoned the sauce, serve the hash on fried sippets.—*Obs.* A cold *goose* may be dressed in the same way, adding a little finely-shred sage and onion to

---

* Fillets cut from the breast of plump, under-roasted ducks (that have been stuffed with chopped young sage and onion before they were roasted), served in hot orange-gravy and the juice that flows from the birds, with cayenne and high seasonings, are esteemed a rare luxury by the skilful gourmand. This is a dish for the solitary epicure, not for a table. Wives, children, and friends have no portion in such dainties. This is indeed the French *Table Salmi*.

the hash-sauce;—or the legs of a goose may be scored, seasoned, and grilled, as directed for a turkey, and served over the hash. Cold *poultry*, *rabbits*, and *game* may all be hashed as above. See that the hash-sauce be well thickened, smooth, and carefully cleared of all fat. Where there is any cold stuffing left, cut it into slices, and serve it warmed in the Dutch oven, round the hashed meat.

532. *To hash cold wild fowl.*—Carve them as at table, and let them soak till hot in boiling gravy thickened with bread-crumbs, and seasoned with salt, mixed spices, a glass of claret, and a spoonful of lemon-pickle or orange-juice. Garnish with fried sippets. For partridges and pheasants use only *white* pepper and *white* wine.—See p. 109.

N.B.—Some *gourmands* dislike bread-crumbs here.

533. *To ragout wild duck or teal.*—Half-roast the birds. Score the breast, but not deeply, and into each indenture put mixed spices and the juice of a lemon. Let the birds lie a few minutes, and then stew them till tender in good brown gravy. Take up the birds and keep them hot; add a glass of wine and three finely-shred eschalots to the gravy, and pour it over the ducks. —*Obs.* This is a dish of very high *gout*, and it is prized accordingly. In carving ducks, whether wild or domestic, after scoring the breast it is an improvement to put a little butter over it, as in shoulder of lamb, and above that to squeeze a bitter orange or lemon. Ducks are also re-dressed as curry, brown ragout, or as a stew-soup. Ducks, and particularly the wild, may be dressed as *civet* of hare.—See also *French Cookery, Salmis*, and No. 29.

534. CHICKEN, RABBIT, AND VEAL, &C. AS CURRY.

THIS common and favourite dish is at once economical, convenient at table, and of easy preparation. All kinds of viands, dressed or raw, may be dressed as curry. The only important rule is, to have good stock; and the sole art consists in hitting the medium in seasoning, or in suiting the tastes of the individuals for whom the curry is prepared.—See *Obs.* p. 190. Cut up the chickens, fowls, rabbits, veal, lamb, &c. &c. into pieces proper to be helped at table, and rather small than clumsily large. Fry this cut meat in butter, with sliced

Spanish or whole button-onions, over a quick fire, till of a fine amber colour. When the meat is thus browned, add nearly a pint of good mutton or veal stock unseasoned; and when this has simmered slowly for a quarter of an hour, or more if the fowls are old, add from two to three dessert-spoonfuls of curry-powder and a spoonful of flour, both rubbed very smooth, and carefully stirred into the sauce. When the curry is just ready, add also a glass of good thick cream, and either the juice of a lemon or a proportionate quantity of citric acid. Skim off all fat, and if the sauce is not rich enough, stir in, before dishing, a small quantity of melted butter. If the sauce be too thick, add a little broth to thin it. Some cooks pound part of the meat and all the scraps to thicken the curry, and also the boiled livers, &c. Others marinade, in lemon-juice and sliced onion, the meat they curry. —*Obs.* Curry may be made of cold chicken, slices of veal, lamb, &c. and is a very acceptable variety at table in place of *toujours* hash, though very inferior to curry of undressed meat. Some cooks add a few small onions that have been cooked in broth; others a few capsicums or a fresh Chili, which is peculiarly acceptable to those who like hot-spiced dishes.—See *Fish-curry,* p. 190.

535. *Curry-balls.*—Take stale bread-crumbs finely grated, the yolk of a hard-boiled egg, and a piece of fresh butter the size of a walnut. Add curry-powder, and, beating these ingredients to a paste in a mortar, make the mixture up into small balls, with raw yolk of egg and a little flour.—See Nos. 301, 355.

536. *To boil rice for curry.*—Pick and soak Patna rice, and boil it quickly in boiling water and salt till it be tender but not soft; drain it, and put it to dry before the fire on a sieve reversed. Either heap it lightly on a dish by itself, or if the dish of curry be small, it may be served round the dish in which the curry is placed in the centre, *en casserole.*—*Obs.* Rice for curry is seldom properly boiled. It is either in a mash, or the grains are quite hard. To avoid both defects some cooks shower cold water upon the boiled rice, and set it to evaporate before the fire, so that every several particle may be distinct, and yet the whole tender enough to eat. When overboiled, the rice may, after draining, be smoothed, brushed over with yolk of egg, and browned in

the oven,—though this necessity ought never to be courted. Handle it very lightly. Spooning spoils it,—toss it lightly up with two forks.—See *National Dishes*.

537. *Hindostanee mode of boiling rice*.—After picking, soak it in cold water a quarter of an hour. Strain and put it into boiling water, which shall rise three inches above the rice. Cover, and boil about six minutes, skimming when necessary. Add a gill of sweet milk for each pound of rice, and in two minutes more remove the pot from the fire; strain without squeezing; return it dry into the pot upon a slow fire, pour over it half an ounce of melted butter, mixed with a spoonful of the hot water in which the rice was boiled, and in six minutes it will be ready for table.—*From a Correspondent*.

538. *Brain-balls and cakes for made-dishes*.—These may be made either for lamb's or calf's-head by the same process. Clear the brains of all the fibres and skins that hang about them, and having scalded them, beat them up in a basin with the yolks of two eggs, a spoonful of bread-crumbs, another of flour, a little grated lemon-peel, and a small dessert-spoonful of finely-shred parsley, and if for calf's-head, a little shred sage and thyme. Put seasonings to the mixture, and a large spoonful of melted butter; and dropping the batter in small cakes, fry them in lard of an amber colour. They may either be served as a garnishing, or as a small side-dish to accompany a dressed calf's-head or lamb's-head.

539. *For balls*.—Roll the above mixture into small balls with more egg and flour.

540. *Croquets and rissoles*.—These little useful dishes differ from savoury patties only in shape. They are all made of cold chicken, sweetbreads, veal, or any nice bit of white meat that is left cold. Mince the meat, season it, and stew it for two minutes in gravy. *Croquets* are minced meat of various kinds rolled up as small sausages, dipped in egg and rolled in bread-crumbs, fried a light brown, and served with nicely-fried parsley. *Rissoles* are made in thin puff-paste, in any form you please, spreading a little of the mince on the paste, and doubling it up like an apple-pasty; or they are served as balls rolled up in paste, and fried, and garnished, with parsley.

541. *Canapés*.—Take the crumb of a large loaf, cut

it in slices the thickness of three quarters of an inch; afterwards cut the slices into any form, and fry them of a nice colour in oil or butter; mince separately the hard yolks and whites of eggs, cucumbers, capers, anchovies, in strips, different fine herbs, small salad herbs, &c. and put them in a little oil; season the *canapés* (i.e. fried bread) with salt, pepper, and vinegar; dress handsomely, and garnish tastefully with hard eggs, ham, beetroot, small radishes, anchovies, capers, cresses, &c. &c. and serve upon dishes for *hors d'œuvres*, i.e. relishes. *Canapés* are also made of skates' livers, and other things.

542. *Pork sausages.*—Mince the fat and lean of pork, keeping out skins and gristles, and season it well with salt, black and Jamaica ground pepper, and chopped sage. Clean and half-fill the guts, and fry the sausages.

543. *Oxford sausages.*—Take equal quantities of veal and pork, mince them, and add a half of the weight of beef-suet; mix and season this well, as directed above, and add a small quantity of the crumb of fresh bread, steeped in water.—*Obs.* A chopped anchovy is an improvement to these sausages. Lemon-peel, grated nutmeg, lemon-thyme, savoury and sweet marjoram, and basil, formerly used for these compositions, are now getting obsolete.

544. *Epping sausages.*—Take equal quantities of young tender pork and beef-suet. Mince them very finely, and season with salt, pepper, grated nutmeg, a sprinkling of sage, and some thin rind of bacon. Roll up with egg, and fry it.—See page 127.

545. *Bologna sausages.*—Take equal weight of bacon, beef, pork, and veal. Mince, and season high with pepper, salt, and sage. Fill a well-cleaned gut and boil for an hour.

546. *Beauvillier's sausages.*—Mince what quantity of fresh pork will be necessary; mix with it equal to a quarter of lard; add salt and fine spices; fill the skins and tie them; hang them in the smoke for three days; then cook them in *bouillon* for three hours, with salt, a clove of garlic, thyme, bay, basil, parsley, and young onions; when cold, serve upon a napkin.

547. *Smoked Scotch sausages, to keep and eat cold.*— Salt a piece of beef for two days, and mince it with suet. Season it highly with pepper, salt, onion, or eschalot. Fill a large well-cleaned ox-gut, plait it in links, and

hang the sausage in the chimney to dry.* Boil it as wanted either a single link or altogether.

548. *Common beef sausages.*—These are made of minced beef, with seasonings, and a proportion of suet. The crumb of a penny-loaf, soaked in water, is allowed to every three pounds of meat, before filling the skins.

549. *Savaloys.*—Take a piece of tender pork, free from skin and gristles, and salt it with common salt and a little saltpetre. In two or three days mince it, and season with pepper, chopped sage, and a little grated bread. Fill the gut, and bake the savaloys for a half-hour in a moderate oven. If to be eaten cold, let them lie a day or two longer in the salt.—*Obs.* Sausage meat may be broiled in a veal-caul, in a cake or flat shape. It may be reddened with a little saltpetre. If to be used immediately, oysters, mushrooms, &c. may be put to sausages to heighten the flavour.—See *Boudin's French Cookery.*

550. DEVILS.

Though devils are often served at supper or luncheon, they are most commonly considered as provocatives and stimulants,—a relish with wine, or a spur to a jaded appetite. Their preparation must accordingly vary with the momentary tastes or necessities of the consumers. The only indispensable attribute of the common familiar cock-crow devil for the *rere-supper*, is scorching heat and tear-compelling pungency. Devils are made of the legs, rumps, backs, and gizzards of cold turkey, goose, duck, capon; and of all kinds of game, particularly the backs of moor-game, which have a peculiarly stimulating bitter; and also of venison, veal, and mutton-kidney, fish-bones, p. 170, and of biscuits or rusks. The meat to be dressed in this way must be scored, that the seasonings may find suitable places of retreat. The seasonings, which consist of salt, pepper, cayenne; and curry, mushroom, anchovy, or truffle-powder, must be administered at the

---

* Some of these sausages wont to be made when a *Mart* was killed: they formed an excellent article of supply for the hill, the moor, or the boat; and in the Hebrides and remote parts of the Highlands they still hold a favourite place in the wide open chimney. Real Bologna sausages labour under the imputation of being made of asses flesh. It is said the celebrated Fetter-Lane sausages owed their flavour and fame to sweet basil.

discretion of the consumer. It is a good mode to have the things seasoned at table, and then sent to the kitchen fire. The devils must be broiled on a strong clear fire, and served in a hot-water dish, or one with a spirit-lamp. When not served *dry* as a relish with wine, the proper sauces for devils, are, grill-sauce, anchovy-sauce, or any very piquant sauce. Dry toasts or rusks are a proper accompaniment to devilled poultry, &c.*

551. *Devilled biscuit.*—Heat the biscuits before the fire, and spread over them the same ingredients, with a little cayenne, as for anchovy-toasts, No. 554. Many other ingredients are used, and also the medicated *Zests* sold in the shops. The anchovy-powder, No. 326, answers well.—See *Le Bon Diable.*—National Dishes.

552. *Sandwiches.*—These are a convenient and econo-mical, but, at the same time, a rather suspicious order of culinary preparations, especially in hotels and public gardens: they are therefore getting into disrepute. Sandwiches may be made of ham or tongue, sliced, grated, or scraped; of German or common pork sausage, cold salted rump, anchovies, shrimps, sprats, potted cheese, or hard yolks of eggs and Parmesan or Cheshire cheese pounded with butter; forcemeat, and potted meat of various kinds, cold poultry, with whatever seasonings, as mustard, curry-powder, &c. &c. are most suitable to the meat of which the sandwich is made. The only particular

---

* The following receipt for the preparation of devils is the best that has yet been disclosed; for in this philosophic and amateur department of cookery profound mystery has hitherto been observed:—"Mix equal parts of common salt, pounded cayenne, and curry-powder, with double the quantity of mushroom or truffle powder. Dissect a brace of wood-cocks (if under-roasted so much the better,) split the heads, divide and subdivide the legs, wings, back, &c. and powder all the pieces with the seasonings well mixed. Bruise the trail and brains with the yolk of a hard-boiled egg, a very little pounded mace, the grate of half a lemon, and half a spoonful of soy. Rub these together till they become smooth, and add a table-spoonful of catsup, a glass of Madeira, and the juice of two Seville oranges. Throw this sauce, along with the birds, into a silver stew-dish to be heated by a lamp. Cover it close, and keep gently simmering, occasionally stirring, until the flesh has imbibed the greater quantity of the liquid. When you have reason to suppose it is com-pletely saturated, throw in a small quantity of salad-oil, and stirring it all once more well together, serve it round instantly." The only remaining direction the writer of this admirable receipt gives, is that as in picking the bones your fingers must necessarily be impregnated with the flavour of the devil, you must be careful in licking them, not to swallow them entirely. These are the French *Tables Salmis.*

directions that can be given, are, to have them fresh-made, and to cut the bread in neat even slices, of any shapes that are fancied, and not too large nor thick.— See *Sweet sandwiches*.

553. *A cheese-sandwich*.—Take two parts of grated Parmesan or Cheshire cheese, one of butter, and a small proportion of made-mustard; pound them in a mortar; cover slices of bread with a little of this, and over it lay thin slices of ham, or any cured meat; cover with another slice of bread, press them together, and cut this into mouthfuls, that they may be lifted with a fork. —*Obs*. An anchovy may be pounded with the mixture.

544. *Anchovy toasts*.—Cut slices of bread as for sandwiches, but keep them larger, and fry them nicely in fresh butter. Spread them with anchovy-butter, or anchovies and butter freshly pounded, and lay some quartered anchovies above all.*

555. *Ramakins*.—Take equal parts of sound Cheshire and Gloucester cheese and of fresh butter, and having crumbled or grated the cheese, beat the whole to a paste, with three or four raw yolks of eggs, and the crumb of a new French roll previously soaked in hot milk. Mix the paste with the whites of two of the eggs first well beaten. Season with a little salt, pepper, and pounded mace. Fill small paper pans, or very small saucers, half full with the mixture, and bake the ramakins in a Dutch oven. Serve them quite hot, which is peculiarly requisite for every relishing preparation of cheese.—*Obs*. This batter is also served over boiled macaroni; or with

---

* *Toasts*.—The old French Cookery possessed an endless variety of *Toasts*, some of which are still worthy of attention; as *Friar's toast*, which was exactly our modern *anchovy-toast* sprinkled over with chopped parsley, eschalot, and capers. *Brittany toasts* were made of chopped salad herbs, with salad-sauce. *Veal-kidney toasts* were rather a luscious mess; the minced kidney seasoned with eschalot and parsley, and mixed with egg and bread-crumbs, was in fact a piquant forcemeat spread on a toast, which was baked and served hot. *Ham-toasts* were made thus: —The slices were soaked to freshen them, in the first place, when this was needful, or the ham was minced. Afterwards they were soaked in a stew-pan in butter and seasonings for a few minutes; the toasts were fried in the same pan. They were drained and dished hot, and a little gravy with pepper, salt, and vinegar poured over them. There were toasts till more *recherché* of fat livers, skate-livers, &c. all appropriate to the *rere-supper* of old convivial times, but scarcely admissible into the cookery of modern, regularly-constituted families.

stewed celery, asparagus, cauliflower, or brocoli. Parmesan or Gruyere cheese will make a more relishing ramakin where expense is not considered.—See *Fondu, French Cookery,* and No. 516.

556. *Pastry ramakins.*—Take any bits of puff-paste that remain from covering pies, tarts, &c. and roll them lightly out. Sprinkle grated cheese over them of any rich high-flavoured kind. Fold the paste up in three, or only double it, but sprinkle it repeatedly with grated cheese. Shape the ramakins with a paste-runner to any shape, and bake and serve them hot on a napkin or as *relishes.* This is almost *Brioche au fromage.*

557. *To dress macaroni in the best way.*—Wash it well, and boil it slowly in water, till it is tender but not soft. Strain it, and add strong well-flavoured stock to it. When quite tender, dish it. Strew it over with grated Stilton or Parmesan cheese, and brown it in a Dutch oven. This dish is fashionably made *en timballe.* The timballe shape is lined with slices of bacon, which are taken off before the moulded macaroni is served, either with a brown sauce, or with gravy in the dish.— *Obs.* Instead of gravy-stock melted butter may be put to it. It may also be covered with ramakin-batter, or boiled with milk instead of water, or stewed in white ragout-sauce, with a little chopped lean ham. The grated cheese may also be mixed up with the boiled macaroni, and having dished it, strew fine bread-crumbs lightly over it, and pour melted butter on the crumbs through a colander. Brown it in a Dutch oven, or with a salamander.—See *Macaroni pudding.*

558. *To pot cheese.*—Cut down half a pound of good sound mellow Stilton, with two ounces of fresh butter; add a little mace and made mustard. Beat this well in a mortar, and pressing it close in a potting-can, cover with clarified butter if to be long kept.—*Obs.* Curry or anchovy powder, cayenne or pepper, may all be added to the cheese.

559. *Toast and cheese.*—Pare the crust off a slice of bread cut smooth, and of about a half-inch in thickness. Toast it, but do not let it wither or harden in the toasting. Butter, and cover the toast with slices of sound fat Stilton, Gouda, or Dunlop cheese of the first quality. Lay the toasts on a cheese-toaster, and notice that the cheese is equally done. Pepper, salt, and made mustard

are to be added at discretion.—*Obs*. The toasts may be covered with the cheese previously grated or chopped, which will facilitate the equal melting of it; or the cheese may be toasted on one side before being put upon the bread.

560. *Cheese-fritters*.—Pound good cheese with bread-crumbs, raw yolks, rasped ham, and butter. Make this into oval small balls, flatten, dip in stiff fritter-batter, and fry them.

561. *Savoury cheese-cakes*.—Take four ounces of butter, four of good grated cheese, four beat eggs, a little cream, salt, and pepper; mix and bake in cases.

562. *Braised cheese*.—Melt some slices of fat good cheese in a small dish over a lamp or over steam. Add butter and pepper, and mustard if chosen. Have ready soft toasts in a hot water-dish or cheese-dish with a hot water reservoir, and spread the cheese on these.

563. *Welsh Gallimaufry*.—Mix well in a mortar, cheese with butter, mustard, wine, flavoured vinegar, or any ingredient admired, *ad libitum*.

564. *A Scotch rabbit*.—Cut, toast, and butter the bread, as in No. 559, and keep it hot. Grate down mellow Stilton, Gouda, Cheshire, or good Dunlop cheese; and, if not fat, put to it some bits of fresh butter. Put this into a cheese-toaster which has a hot-water reservoir, and add to it a glassful of well-flavoured brown-stout porter, a large tea-spoonful of made mustard, and pepper, (very finely ground) to taste. Stir the mixture till it is completely dissolved, brown it, and then filling the reservoir with boiling water, serve the cheese with hot dry or buttered toasts on a separate dish.—*Obs*. This is one of the best plain preparations of the kind that we are acquainted with. Some gourmands use red wine instead of porter, but the latter liquor is much better adapted to the flavour of cheese. Others use a proportion of soft putrid cheese, or the whole of it in that state. This is, of course, a matter of taste beyond the jurisdiction of any culinary dictator. To dip the toasts in hot porter makes another variety in this preparation. Rasped Parmesan is largely used by Italian and French cooks to flavour ragouts and soups, and many dishes of vegetables. It is seldom employed in our insular cookery.

565. *Cheese to serve as a relish.*—Grate three ounces of good mellow cheese, and the same quantity of bread. Mix these with two ounces of butter, the beat yolks of two eggs, some made mustard, pepper, and salt. Mash in a mortar, and spread this paste on small toasts, and cut as sippets. Toast, brown, and trim these, and serve them very hot.*

DIFFERENT WAYS OF DRESSING EGGS AND OMELETS.

566. *To poach eggs.*—Boil and skim spring-water. Put a little vinegar to it. Break the eggs (which should be at least two days laid) with the point of a knife, that the meat may slide gently out without breaking. Take off the stew-pan, and slide them gently into the boiling water, taking care to break their fall. Turn the shell above the egg as you dip it into the water to gather in all the white. Let the sauce-pan stand by the side of the fire till the white is set, and then put it on the fire for two minutes. Take up the eggs with a slice; trim away the broken parts of the white, and serve them on toasts, slices of cold meat, broiled pork-sausages, spinage, brocoli, sorrel; also with veal gravy.—*Obs.* Poached eggs may be served with a sauce of grated ham, shred onions, parsley, pepper, and salt, stewed for ten minutes in weak broth. When ready, thicken and strain

---

* *Toasted cheese.*—This academic, histrionic, and poetical preparation has produced a good deal of discussion in its day. The *Welsh Rabbit*, (by the way, we are inclined to think with a learned friend, that the true reading is *Welsh Rare Bit*,) has ever been a favourite morsel with those gentlemen who think a second supper fairly worth the other three regularly-administered meals of the day. The twenty-eighth maxim of O'DOHERTY is wholly dedicated to this tasteful subject, and his culinary opinions are worthy of profound attention. "It is the cant of the day," quoth Sir MORGAN, "to say that a Welsh Rabbit is heavy eating. I know this,—but did I ever feel it in my own case?—Certainly not. I like it best in the genuine Welsh way, however;—that is, the toasted bread buttered on both sides profusely, then a layer of cold roast beef, with mustard and horseradish, and then on the top of all a super-stratum of Cheshire *thoroughly* saturated while in the process of toasting with *cwrw*, or, in its absence, porter—genuine porter—black pepper, and eschalot-vinegar. I peril myself upon the assertion, that this is not a heavy supper for a man who has been busy all day till dinner in reading, writing, walking, or riding,—who has occupied himself between dinner and supper in the discussion of a bottle or two of sound wine, or any equivalent, and who proposes to swallow at least three tumblers of something hot ere he resigns himself to the embrace of Somnus. With these provisoes, I recommend toasted cheese for supper."

the sauce, and when it is a little cool, cover the eggs with it. They may be poached in butter, or broth.

567. *To fry eggs.*—Carefully break the eggs into a small frying-pan, and have ready some butter fried in another pan to pour over them. Fry them at a good distance from the fire.—See No. 51.

568. *Mushroom and egg dish.*—Slice, fry, and drain some large onions, and a few button-mushrooms. Slice hard-boiled eggs, the yolks and white separately, and either simmer the whole in fresh butter with pepper, salt, mustard, and eschalot-vinegar, or in good gravy. Put in the sliced yolks last, and only let them remain about a minute. Serve very hot, and garnish with curled parsley and a few light rings of the white of the eggs.

569. *Swiss eggs.*—Mix two ounces of grated cheese and two of melted butter with six beat eggs. Season with salt, pepper, shred parsley, and young onions. Cook the mixture lightly in the frying-pan. Brown the upper side with a salamander, and serve very hot.

570. *To butter eggs.*—Beat six eggs well up in a basin. Set three ounces of fresh butter to melt in another basin placed in boiling water. Stir the eggs and butter together; add pepper and salt, and a finely-minced onion, if it is liked. Pour the mixture into a small sauce-pan, and toss it over a slow fire for a few seconds, then pour it into a large basin; *skink* the mixture backwards and forwards, setting it on the fire occasionally, but keeping it constantly briskly agitated till ready. Serve on toasts, or as an accompaniment to salt fish, or red herrings; or serve on a toast, and garnish with sprigs of brocoli.

571. *Scotch eggs.*—Five eggs make a dish. Boil them hard as for salad. Peel and dip them in beat egg, and cover them with a forcemeat made of grated ham, chopped anchovy, crumbs, mixed spices, &c. Fry them nicely in good clarified dripping, and serve them, with a gravy-sauce separately.—*Obs.* Eggs may be boiled half-hard, wrapped in puff-paste, dipped in egg and crumbs, fried and served as a side-dish or supper-dish. Eggs for a small dish may be boiled hard, sliced, and served in a white ragout-sauce, dishing them with a whole yolk in the middle. Curled slips of bacon, toasted sippets, fried parsley, mushrooms, &c. form appropriate accom-

paniments and garnishings to dishes of eggs.—See *French Cookery for other preparations of eggs.*

572. *An omelet.*—Beat up six eggs with salt, pepper in fine powder, a large spoonful of parsley very finely shred, half the quantity of chives or green onions, a small bit of eschalot, if liked, some grated ham or tongue; or if for *maigre* days, to which this dish is considered appropriate, lobster-meat, the soft part of oyster, shrimps, or grated cheese, may be used. Let the several things be very finely minced, and well mixed with the batter, adding a large spoonful of flour and some bits of butter. Fry the omelet in plenty of very hot butter in a nicely-tinned small frying-pan, stirring it constantly till it firm, and then lifting the edges with a knife, that the butter may get below. It must not be overdressed, or it will get tough and dry. Carefully turn the omelet, by placing a plate over it, and return it to the frying-pan to brown on the other side; or, without turning, hold the pan before the fire till the *raw* is taken off the upper side; double it, and serve it very hot.—*Obs.* A more delicate but less relishing omelet may be made by seasoning the batter with lemon-peel, mace, nutmeg, &c. and using neither meat nor fish. Some cooks put a little pulped apple, or mashed potato, to omelets; other flavour them with tarragon and mushroom-powder. Omelets may have grated ham, minced roast veal, kidney, or grated Parmesan cheese, sprinkled over them. In the old French cookery, omelets were garnished with anchovies, fat livers, red herrings, and all the pungent herbs used for toasts. To a simple omelet, the squeeze of a lemon or Seville orange is an improvement. Sweet omelets are made by rolling currant-jelly, or any suitable preserved sweetmeat, in fine pancakes.

573. *Asparagus and eggs.*—Beat three or four eggs well with pepper and salt. Cut some dressed asparagus into pieces the size of pease, and stir them into the eggs. Melt two ounces of butter in a small stew-pan, and pouring in the mixture, stir it till it thicken, and serve it hot on a toast.— Eggs may be made into a pie, using mince-pie meat with the hard-boiled chopped eggs. They may be served as a *vol-au-vent*, or with sippets, &c. Eggs may be filled with a relishing forcemeat, using the hard yolks as part of the *farce.*—See No. 51.

574. *Vol-au-vent.*—Cut with a paste-runner, puff-paste which has got six turns, and been doubled into the shape of the dish in which the *vol-au-vent* is to be served. Lay it on a baking-tin with a ledge, and ornament, and brush it over with yolk of eggs. Open it lightly all round, with the point of a knife, and when baked in a sharp oven, open the cover formerly marked, without breaking the top, scrape out all the inside paste, fill with any white fricassee, as chickens, rabbits, sweetbreads, or with scollops of turbot or cod, fillets of soles, &c., and put on the top.—*Obs.* One main use of a *vol-au-vent* is, that it gives a handsome form to things left cold, which could not otherwise make part of an entertainment for company. For second courses, *vol-au-vents* may be fancifully marked round the border in a wreath of leaves, and have sweetmeats or delicate dressed vegetables served in them.

575. *Edgings to dishes.*—These are made (to serve made-dishes in) of bread, rice, mashed potato, and ornamented pastry edgings; and for sweet dishes served in glass or china, of small drop-biscuit, caramelled fruit, nuts, or almonds, stuck on with candied sugar. These edgings as *casseroles*, *crustades*, *casserolettes*, and other *garnitures*, are most suitable to French dishes.

576. *Bread-borders.*—Take firm stale bread, cut the crumb in slices of the thickness of the blade of a knife; cut those slices into any form; heat pot-top oil in a stew-pan, and put in the sippets; make both white and brown; when they are very dry, drain them, make white paper cases, and put them up separately, according to their form and colour; when they are wanted to garnish dishes, pierce the end of an egg, let a little of the white out, and beat it with the blade of a knife; mix a little flour; heat your dish a little; dip one side of the sippet into the beaten paste, and stick it on; in this manner continue till the border is finished; care must be taken not to heat the dish too much.

577. *Rice casserole, in the French style.*—Pick, wash, and blanch the rice; drain and put it into a stew-pan; moisten it with the top of the stock-pot by degrees as it swells; shake it often, to prevent its sticking, but so gently as not to break it; take care that it is well nourished, that it may be fat enough; put in a little salt; when done, take a piece of bread the size of the

dish it is to be served upon, and mould the rice round this as if it were paste, and fix it well upon the dish; cover the bread with a slice of bacon; put the rice into a mould that has been buttered; cover it; close it well, forming it nicely; mark the cover where it is to be opened when it is done; put it in a very hot oven, let it take a fine colour: when ready to serve, take off the top with care, and empty it by taking out the bread, and fill the space with any *ragout* that is suitable: put on the cover, and send it to table.—See No. 579.

N.B.—This is a fit way to prepare rice for borders. A little of the sauce of the dish to be served may be stirred into the rice.

578. *Crustades, or bread prepared in which to serve ragouts, &c.*.—They are baked in egg or heart-shaped moulds about from six to eight inches long. Scoop out the crumb; fry these crusts or cases in butter or top-fat; drain, dry, and line with *gratin*, and fill with any nice fresh or re-dressed ragout. They are made small also. Moulds of this kind are made in Scotland of potatoes, (waxy ones are best, or a little flour may be added to them.) These *potato-crusts* may be made as Westphalia loaves, No. 225, and filled with any mince, and piled up in the dish as a pyramid. What we call *rolls* and *loaves* are the same as *crustades*.

579. *A casserole*, or rice edging for made-dishes, is thus prepared:—Soak and stew the rice with salt and a blade of mace. If wanted very rich, put butter and the beat yolks of eggs to it when ready. Place it neatly on the dish as an edging; glaze with egg, and set it in the oven for a few minutes before heaping the curry, hash, pillau, or whatever the dish is, in the middle of it. An edging very suitable to any re-warmed ragout, or warmed fish for plain dinners, may be made of mashed potatoes, marking them neatly, browning in the oven, and serving the ragout or fish in the middle.

580. *Fairy butter*.—To six hard-boiled yolks add a half-pound of fresh butter, and the same weight of sifted sugar. Pound this with a spoonful or two of orange-flower-water to keep it from oiling, and squirt it, or rub it through a tightened cloth. It is served over ham and bread for breakfast, and in many ways for garnishing; or by itself, as a little dish garnished with savoury icing —See, also, Nos. 81, 86, 262, and 385.

CHAPTER II.

A COMPENDIUM OF FRENCH COOKERY,

EXTENDED FOR THE NEW EDITION OF

THE COOK'S AND HOUSEWIFE'S MANUAL,

CONSISTING OF RECEIPTS FOR THE MOST APPROVED
FRENCH MADE-DISHES, SOUPS, FISH, SAUCES,
AND PASTRY.

La gloire de la cuisine Française, remplit l'univers entier!
Le Gastronome Francaise

Muse, sing the man that did to Paris go,
That he might taste their *Soups*, and *Sauces* know.
Dr. King.

It will save much trouble to admit at once, that the French are the greatest cooking nation on earth. They, at least, insist that it is so, and perhaps they may be in the right. This much is certain, that in France alone the culinary art is regarded as an exact science, of which every one understands something, and feels pride in his knowledge. The various branches of economy connected with the kitchen are equally well understood; and the art of making the most and best of every thing is diligently practised. The causes of this acknowledged superiority it is not our present business to investigate; our concern being only with those matters in which this confessed excellence consists. But there is one cause of superiority so obvious that it must be mentioned,— namely, the extreme patience and anxiety with which the most restless people in the world upon all other occasions, attend to culinary processes. A French cook will give a half-day to the deliberate cookery of a ragout, which an English one would toss off in a half-hour; and will watch the first *popple* of his stew-pan as if it were the last pulse of life. Any one who has seen a French cook attending to the *velouté*, or pounding the *quenelle*, as if life and death depended on his function, may have some idea of the importance of his art in his own estimation. Another evident cause of French superiority is the comparative plenty of game, fine herbs, and vegetables, mushrooms, truffles, &c.; the cheapness of poultry, and of wines of high flavour; and also, paradoxical as it may seem, the scarcity of fuel in France.

So scientifically is the culinary art understood by our neighbours, that a French kitchen previous to a grand dinner is a perfect arsenal of *consommés*, *gravies*, *glaze*, *roux*, and mixed spices, all prepared in the best and generally in the most economical manner; for, however it may be in this country with those ministers of vanity imported to English kitchens by luxury and ostentation, economy is thoroughly understood in France. Though objections are brought to the high relish of French dishes, we will venture to affirm, that the receipts given in our English Cookery Books, with their heterogeneous mixture of a thousand and one ingredients, are not only more expensive, but less simple, than those of Beauvilliers or Balaire. But if *bonne chere* is so well understood by our neighbours, *bon gout*, in all matters connected with the table, or rather with the *fête*, is their undoubted *forte*. The French are allowed to excel in soups and ragouts, and in the elegant preparations of their sauces. They have also many more and *better* ways of dressing vegetables than are known to us, by which they can, at small expense, add to the variety, fulness, and good appearance of a table. Their modes of cookery, by *braising*, dressing in a *blanc*, or in a *poêle*, and their *farces*, deserve the serious attention of every lover of good cheer. The French have also ever been pre-eminent as a *larding* nation, and as skilful in *glaze*. Now, though we seldom prize *varnished* meat, nor greatly admire *larding*, we do highly value that union of economy with *bon gout* which enables the French to turn every cold left dish to good account, in the well-known elegant varieties of *timballes*, *scollops*, *vol-au-vents*; or by dressing in *casserole* or as *croquets*, &c. This branch of French cookery is worth the attention of every economist; for though one, for example, does not go to the expense of serving a piece of cold turbot as a dressed salad or a *vol-au-vent*, it is excellent to know how the cold fish is best prepared for serving in a plainer style. There is already much French cookery blended with our own, and of late we are taking to the names as well as the dishes. Every modern cook who would thoroughly know her art must study the best French dishes, as modified by English taste and usage; and to do this she must be acquainted with the leading features of the French system. In this chapter, therefore, besides a copious selection of receipts for the best French dishes, we have given the *elements* of French cookery; and, throughout the whole Manual, wherever the French mode seemed to deserve approbation in any particular receipt, the variation has been carefully pointed out to the attention of the cook.

581. STOCK-BROTH, OR GRAND BOUILLON.

Stock-broth is the first step in French as in English systematic cookery. It is made exactly as directed in Nos. 59 and 60 of this Manual.

582. *Grand consommé.*—Take a knuckle of veal, a shin of beef, any fresh trimmings of veal, poultry, rabbits, or game, or an old fowl, or brace of partridges. Cut these in pieces, (except such as you wish to serve as dishes,) and put them into a nice clean stew-pan with a bunch of parsley and young onions, and, if the flavour of foreign cookery is admired, a clove of garlic. Moisten this with fresh broth, and let the meat *sweat* over a slow fire till heated through. Prick it with a sharp-pointed knife to let the juices flow out, and add as much boiling broth as will suit the quantity of meat you have. Skim this, and let it simmer for three hours. Let it settle. Skim and strain it.—*Obs. Consommé*, wholly of poultry or game, to suit dishes of fowl or game, may be made as above without using beef. For such a gravy a little ham is an improvement, but for game *consommé*, a partridge. Always keep in mind, that the flavour of the *consommé* in fine cookery should not be at variance with the flavour of the dish of which it is to form the sauce. For

example, if intended for a dish dressed with mushrooms, which always have a very peculiar and decided flavour, season the *consommé* with mushrooms. *Grand consommé* is the second important step in French cookery.

583. *Blonde de veau,* veal gravy, or *consommé.*— Heat and rub a stew-pan hard with a towel, then rub it with butter. Lay some slices of lean fresh bacon in the bottom of it, and over these four or five pounds of a leg of veal cut into slices. Moisten with a ladleful of *grand consommé,* and in this let the meat *sweat.* When it has catched a golden tinge over a rather brisk fire, prick it with a sharp knife to let its juice flow out; let it sweat for twenty minutes more; when reduced to a jelly of a topaz colour, moisten with boiling broth, (*grand bouillon,* No. 59,) and season with onions, parsley, and mushrooms. Let this boil for an hour, and strain it for use.

584. *Grande sauce.*—See *Savoury brown gravy,* page 233,—it is the same thing.

585. *Sauce Espagnole.*—Put some slices of ham, according to the quantity of sauce you want, into a stew-pan, with double the quantity of sliced veal. Moisten these with a small quantity of *consommé,* and when you have drawn a strong amber-coloured jelly, put in a few spoonfuls more to float this off. [*N.B.*—This is a proper direction for detaching all glaze.] Put in a little more *consommé* of poultry or rabbits, if you have it; if not, some strong *blond de veau.* Season with a little parsley, green onions, a half bay-leaf, two sprigs of basil and thyme, and two cloves. Simmer for a half hour, skim and strain.—*Obs.* This is used for many dishes; it is a favourite general sauce; and, when wanted, is thickened with *roux,* and seasoned with Madeira. It is sometimes made of game, especially when to sauce game.

586. *Velouté,* or *white cullis.*—(See also page 234.) Sweat slowly over the fire some slices of very nice bacon, a knuckle of very white veal, any trimmings of poultry or game you have, and the white part of two carrots, and a bunch of onions. When you have got all the juices out of it, and it is just ready to catch, moisten it with *consommé,* and season with a small faggot of sweet herbs. When all the strength is got from the meat, let the gravy settle, skim it, strain it, and reduce

by quick boiling till it is nearly a jelly. Meanwhile mix three spoonfuls of potato-flour with three pints of cream; and when this boils, pour it to your sauce, and boil till the *velouté* is of a proper consistence and very smooth. Work it well, continually lifting it by spoonfuls and letting it fall, and do this till it is cold, to prevent a skin from gathering on it.

587. *Sauce à la bechamel.*—Take as much *velouté* as you choose, and moisten it with *blonde de veau*. Mix with this a pint of boiling cream, or what quantity you wish, with seasonings fit for the dish you intend to make. See page 239.

588. *Brown Italian sauce,* or *Italienne Rousse, a favourite French sauce.*—Take two spoonfuls of chopped mushrooms, one of parsley, half a one of eschalot, half a bay-leaf, pepper and salt to taste. Moisten with *Espagnole,* and stew the vegetables. Add more pepper, if necessary, and the quantity of *consommé* necessary to bring the sauce to the proper thickness.

589. *Italian white sauce,* or *Italienne blanche.*—Use *velouté* instead of *Espagnole.* This is all the difference between the white and brown Italian sauce.

590. *Sauce à la maître d'hotel.*—Melt a quarter-pound of butter, and thicken it with flour; add in the stew-pan a little scalded and finely minced parsley, salt, pepper, and afterwards a squeeze of lemon. Work it well with a wooden spoon to make it smooth.

591. *Sauce hachée.*—Take of chopped mushrooms and gherkins a spoonful each, half a spoonful of scalded minced parsley, with pepper, salt, and vinegar. Moisten with a little *consommé,* or with brown Italian sauce.

592. *French sauce à la tartare.*—Mix a minced eschalot and a few leaves of chervil and tarragon finely minced with a tea-spoonful of made mustard, a glass of vinegar, and a sprinkling of oil. Stir this constantly, and, if necessary, thin it with vinegar.

593. *Sauce tournée.*—Moisten some white *roux* with *consommé* of poultry or *blonde de veau,* till it is thin. Stew in it a few chopped mushrooms, parsley, and onions. Skim and strain the sauce. For *Roux* see p. 231.

594. *Sauce à la pluche.*—Blanch and drain some large-leafed young parsley and a little tarragon. Put to this

a pint of *velouté* and a half-pint of clear *consommé*. Stir in a bit of butter; work it well to make it smooth. —*Obs*. This is a proper sauce for lamb's stove.

595. *Sauce à l'Allemand*, or *German sauce*.—Thicken *sauce tournée* with the beat yolk of an egg or two, according to the quantity. This sauce is extensively used for dressed meat-dishes.

596. *Sauce à la matelote for fish*.—Take a large pint of brown *roux* heated, or of *Espagnole*; put to this six onions sliced and fried with a few mushrooms, or a little mushroom-catsup, a glass of red wine, and a little of the liquor in which the fish was boiled. Give it a seasoning of parsley, chives, a bay-leaf, salt, pepper, allspice, and a clove. *Skink* it up, (using a large spoon) to make it blend well. Put veal-gravy to it if wanted more rich, or a good piece of butter. Strain it, and if wanted exceedingly rich, add small *quenelles*, (force-meat-balls) made of ingredients proper for a fish-dish, glazed onions and mushrooms, a little essence of anchovy, and a squeeze of lemon. Serve over stewed carp or trout.—*Obs*. This sauce is exceedingly admired by some gourmands, indeed fish served with it is preferred by them to all other ways of dressing fish.

597. *Common sauce à la matelote*.—Take a heaped spoonful of minced parsley, chives, and mushrooms, and give them a fry in butter. Dredge them with flour, and moisten with *consommé* till sufficiently thin. When stewed a few minutes, add to this the beat yolks of two eggs, and take care they do not curdle.—*Obs*. This is a cheap, general, useful sauce for mutton-cutlets, palates, and sweetbreads, as well as for fish. Beauvilliers' *matelote* is made of *Espagnole* reduced, small onions fried in butter, and dressed mushrooms and artichoke bottoms. It is an excellent composition.

598. *Remoulade*.—Pound the hard-boiled yolks of two eggs in a mortar, with a little sour cream, or the raw yolk of an egg, a spoonful of made mustard, pepper, salt, cayenne, one spoonful of vinegar and two of oil. Rub this salad-sauce through a sieve, and it is ready.

599. *Salmi sauce à la Espagnole, a game sauce*.— This is a sauce of high relish. Fry in butter, over a slow fire, three eschalots chopped, a sliced carrot, a bunch of parsley, some bits of ham, and a sprig of thyme.

Let them just catch, and moisten them with Madeira. Let this reduce a little, and add to it any trimmings of the game, and a little *Espagnole*. Let this stew till it is very good; season it with salt and pepper; skim and strain it. This sauce is served over *salmis* of partridge, duck, &c.

600. *Poivrade sauce.*—Cut six ounces of ham into bits, and fry them in butter with a few sprigs of parsley, a few young onions sliced, a clove of garlic, a bay-leaf, a sprig of sweet basil, one of thyme, and two cloves. When well fried over a quick fire, add pepper, cayenne, a little white wine vinegar, and a half-pint of *consommé*. Let it simmer by the side of the fire for a good while, skim it and strain it through a tammy sieve.

601. *Montpelier butter.*—To dressed ravigote add six hard yolks, a spoonful of capers, eight ounces of butter, a clove of garlic, a seasoning of nutmeg, mace, allspice, and tarragon vinegar, and a glassful of salad oil. Pound for eight minutes, then gradually add spinage juice to green the butter. Pound till very smooth; set in ice to firm. This is used in decorating cold dishes of fish, meat, or salads, along with ornamental savoury jellies or aspic.

602. *Dressed ravigote.*—Take a suitable quantity of burnet, chervil, tarragon, and celery, with two leaves of balm. Clean and boil them. Throw them into fresh water, and drain and pound them with a little salad-oil, and vinegar, pepper, and salt. Rub this when sufficiently done through a search.—*Ravigote sauce* is compounded of fine herbs, and is used both cooked and raw.

603. *Cold ravigote.*—This is just a piquant salad sauce. Clean, mince, and pound the above herbs with a few capers and a boned anchovy or two. Pound the whole well with a raw egg, and add a little good vinegar to keep it from clagging. Rub through a search.*

604. *Mushroom-sauce, Beauvilliers' receipt.*—Take two handfuls of mushrooms, wash them in several waters, rubbing them lightly; put them into a drainer; mince them with their stalks; put them into a stew-pan. with the size of an egg of butter; let them fall over a

---

* We cannot here resist the *Ravigote à l'Ude* on which that celebrated *chef* prides himself not a little. Take of Chili vinegar, cavice, catsup, and Reading sauce, each a tea-spoonful, the size of an egg of butter, three spoonfuls of Bechamel, a little cream, salt, pepper, a little chopped parsley blanched, and cayenne.

slow fire, and when nearly done, moisten them with two skimming spoonfuls of *velouté*; let them simmer three-quarters of an hour more; rub them through a search, and finish with boiling cream.— See No. 267.

605. *La Ducelle, Beauvilliers' receipt.*—Mince mushrooms, parsley, young onions or eschalots, equal quantities of each; put some butter into a stew-pan with as much rasped bacon; put them upon the fire; season with salt, pepper, fine spiceries, a little grated nutmeg, and a bay-leaf; moisten with a spoonful of *Espagnole* or *velouté*; let it simmer, taking care to stir it: when sufficiently done, finish it with a thickening of yolks of eggs well beaten which must not boil; the juice of a lemon is not necessary, but may be added. Put it into a dish, and use it for every thing that is served *en papillotes*.

606. *L'Aspic, or savoury ornamental jelly.*—Make the jelly stock of fowls, knuckles of veal and ham, rabbits, or whatever is convenient. Flavour it with vinegar, in which a large faggot of aromatic herbs has been boiled, as basil, burnet, tarragon, and chervil. Season with aromatic spices. Strain the jelly; let it cool; take off the top, and keep back the sediment, and clarify it with the whites of four eggs well whisked in it, and the shells. Continue to whisk it over the fire till it look curdled and white, then draw it to the side of the stove, and throw cloths over it. When quite settled, clear, and bright, strain it off gently, and keep for use in garnishing dishes.—*Obs.* If for moulding, the jelly must be made very stiff. This jelly does for fish, lobster, salads, and dressed dishes of various kinds. If for meat-dishes, the jelly must be seasoned so as best to suit the kind of viands it is to garnish, whether ham, turkey, cold game, &c. It must be run repeatedly through the jelly-bag till clear and amber-coloured.—See No. 174.

N.B.—The other sauces used by the French are either the same as our own that go under similar names, or the difference is pointed out in the receipts given in the Chapter SAUCES.—See *Obs.* Nos. 268, 274, 289, &c.

607. FRENCH SOUPS

SOUPS, under the French names, or, what is the same thing, under a different name, though the same soup, are so common at English tables, that the best part of them will be found in the Chapter Soups. There are still a few entitled to a place here.—See Nos. 68, 72, 63, 64, &c.

608. *Potage au riz, or rice soup.*—Have a strong, clear *bouillon*, (Nos. 59 or 63,) of veal or beef, or of a mixture of these meats, made as directed for stock-broth. Put a sufficient quantity of this, well-seasoned, boiling, into a tureen, in which are two ounces of rice, prepared as directed for Mullagatawny, See. *National Dishes.*

609. *Another way, which makes two dishes.*—Boil a neatly-trussed large fowl or capon in *grand bouillon* with two cloves, two onions, a faggot of sweet herbs, and salt. Skim it well to make the soup clear. Serve the fowl with a little great salt sprinkled on the breast, (*au gros sel,*) and a spoonful of the clear soup about it. Serve the soup on boiled rice, taking out the onions and cloves, and put a little brown beef or veal gravy to it to improve the colour.—See Nos. 66 and 98.

610. *Potage au vermicelli.*—Prepare four ounces of vermicelli by blanching it, and boiling it in broth. Make the soup of *grand bouillon*, of *blonde de veau*, or *consommé*, or a part of each. Let the previously cooked vermicelli boil in it five minutes and no more.—See No. 66.

611. *Potage à l'Italienne, a brown soup.*—Cut young carrots and turnips in scrolls like ribbons; and some white of leeks, and two heads of celery, and three onions in fillets. Fry these in butter; moisten with strong, clear, deep-coloured gravy-stock, and some *blonde de veau.* Season with salt, and serve on toasted crusts soaked in a little broth.—See No. 81.

N.B.—If the roots are old, blanch them. This, in the season, is made a sort of vegetable hotch-potch, with green lettuce and other vegetables.

612. *Potage à la baveau, a clear brown soup.**— Scoop out some yellow turnips the size of marbles with a scooper. Blanch them, and boil them in a clear strong *consommé* with a little browned sugar. Colour the soup deeper with veal-gravy, and serve it on grilled crusts.

613. *Potage au choux, cabbage soup.*—Parboil three firm white small cabbages. Drain them, and *braise* them in top-fat, with a few slices of bacon and seasonings.

---

* The French sometimes brown their carrots and turnips in butter, and rub them through a search for carrot or turnip soup.—See No. 63.

Drain them again of this fat; quarter them, and slide them into the tureen, and over them pour strong well-seasoned boiling beef stock-broth.

614. *German cabbage soup.*—Mince the parboiled cabbage. Stew them in butter, and serve them in strong broth, (No. 63) with toasted bread cut in dice.

615. *Potage printanier, or spring soup.*—Cut carrots, turnips, celery, and onions into small dice. Fry them gently, and drain and boil them slowly in clear veal-broth, with a bit of browned sugar. Boil separately very green asparagus tops, and French beans cut as small diamonds, also very green pease. Mix and serve.

616. *Potage à la Camerani,** by H. J.—For this soup to make it in perfection, the cook must have genuine Naples macaroni, the best Parmesan, and mellow Dutch butter, with two dozen livers of fat pullets, celery, turnip, parsnips, leeks, carrots, parsley, and young onions. Mince the livers, the celery, and the blanched pot-herbs very well, and stew them altogether in butter. Meanwhile boil the macaroni; season it with white pepper, and fine spices, and drain it well. You must now (to do the thing in style) have a soup-dish that will bear the fire: spread over it a layer of macaroni, next a layer of the cooked mince-meat, then a layer of grated Parmesan. Proceed in this order till the soup-dish is filled sufficiently, and end with Parmesan. Place the dish on embers, and let it simmer slowly for an hour.

FRENCH DISHES WHICH ARE SERVED IN TUREENS†
OR SOUP-DISHES, IN THE FIRST COURSE

617. *Civet of hare, a favourite dish.*—Cut the hare into small pieces, and carefully save the blood. Cut some firm white bacon into small cubes, and give them a light fry with a bit of butter. Strain the gravy they

---

* There is an immense quantity of gastrology in our late fashionable novels; not always very judiciously given, nor with very profound or accurate knowledge of that mystery in which we profess ourselves adepts, but with so much apparent good-will, and enthusiasm for the service as to disarm criticism. Among the compositions lauded, with at least as much zeal as knowledge, is M. Camerani's celebrated soup. A dish of this soup has cost five pounds. How can it fail to be good?

† Tureens are now considered old-fashioned: of course, when we say tureen, we mean any form of dish in which soup or sauce is served.

give out, and thicken it with browned flour dusted over it in the stew-pan. Put aside the bits of bacon, and place the cut hare in the stew-pan in the gravy. When firmed with frying, moisten with good broth and a pint of red wine, and season with parsley, young onions, salt, pepper, a few mushrooms or catsup, or mushroom-powder. Let the meat stew slowly till done, and skim off the fat. Now lift all that is good of the hare, and also the bacon that you put aside, into a clean stew-pan. Strain the gravy over this, and now put to the *civet*, the bruised liver, the blood, some small mushrooms and onions ready cooked. Do not let it boil lest the blood curdle. Put the gravy in which the mushrooms and onions were cooked to the civet when it (the gravy) has been well boiled down..—*Obs.* If cooking for palates trained on the continent, add to the seasonings a bay-leaf, a sprig of thyme, and two cloves of garlic. This civet is very similar to the old Scotch hare-soup. Pick out the herbs.

618. *Civet of roe-buck.*—Make this exactly as civet of hare, but without the blood of the animal. Use small cutlets of the neck and breast. It is an admirable way of dressing venison.—See No. 503.

FRENCH MADE-DISHES OF BEEF.

619. *Bœuf à la Flamande.*—See page 275.

620. *Bœuf de chasse*, p. 280; Beef steaks with potatoes, p. 120.

621. *Palais de bœuf à l'Italienne, Beef palates with Italian sauce.*—Rub the palates with salt; parboil and skin them. Cut them into scollops not too large, and stew them slowly in a brown Italian sauce well thickened by a previous boiling down. Add a squeeze of lemon, and serve them.—*Obs.* This will be found an exceedingly good way of dressing palates.—See also Nos. 395, 397, and 406.

622. *Entre-côte de bœuf.*—By this is meant what lies under the long ribs, or those thick slices of delicate meat which may be got from between them. Cut this into narrow steaks. Flatten and broil these, and either serve the steaks *à la bif-tik Anglais*, No. 38, or with *sauce hachée* under them.

623. *Lange de bœuf en miroton.*—Cut a cold skinned

tongue into nice round slices. Heat them in *Espagnole*, with pepper, salt, and a little broth. Dress them hot round a dish, each slice leaning on the edge of the other, which is called *en miroton*. They may be glazed if red.

624. *Langue de bœuf à la braisé.—Tongue braised.* —Clean a large tongue as directed, page 276. Parboil and skin it, and lard it all across with lard, seasoned with cook's pepper. Put it in a stew-pot that will just hold it. Cover it with good broth, and a glass of wine. Season with a bay-leaf and two cloves, two carrots, and three onions, with any trimmings of veal, poultry, or game, you have. Put paper over it, and fire over the lid, and stew it slowly with fire under and over for two hours and a half. Garnish with the roots, and sauce the tongue with the strained gravy seasoned, to which add a little *Espagnole.—N.B.* This is of a very high *gout*, —one of the cloying specimens of French cookery.

625. *Ox rumps in the French manner*, see page 277.

626. *Gras double—or tripe—to dress.*—Take the fattest thick tripe well cleaned, and repeatedly scalded and scraped. Boil it in water two hours, and clean it again: then stew it in a *blanc** for four or five hours. Cut it in lozenges, and serve it in white Italian sauce.

VEAL.

627. *The French manner of dividing and dressing the fillet.*—The fillet is formed of three distinct parts; the large fat fleshy piece inside of the thigh, which the French call the *noix*. Of this they make a principal first-course dish. The piece below this they call the *under noix*, and the side part the *centre noix*. Of the principal *noix* they make a *fricandeau*, or a small roast, by stuffing and skewering this piece, to which in a cow-calf the udder is attached; or they fry it *à la bourgeoise*. Of this part they also make cutlets, and *grenadins*. The *under noix* they use for pie-meat, forcemeat, &c. the

---

* A rich broth or gravy in which the French cook palates, lamb's-head, and many other things. It is made thus:—A pound of beef-kidney fat, minced, put on with a sliced carrot, an onion stuck with two cloves, parsley, green onions, slices of lemon without the peel or seeds; or, if much is wanted, two pounds of fat, and two lemons. When the fat is a good deal melted, put in water made briny with salt; and when done, keep the *blanc* for use.

centre noix, or fat marrowy piece of the fillet next the rump, for *godiveau*, *sauce tournée*, &c. The trimmings and bones help to make *Espagnole*, or any soup or sauce. The part next the rump or *centre noix* is also dressed *à la bourgeoise*, i.e. *fried*.

628. *Noix de veau en Bedeau,—or in the Beadles' fashion.*—Flatten the *noix*, and lard it lengthways with lard, seasoned with minced parsley, green onions, and cook's-pepper. Line a stew-pan that will just hold it with trimmings of veal, and lay slices of white bacon over the *noix* where not larded. Put onions, carrots, parsley, &c. into the stew-pan, and a little *Espagnole* or *roux*. Cook slowly; serve with or over sorrel, spinage, or a *purée* of onions.

A *purée* of onions, turnips, mushrooms, &c. is a pulpy mash or sauce of the vegetable specified, thinned with boiling cream or gravy.

629. *Grenadins de veau,—veal Grenadins.*—These are small slices from the fillet about an inch thick, flattened, and one piece being cut round, the others must be shaped as lozenges to lie round this centre. Lard them, stew them in a pan lined with bacon, and trimmings of veal: season as above; put fire over the pan. Serve on a *purée* of mushrooms, or with sorrel, or endive, dishing the *grenadins* with their points to the centre where the round piece is laid.—See No. 442.

630. *Calf's brains à la Ravigote.**—Skin the brains, and carefully remove all the fibres. Soak them in several waters. Parboil in salt and water, with a glass of vinegar, for ten minutes, and when firm, divide and fry them. Serve with *Ravigote sauce*.

631. *Calf's brains à la maître d'hotel,—a neat corner-dish.*—Boil the brains as above with a little butter in the water; don't fry them. Fry some bread cut like scollop-shells. Dish the brains divided, with the bread between, and cover with a *maître d'hotel sauce. Another* pretty dish of brains may be made by serving very green fried parsley in the middle of the dish, and

---

* We do not conceive these dishes as of much importance; but where there is a table to garnish every day, and a cook to labour, these trifling things may often be found useful. Where good dinners are constantly given, and sauces prepared at any rate, the expense is trifling.

the brains around, *saucing* with browned butter, and a little vinegar.

633. *Calf's ears.*—The French dress these in various ways;—*farced* with dressed forcemeat, with Italian sauce, or *à la Ravigote*. Clean them, cook them in a *blanc*, dip them in eggs and crumbs with seasonings, and fry them of a fine brown colour, or dip in a light frying batter. Garnish with fried parsley. *Fat* sauces would be improper with all such gristly tender meats, as calf's feet or ears, or sheep's or lamb's trotters.

634. *Ris de veau aux mousserons,—veal-sweetbreads, with mushrooms.*—Choose sweetbreads large and white. Soak them and blanch in boiling water till they firm. Cut in nice pieces, and stew them in a little *velouté* with mushroom-sauce,* ready prepared. Boil down the sauce, and, when well reduced, thicken with beat yolks of eggs, and season with a little blanched parsley, nicely minced, and a squeeze of lemon. They are also served with young pease, or mushrooms; or are egged, crumbed and fried. See No. 639.

635. *Calf's liver, with fine herbs.*—Cut a sound white liver into oblong slices an inch thick. Form these into the shape of hearts about two inches broad, dredge them with flour, and put them to fry with onions, mushrooms, parsley previously shred, and stewed in butter, with pepper and salt. Fry all this gently till ready, and dust it with more pepper. Keep the liver hot, put a little broth or gravy to the herbs to moisten them, and stew for three minutes, and serve over the liver which must be dished in order, arranging the bits neatly.—*Obs.* This dish is often served for the *dejeuner à la fourchette*, and must then be highly seasoned, and very hot.—See Nos. 472 and 54.

636. *Blanquettes of veal.*—Cut a cold roast loin or shoulder of veal into small pieces, using only the white part. Trim away the browned outside fat, and mince the veal. Stir it till warm in *velouté* well reduced; but do not let it boil. Thicken with the yolk of an egg or two, and add a squeeze of lemon when ready to serve.—See Nos. 464 and 465.

637. *Blanquettes with cucumbers.*—Cut cold veal as

---

* The French rub this sauce, celery, onion, &c. through a sieve, so that they are all *purées, i.e.* smooth, and of pulpy consistence.

above into scollops, and heat them in *sauce tournée*. Quarter and cut four or five cucumbers also in scollops. Cook these also in *sauce tournée*. Drain them; reduce the strained sauce; thicken it with the beat yolks of two eggs. Put in a little cream, salt, and a bit of sugar. Serve the sauce over the meat and cucumbers.

638. *Blanquettes à la paysanne.*—Prepare the veal as above in scollops. Heat the meat in a reduced *sauce tournée*. Thicken with egg, and season with minced parsley, and, before serving, add a good squeeze of lemon. These may be served in dishes with borders.

639. *Cold sweetbreads.*—Cut them into scollops or square bits. Stew them in strong gravy till heated through. Fry scollops of bread: dish, placing meat and bread scollops alternately, and garnish with fried parsley.

640. *Veal cutlets à la Chingara.**—Cut and trim cutlets from the fillet. Put them into the stew-pan with butter and ham, onions, parsley, carrot, and herbs. Warm in soup a slice of smoked tongue for each cutlet. When the cutlets are enough done, take them out; boil down the stock to a glaze, and put them back. Glaze the slices of tongue. Dish one on each cutlet, shaping them together. Dish them in a round form. Put a little *Espagnole* into the stew-pan, and a bit of butter also; warm in it the remains of the smoked tongue minced, and pour this sauce into the centre of the dish, with the cutlets around.—See pages 126 and 289.

641. *Côtelettes au jambon.*—These are precisely the same as the former, only ham (the prime slices) is used instead of tongue.

642. *Cutlets with fine herbs, or à la Venetienne.*— Chop a handful of mushrooms, two eschalots, a little parsley, and a sprig of thyme. Stew these in rasped bacon and butter; when done, put in, and stew the cutlets over a very slow fire. Add pepper and salt. Skim off the fat carefully. Put in a large spoonful of *sauce tournée* or white *roux*. Thicken with yolks of eggs beat with a little cream. Add the juice of a lemon, which is proper for all dishes made of veal, and a little cayenne.

643. *Loin of cold veal à la Bechamel.*—A loin of

---

* These were the favourite cutlets of the NABOB. JEKYLL preferred cutlets *à l'Italienne*, *i.e.* dipped in butter, nicely broiled, and served with a white Italian sauce.

veal, when used as a *remove*, very often comes back from the table untouched, or with very little taken off it. Make a mince of the fillet or inside of the loin. Cover the loin with buttered paper, and warm it in a Dutch oven. Place it above the stewed *blanquette*, (i.e. mince) and serve with a white sauce.

644. MUTTON.*

Gigot à la Gasconne, or leg of mutton Gascon fashion. —This is a dish of very high *gout* and seldom seen now, but it still has devoted admirers. Lard a leg of mutton with garlic and fillets of anchovies; roast it, and serve with Spanish or garlic sauce.—See pages 81 and 96.

645. *Côtelettes à la Soubise, Soubise mutton-cutlets.* —Cut chops from the ribs, or cutlets from the leg, rather thick than otherwise. Trim off the superfluous fat, and *sweat* them in a stew-pan in strong gravy or butter-sauce, with green onions, parsley, pepper, and salt. When nearly thus cooked, take out the herbs, and reduce the sauce nearly to a glaze. Drain the cutlets. Dish them very hot with the sauce in the middle, and a dozen small onions, cooked as directed, (No. 262.)— *Obs.* Soubise cutlets used to be larded, and *braised* in bacon with all sorts of herbs; but there has been a considerable revolution of late on the side of refinement even in French cookery. They may be served with French beans, or cucumber.

646. *Côtelettes à l'Italienne* and *au naturel.*—These are nearly the same. Cut, trim, and dip the chops in butter and bread-crumbs. Boil them a little. Put pepper and salt over them, then butter and crumbs again, and broil till ready. Press out the fat between folds of hot paper, and serve with *brown Italian sauce.*

647. *Côtelettes à la minute—or in their juice for dejeuners à la fourchette.*—Take rather thin slices from the gigot, as in carving a roast leg. Put them into a thin-bottomed frying-pan in which is hot butter. Turn them continually. Keep them hot by the fire; and put into the pan a little gravy and a few chopped herbs,

* Families in the country, and those who "kill their own mutton," depend so much upon this favourite food, that it is impossible to know too many good ways of dressing it; though, when all is done, none can surpass a roast or boiled leg; hotch-potch, boiled scrag with onion-sauce, or a well-grilled mutton-chop.—P. T.

stewed as for *Venetian* cutlets, No. 642; give this a toss, and skim and serve it round the hot cutlets.

648. *Rognons de mouton, or mutton kidneys.*—These are also served at a *dejeuner à la fourchette*. Skin and split a dozen kidneys without wholly separating them. Pin them out with wire skewers to keep them open; rub them with a little salt and pepper; dip them in butter, and broil first the inside, that, when turned on the grill to be finished, the gravy may be preserved. Dish on a hot plate, with a very little chopped blanched parsley and butter dropped over each.—*Obs.* In France these are also dressed as a mince, stewing the mince in butter, draining and serving it in a well-reduced Italian brown sauce with a very little Champagne.—See pages 277, 299.

649. *Beef-kidneys* are dressed as above, and served at the *dejeuner à la fourchette.*—*N.B.* With brains, kidneys, and liver, always use cayenne.

650, *Haricot brun, or à la bourgeoise.*—Brown mutton chops in the frying-pan. Make a *roux* of the butter in which they were fried, with a little more butter and browned flour. Add a little veal-gravy, or good *consommé*, well seasoned, and some bits of turnip, with parsley and green onions. Skim the sauce often to clear it of fat. Have some turnips scooped into balls ready boiled, as for soup *Baveau*, No. 612. Put them with the chops into a clean stew-pan, and strain the sauce over them. When the sauce looks clear and brown, and the turnips are done, dish the chops round, and serve the sauce and turnip-balls in the middle. Cold mutton haricot the same way.

651. *Hachis de mouton à la Portugaise.*—Prepare the meat as for any hash. Heat it in a thick, well-reduced *Espagnole*, with butter, pepper, and salt. Serve with eggs over it, poached rather hard, and with dressed onions between, *en cordon*, or chainwise.

652. *Minced mutton with cucumbers.*—See page 299.

653. *Pied de mouton à la sauce Robert, sheep's trotters.*—Cook the cleaned trotters in a *blanc* (see note, p. 339.) When slowly stewed till tender, bone them. Roll them in a dressed forcemeat. Dip them in thin frying batter, and fry them.—*Obs.* They may also be stuffed with the forcemeat, and *braised*, and so served. Serve with Robert sauce.—See No. 480.

654. *Pieds d'agneau*, or lamb's trotters, are dressed as above.—See No. 480.

655. *Cervelles des mouton, sheep's brains.*—These are dressed exactly as No. 631, but more pungent seasonings are proper.—*Obs.* Of mutton the French also make *fricandeaux*, *mortadelles*, or large sausages, *grenadins*, and many other dishes.—See *Tongues*, No. 481.

656. *Cochon de lait au moine blanc*, or *en galantine*. —Prepare the pig as directed at page 98, and bone it all except the head and feet; but take care not to break the skin. Make a forcemeat of any degree of richness you choose of veal, beef, suet, calf's udder, &c. Mince basil, thyme, and sage, panada, add some eggs to mix. [Read *Quenelles*, pp. 355 and 356.] Add plenty of spices. Now proceed as directed for *godiveau*. Lay the boned pig on a cloth, and cover it equally with the forcemeat. Rasp some ham over it. Try to keep the pig as near its natural shape as possible. Sew it up. Bind it in a napkin with tape, and boil it in broth seasoned with roots and herbs. When unswaddled, after two hours slow boiling, wipe it dry, and serve with brown *Espagnole*, or if cold, on a napkin.*

657. *Jambon à la broche.*—Take a Bayonne ham, large, fresh, well-selected, and at least twenty pounds weight. Trim it all round. Steep it for two or three days according to the size.—See No. 10. If to be very superior you must steep it in Spanish wine. Spit it, and cover it all over with slices of lard. It must have a slack fire for at least five hours, and be basted incessantly with hot water to freshen it, and dilate the pores, which basting with wine would contract. When nearly

---

* Dr. REDGILL, whose experiments on pig, from first to last, are extremely interesting, totally lost one stuffed pig by overboiling; and had another considerably injured by the sewing tearing the skin. But his final success was triumphant; and he wrote down, as a canon of cookery, that all *stuffed* meats, as pig *à la moine blanc*, haggis, sausage, &c. are not to be boiled by their apparent size, but by their solidity; for forcemeats of any kind will cook in a third or even a half less time than a joint of meat of compact texture. The sewing should be the stitch surgeons use in sewing up wounds. If the cook would avoid the catastrophe of her pig, goose, or haggis bursting, she will boil these important articles on a fish-drainer, that, if an accident do occur, ready help may be administered. Silk thread is more apt to tear the integument than any other thread; the cook should therefore for her purposes use soft thread made of cotton.—See *Pig's cheek—Nat. Cookery.*

ready remove the skin, and cover the surface lightly with fine bread-crumbs.—For *sauce*, boil down the wine in which the ham was steeped, and put to it the juice which will flow from the ham when taken from the spit, and the juice of two lemons. Skim this and serve all hot.*—See Nos. 11 and 12.

658. *Hure de cochon, or pig's face stuffed.*—Make the head as large as you can, by cutting down to the shoulders. Singe it carefully. Put a red-hot poker into the ears. Clean and carefully bone the head without breaking the skin. Rub it with salt, and pour a boiled cold brine over it, with a large handful of chopped juniper-berries, a few bruised cloves, and four bay-leaves, with thyme, basil, sage, a head of garlic bruised, and a half-ounce of saltpetre pounded. Let the head steep in this for ten days, and turn it and rub it often. Then wipe, drain, and dry it, and make a forcemeat for it thus:—Take equal quantities of undressed ham, and the breast of bacon. Season this highly with cook's pepper, and fine spices if you choose. Pound the meat very small, and mix with it some seasoned lard, parsley, and young onions, finely minced. Prove the quality of the forcemeat as directed at page 355. Improve it where deficient. Spread it equally over the head. Roll up, and sew it, and bind it in a cloth, and stew it in a *braise* made of any trimmings and seasonings left, with broth enough to cover it. It will take nearly four hours to cook; and will be still richer if *larded* before it is stuffed. Try to pierce it with a larding-pin. If the pin enters easily it is done. When cool, take off the binding-cloth. Trim the ends of the collared head, and serve it on a napkin.—*Obs.* This dish is well worth the attention of the gourmand and of the country house-keeper. It will keep a long while, and the liquor will make

---

* The above is one of the precious receipts of the Society of the *Caveau Moderne*. If any one choose to attempt this piece of extravagance, a good Yorkshire or Westmoreland ham, well cured, will answer his purpose quite as well. Our *authorities* all speak with enthusiasm of the *Jambon à la Broche*, "un tel rôti est tres superieur a tous ceux que la boucherie, la basse-cour, la poulailler, les fôrets, les plaines, les etangs, et les mers pouvraient nous offrir. Heureux celui qui peut une fois en sa vie manger un jambon à la broche! Il ne plus rien a regretter des sensualitie de ce bas monde!" This dish, even in France, would cost ten crowns.

a savoury pease-soup, boil to a *glaze*, or braise vegetables. Independently of the stuffing, this French mode of curing pig's face is excellent.—See *Pig's cheek, National Dishes*.

650. *To dress cold roast pig à la Bechamel, or in white sauce.*—Carve what remains of the pig into neat pieces, and let these just heat in *bechamel-sauce*, or serve them as *blanquettes i.e.* as a mince.—See No. 636.

FRENCH DISHES OF HARE, POULTRY, AND GAME.

660. *Gateau de lievre,—Hare cake for a second course.* —Prepare the hare as directed at page 113, and save the liver and the blood. Scrape the meat from the skin and sinews, and mince with it the liver, a piece of a calf's liver, and a good piece of the best part of an undressed ham. Pound the whole to a paste with a little cold broth, or with hare or game soup. Add equal to a third part of the whole bulk of rasped lard. Pound the whole well together, with salt, pepper, and young onions, and parsley, previously blanched;—give a seasoning also of a spoonful of brandy, and No. 334. Mix with the pounded meat six or eight eggs one by one, and, if foreign cookery is admired, the expressed juice of a clove of garlic. When the whole is exceedingly well pounded and mixed, line a stew-pan with slices of lard, and put the forcemeat over it to the thickness of an inch and a half, and quite level and smooth. Then put in a layer of lard, pistachios, and truffles, all cut in stripes and neatly laid down like mosaic; then the forcemeat an inch and a half thick. Cover with slices of bacon, and then with paper. Close the pan, and bake the cake slowly for two hours, or for three, if you have a cake of three layers of forcemeat. Let it cool; dip the mould or pan in hot water to loosen the cake, and turn it out. Garnish to your fancy. Serve on a napkin. It makes an excellent dormant dish.— *Obs.* Hare is also dressed as *côtelettes, boudins,* &c.

661. *Rabbits à la Venetienne, i.e. with fine herbs.* —Carve two white young fat rabbits neatly, and fry the pieces in butter with some rasped bacon and a handful of chopped mushrooms, parsley, and eschalot, with pepper, salt, and allspice. Rub a tea-spoonful of flour into a little *consommé*, and pour this into the stew-pan with

the rabbits. Stew slowly till they are cooked; skim and strain the sauce, and serve it hot about the meat, with a seasoning of cayenne and a good squeeze of lemon.—See pages 307 and 308.

662. *Dindon en daube.*—Truss the turkey as for boiling. Have strips of lard seasoned with salt, pepper, and fine spices and herbs. Lard the breast and the thighs. Put slices of bacon in a braising-pan, and place the turkey on it with a cut hock of ham, and a calf's foot broken, the feet of the turkey, five onions, one stuck with four cloves, three carrots, two bay-leaves, three or four sprigs of thyme, a bunch of parsley, and young onions. Lay slices of bacon over the turkey. Moisten with four spoonfuls of melted butter; cover with three rounds of buttered paper, and let it simmer for five hours; take it from the fire, but do not lift it for another half-hour, that it may not get dry. Strain the gravy, and boil it down. Beat an egg well in a sauce-pan, and pour the gravy (or jelly rather) into this. Whip it well; put it on the fire; when just come to boil, place it on the side of the furnace; cover it with a lid which will bear embers over it; let it remain for a half-hour, with embers over; strain again, and with this jelly cover the turkey. *Lievre en daube, the same.*

663. FOWL A LA CHINGARA, *a favourite small gourmand dish.*

CUT a fat white fowl in four, across and down the back. Melt the least bit of butter in a stew-pan, and lay four slices from the best part of an undressed ham in the pan. Lay the cut fowl on this, and stew it very slowly on embers. When done, drain off the fat. Pour over the glaze, which will have formed at the bottom, a little *Espagnole*, and rub in a little cayenne, salt, and pepper. Meanwhile have ready four toasts. Fry them in the fat you poured off the fowl, and dust them with pepper and salt, and serve them between the slices of ham, on each slice of which a quarter of the fowl is to be laid.

664. *Fowls à la Ravigote.*—Roast the fowls, and serve them with *Ravigote-sauce.*

665. *Poulets à la Tartare.*—Roasted young fowls with Tartar sauce.—See Nos. 592, 27.

666. *Fowl à la Campire.*—Slit the breast of a roasted

fowl to let the juice flow out; lay sliced raw onions in the slits, and serve with a brown *poivrade* in the dish.

667. *Poulets aux huitres—young fowls with oyster-sauce.*—Stiffen a quarter of a hundred of oysters in their own strained juice. Then stew them in a little *velouté*, or in two ounces of butter melted, and thickened with a little flour; add white pepper and the squeeze of a lemon, and pour this hot over two roasted fowls, *or* serve the sauce in a tureen separately.—See No. 515.

668. *Fricassée des poulets à la paysanne,—a plain fricassée of chickens.*—Singe two fat white chickens very well, (see note, page 98.) Carve them smoothly with a very sharp knife exactly as at table. Wash them in lukewarm water, and blanch them over the fire a few minutes to firm the flesh. Plunge them in cold water, and then put them into a very nice stew-pan with three ounces of butter, a faggot of parsley and green onions, and a cupful of nicely-trimmed button-mushrooms. When warmed through, and a little tinged with colour, dredge on flour, and add salt, white pepper, and a little of the liquor they were blanched in. Let the fricassee simmer for a half-hour, or more if the chickens are large. Then lift the chickens into another sauce-pan. Skim off the fat, and reduce the sauce they are cooked in by a quick boil, and strain it over them. When about ready to serve, add a thickening of the beat yolks of two eggs.—See pp. 309, 310.

669. *Scollops of cold chicken.*—Mince the cold chickens, and heat in *bechamel-sauce*, dish in scollop-shapes, and serve with a cucumber-sauce.

670. *Rissoles of cold roast chicken.*—Mince the white and good parts. Warm the mince in *velouté* well reduced. Season with mace, white pepper, and nutmeg, and when cold, roll this up into balls the size of good large eggs. Wrap these in paste, and fry and serve them with fried parsley.—See No. 540.

671. *Salpiçons.*—These elegant little dishes are made of any kind of left poultry, or forcemeat, or of the more delicate vegetables, as mushrooms and artichokes, cooked separately, and served together, but in different compartments of the same dish. Salpiçons are usually cooked in *Espagnole*, and neatly dished, with a border,

and division lines of sippets. They may be strewed with crumbs, and browned with a salamander. They are considered *genteel*, and are certainly frugal where cookery is all the cost. They are a variety of the order *rissoles* or hashes.

672. *Salmi de perdreaux, salmi of partridges*.*— Par-roast three or four partridges kept till they have taken a little *fumet*. When cold, skin and carve them. Put them into a small stew-pan, with a bit of lemon-peel, four eschalots, a few bits of dressed ham, seasoning herbs of all kinds that you like, and a dessert-spoonful of peppercorns, with the trimmings of the partridges, a half-pint of *Espagnole*, and two glasses of Madeira. Let this simmer for an hour very gently. Dish the birds, and strain the skimmed sauce hot over them. Serve fried bread with the *salmi*, which must be very hot and high-seasoned to be good for any thing.

673. *Partridge salmi, sportman's fashion.*—Put roasted, or, if done on purpose, half-roasted partridges, skinned and carved, into a sauce-pan with a small glass of eating oil, a large glass of wine, pepper, salt, and the grate and juice of lemon. When just heated through, serve with grilled crusts.—See pages 313, 319.

674. *Salmi of wild duck or teal duck.*—Make a sauce of veal-gravy with cayenne. Simmer the trimmings of the duck in this, and then put in the cold roasted duck, carved and skinned. Simmer till hot. Lift the meat into a small stew-pan. Skim the sauce, and strain it over the meat, adding first more seasoning if needful. Squeeze a bitter orange over the sauce, and serve the dish very hot.—See Nos. 531-2-3.

675. *Eggs à la tripe.*—Peel, slice, and fry in butter, three or four Spanish onions. When done, dust in some flour, and let it catch to a light brown. Put in a little hot milk, salt, and pepper, and let the sauce reduce.† Put to this a dozen small hard-boiled eggs cut

---

* *Salmis* are favourite dishes with epicures, both on account of the excellence of their constituent parts, and their elaborate and piquant composition. They are in fact a species of moist *devils*. For thorough-bred English palates more hot seasonings will be requisite than are used by the French; and this must be attended to.

† *To boil and peel eggs.*—Boil them for fifteen minutes; drop them in cold water; roll them below your hand, and the shell will come off like any other mould.

in pieces. Mix them gently with the sauce not to break the slices. Arrange them neatly in the dish.

676. *Eggs in sauce Robert.*—Proceed as above directed; but brown the onions over a brisk fire, and moisten with soup. Reduce the sauce by boiling. Add a tea-spoonful of made mustard, and stir in the sliced eggs.—See Nos. 567, 568.

677. *Eggs à la maître d'hotel.*—Do these *white* as *eggs à la tripe*, but throw in a good lump of butter and minced parsley.—*Obs.* These dishes, though the best of their kind, seem of little comparative importance; but when the cook, or the mistress of a family, as is often the case, is racked for something to fill up an odd corner, they afford a cheap and ready resource. Eggs dressed in this last way will afterwards make an admirable sauce for poultry, salt cod, ling, &c. &c.

678. *Fondu.*—This is prepared in various ways. Mix grated Parmesan and Gruyère cheese, in equal quantities, or substitute good Gloucester or Cheshire for the latter; add to the rasped cheese about double the weight of cream, melted butter, and beat yolks of eggs; beat the whites of the eggs separately, and having beat the mixture very well, put pepper and a little salt to it, and stir the beat whites lightly in. Either bake the whole in a deep silver or block-tin dish, or in paper cases. Fill only half full, as the mixture will rise very much. Serve very hot in the second course.—See *Ramikins*, No. 555.

FRENCH DISHES OF FISH.*

679. *Court bouillon, for dressing fish.*—Where fish is boiled every day, as in large establishments, this is a very useful broth, as well as in Catholic families during Lent. Season a large gallon of water with salt, three carrots, a bunch of parsley, or roots of parsley and green onions, four eschalots, thyme, basil, two bay-leaves, a half-ounce of peppercorns, and a few cloves. Stew and strain this; as you need it, add wine or vinegar. It

---

* Fish is not nearly so well dressed in Paris as in London or at the Hague. The cooking *au bleu*, *à la Genevoise*, &c. is, in fact, chiefly practised to disguise the want of that first quality of all fish, which *les poissons equivoques* of Paris rarely possess—freshness. The French, however, re-dress fish better than we do, as in *vol-au-vent*, and rissoles, salpiçons, but above all, *au gratin*, No. 688.

will answer repeatedly by being boiled up; and the fish boiled on successive days will enrich it. A piece of butter may be put in at first. It will form a good basis for *maigre* sauces to the fish. This is also called *eau de sel*.

680. *Court bouillon for fish, dressed au bleu.*—Take the same herbs as above, but less in quantity, and fry them a little in butter. Over this, pour two bottles of white and one of red wine, and a little water. In this stew the fish nicely cleaned. This rich and expensive marinade will do repeatedly; water to be added to it when again used.—*Obs.* We consider this receipt useless where fish are to be got fresh. Fish dressed *au bleu* are eat with oil and vinegar, mustard, &c.

681. *Trout or pike à la Genevoise.*—Clean the fish, but do not scale it. Put a little *court bouillon* in a stew-pan with parsley-roots, cloves, parsley, two bay-leaves, and onions, also a carrot if you like. When these have stewed an hour, strain the liquor over the pike or trout in a small oval fish-pan, and add a little Madeira to the liquor. When boiled, drain it, and take off the scales thoroughly; then put it in the pan, with a little of the liquor to keep it moist and hot. Make a *roux* or thickening, and add to it veal-gravy, (or, if for a maigre dish, wine;) season this sauce with bits of mushroom, parsley, and green onions. Let it stew till smooth. Thicken with butter kneaded in flour if needful. Strain the sauce hot over the dished fish, with a squeeze of lemon, and a little essence of anchovy.—*Obs.* For trout use claret or some red wine, with mace and more cloves.

N.B.—*Saumon à la Genevoise* is dressed exactly in this way, which though rich cookery is now more out of vogue than fish served à la matelote. The head of the fish must be bound up to keep it from breaking, which is proper in dressing other fish.

682. *Fillets of haddocks, whitings, or codlings, with maître d'hotel sauce.*—The French dress fish very frequently in *fillets*, cut neatly from the bone the long way on both sides. The practice is good, as it saves a deal of trouble to the eater, the dish looks better, and if the *debris* is put to the stock-pot for fish-soups or sauces, there is no waste. Take the two sides or long fillets clean off the bone. Dry and flour, or egg and crumb them. Fry them, and, when ready, serve under a *maître*

d'hotel sauce, made thus:—Stew in butter a large spoonful of chopped young onions, parsley, and mushrooms, with pepper and salt to taste. This we conceive a useful general receipt.

683. *Fish-pudding, a common and favourite way of dressing cold fish.*—Take any sort of fish. Trim and chop from one to two pounds of it, and season this with chopped onions, parsley, and mushrooms; also salt and pepper; pound this with two raw eggs. Line a pudding-mould with slices of fat bacon, and put in alternate layers of the fish, and of *godiveau*, No. 692. Cover with bacon, and bake for an hour and a half, if the pudding is large. Turn it out; pick off the bacon, and serve with a plain brown sauce poured over it.

684. *To dress fillets of cold pike à la maître d'hotel.* —Cut them neatly. Stew them in butter with pepper and salt. Dish the fillets neatly, and sauce them with a *maître d'hotel* sauce, to which you put a little essence of anchovy.—*Obs.* French cooks serve cold fish, re-dressed, as *vol-au-vents, croquets, salades, boudins,* and in many ingenious modes as to outward shew. See pages 326, and 177.

685. *Matelote de carp à la Royale.*—Clean what number of carp you choose. Cut them into three or four pieces according to the size. Dry these, and stew them very slowly in red wine. Make a *sauce matelote* (see page 333,) but use the wine in which the carp is stewed both from economy and to have the full flavour of the fish. Use also a handful of cleaned mushrooms. Dish the fish, the heads in the middle, and strain the prepared sauce hot over them. Place the small stewed onions and mushrooms dressed in the sauce round the fish, and garnish with the soft roes stewed in vinegar.— *Obs.* This sauce, and all fish-sauces, should be of good consistence, that it may adhere to the fish.

686. *Perches au vin, perches in wine.*—Scale and clean the perch. Cook them in good stock and a little white wine, with a high seasoning of parsley, chives, cloves, &c. Thicken a little of this liquor for sauce. Add to it salt, pepper, nutmeg, and a little anchovy-butter.—*Obs.* Always use white wine with white fish, and red wine with red-coloured fish.

687. *Perch a la maître d'hotel.*—Boil some salt,

pepper, parsley, and chives in water, and in this *bouillon* boil the perch. Drain and dish them, and cover them with a *maître d'hotel sauce*.

688. *Soles,** flounders, and other small flat fish, or fillets of turbot, &c. au gratin.*—Have a flat silver dish, or baking-pan, spread a bit of fresh butter over it. Mince, very finely, parsley, eschalots, mushrooms; season with pepper and salt, and fry the herbs, and lay them in your buttered silver dish. Place your fish neatly cut and trimmed over this, and cover with fine bread-crumbs. Over this stick a few bits of butter; moisten with a little white wine; cook under a furnace, with a few embers, that the *gratin* may get crisp; squeeze lemon over your dish, and serve it very hot. The *gratin* may be browned with a salamander, and fried sippets may be stick over the dish. Small undressed fish may be divided, have the bones taken out, and be baked *au gratin*, arranging the pieces neatly *en miroton.*—No. 623.

689. *Sturgeon à la broche, roast sturgeon.*—Clean and split the fish, or part of a large one. Make a *marinade* of white wine, melted butter, and seasonings, and baste the roasting sturgeon with this. Take for sauce some of the skimmed basting-liquor, a little *espagnole* and veal-gravy, or *roux* and gravy, which may serve as a substitute for *Espagnole* in all kitchens. Boil up, strain, and serve this, and also a *poivrade* sauce.—*Obs.* A sturgeon may be as conveniently baked. Use the *marinade* as a sauce, and let the baking-dish be deep. Baste the fish occasionally. Cold roasted or baked sturgeon may be dressed as directed for turbot, and served in a *vol-au-vent*, a border of potatoes, or of toasted sippets.

690. *Morue à la bonne femme, salt cod in a plain way.* —Prepare the salt fish as directed at No. 161. Have some boiled potatoes in the shape of corks, cut in slices about the size of a shilling, and warm them with the fish in melted butter.

691. *Turbot-roe, a small elegant dish.*—Handle so as not to break the roe; blanch it, and slice and finish

---

* This and canapés of skates' livers are among the *recettes alimentaire* of a celebrated Parisian Society of Gourmands.

in the oven, as a ragout or as a white fricassee. Garnish with lemon.

OF FRENCH FORCEMEAT IN GENERAL.

692. *Quenelles and boudins.*—The French claim supremacy over the whole civilized world in the art of preparing *farces*. Without presuming to question their superiority, it is possible for a cook of ordinary abilities and industry to attain a competent knowledge of this high mystery, without serving a regular apprenticeship at the French stove, provided she give respectful attention to the manner in which foreign artists proceed. The French have reduced the art of preparing forcemeat to fixed principles. As constituents, they have the *godiveau*, the *panade*, the *farce* of fowl, the *gratin*, all cut and dry; and these they laboriously compound, with a degree of patience which goes far to redeem their national character from the charge of fickleness and levity. Of these farces are formed the *quenelle* and *boudin*, a class of preparations which, though made of forcemeat, forms, like our sausages, a distinct order of dishes. The French forcemeats are indeed worthy of the profound attention of every refined epicure, and ought to supplant our home-made crude compounds with all speed. The first element in their composition is the *godiveau, of which also excellent patties may be made.*— Scrape a pound of a fillet of white well-fed veal, and mince a pound and a half of beef-suet, free from all strings, skins, and kernels. Chop a suitable quantity of scalded parsley, young onions, and also mushrooms, to season this meat. Add pepper, salt, allspice, and mace, and pound the whole very well, mixing in three raw eggs at different times, and a little water. When very well pounded, make up a small ball of the *farce*, and boil it in boiling water, to try if it be light, well-seasoned, and good. By this *proof-ball* be guided either in adopting the *farce*, or in adding another egg to give firmness, or more water to liquefy the *godiveau*.

693. *Gratin.*—This *farce* may be made either of the white parts of a fowl, or of veal. Cut a half-pound of the fillet into small bits, and toss them over the fire in butter for ten minutes, with salt, pepper, and herbs. Drain off the butter. Mince the meat, and then pound

it, if for fowls, with the livers parboiled, veal-udder parboiled and skinned, or butter instead of udder, and *panada* (see next receipt.) Have as much butter or veal-udder as of each of the other ingredients, *i.e.* a third of each. Pound the whole together, adding an egg at a time till you have three, as in the *godiveau*. Prove the forcemeat by poaching a small ball of it.

694. *Panada for forcemeats.*—Soak slices of bread in hot milk. Press out the milk when the bread is quite moist, and beat up the bread with a little rich broth or white sauce, and a lump of butter. Stir till this becomes somewhat dry and firm. Add the yolks of two eggs, and pound the whole well together.

695. *Quenelles de volaille, or forcemeat-balls of poultry as a dish.*—Strip off the skin, pull out the sinews, and mince and pound the best parts of young fowls, till the meat will rub through a search. Have one part of this, one of panada, and another of veal-udder, parboiled and skinned. Pound the whole well together, and season with salt, white pepper, and mace. Put raw yolks to the compound, and beat it perfectly smooth. Prove it as directed, No. 692. If not firm enough, add more eggs, one at a time. Make up the *quenelles* of egg shapes, and poach or bake them.— *N.B.* Quenelles may be made of rabbit, partridge, or pheasant, in the same way. Serve with clear gravy. They are considered an elegant dish.

696. *Boudins à la Richelieu, puddings of rabbits or poultry.*—Make a forcemeat of rabbits or poultry, as directed for *quenelles*; but instead of panada use pounded potatoes. Put to the *farce* dressed onions or mushrooms chopped, in any suitable quantity. Spread the forcemeat smooth on the dresser, and with a knife roll it up in small sausages or *boudins*; or mould it to a proper shape, and bake the puddings. Whether boiled or baked, serve with brown Italian sauce.

Boudins may be made of all sorts of game, poultry, also of whitings, craw-fish, &c.

697. *Boudins blanc, an exceedingly good kind of white puddings.*—Cook a dozen small onions in broth. Make a rather dry panada of cream or milk, and pound this with the onions and some pounded sweet almonds. Put to this pig's caul, cut in little bits, some yolks of

eggs, a little cream, the white parts of raw chickens finely minced, with salt and spices. Pound the whole well, and try it by dressing a little in a small pan before you fill the skins. Boil the *boudins* in milk and water, and prick the skins to prevent them from bursting. When wanted, dip them in boiling water to heat, and finish them in a paper-case in a Dutch oven.—See *National Dishes*, No. 739.

FRENCH DISHES OF VEGETABLES, FRUIT, &C.
See also pages, 206-7, 210, 214.

FRENCH cooks claim superiority for their skill and variety in dressing vegetables; and the assumption is in this instance just. Vegetable preparations enter largely into their second courses, usually affording two dishes for an ordinary dinner, and four for a larger one. Great improvements have been made of late, even among ourselves, in preparing the more delicate and showy vegetable dishes; and it is to be hoped that British cooks, besides imitating the French in saucing their cauliflower and artichokes, will soon copy their manner of *braising* cabbages and carrots for homely every-day use.

698. *Asparagus pease for the second course.*—Pick and cut some young asparagus into small equal bits, rejecting what is woody. Boil these *pease* in salt and water, and drain and dry them in a cloth. Then give them a fry in butter with a bunch of parsley and green onions, and a sprig of mint. Dredge flour over them. Put in a bit of sugar, and moisten with boiling water. Give them a quick boil. When boiled down, take out the faggot of parsley and onions, and thicken the sauce with the beat yolks of two eggs, beaten up with cream and a little salt and grated nutmeg.—*Obs.* Melted butter may be used instead of cream.

699. *To dress green pease (the petits pois) for a second course.*—Boil a large pint of the finest green pease in water, with salt and a good piece of butter rubbed among them. When tender, drain them, lifting them out of the colander with your hand that the refuse may be left. Stew them with a faggot of parsley and green onions. The colour will now deepen. Dredge a good deal of flour over them, and stir a piece of butter among them, with salt, a very little grated Parmesan

(if you like), and a knob of sugar dipped in boiling water. Let them get quite dry, and dress them high on the dish.

700. *Sea kale for the second course.*—We do not know that this vegetable is naturalized in France even yet; but after boiling it in plenty of water with salt, French cooks in this country drain it, and serve with *sauce blanche* or *velouté.**—See No. 190.

701. *Artichoke-bottoms en canapés.*—Have the boiled artichokes nicely trimmed, and the *chokes* removed. When cold, fill the bottoms with anchovy butter, and decorate them with pickled capers, gherkins, and beet-root carved, attending to the effect of contrasted colours.—See No. 191.

702. *Artichokes à la Italienne.*—Trim and quarter the artichokes, and boil them in salt and water. Take out the *chokes.* Drain and arrange the quarters with the leaves outwards. Pour a white Italian sauce over them, and garnish with cresses.

703. *French beans à la poulette.*—When boiled, as directed, page 208, very green, drain them. Reduce some *sauce tournée.* Thicken it with beat yolks of eggs, and pour this over the boiled beans.

704. *Windsor beans à la poulette.*—Boil fresh young beans. Stew them, first taking off the coats, and sauce them *à la poulette, i.e.* with *velouté.*

705. *Potatoes à la maître d'hotel.*—Peel boiled potatoes, and turn them the size of thick corks. Cut these in half-inch slices. Put them into a stew-pan with some skinned green onions and parsley, pepper, salt, and butter. Moisten with broth, and toss them till the parsley is cooked.—See p. 220.

706. *Endive for the first or second course.*—Clean the endive by frequent washing, and plunge it head downmost, in salt and water, to draw out those insects which often lodge in the leaves of vegetables. Blanch the heads, drain them, and when cold, chop them fine. Stew them in veal-gravy with salt. When tender, add a little *Espagnole*, and serve with poached eggs for

---

* *Sauce blanche*, i.e. melted butter, is perhaps the most appropriate sauce for all vegetables, but for the danger of its running to oil, which makes *velouté* or cream sauce preferable in nice cookery.

second-course dishes, or under fricandeaux, or with hashed mutton.

707. *Compôte des cerises—preserved cherries.*—To a half pound of clarified sugar put a pound of cherries, of which half the stalk is cut away. Give them a boil of three minutes. Skim, and serve them in a glass dish. Take out the stones and cut away the stalks, if wished.

708. *Pears in sugar.*—Put a clove into the eye of each pear. Throw them into hot water to scald them. Pare and keep them in water to preserve the colour. Boil them in a very thin syrup of a large pint of water to a half-pound of sugar. Add the juice of a lemon, and serve in a glass dish in the syrup.

709. *Another way.*—Divide large pears. Take out the seeds. Blanch them in hot water and lemon-juice to keep the colour white. Pare them. Throw them into fresh water, and give them a few boils in thin syrup before serving them in it.

710. *Apples à la Portugaise.*—Wash and core fine large rennets, but do not pare them. Prick them with a knife, and boil them in thin syrup. Then put them in an earthen dish under a small furnace to brown, basting them with the syrup.

711. *Peaches in sugar.*—Blanch six or eight in hot water that they may peel easily, then give them a boil in syrup, and serve. The French serve all sorts of fruit *en compôte*, which forms tasteful and economical dishes. Serve all these in a *compôte* dish or glass dish.—See *Ornamental Dishes.*

FASHIONABLE FRENCH SMALL PASTRY FOR SECOND COURSES AND SUPPERS, CHIEFLY MADE OF PASTE ROYAL.

712. *Paste Royal to make.*—Put four ounces of butter into a stew-pan with a large glassful of water, two ounces of beat sugar, and a bit of lemon-peel. When the butter is nearly melted, shake some dry flour to it through a fine sieve. Take out the lemon-peel, and with your hand put in as much more flour as the boiling liquid will take, stirring briskly with a wooden spatula or spoon, till it come easily from the sides of the stew-pan. Put it in another pan. Let it cool. Break an egg into it, and stir it well to mix, and afterwards three or four more eggs, till the paste becomes tenacious and

ropy. This is used for many small articles, as *pains à la duchesse, choux, Chantilly baskets*, in short, it may be moulded into any form, according to the ingenuity of the cook. The things made of it, when arranged on paper, may be iced, baked in a moderate oven, and dried before the fire. This paste swells very much, which must be considered in forming the things made of it.

713. *Choux of paste royal.*—Form in the shape of balls larger than children's marbles. Bake in a moderate oven. Dry them, and make a small opening in the side, into which put a little of any sweetmeat you like.

714. *Pains à la Duchesse.*—Make as the *choux*, but flatten them with the rolling-pin to the length of four inches. When baked, slit them open at the end, and introduce the sweetmeat.

715. *Les gimblettes à l'artois.*—Make as the *choux*, but give them a deep dint in the middle before baking. Widen this by turning your finger round it. Sift sugar over them when just done; glaze with a salamander, and put the sweetmeats in the cavity.

716. *Les petits choux, et les gimblettes pralines.**—Make them rather smaller than above directed; and before baking, but when glazed, sprinkle finely-chopped sweet almonds and sugar over them, and garnish with sweetmeats, as the others.

717. *Paste-buttons and Melvilles.*—These may be made better of paste royal than of puff-paste. *Pâte-royale* may, as formerly said, be rolled out, and dressed in any form you choose, serving any preserved sweetmeat neatly upon it.

718. *Chantilly baskets.*—French cooks make these of very small *choux* of *pâte royale*, instead of the ratafia-biscuits used in this country. The method is the same. When the little biscuits or *choux* are quite crisp, have ready some sugar clarified and boiled to crackling height. Stick a small skewer into each biscuit, and dip the edge in sugar. Fix them one by one, as dipt, round a dish that will shape your basket. When one row is done, begin another. The candied sugar will make the biscuits instantly stick. Use rather larger biscuit for

---

* What we would call confected.

the upper tiers, as the basket should widen at the top. Three or four tiers will be enough of height. The handle will be most easily made by sticking the biscuits together round the ledge of a stew-pan, first ascertaining the width of the arch; for really what is ordered in common receipt books, about "throwing over an arch," is easier said than done. An ornamental border of coloured drops of gum-paste may be given to this. Serve any dry sweet you choose in the basket, which should first be lined with tissue-paper.

719. *Bouchées de dames, ladies' lips or kisses.*—Make a paste as for fine biscuits, of six fresh eggs, with six ounces of sifted sugar, and three of potato-flour. Beat this very well; spread it thinly, and bake on paper on a buttered oven-tin for nearly twenty minutes. When fine, stamp out the paste the size of dollars, and glaze with white, rose, or violet-coloured icing, or some of each.—See *To Ice Cakes.*

720. *The twins, or méringues jumeaux.*—Whip the whites of eight eggs to a firm froth, and add to this a pound of fine sifted sugar; *or clarify* and boil it to the second degree. Season with lemon-grate, and beat all very well together. Drop them on paper in the shape of an egg. Sift sugar over them. Bake them in a slow oven. When firm, draw them out, and stick two and two together, and put them to dry before the fire or in a hot closet.—*Obs.* These *méringues* or *gemini* may be made as above, but flavoured with *marasquin* or orange-flowers confected; but they must then be made smaller.

As has been said, an endless variety of trifles is made of paste royal, by purchasing the proper cutters or stamps. Among the neatest are the *petits paniers* and *petits brioches*, of which the proper stamp will direct the forming.—See *Brioche paste.*

721. *A fruit-cake.*—Roll out any bits of puff-paste you have left from more important preparations. Spread marmalade over these. Decorate with paste bands or straws. Glaze the cake with yolk of egg; bake it, and cut it into oblong pieces, and pile them on the dish.— See *Pastry, and Sweet and Ornamental Dishes.*

CHAPTER III.

"There be livers out of England."
Cymbeline.

————————

IT has been remarked, that every country is celebrated for some culinary preparation, and that all national dishes are good. The reason of this is sufficiently obvious: had they not been acceptable to the palate, they never could have either gained or maintained their supremacy. Accordingly, the Spanish *olio*, the Italian *macaroni*, the French *ragout*, the Turkish *pillau*, and, though last not least, in our good love, the *Scotch haggis*, differing essentially as they do, are, nevertheless, all equally good after their kind. We give precedence to the "Great chieftain of the pudding race."

722. *The Scotch haggis.*—Clean a sheep's pluck thoroughly. Make incisions in the heart and liver to allow the blood to flow out, and parboil the whole, letting the windpipe lie over the side of the pot to permit the phlegm and blood to disgorge from the lungs; the water may be changed after a few minutes' boiling for fresh water. A half-hour's boiling will be sufficient; but throw back the half of the liver to boil till it will grate easily; take the heart, the half of the liver and part of the lights, trimming away all skins and black-looking parts, and mince them together. Mince also a pound of good beef-suet and four or more onions. Grate the other half of the liver. Have a dozen of small onions peeled and scalded in two waters to mix with this mince. Toast some oatmeal before the fire for hours, till it is of a light-brown colour and perfectly dry. Less than two tea-cupfuls of meal will do for this quantity of meat. Spread the mince on a board, and strew the meal lightly over it, with a high seasoning of pepper, salt, and a little cayenne, well mixed. Have a haggis-bag perfectly clean, and see that there be no thin part in it, else your whole labour will be lost by its

bursting. Some cooks use two bags, one as an outer case. Put in the meat with a half-pint of good beef-gravy, or as much strong broth, as will make it a very thick stew. Be careful not to fill the bag too full, but allow the meat room to swell; add the juice of a lemon, or a little good vinegar; press out the air, and sew up the bag; prick it with a large needle when it first swells in the pot, to prevent bursting; let it boil slowly for three hours if large.—*Obs*. This is a genuine Scotch haggis; the lemon and cayenne may be omitted, and instead of beef-gravy, a little of the broth in which the pluck was parboiled may be taken. A finer haggis may be made by parboiling and skinning sheep's tongues and kidneys, and substituting these minced for the most of the lights. There are, moreover, sundry modern refinements on the above receipt,—such as eggs, milk, pounded biscuit, &c. &c.—but these, by good judges, are not deemed improvements. Some cooks use the small fat tripes, as in making lamb's-haggis.*

703. *A lamb's-haggis*.—Slit up all the little fat tripes with scissors, and clean them. Clean the kernels also, and parboil the whole, and cut them into little bits. Clean and shred the web and kidney fat, and mix it with the tripes. Season with salt, pepper, and grated nutmeg. Make a thin batter with two eggs, a half-pint of milk, and the necessary quantity of flour. Season with chopped chives or young onions. Mix the whole together. Sew up the bag, which must be very clean, and boil for an hour and a half.†

---

* Mr. Allan Cunningham, in some of his Tales, orders the parboiled minced meat of sheep's-head for haggis. We have no experience of this receipt, but it promises well.

† We have been requested by a correspondent to give the following receipt publicity for the benefit of mankind. The CLEIKUM CLUB have no experience of it, but Dr. REDGILL was willing to stake his reputation upon it untried:—

Calf's-haggis.—"Take the veal-caul (or web of fat), the udder, the kidney, and best part of the pluck. Blanch and boil the udder, and the split kidney and pluck, for ten minutes. When cool, mince them; mince also the caul. Blanch and hash two dozen sprigs of picked young parsley, a few green onions very young, a bit of eschalot, and a few mushrooms, if you have them. Stew the herbs in butter for three or four minutes, and moisten them with a glass of Madeira. When dried, season with salt and pepper. Mix the ingredients, *i.e.* the herbs, and mince. Put them into a bag as other haggis; but for security have

724. *Fat brose.*—Boil an ox-head, sheep's-head, ox-heel, or skink of beef, till an almost pure oil floats on the top of the pot. Have some oatmeal well toasted before the fire, as in making haggis; put a handful of the meal into a basin with salt, and pouring a ladleful of the fat broth over it, stir it quickly up, so as not to run into a doughy mass, but to form *knots*.

725. *Kail-brose* is made as in the above receipt, but of fat broth in which shred greens have been boiled.

726. *Cock-a-leekie.*—Boil from four to six pounds of good shin-beef, well broken, till the liquor is very good. Strain it, and put to it a capon, or large fowl, trussed for boiling, and, when it boils, half the quantity of blanched leeks intended to be used, well cleaned, and cut in inch-lengths, or longer. Skim this carefully. In a half-hour add the remaining part of the leeks, and a seasoning of pepper and salt. The soup must be very thick of leeks, and the first part of them must be boiled down into the soup till it becomes a green lubricious compound. Sometimes the capon is served in the tureen with the cock-a-leekie. This is good leek-soup without a fowl.—*Obs.* Some people thicken cock-a-leekie with the fine part of oatmeal. Those who dislike so much of the leeks may substitute shred greens, or spinage and parsley, for one half of them. Reject the coarse green part of the leeks. Prunes wont to be put to this soup. The practice is obsolete.

---

two bags, one casing the other, in case of a breach. Mix meanwhile the beat yolks of two eggs with a half-pint of rich and highly-seasoned veal or beef gravy, and two spoonfuls of pounded and sifted rusks. Put this into the bag with the other materials, and the squeeze of a lemon, and when sewed up, toss it about to blend them all, and boil in fresh broth if you have it; pricking the bag to let out the air, as in your other receipts."

We find the following directions for *Haggis Royal* in the Minutes of Sederunt of the CLEIKUM CLUB:—"Three pounds of leg of mutton chopped; a pound of suet chopped; a little, or rather as much beef-marrow as you can spare; the crumb of a penny loaf; (our own nutty-flavoured, browned oatmeal, by the way, far better;) the beat yolks of four eggs; a half-pint of red wine; three mellow fresh anchovies boned; minced parsley, lemon-grate, white pepper, crystals of cayenne to taste, —crystals alone ensure a perfect diffusion of the flavour—blend the ingredients well; truss them neatly in a veal-caul; bake in a deep dish, in a quick oven, and turn out. Serve hot as fire, with brown gravy, and venison-sauce."

727. *Balnamoon skink, an Irish soup.*—Clean and cut into pieces two or three young cocks, or fowls. Have one larger neatly trussed for boiling. Boil the cut fowls till the broth is as strong and good as they can make it; but do not overboil the uncut one. Strain the broth, season it with parsley, chives, and young onions chopped, and, if in season, a few tender green pease. Add white pepper and salt, and serve the whole fowl in the tureen, or separately.—*Obs.* This is another variety of the old Scottish *cock-a-leekie*; a dish, which, under some name, is, with whatever modification of seasonings, familiar in every country where a backward system of husbandry renders poultry plenty, and shambles-meat scarce. Without desiring to innovate on these national preparations, we would recommend, for the sake of the ladies' dresses and the gentlemen's toil in fishing it up, that the fowl be carved before it is served in the tureen.

728. *Scotch hotch-potch.*—Make the stock of sweet fresh mutton. Cut down four pounds of ribs of lamb into small steaks, trimming off superfluous fat, and put them to the strained stock. Grate the zest of two or three large carrots; slice down as many more. Slice down also young turnips, young onions, lettuce, and parsley. Have a full quart of these things when shred, and another of young green pease. Put in the vegetables, withholding half the pease till near the end of the process. Boil well and skim carefully; add the remaining pease, white pepper, and salt; and when thick enough, serve the steaks in the tureen with the hotch-potch; trim the fat from the steaks.—*Obs.* The excellence of this favourite dish depends mainly on the meat, whether beef or mutton, being perfectly fresh, and the vegetables being all young, and full of sweet juices. The sweet white turnip is best for hotch-potch, or the small, round, smooth-grained yellow kind peculiar to Scotland, and almost equal to the genuine *Navet* of France. Mutton makes excellent hotch-potch without any lamb-steaks. Parsley shred, white cabbage, aparagus-points, or lettuce, may be added to the other vegetables or not, at pleasure.—See No. 99.

729. *Winter hotch-potch, or German broth.*—This dish may be made of either fresh beef, or of a neck or back-ribs of mutton, or of a mixture of both. Cut four

pounds of meat into handsome pieces. Boil and skim this well, and add carrots and turnips sliced, small leeks and parsley cut down, and some German greens finely shred, and put in only a half hour before the soup is completed. Season with pepper and salt. The quantity of vegetables must be suited to the quantity of meat, so that the soup may have consistence, but not be disagreeably thick. Serve the meat and soup together. Have, if you like, rice or whole pease boiled in it, which last is a great improvement.—*Obs.* The meat may be kept whole and served as *Bouilli Ordinaire*, No. 99.

730. *To make skink, an old Scotch stew soup.*—Take two legs of beef, put them on with two gallons of water; let them boil for six hours, taking care to skim the soup well all the time, as the gravy should be very clear and bright; then strain the liquor from the meat, take the sinewy part of the meat, and lay it aside till your soup is ready to serve up. Cut the sinews about an inch long. Have some vegetables cut, such as carrots, turnips, leeks, onions, celery, lettuce, cabbage shred small, and green pease, when to be had. Blanch the whole in boiling water for ten minutes. Put the whole into the soup, and boil till quite tender. Serve up the sinews in the tureen with the soup. Season the soup with salt and pepper before dishing it.—*Obs.* Herbs may be used in these soups; and white pease (boilers) are by many thought an improvement. Both are cheap and excellent family-dishes.

731. *Plain Scotch fish and sauce, a maigre dish.*— This is, in fact, just a fish-soup. Make a stock of the heads, points of the tails, fins, &c. or where fish is cheap, cut down a small one or two to help the stock. Boil green onions, parsley, and chives in this, and some whole pepper. When all the substance is obtained, strain it. Thicken with butter kneaded in browned flour, but only to the consistence of a soup, and put in the fish, (generally haddocks,) cut in three or divided. Boil the fish ten minutes, and serve them and the sauce together in a tureen or soup-dish.—See pages 180-188.

732. *Scotch fish and sauce, a favourite family dish.*— Proceed as above to make a stock; or use broth of meat if wanted rich, though plenty of butter kneaded in browned flour will make this rich enough. The fish cut

in pieces may also be browned in the frying-pan. Season highly with mixed spices and a half-cupful of catsup. This dish may be enriched with oysters, shrimps, or muscles prepared: or with fish farce-balls. The sauce or soup should be rather thicker than in the former receipt. Serve as above. Some will like celery in this dish.

733. *Friar's chicken.**—Make a clear stock of veal, or mutton-shanks, or trimmings of fowls, or butter. Strain this into a very nice sauce-pan, and put a fine white chicken, or young fowl or two, cut down as for curry, into it. Season with salt, white pepper, mace, and shred parsley. Thicken, when the soup is finished, with the beat yolks of two eggs, and take great care that they do not curdle. Serve with the carved chicken in the soup. —*Obs.* The stock may be simply made of butter, and the meat may be nicely browned in the frying-pan before it is put to the soup. Rabbits make this very well. Some like the egg curdled, and egg in great quantity, making the dish a sort of *ragout* of eggs and chicken.

734. *Minced collops, an economical dish.*—Mince a fleshy piece of beef, free of skins and gristles, very fine, and season it with salt and mixed spices, (that is, kitchen-pepper.) Mix up the collops with a little water or broth; and, having browned some butter in a sauce-pan, put them to it, and beat them well with an iron or wooden spoon to keep them from going into lumps, till

---

* FRIAR'S BALSAM.—We have been favoured by a literary lady with a receipt for making Friar's Balsam, once so highly esteemed in Scotland. The receipt is of value as an antiquarian curiosity, independently of the medicinal virtues of the balsam. After the Reformation, this preparation was, in zealous Protestant families, called "Aromatic Tincture."

"Take 4 oz. of storax, 2 oz. of balsam of Peru, 7 oz. of benzoin, and of myrrh, frankincense, soccotrine-aloes, angelica-roots, and flowers of St. John's-wort, each an ounce. Pound the gums, pulverise the flowers, and put all the ingredients, except the balsam of Peru, into a wide-mouthed bottle or glazed jar, with two English pints of highly-rectified spirit of wine. Cork the bottle or jar very closely, tying it over with bladder and linen, with a waxed packthread. Bury the bottle in the hot dunghill of a stable-yard for a month, taking it up to shake the contents every other day. At the end of four weeks put in the balsam of Peru. Shake the bottle occasionally for three days, and strain off the balsam through a piece of cambric. Keep it in vials well corked and sealed. The pieces of cambric, saturated with the balsam, will be useful for many common purposes of domestic surgery."

they are nearly ready. Put gravy to them, or a little broth made of the skins and gristles, till rather thin.— *Obs.* Minced collops of beef may be dressed like Dr. Hunter's dinner for an invalid, and will be as light. Shred onions will be relished by some persons; also a little made mustard: pickles,* or vinegar, plain or flavoured, is also used. Minced collops will keep some time, if packed in a can and covered like potted meats. Some cooks scrape the meat instead of mincing it: with herbs, chopped eggs, suet, and seasonings, it is then a good forcemeat.

735. *Hare, venison*, and *veal collops* are made as above, using the seasonings appropriate to those savoury preparations.

736. *Potted-head, potted-heels, &c..*—Dress a cow's-head as directed for ox-cheek-soup, page 154, and, when boiled till very tender, cut the meat into small pieces, shaped as directed, No. 460. Strain the gravy; season it very highly with mixed spices and mace, and return the whole into a clean sauce-pan. Boil for some time, and pour it out into stoneware shapes or basins, and when cold, turn it out. This makes a pretty side-dish, dormant dish, or supper-dish. Garnish with a wreath of curled parsley, or sliced beet-root pickled. Cow-heels and calf's-head are potted in the same manner. Season calf's-head with lemon-peel and juice of lemon.

737. *A stoved howtowdie, with drappit eggs.*—Prepare and stuff with forcemeat a young plump fowl. Put it into a *yetling* concave-bottomed small pot with a close-fitting lid, with button-onions, spices, and at least a quarter-pound of butter. Add herbs if approved. When the fowl has hardened and been turned, add a half-pint or rather more of boiling water or broth. Fit on the lid very close, and set the pot over embers. A cloth may be wrapped round the lid, if it is not *luted* on. An hour will do a small fowl, and so in proportion. Have a little seasoned gravy, in which parboil the liver. Poach† nicely in this gravy five or six small eggs. Dress them

---

* Though in all Scotch cookery-books pickles are ordered to be mixed with minced collops and other ragouts, the CLEIKUM CLUB refuse their sanction to the semi-barbarous practice of mingling crude vegetables with hot dressed meat.—P. T.

† This is exactly the French dish *oeufs pochés au jus.*

on flattened balls of spinage round the dish, and serve the fowl, rubbing down the liver to thicken the gravy and liquor in which the fowl was stewed, which pour over it for sauce, skimming it nicely, and serving all very hot.—*Obs.* This is a very nice small dish. Mushrooms, oysters, forcemeat-balls, &c. may be added to enrich it; and celery may be put to the sauce; the spinage may be and often is omitted. Chickens and young fowls are dressed as above, in Germany, with fried eggs; or are steeped in lemon-juice, spices, and parsley, and cut up, fried, and served with fried eggs.

738. *A veal flory, or Florentine pie.*—This Scotch dish is neither more nor less than a good veal-pie, with the addition of some stoned raisins and prunes, minced with beef-suet. Any pie is called a flory, as apple-flory, marmalade-flory, &c.

739. *Scotch white puddings.*—Mince good beef-suet, but not too finely, and mix it with about a third of its own weight of nicely-toasted oatmeal. Season very highly with pepper, salt, and finely-shred parboiled onions. Have the skins thoroughly cleaned, and cut of equal lengths. Fill them with the ingredients, and fasten the ends with a wooden pin or small feather. Boil the puddings for an hour, pricking them as they swell in the pot, to let out the air. They will keep for months in bran or oatmeal. When to be used, warm them through in hot water; then on the gridiron, on oiled paper, or without, and serve very hot.—See No. 697.

740. *Liver-puddings* are made as above, using parboiled liver grated in the proportion of one-fourth; the rest suet and meal, with the above seasonings.

741. *To roast a pig, Scotch way.*—The directions of a thorough-bred Scotch cook, sanctioned by experience, authorize us to recommend that a pig intended for roasting shall be slightly rubbed with melted butter whenever it has warmed at the fire; then quickly dredge every part with fine flour; keep turning the spit continually, but slowly, allowing twenty minutes for each pound weight in the roast; and frequently dredging it, that the skin may have a complete superficies of flour, uniform as on the locks of an antiquated beau of the last century, shrouding the encroachments of Time beneath the *powder* of Fashion. When the pig has performed

the specified revolutions before a clear fire, let the flour be blown off with a small handy pair of bellows; and with a large piece of butter, within a single press of clean linen, rub the skin all over, turning the roast with great deliberation. Persevere in this unction a quarter of an hour, and the pig crackling will be exquisitely crisp. (*From a Correspondent.*)—See also page 97, and *French Mode*, page 345.

742. *Pig's cheek, by a Scotch lady's receipt, equal to Moine blanc.*—Split a large fat head, take out the brains, cut off the ears. Lay the head in water and salt for one day, and boil slowly till the bones will come out. Carefully take off the skin to keep as wrapper for the cheek. Mince the meat while still hot. Season with pepper and allspice (nutmeg and mace if you please.) Press the mince in a pudding pan, very firmly. Put a weight over it. It will get quite firm, and slice like Bologna sausage. It may be kept in a cold *pickle* made of its liquor, with vinegar and salt boiled in it. Serve with vinegar and mustard.—*Obs.* We recommend this confidently to our readers, whether cooks or epicures.—See Nos. 658, 656.

743. *To fry tripe, Scottish fashion.*—This dish is economical, palatable, and agreeable to the eye. The pieces of tripe left after an ordinary stew are quite fit for the present purpose; or, if you are to use tripe just taken from its own jelly, it must be wiped from moisture, and stewed in warm milk, with a small piece of butter and salt. Simmer it slowly till very tender. This should be done in time to let it be thoroughly cold, before the finishing ingredients are added. Make a batter with three eggs well beaten, allowing a spoonful of flour to each egg, and as much milk as will make a thick batter. Season with ginger, onions, or chives, and parsley minced very fine. Cut the tripe in cutlets, dip it in the batter, and fry in beef-dripping. If you find the batter is not thick enough to cover the tripe with a fine brown crust when fried, add a little more flour to it.— See pages 339, 89, 130.

744. *Fine puddings in skins.*—Mince apples and grate biscuit; take an equal weight to these of minced suet. Sweeten this with sugar, and season with cinnamon and grated nutmeg. Moisten the whole with wine,

or any well flavoured liquor, and fill the skins, but not too full, as the bread swells. Boil, and serve hot.—*Obs.* These will keep for a week or ten days, and re-warm. *Another kind* of fine pudding is made of rice boiled in milk, with suet, currants, sugar, and seasonings. The suet in these puddings should not be shred too small, nor yet left in lumps.—See *Boudins*, p. 356.

745. *Scotch black puddings.*—Salt the blood when drawn;* strain it; mix it with a little sweet milk or broth; stir into it shred suet and dried oatmeal, with plenty of pepper, salt, and minced onions. Fill the skins, and boil and broil as white puddings. Savoury herbs may be added.—*Obs.* Blood will curdle if boiled too quick. This national preparation is much superior to the English receipt.—See No. 718.

746. *Oatmeal dumpling, or a fitless cock.*—This antique Scotch dish, which is now seldom seen at any table, is made of suet and oatmeal, with a seasoning of pepper, salt, and onions, as for white puddings, the mixture bound together with an egg, and moulded somewhat in the form of a fowl. It must be boiled in a cloth, like a dumpling.

747. *Crappit heads, or fish with forcemeat.*—The original Scotch *farce* was simply oatmeal, suet or butter, pepper, salt, and onions, made into a coarse forcemeat, for stuffing the heads of haddocks and whitings. Modern CRAPPIT HEADS are farced with the ingredients mentioned in pages 188, 193, or with the fleshy parts of a lobster, or good crab, minced; a boned anchovy, the chopped yolk of an egg, grated bread or pounded biscuit, white pepper, salt, cayenne, a large piece of butter broken down into bits, with beat eggs to bind, and a little oyster-liquor. A plainer and perhaps as suitable stuffing may be made of the roe of haddock or cod parboiled, skinned and minced, mixed with double its bulk of pounded rusks or bread-crumbs, a good piece of butter, shred parsley, and seasonings, with an egg to cement the forcemeat. Place the *crappit* or stuffed heads on

---

* Of all blood that of the hog is thought the richest, and this is always employed in France in their *boudins* of this kind, which are excellent. The blood of the hare has the most delicate flavour of any, but is not to be got in sufficient quantity for puddings.—See *Boudins French Cookery.*

end, in the bottom of a buttered stew-pan; pour the fish-soup gently over them; cover and boil a half hour.

748. *Sheep's-head broth.**.—Choose a large fat head. When carefully singed by the blacksmith, soak it and

---

* This national preparation was wont to be a favourite Sunday-dinner dish in many comfortable Scottish families. Where gentlemen "killed their own mutton," the head was reserved for the Sunday's broth; and to good family customers, and to *victuallers*, a prime tup's head was a common Saturday's gift from the butchers with whom we dealt. By the way, nationally speaking, we ought to say fleshers, as our country-men would, till very lately, have been mortally offended at the designation of "butcher."

Sheep's-head broth is reckoned medicinal in certain cases; and was frequently prescribed as an article of diet by the celebrated Dr. Cullen.

This dish has furnished whole pages to Joe Miller and his right witty contemporaries. In one of the most pleasing pieces of biography that ever was written,—"The Life of Lady Grizel Baillie,"—there is an amusing "Sheep's head anecdote," which at once affords a glimpse of the simplicity of the national manners, and of the dexterity and good sense of the affectionate and very juvenile heroine. Her father, Sir Patrick Home, proscribed after the Restoration, was hidden near his own mansion,—his lady and his daughter Grizel being alone privy to his place of concealment. It was the duty of this young girl, not only to carry food to her father during the night, but to abstract these supplies from the dinner-table, so that neither the servants nor younger children might be aware that there was an invisible guest to feed. Her inordinate appetite and stratagems to procure food became the cause of many jokes at table; and one day, when a sheep's-head—a favourite dish with Sir Patrick—was produced, she had just conveyed the whole into her lap, when her young brother, afterwards Earl of Marchmont, looked up, and exclaimed,—"Mother, mother, look at Grizel; while we have been taking our broth, she has eaten up the whole sheep's-head!"—The consternation of young Home could not, however, exceed that of a learned gentleman, who at present fills a chair in the Edinburgh University, upon a somewhat similar occasion. Before filling his present honourable situation, Professor ——— was for some years a professor in S——— College; and, as might have been surmised, in the lapse of those years of exile, experienced a natural and national longing for that savoury food, which, to a Scotsman, is like his mother's milk. A sheep's-head was accordingly procured by his orders, and sent to the blacksmith's to be singed. The hour of dinner arrived; the chops of the learned professor watered with expectation; when, lo! to his disappointment and horror, the fleshless skull was presented; and, doubly worse, accompanied with the sauce of a bill, setting forth,—"To polishing a sheep's head for Professor ———, one shilling and fourpence!"—Thus making the unfortunate philosopher come down with sixteen shillings Scots money, for being deprived of the exquisite pleasure which he had anticipated in polishing the skull himself.

The village of Duddingston was long celebrated for "sheep's-head," and consequently a favourite resort of the frugal citizens of Edinburgh. Sheep's-head clubs were not unfrequent throughout the country, and "The Tup's-head Dinner" about Michaelmas-day is still a high and appropriate solemn festival with the official dignitaries in certain of our royal burghs.

the singed trotters for a considerable time in lukewarm water. Take out the glassy part of the eyes, and scrape the head and trotters, and brush till perfectly clean and white; then split the head with a cleaver, and take out the brains, &c.; clean the nostrils and gristly parts, split also the trotters, and cut out the tendons. Wash the head and feet once more, and let them blanch till wanted for the pot.

Take a large cupful of barley, and about twice that quantity of soaked white or old green pease, with a gallon or rather more of water. Put to this the head, and from two to three pounds of scrag or trimmings of mutton, perfectly sweet, and some salt. Take off the scum very carefully as it rises, and the broth will be as limpid and white as any broth made of beef or mutton. When the head has boiled rather more than an hour, add sliced carrot and turnip, and afterwards some onions and parsley shred. A head or two of celery sliced is admired by some modern gourmands, though we would rather approve of the native flavour of this really excellent soup. The more slowly the head is boiled, the better will both the meat and soup be. From two to three hours boiling, according to the size of the head and the age of the animal, and an hour's simmering by the side of the fire, will finish the soup. Many prefer the head of a ram to that of a wether, but it requires much longer boiling. In either case the trotters require less boiling than the head. Serve, with the trotters, and sliced carrot round the head. Sheep's-head, not too much boiled, makes an excellent ragout or hash of higher flavour than calf's-head ragout.—*Obs.* The sauces ordered for boiled mutton and cow-heel are well adapted to this dish, if sauce must be had where it is so little required.* For ragout, a sauce may be made of the broth, thickened with butter and flour.

749. *Leek-porridge.*†—Make this as cock-a-leekie,

---

* The reviewer of the first edition of this work in Blackwood's Magazine suggests, that there should be *two heads* and *eight trotters*, which admirable emendation certainly more than doubles the value of the receipt.

† The *Leek* is one of the most honourable and ancient of pot-herbs. It is called *par excellence* "the herb;" and learned critics assert that our word porridge or pottage is derived from the Latin, *porrus*, a leek. "From Indus to Peru," the adoration of the *garlic, onion* and *leek* is universal. The *leek* is the badge of a high-spirited, honourable, and fiery nation

and thicken with toasted or fried bread. Use fewer leeks. Prunes are sometimes put into this composition. They are nearly obsolete.—See No. 726.

750. *Pan-kail, a maigre soup.*—Mince cabbage, Savoys, or German greens; boil them in water, well thickened with oatmeal, and add a piece of butter, salt, &c. *Kail* is also made by parboiling and mashing the greens, putting them to hot pot-liquor, and thickening it with bread or pounded biscuit. Both must be a thick pottage.

751. *Plum-porridge.*—Boil a large shin for six hours, and skim the liquor. Strain off the liquor, and put to it a piece of veal cut from the fillet. Soften the crumb of a penny-loaf in the soup, and beat it smoothly. Thicken the soup with this, and put to it a half-pound of stoned raisins, and a half-pound of stoned prunes, a pound of currants well-cleaned, and some pepper, mace, and grated nutmeg. When the fruit is soft, the dish is ready. A little more bread may be used, if greater consistence is wanted, and the veal may be omitted.

752. *A pillau.*—Stew some rice in broth, or with butter; and season it with white pepper, mace, cayenne, and cloves. Place two small fowls, or a few veal or mutton cutlets, in the centre of a large dish, and lay some slices of boiled bacon beside them. Cover with rice; smooth and glaze the rice with egg, and set the dish before the fire or in the oven, to brown for a while. Garnish with yolks of hard-boiled eggs and fried onions, or use forcemeat-balls.—*Obs.* This is no bad dish, whatever country owns it. A more oriental complexion may be given to this dish by frying the rice in butter, stirring it with a fork till of a light-brown, and then stewing it in broth till soft.*

753. *An olio.*—Boil, in a close-covered pot, a fowl, a couple of partridges, a piece of leg of mutton, a knuckle of veal, and a few rump-steaks; also a piece of good bacon or ham. Brown the meat first; add boiling water; and when it has boiled an hour, add parsley, celery,

—the Ancient Britons. In the old poetry of the northern nations, where a young man would now be styled the *flower*, he was called "the *leek* of his family, or tribe," an epithet of most savoury meaning.

* This is the same dish known in French cookery as *Capons à la Turque,* except that the bodies of the fowls are then stuffed with the boiled rice.

young onions, pease, carrot, turnip, and a bit of garlic, if it is liked, with salt and mixed spices. Serve the whole together, first picking out the bacon. Seasoning herbs may also be used.—See *Pepper-pot*, p. 155.

754. *China chilo.*—Mince a pound and a half of good mutton and four ounces of mutton-suet. Stew this in broth or with butter, and add a pint of green pease, young onions, and a little shred lettuce. Season with salt, cayenne, and white pepper. Heap boiled rice round a shallow soup-dish, and serve the stew or chilo in the middle.—*Obs.* Veal or fowl may be dressed as above. A little curry-powder may be added to the seasoning. The zest of carrots, cut in very small cubes, will supply the place of pease in winter; so will celery.

755. *Pillau of veal.*—Half-roast a breast of veal, and cut it into neat pieces. Season these highly, and stew them in rich gravy. Lay a casserole of rice round a dish, and put the meat in the centre. Cover with more rice, and set the dish in the oven for a short time, having first glazed it with eggs.—*Obs.* Curry-powder may with advantage be used for this pillau; and it may be made of dressed veal. Pillau is also made *baked*, of a mixture of bacon, chicken, and onions, in layers. A fowl, capon, or small turkey, trussed as for boiling, makes an elegant *pillau* dressed as in this receipt; but cover the breast with bacon, which remove before dishing. A hind-quarter of lamb makes a nice *pillau*. Braise the leg, fry the loin in steaks, and treat it as above.

756. *Fricandelle.*—Take one pound of the lean of a leg of veal, half a pound of veal-suet, four rusks soaked in milk, four eggs, leaving out two whites, some onions, pepper, salt, nutmeg, and a lemon-peel; chop all together very fine, and make three balls of it, which you must put into boiling water, and let boil four minutes. Make a gravy of the skin, bones, &c. which must be carefully taken out of the veal. Fry the balls a light-brown in butter, and stew them half an hour in the gravy. Garnish the dish with slices of lemon; thicken the sauce with butter rolled in flour, if thin. It ought to be very thick. (*From a Correspondent.*)—*Obs.* This may be made of beef, or with fowl or game; it may be baked in a mould and turned out.—See No. 692.

757. *Mullagatawny, or curry-soup, as made in India.*

—Have ready pounded and sifted an ounce of coriander-seeds, the third of an ounce of cassia, three drachms of black, and two of cayenne pepper, and a quarter of an ounce of China turmeric; mix them well. This quantity will do either for two chickens, a large fowl, or three pounds of meat. Cut down the meat in small pieces, and let it boil slowly for a half-hour in two quarts of water; then put to it four onions, and three cloves of garlic shred and fried in two ounces of butter. Mix down the seasonings with a little of the broth and rice flour, and strain them into the stew-pan, which must simmer till the soup is smooth and thick as cream. When it is within five minutes of being finished, add the juice of a lemon, or citric acid in the same proportion. Serve the meat and soup in a tureen, and boiled rice, in a hot-water dish.—See No. 82.

758. *To boil rice for this soup, &c.*.—Wash in warm water Patna rice, picking out all the hulls and black particles. Pour boiling water over it, and close the stew-pan, which must be kept in a warm place. In an hour pour off the water, and setting the stew-pan on the fire, briskly stir up the rice with a fork till it dry without hardening.—See No. 536.

759. *Another way.*—Wash a half-pound of rice, and boil it in two quarts of *boiling* water for fifteen minutes. Turn it out to drain through a colander, and dry it by the fire. It must be very lightly handled, and every grain will be separate and distinct. Indeed, rice should never be taken up with spoons, but tossed over into the dish.

760. *The Garbure, a dish of the north of Europe.*—Take a fresh knuckle of ham, a knuckle of veal, and six pounds of the flank piece of beef well beat. Sweat this over a slow fire, with a bunch of parsley, three onions stuck with cloves, and three carrots, putting in a pint of fresh broth at the first. When the meat is well heated, and the juices drawn out, add five or six pints of broth, and stew the whole slowly for two hours. Have some firm white cabbages cleaned, quartered, and blanched, and *braise* them between layers of bacon with a little broth till rich and mellow, when they must be put to the broth; now add sausages, or the legs of salted geese previously dressed. Toast slices of rye-bread, or brown bread as a substitute, and on a bed of this lay the

cabbage, drained of fat, with the ham above it in the middle, and the sausages or geese legs round it. Serve the broth separately as a soup.

761. *German onion beef, or Szwiebel fleish.*—Put six pounds of the thin flank (skinned if you choose) to two quarts of water or weak fresh broth; stew them an hour in a close stew-pan. Add to it the thin rind of two lemons, a quarter-ounce of bruised cloves, two bay-leaves, one dozen black and two dozen Jamaica pepper-corns, in a bit of muslin; add salt; stew a half-hour. Add a dozen large sliced onions, and stew till they are tender. Skim off the fat and thicken the gravy. Boil up. Add what more salt and seasoning is wanted, and dish, taking out the pepper-corns, rinds, and bay-leaves.

762. *Duck with sour-crout, German.*—Braise a half-pound of drained sour-crout with a good piece of bacon, parsley, onions, spices, and sweet herbs, or any fresh *braise* liquor you have. Lay the duck in the middle of it, cover with more slices of bacon; moisten with top-fat, and stew slowly. When about half-done, add some small sausages. Drain the sour-crout when ready to serve, and place the duck over it, with the sausages around.—*Obs.* These dishes are for the first course in place of soups, and must be served in a deep dish.

763. *Provence brandade, an excellent way of dressing salt fish.*—See page 78.—Soak and brush the fish in water (some use lime-water to whiten, but we do not recommend it). Stew it as directed for other salt cod or ling, page 177. Oil a sufficient quantity of butter (or use oil and butter) in a small stew-pan, with chopped parsley and a bruised clove of garlic. Skin and pull the fish to small pieces, and shake them well in the stew-pan to make them melt to a mass in the oil. The stew-pan must be all along vigorously shaken.

N.B.—An easier way of dressing this dish is to pound the fish, and bake it with the butter, in paste or potato-pastry. This is very similar to Dr. Hunter's teased skate, page 178.

764. *Irish stew.*—Having taken the loose fat from a loin or neck of mutton, cut from three to four pounds of it into small well-shaped chops. Flatten and season them with salt and mixed spices. Peel six or eight onions; parboil and skin a quantity of potatoes. Lay

some shred suet at the bottom of a stew-pan, and a half-pint of broth, or melt two ounces of butter. Slice in a layer of potatoes, then a layer of chops, then strew in the onions, then again the potatoes and chops, &c. and let the top be covered with potatoes. A shank or small bit of ham, or a scrape of smoked tongue, or a little sausage meat, is a great addition to this favourite family dish. It must *stove* very slowly, and the pan must be closely and constantly covered. Mashed potato makes an excellent wholesome paste to cover plain meat-pies of all kinds, particularly pies of fat meat.—*Obs.* Some cooks wrap an old napkin round the stew-pan lid, which forms a kind of *luting* in dressing this and other *stoved* dishes. There is a kind of cottage-oven used in Ireland, in form of a wide stew-pan, made of cast-iron, with a lid of the same thickness, on which embers of turf are put. This is placed over other embers, and an equal slow heat is maintained, which dresses a stew, bakes a pudding or a bit of meat, and is found very useful at other times as a cottage-pot. Hunter's-pie is another excellent form of Irish stew, only this is sometimes made of beef-collops instead of mutton-chops; and then the potatoes are always mashed. Place the potatoes, meat, and onions in alternate layers in an earthen-ware pie-dish, and bake them; the top layer of potatoes may be neatly scored, scolloped on the edges, and glazed with eggs, if approved. A fashionable Irish stew is baked in a mould, *en casserole*, and turned out when served.

765. *Irish tripe.*—Cook some onions in milk and water. If large, divide them, and have plenty of them. Add the tripe, cut in stripes, to the onions, and thicken as much of the sauce with butter, flour, and a little mustard, as will sauce the tripe. Serve the onions in it. Vinegar or lemon-juice may be added.—See Nos. 16,56.

766. *Bread and meat, or Koobbé.*—We have been favoured with a receipt for this savoury preparation, which, at sea, in camp, on Indian hunting excursions, and long marches in India, is found to be very convenient. Make a dough with yeast as for bread; when yeast cannot be obtained, use whites of eggs or milk. Roll out the paste very thick, and wrap meat into it (fat meat is best) of any kind, cut and seasoned in any way that is most convenient or agreeable. This dish may be

either boiled or baked. This species of camp-cookery is carried to some perfection in India. It is applicable to all kinds of game, poultry, and meat. Fowls thus cooked, may be stuffed with hard eggs, chopped parsley, oysters, &c.; veal, with a forcemeat; goose, pig, and duck, either with apples or onions, as the sauce is wanted. The stuffed things must be well skewered, or sewed before they are put into the dough, which forms a crust about the meat; thus combining bread, meat, and sauce in one dish.

767. *Milcou, a South American preparation.*—This palatable and even elegant dish is a good deal like the Italian pastes. Potatoes, and a species of pumpkin, are roasted, the pulp taken out and kneaded with salt, and sometimes eggs. This paste is then rolled out, cut into little bits about the size of a dollar, and boiled for a quarter of an hour in milk sweetened.

768. *Le Bon Diable.*—This favourite *bonne bouche*, for which we have obtained the receipt from a lady who has contributed many valuable articles to this work, is thus prepared at Pondicherry:—Score the devil, (whether of duck, goose or turkey,) deeply in all directions; and, seasoning it highly with mixed spices, send it from the table to be broiled. Meanwhile take from each dish at table a spoonful of sauce or gravy, and, stirring this well in a silver sauce-pan over the fire, have it ready boiling-hot to pour over the grill, or *bon diable*, which is then handed round.—*Obs.* The parts usually devilled are the rump, the gizzard, and drumsticks. Soy, lemon-juice, and made mustard may be added to the sauce.—See *Devils* and *Salmis*, pages 319, 350.

769. *Indian Burdwan.*—This eastern preparation is of the English genus, *devil*, or French *Salmi*. It is made of cold poultry, rabbits, venison, kid, game, but is best of the latter. Make a sauce of melted butter with cayenne, or a fresh Chili if possible; a bit of garlic, essence of anchovy, and a sliced Spanish onion. Stew over a spirit-lamp till the onion is pulpy, when the Burdwan will be ready. Squeeze in a lime or Seville orange. Serve round very hot.*

* It would be very easy to swell this section of the MANUAL with a formidable array of uncouth dishes and strange names, with Indian, Syrian,

CHAPTER IV.

Beasts of chase, or fowl, or game,
In pastry built.
Milton.

Chimeras from the poet's fancy flow;
The cook contrives his shapes in real dough.
King.

PASTRY, PIES, PASTIES, PATTIES, PUDDINGS, &c.

770. Savoury pies, made of fresh materials, properly seasoned, and not overdone—their besetting fault—are very generally liked. They are economical, since a good pie may be made of a piece of meat that would neither stew, roast, nor boil, so as to make a handsome dish; and they are convenient at table, since they may be divided and subdivided to any length, with little trouble to the carver. Pies can be made of almost every thing, and they eat better cold than meat dressed in any other way. A *solid pie* is a larder in itself, and is as useful on the moors or at sea as in country situations, where families are liable to the incursions of voracious visitors. The state of the oven should be particularly attended to. Almost every oven has a temperament of its own; and it should never be forgotten, that from the intense degree of heat, and the circumstance of the meat being cut down into small pieces, the process of baking is much more rapid than either roasting or stewing, and in this approaches frying. *Puff-paste* requires a rather smart oven to make it rise light. *Raised paste* must have a quick oven; and paste *iced* must have a slack oven, that the icing, if put on at first, be not scorched before the fruit is sufficiently baked. A few general plain directions may be given; but practice and observation are essential to the proper preparation of pie-crust, and the management of an oven. All pies to be eaten cold must be more highly seasoned than hot ones. Fine crust should have a little sugar, not be *floured* much, and

---

Turkish, and Persian *Yaughs, kabaubs,* and *Cuscussuies,* &c. as modern travellers, and particularly the French, have paid considerable attention to Asiatic cookery; but this we consider mere waste of space, which may be more usefully employed.

should be made in a room of a medium temperature. Have a feather-brush to wipe off superfluous flour. Pastry-cutters of all kinds are bought in the shops.

771. *To make puff-paste.*—Have the best flour, sifted, fresh, and free of damp. Take half its weight, or rather more, of fresh or washed salt butter. Crumble a third part of the butter among the flour, mixing it well, and make it into dough with a proper quantity of water. Throw dry flour on the table to prevent it from sticking, and work it up quickly to a stiff paste by kneading it beneath your hands. Roll out the paste when it is smoothly kneaded, which will be known by pressing it between the finger and thumb. Divide what remains of the butter into four parts. Take the first, break it into bits, and stick it equally over the paste. Strew a little flour lightly on the butter, and clap it down to make it stick; fold up the crust, roll it out, and repeat the process till all the butter is used. The sooner puff-paste is baked after it is made, the lighter it looks, from the folds rising distinctly. Till it is to be used, lay the folds of a wet cloth over it. French cooks give this paste (*feuilletage*) five turns, or more, to make it rise lightly into many leaves. This paste, when for *vol-au-vents,* should get six turns and a half; that is, six turns, and be then doubled up. The more turns the more butter is required. The oven, if possible, should not be opened till puff-paste, or *paté-royale,* is baked; for draughts of cold air always flatten paste.

772. *Cheap raised crust for meat-pies.*—Boil an ounce of lard, and rather more of fresh dripping or butter, in about a pint of water, and make the paste of this. Knead it strongly, and beat it well with a rolling-pin. Let it stand to cool, and then raise the pie; or cut out pieces for the top and bottom, and a long piece for the sides; cement the bottom to the sides with egg, bringing the bottom piece beyond the sides, and pinching both together to make them join closely. Fill up the pie. Put on the top, and pinch it again close to the sides. Small raised pies may be made by lining a tin shape with a sliding bottom with paste on the bottom and sides, and putting on a top.

773. *Common paste for savoury pies.*—To two pounds of good flour take six ounces of butter; break it

down among the flour, and mix it with a couple of beat eggs and a pint of hot water. Knead it smooth, and roll out and double it three or four times. *Cold paste* is made as above, only use cold water.

774. *Rich paste of beef-suet, for common meat-pies.* —Cut the suet in bits, and melt it in water. Strain it into fresh water, and when cold, press out the water, and pound it in a mortar with a little oil, till it come to the consistence of butter. Use this for making pie-crust.—See also No. 44.

775. *Common tart-paste.*—Make as above, only use a little more butter, and a spoonful of sugar, if requisite.

776. *Short crust for preserved sweets.*—To a pound of the finest flour put a half-pound of fresh butter, the beat yolks of two eggs, and three ounces of fine sifted loaf-sugar. Mix this up with hot milk, knead it smooth, and ice the paste when ready. Cream may be used, and less butter.—*Obs.* The more finely the butter is crumbled down among the flour the *shorter* will the crust eat. Those who dislike sweet crust may either entirely omit or use only half the quantity of sugar. The above paste is only employed to line tin pans. This paste may be perfumed by making it of rose or orange-flower water,— almond-paste will enrich it. It may, where suitable, be flavoured with lemon-juice. In this department, like every other, much is left to the taste and discretion of the cook.

777. *Venison-pasty crust.*—Make a paste in the proportion of two pounds of flour to more than a pound of butter, with six beat eggs and hot water. Roll it out three times, double it, and the last time let the part intended for the top-crust remain pretty thick. This paste is adapted to line timballes.

778. *Rice paste for savoury pies.*—Clean and simmer the rice in milk and water till it swell. Cover veal, lamb, chicken, or game pies, equally with a layer of this, using beat egg to make it adhere.

779. *Fine crust for cheese-cakes, or delicate preserved fruits.*—Sift a pound of the best flour, well dried, and mix it well with two ounces of finely-sifted sugar. Beat half a pound of fresh butter to a cream by working it cold with a spoon or knife. Mix the flour and sugar

very gradually with this, and work into it the well-beat whites of three eggs. If the paste is not stiff enough to roll out, put more flour and sugar to it.—See *Paste-Royal, Brioche paste, and Household bread.*

SAVOURY PIES OF MEAT, &c.

780. *To make a beef-steak pie.*—Any tender and well-mixed piece of beef will answer for a pie, though the rump is best. Cut the meat into handsome small steaks; flatten and season them with mixed spices; place fat and lean pieces together, and either roll them up as olives, or place them flat neatly in the dish. Put in either a half-pint of gravy and a small glass of vinegar, or the same quantity of water and vinegar. Let there be enough of fat. A few small cooked onions may be added. —*Obs.* Cut pickles, a little catsup, or other seasonings, may be put to the pie, and either forcemeat-balls or a layer of forcemeat above and below the beef. Some prefer a few oysters. Lay a strip of crust all round the edge of the dish, and then cover it.

781. *Plain veal-pie.*—Cut chops from the back-ribs or breast. Trim off the bones, and season the chops highly with mixed spices and such minced herbs as you choose; add a little gravy drawn from the trimmings, and cover the pie.

782. *A richer veal-pie.*—Proceed as above, but add a few slices of lean bacon, forcemeat-balls and boiled yolks of eggs; or a scalded sweetbread cut into bits, and truffles, morels, or mushrooms, as is convenient or approved. When baked, pour some well-seasoned hot gravy into the pie by removing the top ornament. Then replace it.

783. *A very rich veal-pie.*—Cut steaks from the breast or fillet. Season them with white pepper, salt, mace and cloves pounded, lemon-grate, and a scrape of nutmeg. Cut down and season as above two sweetbreads or a veal-kidney. Lay an edging of paste round the ledge of the pie-dish, and fill it. Put hard-boiled yolks of eggs or the cut sweetbreads, and either some mushrooms or oysters over the meat. Strew in more mixed seasonings, and place a layer of thin slices of ham over the whole. Put in a half-pint of water or gravy, and cover the dish. When ready, remove the top

ornament, and pour in through a funnel a large glassful of good veal-gravy quite hot, and thickened with flour and cream; replace the top.

784. *Veal olive-pie.*—Cut long slices from the fillet, and flatten and season them, having first brushed them with the yolk of an egg. Roll them up neatly as olives, and place them in the dish, making the middle part highest, as is proper in all pies. Fill with water, and cover the dish; or fill with good gravy thickened with cream and flour. A little forcemeat spread on each olive will be an improvement.

785. *Rich veal olive-pie.*—Make a forcemeat of minced veal and a little suet or veal-kidney, a few bread-crumbs, some finely-chopped parsley, lemon-grate, salt, and mixed spices. Work up the forcemeat with the yolks of two eggs, and place a little of it in the middle of each slice of the meat cut for olives. Let the olives be previously flattened and seasoned. Roll them neatly up, and fill up the pie-dish. Make a dozen or more of forcemeat-balls, round and oval, of the remaining forcemeat, and lay them in the dish, with the yolks of four hard-boiled eggs divided, two small pickled cucumbers cut in round and oblong slices, and a few pickled mushrooms. Make a gravy of the bones and trimmings of veal, seasoning it with parsley and onion. Thicken and strain this gravy, and put to it a glass of white wine and the juice of a lemon. Pour this into the pie, and cover it with a good puff-paste.

786. *Calf's-head-pie to eat cold.*—Scald and soak the head, and simmer it for a half-hour in a very little water, with a large knuckle of veal, the rind of a lemon, two onions, a faggot of parsley, and winter savoury, a few white peppercorns, and two or three blades of mace. Take up the head, and when cold, cut it into bits of different forms as directed at No. 460. Peel and cut the tongue into square pieces. Boil the broth in which the head was simmered with a few chips of isinglass till it is reduced to a strong jelly-gravy. Put a layer of thin slices of lean ham in the bottom of the pie-dish; then some of the head and tongue, mixing fat and lean, and forcemeat-balls made of the knuckle; and add hard yolks of eggs cut in two. Strew above each separate layer a seasoning of white pepper, salt, nutmeg, and

lemon-grate. Fill up the dish with the jelly-gravy, and bake the pie.—*Obs.* This pie will keep cold for a fortnight, and slices of it make a very neat side-dish or supper-dish, from the variety of colours and forms.

787. *Calf's-foot-pie.*—Clean and boil two feet till tender, but not slobbery. Mince the meat when cold with suet and pared apples, in the proportion of a third part apples and suet. Mix rubbed currants, sugar to taste, and a quarter-pint of white or raisin wine with the mince. Cover the dish with rich puff-paste. A half-hour or little more will bake this nice pie.

788. *A bride's pie,—a Scotch pie.*—This is just a very nice mince-pie. Chop the meat of two calves' feet, boiled as in the former receipt, a pound of mutton-suet, and a pound of pared apples all separately, till they are fine. Mix them, and add to them a half-pound of picked and rubbed currants, and the same quantity of raisins stoned and chopped. Season with a quarter-ounce of cinnamon in powder, two drachms of grated nutmeg and pounded mace, an ounce of candied citron, and double the quantity of lemon-peel, both sliced thin, a glass of brandy, and another of Madeira. Line a tin-pan which has a slip-bottom with puff-paste, and put the minced meat, &c. into it. Roll out a cover for the pie, which usually has a glass or gold ring concealed somewhere in the crust, and should be embellished with appropriate ornaments and devices, as Cupids, turtles, torches, flames, darts, and other emblematic devices of this kind.

789. *A mutton-pie.*—Cut the back-ribs or loin into handsome chops; chop off the bone, flatten and season the chops with pepper and salt. Place them neatly in the dish; fill it up with gravy or water, and strew parsley and a minced onion over the meat.*.—*Obs.* Mutton or veal pie may be seasoned with curry-powder. Mutton or veal may be made into small raised pies of an oval or other shape, and re-warmed in a Dutch oven when wanted for hot suppers or luncheon. A *Squab-pie* is made of mutton chops, cut apples, and shred onions, with spices and a little sugar.

790. *Lamb-pie.*—This is made of either the loin,

---

* A corresponding member of the Cleikum Club recommends sauce Robert for mutton-pie, but made without lemon-juice.

back-ribs, or breast, *not too fat*, cutting out the bone if wished, but always leaving the gristles. Do not season this delicate meat over highly. Put a little jelly-gravy in the dish if the pie is to be eat cold, in which state a lamb-pie is exceedingly good. Hard eggs may be added.

791. *Pigeon-pie.*—Clean and season the pigeons well in the inside with pepper and salt. Put into each bird a little chopped parsley mixed with the livers parboiled and minced, and some bits of butter. Cover the bottom of the dish with a beef-steak, a few cutlets of veal, or slices of bacon, which is more suitable. Lay in the birds; put the seasoned gizzards, and, if approved, a few hard-boiled yolks of egg into the dish. A thin slice of lean ham laid on the breast of each bird is an improvement to the flavour. Cover the pie with puff-paste. A half hour will bake it.—*Obs.* It is common to stick two or three feet of pigeons or moorfowl into the centre of the cover of pies as a label to the contents, though we confess we see little use and no beauty in the practice. Forcemeat-balls may be added to enrich the pie. Some cooks lay the steaks above the birds, which is sensible, if not seemly.

792. *Moorfowl-pie.*—If the birds are small, keep them whole; if large, divide or quarter them. Season them highly, and put plenty of butter into the dish above and below them; or put a beef-steak into the bottom of the dish. Cover the dish with good puff-paste, and take care not to bake the pie too much. A hot sauce made of melted butter, the juice of a lemon, and a glass of claret, and poured into the pie when to be served hot, is an improvement, and does not overpower the native flavour of the game. *Woodcocks* and *snipes*, when very plentiful, are sometimes made into pies. Clean the intestines, which are so highly prized. Parboil and pound them with seasonings, scraped lard, chopped herbs, and truffles. Stuff the birds with this forcemeat.—*N.B.* Carefully take away the gall-bag.

793. *A hare-pie.*—Cut up the good parts of a hare; season and put them in a pie-dish with plenty of butter; or if to be very rich, forcemeat-balls and yolks of hard-boiled eggs. If to eat cold, which this pie does very well, fill the dish with a jelly-gravy when the top is taken off.

794. *Chicken-pie.*—Cut up, as for helping at table, as

many young fowls as the size of your pie requires. Season the joints with white pepper, salt, and a little mace and nutmeg, all in fine powder. Put the pieces into the pie-dish, with thin slices of fresh ham or veal chops, or veal udder. Forcemeat-balls, layers of forcemeat, and yolks of hard eggs, may be added at pleasure. Make a good gravy of knuckle or scrag of veal or shanks of mutton, seasoning it with white peppercorns, onions, and parsley. Strain this gravy, which must be boiled to a jelly, and put it to the pie. Cover with a rich puff-paste; and bake the pie, if large, for an hour and a quarter.—*Obs.* The chickens may be stuffed, if small, and laid on forcemeat. This pie, and all pies, may be made plainer at the discretion of the cook.

795. *Giblet-pie.*—Clean and stew the giblets in broth, with peppercorns, onions, and parsley. When tender, take them up, and when cold, cut them in a few neat pieces. Lay a beef-steak in the bottom of a small pie-dish, or a layer of forcemeat made of seasonings, minced veal or beef, and a little ham. Put in the cut giblets, and strew in shred onion. Strain the liquor over them in which they were stewed, and place a few boiled potatoes sliced above all. Cover with a common crust, or for a plain dish with mashed potatoes.—*Obs.* A giblet-pie is sometimes made with a pudding composed of the blood of the goose or ducks strained, a little boiled rice, suet and onion shred fine, with pepper and salt. Keep the skin of the neck of the goose, and stuff it with this. Close the pudding at both ends, turn it round, and place it in the centre of the pie.

796. *Rabbit-pie.*—This may be made as directed for chicken-pie; or more plainly as giblet-pie, making a forcemeat of the livers parboiled, chopped parsley, and anchovies, or eschalot, pepper, salt, and a little butter or shred suet. A few thin slices of well-flavoured bacon will grealy improve a rabbit-pie.—*Obs. Rabbit-pie* may be made with onion-sauce; but first parboil the onions to take off the excess of their flavour.

797. *Partridge-pie.*—Clean and truss four, or, if large, three partridges, cutting off the legs at the second joint. Season with pepper, salt, and chopped parsley.* Place

---

* French cooks chop the livers with parsley, and stuff with this. They

a veal and ham forcemeat, or slices of veal and ham, at the bottom of the dish, then put in the partridges, with a good many bits of butter stuck about them, and either a few scalded button-mushrooms or a glassful of mushroom-catsup. Cover the ledge of the dish with stripes of paste, and then put on the cover. About an hour will bake this pie.

798. *A goose-pie.*—This is generally made in a raised crust. For a common pie, quarter or cut the goose into eight pieces; season, and bake it with plenty of butter. Two *green geese* will make a still better pie. They may be baked with either a plain paste or a layer of mashed potatoes laid over the baking-dish and neatly marked. They may be previously braised.

799. *A Christmas goose-pie.**.—Bone and season highly a goose and a large fowl. Stuff the latter with forcemeat made of minced tongue or ham, veal, parsley, suet, pepper, and salt, with two eggs, or No. 516. Stew them for twenty minutes in a little good broth in a close stew-pan. Put the fowl within the goose, and place that in a raised pie-crust, filling up the vacancies with forcemeat or slices of parboiled tongue or pigeons, partridges, &c. Put plenty of butter over the meat. This pie will take three hours to bake. It will eat well cold, and keep a long while.

800. *Perigord-pie.*—This is a dish which can scarcely be ever prepared in this country, where truffles are scarce, and very inferior to those of France. The Perigord-pie is, however, so celebrated, that it would be unpardonable to treat it with neglect. Truss as for boiling six partridges. Singe and wipe them. Season them with salt, pepper, and mixed spices, minced parsley, and

---

also *barde* the birds with seasoned lard. Partridges done thus make an admirable cold pie in a raised crust.

* This receipt still keeps its place in cookery books, though the pie itself is now as rare as the capercailzie or the wild boar. Still in the north of England we hear of the *wains* groaning about Christmas-tide, under the load of these pies. At such times the hostess of a well-frequented inn, of the old school, will construct a pie of circumference rivalling her own; and the county newspaper will record its dimensions. But Yorkshire pie is a mere joke to those with which a German baron or Italian noble was wont to regale his vassals. A bullock the outwork, —containing a deer, which contained poultry or game, which contained ortolans and quails, which contained oysters and crawfish; and all boned and seasoned. How magnificent a *piece de resistance*! Such was the cookery of the feudal age.

young onions, and lard them. Brush, wash, and peel
two pounds of truffles. Hash the small and broken ones;
and pound them with the livers of the partridges and a
fat goose-liver, or fat livers of poultry, or a piece of veal-
udder parboiled. Mince all these things, and pound
them in a mortar, adding raw egg, as directed for
quenelles, pages 355, 356. Season this forcemeat very
highly. Cut open the trussed partridges at the back,
and stuff each of them with the forcemeat, and some
whole truffles. Bake them in a raised pie-crust, either
round or oval shaped, lining the crust with slices of bacon
and forcemeat.

801. *Venison-pasty*.—A modern pasty is made of what
does not roast well, as the neck, the breast, the shoulder.
The breast makes the best pasty. Cut it into little bits,
trimming off all bone and skins. Make some good gravy
from the bones and other trimmings. Place fat and
lean pieces of the meat together; or, if very lean, place
thin slices from the firm fat of a leg or a neck of mutton
along with each piece. Season the meat with pepper,
salt, pounded mace, and allspice. Place it handsomely
in a dish, and put in the drawn gravy, a quarter-pint of
claret or port, a glassful of eschalot vinegar, and, if liked,
a couple of onions very finely shred. Cover the dish
with a thick crust, No. 777.—See pages 129, 304-5.
—*Obs*. This is a dish in which ornament is not only
allowable but is actually expected. The paste decorations
are, however, matters of fancy. Before the pasty is
served, if the meat be lean, more sauce made of a little
red wine, gravy, mixed spices, and the juice of a lemon,
may be put in hot. A common fault of venison-pasty
is being overdone. An hour and a half in a moderate
oven is fully sufficient for baking an ordinary-sized pasty;
an hour will do for a small one. Some cooks marinade
the meat in the wine and other seasonings for a night, or
for some hours previous to baking. This, no doubt,
imbues the venison with the flavour of the seasonings,
but at the same time drains off the juices, and hurts
the natural flavour of the meat, so that we would rather
discountenance the practice. A *mock venison-pasty* is
made of a breast of mutton soaked in claret, vinegar and
spices, for a night before dressing.

802. *Rook-pie*.—Skin the young birds; cut out the
back-bones; season them with pepper and salt. Lay a

beef-steak in the bottom of the dish, and pour a good deal of thickened melted butter over the birds. Cover with a common crust. A hour and a quarter will bake them.

N.B.—For *Savoury fish pies*, see pages 191, 193.

FRUIT-PIES, &c.

FRUIT-PIES require a light and rich crust. Fruits that have been preserved are generally baked in an open crust, and are ornamented with paste-bars, basket-work, stars, &c. Preserved fruit need not be put in till the crust is baked, as the oven often injures the colour of preserved things.

803. *Apple-pie.*—Wipe, pare, core, and slice the apples. Lay a strip of puff-paste round the edge of the dish. Put in a layer of the sliced fruit, then sugar and whatever seasonings you use. A mixture of quince greatly improves the flavour. Proceed in this manner till the dish is heaped, keeping the fruit highest in the middle. Cover it with puff-paste, and ornament the top with leaves, flowers, &c.—*Obs.* A variety of apples are used for baking, though russetings, Ribstone pippins, golden pippins, and such as are a little acid, are esteemed the best. Apple-pie is generally seasoned with pounded cinnamon and cloves, lemon-grate, quince marmalade, candied citron or orange-peel. If the apples have become dry and insipid, the parings and cores may be boiled with a stick of cinnamon, and the strained liquor added to the pie. Apple-pie is liked best hot. It is eat with plain cream or made-cream. It was wont to be *buttered*, and this is still the practice in some provincial situations in England, though *buttered* pease and buttered apple-pie, for some reason which we do not comprehend, have latterly come to be considered ungenteel, if not absolutely vulgar. *Buttering* is performed by putting a piece of butter into the hot pie when it is cut open. Apples must be thrown into plenty of water as they are pared, or they will become black.

804. *Ripe fruit pies.*—*Black cherries* and *currants, damsons, plums* of all kinds, *currants,* or *raspberries* and *currants mixed, apricots* and *gooseberries,* are all made into fruit pies. Place the fruit, picked and washed in a flattish pie-dish, raising it high in the middle. Allow enough of sugar, and cover with a rich light paste, which fruit pies require more than those made of meat.

805. *Gooseberry-pie.*—Top and tail as many unripe gooseberries as will fully fill your dish. Line the dish, or merely border it with paste. Put in the fruit, and plenty of moist sugar, and cover the pie with good puff-paste. The gooseberries may be first stewed in the sugar.—*Obs.* As all fruit goes on to ripen, it requires more sugar till fully ripe.

806. *Rhubarb-pie.*—Peel off the skin from stalks of young rhubarb, and cut them slantwise into bits of about an inch and a half. Stew them slowly in sugar, or in butter, and a little water, till soft: mash, sweeten, and make them into a covered pie or open tart.—*Obs.* Gooseberry, apple, rhubarb, and other fruit pies, eat very well cold; or the fruit may be stewed and sweetened for common use, without further preparation. Fresh good cream is a very great improvement to all fruit pies and tarts. The next best thing is plain custard. In England the cream is often sweetened, thickened with beat yolks of eggs, and poured over the fruit. In Scotland cream for tarts is usually served either plain or merely whisked; or served over the stewed fruit whipt.

807. *Fruit tarts of preserved fruits.*—These are made of all sorts of marmalades, jams, and preserved small fruits. If apples, pare, core, and quarter them. Stew and mash them, and sweeten them with fine beat sugar. Season with the squeeze of a lemon, a little beat cinnamon, an ounce of candied orange-peel, and a little white wine or cider. Cover a flat dish with tart-paste, and place a broad rim of puff-paste round the edges. Bake the paste, and put in the jam, either when it is ready, or a few minutes before. Paste stars, flowers, &c. may be cut out, and baked on tins to ornament the top; or if the fruit is put in at first, it may be covered with paste trellis-work.—*Obs.* Tarts of preserved fruit, when much ornament is wanted, are served under a paste *croquante*, or an ornament of sugar boiled to caramel; but as this is rather the business of the professed confectioner than of the practical cook, and cannot be taught without actual experiment, we pass it over.

808. *Small tarts and puffs of fruit.*—Line very small patty-pans, either oval or round, with puff-paste, and pare the paste neatly. Put in a little of any kind of jam or marmalade, and either cross-bar the tarts with paste-straws,

or wreathe paste-straws round them.—*Obs.* This, or making little patties or pastry ramekins, is a very good way of using any bit of paste that is left over from a large pie or tart.

809. *Small Puffs.*—Roll out puff-paste of nearly a half-inch thick. Cut it into pieces about five inches wide, to have, when doubled, the form of squares, triangles, crescents, &c. Place a little jam of any kind on each, and double them up. Wet and pinch them close at the edges with a fluted paste-runner, and bake them on tins, with paper below.

810. *Cranberry-tart.*—This may be made either of fresh or preserved cranberries. Season with beat cloves and cinnamon. Put in a sufficient quantity of sugar. Cover with a puff-paste, and serve with cream, which to this dry fruit is indispensable.

811. *Prune-tart.*—Wash and scald the prunes; take out the stones, and either bruise them, and take some of the kernels to add to the tarts, or not, as you choose. Put sugar to taste to the fruit, and bake it as a tart or pie.

812. *To ice tarts.*—Beat the white of an egg very well, and with this brush the paste with a feather, either at first, or when *half baked*, which prevents the icing from becoming scorched in the oven. When brushed well over with egg, sift fine sugar, beat to an impalpable powder, over it. A heavier kind of varnish for some things is made of beat yolks of eggs and melted butter, —See, *for other Icings, Cakes.*

813. *Common glazings for paste.*—Sugar and water. Yolk or white of egg beat up with water, white of egg and sugar sifted over. Yolk of egg and melted butter.

814. *Mince-Pies.*★—These are made in an endless variety of ways. Indeed every family receipt-book teems with prescriptions. We select what is, after experiment and mature consideration, considered the best formula. Par-roast, or bake slightly, a couple of pounds of the fine lean of good beef or tongue. Mince this, or scrape it. Mince also two pounds of fresh suet, two of apples,

---

★We recommend to every young housekeeper to adopt in this favourite preparation the receipt of her own grandmother. This ought to produce the best Christmas-pies.—P.T.

pared and cored, three pounds of currants, rubbed, picked, and dried, and a pound and a half of good raisins stoned. Let the things be separately minced till fine, but not so fine as to run together; then mix them with a pound of beat sugar, and add a tea-spoonful of salt, a half-ounce of ground ginger, the same weight of allspice and bruised coriander-seeds, some beat cloves, two nutmegs grated, the juice and grated rind of two lemons and of two Seville oranges, half a pound of candied lemon and orange-peel, and a quarter-pound of candied citron sliced. Mix the seasonings equally with the meat. Keep the minced-meat closely pressed in cans, in a cool, dry place. Put a half-pint of brandy, or pine-apple rum, into a basin, with double that quantity of Madeira or sherry, and a half-pint of orange-flower water. When to be used, cover pans of any size, small saucers, or a small pie-dish, with puff or plain paste, and moisten the meat, if hard, with a little of the wine and brandy, and fill the pies. Put a cover of puff-paste over them, or if a plain paste, ice it. Pare the edges neatly, and mark the top with a paste-knife. Half an hour of a moderate oven will bake them. Slip them out of the tins, and serve them hot.—*Obs.* Mince-pies may be made cheaper, and yet very good, by substituting gravy for wine; or by using home-made wine, (ginger-wine is best,) by lessening the quantity of expensive fruits and spiceries, and taking any bit of lean dressed beef the larder affords, or a piece of the double tripe boiled, minced fine.

815. *Superlative mince-pies.*—Rub with salt and mixed spices, a fat bullock's tongue. Let it lie for three days, and parboil, skin, and mince or scrape it. Mince separately three pounds of Zante currants, picked, plumped, and dried, a dozen of lemon pippin apples pared and cored, and a pound of blanched almonds, with a few bitter ones. Mix the mince, and add a half pound of candied citron and orange-peel minced, and an ounce of beat cinnamon and cloves, with the juice and grated rind of three or four lemons, half an ounce of salt, and the same quantity of allspice, a quarter-pound of fine sugar pounded, and a pint and a half of Madeira, the same quantity of brandy and orange-flower water. Line the pans with a rich puff-paste, and serve the pies hot with

burnt brandy.—*Obs.* The brandy should be burnt at table as it is used. Though the mince-meat will keep good for some time, it is best not to be too old. The fruit, suet, and wine may be added when the pies are to be made, as the suet and raw apples are apt to spoil, and the dried fruits, though in less danger, do not improve by keeping in this state. Mince-pies warm up very well in a Dutch oven, or in a slow oven, or before the fire.

816. *Common apple, gooseberry, or rhubarb pasties or turn-overs.*—Make a hot crust with dripping or lard melted in boiling water; roll it out quickly, and cut it so as to be of a semicircular form when turned over. Lay stewed apples, rhubarb, or scalded gooseberries, in the crust, with moist sugar to sweeten; add, if apples, quince, lemon-peel, or cinnamon. Cut the edges, double up and pinch the crust, and bake the pasties in a moderate oven. If there be icing at hand they may be iced..—*Obs.* This is a cheap preparation, and a greater favourite with young persons than those that are more delicate and expensive.

PUFFS.

THESE are called apple-puffs, lemon-puffs, cheese-puffs, egg-puffs, &c. from the principal ingredient in their composition.

817. *Apple-puffs.*—Stew, or roast apples till they will peel and pulp dry. Mix them with good beat sugar and finely-chopped lemon-peel. Bake them in thin sweet paste, in a quick oven. They are best when made rather small.

818. *Lemon or orange-puffs.*—Grate down three quarters of a pound of refined sugar, and mix it well with the grate of three lemons, or two Seville oranges. Beat the whites of four eggs to a *solid-looking* froth, and putting this to the sugar, beat the whole together without intermission for half an hour. Make this batter into any variety of shapes, and bake it on oiled paper laid on tin plates, in a moderate oven. When cold, take off the paper. There are fifty other little things made of pastry and bits of sweetmeats, which cannot be enumerated here, as *sweet sandwiches, gimbelettes, &c.*

SAVOURY PATTIES

PATTIES are an elegant, though secondary class of culinary preparations, and are as much admired by the economist as the gourmand. Where dinners have been given, or are in course of preparation, it is easy to make a dish of savoury patties, with small trouble and almost no expense. Patties are made of a variety of things, as cold veal, fowl, rabbit, hare, lobsters, oysters, &c. They admit of all manner of seasonings, and must be nicely minced and served.

819. *To make crust for savoury patties.*—Roll out a thin puff-paste, and line the patty-pans. Cut out the tops on paper, with a tin stamp in form of a star or any handsome shape. Mark the tops very neatly, and lay a piece of paper crumpled up into the lined patty-pan, to support the top when baking, and then put on the top. Bake the patties, and ice them. When to be served, take off the tops and pick out the paper, fill up with a hot mince, and put on the tops neatly, taking care not to fill the patties so full as to run over.—*Obs.* This plan of baking the crust separately will, on trial, be found much superior to filling them at the first. The icing may be omitted.

820. *Chicken and ham patties.*—Skin and mince very finely, the breast or white fleshy parts of a cold chicken, and about half the quantity of lean ham, or of tongue highly flavoured. Have, in a nice small sauce-pan, a little good veal-gravy drawn from bones or trimmings, or the jelly of roast veal or lamb, thickened with a bit of butter rolled in flour; add a little grated lemon-peel, white pepper, salt, a very little cayenne, and a tea-spoonful of lemon-juice. Stir the mince in this till quite hot, and fill up the patties, which are best baked empty, as the minced meat hardens in the baking.

821. *Egg and ham patties.*—In these *bread* is used for paste, or they are served *en crustades*. Scoop out the thick part from slices of a stale loaf; shape the *crustades*, and fry of a gold-colour; drain and fill with ham, prepared as directed for chicken and ham patties; lay a nicely poached egg on each.—*Obs.* This is a nice ready supper-dish.

822. *Rabbit and hare patties.*—Mince the best parts

of a cold roast rabbit or hare, very fine, with a little finely shred mutton-suet. Draw a gravy from the bones, or take any other good gravy; thicken it with butter and flour, and season with salt, cayenne, pepper, nutmeg, mace, the grate of half a lemon, and a very little red wine, or any suitable flavoured vinegar. Stew the mince, and fill the patties as above directed.—*Obs.* If there be any stuffing of the hare left, it will make, when minced, a good addition to the patties, as will all the native gravy left about veal, hare, &c. Patties may be made by frying, either for a dish or a garnish.

823. *Oyster-patties.*—Prepare the paste for these patties as in No. 819, and wash in their own liquor, and beard as many small oysters as will make a dozen of patties. Strain the liquor, and put to it an ounce of butter rolled in flour. Cut the oysters, if large, into small bits, and stew them in this with a little salt, mace, and white pepper, the grate of half a lemon, and, if liked, a little cayenne. A spoonful of thick cream may be added. Put this hot into the patties when ready to serve. Some good cooks put a little hashed parsley to the oysters, with salt and pepper, and no other seasoning.

824. *Lobster-patties.*—Chop the meat of the tail and claws of a boiled hen-lobster. Pound a little of the spawn in a mortar, with a half-ounce of butter crumbled, a little veal jelly gravy, or butter, and a spoonful of cream; add a seasoning of cayenne, mace, salt, a little essence of anchovy, and a tea-spoonful of lemon-grate. Stew the lobster meat in this for a few minutes, adding a spoonful or two of water if over thick, and a very little flour to give consistence to the gravy. Fill the patties with the hot stew when they are ready to serve.

825. *Oyster and mushroom patties.*—Take two parts of stewed oysters, and one of fresh mushrooms, cut them separately into small dice. Fry the mushrooms in butter and flour. Moisten this with gravy, the oyster-liquor, and a little cream. Season with salt, nutmeg, pepper, and cayenne. Stir in the oysters, and fill the patties.

826. *Turkey-patties.*—Mince the white part, and a little grated ham. Stew this in a little good gravy, or

melted butter. Put a spoonful of cream to the mince, and season with white pepper, salt, and mace.

827. *Veal and ham patties.*—Make and season them as chicken and ham patties.—No. 820.

828. *Beef-patties or podovies.*—Shred a tender under-done piece of lean roast beef with a little of the firm fat. Season with pepper, salt, onion, an anchovy boned and chopped, and a very little eschalot or Chili vinegar. The podovies may be made either by putting the mince into hot paste like apple-pasty, and frying them, or be baked in patty-pans in a good plain crust made of dripping or lard.—See *Godiveau*, No. 692.

829. *To prepare meat for small pies for suppers and hot luncheons; or for patties.*—Take in the proportion of a pound of fillet of veal, a pound of beef, and a half-pound of suet. Mince the meat roughly, and the suet less than the meat. Season with salt, pepper, and allspice. The meat thus prepared will keep some days if pressed into a pot. When to be baked in saucers, or as little raised pies or patties, add a little hashed parsley. Or bake the pies, and heat them when wanted.

830. *Sweet patties.*—Mince the boiled meat of a calf's-foot, three apples, and a little candied orange and lemon-peel; add fresh lemon-grate, and the juice of a lemon, a little fine sugar, a small glass of sweet wine, a little nutmeg, the chopped yolk of two hard-boiled eggs, and, if wished, a little shred mutton-suet or marrow. Bake the patties in puff-paste. *Patties* may be made like mince-pies, and seasoned in an endless variety of ways. They may be made as *turn-overs*, and fried in plenty of lard or dripping. They are also a simple and favourite family-dish when baked as *turn-overs* on tins.

PUDDINGS.

ANY tolerable cook, however young in the art, may compound a good pudding by attending to the following simple rules and plain directions. Attention is all that is required, and a little manual dexterity in turning the pudding out of the dish or cloth in which it has been dressed. Let the several ingredients be each fresh and *good* of its kind, as one bad article, particularly eggs, will taint and destroy the whole composition. Have the pudding-cloths washed, boiled in wood-ashes, and always laid by quite dry after using. Puddings ought to be boiled in an open pot, in plenty of water, which must be kept on a quick boil; or baked in a quick but not scorching oven. A pudding, in which there is bread, must be tied up loosely, to allow room for swelling. A batter-pudding ought to be tied up firmly. Eggs for puddings must be used in greater quantity when of small size. The yolks and whites, if the pudding is wanted particularly light and nice, should be strained after being separately well beat. The several ingredients, after being well stirred together, should have a little time to stand, that the flavours may blend. The common fault of boiled puddings, which are often solid bodies, is being underdone. Baked puddings are as often scorched. Puddings may be steamed with advantage, placing the mould or basin in the steamer. When the pudding-cloths are to be used, dip them in water, and dredge them with flour. When a pudding begins to set in the oven, stir it up to prevent the fruit, &c. from settling down to the bottom; and if boiled, turn over the cloth in the pot for the same reason, and also to prevent it from sticking to the bottom. As the water wastes, fill up the pot with boiling water. When the pudding is taken out of the pot, dip it quickly into cold water, and set it in a basin of its size. It will then more readily separate from the cloth without breaking. Some cooks, in seasons of scarcity, recommend *snow* in place of eggs. We do not pretend to understand the philosophy of this prescription;—to be sure snow, as it falls, does look something like beat white of eggs, and from the quantity of air contained in it, may help the pudding to rise. This is all that it can do. *Small beer*, when fresh and yeasty, is a better substitute; but the pudding or dumpling should be allowed to rise for some time after the beer is put in, before it is cooked. Care must be taken to mix batter-puddings very smoothly. Let the flour be gradually mixed with a very little of the milk, as in making mustard or starch, and aftrwards strain the batter through a coarse sieve. Raisins, prunes, and damsons, for puddings, must be carefully stoned; or sultanas may be used in place of raisins. Currants must be picked, and plumped in hot water, or, which is better, rubbed in a cloth and plumped before the fire; almonds must be blanched and sliced; and in mixing grated bread, pounded biscuit, &c. with milk, pour the milk on hot, and cover the vessel, which is both better and easier than boiling. Mutton-suet for puddings is lighter than that of beef; but marrow, when it can be obtained, is better than either. A baked pudding for company has often a paste-border or a garnishing of blanched and sliced almonds about it; if boiled, it may also be garnished in various ways. The best seasoning for batter puddings is conserve of Seville orange, lemon-rind, and orange-flower-water. Spirits, and even wine, are every day less used, both from taste and economy. *Pudding-sauces*, see p. 246. The degree of sweetness and the flavour of all puddings must be determined by taste.

831. *A common plum-pudding.*—Take six ounces of shred suet, four of dry flour, two of stoned raisins, three of picked and plumped currants, a little allspice and nutmeg, or cinnamon. Thin this with beat egg and a little milk, and put in either a glass of sweet wine or a half-glass of rum or brandy, and sugar to taste. There are a thousand other ways of making a plum-pudding.—*Obs.* The wine or spirits may be spared, and the pudding flavoured with distilled waters, as rose-water, peach-water, orange-flower-water, &c.

832. *A superfine plum-pudding.*—Take four ounces of pounded pudding-biscuit, and two ounces of the best flour, or of good common biscuit, a half-pound of bloom or muscatel raisins stoned, the same quantity of fresh Zante currants picked and plumped, and a half-pound of suet stripped of skins and filaments, and shred; a small tea-spoonful of nutmeg grated, a quarter pound of fine beat sugar, a drachm of pounded cinnamon, and two blades of mace; three ounces of candied lemon, orange and citron peel, sliced, and two ounces of blanched almonds roughly chopped. Beat four eggs well, and put to them a little sweet milk, a glass of white wine or brandy, and then mix in the flour and all the ingredients. Tie up the pudding firm, and boil it for four hours, keeping up the boil, and turning the cloth. Serve pudding sauce. —No. 305.—*Obs.* Plum-pudding will keep cold, and re-warm when wanted, in slices, in the Dutch oven or

frying-pan. A plum-pudding with meat, may be made either according to the receipt for *minced-pies*, or *a bride's-pie*, adding eggs and milk enough to thin it.

833. *Marrow-pudding.*—Grate as much bread as will fill a large breakfast-cup quite full. Put it into a jug, and pour nearly a quart of boiling sweet milk or thin cream over it, and let it swell and soak, while you shred a half-pound of marrow or suet, and beat up four large or six small eggs. Have two ounces of raisins stoned, and two ounces of currants picked and plumped. Sweeten the pudding to taste, and season it with a very little grated nutmeg, and a tea-spoonful of cinnamon in powder. Cover a stoneware flat dish on the edge with strips of puff-paste, and mark it neatly in leaves. Bake the pudding in this dish, or plainly in a deep dish.—*Obs.* A few cut almonds, or a little candied citron or orange-peel may be put to this pudding for variety. A little finely-sifted sugar may be strewed on the top, which makes a good veil to puddings when unluckily scorched in the oven; or a few blanched almonds sliced may be stuck round it for ornament. In a flat dish twenty-five minutes will bake it. It will require a half-hour in a deep dish; or *it may be boiled* in a pudding-shape. This pudding will keep and cut in firm slices, which may be broiled or heated in a Dutch oven. A *suet-pudding*, a *baked plum-pudding*, and a *fat-pudding*, are made exactly as the above, only the quantity of fruit may be varied at pleasure, or cheaper fruit substituted.

834. *A hunter's pudding.*—This is nearly a plum-pudding. Stone a pound of raisins, and chop them, shred a pound of suet, clean a pound of currants, grate the rind of a lemon over this, and mix up six beat eggs with a pound of flour, a quarter-pound of sugar, and what milk will make a stiff batter. Season with a salt-spoonful of Jamaica pepper, and the same quantity of nutmeg; and add candied citron and orange-peel, if you like. Boil for six or seven hours in a cloth or mould, and serve with pudding sauce.—*Obs.* This pudding will keep a long while, and in this its utility consists; it may either be broiled in slices, or warmed up in a fresh cloth. It will take a long time to get hot quite through if warmed whole.

835. *Bread-pudding.*—Pour a large pint of boiling

milk over what will fill a breakfast-cup of bread-crumbs. Let them soak covered till cold, and mash smooth with a spoon. Sweeten this to taste. Add to it four or five eggs well beat, and season with cinnamon or nutmeg. Stir in two ounces of currants picked and plumped, or a few cut raisins; or the pudding may be made very rich by the addition of blanched and chopped almonds, candied citron, and orange-peel, with raisins and currants. Boil it in a basin, or bake it in a dish. Pounded sweet or plain biscuit may be used instead of bread-crumbs. *A brown bread-pudding* is made as above, but more plainly, and also a *save-all* or *crust-pudding*. Small bread-puddings may be baked in little buttered cups.

836. *Rice-pudding.*—Wash well in several waters, and pick a half-pound of the best rice. Boil it slowly in a little water for a few minutes, pour off, and put a pint and a half of milk to it, with a roll of lemon-peel. Stir it constantly, to prevent it from sticking. When quite soft, pour it into a dish, and mix two ounces of fresh-butter, or of nicely-shred suet with it; and when cold, three or four beat eggs, sugar to taste, and a seasoning of cinnamon or nutmeg. Cover the edges of a flat pie-dish with paste cut into leaves, and bake the pudding in it. A few currants may be put to it. This pudding may be thinned with milk and boiled in a cloth; or it may, allowing a double quantity of suet, be filled into skins and so boiled. Chopped apples, stoned prunes, &c. may be put to this pudding; and it may be made of ground instead of whole rice.* When candied peel is used, this takes the name of a Patna-pudding.

837. *Delicate small rice-puddings.*—Prepare four ounces of rice as above directed, and put to it three ounces of fresh butter, and a half-pint of cream. When cold, mix in sugar to taste, and six well-beat yolks of eggs, with three whites, grated lemon-peel, and a little cinnamon. Butter small cups, and putting into each a few slices of candied citron, fill very nearly full, and

---

* We have seen wheat, struck in the same manner as pot or pearl barley, substituted for rice, in making puddings. It is much cheaper, can be had fresh at all times, and is by many persons thought better than rice. Rice, chopped suet, molasses, skim-milk, and ginger, will make a good cheap pudding.—P. T.—*See Cheap Dishes.*

bake them. Dish and serve them hot with sweet sauce in a boat.

838. *Castle-puddings*.—Take the weight of two eggs in flour, butter, and sugar. Set the butter in a basin before the fire till half melted; beat it to a cream; beat the two eggs for ten minutes, and then mix them gently with the butter, then the sugar, then the flour; add nutmeg and grated lemon-peel; bake in cups for twenty minutes in a slow oven.

839. *Sago-pudding*.—Wash in several waters, and boil four spoonfuls of sago in a quart of new milk. Sweeten to taste, and season with cinnamon, lemon-peel grated, and a scrape of nutmeg. Add, when cold, four eggs well beat, and bake in a dish with a cut paste-border.—*Obs.* The sago may be first boiled in water, and then have wine and lemon-peel put to it, with some beat butter, and no milk.

840. *A millet-pudding*.—Wash four ounces of the seeds, and put to them a pint and a half of hot new milk, and two ounces of butter, sugar to taste, a little ginger and nutmeg, and whatever other seasonings are fancied. When the milk is cold, add three eggs beat. Some finely-shred mutton-suet will be no bad improvement, and a little brandy or pine-apple rum.

841. *Rich macaroni-pudding*.—Simmer the macaroni in milk and water till tender, add new milk to thin it; and when cold, add three beat yolks of eggs. Season with nutmeg, cinnamon, and a little almond-flower-water or noyeau, and sweeten with fine sugar. A little ginger-wine or raisin-wine is an improvement. A layer of orange-marmalade, or apricot-jam, in the centre of the pudding, is an excellent addition; or plums or prunes stoned and plumped, with shred marrow finely beat, mutton-suet and sugar, may be placed in a thick layer over the macaroni. Stick blanched almonds, sliced long-ways, round the edges. It may be steamed or baked.

842. *Parisian macaroni-pudding*.—Wash six ounces of macaroni, and simmer it in water till it is tender, but not soft. Strain it off; beat up five yolks, and two whites of eggs. Stir into them a very little salt and pepper, and a half-pint of good sweet cream. Mince, but not too finely, the skinned breast of a cold fowl, or rather less of dressed lean ham. Grate about an ounce

and a half of Parmesan cheese over the mince, and mix the whole ingredients well together with the macaroni. Butter and fill a melon-shaped or other pudding-dish, and expose it to the steams of boiling water till thoroughly done. Turn the pudding carefully out, and serve it hot, with a strong clear gravy flavoured with onions, parsley, and, if the flavour of the French cookery is admired, a little tarragon.—*Obs*. This, by gourmands of experience, is considered as out of sight the best modern preparation of macaroni, sweetened dishes of this paste being considered by them as only fit for boys and women. More cheese may be employed.—See No. 557.

843. *Vermicelli-pudding*.—Boil three ounces of soaked vermicelli till soft, in a pint and a half of new milk, with fine sugar to taste, a stick of cinnamon, and a bit of lemon-peel. Stir in, when cold, the beat yolks of four eggs with two of the whites, and bake the pudding in a dish with a paste-border.

844. *Custard-pudding*.—Bet up the yolks and whites of from four to six eggs separately. Mix the yolks with a pint and a half of rich new milk into which two or three spoonfuls of flour have been rubbed. Sweeten the mixture to taste, and add cinnamon and lemon-grate. When just ready to dress, stir in the beat whites of the eggs, and a little orange-flower-water. Boil the pudding for a half-hour in a buttered basin, with a floured cloth tied tightly over it; or bake it for twenty minutes. Grate sugar over the top, or put bits of red currant-jelly neatly round it.

845. *Batter-pudding*.—Mix three or four ounces of flour with a little milk, and add a pint more of milk to it. Put a piece of butter the size of a small egg to this, and put it on the fire, stirring constantly till it thickens. When cold, add the beat yolks of four eggs, and a little ginger and grated lemon-peel. Boil in a buttered basin, and serve hot with a sweet sauce, or along with meat.—*Obs*. A little orange-marmalade or conserve is a great improvement to this and to all batter-puddings; but not if served with meat. Instead of wheaten-flour, potato-flour, ground rice, or arrow-root may be used.

846. *Almond or ratafia pudding*.—Blanch, cut down, and beat in a mortar to a paste, a half-pound of sweet and a half-ounce of bitter almonds, with a spoonful of

orange-flower-water or pure water. Add to this paste
three ounces of fresh butter melted in a glass of hot
cream, four beat eggs, sugar to taste, a scrape of nutmeg, and a little brandy or curaçoa. Bake this in small
cups buttered, or in a dish, and serve with a hot sauce
of wine, sugar and butter.

847. *Other almond-puddings*.—Beat half a pound of
sweet and a few bitter almonds with a spoonful of rose-
water. Then mix four ounces of butter with two spoonfuls of cream warmed in it; four eggs, a spoonful of
brandy, and sugar and nutmeg to taste. Butter some
cups, half fill them, and bake the puddings. Serve with
butter, wine, and sugar.

848. *A baked almond-pudding*.—Beat, as above, six
ounces of sweet and a dozen bitter almonds, and mix the
paste with the beat yolks of six eggs, four ounces of
butter, the grate and juice of a large lemon, a pint and
a half of cream, and a glass of white wine. Add sugar
to taste, and bake in a dish, with a neatly-cut paste-
border. Ornament the top with sliced almonds or citron.

849. *Orange-pudding*.—To the grated rind of a large
Seville orange put four ounces of fresh butter and six
of pounded fine sugar. Beat this in a mortar, and
gradually add eight well-beat eggs. Scrape a raw apple
into the mixtures, and put it into a dish lined with paste
and neatly scolloped on the edge. Cross-bar it with
paste-straws, and bake till the paste is done. It may
have three sponge biscuits, soaked in milk, put to it.—
Obs. Less of the above mixture will do for an ordinary-
sized pudding, as this high-flavoured composition goes
far. Candied orange-peel beat to a paste makes a very
fine pudding when used as above.

850. *Lemon-pudding*.—Melt half a pound of sugar
and six ounces of fresh butter together, and when cold,
add six eggs very well beat, (leaving out three of the
whites,) the juice of one lemon, and the grated yellow
rind of two. Mix them all well, and bake in a puff-
paste neatly marked on the edges.

851. *An apple-pudding*.—Pare and grate three quarters
of a pound of juicy applies. Put to them six ounces of
butter beat cold to a cream, four beat eggs, two pudding-
biscuits pounded, the rind of a lemon grated, sugar
to taste, a spoonful of brandy, and another of orange-

flower-water. Bake in a puff-paste marked in leaves round the border, and, when done, strew candied lemon or orange peel sliced over the top.—*Obs.* Any good sweet biscuit may be used, or grated bread. A little lemon-juice or cider may be added if the applies are too mellow.

852. *A Swiss apple-pudding.*—Place an alternate layer of sliced apples and sugar, with a very thin layer of rusks pounded and soaked in milk. Finish with the pounded rusks, and pour melted butter over the pudding. Grate sugar over it when baked.

852. *An excellent apple-pudding.*—Pare, core, and stew the apples in a small stew-pan, with a stick of cinnamon, two or three cloves, and the grated rind of a lemon. When soft, sweeten them to taste. Pulp them through a sieve, and add the beat yolks of four eggs, a quarter-pound of butter, the grated peel and the juice of a lemon. Mix the ingredients well, and bake for a half-hour in a dish lined with good puff-paste.

854. *Nottingham pudding.*—Pare and core six large apples. Fill the hearts with moist sugar and a little cinnamon. Place them in a pie-dish, and pour a light batter-pudding, suitably seasoned, over them, and bake till the apples are ready,—about three quarters of an hour.

855. *Apricot, peach, or nectarine-pudding.*—Pour a pint of hot cream over what would fill a cup of bread-crumbs, and cover the jug. When cold, add the beat yolks of four eggs, a glass of white wine, and beat sugar to taste. Scald till soft a dozen large apricots. Cut them, take out the kernels, and pound the whole in a mortar. Mix them with the other ingredients, and the beat whites of two of the eggs, and bake in a dish with a paste-border.

856. *Gooseberry-pudding.*—Stew green gooseberries till they will pulp through a sieve. When cold, pulp them, and add to them six ounces of butter, four ounces of sugar-biscuit, pounded sugar to taste, four beat eggs, and a glass of brandy. Bake in a dish with a paste-border.—*Obs.* Excellent patties, and small pasties or turn-overs, may be made of this material.

857. *Newmarket or bread-and-butter-pudding.*—Boil a pint and a quarter of good milk for a few minutes,

with the rind of half a lemon, a stick of cinnamon, and a bay-leaf, or a spoonful of almond-flower-water. Put in fine sugar to taste, and as the milk cools mix it gradually with the well-beat yolks of six eggs, and three of the whites separately beaten. Cut and butter with fresh buttered slices of bread of about a half-inch thick. Place these in a pudding-dish, and then a layer of cleaned currants with a few raisins stoned and chopped, then again bread, and then fruit; but have the top layer of buttered bread. Pour the custard through a five sieve over this; let it soak for an hour or two, and bake it for a half-hour.

858. *Chancellor's or cabinet-pudding, a very delicate pudding.*—Boil a pint of cream with a bit of lemon-peel, and some fine sugar, and pour it hot over a half-pound of newly-baked Savoy biscuit. Cover the dish. When the cream is soaked up, add the yolks and whites of eight eggs, separately well whisked. Bake the pudding, serve with custard-sauce. Dates, plums, or raisins may be added, and also minced marrow, almonds, and grated citron.

859. *Ginger-pudding.*—Season a *Chancellor's* pudding with two ounces of wet preserved ginger. Steam it in a shape.—*Obs.* The fruit in these puddings should be arranged in form round the mould to look well when the pudding is turned out.

860. *College-puddings.*—Beat six yolks and three whites of eggs, and mix them to a smooth batter with three heaped spoonfuls of flour, a little ginger, and half a nutmeg, with pounded loaf-sugar to taste. Add four ounces of shred suet, four of picked currants, and an ounce of candied orange-peel and citron sliced. Bake in patty-pans, or fry these small puddings, making them up of an egg-shape. Serve with pudding-sauce and sliced lemon.—*Obs.* Bread-crumbs or pounded biscuit may be used instead of flour when the pudding is to be baked. For all puddings bread is much lighter than flour, and more suitable to delicate stomachs.

861. *Puddings in haste.*—Mix shred suet with grated bread, a handful of currants, the yolks of four eggs, and the whites of two. Add grated lemon-peel and ginger. Mix, and roll this in little balls (the size of a small egg) with flour. Have ready a pan of boiling water, and slip

them in. When done they will rise to the top. Serve with pudding-sauce.

862. *Northumberland puddings*.—Make a thick batter by boiling and sweetening milk and flour. When cold and firm, mash it up, and add to it four ounces of melted butter, the same weight of currants, two ounces of candied lemon and orange-peel sliced, and a little brandy if liked. Butter tea-cups, and bake the puddings in them for fifteen minutes. Turn them out on a dish, and pour wine-sauce over them if to be eat hot. If to make a cold ornamental supper-dish, omit the wine-sauce, and garnish with red currant-jelly.

863. *Dutch pudding, or Albany cake*.—Mix two pounds or rather less of good flour with a pound of butter, melted in half a pint of milk. Add to this the whites and yolks of eight eggs separately well beaten, a half-pound of fine sifted sugar, a pound of cleaned currants, and a few chopped almonds, or a little candied orange-peel sliced fine. Put to this four spoonfuls of yeast. Cover it up for an hour or two, and bake it for an hour in a wide flattish dish. When cold it eats well as a cake.*

864. *A Welsh pudding*.—Melt a half-pound of butter by setting it in a basin floating in hot water, and gradually mix it with the beat yolks of eight eggs, and the whites of four. Sweeten with fine pounded sugar, and season with the grate of a lemon and a little nutmeg. Bake in a dish with an ornamented paste-border; and when ready, stick slices of citron or candied orange-peel round the edges.

865. *Amber-pudding*.—A quarter-pound of fine sugar sifted, the same quantity of melted butter, the beat yolks of six eggs. Mix well, and season with half a grated nutmeg. Line the dish with puff-paste, and bake for a half-hour.

866. *A George-pudding*.—Boil as for rice-pudding four ounces of rice with a roll of lemon-peel. Mix this, when drained dry, with the pulp of a dozen boiled, roasted, or baked apples, well beaten. Add the beat yolks

---

* This is the *bonne bouche* at the substantial rural tea-parties of the State of New York. The feast, begun with fried eggs and bacon, ends with buck-wheat cakes and the above preparation.

of five or six eggs, sugar to taste, and a little cinnamon, with two ounces of candied orange and citron-peel sliced. Line and butter a basin or mould with paste, (not too thick,) and pour the pudding into it; then gently stir in the whites of the eggs beaten to a strong froth. Bake the pudding for more than a half-hour, and serve it with a hot sauce made of wine, sugar, the yolk of an egg, and a bit of butter.

867. *Cream-sauce for puddings.*—Sweeten thin cream, and season either with nutmeg, cinnamon, or lemon rind, as best suits the pudding. Boil the cream with a bit of butter and a little rice-flour. Skink it well, and keep it hot by plunging the dish in hot water. When ready to serve, add a glass of sweet wine. Boil it up, and pour over the pudding.—See page 246.

868. *A French fruit-pudding, or Charlotte.*—The preparations known here by this name are much admired on the continent, and particularly in France, where the solid, lumpy, and doughy English pudding, and fat pie or tart crust, are not so much esteemed as they are at home. *A Charlotte—a French fruit-pudding*, or by whatever other name it be designated, may be made of any kind of fruit, or of a mixture of such as blend well, as apricot and apple marmalade. Cut smoothly, slices of bread of nearly half an inch in thickness. Butter them richly on both sides, and cover the bottom and sides of a buttered pan with them, cutting the bread into dice or long slips, to make the whole joint or dove-tail compactly. Fill up the dish with apples, stewed and seasoned as for an apple-pudding, No. 853. For the top, soak slices of bread in melted butter and milk. Cover the apples with these soaked slices. Butter them, and keep them pressed down while baking in a quick oven with a plate and a weight placed on it.—*Obs.* This, turned out of the shape when baked, is sometimes called *an apple-loaf.* Any kind of preserved or ripe fruit may be used instead of apples. A few thin slices of bread soaked and buttered thus make a good crust to a rice or other pudding.

869. *Yorkshire pudding, to bake under a roast.*—Mix four ounces of flour very smoothly with a pint and a half of milk, four beat eggs, and a little salt, and also ginger if liked. Butter a shallow tin pan; pour the

batter into it, and place it below the roast. When settling, stir up the batter; and when browned on the upper side, turn over the pudding, first drawing a knife round the edges to loosen it. Brown the other side. It should be about an inch thick when done. This is the favourite English accompaniment to a sirloin of beef, or a loin of veal or mutton; finely-minced parsley, eschalot, onion, and also suet well beat, may be added. This pudding, if for roast pork, should have a little minced sage. It may be cut in strips.

870. *Potato-pudding, to go below a roast.*—Peel, boil, and mash the potatoes, with a little milk, salt, pepper, and a finely-shred onion if approved. Dish and score this, and set it below the roast to catch the dripping, and to brown.—See No. 19.

871. *Potato-pudding with meat.*—Mash the potatoes; thin them with milk, and season as above. Cut either fat beef, mutton, or pork, into very small bits, and season these well with salt, pepper, allspice, and shred onion. Place a layer of meat at the bottom of a baking dish, then potatoes, and proceed thus till the dish is filled. Pour all the potato-batter that remains equally over the top, and stick some butter over that. Bake of a fine brown, covering with paper to prevent scorching.— See No. 764.—*Obs.* This dish is in no material respect different from baked Irish stew. The meat may be kept in steaks; and the pudding is then called a *rump-steak pudding*. Chicken or veal, with curry seasonings, may be dressed as above, using a batter of boiled rice. A *mutton-pudding* is also made with potatoes as above.

872. *Kidney-pudding, or dumpling.*—Split, soak, and season one or two ox-kidneys. Line a basin with a hot paste, made of suet, flour, and hot milk. Put in the kidneys with a little shred onion and suet, and pinch in the paste; cover with a cloth, and boil for two hours.— For *blood-puddings* and *white-puddings*, see *National Dishes*; and *French Cookery* for several excellent meat puddings.

873. *Pease-pudding*, see p. 147. *Sauces for puddings*, pages 245-6, and No. 867.

DUMPLINGS.

DUMPLINGS are made of all sorts of fruit, either fresh

or preserved, and also of meat and other things. They are convenient, and sometimes economical, though not particularly elegant, and far from being of easy digestion. The boiled paste of dumplings is dough in its heaviest form,—yeast will lighten it and save eggs.

874. *Suet-dumplings.*—Chop from four to eight ounces of suet fine, and take double the weight of flour and grated bread. Beat two or three eggs with a glassful of milk. Mix all well together, and put a little salt and allspice to the mixture. Work it up into the shape of large eggs, and tie each up separately in a puddingcloth dredged with flour. Boil three quarters of an hour. These are eat hot along with meat, or alone with butter and vinegar.

875. *Plum, apple, currant, raspberry-jam, strawberryjam, gooseberry, or damson dumpling.*—Line a buttered tin basin with a plain crust, and fill with the fruit, either preserved or prepared, as for pies and puddings. Pinch in the paste, tie a floured cloth over the basin, and boil from two to three hours, and turn it out.

876. *Norfolk dumplings.*—Make a very stiff batter with flour, a little milk, three eggs, and salt. Work this up into balls of the size of small turkey eggs, and roll them in flour, and boil them in water, or along with meat: *or* drop the batter from a spoon into water that boils fiercely. Boil them for ten minutes, drain and serve them hot. Currants and sweet spices may be mixed with suet or batter dumplings.

PANCAKES AND FRITTERS.

THESE articles make an economical and genteel addition to small dinners, and have the advantage of being quickly forthcoming upon any emergency.

877. *Common pancakes.*—Beat from four to eight eggs, according to the number of pancakes wanted, and put in a spoonful of flour for every egg, with sugar, ginger, and a little nutmeg. Stir in milk enough to reduce this to a thick batter. Make a small frying-pan hot, melt a little butter in it, pour it out, and wipe the pan; or rub it with a buttered cloth. Put in a very small piece of butter, and when it froths, a ladleful of batter;—toss round the pan to diffuse this equally. Run a knife round the

edges, and turn the pancake. Brown very lightly on both sides, double them up to keep hot. Serve a few at a time, with grated sugar and sliced lemon, or roll them lightly up as a collar.

878. *Fine pancakes.*—Beat six eggs, add a pint of cream, and three or four ounces of butter, if they are wanted rich. Use rice-flour, or a proportion of it, and sweeten with sugar, and season with nutmeg, cinnamon, or lemon, as is most agreeable. Sift sugar over them as they are fried.*

879. *Irish pancakes.*—These are made as above, with more flour and sugar.

880. *Rice-pancakes or fritters.*—Boil four ounces of rice-flour in a quart of cream, or very good milk, till it is as thick as pap. Stir in a quarter-pound of sugar. When cold, mix four spoonfuls of flour, a little salt, and eight beat eggs, thoroughly together. If not stiff enough, add more flour and sugar, and fry the batter either as fritters or pancakes. Serve with a little melted butter, wine and sugar, poured into the dish.

881. *Batter for fritters and for frying.*—Put a half-pound of sifted flour into a dish, with salt, a little melted butter, and the yolks of two eggs. Moisten and work up this with worts, or fresh yeasty beer, till it is of a proper consistence. Have the whites of the eggs well whipt, and work them into the paste, which should be made hours before it is used. Water or wine may be used instead of beer: milk is often used. Top-fat makes the best frying material for fritters, and next to it the soft kidney-fat of beef, or dripping.

882. *Good plain fritters.*—Mix minced apples rolled in sugar with a little finely-shred suet and stiff pancake-batter or fritter-batter, as above described. Drop this in proper quantities into boiling dripping, and fry the fritters; *or* a few picked currants may be stirred into

---

* In the CLEIKUM, and probably in some other old-fashioned inns and Scottish families, pancakes were wont to be served with a layer of currant-jelly between the folds,—a practice for which much might be said by those familiar with it. Is not this the *omelette à la Celestine* or *au confiture*, of our old allies, still lingering in remote places of the country? Pancakes are still better with apricot marmalade.—P. T.

the batter, and dropt in spoonfuls into the boiling dripping.

883. *Apple-fritters.*—Put a little additional flour to common pancake-batter. Peel and core large apples;* cut them in slices, dip them in the thick pancake-batter, and fry them in lard, or good clarified dripping. Drain and dish them neatly above each other, and grate sugar over them; *or* drop batter into the boiling fat in the frying-pan, then a slice of apple, and drop more batter over that.—*Obs.* Fritters are best served on the folds of a damask napkin. They may be made of ripe or preserved fruits of all kinds, and are then called *Italian.* The batter may be seasoned with wine. Whole apples may be pared, cored, and baked, dipped in batter, and fried as fritters, &c.—See Potato-fritters, p. 220.—*Oyster-fritters*, p. 202.

CHAPTER V.

CREAMS, JELLIES, SWEET DISHES, PRESERVES, AND ORNAMENTAL CONFECTIONARY.

Make your transparent sweetmeats truly nice,
With Indian sugar and Arabian spice;
And let your various Creams enriched be
With swelling fruit just ravished from the tree.
DR. KING.

WHERE there is a good confectioner at hand, it will in general be not only more convenient, but as cheap, to purchase a great part of the smaller articles used for *desserts* and *suppers*, as *wafers*, little *soufflé* cakes, *Bouchées des dames*, and the many fanciful trifles made of *paste-royal*. Even moulded creams, jellies, and preserved fruits of the finer kinds, where they are not often used, will be often obtained as cheap, and in better style than they can be prepared in small families. But this department of the culinary art, besides affording a pleasing variety to the domestic business of ladies, often in

---

* French cooks steep rennets for fritters in brandy and cinnamon, or some liqueur, before dipping them in the batter. They make fritters of all sorts of fruits, first *half-baking* the cored apples or apricots.

the country becomes a necessary branch of knowledge. We have therefore given a copious selection of receipts in ornamental confectionary, according to modern and fashionable practice.

Beginners in confectionary, as in cookery, are often at a loss to know how much of a receipt must be followed according to the letter, and how much understood in the spirit only. Like the *Malade Imaginaire*, when ordered to walk across the room, they are miserable from not knowing whether to take the breadth or the length of it. In general this is of small consequence, provided they do walk either way.

ICES, CREAMS, JELLIES, &c.

CREAMS are either shaped in a mould, and turned out, and garnished with myrtle or other flowers, or served in a glass dish, or in little glass cups. For creams and jellies moulded to shapes, *freezing* is necessary if you would make sure of having the shape fine and entire. If too rich in syrup, cream-jellies won't freeze. If too *watery*, they will set in a kind of dissolved ice. It is a good method to freeze the mixture so far before filling the moulds. *Isinglass* also must be put in considerable quantity to all things of this kind that are made in shapes; but if served in a dish or little cups, only eggs are used, and no isinglass. Melt slowly, in a little water, the isinglass to be used; and after adding it try a little of your cream or jelly in a small shape or orange-skin, to see if it be strong enough to take and keep a shape. Moulds are best of earthenware; pewter or tin ones give red jellies a bad colour. Moulds should come in pieces.

All creams are made nearly in the same manner, the chief difference arising from the flavouring ingredient, which generally gives the name, as *coffee, chocolate, tea, vanilla, &c.* Though creams certainly look handsomer when moulded and iced, they are not better than when served in glass cups, from the greater quantity of isinglass in them, and the absence of eggs.

The yolk of one fresh egg to every cupful is a good rule in making creams and custards to be served in cups, but many more are often used for moulds. A little grated nutmeg, or cinnamon, should be sprinkled over *creams* served without being freezed. The exact quantity of isinglass necessary can only be known by experiment at the time of making the cream, this commodity varies so much in strength. For a large mould the material must be stiffer, to keep shape, than for a small one.

884. *To freeze creams and jellies.*—There are various ways of procuring ice; the cheapest is to buy it of nature's making, and to have a necessary apparatus for preserving it after you have got it. Break the ice in a proper ice-bucket, and strew a handful of salt amongst it. Take it from the sides occasionally. Place your mould over the ice, and bury it amidst ice, but take care that the cream or jelly be quite cold, else it will melt the ice instead of being frozen itself. Let it remain till wanted for the table. Then dip a towel in hot water, and rub it quickly round the mould, to detach your jelly or cream, and turn it carefully upside down. You must use a towel dipped in hot water to turn out every thing made in a mould, (as puddings, &c.) whether iced or hot.—*Obs.* Several ices, if left, by the addition of rum or brandy, will make very agreeable sorts of beverages.—See *Punch de la Romaine.*

885. *Italian cream.*—Take two parts of sweet cream and one of milk, about a quart in all. Boil this, and infuse in it four ounces of fine sugar, and the thin rind of a lemon, or two if small. When flavoured, add the beat yolks of eight eggs, and beat the whole well. Set it on the fire to thicken; and when this is done, put in a little strained melted isinglass, (about a half-ounce; more afterwards if necessary;) whip it well; strain it through a lawn-sieve, and try a little in a small mould, before filling the mould.

886. *Italian cream, another way.*—Whisk up a pint or rather more of the richest cream, the yellow rind of a lemon rubbed off with sugar, the juice of the lemon, and more fine sifted sugar to sweeten the cream to taste. Put to this, when well whisked, an ounce of isinglass dissolved by boiling-hot water, and strained. Beat these together well, and season with noyeau, or curaçoa, if liked. Fill the shape, and when frozen, turn out, and garnish according to fancy.—*Obs.* This, with little variation, is the preparation called *Italian cheese.*

887. *Ginger-cream, an elegant cream.*—Four ounces

of preserved ginger sliced fine; three spoonfuls of the syrup; five beat yolks of eggs, and a pint and quarter of cream, Imperial measure. Boil and whisk till cold. If sugar is wanted add the finest, then isinglass; freeze the cream. This may be flavoured with a tincture of ginger.

888. *Coffee-cream.*—Boil equal quantities of fresh cream and milk. Season with sugar and a particle of salt. Roast two ounces of good coffee-beans, or refresh the same quantity of those already roasted, and throw them hot into the cream, or you may use a strong clear tincture, by infusing good coffee. When cold, add the beat yolk of an egg for every cupful, strain it twice or three times; and place the cups in a wide pan of boiling water, which will cover them half-way up. Cover the pan, and put embers over the lid, to keep the vapour from falling down. If for a shape, set the cream and eggs on the fire to thicken, put isinglass to it, and fill the mould.

889. *Whipt coffee-cream.*—Infuse two ounces of coffee, so as to have a breakfast-cupful of a strong tincture. Whip a quart of sweetened cream, and lay aside the froth as it rises, on a sieve reversed, to drain. Add the white of an egg if it will not rise well. Boil the remaining cream, and put it to the beat yolks of three or four eggs, and the clear coffee-tincture. Serve it in a glass dish and the whip over it.

N.B.—Whips will be easier made if the cream, where convenient, is whisked over ice.

890. *Another coffee-cream.*—Have a pint of clear jelly of calves'-feet, free of blacks and fat. Clear a large cupful of strong coffee with isinglass till bright and deeply brown. Mix it with the jelly; add a pint of good cream and fine sugar to taste; and after mixing well, boil up for a few minutes till you have a weak jelly. This is an easily-made and favourite cream.

891. *Ratafia-cream.*—Mix a quarter-pint of ratafia or noyeau with the same quantity of mountain wine, sugar to taste, and the juice of a lemon and of a Seville orange. Whisk this with a pint of good cream, adding more sugar if necessary, and fill the glasses. *Ratafia-cream* may also be made of the beat yolks of four or five eggs, with a quart of cream and two glasses of brandy scalded together (but not boiled) over the fire. If moulded, add

isinglass, and proceed as for other creams made in shapes.

892. *A plain cream.*—Boil a pint of milk and one of cream, with two bay-leaves, a bit of lemon-peel, fine sugar to sweeten, a dozen almonds, and three bitter ones, beaten to a paste with orange-flower-water. Thicken with a little rice-flour rubbed with milk, and give it a scald. When cold, put a little lemon-juice to the cream, and fill the glasses or cups. A little nutmeg or cinnamon may be strewed over this and other creams in cups.

893. *Orange-cream, an elegant cream.*—Wipe with a wet towel, and grate and put aside the thick coarse parts of a Seville orange-rind; then pare and boil the skin till soft, changing the water. Beat this in a marble mortar, and put to it a spoonful of ratafia, the juice of the orange strained, four ounces of fine sugar, and the yolks of four eggs. Beat these ingredients thoroughly well together for a quarter of an hour, and then by degrees mix them with a pint of cream that has boiled; keep beating till the whole is cold; then put it into custard-cups, and set these in a kettle of boiling water. Wipe the cups, let the cream thicken by cooling, and garnish with thin parings of preserved orange-chips.—*Obs.* By the addition of isinglass this cream may be made in a shape.

894. *Lemon-cream.*—Make as coffee-cream, but use lemon-rind instead of coffee, to give the flavour.—*Obs.* Every variety of cream may be made in the same manner, only changing the flavour, as *pistachio cream* of the nuts, *chocolate* and *tea* creams, by employing an infusion as in coffee. *Orange-flowers* make an elegantly flavoured cream.

895. *Canary or sack cream.*—To a half-pint of cream add one of sweet milk, and sweeten; put to this the beat yolk of an egg or two, a bit of lemon-rind, and a glass of wine. Stir over the fire, but take care it does not curdle. Serve in glass cups, with nutmeg grated over, and bits of toast, or small light biscuits along with it.

CREAMS OF PRESERVED OR FRESH FRUITS.

896. *Raspberry or strawberry cream, not iced.*—Mash the ripe fruit, and boil down the drained juice with fine sugar. Have a strong whip made of sweetened cream. With what remains of the cream, mix the beat

yolks of eggs, and when cold, mix the fruit with this, and serve the whip over it.—*Obs*. This will make equally well of preserved jellies or jams, by freeing the latter of all seeds and skins; *or* it may be made in a shape by mixing an ounce of melted isinglass with a quart of cream, straining it, and when cool, adding the fruit-syrup, and filling the mould. It is very good made of the pulp of apples, plums, or apricots, but changes its name.

897. *Pine-apple-cream*.—Infuse the rind of a pine-apple in boiling cream, and proceed as in other creams, only this cream is almost always moulded and freezed.

898. *Cocoa-nut-cream*.—Use a strong infusion of grated cocoa to flavour.

N.B. This is a favourite flavouring ingredient in the colonies for puddings, &c. It is thought to give the laurel-leaf flavour, and has no pernicious quality.

899. *To ice fruits, creams, jellies, &c.*.—Proceed as before directed for freezing creams in moulds. It is necessary that creams and fruits served with the name of iced, should be thoroughly done; to be so, let them be long enough in the freezer, and only fill the glasses when they are wanted at table. All sorts of fruits may be iced.

900. *Strawberry ice-cream*.—Mix the fruit-juice, strained and sweetened in the proportion of a pound to a pint of whipped cream. If to be moulded to a shape, add a little melted and strained isinglass; if in small glasses, this is not necessary.

901. *Raspberry ice-cream*.—Make as above.

802. *Apricot ice-cream*.—Peel, stone, and pound the apricots with a little sugar. Press the mash through a tammy-sieve, with a wooden spoon. Mix it with sweetened whipt cream; put a little melted isinglass to it; whip the whole over ice till it is thoroughly blended; then fill the mould, and place it in the ice-bucket.

N.B. We must again notice, that the necessary quantity of isinglass to make creams take a shape can only be ascertained by experiment.

903. *Imitation of fruit ice-creams* is made by tinging blancmange with beet-root or prepared cochineal.

ICE WATERS.

In these water is generally substituted for cream—

there is a great variety of them made much in the same way. Spirits will make them into good punch. They are just in fact the prepared sherbet.

904. *Lemon water ice.*—Take the zest of six fresh lemons off on lumps of sugar. Scrape this off; add to it half a pint of lemon juice, and one pint of syrup. Strain and freeze.—*Orange water ice the same.*

905. *Tamarind water ice.*—A pound of tamarinds, a quarter pint of syrup, a little lemon juice, a pint and quarter of water; rub through a sieve, and freeze.

906. *Negus ice.*—A bottle of port wine, half a nutmeg grated, the zest of a lemon rubbed off on sugar, a pint of syrup or more to taste:—freeze this.

907. *Pine-apple water ice of fresh or preserved fruit.*—Take a half-pint of pine-apple syrup, the juice of three lemons, a pint of water, and a few slices of pineapple in dice,—freeze. For fresh pine-apple, take a pint of syrup to a pound of grated fruit, and half a pint of water; rub through a sieve and freeze.

JELLIES TO BE SENT TO TABLE IN A SHAPE.

CLARIFY the sugar you use, whether the jelly is boiled or worked cold; for although the main excellence of these jellies is no doubt the flavour, their most obvious qualities are colour and transparency. The former depends on the materials employed and on the manner of preparing; the latter in a great measure upon the straining of the jelly. The utensils should all be brightly clean, the moulds of earthenware, (as metal will turn jellies of red fruits to a dingy purple,) and the spoons silver or wood. Unless the moulds are set in ice, the cook will often be disappointed of an entire shape.

908. *Calves'-feet jelly.*—It is best to make the plain jelly the day before the dish is wanted. Clean and slit four calves'-feet, and boil them slowly in five quarts of water till rather more than the half is wasted. Skim the stock, strain it off, and when cold and firm, remove the top-fat and the sediment. Put this jelly-stock, when wanted, into a nice preserving-pan, with white sugar to taste, the thin peel of two lemons, and the juice of from four to six; a half-bottle of Madeira or Sherry, the whites of six eggs well whisked, and the shells crushed and thrown into the pan. Stir this well together, and

set the pan on the fire, taking care not to agitate the jelly after it begins to heat. Let it boil slowly for from twelve to fifteen minutes, then throw in a little cold water, and let it boil another five minutes. Set the pan, with a flannel cloth thrown over it, to settle for a half-hour, pour the jelly into a flannel jelly-bag, and strain till it be perfectly pellucid.

N.B.—If you have any doubts of your jelly not keeping the shape, add a little melted isinglass.—*Obs.* This jelly may be made of cow-heels, or a proportion of them; and it may be flavoured with many things, some of them cheap substitutes for what is ordered above. *Curaçoa, noyeau,* or *ginger-wine,* may be substituted for wine, or less wine may be used, and a little good vinegar or verjuice does for part of the lemon-juice. Some very great economists even substitute porter or ale for wine, and flavour with coriander-seeds, allspice, cinnamon, and cloves. Finely-flavoured ale is indeed an excellent substitute, but it must not be too much hopped.

909. *Madeira wine jelly.*—Make this precisely as calves'-feet jelly, but with more wine, and a glass of brandy after the jelly is clarified; and as this diminishes the strength of the jelly, a little melted isinglass to give firmness. The philosophers of the stove allege that jellies broken, *i.e.* roughed, eat better than those in shape, the admission of air heightening the flavour.

910. *Orange-jelly.*—Take twenty oranges, infuse the rind of six in a basin with boiling water. Divide and squeeze the whole number, as in making orange-marmalade. Clarify a pound and a quarter of sugar, and when it has reached the second degree, (see *clarifying,*) put in the strained juice, and the strained infusion of the rind. Let it come to the point of boiling, but not boil. Skim it, and run it through a jelly-bag. If the oranges are too ripe, use a fourth part bitter oranges, or a couple of lemons, with their rind infused. Add clarified isinglass. First try the jelly in a small mould, then fill the moulds.—*Obs.* The colour should be a pale topaz; a few blades of saffron will improve it.

911. *Lemon-jelly.*—Make this exactly as the above, but use more sugar, and take care that all the lemons are quite fresh. Much less fruit may do, and the zest may be saved, rubbed off on sugar, for other purposes.

912. *Apple-jelly*.—Pare as many juicy apples as you will want, and slice them into a little water. Boil them to a mash, drain them through a jelly-bag, and take equal weight of sugar, boiled to blowing height. Boil for ten minutes, seasoning with the grate and juice of two or more lemons. Mould and freeze.

913. *Peach-jelly*.—Peel, divide, and stone eighteen peaches. Break the stones, and take out the kernels. Boil the peaches and bruised kernels in clarified syrup for a quarter of an hour. Season it with the juice and grate of four fresh lemons. Run it through a jelly-bag, add an ounce of strained melted isinglass, and fill the mould, which must be plunged in ice.

JELLIES OF RED FRUITS IN SHAPES.

MAKE all these with isinglass purified, and do not boil them so long as jellies for preserving, as the colour will suffer. One direction will do for all.

914. *Raspberry-jelly for a shape*.—Put fresh-picked fruit into an earthenware mortar, with sifted sugar. Mash them well. Put in a little water, run this through a jelly-bag, and stir in what you think a sufficient quantity (about an ounce to the quart) of melted cold isinglass. Fill your mould.—*Obs.* Strawberry, red currant, and cherry jelly, are all made as above—only for cherries add a little lemon-juice; and also for the other fruits if mawkishly sweet with over-ripeness.

915. *Hartshorn-jelly*.—Simmer a half-pound of the shavings in two quarts of water till the half is wasted. Strain and boil up the jelly with the thin rind of three sweet oranges and three lemons. When cool, add white sugar to taste, the juice of the fruit, wine, and the whites of six eggs well whisked up. Let it just come once more to boil, without stirring it, and run it through a jelly-bag till quite clear. A pinch of saffron to tinge with colour may be added.

916. *Venus's jelly*.—Make as hartshorn-jelly; tint this rose-colour with cochineal, and flavour with Madeira. This is a fashionable jelly.

917. BLANCMANGE.

PICK and boil two ounces of isinglass for a quarter of an hour in a quart of milk or sweet cream, with the thin rind of a small lemon, sugar to taste, and a blade of mace. Blanch, split, and pound, six bitter almonds, and two dozen sweet ones, with a little rose-water, or plain water, to prevent their oiling, and stir the paste gradually into the hot milk. Strain through a fine-lawn sieve or napkin into a basin, and let it settle for a good while, that the sediment may fall. Pour it again clear off from the sediment, and fill the moulds. It is sometimes difficult to take out, and dipping the mould in hot water destroys the fine marble-like surface. Rub it with a towel dipped in hot water, raise it from the edges with a fruit-knife, and then use the fingers to get it out. Garnish with flowers, &c. &c.

918. *Blancmange as in France.*—Make the stock of calves'-feet well blanched, or of white fish, as skate, or of feet of poultry. Season it with lemon-peel and coriander-seeds. In other respects make it as above; but use as little isinglass as possible.—*Obs.* This is a sensible receipt. Our English blancmange is, in fact, just almond-cream.—*Rice blancmange,* No. 952.

TRIFLES.

919. *An elegant trifle.*—Whisk in a large bowl, the day before you make the trifle, a quart of good cream, with six ounces of sifted sugar, a glass of white wine, the juice and fine grate of a lemon, and a few bits of cinna-mon. Take off the froth as it rises, with a sugar-skimmer or silver fish-trowel, and place it to drain on a sieve reversed over a bowl. Whisk till you have enough of the whip, allowing for what it will fall down. Next day place in a deep trifle-dish, six sponge-cakes broken, or rice trifle-cake, or remnants of any good light cake cut down, a dozen ratafia-crop-biscuits, and some sweet almonds blanched and split. Pour over them enough of white wine, or ginger-wine, to moisten them completely, and add a seasoning of grated lemon-peel, and a thin layer of raspberry or strawberry jam. Have ready a rich and rather thick custard, and pour it over this to the thickness of two inches. Heap the whip above this lightly and elegantly, and garnish with a few sprigs of light flowers of fine colours, or a few bits of very clear currant-jelly stuck into the snow-white whip, or a sprinkling of Harlequin-comfits.

920. *Gooseberry or apple trifle.*—Scald, pulp, sweeten, and season the fruit, if apples, with cinnamon or lemon grate; mix it over the fire with a thin custard: put it into the trifle-dish, and, when cold, cover it with a whip made the day before, as no whip will be *solid* unless it has stood a good while. There need be no cream put to the fruit pulp.

CUSTARDS.*

921. *Custard for a centre dish,—Scotch.*—Make a strong whip of sweetened cream, and have a little of the same cream tinged with cochineal before it is whipt. Heap the white whip over a rich custard, and drop the pink-coloured froth fancifully round that. Garnish with bright green and scarlet preserved fruits, to contrast the colours.

922. *Almond-custards.*—Blanch and pound nearly a half-pound of sweet and a half-ounce of bitter almonds, using a little rose-water to prevent them from oiling. Sweeten a pint or rather more of boiling sweet-milk and another of cream, and mix these gradually with the beat yolks of six eggs, stirring them well as they cool. Rub the almond-paste through a sieve to this, and set it over the fire to thicken, carefully stirring it. Pour it into a jug, and stir till it cools. Instead of boiling, this may be baked in cups, or in a dish with an elegantly-cut paste-border. Flour of rice may be used instead of almonds: these are then called Rice-custards.

923. *Baked custards.*—Boil and sweeten with fine sugar a pint of milk, and another of cream, with a stick of cinnamon and a bit of lemon-peel. When cool, mix in the beat yolks of six eggs. Pick out the cinnamon and lemon-peel, fill the cups, and bake for ten minutes.

924. *Lemon custards.*—Beat the yolks of eight eggs as well as if for a cake, till they are a strong white cream. Mix in gradually a pint of boiling water and the grated rind and juice of two lemons. Sweeten to taste, and stir this one way over the fire till it thicken, but do not let it boil. Add a little wine and a spoonful

---

* Our custards are almost the same thing with the French *frangipane*, an old word of our own; or the *creme patisserie*, with which they eat *tourtes* or *tarts*.

of brandy when the custard is almost ready. Stir till cool. Serve in cups, and grate nutmeg over.

925. *Excellent common custards.*—Boil a quart of new milk with sugar, a bit of cinnamon and lemon-peel, and a bay-leaf. Mix a spoonful of rice-flour with a little cold milk and the beat yolks of six eggs. Stir the whole together into the boiling milk in a basin, and then let it thicken over the fire, but not boil. Pour it into a cold dish, and stir one way till cool. A very little ratafia, curaçoa, or peach-water, may be put to flavour these custards. Grate a little nutmeg, or strew a little ground cinnamon lightly over the top of the cups.

926. *Cheesecakes.*—These are just various pudding ingredients, more or less rich, baked in paste. Mix with the dry beat curd of a quart and a half of milk, a half-pound of picked currants, white sugar to taste, and also pounded cinnamon, the beat yolks of four eggs, the peel of a lemon grated off on lumps of the sugar used for sweetening, a half-pint of scalded cream, and a glass of brandy. Mix the ingredients well, and fill patty-pans lined with a thin light puff-paste nearly full. Twenty minutes will bake them in a quick oven. They may be iced.

927. *Almond-cheesecakes.*—Blanch and pound a quarter of a pound of sweet almonds and eight bitter ones with a glass of common or of orange-flower-water. Add four ounces of sugar, a quarter-pint of cream, and the whites of two eggs beat to a froth. Mix and fill small patty-pans; or these almond-cheesecakes may be made merely mixing a few beat almonds with cheesecakes— No. 926.—See *Savoury cheesecakes*, No. 561.

928. *Lemon or orange-cheesecakes.*—Grate the rinds of three lemons, and squeeze their juice over three sponge-biscuits soaked in a glass of cream. Add to this four ounces of fresh butter, four of fine sugar, and three eggs well beaten. Season with cinnamon and nutmeg. Mix the whole ingredients thoroughly, and bake in small pans lined with a light thin paste. Lay a few long thin slices of candied lemon-peel along the top before baking.

929. *Whipt syllabub.*—Make a strong whip as directed for trifle; or in making a trifle a little of the whip may be saved, or may even be applied to this use after it has done duty on the trifle. Mix a large pint of rich sweet cream with a half-pint of sweet wine,

sifted sugar to taste, the juice and fine grate of a lemon, and a little cinnamon. Stir this briskly, and fill the glasses within a half-inch of the brim. With a spoon lay a little of the whip lightly on the top of each; or a whip may be got by whisking the above materials, and draining the froth on a sieve as long as possible before the syllabubs are wanted.

930. *Windsor syllabub.*—Pour a bottle of sherry or port into a deep china or glass bowl; sweeten it well, and season it with pounded cloves and grated nutmeg. Milk from the cow nearly double the quantity of milk over it, and stir it up.

931. *Staffordshire syllabub.*—It is made as above, substituting cider with a little brandy for the wine.

932. *Somersetshire syllabub.*—Sweeten a pint of port, and another of Madeira or sherry, in a china bowl. Milk about three pints of milk over this. In a short time it will bear clouted cream laid over it. Grate nutmeg over this, and strew a few coloured comfits on the top if you choose.

933. *Curds and cream.*—When the milk is curdled firmly, fill up a melon-shape or Turk's-cap-shape, perforated with holes to let the whey drain off. Fill up the dish as the curd sinks. Turn it out when wanted, and serve in a glass dish with cream; or a whip may be poured about the curd, which may be made firm either by squeezing or standing long to drain; or having drained it well, rub through a search, and pour cream over it. Garnish with red currant-jelly or barberries.

934. *Clouted cream.*—Season a quarter-pint of new milk with two blades of mace, and put to it a large glass of rose-water. Strain and add to this the beat yolks of two eggs. Stir the mixture into a quart of rich cream, and let it scald, stirring it all the while. The rose-water may be omitted when this is to be eaten with fruit.

935. *An egg-cheese, or curd-star.*—Boil and season with cinnamon and lemon-peel a quart of milk or cream, and put to it eight eggs well beat, and a very little salt. Sweeten and season with orange-flower-water, wine, or any seasoning that is preferred. Stir and let this boil till it curdles, and till the whey is completely separated; then drain it through a sieve, and put it into a star-mould or other shape, that has holes to let the whey

drain wholly off. When firm, turn it out, and serve with cream, custard, or wine and sugar with or around it.

936. *Wassail-bowl, a centre supper-dish.*—Crumble down as for trifle a nice fresh cake (or use macaroons or other small biscuit) into a china punch-bowl or deep glass dish. Over this pour some sweet rich wine, as Malmsey Madeira, if wanted very rich, but raisin-wine will do. Sweeten this, and pour a well-seasoned rich custard over it. Strew nutmeg and grated sugar over it, and stick it over with sliced blanched almonds.—*Obs.* This is, in fact, just a rich eating posset. A very good wassail-bowl may be made of mild ale well spiced and sweetened, and a plain rice-custard made with few eggs. The wassail-bowl was anciently crowned with garlands and ribbons.

937. *Devonshire junket.*—Milk the cow into a bowl in which a little rennet is put. Stir it up when full; and when firm pour over it scalded cream, pounded sugar, and cinnamon.

SWEET DISHES OF APPLES, &c.

938. *Gooseberry-fool.*—Put the picked fruit and a glass of water in a jar with a little moist sugar, and set the jar over a stove, or in boiling water, till the fruit will pulp. Press it through a colander, and mix the pulp by degrees with cream or with common plain custard made with very few eggs.

939. *Apple-fool.*—This is made as above. The fruit may either be mixed with sweetened milk thickened with eggs, or with plain custard or cream.

940. *Buttered apples.*—Pare and core pippins or rennets. Stew in thin syrup as many as will fill your dish, and make a mash or marmalade of the rest. Cover the dish with a thin layer of the marmalade. Place the apples on this, with a bit of butter in the heart of each. Lay the rest of the marmalade into the vacancies. Glaze with sifted sugar, and give them a fine colour in the oven.

941. *Apples in rice.*—Prepare apples as above; but instead of apple-marmalade use seasoned and buttered rice. Glaze and brown as above.

N.B. These are cheap and excellent preparations. For preparing the rice, see *Gateau de riz*, p. 445.

924. *To bake pears.*—Pare, core, and, if large, divide them. Bake them in a stoneware dish with sugar, bruised cloves, a little sweet wine, and grated lemon-peel. The oven should be rather slow.—See Nos. 710, 983.

943. *To stew pears.*—Prepare and season them as above, and pack them in a new block-tin saucepan with a little water or wine. Cover them close, and let them stew slowly for three hours.—See Nos. 708, 984-5.

944. *Black caps.*—Pare, divide, and core some large juicy apples. Serve with a sauce of wine, water, and sugar, seasoned with cloves and cinnamon.—*Obs.* Genuine *black caps* are neither pared nor divided; they are merely cored, the holes stuffed with sugar and seasonings, and the apples stewed very slowly in sweet wine in a close-covered tin pan. The tops are then blackened with a salamander, which gives the name.—See also *French dishes of fruit, and preserves of pears and apples,* pages 435-6-7, and 359.

945. *Chartreuse de pommes,—Beauvilliers' receipt.* —Take a score of rennets; peel them, and with a very small corer take off all the pulp about the heart; when there is enough cored to fill the *Chartreuse* mould, mince the rest of the apples to make a marmalade; equalize all the little apples, or pieces that have been cut out with the apple-corer; make a little saffron-water; put a little sugar to it; throw in a third of the small apples; give them a slight boil, take them off, and drain; do another third in cochineal, and the last in a syrup of white sugar, with an equal quantity of angelica as of each of the apples; cover the mould with white paper; make any design in the bottom with the red, green, yellow, and white apples; fix them tastefully all round the mould to the top, and fill it up with the marmalade: it ought to be firm and without any void. When ready to serve, turn up the mould upon the dish, and take off the paper.—*Obs.* At grand dinners dressed in the French style roots are cut in forms, and served in the above way.

946. *A dish of snow, or snow-cream.*—Stew and pulp a dozen of apples; beat, and when cold stir this into the whites of a dozen eggs whisked to a strong froth; add a half-pound of sugar sifted, and the grate of

a lemon. Whisk till it becomes stiff, and heap it in a glass dish.

SWEET DISHES OF RICE AND FLUMMERY.

947. *Snow-balls.*—Swell a half-pound of rice in water with a roll of lemon-peel till tender, and drain it. Divide it into five parts, and roll a pared apple cored, and the hole filled with sugar and cinnamon, into each heap, tying each up tightly in separate cloths. Boil for an hour, untie, and serve with pudding-sauce.

948. *Buttered rice.*—Swell the rice till tender in new milk. Pour off the thick milk, and add melted butter, sugar, and cinnamon. Serve hot. For croquets of rice, see observations on *Gateau de riz*, page 445.

949. *Oatmeal flummery.*—Put finely-ground oatmeal to steep in water for three days. Pour off the thin of the first water, and add more water. Stir up, strain, and boil this with a little salt till of the thickness wanted, adding water at first if it be in danger of getting too stiff. A piece of butter is an improvement, and a little white sugar. Serve in a basin with milk, wine, cider, or cream.—*Obs.* This, if allowed to stand to become sour, is neither more nor less than Scotch *sowens*, and an excellent dish it is.

950. *Rice flummery.*—Mix a couple of spoonfuls of rice-flour with a little cold milk, and add to it a large pint of boiled milk sweetened and seasoned with cinnamon and lemon-peel. Two bitter almonds beaten will heighten the flavour. Boil this and stir it constantly, and when of proper consistence, pour it into a shape or basin. When cold turn it out, and serve with cream or custard round it; or with a sauce of wine, sugar, and lemon-juice.—This differs in nothing from rice blancmange, except that rice-flour is used instead of unground rice.

951. *French flummery*, or *yellow flummery, &c.* may be made as directed for blancmange, using well-beat yolks of eggs instead of cream. Colour with saffron. It may be made either in cups or in a mould of any shape.—*N.B.* Seldom made.

952. *Rice blancmange.*—Swell four ounces of rice in water; drain and boil it to a mash in good milk, with sugar, a bit of lemon-peel, and a stick of cinnamon. Take care it does not burn; and when quite soft, pour

it into cups, or into a shape dipped in cold water. When cold, turn it out. Garnish with currant-jelly or any red preserved fruit. Serve with cream, or plain custard.

953. *Mille feuilles, Italian pyramid, puits d'amour.* —This is the self-same thing with these, different names. A good puff-paste, rather thick, must be stamped out with tin stamps, or any ingenious substitutes, into a number of pieces, each less than the other, the base being of the size of the plate in which the pyramid is to be raised, and the others gradually tapering pyramidally. Bake the pieces of paste on paper laid on tins, and ice them. Pile them up, laying raspberry and other jams of different colours on the edges, and a bunch of small preserved fruit or some other ornament to crown the pile.

954. *Another way, from Beauvilliers.*—Take puff-paste, and roll it out as above; cut it with figured paste-cutters of different sizes; cut them equal in number, the large and small; put the large upon a leaf; wet them with water, and put a small one on each large one; with the point of a knife cut them out in the middle the size of a thimble; put them into the oven, and when nearly done powder them with sugar; take out the cut middle, replace it with sweetmeats, and serve.

SOUFFLES.

955. *Soufflé of ground rice.*—Bleach two spoonfuls of rice-flour, as directed for potato-flour, No. 232, and dry this quantity. Boil it slowly with a half-pint of sweet milk. To a little of it in a basin put the beat yolks of four eggs, and mix them well. Sweeten this, and cook the whole for a few minutes over the fire, as in making custard. Cool this, and gently pour into it the whites of six eggs beaten to a snow. (If they are not well beaten the soufflé will never rise.) Put the whole into a soufflé-dish, and bake it in a rather slack oven.

956. *Soufflé of potato-flour.*—Mix a large spoonful of potato-flour and one of sifted sugar, with as much boiled milk or cream as will make a thick batter of them, or a thin paste. Flavour this with rose-water, orange-flower-water, coffee, or chocolate, as you please, and name the soufflé accordingly. Work into this the beat yolks of six eggs, and afterwards gently add the

whites, beat to a snow. Bake the soufflé, and glaze it if you please. This dish is susceptible of many forms; it may be coloured with saffron, &c. The whipping of the eggs and the state of the oven are the main points.

957. *Omelette soufflé.*—Beat separately, and strain the whites and yolks of six eggs. Sweeten the yolks, and perfume with orange-flower-water or lemon peel. Beat the whites again to a strong whip, and stir lightly into the yolks. Melt a bit of fresh butter in an omelet-pan, and pour in the mixture. Cook it over a slow fire not to scorch. Turn it carefully out. Dredge fine sifted sugar over it, and set in the oven to rise.—*Obs.* All *soufflés* must be instantly served when ready, or they will flatten. They may be flavoured in many ways.

958. *Soufflé of apples in a rice-border.*—Prepare the rice as for *Gateau de riz*, but keep it thicker by using less milk. Raise the border three inches round your dish, egging the edge to make it adhere. Make it smooth and of a neat form. Mix with new-made apple-jam, very sweet, the beat yolks of six eggs, and two ounces of butter. Stir this over the fire to cook the eggs. To this put the whites of eight or ten eggs whisked to a snow. Mix gently. Fill the dish, and bake in a moderate oven till the soufflé rises light.

OBSERVATIONS ON SWEETMEATS AND PRESERVES.

To preserve the fruits that are in common use, and to make those sweetmeats which are oftenest wanted in private families, is justly considered a point of good housewifery; for these common things may be both cheaper and more nicely done at home than where they are manufactured by wholesale for the market. A little care and practice will soon give the cook or mistress of a famility sufficient skill to prepare the sugar for these things,—attention and cleanliness do the rest. The sugar for preserves ought, generally speaking, to be of the first quality. It ought also to be in sufficient quantity, for it is short-sighted economy to make paltry savings, at the risk of injuring commodities which are always costly, however they may be managed. Never squeeze the fruit too much. Take merely the juice that flows freely; and use what remains for made-wine, coarse jams, or black butter. Unless preserves are bright, and of a fine colour, they lose half their value; and this they never will be if the fruit is squeezed till the seeds are broken. Let the jelly-bags and sieves be dipt in and wrung out of hot water before using them, or they will absorb a great quantity of the jelly. Sweetmeats are most safely kept in small pots of earthenware, or small stone jars, with papers steeped in brandy put over them as soon as they are cool, and a layer of sugar sifted either above or below these papers, or both. This sugar is well bestowed, and it can be afterwards used in making other preserves. To keep stone fruit, melted mutton-suet is sometimes poured over it, which is certainly an efficacious method of excluding the air, though not very pleasant otherwise. Presses lined with wood, shelves, pantry-drawers, or any place that is perfectly dry, and, if possible, not too warm, are best suited for keeping preserves. Brass and copper-pans, scoured till brightly clean, are still much used for making preserves; but a vessel of double block-tin, or of iron very thickly tinned, if kept for jellies and sweet things, answers very well, and is far more safe, particularly for the coarser jams, which being generally made with a short allowance of sugar, require long boiling. Sweetmeats are best when rather quickly boiled, that the watery parts may be driven off without a process continued so long as to injure the colour of the fruit.* The shade of colour may be varied in many ways by using white currants to lighten, or black to deepen the colour, or by white or red raspberry-juice. Fruit-jellies may be made without boiling at all, by merely stirring the sugar finely beaten and sifted into the juice of the fruit. But though the flavour is preserved, they look muddy and eat harshly. It is a good plan to have a sieve, spoons with holes, and two pans of different sizes, kept wholly for preserves and sweet dishes, as the least taint of other things will at once destroy these delicate preparations. Sweetmeats and preserved fruits ought to be looked at several times during the first month; and if mouldiness gathers on them which is not occasioned by external damp, jellies

---

* This, we believe, is a culinary heresy, but we avouch it.

and jams, and the syrup of preserves, must be boiled over again till the jelly is firm, and the watery particles are wholly evaporated. Coarse glass vessels keep preserves well, and are perhaps cheaper in the end than earthenware ones.

OF BOILING SUGARS FOR PRESERVES.

CONFECTIONERS reckon several degrees in preparing sugars, from a simple *clarified syrup* to *caramel*.

959. *To clarify sugar*.—To every pound of broken sugar take a quarter-pint of water, and the half of the white of an egg beat up, or less egg will do. Stir this up till the sugar dissolve, and when it boils, and the scum rises strong and thick, pour in another quarter-pint of cold water to each pound. Let it boil, edging the pan forward from the stove till all the scum is thrown up. Set it on the hearth, and when it has settled take off the scum with a sugar skimmer, and lay this on a reversed hair sieve over a dish, that what syrup is in it may run clear from it. Return the drained syrup into the pan, and boil and skim the whole once more.

960. *Candied sugar—first degree*.—Boil sugar, clarified as above, till it rises in the pan like clusters of pears; or try between the finger and thumb if it have tenuity enough to draw out into a thread.

961. *Blown sugar—second degree*.—Boil candied sugar till on dipping the skimmer into the syrup, and blowing through the holes of it, the sugar forms into bubbles.

962. *Feathered height—third degree*.—Boil sugar of the second degree for some time longer, and dip the skimmer in the pan. Shake off the sugar, and give the skimmer a quick toss, when, if enough done, the sugar will fly off like snow-flakes.

963. *Crackling sugar—fourth degree*.—Boil *feathered* sugar till on dipping a stick into the pan, and dipping it afterwards in cold water, the sugar will immediately become hard.

964. *Caramel sugar*.—Boil crackling sugar till on dipping a stick into it, and then into cold water, it hardens and snaps like glass.—*Obs*. This last makes a very elegant cover for sweetmeats, when prepared thus:—

Set the pan with the caramel sugar instantly into a vessel of cold water. Have the caramel-moulds oiled with almond-oil, and with a fork or spoon spread fine threads of the caramelled sugar over them in form of net-work or chain-work. All sorts of fruit may be *caramelled*, whether fresh or preserved. They must be washed free of sugar, if preserved, and dried in both cases. The process is, however, troublesome, and seldom succeeds but under the hands of thorough-bred confectioners, to whom, in general, all highly ornamental affairs should be left. If families can afford ornament, they must not grudge the cost of having it well executed.

FRUIT-JELLIES.—See *also* pages 419-20.

965. *Red-currant jelly.*—Let the fruit be good of its kind, fully ripe, and gathered on and after a dry day. Strip it off the stalks; weigh it, and clarify and boil to the second degree an equal weight of refined sugar. Put the fruit to this in the preserving-pan. Skim and boil for fifteen minutes. Skim again, and run the jelly through a hair sieve, pot it, and when cold paper it up. What remains in the sieve will make pies, or mix with any common jam, and the jelly will be far more delicate from avoiding all squeezing.—*Obs.* A small proportion of raspberries will greatly improve the flavour of the jelly. It may be made paler by the mixture of a fourth or third part of white currants; or white raspberries may be used. This jelly may be made with much less boiling, or no boiling, as it may be worked cold as it is technically termed; but though this method is very suitable for jellies made to serve in shapes—for immediate use in desserts—it does not, in our opinion, or by our experience, answer for preserving long.

966. *White-currant jelly.*—Make as above, or squeeze the fruit and strain the juice. Use only a silver skimmer and the finest sugar, and boil only five minutes, as the delicate colour of this sweetmeat is very easily injured. Run it twice through a jelly-bag if necessary. Apple-jelly, or white raspberry-juice may be put to this preserve.—*N.B.* Have the sugar high-boiled.

967. *Black-currant jelly.*—Pick the fruit and scald it in a jar set in boiling water. Add a little water to it,

and squeeze the hot fruit through a sieve. To every pint of the juice allow a pound of sugar and a little water, and boil and skim for twenty minutes.

968. *Another way*.—Clarify the sugar, and put the fruit to it. Let it boil for twenty minutes; run off some of the jelly through a sieve, and keep the rest as jam for common tarts, &c.: if for sore throats, a little spermaceti may be added, or a little calf's-feet jelly.

969. *Gooseberry and cranberry jellies*.—Clarify an equal weight of sugar with that of the fruit. Boil the fruit for twenty minutes, and run the jelly through a sieve, allowing a little to remain to make a coarse jam, which may be seasoned with spices and used for dumplings and pies.—*Obs.* Where cranberries are gathered in this country, good country housewives put cinnamon to those they preserve for tarts. Cloves or mace would be more suitable.—See p. 392, and *Cranberry gruel*.

970. *Raspberry-jam*.—Take four parts of picked raspberries and one of red-currant juice, with equal weight of sugar. Put on half the sugar with a little water. Skim this and add the fruit. Boil for fifteen minutes, add the other half of the sugar, and boil for another five minutes, and when cold pot the jam. This and all other jams may be made with less sugar, if they are longer boiled; but both colour and quality will suffer in the process, and less boiling will serve if the sugar is previously high boiled.

971. *Strawberry-jam*.—Gather fine scarlet strawberries quite ripe. Bruise them, and put about a sixth part of red-currant juice to them. Take nearly an equal weight of sugar sifted, and strew it over them in the preserving-pan; boil quickly for fifteen minutes; pot, and cover with brandy papers.—See No. 994.

972. *Gooseberry and black currant jam*.—Take equal weight of pounded lump-sugar and picked fruit. Strew the sugar over the fruit in the preserving-pan and put a little water into it. Boil and skim. Lift a little of the juice and fruit when the fruit is boiled for about twelve minutes, and set it to cool on a plate. If the juice runs off, the jam must be boiled longer. If it jellies, though slightly, it is enough. *This is a test for all jellies.*—*Obs.* To get rid of some of the numerous

seeds of the hairy red gooseberry, take up the syrup as it boils with a gravy-spoon, and run it through a small sieve, and return it to the pan.

973. *Apricot and plum jam or marmalade.*—Stone and skin the fruit. Scald it with a little water in an earthenware or stone vessel. Rub it through a coarse sieve, or mash it in a bowl. Take equal weight of pulp and pounded loaf-sugar, and boil the jam for fifteen minutes in a preserving-pan, stirring and skimming it. The bruised kernels of the fruit, or a few bitter almonds blanched and bruised, may be put in to flavour the jam. *Peach, nectarine,* and *quince* jam, for puddings and tarts, may be made in the same manner.—*Obs.* Jams should be quickly boiled to retain a good colour, and care must be taken that the thicker sorts do not stick to the pan.

974. *Scotch orange-chip marmalade.*—Take equal weight of fine loaf-sugar and Seville oranges. Wipe and grate the oranges, but not too much. [The outer grate boiled up with sugar will make an excellent conserve for *rice, custard, or batter puddings.*] Cut the oranges the cross way, and squeeze out the juice through a small sieve. Scrape off the pulp from the inner skins, and pick out the seeds. Boil the skins till perfectly tender, changing the water to take off part of the bitter. When cool, scrape the coarse, white, and thready part from the skins, and trussing three or four skins together for despatch, cut them into narrow chips. Clarify the sugar, and put the chips, pulp, and juice to it. Add, when boiled for ten minutes, the juice and grate of two lemons to every dozen of oranges. Skim and boil for twenty minutes; pot, and cover when cold.—*Obs.* There are various ways of making this favourite marmalade. The half of the boiled skins may be pounded before they are mixed; and if the chips look too numerous, part of them may be withheld for pudding-seasoning. The orange-grate, if a strong flavour is wanted, may either be added in substance, or infused, and the tincture strained and added to the marmalade when boiling. Where marmalade is made in large quantities for exportation, the various articles are prepared and put at once into a thin syrup, and boiled for from four to six hours, and potted in large

jars. Orange-marmalade may be thinned with apple-jelly, or when used at breakfast or tea, it may be liquefied *extempore* with a little tea.

975. *Smooth orange-marmalade.*—This is made as above, only the skins, instead of being cut into chips, must be pounded in a mortar, and gradually mixed with the syrup,—withholding a part if the marmalade be in danger of becoming too thick.

976. *Transparent orange-marmalade.*—Use the juice and pulp of the fruit only. Wash the latter in a very little water, and strain this to the juice. Take a pound or rather more of refined sugar to the pint of juice, and boil it to the second degree. Put the juice to the syrup, and boil and skim well for twelve minutes. —*Obs.* Use the skins for candied orange-peel, No. 1000.

Lemon marmalade may be made as above, but is seldom seen.

977. *Apple marmalade.*—Pare and core the apples. Set them in a slow oven all night. Next day boil them, sweetened, and seasoned with lemon-peel, &c. according to your taste.

978. *Black butter for children, a cheap preserve.*— Pick currants, gooseberries, strawberries, or whatever fruit you have: to every two pounds of fruit put one of sugar, and boil till a good deal reduced.

979. *To preserve damsons for pies.*—Have equal to the weight of fruit of clarified sugar. Boil any of the broken damsons in this; and then add the whole quantity, and boil till it jellies. Pot the *compôte*, and tie paper over the pots. Keep them in a dry place.

980. *Another way.*—Put the fruit in Dutch stone jars, place the jars in boiling water up to their necks, and scald the fruit by this means for an hour. Next day fill up the jars with cold water, and cover them.

N.B.—We place small faith in this receipt, but it is often given.

981. *Cheap method of preserving fruit for puddings.* —Pare apples, pears, plums; or pick whatever sort of small fruit you have, and place it in a stone jar, with as much Lisbon or brown sugar as will sweeten it. Bake in a cool oven till done. It will eat with rice or with bread, make small pasties, &c.

982. *To preserve fruit without sugar, for pies, puddings, &c.*—Gather Morello cherries, greengages, currants in bunches, green gooseberries, &c. not over ripe, and pick them as soon and as gently as possible. All bruised ones must be laid aside. Drop them softly into wide-mouthed short-necked glass bottles, and shake the bottles gently that the fruit may lie compactly. Stop the bottles with good corks, and set them in a slow oven till the fruit begins to shrivel. Take them out of the oven, and in a little while make the corks firm, dip them in bottle-rosin, and keep till wanted.—*Obs.* We do not pledge ourselves for this receipt.

RECEIPTS FOR BEAUTIFUL PRESERVES AND COMPÔTES, FOR DESSERTS, &c. &c.

983. *Jargonelle pears.*—Take large, finely-shaped pears, and pare them very smoothly though thinly. Simmer them in a thin syrup, and let them lie in this syrup in a covered tureen or basin for a day or two. See that they are covered with the syrup. Drain off the syrup, and put more sugar to it. Clarify it, and simmer the pears in it till they look transparent. Take them up, and pour the syrup over them. About a fourth more sugar than the weight of the fruit is the requisite quantity in all.—*Obs.* The syrup may be seasoned with the juice of lemons. The pears may either be served dry by drying them in the sun, or in a slow oven when wanted; or served in the syrup, which is better and more economical, as the fruit that is not used can be potted up afresh. If the seeds of this and of all preserved fruits are picked out, which may be done by an opening at both ends that will allow an ivory bodkin to be introduced, they will keep much better. Large, finely-shaped pears of any kind done in this way, and *iced white*, as directed, No. 1005, look exceedingly well. Pears are preserved *red*, by putting a grain or two of pounded cochineal into the syrup, and pouring red gooseberry or currant jelly over them.—See *French Compôtes*, p. 329.

984. *Preserved apples, or, en compôtes.*—Clarify fine sugar, and boil nicely-pared and cored pippins in it, with a little lemon-juice and lemon-rind. Serve in a glass or china dish, with the syrup about them, and

garnish with bunches of preserved barberries, or sprigs of myrtle.—See p. 539.

985. *Red apples* served in jelly are made nearly as above. Pare and core the most beautiful pippins you can get, but leave the stalks. Throw them into a pan of water to keep the colour good; boil them in a very little water, and turn them. Mix cochineal with the water. When done, dish them heads downmost, and put sugar to the red water, with the rind of a lemon, and boil it till it jellies. Strain it, and when cold scoop it up neatly with a tea-spoon, and lay it among the apples in heaps, like *roughed* calf's-feet jelly. Garnish with sprigs of myrtle, rings of lemon-rind, &c. Isinglass may be added if the jelly is too weak.

986. *Oranges in sugar, a pretty little dish.*—Skin four or five oranges, carefully remove all the scurf and thready parts. Cut them in round slices, and dress them in a small glass dish in hot syrup. Garnish with sprigs of myrtle.

987. *To preserve apricots.*—Always choose the finest fruit for preserving. Stone and pare the apricots, keeping them as firm and entire as possible. Take above their own weight of pounded sugar, and strew it over them for a night, laying the slit part upmost to keep in the juices of the fruit. Break the stones, and blanch what are good of the kernels. Simmer the whole gently till the fruit looks transparent. Skim carefully, and lift out the fruit into pots, pour the syrup and kernels over them, and cover when cold;—*or* they may be preserved in apple-jelly; or *greened*, by putting a bit of alum, about the size of a large nutmeg, into the water in which they are alternately scalded and cooled, till they take the desired colour. *Peaches* and *greengages* may be preserved as above.—*Obs.* Sugar for preserved fruit must be boiled to the second or third degree. The fruit should be looked at for the first month, and, if needful, the syrup may be boiled up, allowed to cool, and again be put over them. If you put them into fresh syrup, and use the first for pies, apple-marmalade, &c. the fruit will be better preserved, and the loss nothing.

988. *Magnum bonum plums.*—Do them as directed for apricots, and be sure that the syrup is well clarified and well skimmed, and that the first simmering is slow and short, or else, instead of looking clear and plump,

the fruit will shrink and shrivel in spite of whatever may be afterwards done to plump it.—*Obs*. A bit of the stalk left is by some thought an improvement to the appearance of those preserved fruits.

989. *To preserve red gooseberries*.—Clip off the top of each berry, and take weight for weight of fruit and sugar. Clarify the sugar, and put the fruit to it, having made a slit with a needle in each berry, to let the sugar penetrate the fruit. Skim well, and when the skins look very transparent, take up the fruit with a sugar-skimmer into glasses or pots. Boil the syrup till it will jelly, (if the fruit were boiled so long it would become leathery,) strain it through a fine sieve, and pour it on the berries. This is a cheap and beautiful preserve, either served as a tart with a croquante cover, or in a glass dish. *Green Gascoignes* may be done in the same manner, first *greening* them, as directed for pickles, with alum and vine or cabbage leaves, though this at best is, we confess, a suspicious process. The seeds must be picked out of those green gooseberries with a needle, or they will not look nor keep nearly so well.

990. *To preserve cherries*.—Take a fourth more of sugar than of Morello cherries. Cut the stalks; take out the stones with a silver toothpick or bodkin as gently as possible; or, if this be too troublesome, prick the fruit with a needle. Clarify the sugar, and put to it a half-pint of red or white-currant jelly; and when this has boiled for five minutes, put in the cherries, and let them simmer till they look bright.

991. *Dried cherries*.—Take out the stones, and give the cherries a slow boil in a thin syrup. Let them remain in this for a day, and scald them again and again, making the syrup gradually richer. When they look bright and plump pot them up in the syrup; and when wanted, drain and dry them on a stove or wire sieve, or in a very cool oven. *Cherries, peaches, apricots, &c.* may be preserved in brandy with great ease. Prick them with a needle, and drop them into wide-mouthed bottles, with some fine sugar. Fill up with brandy, and cork and place the bottles in a hot-water bath or cool oven for some hours.

992. *Cherries en chemise, a very pretty little dish*. —Take the largest ripe cherries you can get. Cut off

the stalks with scissors, leaving about an inch to each cherry. Beat the white of an egg to a froth, and roll them in it one by one, and then roll them lightly in sifted sugar. Lay a sheet of paper on a sieve reversed, and laying them on this, set them on a stove till they are to be served.—*Obs.* The same may be done with bunches of currants, strawberries, hautboys, &c. Fruits *en chemise* look well and cost little.—See No. 707.

993. *Cucumbers, a beautiful preserve.*—Lay fine-shaped cucumbers in a weak pickle of salt and water for two days, and then for the same length of time in fresh water, changing it twice. *Green* them as directed for pickles, p. 264, and strew a bit of alum over them to assist the process. When alternately scalded and cooled till they look of a fine green, boil them for a few minutes in water with fresh leaves above and below them, and when cool, cut a bit out of the flat side, and scrape out the seeds and pulp. Dry the cucumbers gently in a cloth, and put into the inside a seasoning of bruised cloves, sliced ginger, thin lemon-rind, mace, and a few white peppercorns. Tie in the bit cut out with a piece of narrow tape. To every pound of fruit have clarified a pound of sugar, and when cold pour it over them. Press them down with a plate on which a weight is placed, that they may be covered; and when they have soaked two days, boil up the syrup, adding one-half more of clarified sugar to it. Repeat the soaking of the fruit, and boiling up of the syrup three times during a fortnight, and, last of all, add to it the juice and fine grate of two lemons for every six cucumbers, and boiling them in it for ten minutes, pot them up. They may be preserved by a more simple process, by cutting them in quarters, but look best when done whole and served in a glass dish, with a little syrup round them. A little pine-apple rum put to the syrup gives the flavour of West India sweetmeats. *Melons* are preserved in the above manner.—*Obs.* The great art in preserving is to avoid having the syrup too rich at first, which would infallibly shrivel the fruits, particularly if they be boiled in it, or have it poured hot over them.

994. *To preserve strawberries.*—Sprinkle sifted fine sugar, equal to half their own weight, over the finest fruit of the scarlet kind, not over ripe. When they

have lain in this for a night, take as much sugar again; or, in all, equal weight to the fruit, and with currant-juice make it into a thin syrup, and simmer the fruit in this till it will jelly. Serve either as an iced cream, or in a glass dish.

995. *To preserve carved oranges whole.*—Choose large well-shaped and well-coloured smooth oranges. Rub them hard with a towel; and then, with a sharp penknife, or the knife made for this purpose; carve the rind in deeply-indented leaves, or in groups of dancing-nymphs, &c. &c. according to your fancy (to do this well the thing must be seen.) Boil them thus carved, in plenty of spring water, and when quite soft take them up and drain them. Cut a piece out of the top with a sharp knife, and with a mustard-ladle scoop out all the pulp, seeds, and fibres. Boil them *filled* with and floated in clarified syrup for forty minutes. In four days repeat the boiling for twenty minutes. Do this four times. Last of all boil the syrup candy-high, adding more syrup, and keep the oranges well covered with it. If the colour fall, boil them up, and add fresh syrup.—*Obs.* Several pretty dishes are made with preserved oranges. They may be filled with rich custard, with calves'-feet jelly, or other jellies, or with a mixture of beat almonds, sugar, cream, and seasonings.—See *Oranges in sugar*, page 437.

TABLETS AND CONFECTIONARY DROPS.

A few receipts in this department may be useful in most families, as these things are cordial and sometimes even medicinal, and may be easily and very cheaply prepared at home.

996. *To make cinnamon, lemon, horehound, or ginger tablet.*—Take either oil of cinnamon, fine sifted China ginger, essence or grate of lemon pounded, in the proportion wanted for flavouring the article to be made. Two drops of oil of cinnamon, a half-ounce of ginger, or the grate of two lemons, is a medium quantity to a pound of sugar. Mix the flavouring ingredient very well with the boiling sugar, and pour it out when boiled candy-height, on a marble slab or stone previously rubbed with sweet oil. Mark the tablet quickly in small squares with a roller and knife. *Drops*

may be made with the same material, dropping it regularly on paper, and taking the drops off with a knife when firm. Any kind of *sugar-drops* may be made by using different flavouring ingredients to moisten the sugar; as for example, for *coffee-drops* use a little strong, clear tincture of the coffee-berry; for *clove-drops*, essence of cloves; for *peppermint-drops*, essence of peppermint.

997. *Fruit pastes.*—Oranges, apples, cherries, pears, raspberries, &c. may all be made into paste. Boil the pared fruit with clarified sugar to a thick marmalade. Season it, mould it into thin cakes. Dry these in a stove. The pastes must be small, but of any form or variety of forms; they may be ornamented by having the impress of some of the Wedgewood-ware seals, groups from the antique, pressed upon them while still moist.

998. *Ratafia-drops.*—Blanch and pound, with an ounce of fine sugar and a little water, four ounces of bitter and two ounces of sweet almonds. Add to the paste a pound of sugar, the whites of two eggs, and a little noyeau. Beat the whole well, and when light, drop the batter from a biscuit-funnel on paper, of the size of pigeons' eggs, and bake on tins.

999. *To make barley-sugar.*—Clarify, and boil sugar to the fourth degree, or *crackling* height, and when nearly boiled enough, add to it lemon-grate, a drop of citron-oil, or a little beat spermaceti, according to the sort of barley-sugar wanted. Rub a slab with oil, and when the sugar is ready, dip the pan in cold water for two minutes, and then pour it out on the slab. Cut the sugar into slips, and while hot twist it if you choose. Care must be taken in boiling sugar to this height, that it does not burn nor fly over; to prevent which, a small bit of butter may be thrown in to check the violent ebullition:—add a little lemon-juice if it be in danger of *graining*. This may be made as small lozenges or drops.

1000. *Candied orange and lemon-peel.*—Soak the peel of lemons or Seville oranges first in salt and water, and afterwards in fresh water, till their acrid taste is gone. Dry them, and boil them till tender in a thin syrup; afterwards in a stronger syrup boiled higher; next drain and dry them for use.

1001. *Rose soufflé cakes.*—Pick a handful of rose-leaves, and give them a boil in a syrup made of a pound of sugar. Have ready an icing made of two ounces of sugar, and the white of an egg well beat up and tinged with cochineal. Stir a spoonful of this into the syrup till it rises; fill the small moulds, and bake.—*Obs*. Confectioners use carmine or lake-powder for rose-coloured cakes, and so have rose soufflé cakes in full bloom all the year round.

1002. *To make devices and ornaments in sugar*.— Make a paste of the finest loaf-sugar and gum tragacanth steeped in rose-water, or any flavoured-water, and mould and colour the ornaments as best suits the purpose for which they are intended; as rose with cochineal; yellow with gamboge; green with spinage-juice.

1003. *Nougat in the French style*.—Blanch a half-pound of almonds and six bitter ones. When the peel is off cut them into dice. Dry them thoroughly before the fire or in an oven, but do not let them brown much. Put a half-pound of superfine sifted sugar, in a small preserving-pan over a very slow fire, without a drop of water. When it is melted throw in the dried almonds quite dry. Stir and turn out the paste as it will now be on a mould rubbed with oil or butter, or on a marble slab. It must be quickly worked or it will harden. It may be made in a variety of forms. If flat, press it quickly with an oiled rolling-pin, and cut it up in oblong slips. Cinnamon or small white nonpareil comfits may be strewed over the surface while hot.—N.B. *Nougat should be left to the confectioner*.

OBSERVATIONS ON CAKES.

Before beginning to make any sort of cake, have sugar beat and sifted; flour of good quality dry and sifted; the fruit stoned, or picked and washed, or rubbed in a towel; the lemon-peel pared, or beat to paste in a mortar, with a little cream; the butter, when this is used for light cakes, beaten cold to a cream; and, above all, have the eggs, yolks and whites, separately well beaten. A large tin basin answers best for this purpose, as the yolk or butter can in this be heated a little over the fire while the whisking is going on, which assists the process. It is a good test of beat eggs when they are so thick as to carry the drop that falls from the whisk. If the eggs are not properly managed at first, it is difficult to raise them to a cream afterwards. It ought to be remembered that eggs, besides enriching cakes, are intended to supply the place of yeast. When the several ingredients are well mixed, they ought immediately to be put into the oven, that the fruit may not sink: If, however, yeast is used, the cake must stand for some time to rise. Yeast should be sweet and thick. It may be improved by blanching it with water, allowing it to settle, and then pouring the water off. The thing next to be attended to is the state of the oven. It must not only be thoroughly heated previously, but have a quick heat when the cake is put in. Folds of paper ought to be put about cakes when put into the oven, lest the top get scorched. Plunging a large knife into the heart of a cake, and drawing it quickly out, is the best mode of judging whether it be ready. If not enough, the blade of the knife will be glary, and the cake must be instantly returned to the oven. The heat ought to be kept up throughout, by adding fresh fuel occasionally till the cake is drawn; but, above all, attention must be given till it is once properly raised. Cakes ought to be kept in a dry place, wrapped up and set in a close jar to keep them from hardening. They will keep thus a very long time. They may be heated on the hob or in a slack oven to refresh them, when used.

1004. *To ice and glaze pastry and cakes.*—This is done with the white of eggs and sugar; and in a common way is a very simple process. *Yolks* of eggs glaze cakes the most effectually, but sifting fine sugar over little cakes and biscuits before they are put into the oven, or when half-baked, will do them well enough.— See also p. 392.

1005. *To ice or frost a bride's-cake,* or *very large plum-cake.*—To a half-pound of fine sifted sugar put the whites of two eggs, beaten with a little orange-flower-water, or simple water, and strain. With this whisk the sugar for a long time, till it is quite smooth. This may be tinged with the juice of strawberries or currants, or with prepared cochineal. For a bride's-cake confectioners use lake or cochineal. Lay the icing equally on large cakes with a flat spoon. Brush small ones with a few feathers dipt in the mixture. Lemon-juice well beat with the sugar and white of eggs will make a white icing. No other *white* icing is admissible, yet vile ingredients are sometimes used.

1006. *A plain pound-cake.*—Beat a pound of cold butter to a cream, and put to it nine eggs well beat. Beat them together till well mixed and light; and put to them a little shred lemon-peel, or a few blanched almonds chopped, sugar, and a pound and a quarter of dried and sifted flour. Bake in a pan for an hour, in a rather quick oven; *or* two small cakes may be made of the same ingredients.—*Obs.* This may be made a *plain plum-cake*, by putting to it a half-pound of currants, a few raisins, and a half-pound of candied lemon and orange-peel, with nutmeg and cinnamon to taste. This may also be converted into a *fine seed-cake*, by adding caraway and coriander seeds to the plain cake.

1007. *A plain plum-cake.*—Use as much flour, butter, and sugar, as are ordered in the next receipt, but take only half the quantity of fruit, candied peel, and eggs. Season with cloves and nutmeg. Melt the butter in a half-pint of hot cream. Mix with the beat eggs three spoonfuls of good yeast. Put the whole together; and if the stuff be too thick, add a little sweet wine to it, or more cream. Pour it into a buttered pan, and let it rise before the fire before it is put into the oven, which should be strongly heated.

1008. *A very rich plum-cake.*—Take equal weight of currants and flour; about a pound of each will make a cake of good size; a pound and a half will make a large one. Beat twelve ounces of fresh butter to a cream. Beat also sixteen eggs to a cream with a whisk in a tin-pan, and set them over the fire with a pound of sifted sugar, whisking all the time. When warm take them off, and continue to beat till they are cold, when the butter must be well mixed with them; and then the currants, which should be previously picked, dried in a cloth, and rubbed in flour. Put to this a half-pound of candied citron, lemon and orange-peel cut in long bits, a half-ounce of bitter almonds beat to a paste with a little sugar, two ounces of sweet almonds blanched and cut the long way, half an ounce of pounded cinnamon and mace, and a little curaçoa, or any highly-flavoured liqueur, or plain brandy. Paper a hoop, and pour in the cake.*

1009. *Rice-cake.*—Mix half a pound of sifted rice-flour with a half-pound of loaf-sugar sifted, and put this to six eggs well whisked and strained. Season with a little ratafia and orange-flower-water, and a drop or two of essence of lemon, or some finely-grated rind of lemon. Beat the whole together for twenty minutes, and fire in a quick oven.—*Obs.* This is an excellent cake for a trifle, but it will not keep long. A small proportion of wheat-flour may be mixed with the rice-flour.

1010. *A fine seed-cake.*†—Take a pound and a half of flour, and sixteen eggs well whisked. Mix with them a pound and a half of fine beat sugar, and whisk them well together. Throw in a half-pound of cut candied citron, lemon, and orange peel, and four ounces of almonds blanched and cut. Mix this with a pound and a half of dried flour, and twelve ounces of butter beat to a cream. Season with cinnamon and cloves, and throw in a few caraway-seeds. Smooth the top of this (and every sort of cake) when put into the hoop, and throw sugared caraways over it.

1011. *A common seed-cake.*—Mix a half-pound of beat white sugar with two pounds of flour in a large bowl or pan. Make a hole in the centre, and pour into it a half-pint of lukewarm milk, and two spoonfuls of yeast. Mix a little of the surrounding flour with this, and throwing a cloth over the vessel, set it in a warm place for an hour or two. Add to this half a pound of melted butter, an ounce of caraway-seeds, a little all-spice, ginger, and nutmeg, and milk sufficient to make the whole of a proper stiffness. Butter a hoop, and pour in the mixture. Let it stand a half-hour at the mouth of the oven to rise, and then bake it.

1012. *Rice-cake for the centre of a table,—the French gateau de riz.*—Prepare the rice as for a casserole (see page 326), and for four ounces take a

---

* Sal volatile is sometimes used to make cakes rise, or more properly to prevent them from flattening, by keeping the batter, &c. from oiling.

† "When," says ancient Trusser, "the wheat-seed is put into the ground, the village is to be treated with *seed-cake*, pasties, and frumentie-pot."

quart of boiled cream, in which the peel of a lemon has been infused. Let them soak till the rice has absorbed all the cream, and is swelled. Sweeten this with fine sugar, and season with essence of lemon. When cool add the beat yolks of eight eggs, the whites well whisked by themselves, and also a good piece of butter. Then pour four ounces of melted butter into the mould, and turn it round and round till the cooling butter adheres in a coat to all sides of it. Next cover the mould with fine bread-crumbs; and this done, pour in the cake. Bake it for an hour in a moderate oven, turn it upside down on the dish, and garnish it with flowers, &c. &c.— *Obs.* If any of the material is left after filling the mould, roll it up in the shape of corks, dip them in butter, and fry as fritters. Dressed round fried parsley, they are called *croquets of rice.* A dozen sweet and a few bitter almonds may be put to this cake; and it may be made of vermicelli, or served as a pudding, with a custard-sauce.

1013. *Scotch diet-cake.*—Take a pound of fine sugar sifted, the same weight of eggs very well whisked, and mix and beat these together for twenty minutes. Season with lemon-grate and cinnamon. Stir in very smoothly three-quarters of a pound of sifted flour. This is a very light cake, and will bake quickly. It may either be iced, or have sifted sugar strewed over it before baking.

1014. *Scotch short-bread.*—To the fourth of a peck of flour, take six ounces of sifted sugar and of candied citron and orange peel, and blanched almonds, two ounces each. Cut these in rather large slices, and mix them with the flour. Rub down among the flour a pound of butter in very minute bits, and melt a half-pound more, and with this work up the flour, &c. The less kneading it gets the more *short* and crisp the cakes will be. Roll out the paste into a large well-shaped oval cake, about an inch and a half thick, and divide this the narrow way, so as to have two cakes somewhat the shape of a Gothic arch. Pinch the cakes neatly at the edges, and mark them on the top with the instrument used for the purpose, or with a fork. Strew caraway-comfits over the top, and a few strips of citron peel. Bake on paper rubbed with flour. The cakes may be squares, or oblong figures.—*Obs.* Plainer short-bread may be made by using less butter and no candied peel. The whole of the butter may be melted, which makes the process easier. Chopped almonds are used in larger quantity for very rich short-bread.

1015. *Savoy or sponge biscuit*.—Whisk twelve eggs till white and thick, and mix with them a pound of sifted sugar. Beat these very well together, and then gradually mix in a half-pound of flour, a seasoning of essence of lemon, or lemon-grate, and a little orange-flower-water. Butter a melon or Turk's-cap mould, and fill it within two inches of the top. Bake for three-quarters of an hour, and when ready, take out the cake, shaking the mould to loosen it. *Sponge-biscuits* of the same material are baked in small tin shapes, and iced or glazed with sifted sugar.—*Obs*. These light cakes, or the remains of them, are well suited to puddings or trifles.

1016. *Macaroons.**—Blanch and pound with the whites of four eggs a pound of Jordan almonds. Add to this two pounds of fine sugar, and pound these ingredients to a paste; then put in eight more whites of eggs. Beat the whole well together; fill a biscuit-syringe, and squirt the macaroons on wafer-paper, and fire them slowly on tins. *Ratafia-cakes* may be made as above, by using one half bitter almonds. Drop the biscuit from a knife, instead of a squirt, if you have no squirt. Rice-flour is sometimes substituted for part of the almonds.

1017. *Plain gingerbread*.—Mix with a pound and a half of flour four ounces of butter, four of brown sugar, a half-ounce of ground ginger, and some allspice. Make this into a paste with two ounces of hot treacle, and shape and bake the cakes.

1018. *Fine gingerbread*.—Two pounds of flour, a half-pound of brown sugar, a half-pound of candied orange-peel cut into bits, an ounce of ground ginger, half an ounce of caraway-seeds, cloves, mace, and some allspice. Mix with these a pound and a half of treacle, and a half-pound of melted butter. Mix the ingredients

---

* An endless variety of small biscuit is made in the manner of macaroons, as light lemon-biscuit, by using grated peel and the yolks of three eggs, chocolate biscuit, orange and common biscuit, judges' biscuit, *i.e.* biscuit for hungry lawyers, &c. &c.

well together, and let them stand for some hours before rolling out the cakes. The paste will require a little additional flour in rolling out. Cut out the cakes, mark the top in diamonds with a knife, and bake them on tin plates.

1019. *Gingerbread or spice-nuts* may be made out of the above paste, but a little more of the ginger and other spices should be employed, and a little more flour. Drop from a spoon and bake on paper.—*Cayenne* rather improves gingerbread.—P. T.

1020. *Wine biscuit.*—Have a pound of the finest flour, "thrice-bolted," dry and sifted. Rub down among it three ounces of butter; add sugar, and salt to taste. Make a dough of this with warm good milk, and a spoonful of yeast. Knead it quickly up, and let it repose an hour. Roll out, and stamp and prick the biscuits with a dabber. Bake in a quick oven.

1021. *Imitation of Leman's* biscuit.*—To the above dough put a bit of volatile salt. Roll out, and mould in the form of Leman's biscuit in square and oblong figures, and balls flattened. Prick and fire them lightly.

SMALL TEA-CAKES.†

1022. *Good tea-cakes.*—Rub four ounces of butter

---

* While the house of the great Leman flourishes in London, and that of the not less famous Littlejohn in Edinburgh, we would say *buy* biscuits and *rusks*, and you will be sure to have the best.—W. W.

† The greatest difficulty we have experienced in correcting the various editions of this immortal work has been in restraining the headlong torrent of our extensive culinary knowledge within reasonable bounds—what to tell, and what to suppress,—not when to begin, but where to have done prescribing, is our stumbling-block. We confess a strong natural leaning to the side of plenty—nay, of abundance—and of good-nature. If the solitary gourmand have his *salmi*, his *rogons*, his "*soupe à la Camerani*," who would deny to the spinster her cordial waters, and the petticoat-tails that grace her tea-table; or to the schoolboy his mince-pie and "hot cross-bun." Besides, at our *table d'hote* every variety of guest expects to find what will suit both his palate, his purse, and his humour. "We always," says the chief of Modern Reviewers, "fancied the description of Harriet Byron's wedding-clothes (in Sir Charles Grandison) superfluous, till we found that two young ladies of our acquaintance had copied out the whole passage for their private entertainment." We quote from memory, but this is the idea,—and this must be our apology for the superfluous variety of our *puddings, cakes, liqueurs,* and even *sauces*,—the half of the number here noticed cannot be used in any single family, yet, for the many families into whose hands our work may fall, it is requisite that they should all be known.—P. T.

into eight ounces of flour, and mix with this six ounces of cleaned currants, the same of beat sugar, and three beat eggs. Make this into a paste, and roll it out about a half-inch thick, and stamp out the cakes of any size you please with an inverted wine-glass, ale-glass, or small tumbler, by running a paste-cutter round the glass. Dust the top with sugar, in which, for all these small cakes, a few finely chopped almonds may be mixed.

1023. *Tunbridge-cakes.*—Make them as above, of any size you please, and strew caraway-comfits over.

1024. *Shrewsbury cakes.*—Beat half a pound of cold butter to a cream, and mix with it six ounces of sifted sugar, eight ounces of flour, a few caraway-seeds, and some pounded cinnamon, two eggs beat, and a little rose-water. Roll out the paste a quarter of an inch in thickness, adding a little more flour if necessary, and stamp out the cakes of any shape or size that is liked.

1025. *Bath cakes and buns.*—Roll half a pound of butter into a pound of flour, and add four beat eggs and a glassful of yeast. Set this before the fire to rise; then add four ounces of sifted sugar, and a few caraway-seeds. Roll the paste into thin sheets, and stamp them out. Bake them on tins. They should rise very light. —*Obs.* This is made into BATH-BUNS by moulding the paste in the shape of buns, and strewing a few sugar-caraways over the tops. These Bath-buns are almost the same preparation as the *Brioche* cakes so much eaten and talked of in Paris.—See page 455.

1026. *Scotch petticoat-tails.*—Mix a half-ounce of caraway-seeds with the fourth of a peck of flour. Make a hole in the middle of the flour, and pour into it twelve ounces of butter melted in a quarter-pint of milk, and three ounces of beat sugar. Knead this, but not too much, or it will become tough; divide it in two, and roll it out round rather thin. Cut out the cake by running a paste-cutter round a dinner-plate, or any large round plate. Cut a cake from the centre of this one with a small saucer or large tumbler. Keep this inner circle whole, but cut the outer one into eight *petticoat-tails*. Bake all these on paper laid on tins, serve the round cake in the middle of the plate, and the *petticoat-tails* as *radii* round it.

1027. *Queen's cakes.*—Make these as pound-cake or plum-cake; but bake in small saucers, or in the fluted tins made for the purpose.

1028. *Cinnamon-cakes.*—Whisk six eggs with a glass of rose-water; add a pound of sifted sugar and a quarter-ounce of ground cinnamon, with flour enough to make a paste. Roll this out, and stamp it into small cakes. Bake them on paper. They may be iced, or have sifted sugar strewed over them.

1029. *Sugar tea-cakes.*—Make a paste with a pound of flour, twelve ounces of sifted sugar; the yolks of two eggs, a little nutmeg or cinnamon, and a glass of orange-flower-water. Roll it out thin, cut with a stamp or glass inverted, strew sugar over the cakes, and bake.

1030. *Derby short-cakes.*—Rub down a pound of butter into two pounds of flour, and mix with this a half-pound of beat sugar, an egg, and as much milk as will make a paste. Roll this out thin, and cut out the cakes in any form. Bake on tin plates for about ten minutes. They may be iced, or have sifted sugar strewed over them.

1031. *Kent drop-cakes.*—A pound of flour, a half-pound of butter, the same of sifted sugar and currants. Make this into a paste with two eggs, two spoonfuls of orange-flower-water, a glass of brandy, and one of sweet wine. Mix up quickly, and drop the batter through a biscuit-funnel on floured tins, and bake for five or six minutes.

1032. *Rout-cakes.*—To the beat yolks of twelve eggs put a half-pound of butter to beat to a cream, half a pound of sifted sugar, the fresh grate of a lemon, and twelve ounces of flour dried. Season this with a little orange-flower-water, or a few pounded almonds. When very well mixed, pour the cake into a paper-mould. Let it be scarcely an inch thick; bake it, and when cool ice it, and cut it with a sharp knife and ruler into squares, lozenges, diamonds, &c. Moisten the edges of these morsels with sugar, and crisp them before the fire.

1033. *Common buns.*—Mix two pounds of flour and one of beat sugar. Make a hole in the middle of the flour, and put in a glassful of thick yeast, and half a pint of warmed milk. Make a thin batter of the surrounding flour and the milk, and set the dish covered before the fire till the leaven begins to ferment. Then put to the mass a half-pound of melted butter, and milk enough to make a soft paste of all the flour. Cover this with a dust of flour, and let it once more rise for half an hour. Then shape the dough into buns, and lay them apart on buttered tin plates in rows to rise for a half-hour. Bake in a quick oven.

1034. *Cross-buns* are made of the same sort of dough, with the addition of a little more sugar, and a seasoning of cinnamon, allspice, and mace. They must, when moulded, have the figure of the cross impressed on them with a stamp. *Seed-buns* are also made as above, with the addition of caraway-seeds. They may be baked in pans, and glazed.

1035. *Plum-buns.*—Mix with the dough of common cross-buns, currants, candied orange-peel, blanched almonds chopped, and a seasoning of cinnamon and mace. Mark them round the edge when moulded, and bake as common buns.

1036. *A Scotch Christmas bun, from Mrs. Fraser's Cookery.*—Take half a peck of flour, keeping out a little to work it up with; make a hole in the middle of the flour, and break in sixteen ounces of butter; pour in a mutchkin (pint) of warm water, and three gills of yeast, and work it up into a smooth dough. If it is not wet enough, put in a little more warm water; then cut off one-third of the dough, and lay it aside for the cover. Take three pounds of stoned raisins, three pounds of cleaned currants, half a pound of blanched-almonds cut long ways; candied orange and citron peel cut, of each eight ounces; half an ounce of cloves, an ounce of cinnamon, and two ounces of ginger, all beat and sifted. Mix the spices by themselves, then spread out the dough; lay the fruit upon it; strew the spices over the fruit, and mix altogether. When it is well kneaded, roll out the cover, and lay the bun upon it; then cover it neatly, cut it round the sides, prickle it, and bind it with paper to keep it in shape; set it in a pretty quick oven, and, just before you take it out, glaze the top with a beat egg.★

★ Every country-town, village, and rural neighbourhood in England, Scotland, and Ireland, has its favourite holiday-cake, or currant loaf, under some such name as "Lady Bountiful's loaf," "Mrs. Notable's cake," "Miss Thrifty's bun," &c. &c. We do not pretend to give

1037. WAFERS.

THERE are *wine, butter, cream, brandy, Flemish, Spanish,* and *almond* wafers. The latter is the sort commonly made. Mix in equal quantities dry flour and sifted sugar. To every six spoonfuls of this which you mean to use, allow three eggs. Beat the mass, and flavour it with lemon, orange-flower-water, or mace. Put a very little fresh yeast to it if you have it, and moisten it down to a thickish batter with good cream. Work the ingredients well, and let the whole settle a while. When wanted, rub the irons for making wafers with fat bacon, or with fine wax. A tea-spoonful of the batter will make one wafer. Turn the iron round as it bakes over a brisk fire. While hot roll them round a wooden short roller; when cold, sprinkle them with sugar, and serve. *Brandy scrolls* the same, but season as No. 1019.

HOUSEHOLD BREAD, &c.

1038. *Common wheaten bread, nearly on Cobbett's plan.* —Put a bushel of flour into a trough. Make a deep hole in the middle of the heap, and take for a bushel of flour a pint of good yeast, and stir it well up with as much milk-warm water. Pour this into the hole made in the flour; then take a spoon, and work it round the edges of this body of moisture, so as to bring into it by degrees flour enough to make a thin batter, which must be well stirred for a minute or two. Throw a handful of flour over the surface of this batter, and cover the whole with the folds of a cloth to keep it warm. Set it by the fire, regulating the distance by the state of the weather and season of the year. When the batter has risen enough to make cracks in the flour form the whole mass into dough thus:—Begin by strewing six ounces of salt over the heap; and then beginning round the hole containing the batter, work the flour into the batter, pouring in milk-warm soft water or milk as it is wanted. When the whole mass is moistened, knead it well, that the fermented paste may be duly mixed with the whole mass.

---

receipts for all these—the formula is endless—and they are all good.— The receipt, *Brade breachd,* page 454, is nearly the substance of all of them. That they be well raised and well fired is all besides of any importance. They should be baked in a dome-shaped fluted mould or Turk's-cap, but look still more *imposing* at holiday times, formed like large respectable household loaves.

Mould the loaves; let them rise for twenty minutes, and put them into the oven, which should be previously heated. The loaves will require a length of time to fire proportioned to their size. To boil the water in bran is a saving of flour. Stale bread may be refreshed by placing it for an hour in a cool oven.

1039. *To bake breakfast rolls*.—To two pounds of flour put a spoonful of salt, a quarter-pint or less of fresh yeast, and as much warmed milk and water as will make a batter. Stir this well till it is smooth, and let it stand covered before the fire to rise for two hours, if you have time to wait so long. Add as much more flour into which you should have rubbed down what butter you mean to put to the rolls. Work the dough, divide it, and mould the rolls; fire them on tins, and rasp, and keep them covered to keep soft.

1040. *Manheim rolls,—a French receipt*.—Break two raw eggs among six ounces of flour, with two ounces of sifted sugar. Mix this to a paste, and add half an ounce of anise-seeds in powder. If the paste be too wet, put in more flour. Make this kneaded paste level, and cut it into rolls about twelve inches long and two broad. Bake them on a buttered tin, and glaze with the yolk of an egg. Cut them when done into very small cakes.

1041. *Muffins*.—A pint of hot milk, a quarter pint or rather less of fresh small beer yeast. Stir in flour to make this a batter. Let it repose covered in a warm place to rise. Add a little more milk, two ounces of butter, rubbed in flour, in very small bits, and add flour enough to make a dough. Mix, cover, and let it repose a half-hour; then knead, break and mould the dough into muffins. Let them repose once more after this operation for a quarter of an hour, and then bake them.

N.B. These at a pinch may be baked on the Scotch *girdle*, or in a thick-bottomed frying-pan, or the cottage-oven pot.

1042. *Brown bread* is made as 1038, with coarse flour, or a proportion of sheelings added to flour.

1043. *French bread*.—All sorts of fine bread baked with milk, eggs, and butter, receive this name. To a half-peck of the finest flour put a quart of lukewarm milk, a little salt, a quarter-pound of melted butter, and a half-pint of bleached yeast; whisk the fluids together, and add two or three beat eggs; mix the flour with this, handling it as little as possible; let the dough rise, and mould the bread into rolls, cakes, &c. Bake on tins in a quick oven, and rasp the loaves.

1044. *Sally Lunn cakes.*—Make them as French bread, but dissolve some sugar in the hot milk. Mould into the form of cakes. A little saffron boiled in the milk enriches the colour of these or any other cakes.

1045. *Yorkshire cakes* are made as above, only moulded smaller.

1046. *Irish Brade breachd.**—To as much flour as

---

* This Irish word signifies spotted or freckled. This mottled loaf is the holiday-cake of Munster.

NOTE.—*Brioche paste.*—Every one who has had the happiness of seeing Paris, has, of course, paid for it in many ways besides by being deafened with shrill cries of "*Brioches.*" "*Gateaux de Nanterre,*" &c. The *brioche paste* is notwithstanding the first-rate article of its kind in Europe when properly prepared, and by a variation in the shapes of the *Gateaux* and a few additions, it may be produced in fifty forms of cakes. It is made (in the best way) in the following manner and proportions:— Have four pounds of dry fine flour, take one-fourth of this to make the *leaven* in this manner; make a hole in the centre of the pound of flour, into this pour a small wine-glassful of sweet yeast, and over this as much hot water as will make up a rather thick leaven. Set this covered before the fire, making a few transverse incisions in the surface. Give it fifteen or twenty minutes to rise. Then *leaven* the remaining flour thus:— Throw a little beat salt, and some sugar, both melted in water, over the flour. Make a hole in the middle of it. Crumble down two pounds of butter, and break a dozen eggs into it. Knead it up quickly, once and again till well mixed, and pour the *leaven* equally over it. Divide it into pieces, which knead and toss about, changing their place continually to blend the whole materials equally and well. Next beat up the whole together, and keep the *brioche paste* in a medium temperature (according to the state of the weather) rolled up in a cloth, dusted with flour, and spread over any earthen-ware or other deep vessel. Next day (for it works the better for lying a night over) break and mould the paste into any form you please, large or small. By the addition of currants or sugar, you have sugar-loaves and *Gateaux de Nanterre.* Add currants and fine stoned raisins, and you have the *Gateaux de Compeigne.* Tinge the paste with saffron diluted in water, and add a glass of Madeira or sweet wine, and by moulding in proper shapes you have *Babas.* The moulds should be buttered; and care must be taken that the *babas* are not scorched a-top as the colour is of consequence. A still better preparation is *Brioche au Fromage,* made by strewing well-flavoured Swiss, Italian, or English cheese in dice into the paste before baking it. The *brioche* cakes are generally made with a head and sole or flat part like our buns. These are separately shaped in the hand and then stuck together; a smaller top or button of the paste is clapped on above all, and the top a little dinted in. The cakes are brushed with eggs beaten, and baked in a quick oven. If large, *brioche* cakes, like all cakes, require a steady, but not quick heat, else they will scorch before getting baked to the heart.— By H. J. *Ecuyer tranchant* to the CLEIKUM CLUB.

will make two quartern-loaves put a half-pound of melted butter. Make the dough with fresh yeast, and when it has risen, mix in a half-pound of beat sugar, a half-pound of currants, picked, cleaned, and dried; the same quantity of stoned raisins; a few sweet almonds blanched and chopped, and some candied orange-peel sliced. Mould and bake the loaves. They may be of any size.

1047. *Yeast.*—There are many ways of preparing yeast, but no yeast is to be compared with that made of fresh worts. Yeast is made of the flour of pease, rye, potatoes, and wheat, mixed with sugar and water, and afterwards fermented with good fresh yeast. Bad yeast may be improved by mixing in it flour and sugar, with a little warm water, or by bleaching it; that is, beating up the yeast with water equal in quantity to itself, and the white of an egg to each quart of yeast. In twelve hours pour off the thin. What remains will be an improved yeast. Strain all yeast put to flour.

1048. *Russian yeast,—the best substitute that we know.* —Make a thick wort of ground rye or malt, and for a gallon of this take three ounces or more of leaven, and dissolve it in a little of the wort. Mix the whole, and add a half-pound of ground malt; shake the mixture for some time, and in half an hour add two large spoonfuls of good yeast; cover for forty-eight hours, and the whole will be good yeast.

1049. *Another substitute.*—To a pound of good mashed potatoes, of the mealy kind, put two ounces of brown sugar. Pulp the potatoes through a colander, and mix them with hot water; add two or three spoonfuls of good yeast. This is not so strong as beer-yeast, but it does for household-bread by using more of it. In the country, this substitute, as it is easily obtained, will be found particularly convenient.

1050. *Camp yeast.*—Make a thin gruel of a gallon of spring water, with flour of rye, wheat, or pease; boil it, stirring it well for twenty minutes. Add to this a half-pound of raw sugar, and when as cool as new milk, put a quarter-pint of fresh yeast to this, and let it ferment, covered before the fire, or in a warm place. Pour off this part. Keep bottled a few spoonfuls of this to ferment the next quantity wanted. A quarter pint will do for four quartern-loaves.

PART FOURTH

CHAPTER I.

O, Girzy, Girzy, when thou go'st to brew,
Consider well what you're about to do;
Be very wise, very sedately think
That what you're going now to make is drink:
Consider who must drink that drink, and then
What 'tis to have the praise of honest men.

LIQUEURS, CORDIALS, HOME-MADE WINES, BEERS, AND
MISCELLANEOUS RECEIPTS.

THE best basis of all liqueurs is pure rectified spirit, or uncoloured proof brandy or whisky,—provided the latter have no smoky or *peat-reek* flavour. Some fine liqueurs require to be distilled; but, as this is a troublesome process, they are generally made in small families, by infusion, which succeeds very well. *The syrup employed must be clarified as for preserves.* Sometimes capillaire-syrup is used, but this, in most cases, is an unnecessary expense.

1051. *Curaçoa.*—Infuse three drachms of sweet oil of orange-peel with a pint of rectified spirits and a pound of clarified syrup. *Another way.*—Infuse five ounces of the dry peel of bitter oranges, beat to a paste with a little sugar, in a quart of pure spirit and a pound of clarified sugar. Let the mixture stand for a week in a warm place, and strain it off, first through a jelly-bag, and then patiently through filtering-paper.

N.B.—This is the mode of clearing all liqueurs and cordials, when straining is not sufficient to clear them.

1052. *Noyau.*—To a quart of pure brandy, or aquavitæ, put six ounces of clarified syrup, one ounce of French prunes, with the kernels broken, two ounces of sound peach, nectarine, or, what is better, apricot kernels bruised; a few grains of celery-seed, and a *flavour* of essence of lemon or bitter orange. Infuse for ten days or more, and filter, adding a half-pint of water.

1053. *Scotch Noyau, a very pleasant compound.*— Two quarts of proof-spirit, a pint and a half of water, a pound and a half of clarified syrup, six ounces of sweet and four of bitter almonds, blanched and chopped. Infuse for a fortnight, shaking the compound occasionally, and filter. Lemon-juice may be added.

1054. *Strong cinnamon cordial.*—Pour about sixpence worth of oil of cinnamon on a few knobs of sugar, and rub them well together. Mix this with two quarts of spirits and a pound of hot clarified syrup. Shake well, and let this infuse for a few days, and then filter it for use. Water may be added at pleasure to reduce the strength.—*Obs.* This may be made of cinnamon in substance. Use for this quantity about the eighth of an ounce, and the rind of a quarter of a lemon. This and other compounds may be coloured with burnt sugar; but if well filtered, they look better colourless and bright.

1055. *Citron cordial, a high-flavoured and excellent compound.*—Take yellow rinds of citrons, six ounces; of orange-peel, four ounces; a nutmeg bruised, and a pint and a half of clarified syrup. Mix with two quarts of spirits for ten days, keeping the vessel in a warm place. Filter as directed No. 1051.

1056. *Clove cordial.*—Take of bruised cloves and cassia-buds, a quarter of an ounce each, and a dozen Jamaica peppercorns. Infuse the spices in hot water, and keep the bottle by the fire, close stopped, for a night or two. Strain this to three pints of proof-spirit, and add syrup to taste. Filter, and colour with burnt sugar, or a bit of cochineal. Mace or nutmeg, bruised, may be added to Clove cordial. It is grateful and tonic.

1057. *Barbadoes water.*—To two quarts of proof-spirit add syrup to taste, two ounces of fresh orange-peel, four of lemon-peel, and a few bruised cloves. Infuse for ten days and filter.

1058. *Crême d'Orange, a delicious cordial.*—Over a dozen oranges, sliced, pour three quarts of rectified spirit, and a pint of orange-flower-water. Close the vessel carefully; and in ten days add five pounds of clarified syrup, a quart of water, and a half-ounce of tincture of saffron; close the vessel again, and in a fortnight strain off the liquor through a jelly-bag; when it has settled, pour it from the lees and bottle it.—*Obs.* The lees of liqueurs make an excellent addition to those puddings and cakes for which spirits are ordered.

1059. *Crême d'Absinthe, by M. Beauvilliers' receipt.* —Take in the proportions of twelve pints (old measure) of French brandy and two of water; a small handful of fresh wormwood, or a large half-ounce of the dried herb, a quarter-ounce of cinnamon, and a drachm of mace. Infuse for some days, and, if convenient, distil the compound. If not, infuse in a warm place for a fortnight, strain the liquor, and add a pound of sugar made into clear syrup, with five pints of water.—*Obs.* This *liqueur*, or a glass of Madeira or of rum, forms the *coup-de-milieu* at a *knowing* French dinner; and by its stimulating bitter enables the gourmand to renew the flagging contest.

1060. *Common ratafia.*—Take an ounce of bruised nutmegs, a half-pound of bitter almonds, blanched and chopped, and a grain of ambergris, well rubbed with sugar in a mortar; infuse in two quarts of proof-spirit for two weeks, and filter.

1061. *Red ratafia.*—Six pounds of the black-heart cherry, one of small black cherries or geens, and two of raspberries and strawberries. Bruise the fruit, and when it has stood some time, drain off the juice, and to every pint add four ounces of the best refined sugar, or of syrup, and a quart of the best brandy. Strain through a jelly-bag, and flavour to taste with a half-ounce of cinnamon and a drachm of cloves, bruised and infused in brandy for a fortnight before, or with cloves alone.

1062. *Cherry brandy or whisky.*—Pick morello, or black cherries, from the stalks, and drop them into bottles, till the bottles are three-quarters full; fill up with brandy or whisky. In three weeks strain off the spirits, and season with cinnamon and clove mixture, as in last receipt, adding syrup to taste. Ratafia should not be sweet. A second weaker decoction may be obtained by pouring more spirits on the fruit.

1063. *Black-cherry brandy.*—Put, to three quarts of brandy, four pounds of stoned black cherries;—bruise the stones, and add them to the mixture. Infuse for a month;—filter, and add the flavouring ingredients and syrup, as directed above. A second infusion may be made, which will require more seasoning than that first drawn.—*Obs. Perfumes* are out of place in compounds of this kind. The blossoms of the sloe, infused for six weeks, makes a sort of ratafia.

1064. *Raspberry brandy* is made precisely as above, and, if strong of the fruit, is best without any other flavouring ingredient.

1065. *Usquebaugh, the Irish cordial.*—To two quarts of the best brandy, or whisky without a smoky taste, put a pound of stoned raisins, a half-ounce of nutmegs, a quarter-ounce of cloves, the same quantity of cardamoms, all bruised in a mortar; the rind of a Seville orange, rubbed off on lumps of sugar, a little tincture of saffron, and a half-pound of brown candy-sugar. Shake the infusion every day for a fortnight, and filter it for use.—*Obs.* Not a drop of water must be put to Irish cordial. It is sometimes tinged of a fine green with the juice of spinage, instead of the saffron tint, from which it takes the name (as we conjecture) of usquebeæ or *yellow-water.*

1066. *L'Eau de la Vie.**—This liqueur is very pleasant, and in quality so similar to verder or milk punch, Norfolk punch, lemon brandy, &c. that it is almost unnecessary to give any other receipt for these compounds than the rhyming one subjoined.

---

* *L'Eau de la Vie.*—The following rhyming receipt for compounding this pleasant liqueur is communicated by a lady, who has contributed to this volume many useful and some rare receipts:—

"Grown old, and grown stupid, you just think me fit
To transcribe from my grandmother's book a receipt;
And comfort it is for a wight in distress,
To be still of some use:—he could scarce be of less.
Were greater his talents, fair Anne might command
His head—if more worth than his heart or his hand.
Your mandates obeying, he sends with much glee,
The genuine receipt to make *l'Eau de la Vie.*
Take seven large oranges, and pare them as thin
As a wafer, or, what is much thinner, your skin:
Six ounces of sugar next take, and bear mind,
That the sugar be of the best double-refined.
Clear the sugar in near half a pint of spring-water,
In the neat silver sauce-pan you bought for your daughter.

1067. *Glasgow   punch.—(From   Peter's   Letters.)*
"The sugar being melted with a little cold water, the
artist squeezed about a dozen lemons through a wooden
strainer, and then poured in water enough almost to fill
the bowl. In this state the liquor goes by the name of
sherbet, and a few of the connoisseurs in his immediate
neighbourhood were requested to give their opinion of it
—for in the mixing of the sherbet lies, according to the
Glasgow creed, at least one-half of the whole battle. This
being approved by an audible smack of the lips of the
umpires, the rum was added to the beverage, I suppose,
in something about the proportion of one to seven. Last
of all, the maker cut a few limes, and running each
section rapidly round the rim of his bowl, squeezed in
enough of this more delicate acid to flavour the whole
composition. In this consists the true *tour-de-maître* of
the punch-maker."—See *Regent's punch*, No. 1076.

Glasgow punch is made of the coldest spring water
newly taken from the spring. The acid ingredients
above mentioned will suffice for a very large bowl.

1068. *Punch à la Romaine.—*Make a good lemon
ice, as for a dessert, (or take any left.) To one quart of
ice put the whites of three eggs, well beaten, and rum
and brandy till the ice liquefies. The proportions three-
parts rum to one of brandy, the strength to taste. To
this put a cup of strong green tea, and a little champagne.
—See p. 418.

1069. *Bishop hot or iced.—*The day before the liqueur
is wanted, grill on a wire-grill, over a clear slow fire, three

---

Then the fourth of a pint, you must fully allow,
Of new milk, made as warm as it comes from the cow.
Put the rinds of the lemons, the milk, and the syrup,
In a jar, with the rum, and give them a stir up.
A full quart of old rum (French brandy is better,
But we ne'er in receipts, should stick close to the letter;)
And then, to your taste, you may add some perfume,
Goa-stone, or whatever you like in its room.
Let it stand thus ten days, but remember to shake it;
And the closer you stop it, the richer you make it.
Then filter through paper, 'twill sparkle and rise,
Be as soft as your lips, and as bright as your eyes.
Last, bottle it up, and, believe me, the Vicar
Of E——— himself never drank better liquor.
In a word, it excels, by a million of odds,
The nectar your sister presents to the gods!"

smooth-skinned large bitter oranges. Grill them of a pale brown. They may be done in an oven, or under a furnace. Place them in a small punch-bowl, that will about hold them, and pour over them a full half-pint from a bottle of old Bourdeaux wine, in which a pound and a quarter of loaf sugar is dissolved. Cover with a plate. When it is to be served next day, (though it may lie over two or three days,) cut and squeeze the oranges into a small sieve placed above a jug, containing the remainder of the bottle of wine previously made very hot. Add more syrup if it is wanted. Serve hot in large glasses; or in summer it may be iced. Bishop is often made of Madeira in England, and is perfumed with nutmegs, bruised cloves, and mace. It ought, however, to be made of old generous Bourdeaux wine, or it fails of its purpose as a tonic liqueur. It is reckoned highly stomachic, and is served at French dinners, *savans et recherchés*, either as the *coup-d'apres*, or after the dessert.—See *Absinthe* No. 1059.

1070. *Norfolk punch.*—Pare thirty-two dozen Seville oranges, and the same number of lemons. Infuse the peel for two days in a large bottle or jar, with a gallon of brandy, (or flavourless whisky,) a little reduced in strength. Clarify in a gallon of water, four pounds of sugar. When cold strain the brandy (which will now be a tincture) to this. Add the juice of the oranges and lemons to this, previously strained and bottled, when the peel is taken off. Cask the liqueur, or put it in a jar. Stop it well. In six weeks it may be gently poured, or drawn off and bottled. A tincture of bruised nutmegs and cloves may be added to this compound.

1071. *Milk punch.*—Rub off on lumps of sugar the zest of a dozen lemons. Pare off what you do take off on the sugar, but take none of the white. Infuse in two quarts of brandy reduced. Strain off in two days, and add of clarified syrup two pounds, and of water two quarts, with a half pint of hot new milk. Strain through a jelly-bag, and keep in a close-stopt jar, or small cask, till it fine, which will be in six weeks or less.—*Obs.* This cordial is rather getting into desuetude. It may be made *extempore* by adding a little hot milk to lemonade, and straining through a thick jelly-bag.

1072. *To mull wine.*—Boil the spiceries (cinnamon,

nutmeg grated, cloves, and mace,) in any quantity approved, in a quarter-pint or better of water; put to this a full pint of port, with sugar to taste. Mix it well. Serve hot with toasts or rusks.—*Obs*. The yolks of eggs were formerly mixed with mulled wine, as in making custard or egg-caudle, and many flavouring ingredients were employed which are now discarded.* Lemon or orange juice may be added, and the water may be strained off from the spices. Ale or porter may be mulled as above.

1073. *Wine-whey.*—Boil, in a small sauce-pan a half-pint of new milk, and pour as much sherry or other wine to it as will curdle it. Take the pan off the fire, and when the curd sinks pour off the whey. Sweeten it with good sugar, and with hot water reduce it to any degree of strength that is wanted. *Vinegar whey, cream of tartar, lemon, mustard-seed, and alum whey, &c.* may be made as above.

1074. *Scotch hot pint.*—Grate a nutmeg into two quarts of mild ale, and bring it to the point of boiling. Mix a little cold ale with a considerable quantity of sugar and three eggs well beaten. Gradually mix the hot ale with the eggs, taking care that they do not curdle. Put in a half-pint of whisky, and bring it once more

---

* Hot spiced wines.—A variety of these delicious potations were in use so late as the beginning of the sixteenth century. The old metrical romances are full of allusions to these favourite compounds, and particularly to the *hyppocras, sack,* and *clary*. The first of these, which took its name from the bag through which it was strained being called "Hippocrates' sleeve," was made of either white or red wine with aromatics, such as ginger, cinnamon, and aromatic seeds, and sugar. *Clary* was made from claret, with honey and aromatics; and *sack* from the wine of that name. This medicated *vin de coucher* was used as a composing draught, or "nightcap," and also drank at the conclusion of a banquet. "Of these spiced wines," says Le Grand, in his Vie Privée de François, "our poets of the thirteenth century never speak without rapture, and as an exquisite luxury. They considered it the masterpiece of art to combine in one liquor the strength and flavour of wine, with the sweetness of honey, and the perfume of the most costly aromatics. A banquet at which no *piment* was served would have been thought wanting in the most essential article." The only kind of these delicious beverages still in use, besides our common mulled wine, is *Bishop*, that bewitching mixture made of Burgundy oranges and spices, with sugar.—See receipt *Bishop*, p. 460.

When this compound is made of Bourdeaux wine, it is called simply *Bishop*; but, according to a German amateur, it receives the name of *Cardinal* when old Rhine wine is used; and even rises to the dignity of *Pope* when imperial Tokay is employed.

nearly to boil, and then briskly pour it from one vessel into another till it becomes smooth and bright.*

1075. *Bitters, an excellent tonic.*—Take of juniper-berries two ounces, of gentian-root one ounce and a half, of coriander-seeds a quarter of an ounce, or orange-peel a quarter of an ounce, of calamus-aromaticus a quarter of an ounce, of snake-root a drachm, and of cardamom-seeds a half-drachm. Cut the gentian-root into small pieces, pound the other ingredients in a mortar, and put the whole into a large bottle or jar with five bottles of the best malt-whisky of the strength of glass-proof, or 15 per cent. below hydrometer-proof. Shake the bottle a little when the ingredients are first put in, but not afterwards. Let it stand for twelve days carefully corked, and then strain it off, and bottle it for use.—*Obs.* Gin or brandy may be substituted for whisky; whatever spirit is used must be reduced to the strength of glass-proof. Sherry may be used for spirits.

1076. *The German vermoute, or wormwood-wine.*—Infuse two tea-spoonfuls of the extract of wormwood in a quart of St. George, a celebrated Hungarian wine. Any rough white wine will probably answer the same purpose.—See No. 1059.

1077. *To make sack-posset.*—This is made either of good cream and grated sweet biscuits, or of beat eggs and milk instead of cream. Boil the cream or milk, sweeten it, and season with cinnamon and grated nut-meg. Warm the wine (Canary, *alias* sack) in a separate vessel, and stir it gradually into the milk; then pour it quickly from one vessel into another till perfectly smooth: this is especially requisite if made with eggs.—See *Wassail bowl*, page. 425.

1078. *Ale-posset.*—Boil a pint of new milk with a slice of toasted bread, sweeten and season a bottle of mild ale in a china basin or dish, and pour the boiling milk over it. When the head rises serve it.

1079. *Regent's punch.*—A bottle of champagne, a quarter-pint of brandy, a glassful of *veritable Martinique*:

---

* This beverage, carried about in a bright copper-kettle, is the celebrated new-year's-morning *Het Pint* of Edinburgh and Glasgow. In honest Aberdeen, half-boiled sowens is used on the same festive occasion. In Edinburgh, in her high and palmy state,—her days of "spice and wine," while she yet had a Court and a Parliament, while France sent

With this mix a pint or more of a strong infusion of the best green tea strained, and capillaire or simple syrup to taste.—*Obs*. Other liqueurs may be used with this compound, and also a flavouring of aromatics first infused and strained.—See No. 1068.

1080. *The Pope's posset*.—Sweeten and boil a bottle of white wine. Have a half-pound of sweet almonds, with a few bitter, blanched, pounded, and boiled in water, and ready strained. Mix the boiling-hot ingredients, beat them well up together.

1081. *A cool tankard*.—Put two glasses of sherry and one of brandy into a jug with a hot toast and sugar. Pour a bottle of fine ale over it; stir with a sprig of balm, and let it settle for a half-hour.

1082. *Athole brose*.—Mix with a cupful of heather-honey, two cupfuls of whisky, *alias* mountain-dew, or in this proportion; brandy and rum are also used, though the combination they form with honey cannot be called *Athole brose*. The yolk of an egg is sometimes beat up with the brose.

1083. *Auld man's milk*.—Beat the yolks and whites of six eggs separately. Put to the beat yolks, sugar and a quart of new milk, or thin sweet cream. Add to this rum, whisky, or brandy to taste (about a half-pint.) Slip in the whipped whites, and give the whole a gentle stir up in the china punch-bowl, in which it should be mixed. It may be flavoured with nutmeg or lemon-zest. This morning dram is the same as the egg-nog of America.

1084. *Lait sucré*.—Boil fine sugar in milk, and flavour with lemon. This is a refreshment fit for children's balls, and is so used in France.

1085. *Eau sucré*.—Sugar in boiling water. This is a frugal beverage much used by French ladies, and is considered soporific.

1086. *Rum shrub*.—This is made in the easy way by adding the juice and an infusion of the rind of Seville oranges to rum, with a little syrup and plain water or orange-flower-water. Honey, raisin-wine, porter, citric acid, &c. are employed in compound shrub.

---

her wines, and Spain, Italy, and Turkey fruits and spices, a far more refined composition than the above was made by substituting light white wine for ale, and brandy for whisky.—W. W.

1087. *Brandy shrub* is made in the same manner. It is best to buy these compound liquors rectified and distilled.

1088. *Currant shrub,—white or red,—*is made by putting the juice of the fruit to rum or brandy, in the proportion of a pint of juice, or less, to a quart of spirits, and adding syrup to taste. It must then be filtered.

1089. *Lemonade.*—This agreeable beverage wont formerly to be fermented,—now the process is more simple. Take any number of lemons, suitable to the quantity of liquor wanted; pare them as thin as possible; then rub the surface with knobs of refined sugar, to extract all the zest; put the saturated sugar and half the parings into a basin, and squeeze the lemons over it. Add the best refined sugar to taste. Hot water, (and a little boiling milk, if approved,) must be added, in the proportions wished for: three quarts to two dozen lemons is a fair quantity, using the whole juice, but only half the rinds. Skim the liquor when well mixed, and run it through a jelly-bag previously dipped in hot water and wrung. Bottle it.—*Obs.* Orangeade is made as above.

1090. *Portable lemonade,—very useful on voyages or in the country.*—Take of tartaric. acid one half-ounce, refined sugar three ounces, essence of lemon half a drachm. Pound the tartaric acid and sugar very well in a marble mortar, and gradually pour the essence upon the mixture. Mix the whole very well, and paper it up for use in twelve separate parcels; each of which, when mixed with a tumbler of wter, will make a very pleasant and refreshing draught. Lemonade may also be made extempore with the concrete of lemon acid and syrup.

1091. *Capillaire.*—Beat up six eggs and their shells with sixteen pounds of loaf-sugar; put to this three quarts of water; beat the whole mass, and boil it twice, and skim it well. Perfume with orange-flower-water, or *eau de milles fleurs.*—*Obs.* This syrup answers well for sweetening liqueurs, or, with a little lemon-juice and water, makes a pleasant summer-draught.

1092. *Another way.*—Infuse what quantity of American capillaire is wanted in boiling water; sweeten with clarified syrup; strain, perfume if you choose, and bottle.

1093. *Aromatic tincture.*—Take an ounce of bruised cinnamon, and an ounce of the seeds of the lesser cardamom; take also an ounce of bruised ginger, two drachms of long pepper, and a quart of spirits. Infuse this for a fortnight, keeping it in a warm place, and strain for use. Two or three tea-spoonfuls may be taken in a little capillaire, or *eau sucré*, or in wine with a little water or without. This tincture is cordial; and, in cases of indigestion and languor, is considered restorative.

BRITISH OR HOME-MADE WINES.

"Of wine may be verified the merry induction, that good wine maketh good blood, good blood causeth good humours, good humours cause good thoughts, good thoughts bring forth good works, good works carry a man to Heaven; *ergo*, good wine carrieth a man to Heaven."—*Howell*.

THOSE families who make wine in any quantity will find it useful to procure a treatise on this branch of domestic economy alone. Several of those, well deserving of notice, have lately been published. We shall, however, give receipts for making and ordering the best and most admired sorts of wine in sufficient variety to suit most private families.

1094. *General important observations.*—The fruit ought to be gathered before it is *dead* ripe, and in dry and sunny weather, which will greatly improve the quality and flavour of the wine. All fruit that is unripe or spoiled should be picked out with care, as one ill-flavoured berry will taint the juice of three dozen of good ones. The fruit must be carefully bruised and put into the softest water and sugar. The more carefully the husks and seeds are excluded, the better will the wine be in flavour and salutary qualities. The less water that is used the richer will be the wine; and the more the fruit-juice, and the less the sugar employed, the more will the vinous taste and flavour predominate. Two or three days are generally enough for the white wines to ferment in the vat. Red wines require a day or two longer. Fermentation may be hastened by agitating the liquid, and raising the temperature of the place in which the vat is placed. When the wine has undergone this process it must be *cleared* by being put into hair-bags, and strained in a wine-press, or strained through a canvas-bag. [Sieves are used in the small scale of wine-making, and are convenient in small families.] The casks are then filled till within an inch of the bung-hole, which should be slightly covered over. The casks must be set in a cool place; and now another fermentation comes on, called the *spiritous*, which will throw off the feculence that remains in the *must*, and greatly purify the wine. When this second fermentation has abated, the spirits ordered for the wine should be added, and the cask filled up and bunged. In six weeks or more the cask must be pegged, to see if the wine is bright, and if so, it must be carefully *racked* off from the lees into another cask. The best method is this:—Bore a hole about half way up the cask, and use a small quill to draw off the purest of the wine. Now bore a hole a little lower down, and if what is drawn off be not so bright as the first drawn, do not mix them. The lees may be filtered. The best qualities of home-made wines (for they never will have the flavour of grape-wines) consist, after all, in colour and brightness; so that it is of great importance to have them carefully *racked*. When not perfectly translucent on a first racking, the wine must be racked a second and even a third time, and *fined*. Wine should be bottled in clear settled weather. The bottles must be new, or at least perfectly clean, and great attention must be paid to the corking.—See *Bottling*.

A variety of things are used for perfuming wines; such as sweet herbs, peach-leaves, sweet bay-leaves, almonds, kernels of fruit, bergamot, cloves, ginger, &c. &c. Brandy will enrich wines: it ought, when added, to be previously mixed with honey or syrup. Flat wines may be enlivened by adding raisins bruised, mixing first a little spirits with them. The addition of good wine will better answer the same purpose. Wine is very apt to ferment over much; this may be checked by removing it into a cool place, putting a little spirits to check it, and making the bung fast, so as to exclude all air. We would recommend, as a certain means of making the fermentation sure, whether of wines or beers, to commence the process with a quart of the cooled liquor in a small vessel. This may be gradually increased to two or three quarts, and then put to the whole contents of the vat which you wish to ferment. By this means less yeast will do, and the process will be more certain.

This rule is applicable to ginger-beer and to every sort of fermented liquor. After fermentation is over, be sure the cask is kept quite full and close bunged. The sooner wine is bottled after it has *fined* the more it will sparkle; we do not say it will be the better wine.* A good judge will choose a *creaming* rather than a sparkling wine.

1095. *Best white gooseberry champagne.*—To every Scotch pint of ripe white gooseberries mashed, add a quarter and a half of milk-warm water and twelve ounces of good loaf-sugar bruised and dissolved. Stir the whole well in the tub or vat, and throw a blanket over the vessel, which is proper in making all wines, unless you wish to slacken the process of fermentation. Stir the ingredients occasionally, and in three days strain off the liquor into a cask. Keep the cask full, and when the spiritous fermentation has ceased, add, for every gallon of wine, a half-pint of brandy or good whisky, and the same quantity of Sherry or Madeira. Bung up the cask very closely, covering the bung with clay; and when *fined*, which will be in from three to six months, rack it carefully off, and rack it again if not quite bright.

N.B.—The fruit here should be rather over ripe. A very excellent white-currant wine may be made by this receipt, or a wine of white gooseberries and white currants mixed.

1096. *Red gooseberry wine.*—Take equal measure of water and bruised fruit, or more of the fruit if it be plentiful. To every twenty pints (Scotch) of the mixture add fifteen pounds of good loaf-sugar, and a pound of sliced beet-root. When casked and fermented, add a quart or more of brandy.

1097. *British Rhenish.*—To every gallon of fresh apple-juice, add two pounds of loaf-sugar. Boil and skim this till quite limpid. Strain it. Ferment it as other wines; and when the head flattens, rack it off clear, and tun it. Next season rack it off again; add a pint of brandy to every three gallons.—*Obs.* This is a highly-reputed wine, but we have no actual experience of its qualities.

---

* A French gentleman has lately announced a method of ripening wines in a few weeks, by merely tying parchment or bladder over the necks of the bottles. Spirits we have seen mellowed in the same manner.

1098. *Red currant wine.*—To twenty Scotch pints of water put thirty-six Scotch pints or more of red currants, and one pint of raspberries. When these have fermented, add twenty pounds of good sugar, and, after the wine is casked, two pints (if you choose) of brandy. This will make eighteen gallons of wine.

N.B.—The Scotch pint is two quarts. Red tartar in fine powder, and a pound and a half of sliced beet-root, may be added to the above to deepen the colour. The hull of the black currant boiled, and the liquid strained and used as part of the water, answers very well for the purpose of deepening the colour of dark red wines.

1099. *A cheap wine of mixed fruit.*—Take equal measure of water and such fruit as you can get; such as raspberries, cherries, strawberries, gooseberries, and currants, either black, red, or white. Strain and ferment, adding fifteen pounds of treacle or coarse sugar for every twenty gallons. Perfume with a quarter-pound of ginger, and a handful of sweet marjoram and lemon-thyme. Add two quarts of whisky.

N.B.—A more delicate *compound wine* may be made by using loaf-sugar and brandy; the colour may be enriched by red tartar.

1100. *Elder-flower wine, or English Frontignac.*— Whisk six whites of eggs in six gallons of water, and put to this sixteen pounds of good loaf-sugar. Boil and skim it well. Put to the boiling liquid eight pounds of the best raisins chopped, and a quarter-peck of elder-flowers. Infuse these, but do not boil them. When cool, put a quarter-pint of yeast to the liquid, stirring it well up. Next day put in the juice of four lemons and the thin rind. Let it ferment in the open vessel for three days, and then strain and cask it.—*Obs.* This wine, if properly managed, resembles Frontignac.

1101. *Elder-wine*, made of the elder-berries, is a rich and expensive preparation. It is made in the proportions of three pounds of sugar and three pints of elder-berry juice to the gallon of water, enriched with chopped raisins, and perfumed and flavoured with ginger, nutmeg, cloves, &c. An excellent but very expensive *Elder-wine* is made by using equal weight of water and Malaga raisins and sugar, and an eighth part elder-berries; and flavouring with cinnamon, cloves, mace, and ginger.

Elder-wine is the pride of many English housewives, and no expense nor pains are spared in its preparation. Mulled, or as negus, it forms a very pleasant beverage. It may stand in the cask till February to fine before being bottled, and is best relished hot and spiced as No. 1072.

1102. *Orange-wine.*—Dissolve twelve pounds of loaf-sugar in six gallons of water, in which the whites of a dozen eggs have been whisked. Whisk the whole, and boil and skim it. When nearly cold, put into it six spoonfuls of yeast, and the juice of a dozen lemons. Next morning skim off the top, and add the parings of the lemons and the juice and yellow rind of four dozen Seville oranges. Ferment for three days, and cask the wine.

N.B.—This wine may be improved by substituting honey for one-third of the sugar. It may be enriched by the addition of some of the high-flavoured wines, and perfumed with ginger, bitter almonds, bergamot, citron, peach-leaves, &c. &c. The whole of the orange-rind is by some thought to give too decided a flavour; less may be used at pleasure, and the rest made candied chips.

1103. *Orange and lemon-wine of raisins.*—Take two pounds of loaf-sugar, one pound of Malaga raisins, and the juice and peel of a Seville orange, to each gallon of water. Add the orange-juice when the wine is nearly done fermenting. *Lemon-wine* is made in the same manner, using the lemon in rather greater quantity than the orange.

1104. *Parsnip-wine.*—To every four pounds of parsnips, cleaned and quartered, put a gallon of water. Boil till they are quite soft, and strain the liquor clear off without crushing the parsnips. To every gallon of the liquor put three pounds of loaf-sugar, and a half-ounce of crude tartar. When nearly cold, put fresh yeast to it. Let it stand four days in a warm room, and then bung it up.

N.B.—Parsnip-wine is said to surpass all the other home-made wines as much as East-India Madeira does that of the Cape. So much is said for it, and on good authority, that it certainly deserves a trial. Horseradish-wine is made as above, and is recommended for gouty habits. In Ireland a pleasant table-beer is made from parsnips brewed with hops.

1105. *Ginger-wine, a pleasant cordial wine.*—To ten gallons of water, in which fifteen pounds of loaf-sugar have been dissolved, put the beat whites of a dozen eggs; whisk this well, and boil and skim it; then put to it twelve ounces of the best white ginger scraped and bruised. Boil the whole a half-hour in a covered boiler, to extract the flavour. When the liquor is nearly cold, put a glassful of fresh yeast into the tub. Let it ferment for three days at least, and on the second add the thin parings of four Seville oranges and six lemons. Cask it, and bottle off in six weeks or when bright. This wine may be aromatized, as it is called, by allspice, a few cloves, some mace, cinnamon, and nutmegs, bruised and infused in brandy: the strained infusion must be put to the wine just before it is bottled.—*Obs.* Ginger-wine, an insipid sort, is sometimes made without being fermented; and in the cheap wholesale way, allspice, and cayenne are used to flavour and give poignancy.

1106. *Birch-wine.*—To every gallon of the sap of the birch-tree, boiled, put four pounds of white sugar, and the thin paring of a lemon. Boil and skim this well. When cool, put fresh yeast to it; let it ferment for four or five days, then cork it. Keep the bung very close, and in four months rack and bottle it.

N.B.—The pith must be carefully corked up when it is drawn off from the trees, till it is to be used. Less sugar will answer. This is sometimes made with a third part raisins, and flavoured with almonds.

It ought to be remembered, that in currant and gooseberry wine fermentation is spontaneous; no yeast is employed or required.

BEERS AND OTHER HOUSEHOLD BEVERAGES.

1107. *White spruce-beer.*—To five gallons of water put seven pounds of loaf-sugar, and three-fourths of a pound of the essence of spruce. Boil and skim this. Put it into a vessel, and, when nearly cool, add fresh yeast (about a half-pint or less.) When the beer has fermented for three days, bung the cask, and in a week bottle it off.

N.B.—For *Brown spruce* use treacle or coarse brown sugar, instead of loaf-sugar.

1108. *Ginger-beer of a superior kind, for keeping.*— Take four pounds of loaf-sugar, four ounces or more of bruised ginger, and four gallons of water. Boil for a half-hour, and skim this. Slice two lemons or more into a tub, and put to them one ounce of cream of tartar. Pour the hot liquor over this, and when cool, add a half-pint or rather less of fresh beer-yeast. Let this work for three or four days. Strain it off clear from the lees into a cask, and add to it, if it is to be kept, a half-pint of brandy. Bottle in a week or ten days, and wire the corks.—*Obs.* With four times the quantity of cream of tartar this makes *aerated* ginger-beer.

1109. *Common ginger-beer.*—Make as above, but take a third less sugar, (brown sugar will do,) and no lemons nor brandy. Ferment for two days, and bottle for use. A little cayenne or allspice is a cheap substitute for part of the ginger. The above compositions are sometimes called Imperial, ginger-pop, &c.

1110. *Treacle-beer, a table beer.*—Boil, for twenty minutes, three pounds of molasses, in from six to eight gallons of soft water, with a handful of hops tied in a muslin rag, or a little extract of gentian. When cooled in the tub, add a pint of good beer-yeast, or from four to six quarts of fresh worts from the brewer's vat. Cover the beer (and all fermenting liquids) with blankets or coarse cloths. Pour it from the lees and bottle it. You may use sugar for molasses, which is lighter.

N.B.—This is a cheap and very wholesome beverage. A little ginger may be added to the boiling liquid if the flavour is liked.*

ON BOTTLING LIQUORS, AND ON CORKS,
BOTTLE-WAX, &c. &c.

"The penny-wise and pound-foolish" principle is not shown in any department of domestic management more decidedly than in the purchase of corks. These should always be of the best cork-wood, whether for pickles,

---

* Excellent plain directions for brewing ale and beer of malt, on the small scale, suited to families in the middling and lower ranks of life, are given in Cobbett's Cottage Economy.

catsups, made-wines, or even the cheapest commodities. Bottles are best when new; but, if well kept and thoroughly cleaned, they will continue to answer quite well. They should always be washed when set away empty, and kept with the head downmost. Bottles that have contracted a bad smell may be fumigated by a lighted match after they are well brushed and washed. Wash and drain them again. The shot used for cleaning bottles should be carefully removed before they are filled. Bottle-wax is sold ready prepared, or is easily made thus:—

1111. *Bottle-wax.*—A pound of rosin, a pound of bees-wax, and a half-pound of tallow. Mix with this red or yellow ochre, soot, or Spanish whitening, whichever colour you want. Melt it carefully, stirring all the while. If likely to boil over, stir with a candle-end, which will allay the ebullition.

112. *To prevent liquors from having a corked taste.*—Dip the corks in a varnish made of equal quantities of purified wax and suet melted together, and repeat the dipping till the cork is covered with the mixture.

N.B.—We are not sure of this prescription. It will prevent a worked taste; but, by contracting the fibres of the work, will it as effectually exclude the external air?

CHAPTER II.

MISCELLANEOUS RECEIPTS, PREPARATIONS FOR THE SICK, AND CHEAP DISHES.

Good broth with good keeping do much now and then;
Good diet with wisdom best comforteth men;
In health to be strong shall profit thee best;
In sickness hate trouble, seek quiet and rest.
Thomas Trusser's good Huswifely Phisick.

1113. *Rice milk.*—Wash the rice, and pick out the black parts. If milk is plentiful, it may be boiled in milk; if not, boil it in water to plump and soften it, and when the water is wasted put in the milk; take care that it does not stick to the sauce-pan. Season with sugar and a bit of cinnamon boiled in the milk. Currants and grated nutmeg are sometimes used with rice milk; and the milk is made first thin, and then thickened to a caudle with beat egg and flour.—*Obs*. Where boiled rice and milk is frequently used as an article of diet, as in some nurseries and boarding-schools, the addition of a little roughly-shred beef or mutton suet boiled with it, will not only render it more nutritious, but more wholesome. A bit of lemon-peel will give zest.

1114. *Saloop milk* is made as above; but, from its native flavour, saloop does not require so much, nor indeed any seasoning.

1115. *Sago milk*.—Soak the berries in water for an hour before boiling; or boil first in water for two or three minutes, which water pour off. Boil a large spoonful in a quart of new milk. Sweeten and season to taste.—*Obs*. The foregoing milks may be made of ground rice and saloop, using the flour in smaller quantity.

1116. *Hatted kit*.—Where this cooling and healthy article of diet is in constant use for children or delicate persons, a kit with a double bottom, the upper one perforated with holes, and furnished with a fosset and cover, should be got. In this vessel put in the proportion of two quarts fresh good butter-milk, and a pint of milk hot from the cow. Mix well by jumbling; and next milking add another pint of milk, mixing all well. It will now firm, and gather a *hat*. Drain off the whey whenever it runs clear, by the spigot; remove what of the top or *hat* is necessary, to take up the quantity wanted. This dish, to present at table, may be moulded for an hour in a perforated mould, and strewed over with a little pounded sugar, and then nutmeg or cinnamon. The kit must be well sweetened every time it is used with lime-water or charcoal; and too much should not be made at once, it gets so rapidly very acid. A slight degree of coagulation assists digestion, but milk highly acidulated is not wished for in this dish.

1117. *Another and easier way*.—Pour a quart of very hot new milk over two quarts of fresh butter-milk. Let it repose. When firm take off the surface, and drain the rest in a milk-sieve, or mould it if you choose. Serve cream in a jug.

1118. *Corstorphine or Ruglen cream*, or *Lappered milk*.—Pour a quart of new milk into a jar. On this, next morning, pour another, and mix well: at night do the same; and next day beat up the thickened milk with moist sugar. This cooling preparation is patronized by Sir John Sinclair. It may be made like *hatted kit*, of mixed butter-milk and sweet milk.—Indeed there is a learned controversy on the genuine preparation; as well as whether its invention really belongs to Corstorphine near Edinburgh, or to the village of Rutherglen in the neighbourhood of the western metropolis.

1119. *Sour milk crowdie*.—Pour fresh good butter-milk into finely-ground oatmeal, till as thin as pancake-batter. Stir the mixture.

1120. *Sago,—also a supper-dish*.—Soak the berries, changing the water. Simmer with a bit of lemon-peel till the berries look transparent. When nearly done, add aromatic spices, (*i.e.* nutmeg, mace, and cloves,) to taste, with wine and sugar. Give the whole a boil up before dishing it.—*Obs.* Sago and patent cocoa, pounded in equal quantities, and a spoonful boiled in milk, with sugar to taste, make a nutritious breakfast.

1121. *Arrow-root jelly*.—This may be prepared with either water, milk, or white wine and water, according to the purpose for which it is wanted, and sweetened and seasoned to taste. Rub two tea-spoonfuls of the flour well with a little cold water, as in making starch, and pour over it a pint of the boiling liquid to be used. Stir it the whole time it is on the fire. Three minutes will dress it.—*Obs.* This jelly, made in a shape and turned out, makes a light and pretty supper-dish, garnished with bits of red-currant jelly, or may serve for luncheon to young persons and children. Potato-flour is done in the same way, but it must be boiled longer to be good or safe. Arrow-root need not be boiled, and often is not, though best so cooked.

1122. *An Indian Curry*.—Take a clove of garlic and a small onion; bruise them in a mortar, with three tea-spoonfuls of the powder, described below, and a tea-spoonful and a half of salt. Slice another onion, and fry it in a stew-pan with a good piece of butter. Let it fry till the onion is brown. Pick out the shreds of onion, and put the mixed ingredients into the pan with a tea-

spoonful of good butter-milk, or soured cream; add to
this a young fowl skinned, and carved into joints; and
simmer till it is ready, stirring the whole quickly.

1123. *The curry-powder.*—One tea-spoonful of powdered white ginger, two of coriander-seeds. Half a one
of turmeric, a quarter one of cayenne; acid to be added
at pleasure to the curry when nearly ready.

1124. *Vegetable marrow.*—Parboil the fruit. Take
it up; and when cool enough to handle, cut a longi-
tudinal piece reaching to the heart of it; and draining
out the moisture from the fruit, replace the piece cut
out, and fasten it with thread. Boil in water with salt,
till on probing it is found that the marrow is thoroughly
done. It may be either served whole or divided on a
toast, with melted butter poured over; or mashed with
cream and butter; or treated as at Nos. 203-4.

1125. *Meat cubbubed,—a good dinner for an invalid.*
—Cut veal, beef, or mutton, lean but juicy, into small
bits. Beat them slightly; run them on wire skewers,
and fasten these to the small whirling wire-jack. Baste
well with their own dropt gravy, using a little butter at
first; dust with salt when ready, and pepper or curry-
powder, at discretion. Serve either with grilled toasts
or dry rice.

N.B.—A chicken or rabbit may be skinned, quartered,
and done as above. *Cubbubed curry* is made as any
other curry, but half of the meat is pork, fresh or
pickled, and more garlic and turmeric than are ever
employed in our cookery. Fresh pork in any form of fry
or curry is not relished in this country, and is seldom
seen, save perhaps, of necessity, on board of ship. If for
a landward dinner, we would recommend a large
allowance of acid.

1126. *Gloucester jelly for invalids.*—This is made of
equal parts of rice, sago, pearl-barley, hartshorn-shavings,
and eringo-root; four ounces of the ingredients to nearly
two quarts of water. Simmer slowly for an hour, and
strain it. The jelly may be dissolved at pleasure in
milk, wine, soup, &c. and is reckoned nourishing and
light.—*Obs.*. This is sometimes called *Dr. Jebb's Restorative Jelly.* It makes a good breakfast for invalids, when
warmed in milk and sugar.

1127. *Dr. Hunter's dinner for a delicate person.*—

"Cut a piece of veal into slices, beat, and put these into an earthenware can with plenty of stewed turnip. Cover the vessel, and let it stand up to the brim in boiling water, Add salt and pepper, and serve when done. This simple dish, says the learned Doctor, contains all the juices of the veal, with the addition of saccharine matter afforded by the turnip. The Romans were acquainted with this mode of cookery; it was what they meant by *per duplex vas coquere*." Beef may be dressed thus:— Soups of sheep's-head, or trotters, or calf's-feet boiled slowly to a weak jelly, are excellent invalid dishes in many cases. They should be served with grilled toasts, [No. 81,] which are often acceptable to a stomach too delicate to bear other food.

1128. *Barley-water*.—Wash common or pearl barley, and take in the proportion of an ounce to a quart of water. Give it a boil for a few minutes in a very little water, and strain off this, and take fresh water, which will make the barley-water lighter and of a better colour. Boil it down one-half when it is strained. Lemon-peel and sugar may be added; or a compound draught made, by adding to every pint of the decoction an ounce of stoned raisins, a quarter-ounce of sliced liquorice-root, and three or four figs. With lemon-juice it is less cloying and more grateful to the sick. Currant-jelly answers very well mixed in barley-water.

1129. *Panada*.—Slice the crumb of a loaf very thin, and soak or boil it gently in water; when soft, beat it well, and add sugar and wine, or a little rum. A little butter may be added to it.—*Obs*. Panada may be made of chicken-broth instead of water, and seasoned with a little mace, or a bit of lemon-peel.

1130. *White caudle*.—Mix two large spoonfuls of finely-ground oatmeal in water, two hours previous to using it; strain it from the grits and boil it. Sweeten, and add wine and seasonings to taste. Nutmeg and a little lemon-juice answer best for seasoning.

1131. *Brown caudle—the Scotch ale-berry,*—is made as above, using mild sweet small beer instead of water.— *Obs*. Caudle may be made of rice-flour or wheat-flour, with milk and water, sweetening it to taste.

1132. *Beef-tea*.—Cut a pound of lean, fresh, juicy beef into thin bits, and pour a quart or better of hot water over it; infuse this for a half-hour by the fire, and then let it boil up quickly with a little salt, and take off the scum. Boil gently for a half-hour, and let it settle. Pour carefully from the sediment, or strain it. Beef-tea is sometimes made by simple infusion, but this is a rather disgusting preparation to most people.— *Veal* or *Chicken tea* are made in the same way as beef-tea.

OF COFFEE.

1133. *Coffee by the Imperial percolator.*—*P. S. Touch-wood's method.*—Pour some boiling water into the percolator, and let it remain till the metal of the pot is thoroughly heated. Put the coffee-powder into the proper receptacle, between the perforated bottoms of the upper and under cylinders. Pour out the hot water from the pot, and put into the upper cylinder of the percolator as much boiling water as will completely saturate the coffee-powder—a small tea-cupful will be sufficient. In about a minute, fill the cylinder with boiling water; place the percolator by the fire, or over a hot water dish, and, when the water has filtered through, pour in again as much as will make the coffee required.

N.B. This process may appear tedious in detail, but nothing is more simple and easy in daily practice. In about five minutes coffee may be made for four or five persons. When the filtered coffee is poured into a small vessel, brought to the boiling point, and again returned to the cylinder and filtered a second time, it is exactly the coffee of the Society of Gourmands. But unless the operator is very careful not to let the smallest ebullition take place, the delicate aroma will be evaporated, and the flavour of the coffee destroyed.

1134. *Coffee by the receipt of the authors* of the *Code des Gourmands,* adopted by the members of the *Caveau Moderne, and communicated to the Cleikum Club.* It is given in their own words,—"Apres avoir nous-même experimenté en cent façons, nous avons fini par nous arrêter à la manière suivante qui nous donnons *pour officielle.*

"On brûle séparément, et soi-même, une partie de café Martinque vert, une café Bourbon, une Moka. [La bonté de la liqueur depend specialement du degré de torrefaction; la moindre négligence à cet égard altère le parfum du café. Brûle à point, le grain doit être *alezan clair*. Il vaut mieux brûler moins que plus, l'inconvénient subsiste dans les deux cas, mais dans le premier il est moins désastreux.] On opère ensuite le melange, et on reduit le tout en poudre, pas trop fine. Puis on opère d'après le système de la cafetière Dubelloy qui consiste à verser l'eau bouillante sur le café placé dans un vase à doubles fonds, percés de très-petits trous. L'eau s'ecoule chargée de toute la partie essentielle. On la met alors sur le feu jusqu'à ebullition, on la repasse de nouveau dans l'appareil, et l'on obtient un café aussi clair aussi bon qu'il se puisse fair." It is added, "Celui qui a le gosier pavé et peut avaler toute bouillante cette delicieuse boisson de doit plus envier l'ideale ambroisie."*

1135. *To make coffee, Buonaparte's way.*—Put the ground coffee into a vessel with a strainer, and pour the

---

* The French, if not the most skilful coffee-brewers in the world, which perhaps they are, celebrated as the coffee of Germany is, are at least its most devoted swallowers. Their Voltaire, and their Napoleon were the greatest coffee-bibbers of modern times. This beverage was called the hypocrene of Voltaire. One of the most agreeable passages of De Lille is devoted to its praise, at once a recipe and an eulogy. He has done for it what Cowper has done for Tea in England.

> Il est une liqueur au poète bien chère,
> Qui manquait à *Virgile*, et qu'adorait Voltaire;
> C'est toi, divin *Café*, dont l'aimable liqueur,
> Sans altérer la tête, epanouit le coeur!
> Ainsi, quand mon palais est émoussé par l'age,
> Avec plaisir encore je goûte ton breuvage.
> Que j'aime à préparer ton nectar précieux;
> Nul n'usurpe chez moi ce soin delicieux;
> Sur le réchaud brûlant, moi seul, tournant ta graine
> A l'or de ta couleur fais succéder l'ebène
> Moi seul, contre la noix qu'arment ses dents de fer
> Je fais, en le broyant, crier ton fruit amer
> Charmé de ton parfum, c'est moi seul qui, dans l'onde,
> Infuse à mon foyer ta poussière féconde;
> Qui, tour-a-tour, calmant, exitant tes bouillons,
> Suis d'un oeil attentif tes légers tourbillons.
> Enfin, de ta liqueur, lentement reposée,
> Dans le vase fumant la lie est déposée;
> Ma coupe, ton nectar, le miel Americain
> Que de suc des roseaux exprima l'Africain,
> Tout est prêt:—du *Japon* l'émail reçoit tes ondes,
> Et seul tu réunis les tributs des deux mondes.
>   Viens donc, divin nectar! viens donc; inspiré moi:
> Je ne veux qu'un désert, mon *Antigone* et toi!

water on it perfectly cold; plunge this vessel into another filled with boiling water, which must be kept at the boiling-pitch till the process is completed. This method is thought to preserve the flavour of the coffee.

1136. *Parisian coffee, as made by M. Dubelloy.*— Take, when the coffee is needed, nearly four ounces of the best powder recently prepared, and put it, with a very little shred saffron, into a *Grecque.*★ Pour in boiling water till it bubbles up through the strainer, and then close the vessel and place it near the fire; and as soon as the whole water is passed through the coffee is made.

1137. *To make coffee, by a simple and good method.*— Pour boiling water in the proportion of six cupfuls to one cupful of freshly-ground coffee, but double the coffee if for foreigners. Let this be on the point of boiling for two or three minutes, held over the fire, and taken off at pleasure, so as to keep up the temperature, but not to permit any violent ebullition. Pour out a cupful two or three times, returning it; and set the coffee-pot on the hob to keep hot, while the coffee clears.†—*Obs.* By attending to the above simple receipt, if the coffee-powder is good, and not ground too finely, no isinglass, whites of eggs, &c. will be required to clear it. The bad quality of English coffee is become a sort of national reproach. Its capital defect is a want of material, or that material having either lain too long in powder, or in roasted berries. Coldness is the reproach of our coffee

---

★ An utensil which is used in Paris, similar to our Imperial percolator.

† If the hob is too hot, the coffee will never clear. It will spoil from being kept nearly boiling. The receipts for making coffee, which are given in cookery-books, must completely drive off the flavour of the berry from the length of time that the coffee is directed to be boiled. Flour of mustard, in the proportion of a small tea-spoonful to the ounce of powder, is thought by some persons to improve the flavour, and is reckoned good in gouty as well as rheumatic habits. Coffee made before-hand, and heated up for use, is ever a vile slop, detested by every coffee-drinker, and every one else who has the taste of his mouth. Where coffee must be got ready for travellers, sportsmen, and others, before servants can reasonably be expected to be astir, the Essence is valuable; but if coffee is prepared over-night, let it be of triple strength, and reduced by water or milk. Some modern amateurs in coffee like the cream (rich and thick) a little sourish, beat up with the sugar in the cup to keep it from curdling, before the hot coffee is poured in. To those whom habit has brought to relish the peculiar flavour of the Essence, it will give somewhat of that taste.

even more than muddiness. The coffee-berries ought also to be of proper age, as the quality of the raw berry improves by keeping for three or four years. Good cream is essential to good *English coffee*. Lisbon sugar, or pounded white candy, is often ordered. We can see no reason for this, except that they dissolve quickly, notwithstanding the cream being usually poured into the dishes before the hot coffee.

Coffee, like tea, promotes watchfulness; indeed some persons cannot sleep after drinking it in an evening. It is considered good for asthmatic patients. A mixture of made-mustard in coffee, is reckoned good for rheumatic persons. Coffee is also considered beneficial in dull headache. Roasted acorns, beech-mast, rye, pease, beans, &c. &c. are all used as substitutes for coffee; and by frugal French families chicory put to the coffee grounds, and boiled up afresh, is allotted to servants and young members of the household.

1138. *Café à la créme.*—Make very strong, clear coffee. Add boiled cream to it, and heat them together. It is always proper to boil the milk or cream for coffee separately.

1139. *Coffee-milk.*—Boil coffee-powder, according to the strength you want it, in new milk, for five minutes. Allow it to settle and pour it off, or clear it with a few bits of isinglass. It is safer to boil the milk first.

1140. *Essence of coffee* is convenient and even useful in particular situations; but, besides being expensive, can never be compared with fresh well-made coffee, of good well-roasted berries. A tea-spoonful is put into the cup, and boiling water poured on.

1141. *Chocolate, to make.*—Boil equal quantities of good new milk, and water. Scrape down the chocolate according to the strength and quantity wanted, and take the milk and water off the fire. Throw in the chocolate and sugar, and mill it well and rapidly, that it may be served with the froth on it, and completely blended with the milk.—*Obs.* Chocolate is sometimes made in gruel for delicate persons. Where much is used, it is thought an economical plan to make a pint of very strong chocolate, and to boil up a couple or three or four spoonfuls of this, in milk, water, and sugar, as it is wanted, milling it well. It is best fresh-made if possible.

1142. *Waters, for cooling draughts, of preserved or fresh fruits.—lemon-water and orange-juice water.* —Pour boiling water on the preserved or sliced fresh fruit, or squeeze out the juice, boil it up in a little thin syrup, and put water to it as it is wanted. *Apple-water* is made as above.—A tea-pot or covered jug should be used when those drinks are made by infusion. *Cucumber and melon waters.*—The water in which cucumber is cooked, may have any odd bits and parings of the cucumber put to it and be boiled up, strained and sweetened for a cooling draught—water flavoured with melon the same—all these may be iced if agreeable.

1143. *To stew prunes.*—Put them in a nice small sauce-pan with very little water, and stew till soft, but not to a mash. The stones may be broken, and the kernels put to the stew.

1144. *Gruels of fruit.*—Boil in thin gruel, currants, black or red, or cranberries, in their juice, with sugar and nutmeg to taste, or use the jam of those fruits.

1145. *Oatmeal gruel, in the best manner, as made in Scotland.*—Take very finely-ground oatmeal, of the best quality. Infuse as much as you wish in cold water for an hour or two. Stir it up, pour it from the grits, or strain it, and boil slowly for a long time, stirring it up.* Add a little salt and sugar; with any addition of wine, rum, fruit, jelly, honey, &c. &c. you choose. This gruel will be quite smooth; and when cold will form a jelly. With a toast, it makes an excellent luncheon or supper-dish for an invalid. It may be thinned at pleasure.

1146. *Sweet orange or lemon juice.*—When you make candied chips, preserve the strained juice, by boiling it with an equal weight of fine sugar. It is a great addition to gruel or barley-water, and will be very useful for gargles in fevers and cases of sore throat, &c.

1147. *Toast and water.*—An hour or more before it

---

* The English language is very deficient in terms descriptive of culinary processes. The Scotch retain the word "to skink" in defining the process of continually lifting high a sauce or gruel by spoonfuls, and rapidly letting it fall back into the pan. The French language, which is peculiarly rich in culinary terms, calls what is signified above by stirring, to *vanner* a sauce or soup; and to see a French cook, thus engaged at the stove with the *veloute*, or sauce *à la Lucullus*, an Englishman might well suppose that life and death were depending on a process for which *his* language has no name.—P. T.

is wanted, toast some thin slices of bread on both sides very carefully. Pour cold water over the bread, and cover the jug:—or use boiled water, which many prefer, allowing it time to cool.

1148. *Artificial asses' milk.*—Take eringo-root, sea-holly, and pearl-barley, each half an ounce; liquorice-root three ounces; water one quart; boil the mixture over a slow fire, till the full half is evaporated. Strain, and when cool, add an equal quantity of fresh cow's milk.

1149. *Fumigating mixture for sick chambers.*— Two ounces of *salt* dried, two ditto of *nitre*. Mix and put to them in a stoneware basin or plate, a half-ounce of water, and the same quantity of good *sulphuric acid*. Remove all polished-metal articles from the room, as the vapour would rust them, and close all doors and windows. To procure more advantage, when the process appears to cease, place the basin on hot sand.

1150. *Poultices and fomentations.*—These things are usually made in the kitchen, and a knowledge of their proper preparation is of importance to every cook or housekeeper in some part of their lives. *Poultices* are generally bread-crumbs soaked and boiled in milk, water, or a preparation ordered by a medical man. They are also made of lintseed-meal, oat and barley meal, yeast, and grated carrot, turnip, &c. They should be made as clean as possible, and they must be well boiled, soft, large enough, and, if to promote suppuration, applied hot. They must be renewed as frequently as they harden, and should always be fresh made. It is good practice to put oil or lard on the surface of the poultice. Nice persons stitch poultices in a fold of thin muslin.

1151. *Fomentations.*—These are generally made of the leaves or flowers of plants, as chamomile-flowers, mallows, elder-flowers, poppy-heads, wormwood, &c. They are best made by infusion in boiling water kept hot near the fire; but the vegetables may also be boiled. Fomentations are generally applied by dipping flannel (about a square of flannel) into the boiling decoction, and wringing it quickly out. The hot vegetables are also applied in substance in the folds of a cloth; but this is more of the nature of a poultice than a fomentation.

1152. *The proper medium temperature of baths.*—

The tepid from 86° to 97°, the HOT BATH from 97° to 108°, the VAPOUR BATH from 100° to 180°.

1153. *Cheap substitute for a water-filter.*—Lay a thick bed of pounded charcoal at the bottom of a large common earthen flower-pot, over this lay a bed of fine sand about four inches thick. Make all compact, and suspend the pot over any receiving vessel. A bit of quick-lime thrown into a water puncheon, will be useful in purifying water. Agitating the water and exposing it to the air, will both soften it and help to keep it fresh. Water, if muddy, may be strained through a common sieve, in which a cloth and sponge, or layer of fine sand or charcoal is placed.

PREPARATIONS FOR THE DRESSING-ROOM.

1154. *Pot pourri.*—Put into a large china jar used for this purpose, damask and other single roses, buds, and blown flowers, as many as you can collect; add to every peck of these, a large handful of jasmine-blossoms, one of dame violets, one of orange-flowers; orris-root sliced, an ounce; benjamin and storax, each an ounce (many dislike these); two or three handfuls of clove gilly-flowers, red-pinks, and lavender-flowers, cloves, nut-megs, thyme, rind of lemon, balm of Gilead dry, and a few laurel-leaves. Chop all these, and mix them well with bay-salt. Cover the jar; stir occasionally. The various ingredients may be collected in succession as they flower. To these are added woodroof, jonquil-flowers citron, and many other things.

1155. *Eau de Cologne.*—Take the essence of bergamot, lemon-peel, lavender, and orange-flowers, of each an ounce, essence of cinnamon half an ounce, spirit of rose-mary, and of the spiritous water of Melisse, of each fifteen ounces, strong alcohol seven pints and a half. Mix the whole together, and let the mixture stand for the space of a fortnight; after which introduce it into a glass retort, the body of which is immersed into boiling water, contained in a vessel placed over a lamp, while the beak is introduced into a large glass retort well luted. By keeping the water to the boiling point, the mixture in the retort will distil over into the receiver, which should be covered over with wet cloths. In this manner will be obtained pure Eau de Cologne, at one-fourth the selling price.

N.B.—The above receipt is given on the authority of Dr. Granville, who, lately at Cologne, took some pains to learn the component parts of this favourite accompaniment of an elegant toilet. Only 38,000 bottles of the water are made at Cologne in the year, so that probably two thirds of the commodity sold as such, is made by a process far inferior to the above.

1156. *A cheap perfume.*—Dip fine cotton wool, such as jewellers use, in olive-oil, and spread it in thin layers over jasmine-flowers, and rose-leaves, in a jar or glass vessel. In a week squeeze out the perfumed oil into a vial for use, and keep the scented wool to perfume clothes, presses, &c. &c.—*Obs.* One of the most effectual *perfumes* is fresh-burnt charcoal, as it destroys bad odours, while more elegant preparations only subdue the smell.

1157. *Thieves' vinegar.*—Take an ounce of the tops of wormwood; rosemary, sage, mint, and rue, of each half an ounce; flowers of lavender, two ounces; aromatic gum, cinnamon, cloves, nutmegs, and fresh garlic, two drachms of each; half an ounce of camphor, and eight pounds of red vinegar: beat all the ingredients well, and put them into a proper earthen jar, and pour the vinegar upon them; the garlic ought to be sliced. After stopping the jar, put it in the sun or in a hot place, such as a sand-bath, for three or four weeks; wring out the ingredients, and filter through filtering paper; the camphor must be dissolved in a little spirits of wine. This vinegar, like all perfumed liquids, ought to be kept closely corked.

1158. *Rose vinegar for salads, or for the toilet.*—Put a quarter of a pound of rose-leaves to four pints of good vinegar, and some roots of the Florence lily. Infuse till a fine tincture is obtained, and strain off the infusion.

1159. *Lavender vinegar—French.*—To every pint of the best champagne vinegar put half an ounce of fresh lavender-flowers, and the thin rind of a lemon. Infuse for twenty-four hours in a stone-jar, then take the jar and set it over hot embers to digest for ten or twelve hours. Filter and bottle it, dipping the corks in wax.

1160. *Honey-water for the hair.*—Mix three drachms of tincture of ambergris, and one of tincture of musk, with a little spirit of wine. Afterwards add a pint of spirit of wine, or strong spirits, and shake all well and often.

1161. *Cold cream for the skin.*—Take two ounces of oil of sweet almonds, a drachm of white wax, and one of spermaceti. Melt them in an earthen pipkin, and stir in a mortar till quite smooth and cold. Add orange-flower or rose-water till the mixture is as thin as double cream. Keep in a gallipot covered with leather.

1162. *Lip-salve.*—Put four ounces of the best olive-oil in a bottle, with a half-ounce of picked alkanet-root; stop the bottle, and set it in the sun till the oil is coloured; strain it into an earthen pipkin in which an ounce of white wax and one of clarified mutton-suet are placed; melt this by the fire, and perfume with a drop of oil of rhodium, or bergamot, or lavender; pour it off the sediment into very small gallipots.

1163. *Paste for chopped hands.*—Make a paste of fresh lard, honey, yolks of eggs, and a little of the fine dust of oatmeal or of bean-flour: it may be perfumed with a drop of essence of lemon.

CHEAP DISHES AND COOKERY FOR THE POOR.

WE are convinced that the art of preparing cheap dishes is much better understood by the intelligent poor, than by those who assume the task of instructing them. It is not, therefore, for the direct use of the poorer classes, but for the information of those who, from charitable motives, are anxious to devote part of the abundance with which Providence has blessed them to their humble brethren, that this section is added to the Cook's Manual.

There is not a family of any consideration but might distribute at least three or four gallons of soup a week to their poor neighbours, with almost no additional expense, and only a little personal trouble to the cook or kitchen-maid. There is much waste in all families, which, by a slight degree of attention, might be avoided, and turned to good account, not only in supplying the wants of the poor, but in improving the domestic habits of young female servants, and qualifying them to be managers when they shall come to be poor men's wives.

Without wishing to encourage habits of dependence, much less of beggary, benevolent persons will find in all neighbourhoods, old men and women, and orphan children, to whom the certainty that on even one day of the week they may look forward to a warm and comfortable meal, will be no small blessing. Those benevolent individuals who actively interest themselves in bettering the condition of the poor, seldom fail to enjoin them to go to church. Were this injunction coupled with a comfortable Sunday's dinner of warm stew-soup, to such as need this kindness, the advice would not prove the less efficacious. For an expense of two shillings per week, any benevolent individual may dine ten old women or men every Sunday of the year, even allowing that none of the waste of his kitchen were applied to this purpose, but that every article were purchased.

In speaking of dishes for the poor, it is at once proper to say, that we have no idea of human life in grown persons being sustained in comfort and physical energy without a due proportion of animal food; nor do we conceive that, with any better diet than the miserable unchanging meal of the Irish and Highland peasantry, or the rice of the feebler tribes of India, there is any hearty food more really economical than cheap stew-soups of meat or fish, with a proper mixture of vegetables, roots, and farinaceous seeds. But this mode of cookery is not only the cheapest, it is also the most savoury in which food can be prepared. The worst feature in the domestic management of the poor—we speak not of drinking—is the universal and excessive use of tea, and they must either swallow this a coarse half-sweetened pernicious decoction, without the milk, buter, meat, &c., which can alone render it a nourishing meal, or spend on it a share of their earnings, which must be subtracted from better purposes. The tea-pot drains the soup-pot;—the price of the materials of a coarse unsatisfying breakfast would nearly purchase enough of meat, vegetables, and barley, or pulse, to make a hearty and comfortable family-dinner. Were soup or gruel substituted for tea, and for those sickening and abominable slops called British coffee, as is the practice with decent families on the continent, and, till of late years, was the custom of the Highlands of Scotland and Ireland, the change would be still better; as the meat, either cold, or rewarmed in a little of the soup, would afterwards furnish dinner. The objection made to the old hearty breakfast of the Lowlands of Scotland, oatmeal porridge, to the *burgou* of the navy, the *stir-about* of Ireland, and *hasty-pudding* of the North of England, as heavy fare for females and sedentary mechanics, could not be brought against a light soup merely thickened with oatmeal, and eaten with bread. The increase of soup-shop, and even of places for the early sale of coffee and saloop, will be found one of the most effectual means for the suppression of dram-shops; for there can be no doubt that there are in large towns, thousands on thousands of poor persons, market-women, barrow-women, and dealers in all sorts of small wares, who, were a pint of warm soup and a penny-loaf as easily come by at the corner of every street as a glass of gin, would, at least in the beginning of their career, prefer the former.*

Besides the receipts for CHEAP DISHES subjoined, there are many scattered throughout the work, as stew-soup of *bullock's-heart; sheep's-head* broth in a plain way; *rice and milk with suet; plain Scotch fish and sauce; Scotch haggis; pan-kail; pease-soup; potato-soup* in which dripping is substituted for butter; *ox-tail* and *ox-head* soup and *ragout; baked herrings; kidney-collops;* white, blood, and liver puddings, *muscle* or other cheap shell-fish soups, *calecannon* enriched with dripping; Scotch *kail-brose*, and many other things.

In treating of cookery for the poor, however briefly, it would be wrong to pass over the potato-flour, of which so much has lately been said and written. Of its uses and excellence in its own place, we have no doubts whatever, though we cannot just yet believe that in potato-flour an universal panacea is discovered for human misery. The manner in which potato-flour is made, is shortly described at page 222. But it is now prepared for sale in considerable quantities, and if it prove as really cheap, nutritious, and agreeable, as is alleged, there is no doubt of its success. People are in general quite alive to their true interests, whether of purse or palate. To the mode of cooking potato-flour as promulgated by its most zealous patrons and *proneurs*, we however decidedly object. *Their pudding* is in fact *raw* potato-glue, if boiling water is merely poured over the flour. This might do for genuine arrow-root, or for oatmeal, but not for crude potato-mucilage. We give the subjoined *formula* as an improvement: *Mix the flour* as in making starch; pour boiling water over it, and boil it from five to eight minutes, stirring constantly. If boiled in milk, or milk and water, with a little sugar, it will make a very agreeable mess either for breakfast or a light supper—where suppers are taken.

---

* It is not easy to hear the stern denunciations of gin, and of the profligacy of the lower classes, proceeding from one of those well-fed, well-clad moralists, who never indulge in any thing save sound old port, or the best of malt-liquor, without calling to mind one of the pictures of him, whose sagacity in detecting the manifold weaknesses of the human heart, and penetrating to its most hidden springs, is only excelled by his indulgence in judging of its wanderings and weaknesses. The Antiquary is expressing his hope to the fish-woman, that the distilleries, then stopt, may never work again. "Ay, ay," said Maggie, "it's easy for your honour, and the like o' you gentle folks, to say sae, that ha'e stouth and routh, and fire and fending, and meat, and claith, and sit dry and canny by the fireside; but an ye wanted fire, and meat, and dry claise, and were deeing o' cauld, and had a sair heart, whilk is warst ava, wi' just tippence in your pouch, wad na ye be glad to buy a dram wi't, to be eilding and claise, and a supper, and heart's-ease into the bargain, till the morn's morning?"

"It's even too true an apology, Maggie," said Monkbarns.

CHEAP DISHES.

SOME of the subjoined receipts were published during a period of scarcity. They are equally applicable now, as the preparations, besides being frugal, are savoury and healthful. They are attributed to a lady whose eloquent pen has been usually devoted to the highest and most sacred subjects, but who has not disdained to employ her talents in improving the manners and increasing the domestic comforts of the humblest of her brethren—Mrs. HANNAH MORE. The rest are original.

1164. *Cheap rice milk.*—A quart of skim milk, a quarter of a pound of rice, with sugar, and a little Jamaica pepper, will make a cheap and dainty dish. Swell the rice first with water.

1165. *Rice pudding.*—Two quarts of skim milk, a half-pound of rice, and two ounces of brown sugar.

N.B.—A little shred suet, and a very little ginger, will make this excellent.—*Ed.*

1166. *Mrs. White's cheap stew.*—"I remember," said Mrs. White, "a cheap dish, so nice that it makes my mouth water. I peel some raw potatoes, slice them thin, put the slices into a deep frying-pan, or pot, with a little water, an onion, and a bit of pepper. Then I get a bone or two of a breast of mutton, or a little strip of salt pork, and put it into it. Cover it down close, keep in the steam, and let it stew for an hour."

1167. *Herring and potatoes.*—Take two or three pickled herrings, wash and put them into a stone jar, fill it up with peeled potatoes and a little water, and let it bake in the oven till it is done. [This dish is made in Scotland in a close-covered pot by boiling. Place the herrings upmost.—*Ed.*]

1168. *Stew-soup.*—Two pounds of beef, four onions, ten turnips, half a pound of rice, a large handful of parsley, thyme, and savoury; some pepper and salt; eight quarts of water. Cut the beef in slices, and after it has boiled some time, cut it still smaller. The whole should boil gently about two hours on a slow fire. If fuel be scarce, it may be stewed all night in an oven, and warmed up next day. You may add oatmeal and potatoes. Grey pease will be a great addition.

1169. *Another.*—Take half a pound of beef, mutton, or pork, cut it into small pieces; half a pint of pease, four sliced turnips, six potatoes cut very small, two onions or leeks, put to them seven pints of water. Let the whole boil gently over a very slow fire two hours and a half. Then thicken it with a quarter of a pound of oatmeal. After the thickening is put in, boil it a quarter of an hour, stirring it all the time; then season it with salt and pepper.

1170. *Stew-soup of salt meat.*—Take two pounds of salt beef or pork, cut it into very small bits, and put it into a pot with six quarts of water, letting it boil on a slow fire for three-quarters of an hour; then put a few carrots, parsnips, or turnips, all cut small; or a few potatoes sliced; a cabbage, and a couple of carrots. Thicken the whole with oatmeal. Season with salt and pepper.—See Bullock's Heart Stew, No. 405.

1171. *Cheap soups.*—The following soup Mrs. Sparks sold every Saturday in small quantities.—A pint of the soup, with a bit of the meat warmed up on a Sunday, made a dinner for a grown person.

An ox-cheek, two pecks of potatoes, a quarter of a peck of onions, one ounce of pepper, half a pound of salt, boiled altogether in ninety pints of water, till reduced to sixty; any garden-stuff may be thrown in.

Friendly hints, by the same writer.—*The difference between eating bread new and stale is one loaf in five.*

If you turn your meat into broth, it will go much further than if you roast or bake it.

If you have a garden, make the most of it. A bit of leek, or an onion, makes all dishes savoury at small expense.

If the money spent on fresh butter were spent on meat, poor families would be much better fed than they are.

If the money spent on tea were spent on home-brewed beer, the wife would be better fed, the husband better pleased, and both would be healthier.

Keep a little Scotch barley, rice, dry pease, and oatmeal in the house. They are all cheap and don't spoil. Keep also pepper and ginger.

1172. *Mrs. White's breakfasts.*—"Neighbours," said Mrs. White, "a half-pennyworth of oatmeal, or groats, with a leek or onion out of your own garden, which costs nothing, a bit of salt, and a little coarse bread, will breakfast your whole family. It is a great mistake at any time to think a bit of meat is so ruinous, and a great load of bread so cheap. A poor man gets seven or eight shillings a week; if he is careful he brings it home. I dare not say how much of this goes for tea in the afternoon, now sugar and butter are so dear, because I should have you all upon me; but I will say, that too much of this little goes even for bread, from a mistaken notion that it is the hardest fare. This, at all times, but particularly if bread is dear, is bad management. Dry pease, to be sure, have been very dear lately; but now they are plenty enough. I am certain, then, that if a shilling or two of the seven or eight was laid out for a bit of coarse beef, a sheep's-head, or any such thing, it would be well bestowed. I would throw a couple of pounds of this into the pot, with two or three handfuls of grey pease, an onion, and a little pepper. Then I would throw in cabbage or turnip, and carrot, or any garden-stuff that was most plenty; let it stew two or three hours, and it will make a dish fit for his Majesty. The working men should have the meat; the children don't want it; the soup will be thick and substantial, and requires no bread."

1173. *Another cheap soup.*—Two pounds of shin of beef, or ox-cheek, a quarter-pound of barley, a half-pennyworth of parsley and onions, with salt, will make four quarts of good soup. A few potatoes, or any cheap vegetable, may be added.

1174. *Bean pudding.*—Boil, skin, and pound beans with pepper and salt, and a piece of butter and dripping. Tie the pounded mass into a floured cloth, and boil.

1175. *Bean pudding, to eat with bacon or pickled pork, hot pig's cheek, &c.*—Boil and skin the beans, or take any left. Pound them with pepper and salt, and, if you like, a piece of butter, melted suet or dripping. Put them in a buttered tin basin. Tie a pudding cloth round, and boil in water, or better with the pork, for from a half-hour to three quarters. Undo the cloth; let the pudding cool and firm for a minutes; then place the basin inverted on a dish, and turn it out.

1176. *Cheap pease-pudding.*—To a pound of pease

boiled for pudding, add two pounds of mashed potato, with drippings of any kind.

1177. *Cheap casserole of potato, in which cheap mince or stew may be neatly served.*—Mash the potatoes with a little milk, and a bit of butter, with salt, and a *point* of finely shred onion if you like. Border a flat dish thickly with this, and mark it, and place a layer of potatoes over the dish; brown in the oven or before the fire, and scoop out the centre, and serve in it hashed beef-heart, kidney-collop, salt, or other fish warmed up, &.

1178. *Milk porridge.*—Stir oatmeal into boiling skimmed milk as in making stir-about. Eat with milk.

1179. *Ox-liver*, sound and fresh, sliced, steeped for some hours in salt and water, and fried with fat bacon, parsley, onions, and allspice, makes a good cheap dish.

1180. *Stew soup* may be made of the rich liquor in which tripe is boiled, with rice or potatoes, parsley, and onions; of the same liquor a *jelly* is often made for the great.

The *culinary* utensils of the poor are of great importance.* Every family ought to have a cheap and small steamer of a substantial kind, fitted to the metal pot, which serves either for boiling or baking. In baking a pudding or meat, the thick metal lid of this sort of pot is first made hot and laid on the hearth, and the pot is turned upside-down over it; turf embers are placed all around or over this little oven, in which meat with

---

* *Economical Maxims of ancient Trusser, the first English writer on Domestic Economy, and author of "The Points of good Husbandry and Housewifery."*

"Save wing for a thresher when gander doth die;
Save feathers of all things the softer to lie;
Much spice is a thief, so is candle and fire;
Sweet sauce is as crafty as ever was friar;
Save droppings and skimmings whatever ye do,
For medicine, for cattle, for cart and for shoe."

From the maxims of this worthy, it would appear that the jolly English yeoman of the 16th century, fared fully as well as the gentleman farmer of the 19th—so far as substantials go—and his servants a great deal better. For the yeoman and his household's Lenten diet, Trusser recommends red herrings and salt fish. At Easter, veal and bacon; and at Martinmas, when dainties were no longer to be had, contentment with salted beef. At Midsummer, when mackerel went out, there was fresh beef and *salads*; at Michaelmas, fresh herrings and old crones,

potato-pastry, fish-pie with potato, rice-pudding, or any dish may be cooked. The lid may be laid over embers in the grate, and the pot inverted over it.

CHAPTER III.

OF SALTING MEAT, TONGUES, HAMS, MAKING CHEESE, FATTENING POULTRY, PRESERVING BUTTER, EGGS, &c. &c.

MEAT should either be salted before the animal heat has left it, or be allowed to hang for a few days, to become tender. It should be wiped free of moisture, blood, &c. and have the kernels and pipes taken out. As a general rule, which is too little attended to, meat should first be rubbed with about the half of the salt ordered; and, after lying a day or two to disgorge, have the remaining half rubbed in. This *twice salting*, from the effectual rubbing and mixing it causes, will be found an excellent method, not only for meat, but for butter and fish. Bay-salt is imagined to give meat a better flavour than any other salt. It is thought sweeter than manufactured salt, from being dried by the gradual action of the sun. There are various modes of purifying salt for preserving meat, butter, and fish, but they are too complicated and troublesome for domestic use. The Dutch,

---

(sheep;) at All Saints, pork and pease, sprats, and sparlings; and at Christmas, in Old England! Merry England! all good cheer and play; with good drink, a rousing fire in the hall, brawn, puddings, and sonse, and mustard withal; beef, mutton, pork, and minced pies of the best; pig, veal, capon, goose, "turkey and the chine;" cheese, apples, nuts,—and, to crown all, "jolly carols."—Peace be with thy memory, Thomas Trusser.

From the same judicious person we learn that in those Catholic times, it was customary, and of ancient prescription, that twice a week the farmer should give his servants roast meat, namely, on Thursday and Saturday evening. He, at the same time, restricts the yeoman and franklin's family dinner to three dishes, "which, being well dressed, will be sufficient to please your friend and grace your hall." Servants are ordered to bed at ten in summer and nine in winter, and to rise at four in summer and five in dark mornings. There are to be fritters and pancakes for dinner on Shrove-Tuesday; and on WAKE DAY, the vigil of the saint to whom the parish church is dedicated, "when every wanton may dance at her will," the oven is to be filled with flaunes. The seed-cake is to grace the end of seed-time, and the harvest-home goose never to be neglected.—Why does not Mr. Cobbett give us a new edition of ancient Trusser?

who are celebrated for the mild mellow flavour of their butter and fish, often refine the salt by boiling it up with whey; and this method is quite practicable in any dairy. Heating and pounding the salt facilitates the salting of meat. Sugar is an admirable ingredient in curing meat and fish. Without making them salt, it preserves and keeps them mellow. Some recommend that the meat should be first rubbed with sugar for some days, and then salted. Saltpetre dries up meat so much, that it is daily less and less employed. Much less of it will colour meat, or sausage meat, than is imagined: or sanders-wood will give the red colour. Crude sal ammonia is an article of which a little goes far in preserving meat, without making it salt. All troughs and tubs in which meat is cured ought to be kept closely covered with several folds of blanket, or something of the kind. Meat, till it be taken out to hang up, should be kept covered with pickle, and rubbed, basted, and turned in the troughs, at least once a day;—the doubled parts ought to be looked at, and rubbed; and if any mouldiness gather on the meat in any stage of curing, it must be carefully taken off. If the brine become rank with blood and slime, it must be boiled up, skimmed, and, when cold, poured over the hams; or now, that salt is so cheap, a fresh brine may be made. Bruised juniper-berries, coriander-seeds, sweet herbs, pounded or not, and all sorts of aromatic spices, may be added to hams, tongues, rumps, and sausage meat; also garlic; but this must all be left to the discretion of the cook.

1181. *To cure hams*.—Choose the short thick legs of clean-fed hogs. Those which are just old enough to have the flesh of firm texture, and which have roamed at large in a forest, are far the best. To each large ham, allow half a pound of bay-salt, two ounces, or even more, of saltpetre, eight ounces of coarse sugar, and a half-pound of common salt, with four ounces of Jamaica and black pepper, and one of coriander-seeds. Pound the ingredients, and heat and mix them well; but first rub in about six ounces of the salt and the saltpetre, and, after two days, the rest of the salt and the spices. Rub for a long half-hour. Lay the hams in the trough;—keep them carefully covered, and baste them with the brine every day, or oftener;—turn them occasionally, and rub with the brine: make more brine, if necessary. *Bacon* and *pig's face* are treated as above.—(*See pp.* 370, 346.) The latter is the better of being pressed down with a weight. Some persons use weights for all cured meat, to keep it below the brine. Hams are *spiced* thus by using aromatic spices and sweet herbs in curing. Smoking with green birch, oak, or the odoriferous woods, as juniper, &c. is an immense improvement to all dried meats.

1182. *To cure hams,—M. Ude's receipt.*—As soon as the pig is cold enough to cut up, cut out the round bone from the hams. Rub well with common salt, and drain for three days. Then dry the hams; and for two of eighteen pounds each, take a pound of moist sugar, a pound of salt, and two ounces of saltpetre. Mix and rub the hams well with it. Put them in a trough, and treat as other hams; but in three days pour a bottle of good vinegar over them. They will be ready in a month, when dry as usual. "This," says the venerable *chef* of Crockford's, "is superior to a Westphalia ham." We are sure, that if smoked, it is as well cured.

1183. *Beauvilliers' hams.*—Make a pickle with water and wine lees to suit the size or number of hams and flitches, and add all sorts of sweet herbs—as sage, basil, thyme, bay, juniper-berries, salt, and saltpetre. Steep for some days, and strain and put in the meat. Let the hams lie a month, drain, wipe, and smoke them. When smoked and dry, rub with wine and vinegar to keep off flies. *Tongues* of hogs may be cured in the same pickle, dried, and smoked in skins. They are cooked in small wine and water, with herbs, and served cold. [If the hams were rubbed with salt, and drained for a day or two, the receipt would be excellent.—*Edit.*]

1184. *General easy receipt* for curing hams or bacon of 14 lbs. weight, or in the proportion. Two ounces of saltpetre, three quarters of a pound of treacle, five ounces of salt, five of bay salt, one of ground black pepper, one of Jamaica pepper. Mix the articles, and rub the hams well. Turn and rub every day for a month. Hang the hams in a canvass bag in a dry place. Smoke them if convenient; they will keep for years.

1185. *Mutton-hams.*—Proceed as at No. 1181, using for one ham a fourth of the salt, but a half of the spices and sugar. Rub the ham very well with the *hot* pounded salts.—*Obs.* Ram-mutton, though disliked at table, is, when good, thought to make the best-flavoured hams. In the Highlands, dried junipers are used in curing mutton-hams. No sort of meat is more improved by smoking with aromatic woods than mutton. Mutton-hams, when they are once dried, will keep long enough, but scarcely improve after six months.

1186. *Tongues, to salt.*—Cut off the roots, and steep them in a weak brine; afterwards salt them with common salt. [The roots eat very well with greens, or will make pease-soup, stew, or Scotch kail.] Scrape and dry the tongues; rub them with a little common salt and saltpetre; next day rub them very well with salt and brown sugar. Keep them covered with pickle for a fortnight; smoke and dry them.—*Obs.* When many tongues are salted, use a sinking-board and weights, to keep them below the brine. They may be spiced as No. 1281.

1187. *To salt a round or rump of beef.*—A rump of twenty-five pounds will take two ounces of saltpetre, eight of sugar, four of pepper, half a pound of bay-salt, and as much common salt. Rub the meat very well with the mixed salts and spices; turn it on all sides, and rub it. Baste and rub with the brine every day for a month. It may either be hung and dried, or boiled out of this pickle.—*See pp.* 80, 279, 280, for beef cured in various ways with spices.

1188. *To cure geese.*—In Languedoc and other parts of France, where land is of small value, and geese are plentiful, much of the winter-food of *genteel* provincial families depends on these birds. As the information may be found useful in Ireland, and remote parts both of England and Scotland, we shall detail the French method of proceeding:—When the geese are very fat, about the end of autumn, they are killed, and the wings and legs cut off, leaving as little flesh on the body as possible. The legs are partly boned; and for every five geese a half-ounce of saltpetre is mixed with the necessary quantity of common salt, with which the legs and wings are well rubbed, and laid for twenty-four hours in a pan with savoury herbs. Meanwhile all the fat is collected from the bodies and intestines, and boiled down as lard over a very slow fire, strained, and put to cool. The legs, wings, and the body cut in pieces, are in twenty-four hours taken from the salt, passed through fresh water, and stewed over a very slow fire till the flesh will pierce with a straw. They are then taken out, and, when cold, packed in jars, and the melted fat poured over them. When cold, parchment, or paper and bladder are tied over the jars. A French family has, from this stock of winter-provisions, the power of having a *ragout* of a leg or wing, heated in a little of the jelly and fat in which the meat is preserved; or a *soupe* of a neck, back, or pinion, with the mere addition of herbs, vegetables, and suitable seasonings. The relish is very high; and French cooks speak with rapture of this savoury and economical mode of cooking geese. Young pigs may be treated in the same manner, but their relish is not nearly so high. If the fat of geese be thus esteemed by our continental neighbours, there is certainly in this department much waste in English kitchens.

1189. *To salt a yule mart, or whole bullock.*—The following approved receipt has been communicated to us for salting meat for family-use, in those families in the country where a winter-store, or *mart*, is still annually cured:—Take as much spring-water as you think will cover the pieces of meat, and, with Liverpool salt,* or bay-salt, make of this water a pickle so strong as to float a potato. Stir till the ingredients are dissolved; and afterwards boil the pickle till all the scum is thrown off. When quite cold, pour it over the meat in the salting-tub or *beef-stand.*—*Obs.* The meat, and all meat or vegetables salted, must be wholly and constantly covered with the pickle, by occasionally adding fresh supplies as it wastes, and using a sinking-board. If the pickle becomes turbid, and a scum gather on it, either pour it off, and boil and skim it well before returning it, when cold, to the meat, or use a fresh pickle, which may now be afforded cheaply, and is perhaps better, because purer than the original liquor boiled up. Meat preserved in this way is never disagreeably salt, and will keep for a long time. A little saltpetre boiled with the pickle will tinge the meat, and if it is rubbed with salt and suffered to drain from the blood for a day and night, it will keep

---

* Rock salt, called Liverpool salt in the north-west of Scotland and in Ireland, because it comes from that port.

the better. If meat is not liked so salt, substitute sugar for one-third of the salt.

1190. *An excellent general pickle for meat, hams, tongues, &c.*.—Take in the proportion of six ounces of salt and four of sugar to the quart of water, and a quarter-ounce of saltpetre. Rub the meat with salt, let it drain for two days, and pack it, and over it pour the pickle, first boiled, skimmed, and cooled. Herbs and spices *ad libitum.**

1191. *To salt beef for immediate use, and to make soup of.*—For this purpose we prefer the thin flank, what is in Scotland called the nine-holes, the runner and the brisket. Cut it, as suitable, into pieces of from three to seven pounds. Rub heartily with dried salt. Cover up the meat. Turn it over occasionally, (to have it covered with brine) and in a week it will eat well as plain bouilli with roots, and make a good Scotch soup. From that time to six weeks it will eat with greens, and the pot-liquor make, or help to make, potato or pease soup.

1192. *Mutton, either ribs or breast*, may be salted and served boiled with roots, making at the same time potato soup, seasoned with parsley or celery. A *boiled leg salted* a week is esteemed, with carrot and turnip, before a fresh one, by many excellent judges. The *Collier's Roast*, a favourite dish with many persons, is a leg of mutton salted for a week, roasted and served with mashed turnip, or browned potatoes.

1193. *To cure bacon in flitches, or whole sides.*— (See note, page 98.)—When all the lard is removed, and the tail, ears, pettitoes, &c. taken away, rub the skin side of the meat, long and briskly with warmed salt in abundant quantity. Rub about the shoulders and hams very well, as these are so thick. The pig should either still retain the animal heat, or hang (which we like better ere handling) two days, to get tender. Turn the thoroughly rubbed meat, and strew a thick bed of salt

---

* Various ways of hastening the process of rendering meat fit for cooking are proposed. Some recommend burying in the earth; others hanging the meat or poultry in a fig-tree. A high but equal temperature appears the most rational plan. Cover the meat with a thin cloth, and leave it as long as is wished for, or convenient, near the kitchen fire, or in a cold oven. If, however, the temperature be too high the meat will be rather hardened than improved.

in which a small quantity of saltpetre is mixed, over the whole inside. Press this down close everywhere. Throw folds of blanketing over the meat, on the table or trough, and place a gentle weight over it. Let it lie a week basting with brine. Then rub afresh the outside stoutly and long, and with fresh salt, cover the inside; let the meat lie thus for ten days, and then drain, roll in bran, or coarse barleymeal, and hang it up in the kitchen. When thoroughly dry, remove to a dry place to hang till wanted. It may be smoked.

1194. *Rapid salting.*—Lay a piece of meat rubbed well over with salt, over a vessel with water on two or three twigs. Lay salt thickly over the meat. The attraction of the water will melt the salt, and accelerate the salting of the beef.

N.B.—We have no experience of this mode of salting. It is evident that the meat thus treated must either be used immediately, or plunged in pickle.

1195. *To smoke hams and fish on the small scale.* —Drive the ends out of an old puncheon or cask. Invert it over birch or juniper branches, or a heap of sawdust of green hardwood, (oak is best,) in which sawdust a bar of red-hot iron is buried. Hang the tongues, hams, &c. on sticks across the cask, and cover it to confine the smoke, giving a very little air, that the material may smoke and smoulder slowly, but not burn.

N.B.—Most neighbourhoods command a corn-kiln, in which hams may be smoked and dried tolerably well.

1196. *To cure butter in the best manner.**—Having

---

* On a former occasion, we complained of the small attention given by the Farmer's Magazine, or in the printed Transactions of the Highland Society, to the homely processes of making butter and cheese, and the curing of bacon. This grievance no longer remains. During the last few months, we find, in the QUARTERLY JOURNAL OF AGRICULTURE, the report of a series of experiments instituted by the Highland Society, under the superintendence of the late Dr. John Barclay and Mr. Alexander Allan; and, more recently, under that of Mr. John Ballantyne, cheesemonger, Hanover Street, which must be interesting to all practical persons. The experiments were to ascertain, what should be the exact temperature of cream to afford butter of the best quality, and in greatest quantity. Dr. Barclay's experiments were five in number, Mr. Ballantyne's six; the result in both cases was very nearly the same. The mean temperature of cream, when put into the churn, is best at about 53°; but

washed and beat the butter free of butter-milk, work it quickly up, allowing a scanty half-ounce of pounded salt to the pound. Let the butter lie for twenty-four hours, or more, and then for every pound allow a half-ounce of the following mixture:—Take four ounces of salt, two of loaf-sugar, and a quarter-ounce of saltpetre. Beat them all well together, and having worked up the butter very well, pack it for use in jars or kits:—or use more sugar and less salt.—*Obs.* We confidently recommend this method of *twice salting* butter, which only requires to be known to come into general use. It effectually preserves the butter, without so much salt being employed as to give it a briny and disagreeable taste. Summer-butter requires a little more salt than what is cured in autumn; but the above proportions are used in some of the best-managed dairies in Scotland, though less might preserve the butter. Instead of strewing a layer of salt on the top, which makes a part of the butter useless for the table, place a layer of the above mixture in folds of thin muslin, stitch it losely, and lay this neatly over the top, which will effectually exclude the air. The turnip-flavour is a general complaint against butter made in winter and spring. Many experiments have been made, but we fear it is not possible wholly to remove this offensive taste. It may, however, be much ameliorated

---

may range from 50° to 57°. The lower the temperature, the longer churning is required. In Dr. Barclay's first experiment, the cream taken at 50° rose in two hours' churning to 56°; and at four hours, when the operation was complete, to 60°. Each gallon of cream yielded two pounds of butter of the first quality. At high temperatures, the quality was inferior, and the quantity less. When put in at a temperature of 66°, the cream rose in the churn to 75°, and the butter was very inferior in quality and appearance; and from the same quantity of cream as on the former experiments, (fifteen gallons of cream) yielded four and a half pounds less of butter. We learn from these experiments, that if the temperature be below 52° the butter will be apt to suffer from the tediousness of the process of churning; if above 60°, it will be in danger of becoming what in Scotland is called *bursten* butter. From a communication made to Sir John Sinclair by Mr. Vandergoes, President to the Board of Agriculture of South Holland, we learn, that the Dutch butter is made wholly of cream, and that no ingredient is used in curing save salt,—"a pickle renewed from time to time."—*See Quarterly Journal of Agriculture, No. IV.* If the half, or part of the milking, is used sweet, or for making cheese, the half first milked should be taken, as the last quantity is ascertained to yield more cream. Summer cream yields rather less butter than that of the autumn months, even at the same temperature; and August or September butter should be preferred for storing.

by mixing nitre, dissolved in water, with the milk, in the proportion of an ounce of nitre to ten gallons of milk. To give the cattle a little straw previous to their feed of turnip is a method employed in some places for preventing the turnip-flavour.

1197. *Butter, as made in Dumbartonshire.*—The subjoined receipt, which is excellent in a plain and rational way, is taken from the FARMER'S MAGAZINE. No process is so effectual in salting butter as working it *with the hand* as here directed. We may premise, that butter-*kits* are best preserved for the next salting season, by being allowed to stand *unwashed*, with any bits of butter that may adhere to the sides, and any pickle that is left. When to be used, clean the kits well by scouring and scrubbing with salt. If old-smelled from rancid butter, fill them with fresh earth for a day or two before cleaning them, which will freshen and sweeten the vessels. Dutch stone-jars, that hold from 10 to 15 lbs. are very useful for preserving butter, and twenty other domestic purposes, and are far cheaper in the end than our brown coarse jars.

"My cows are milked at eight in the morning and at eight in the evening; and the number kept is from ten to twelve. Each cow's milk is strained, either by itself, into a dish of wood, or two put together, according to the size of the dish. As soon as milked, it is set upon shelves of wood in a dairy or milkhouse, where it stands in general as follows, viz. the evening milk thirty-four hours, and the morning milk twenty-two hours; when the cream is skimmed off, and put into a vessel which holds one week's cream; and the milk is then made into cheese, which sells from 6s. to 7s. per stone. The churn is something like a large barrel, which stands upon a frame made for the purpose; the inside work being driven round with a handle, the same as a pair of common fanners. The butter is made generally once a week; and in the morning previous to that operation, the churn is filled with boiling water, when the inside work is driven a few times round, and then the opening side of the churn is turned down to let it out, the work being kept going round till the water be completely discharged, in order to throw out any sand or dust that might fall to the bottom, if the water was allowed to settle and run out of itself. The cream vessel is then brought, and the cream put into the churn, where it is wrought till the butter is separated from the milk; when it is taken out into a clean vessel, and the milk well wrought out of it. A corn-sickle is then drawn through the butter, several crossways, in order to take out any hairs that may remain it it; and if any other motes appear, they also are taken out. This part of the work is generally done with the butter among clean spring water, as the water keeps it from turning soft, and washes away any milk that may remain.

"The butter is then weighed; and for every stone, ten ounces of salt are taken (after having all the motes carefully picked out) and mixed with it. The salting process is carefully performed with the hand; as I have always found, that if salt is not properly mixed and incorporated with the butter at the time of salting, it never keeps so well. I am very particular in this part of the work, the salt being weighed with the same weight the butter is weighed with. In May and June, each stone of butter will take one ounce of salt more; and after the middle of August, it takes one less than the above-mentioned quantity. The butter thus salted is put into a clean well-seasoned kit, and a handful of salt shaken on the top, which keeps it from turning mouldy, or winding, till next week, when the butter is again made as above, and put into the same kit, on the top of what was put in the week before, without stirring it, and a handful of salt shaken upon the top. The same process is continued weekly till the kit is full; after which it is covered up, and set aside till my customer sends for it. It may be proper, however, to examine the kit occasionally, to see that it does not let out the pickle; as butter standing without pickle soon spoils. Indeed, butter salted in this way does not require pickle poured on it, unless the kit is defective.

"I never use saltpetre, since butter made as above always retains the same sweet taste till used, which generally happens within twelve months after it is made."

N.B.—In this butter there are twenty-four pounds to the stone, and twenty-two ounces to the pound.

1198. *To freshen salt butter.*—Churn it anew in sweet milk,—a quart to the pound. It gains in weight.

1199. *To improve rancid butter.*—Wash it, melt it gradually, skim it, and put to it a slice of charred toast, or some bits of charcoal.*

1200. *To roll butter for a cheese-course, or for breakfast, and to garnish supper-dishes.*—Have two wooden, fluted spoons, such as are used for lifting butter. Wash and boil them as often as wanted. Dry them well, and rub them with a bit of butter to clean them perfectly; then, between them lightly roll up bits of butter in form of corks, fir-cones, small pine-apples, shells, &c. Butter is used in many ways for garnishing salads of meat or fish, ham, eggs, anchovies, &c. It looks best when squirted in little tufts, or like delicate coral branches, or open lace-work, or fine basket-work.

1201. *To scoop butter.*—Heat the tea-spoon or scooper in warm water in cold weather. Scoop quickly, and heat again and again if needful.

OF MAKING CHEESE.

MANY parts of our island, from the delicate quality of the natural pastures, ought to furnish the very best cheese. We can indeed perceive no good reason why the cheese of Scotland and Wales should not equal in flavour that of Switzerland and Lombardy. Considerable improvements have already been made in this tardy branch of our rural economy; but, notwithstanding the zeal with which the Highland Society has lately taken up this subject, the range of improvement is still limited. Though one occasionally sees very excellent cheese in private families, little that is very good comes to market, except the Ayrshire cheese, and it is not, after all, a very

---

* On the continent butter is cured by putting it, when well freed of the milk, over a slow charcoal fire in a preserving pan. It is carefully skimmed and suffered to boil for a few minutes, and then stored in potting-cans made very close. Butter is sometimes clarified as above, and preserved by melting about an ounce of honey to the pound with it. It keeps well if potted, and answers admirably for sweet crust, cakes, and short-bread. In the East butter is melted in the sun, and kept in skins like wine. The Icelanders allow their butter to become *sour*, and seldom use it either fresh or salted. With them, butter, like wine in other countries, is chiefly valued for its age. One pound of old sour butter (*Surt smære*) is reckoned worth two of fresh. The same people cook their meat in sour whey, esteeming the broth thus made the better half of the dish. They keep sour whey in casks as one of their favourite dainties.

delicate cheese for the table.* The low price that cheese gives in those remote parts of the country, where the milk most resembles that from which the Swiss and Parmesan cheese is made, makes the farmer's wife still consider all the sweet milk that goes to her cheese as so much butter lost; and it will take a few more premiums, and a few more years, to convince those goodwives, that a shilling got for cheese will go quite as far as one got for butter, and often be more conveniently obtained. Skim-milk cheese never can be very good. At least one-half of the milk used should be fresh from the cow. Another capital error is making the milk too hot, and then employing too much rennet, which makes the curd tough and hard, however rich its basis may be. The quality of the rennet is also of much importance. The more gently the curd is separated from the whey, the milder will the cheese be. Made in a cylindrical form, it will eat more mellow than if moulded in a broad flat shape. Particular attention must be given to the cheese in the *winding* or drying. The wrapping-cloths must be changed very frequently, that the cheese may dry equally. The salting is also of importance; and, in preference to either salting the curd, or rubbing the new cheeses, some recommend cheeses being steeped in pickle. We have doubts on this, and no experience of it, and would prefer salting the curd to any mode. A sort of cheese for the table of very high *goût*, an almost Tartarian preparation, is made in the north by allowing the milk to become sour, and to coagulate of itself, which gives a flavour even more pungent than that of goat's-milk cheese. Cheese should be kept in a cool and rather damp place, wrapped in a damp cloth, and placed in a covered jar. It should always be presented at table wrapped in a small damask napkin, from economy as well as neatness. The surface of cheese, particularly a cut cheese, when to be kept, should be rubbed with butter or lard. Dried pieces, when they cannot be presented at table, may either be grated down, to eat as a homely

---

* Since our first edition was published in 1826, considerable improvements have taken place in cheese-making. Some capital specimens were exhibited last year in Ballantyne's, Hanover Street; and we place great hopes on BLACKWOOD'S QUARTERLY JOURNAL OF AGRICULTURE for many improvements, both in butter and cheese.

kind of Parmesan, or used in macaroni, &c. The offensive mould which gathers on cheese may easily be distinguished from "the blue,"—the genuine *ærugo*, which stamps its value,—and must be carefully wiped off. The production of mites may be checked by pouring spirits on the affected parts. The addition of butter to the curd, or of lard rubbed into the new cheeses, is employed to enrich the quality and mellow the cheese. Chopped sage, or the expressed juice of young red sage, caraway-seeds, &c.,* are employed to flavour cheese, and various substances are used to heighten the colour. Of these saffron and arnatto are the most inoffensive. Housewives, who make this branch of economy their study, will find many observations worthy of attention in Arthur Young's Tour in France and Italy, a few in the Farmer's Magazine, and in the Papers of the Bath Society. We merely subjoin a few receipts which are not in general circulation, though of approved merit.

1202. *Rennet or yearning to make.*—Rennet is useful even where there is no dairy, as whey is often wanted, and with a little rennet a cheap elegant second-course or supper-dish for warm weather may be furnished, and an agreeable variety given to the milk diet of schools, nurseries, and invalids. Rennet is generally made of the stomach or *maw* of the calf, but also of that of pigs and hares, and of the membrane which lines the gizzards of fowls and turkeys. This last makes the gallino rennet of Italy. Some plants are also used as rennet, as lady's bed-straw, an acrid species of thistle and artichoke.

Take the stomach of a new-killed calf, of from a week to a month old. Remove any crude food or straws found in it, but not the curdled milk. Put a handful of salt into it. Sew and roll up the bag, and lay it in a jar, and strew another large handful of salt over it. Cover and keep in this pickle for ten days, then drain, wipe, and paper it up, or cover with a thin cloth, (a ceremony few of our goodwives observe,) to dry near the kitchen fire. It generally hangs from the spring of one year till another. When rennet is wanted in large quantities for

---

* To the herb melilot which grows in abundance in some of the cheese districts of Switzerland, is ascribed the peculiar flavour of the Swiss cheese, as Cheshire made at particular seasons is fancied to owe its fine flavour to the wild radish.

large dairies, a whole dry maw is cut into pieces at once, put in a jar with a handful of salt, and has from six to nine pints of boiling whey, cooled to summer-heat, poured over it, according to the age of the calf, four weeks being the age at which it yields more rennet than either when younger or older. The *steep*, as it is called, is then strained and bottled for use, a glass of spirits being sometimes added to each bottle to increase its effect, and make it keep well. A small quantity of water, with salt, is again poured on the maw, and allowed to steep for two more days, and strained and added to the other. In the small way, for family use, a bit of the bag from the pickle may be steeped in lukewarm water, and will repeatedly give rennet; or a bit of the dried maw may be steeped as above. *Gallino rennet*:—When cooking fowls or turkeys, keep the skins that line the stomachs or gizzards; clear them of pebbles and other matters; and salt, dry, and steep as above, a few bits the night before rennet is wanted.

1203. *Temperature of milk to put in the rennet.*— From 90° to 96°. The rennet may in temperate weather be put to the milk from the cow, if not allowed to get cool, and the cheese will be the finer; on the average three quarts of milk will yield one pound of cheese. Cover the pan or dish in which milk is set to coagulate, and do not disturb it for a half-hour or more.

1204. *To colour cheese and butter.*—The arnatto is prepared in cakes, in London, for the use of the dairy, but will do very well as bought in the shops. Tie it up, when reduced to powder, in a bit of muslin, and use it in the milk for cheese, precisely as laundresses do blue in tinging linen, till the desired shade of colour is obtained. For butter infuse the arnatto in a little milk, and put the tincture to the cream. Cheese is tinged *green* with juice of spinage; flavoured or slightly tinged with the expressed juice of the red sage.

1205. *British Parmesan.*—Heat the day's milk to little more than blood-heat; and after it has settled put in the yearning. When it has stood for an hour or more, the coagulated milk is to be placed on a slow clear fire, and heated till the curd separates of itself. When separated, throw in cold water to reduce the temperature, and quickly collect the curd in a cloth, gathering it up at the corners. Place it in a deep cheese-hoop, and press it as other cheese. Next day it will be firm enough to turn. Let it dry slowly and gradually, often (at first almost every hour) changing the wrapping-cloths. Rub it with salt daily, for three weeks, or plunge it in pickle for a few days. The curd for this or any other cheese may be coloured with a little saffron or arnatto, by putting a tincture of them, extracted in milk, to the milk when to be curdled.—See also No. 1204.

1206. *Scotch imitation of Stilton.*—To the morning's milk add that of the previous evening, either skimmed or with the cream, as you intend to make a very rich cheese or one of inferior quality. Do not heat the milk too much, and employ no more yearning (or rennet) than will barely serve to curdle it.* When fully coagulated, gently, and without much handling or breaking, place the curd in a deep sieve or net, and afterwards, when firm enough to lift, in a hoop. Afterwards steep the cheese in pickle; then dry it, changing the binders very frequently. All fine cheese should be rubbed and turned every day for the first two months.†

1207. *Imitation of Double Gloucester.—Receipt by which the specimen was made, for which the Highland Society gave their first premium.*—This specimen was what is called a *one meal cheese*, that is, made of the milk obtained at one milking. The morning's milking is reckoned the richest. Strain the milk into the tub. Colour it with arnatto as above described. Put the rennet to it. The quantity of rennet must be proportioned to its strength. In ordinary circumstances a spoonful will

---

* If the cream is used, which, for a prime cheese, it should be, skim it off; and heat, and have hot in readiness, as much of the skim-milk as, with the fresh milk hot from the cow, will make the whole warm enough for the rennet; then pour back the cream. Mix and add the rennet.

† In Inverness and Ross-shires, there is a rural breakfast article called *crowdie*, not the common composition, oatmeal and water or milk, but made thus:—Take two parts fresh sweet-milk curd, and one of fresh butter. Work them well together, and press them in a basin or small shape, and turn it out, when it will slice nicely. When whey is much used for drink in hot weather, the curd may be usefully thus disposed of. It is eat with bread and butter, and keeps a long time, if *gout* is liked. This preparation, when the curd is well broken and blended with the butter, is sometimes made up in deep narrow cogs, or wooden moulds, and kept for months, when it becomes very high-flavoured though mellow. The celebrated Arabian cheese is made in the same way in vats, and both are uncommonly fine. These preparations deserve trial. In the Lowlands this is sometimes seen, but is not kept, and is, for this reason, called a *one day's cheese.*—P. T.

coagulate twenty quarts of milk. When the curd has set, press off the whey with skimmers; and next press the curd to the sides of the tub till it get firm. Cut it into cubes of an inch; and, gathering it into a cloth, place it in the sieve or hoop, which should have a cover fitted to slip down within, on which place a weight of a half hundred to press it moderately. Let it at this time stand near the fire. When drained, which will be in about twenty minutes, cut the curd still smaller than before, and place it as before in the hoop for another twenty minutes, and near a fire. Next put it into the tub, and mince it into very small bits with the three-bladed knife used for this purpose in dairies, or any substitute. Now salt the curd, which must be done to taste, and mix the salt well with it; and, gathering, bind it up into the sort of cloth used in dairies. Place it in the chessel in the cheese-press for a day or more, changing the cloth or binder as often as it gets wet. When the cloth remains dry, the cheese may be presumed dry. For some weeks after, turn frequently. Rub the cheese, and, if you like, wash it moderately with warm whey. In this experiment 100 quarts of milk produced a cheese of thirty pounds. It was made in the dairy of James Bell, Esq. of Woodhouselees.

N.B. Slips of the elder, placed on cheese racks, are said to keep away the blow-fly.

1206. *Best Dunlop cheese.*—As soon as the milk is taken from the cows, it is poured into a large pail, or pails, and, before it is quite cold, the substance called the *sleep, i.e.* rennet, is mixed with it. When it is sufficiently coagulated, it is cut transversely with a broad knife made for the purpose, or a broad three-toed instrument, in order to let the curd subside, and to procure the separation of the whey from it. When this separation is observed to have taken place, the curd is lifted with a ladle, or something similar, into the *chessel,* (for it is to be observed, that where a proper attention is paid to the making of these cheeses, no woman's hand ought ever to touch the curd, from the milking of the cow to the finishing of the whole,) where it remains a few hours, till it has acquired something of a hardness or consistency. It is then taken out of the cheese-press, and cut into small pieces, with the instrument above-mentioned, of the size of one or two cubic inches, after which it receives the due proportion of salt, and is again replaced in the *chessel*, and put into the press, where it remains a few hours again. Then it is taken out a second time, cut as before, and mixed thoroughly, so as every part may receive the benefit of the salt; and, for the last time, it is put into the cheese-press, where it reamins until replaced by its successor. After this is done, it must be laid in a clean and cool place, till sufficiently dried, and fit to be carried to market; great care is to be used in frequent turning and rubbing, both to keep the cheese dry and clean, and to preserve it from swelling and bursting with the heat, vulgarly "fire-fanging." When these cheeses are properly made and dried as they ought to be, they have a rich and delicious flavour.

N.B.—This, and all sorts of cheese, may be pricked with a bodkin, to allow the escape of the air, which, if left, forms what are called *eyes* in cheese.

1209. *A rich cream-cheese, without rennet.*—Dr. HUNTER.—Take any quantity of cream, and put it into a wet cloth. Tie it up, and hang it in a cool place for seven or eight days. Then take it from the cloth and put it into a mould (in another cloth,) with a weight upon it for two or three days longer. Turn it twice a day, when it will be fit for use.

1210. *Imitation of Shap Zigar.*—This is made by flavouring the curd with the expressed juice of melilot, and *greening* it with juice of spinach. Press it hard, and dry it slowly, that it may be thoroughly dry, and fit to rasp. If made of ewe or goat's milk the imitation will be very close.

1211. *To fatten poultry for the table.*—Keep the fowls clean, warm, and dry. Mix together for their food, oat and pease meal, with mashed potatoes, and a little kitchen-stuff. Have their food always fresh and in plenty, but do not cram them. Rice swelled in sweet skimmed milk is liked to fatten fowls by those who value the colour as much as the quality. In France they are fattened on barleymeal with milk, or on buckwheat. Young pullets are used at any age, but, for the more delicate purposes of cookery, they are best at the age of seven or eight months. Darkings white, and Polanders black, are good *layers*, and approved for the table. Turkeys are fed as above; or on stewed barley, with the part of wheat-flour called in Scotland paring-meal, mixed with it. If Cobbett's Indian corn succeed, as we hope it may, we shall have another admirable article for fattening poultry.

To keep hens laying in winter, the French give them nettle-seed and hemp-seed. In establishments where much attention is paid to poultry, besides taking great care to keep them clean and warm, which is necessary to the thriving or fattening of every animal, they are fed with toasts and ale, barley, sodden and steeped in fresh beer, or messes of peasemeal or rye-flour. The Malay or Chittagong fowls have for some years been favourites in Scotland. They are a handsome variety.

1212. *Eggs to preserve.*—They should at all times, either when bought in, or gathered from the nests, be rubbed with butter. A minute will go over two dozen, and this simple process will generally be enough to preserve them as long as is required in private families, and even when to be exported from Ireland, Orkney, Jersey, and the many places from which eggs are now sent to the markets of our great cities. They may also be preserved by a solution of lime, salt, and cream of tartar, poured over them in the keg in which they are packed. In England, old-fashioned housewives, after smearing, hang eggs in a net, which is turned up-side-down daily. To keep for plain boiling, they may be parboiled one minute, or have boiling vinegar repeatedly poured over them.

1213. *Another way.*—Dip them in a solution of gum-arabic, and pack in dry pulverized charcoal.

1214. *To run honey.*—Gently loosen the combs. Separate the best pieces to keep and serve in the comb, if wished. If not, place these singly on open wire frames, laid over a jar, opposite the fire, (an open corn-sieve will be a good substitute for a frame.) Cut the pieces of comb with a long knife twice, horizontally; then slice them down as it were into chequers, to permit the honey to flow. When drained completely on one side turn over the other. The liquid honey is then to be run through a canvass jelly-bag, made of the stuff used in dairies, and hooked on a stand in the usual manner of running jellies; the jar placed under the bag, when full, must be closely *bunged* up. The pure or virgin combs being thus disposed of, the inferior sort are to be treated in the same manner, and the refuse obtained by wringing the bags and scraping the frames and jars may be turned to account in vinegar, adding double its weight of water, or with hogs lard as a paste for chopped hands. *Honey-comb, to keep entire*, the finest pieces are selected, handled as gently as possible, papered and kept in a wide jar, set aslant and covered.

N.B.—Those who have even but three or four hives would do well to consult Loudon's Gardener's Dictionary, which contains the substance of all that is known on the subject of bees, whether theoretically or practically; or the *Bee-Preserver*, a little work by a Swiss clergy-man, M. de Gelieu, lately translated by a lady.

CHAPTER IV.

A SELECTION OF USEFUL MISCELLANEOUS RECEIPTS FOR CLEANING AND PRESERVING FURNITURE, CLOTHES, &c.

1215. *To scour carpets.*—Dust the carpet well, and if large, pick it asunder into two or more pieces. Have those first well rinsed, in running water if possible, and then scoured in a ley made of boiled soap. Repeat this if necessary. Next rinse the pieces, and, last of all, put into a tub of clean water a large table-spoonful of oil of vitriol, which will brighten the colours and keep them from running. Choose a dry windy day to scour carpets, as remaining long wet will injure the colours. If there are any greasy spots, let them be rubbed with soft or boiled soap before the carpet is wet. Hearth-rugs are done in the same way.—*Obs.* Carpets may be washed stretched on a clean floor, using sponge and soap-leys, and afterwards rinsed and dried. Nail them tightly out when again laid down. They may also be scoured with a bullock's gall mixed in a pail of water, or with Fuller's-earth, and then be rinsed.

1216. *To wash chintz, furniture, shawls, &c..*—Choose a good drying day before you wet the chintz. Dust the things well, by shaking and brushing, and wash them quickly out in cool lathers ready made up with boiled white or mottled soap. Two, or at most three lathers will do them. Rinse in cold spring-water in which starch and a little oil of vitriol has been dissolved, which, without injuring the fabric, will fix and brighten the colours, and prevent them from running. Shake the things very well, and repeat this occasionally till they are dry.—*Obs.* Rice-water is now very much used for fine printed calicoes and chintzes. *It is used thus:*— Boil a pound of rice in five quarts of water, and when cool enough, wash the chintz in this, using the rice for soap. Have another quantity ready, but strain the rice from this, and use it with fresh warm water, keeping the rice-water strained off for a third washing, which, at the same time stiffens the chintz, and brightens the colours.

1217. *To clean printed calico furniture.*—Shake and brush it with a long-haired brush, rub with clean flannel, and fold it carefully in large folds. Crumb of bread will also clean it.

1218. *To scour blankets.*—Boil a pound of good mottled soap, and put as much of it into a tub as with a solution of pearl-ashes will be enough to make a strong lather. Pour hot water over, and wash the blankets till the lather becomes useless. Repeat this till a clear lather comes off them. Less soap may be used the second time, and very little the last time; but the water must be as hot as possible, and the blankets fully covered with it, else they will thicken. Shake well while drying. Every thing in drying should be well shaken and stretched—Linen to make it mangle well—woollens to keep them from thickening, and to raise the pile.

1219. *To wash silk stockings.*—Wash in white-soap ley and hot water, and scald them in the same. Rinse in cold water, and dip them in water in which a drop of blue or a bit of cudbear or pink dye is put, according to the tinge wanted. Rub them till dry with clean flannel; if well polished no mangling is required, and the lustre is brighter.

1220. *To take spots of paint from cloth and silks.*— Dip a pen in spirit of turpentine, and touch the spot as soon after it is stained as possible. When dry, rub the place.

1221. *To take greasy stains out of silk.*—Scrape French chalk over the spot, and repeat this till the grease comes out, then rub off the chalk.

1222. *To take out iron-moulds.*—Hold the spot stretched wet over a jug of hot water, and rub it with salt of lemons, or juice of sorrel, and salt; then wash it immediately, lest the acid injure the fabric of the cloth.

1223. *To take out stains of wine, fruit, &c.*.—Wash well, rub with starch, and expose the linen to the sun till the stains come out. Exposing the spot, slightly wetted, to the fumes of burning sulphur for an instant, will remove these stains. A common match will answer the purpose.

1224. *To remove mildew.*—Rub the spots with soap, and scrape some fine chalk over this. Rub it in, and expose the cloth to the sun. Repeat this till the spots disappear.

1225. *Clothes'-closets.*—These small useful apartments should be lined with wood very closely fitted; furnished with shelves and wooden pegs, on which to suspend ladies' dresses, and things which folds would injure. Turpentine, cedar-shavings, Russia leather, &c. should be strewed about them, and glazed linen curtains should be drawn closely round the shelves; on which pieces of charcoal wrapped in muslin may be laid. Modern wardrobes are better than these; but, unluckily, though their price might not be grudged, few bed-chambers are large enough conveniently to hold them. *Bonnet-boxes*, whether of pasteboard, wood, or tin, let them be roomy, and furnished with a pin in the centre, on which to hang the head-dress.

1226. *Fur,—to preserve.*—Sew the articles closely up in linen of a close texture, with camphire or Russia leather about it. Air them occasionally before the fire.

Another way.—Keep in tin-plate boxes closely shut.

1227. *Ink-spots.*—Wash these immediately, first in cold water, then in soap and water. Use also lemon-juice or vinegar. Oil of vitriol will take ink from mahogany. Rub it quickly out, and put a little oil on the spot lest it whiten.

1228. *To clean marble slabs and chimney-pieces.*—Mix verdigris and pumice-stone with new-slaked lime in soap-ley. Make a paste of this mixture, and rub one way with a woollen rag. Wash, and repeat this till the strain comes out.

1229. *To clean papered rooms.*—Clear away the

dust with bellows and a long hair-brush; cut a stale loaf into eight pieces; and, beginning at the top of the wall, rub downwards in even strokes, as if laying on paint.

1230. *To clean paint.*—Brush off the dust; and, with ox-gall and whitening, scour the paint, rubbing it hard to restore the gloss; or use mottled soap made into a strong ley, if the only object is to clean.—*Obs.* Sponge is peculiarly well suited for this, and, indeed, all domestic purposes of cleaning, whether dishes, plate, floor-cloths, mahogany, &c. &c.

1231. *To take grease from papered walls or books.* —Apply dry hot flannel to the spot, then rub it over with hot spirit of turpentine. Repeat this till the grease is removed. If turpentine would injure the colours in the paper, lay several folds of blotting-paper on the spot, and apply a hot iron over that, till the grease is absorbed by the blotting-paper—*or* cover with French chalk.

1232. *To clean floor-cloths.*—Sweep and rub them; then wash with soap-ley, using sponge or flannel, but do not wet them much. Rub hard up with dry flannel. A little wax may be rubbed in, which both improves the appearance and preserves the surface.

1233. *To polish furniture.*—Nothing improves mahogany so much as daily brisk rubbing; but various preparations are in use. Break down two or more ounces of bees'-wax, and melt it in an earthen pipkin, take a half-pint of oil of turpentine, an ounce of alkanet-root, and a very little rose-pink; pour this on the wax when ready to boil; stir it up, and let it cool; rub a very little on furniture (previously cleaned,) and polish with dry flannel, *or* use merely one ounce white wax and two of turpentine.—*Obs.* Lintseed-oil, cold-drawn, was wont to be used for mahongany; but the taste of the day is for light-coloured furniture, and, accordingly, oil which deepens the colour rapidly is not so much used. Two parts lintseed-oil, with one of turpentine, make a good composition for dining-tables. Wax prevents the action of the light, and keeps wood of a lightish colour for many years. Various pastes and varnishes are sold to colour and polish mahogany, which, with the exception of wax, if we wish to preserve the wood of its first colour, or of oil to polish, we conceive of little utility, farther than as they may contribute to beguile the toil of the fair polisher.

1234. *To polish mahogany, &c. in the Italian manner.*
—Clean and cover the wood with olive-oil. Melt gum-arabic in spirits of wine, and polish the wood hard with this, which gives a beautiful varnish.—*Obs.* Pieces of old soft beaver-hats, and of soft smooth cork, are very useful in rubbing furniture.

1235. *To preserve polished steel.*—Smear with mutton-suet, and dust over with unslaked lime. A paste of lard or fowl's-grease, camphire, and black-lead, will also preserve steel. Caoutchouc-varnish is the most effectual coating for steel, but it is too expensive for common domestic purposes.

1236. *To clean steel grates.*—Rub the bars clean while still warm, if it be possible; then clear with emery-paper, or polish by hard rubbing, using a little dry emery, or finely-pounded Bath brick. When very dirty, a thin paste, made of emery and boiled soap, will be found useful. Pastes for brass are now sold very reasonably.

1237. *To clean brass grates, fire-irons, &c.*—Make a smooth paste of rotten-stone (pounded finely and sifted) and sweet oil. Keep in a tin box; rub on, if hard using a drop of oil, and cleaning with a linen rubber; polish with leather.

1238. *To clean knives and forks.*—Use a board covered with leather. Bath brick is the best thing known for cleaning knives. Wash off the grease and dry the knives as soon as they come from table; but do not use water too hot. On a wooden board two may be cleaned at once, taking one in each hand, holding them back to back, and rubbing in different directions. Wipe forks well, and plunge the prongs into a jug or other small vessel filled with Bath brick-dust or fine sand, which may be kept compact by a mixture of damp moss. Clean between the prongs with a piece of leather tied to a stick; wipe off all dust, and rub them up.

1239. *To clean plate and plated articles.*—Clean the plate very well, using a sponge, with soap-ley and boiling water, and brushing all the carved places. Dry and rub with plate powder, or the very finest whitening either wetted with spirits or dry. Polish with the hand, soft leather, or hare's-foot. The longer plate is rubbed the brighter it will look. Brush the powder carefully from all the carved places. Plated goods should be kept in flannel or baize, or buried in dry bran, never allowed to get damp or dirty, nor be rubbed more than can be avoided. Spirit of wine, or strong spirits, is the best thing to clean them with. When candlesticks are smeared with wax or grease, do not scrape, but pour boiling water on the parts before cleaning them. Have brushes of soft texture and different sizes for plate.

1240. *To clean pewter vessels and tin covers.*— Keep these always free of damp by wiping and drying them before the fire after they are used. Polish with the finest whitening and sweet oil, not water.

1241. *Directions for cleaning Britannia-metal goods.* —Take a piece of fine woollen cloth; upon this put as much sweet oil as will prevent its rubbing dry;—with this rub them well on every part—then wipe them smartly with a soft dry linen rag until they are quite clean, and rub them up with soft wash-leather and whitening. This simple method will preserve the colour as long as the articles endure.—*Obs.* Washing them in boiling water and soap, just before they are rubbed with wash-leather and whitening, would take off the oil more effectually, and make the carving look brighter.

1242. *To preserve gilding.*—In summer it may be covered with slips of soft writing-paper. Never rub gilding. Use the bellows and a long soft hair-brush; or, if this will not do, a piece of wadding or some cotton-wool. Frames properly gilt will, however, stand cleaning with hot spirits of turpentine, applied with sponge.

1243. *To clean looking-glasses and plate glass.*— Wash with warm water and sponge; then wash with spirits, and dust the glass with powder-blue in a rag, and rub it up with a piece of soft calico, and afterwards with an old silk handkerchief.

1244. *To wash wine-decanters.*—Use lukewarm water, a few bits of soap, and a little pearl-ashes, with sponge tied to the end of a stick to rub off the crust that forms on the glass. Rinse and dry them thoroughly. If stoppers are fixed, dip a towel in hot water, and wrap it round the neck of the bottles. Repeat this till they loosen;★ or drop a little sweet oil on the necks of the bottles, and leave them before the fire to expand, when the stopper will loosen.

★ We owe this direction to Dr. Hope's Lectures on Chemistry to the ladies of Edinburgh.

1245. *To clean Japanned goods.*—Wash with sponge, using soap and warm water, and rub up with a dry cloth. If the things still look greasy, dust a little powder-blue or fine whitening on them, and rub them again. Oil will take marks out of *paper-trays.* *Urns* ought to be well dried, rubbed when brought from the table, and kept covered with a woollen cloth.

1246. *To get oil out of wood and stone.*—Mix Fuller's-earth with soap-lees, and scour the places repeatedly with this.—*N.B.* Fuller's-earth does well for cleaning very dirty passage and stair carpets.

1247. *To take rust out of fire-irons.*—Cover with sweet oil, rubbing it hard in, and next day rub with powder of unslaked lime till the rust is removed, or emery will do very well. Rub with a spongy piece of wood.

1248. *To clean china and glass.*—Use pearl-ashes or Fuller's-earth in fine powder, and rinse in fair water, and polish the things well.

1249. *To take stains out of mourning dresses.*—Boil a handful of fig-leaves in two quarts of water, till reduced to a pint. Strain and apply this with sponge.

1250. *An excellent shoe-blacking.*—Eight ounces of ivory-black, six of treacle, two of spermaceti or sweet-oil, and three pints of coarse vinegar or alegar; a quarter-ounce of vitriolic acid may be added. These things must be well mixed. The vinegar made hot should be poured over the other ingredients, or the composition may be boiled.

1251. *Liquid Japan blacking.*—Mix with four ounces of ivory-black, a large spoonful of sweet oil; then put to these two ounces of sugar and a little vinegar; make a paste of the blacking. Add a half ounce of sulphuric and the same of muriatic acid, and nearly a pint of vinegar. Mix them well. With less acid the polish will not be so bright, but it will be more safe for the leather.

1252. *To extinguish fire in female dresses.*—So many fatal accidents arise from light dresses catching fire, that every MANUAL intended for females should contain the following necessary cautions:—1. Let it be early and diligently impressed upon the mind of every female, that flame uniformly tends upwards; that every article of her dress will consume much more rapidly if held upright, then if laid along the floor; and that her life may depend on her presence of mind, should her clothes unhappily catch fire. 2. Give instant alarm by pulling the bell, (which is generally near the fire-place,) by screaming, or any other means; but, if possible, avoid opening the door; for both the movement of the fire, and the current of air admitted, will increase the rapidity of the flames. 3. The alarm may be given while the female is at the same instant sitting down by the rug, attempting to tear off the articles of dress which are on fire, and rolling herself in the rug or carpet. If the latter is nailed down, she may easily, when on the floor, tear it up. She may also catch at any piece of baize, or vessel of water within reach; and, if very active, may even turn her clothes over her head, to her shift, and thus arrest the progress of the flames. 4. The most ready and effectual assistance a spectator in general can give, will be to turn the clothes of the sufferer to her shift over her head, and hold them firm thus, till wrappers, cold water, &c. are procured. 5. A man may quickly strip off his coat and wrap it round the female. 6. Let the sufferer, even if she fail to pull away the burning articles, or to extinguish the fire by rolling on the floor, and wrapping herself in the hearth-rug (which is generally always ready,) still protect her bosom and face, by lowering her face and crossing her hands and arms over those parts. 7. A piece of green or scarlet baize, called a *fire-extinguisher,* is kept in some sitting rooms and nurseries, and should be in universal use while thin muslin and cotton dresss continue to be worn. As its name and uses are familiarly known, though it serve as a table or piano-forte cover, it can be instantly seized on an emergency. 8. If, in spite of all exertions, the person is injured, let one assistant or the sufferer herself throw cold water plentifully over the parts, while another supplies water, and a third cuts off the clothes. Continue the effusion, or apply wet cloths constantly to the parts—if they cannot be wholly immersed in water —till medical advice is obtained.

Table of the Average Time required for Boiling, Roasting, and Frying different quantities of Meat, Fish, and Vegetables.

BOILING.*

A salted round of eighteen pounds, four hours.

Edge-bone, of ten to fourteen pounds, three hours.

Brisket, of ten pounds, three hours.

Ham, of twelve to sixteen pounds, simmer five hours.

Tongues, two hours if fresh; if salt, from three to four hours.

Leg of mutton, of nine pounds, simmer for three hours.

Neck of mutton, from five to seven pounds, two hours.

Shoulder, of seven pounds, two and one half hours.

Leg of lamb, five pounds, simmer one hour and twenty-five minutes.

Neck of lamb, three pounds and a half, one hour and quarter.

Leg of pork, of six to eight pounds, two and a half hours.

Hand or spring of pork, five to six pounds, two hours.

Piece of bacon, from three to four pounds, one and half hour.

Neck of veal, five pounds, two hours.

Breast of veal, seven pounds, simmer two hours and half.

Knuckle, from five to seven pounds, two hours and a half.

Calf's head, unskinned, simmer three hours.

Pig's cheek, two hours.

Pig's feet, three hours.

Tripe to simmer from six to eight hours.

Small hen turkey, from one to one and half hour.

Fowls, if large, one hour.

Rabbits from one to one hour and twenty minutes.

Chickens from twenty minutes to a half hour.—Partridges a half hour.—Pigeons twenty minutes.—Pheasants from an hour to an hour and quarter, according to the size and age.

---

* By boiling, we mean simmering slowly; keeping the meat at the boiling point, without any violent ebullition. Potatoes, artichokes, carrots, and other things, must be *probed* to try if they be done.

Greens and Cabbage, quick boiling, twenty-five minutes.

Artichokes, thirty-five minutes.

Green pease, from fifteen to twenty minutes.

Turnips and carrots, from fifteen to fifty minutes, according to age and size.

French beans, thirty minutes.

Broccoli and cauliflower, from twelve to fifteen minutes.

Asparagus, from twenty-five to thirty minutes.

Beet-roots, two hours and a half, or more.

Parsnips, thirty-five minutes.

Spinage, from ten to fifteen minutes.

Jerusalem artichokes, peeled, from twenty-five to thirty minutes.

A turbot, of ten to fourteen pounds, an hour and twenty minutes of simmering, after it boils.

Cod's head and shoulders, an hour from the time it is put on with cold water and salt.

A salmon, or large jole, an hour from the time it is put on with cold water and salt.

Slices of salmon, or cod, crimped, from twelve to fifteen minutes.—Eels and small flat fish are soon boiled.— Haddocks, whitings, soles, &c. according to their size. Soles, put on with boiling water, from ten to fifteen minutes; their texture does not require long cooking.

Herrings and mackerel, from ten to fifteen minutes.

Lobsters and crabs, about thirty minutes, if of average size.

Skate from twelve to twenty minutes, simmering.

ROASTING.

A sirloin, from fifteen to eighteen pounds, four hours.

Ribs, same weight, three and a half hours.

Collared ribs, three and a half hours.

Haunch of venison, from three to four hours.

Haunch, if in paper and paste, from four to five hours.

Leg of mutton, of eight to ten pounds, from two to two and a half hours.

Shoulder of eight pounds, two hours.

Fillet of veal of ten pounds, stuffed, three hours.

Brisket of veal of eight pounds, two hours.

Loin of eight to nine pounds, two hours.

Leg of lamb of six pounds, one and a half hours.

Loin of three to four pounds, one hour and a quarter.

Leg of pork, of eight pounds, two hours and three quarters.

Loin of pork, of six pounds, two hours.

Goose, from one hour and half to two hours.

Green goose, fifty minutes to an hour.

Ducks, fifty minutes.

Hare, an hour and quarter to an hour and half.

Large turkey, from two and a half to three and a half hours.

Leveret, fifty minutes.

Rabbits, large, one hour.

Wild duck, thirty-five minutes.

Partridges, large, thirty-five minutes.

Pigeons, from twenty to twenty-five minutes.

Chickens, from twenty to fifty minutes, according to the size.

Black cock, from an hour to an hour and quarter.

Pig, from an hour and quarter to two hours, according to the size.

Large fowl, sixty-five minutes.

Ox-heart, stuffed, if large, two hours and a half.

Calf's-heart, one hour.

Grouse, thirty-five minutes.

> N.B.—In frosty weather, a few minutes more to be allowed.

FRYING.

Soles, from six to fifteen minutes, according to size.

Slices of cod, or salmon, or turbot, or any large thick fish, fifteen minutes.

Fillets, rolled up circularly, fifteen minutes.

Herrings, whitings, and small haddocks, from eight to twelve minutes.

Small whitings and flounders, eight minutes.

Skate, ten minutes. Eels, twleve minutes.

Tripe, in batter, seven minutes.

Perch and smelts, if small, five minutes.

Oysters, for garnishing, three minutes.

Pancakes, from three to four minutes.

Fritters, in batter, the fruit previously stewed or roasted, five minutes.

Fritters of fresh-sliced apples, in batter, eight minutes.

Rissoles and croquets, of mince meat, five minutes.

Potatoes, in slices, three minutes.

Eggs, three minutes.

NOTICES OF THE PRINCIPAL MEATS, FISH, AND VEGETABLES, IN SEASON IN THE DIFFERENT MONTHS OF THE YEAR.

JANUARY.

Beef and mutton, which are to be had good all the year round, are both prime in this month, though they begin to get dearer than in the fall of the year; veal to be had good, but dear at this season; house-lamb and pork generally both dear. *Poultry*—Turkeys, geese, ducks, fowls, pullets, tame pigeons, wild ducks, hares and rabbits, plentiful; the latter about the cheapest. *Fish*—Turbot, holibut, skate, cod, haddocks, soles, plaice, flounders, oysters—prime turbot is now scarce; lobsters and crabs hardly to be got at this time; prawns plentiful. *Vegetables*—The same sorts of vegetables are in season, with little variation, from the beginning of November till the end of February: they are Savoys, cabbage, and greens of all the sorts, Brussels sprouts, broccoli, sulphur-coloured and purple; spinage, leeks, onions, beet-root, parsnips, turnips, celery, carrots, potatoes, cresses, parsley, cucumber, endive, and forced asparagus, and mushrooms. *Fruits*—A variety of apples, pears, and filberts, walnuts, oranges, and all the dried fruits, now plentiful and excellent.

FEBRUARY.

Meat the same as in January, but veal and house-lamb generally rather cheaper. *Fish* the same, but cod and haddocks fallen off; lobsters more plentiful; barbel and dace got. *Fowls* and *Game* the same, and spring chickens and ducklings in addition, but always enormously dear. Pea and guinea fowl now come in and continue till July. *Vegetables* the same, and in addition forced beans, and salad herbs.

MARCH.

Meat as in January, and grass-lamb; house-lamb now cheaper; and mountain-mutton, which begins to fall off about mid-winter, now not so good, particularly in severe seasons; veal gets cheaper. Poultry the same as last month's; no hares, close-time till September; green geese, ducklings, tame pigeons, (cheaper;) wild pigeons; Moor-game close. *Fish*—Salmon is now got, but dear,—indeed it is to be had in London almost the whole year round. Fish, in an open spring, are plentiful about this time, but still more so in April; mackerel, shrimps, and prawns, are now seen. *Vegetables*—Forced cucumbers, young turnips, and turnip tops, spinage, broccoli, radishes, and forced salad herbs.

APRIL.

Meat of all kinds.—Veal and lamb get cheaper. Poultry same as last three months. Leverets to be got towards the end of the month; young fowls, with eggs, and turkey-poults, but extravagantly dear. *Vegetables* same as the last months, with chervil and lettuce: vegetables now begin to get cheaper. *Fruits*—Green gooseberries and rhubarb for tarts. White fish plentiful.

MAY.

The same in meat as the preceding months, and about Whitsuntide buck-venison comes in season. *Fish*—Turbot, lobster, trout, salmon, eels, and plenty of the smaller white fish in favourable weather; oysters go out of season till August, and cod is not liked from about Lady-day till Midsummer, or later. *Vegetables* of all kinds as before, with forced pease and early potatoes; sea-kale, saladings, and carrots, are now obtained of natural growth.

JUNE.

Meat of all kinds, and generally begins to get cheaper. *Fish*—Salmon, turbot, skate, holibut, lobsters, soles, eels, in high season, and getting cheaper. *Vegetables* in great plenty and variety, and cheaper; early cauliflower got, asparagus plentiful, and about the cheapest towards the end of the month. *Fruits* in fine seasons are strawberries, early cherries, melons, and forced peaches and apricots; also apples for tarts.

JULY.

Meats of all kinds.—Lamb and veal cheap. Poultry of all kinds as before, and also plovers and wheat-ears. Leverets, turkey-poults, and ducklings, are now worth eating, and cheaper. Wild-ducks are often got about this time. *Fish* is now good of all kinds, save oysters; and the rarer sorts, as turbot and salmon, are about the cheapest. *Vegetables* of all kinds good and plentiful, as cauliflowers, pease, and French and Windsor beans. *Fruits*—All the small fruits at their best, also early plums, apricots, melons, cherries, and pine-apples.

AUGUST AND SEPTEMBER.

Meat of all kinds, and cheap.—Mountain-mutton now excellent. Grass-lamb growing coarse. Veal scarcer. Poultry as before; with moor-game of all kinds after the 12th of August, and partridges and hares from the beginning of September. Geese and ducks now full-grown. *Fish*—Cod becomes good,—turbot goes rather out, as does salmon. Fresh-water fish now plentiful, as pike, carp, perch, and trout. Herrings, which are in season from July till March, are now excellent. *Fruits* of all kinds plentiful, as peaches, plums, nectarines, grapes, melons, filberts, pears, apples: retarded small fruits still seen; also quinces, morello cherries, and damsons. Mushrooms most plentiful at this time, also cucumbers.

OCTOBER.

Meat as before, and doe-venison. Pasture-fed beef and mutton are probably at the best in this month. Poultry and game in all variety, but young fowls get dearer. Pheasants now got, and generally wild pigeons, snipes, and wild ducks, begin to appear. *Fish*—Cod, haddocks, brill, tench, and all sorts of shell-fish. Oysters, which come in at London in August, and at Edinburgh in September, are now excellent. *Vegetables*. Beans, broccoli, and cabbage of all kinds; beet, onions, leeks, turnips, carrots, lettuce, cresses, chardoons, endive, celery, skirrets, cucumbers, spinage, and dried herbs; asparagus gets rare. *Fruits*—All sorts of apples and pears, nuts, walnuts, chestnuts, grapes, and retarded gooseberries.

NOVEMBER AND DECEMBER.

Meat—Beef and mutton prime. House-lamb and veal. Sucking-pig. Buck-venison goes out. *Fish*—All good about this time. Salmon dear. *Poultry* gets very dear in large towns about this season, but is to be got of all kinds; also woodcocks and snipes, mallards and sea-fowl.

It is, however, quite impossible rigidly to fix the seasons of provisions, and much less their price. Meat, generally speaking, is cheapest in the latter end of autumn, and dearest in spring. Beef is found prime all the year round, but small natural pasture fed beef is at the best in October; so is hill-mutton: both fall away in the winter, and are lean in spring. Veal is good from Christmas till after Midsummer, and is cheapest about May and June. It is always rather dearer in proportion than lamb. House-lamb is less liable to variation, in fact, than other meat; it is seldom cheap, and always very dear till after Christmas. Grass-lamb is one of the few things that is at its best when dearest. In July and August it becomes cheap, but coarse. Pork, as it varies much in quality, also varies in price, from local situation. It is always dear in London. Poultry is found cheapest in great towns in the end of summer; and, in remote places, about Christmas, or before spring. Wild-fowl and sea-birds, like fish, depend wholly on the supply. Eggs are dearest just before Christmas, and cheapest about Easter. Vegetables, except perhaps young peas and early small salad herbs, are always best when cheapest, that is, in June, July, and August. They are often cheap in spring, when the gardeners clear their grounds to receive fresh crops. Eschalots and carrots to store, and beans, cabbage, and cucumbers to pickle, will be best bought in August and September. Onions, potatoes, and turnips, in October. Beef and mutton may be cured for winter-store, or for hams, with most advantage at the beginning of November, both from quality and price. Fruits ought also to be preserved when their several kinds are at the best and cheapest, as pines, plums, and melons, about August; oranges in February, &c.

GLOSSARY

MORE UNFREQUENT CULINARY TERMS, FRENCH AND ENGLISH.

It has been suggested that a short Glossary is a necessary accompaniment to this volume, intended, as it is, for the instruction of the young, as well as the information of the more experienced cook. Instead, however, of elaborate definitions, we shall, in most instances, merely refer to the page at which the dish or process signified is fully explained.

Blanch, to, to soak meat or vegetables in hot water, also to scald them, or give them firmness or whiteness, by a short rapid boil.

Blanc, a rich stock, in which tripe is stewed, note p. 339.

Blanquettes, minced dishes, see p. 341.

Barding, covering with thin lard birds or meat to be dressed.

Boudin, any French pudding, used in this work only to signify puddings of meat or fish, p. 356.

Bouilli, boiled meat of any kind, but generally said of boiled beef.

Bouillon, broth or boiled liquor of many kinds, pp. 136, 330.

Bouillon, Court, a liquor for boiling fish, p. 351.

Braise, to, see page 300.

Braises, dishes braised or cooked in a braise, p. 288.

Brisket, the breast of beef, veal, or lamb.

Casserole, an edging, border, wall, or encasement of rice, paste, or mashed potatoes, in which meats are said to be served *en Casserole,* pages 326-7.

Chops, slices of meat, generally cut from the ribs of mutton, pork, or lamb, and generally with a bit of bone.

Citric acid, lemon acid.

Civet, a dark thickish stew generally of hare or venison, p. 337.

Clarify, to, to refine, to purify by boiling, skimming, straining, or filtering, pages 431, 232, 124.

Collar, to, to bone, season, and roll up meat or fish before dressing.

Crimp, to, said of fish cut into fillets or slices, as cod, salmon, skate, or turbot, when very fresh, and boiled rapidly, till crisp and curdy.

Crumb, to, to stew with or dip meat, fish, &c. in bread-crumbs.

Cullis, the French *Coulis*, a rich gravy, the basis of sauces, pp. 233, 331.

Cutlets or *Cotlettes*, slices of veal, mutton, venison, or salmon, thinner and smaller than chops, and generally without bone.

Daubes, an order of French dishes dressed *en Daube*, p. 348.

Dejeuner à la Fourchette, or fork breakfast, a breakfast at which the use of forks is required from solid dishes being served, p. 75.

Dormants, said of dishes which remain from the beginning to the end of a repast, as the cold pies, hams, or potted meats placed down the middle of a table at large entertainments.

Dormant, a, a centre-piece which is not removed, and which is commonly used by the French, who never change the table-cloth.

Drappit eggs, eggs poached in sauce, page 368.

En compote, things served in syrup, generally fresh fruits, pages 359, 436.

En chemise, fruits rolled in pounded sugar, or frosted with it. p. 438.

En croustade, said of things served in crusts, or crust shapes, p. 327.

    N.B.—In like manner French dishes are said to be *à la Maitre d'Hotel*, *à l'Espagnole*, *à la Venetienne*, &c. from the sauces with which they are dressed or served.

En papillotte, generally said of every thing served in twisted paper, as salmon and mutton cutlets Maintenon, Nos. 445, 474.

Entrées, the French term for their first-course dishes.

Entrees de Desserte, dishes made of cold left meats.

Entremets, the French term for second-course dishes.

Fillets, things cut sharply into stripes, as breasts of poultry, fish, French beans, and many other things, No. 682.

Forcemeat, or *Farcemeat*, stuffing in general, whether for meats, poultry, fish, balls for soup, pies, &c.

Force, to, or *farce*, to stuff with forcemeat.

Garnish, any thing useful, relishing, or ornamental, served around, or along with dressed meats.

Garnish, to, to decorate, to ornament, Note, pp. 17, 52.

Gigot, the French and Scottish term for the leg of mutton or lamb, as distinguished from the loin.

Glaze, the rich juices of meat thickened by boiling and evaporation to a jelly, or robb.

Glaze, to, to cover meats with glaze, p. 271.

Godiveau, a French forcemeat, p. 355.

Gratin, a French forcemeat, generally of poultry, *ib.*

Gravy, generally in England understood to mean the juices of roasted meat, and also stock.

Haricot, so called from the French word for beans, with which it was originally made; now often understood of any ragout or thick stew of beef, mutton, or veal, cut in pieces, and dressed with vegetables and roots, No.s 650, 444, 467.

Herbs, savoury or fine, are parsley, mushrooms, chives, rocambole tarragon, &c.

Herbs, sweet, are lemon-thyme, mint, basil, bay-leaf, &c. &c.

Hotch-potch, any thin stew, or stew-soup, of meat cut in pieces, with fresh vegetables; also the name of a Scottish national dish, see pages 365, 277.

Kitchen-fee, dripping, probably called kitchen-fee in Scotland from being formerly the perquisite of the cook.

Lard, to, to enrich meats, poultry, &c. by introducing stripes of lard into them with an implement or sort of needle used for that purpose; also said of introducing parsley, &c. in this manner.

Lardons, strips of lard.

Liaison, a thickening, generally of beat eggs, sometimes of cream, intended to *tie* or connect the component parts of a dish.

Maigre:—Preparations of all kinds if made without butcher's meat, poultry, or game, and cooked merely with butter, where lard or dripping might at other times be proper, are *maigre,* in opposition to *gras.*

Maigre dishes, dishes used by Roman Catholics on the days when the Church forbids flesh-meats; comprehending all fish and vegetable pies and soups, puddings, fruit-pies, egg-dishes, omelets, fritters, macaroni, all preparations of fish, cheese-dishes, fish-sausages, and all creams, jellies, and confectionary, also dressed vegetables, pickles, and preserves, cakes and biscuits.

Marinade, a, a compound liquor of various kinds, generally made of wine or vinegar, with herbs and spices, in which fish or meats are steeped before they are dressed to improve their flavour or quality.

Marinade, to, to steep in a marinade, as No. 22, and Obs. No. 112.

Panade, a batter for mixing with forcemeats, anciently employed for basting, p. 356, Note 94.

Patties, corrupted from the French *patés,* very small hot savoury pies, served at dinner, hot luncheons, or suppers, pp. 396-7.

Puree, a, a pulpy mash of onions, celery, turnips, mushrooms, chestnuts, &c. thinner than a mash, but thicker than a sauce, over which meats are often served in French Cookery.

Poele, to, to cook meat in a particular kind of rich broth, Note 298.

Probe, to, to pierce to the heart or inside of butter, cheese, hams, &c. with a *probe,* to try their qualities by sight or smell;—also, to try if potatoes, turnips, gourds, &c. are enough boiled.

Refresh, to, to steep or soak meats and particularly vegetables in plenty of pure water, changing it, or letting it flow off; as spinage, when boiled, is often held in a colander, under the water-cock, before being finished, to *refresh* it.

Reduce, to, to boil a sauce or soup rapidly down to a jelly, or till it become rich and thick.

Roux, thickening, white and brown, p. 231.

Salads, cold dressed dishes of many things, but in modern England generally said of vegetables only, p. 222.

Sandwiches, a class of relishing, convenient preparations, named from the inventor, p. 319.

Scallops, small dishes of various kinds, so called from being served either in real scallop-shells, or little shapes resembling them, Nos. 178, 669.

Sippets, little bits of bread cut in various shapes, and soaked in stock, toasted or fried, to serve with meats as garnishings or borders, pp. 131 and 326.

Skink, a thin broth; also the leg or shin of beef from which such broth is generally made.

Stock, broths of various qualities prepared before-hand of different materials, as the basis of soups and sauces, and often called gravy.

Sweat, to, to expose meat, cut or whole, to a slow steady heat, to extract its juices with little water.

Test, to, to cook a little of any farce or other thing, in order to prove its quality, page 355.

Tendrons, (sometimes *tendons,*) the french term for the gristles of veal or lamb.

Vanner, to, the French term for working a sauce smooth, by rapidly lifting it up in spoonfuls, and letting it fall as rapidly, for a length of time.

Vol-au-vent, an elegant French mode of serving meats, particularly things dressed anew, as cold turbot, chickens, rabbits, p. 326;—also a mode of elegantly serving second-course dishes.

N.B.—The measure used in this volume is the Imperial measure,— the weight the lb. avoirdupois.

INDEX